Advanced Structured Prediction

Neural Information Processing Series

Michael I. Jordan and Thomas Dietterich, editors

Advances in Large Margin Classifiers, Alexander J. Smola, Peter L. Bartlett, Bernhard Schölkopf, and Dale Schuurmans, eds., 2000

Advanced Mean Field Methods: Theory and Practice, Manfred Opper and David Saad, eds., 2001

Probabilistic Models of the Brain: Perception and Neural Function, Rajesh P. N. Rao, Bruno A. Olshausen, and Michael S. Lewicki, eds., 2002

Exploratory Analysis and Data Modeling in Functional Neuroimaging, Friedrich T. Sommer and Andrzej Wichert, eds., 2003

Advances in Minimum Description Length: Theory and Applications, Peter D. Grünwald, In Jae Myung, and Mark A. Pitt, eds., 2005

Nearest-Neighbor Methods in Learning and Vision: Theory and Practice, Gregory Shakhnarovich, Piotr Indyk, and Trevor Darrell, eds., 2006

New Directions in Statistical Signal Processing: From Systems to Brains, Simon Haykin, José C. Príncipe, Terrence J. Sejnowski, and John McWhirter, eds., 2007

Predicting Structured Data, Gökhan Bakır, Thomas Hofmann, Bernhard Schölkopf, Alexander J. Smola, Ben Taskar, and S. V. N. Vishwanathan, eds., 2007

Toward Brain-Computer Interfacing, Guido Dornhege, José del R. Millán, Thilo Hinterberger, Dennis J. McFarland, and Klaus-Robert Müller, eds., 2007

Large-Scale Kernel Machines, Léon Bottou, Olivier Chapelle, Denis DeCoste, and Jason Weston, eds., 2007

Learning Machine Translation, Cyril Goutte, Nicola Cancedda, Marc Dymetman, and George Foster, eds., 2009

Dataset Shift in Machine Learning, Joaquin Quiñonero-Candela, Masashi Sugiyama, Anton Schwaighofer, and Neil D. Lawrence, eds., 2009

Optimization for Machine Learning, Suvrit Sra, Sebastian Nowozin, and Stephen J. Wright, eds., 2012

Practical Applications of Sparse Modeling, Irina Rish, Guillermo A. Cecchi, Aurelie Lozano, and Alexandru Niculescu-Mizil, eds., 2014

Advanced Structured Prediction, Sebastian Nowozin, Peter V. Gehler, Jeremy Jancsary, and Christoph H. Lampert, eds., 2014

Advanced Structured Prediction

Edited by

Sebastian Nowozin, Peter V. Gehler, Jeremy Jancsary, and
Christoph H. Lampert

The MIT Press
Cambridge, Massachusetts
London, England

MIT Press books may be purchased at special quantity discounts for business or sales promotional use. For information, please email special_sales@mitpress.mit.edu

This book was set in LaTeX by the authors and editors. Printed and bound in the United States of America.

Library of Congress Cataloging-in-Publication Data

Advanced structured prediction / edited by Sebastian Nowozin, Peter V. Gehler, Jeremy Jancsary, and Christoph H. Lampert.
     pages cm. - (Neural information processing series)
Includes bibliographical references and index.
ISBN 978-0-262-02837-0 (hardcover : alk. paper) 1. Machine learning. 2. Computer algorithms. 3. Data structures (Computer science) I. Nowozin, Sebastian, 1980– editor.
Q325.5.A295 2014
006.3'1-dc23
                    2014013235

10   9   8   7   6   5   4   3   2   1

Contents

Series Foreword   xi

Preface   xiii

1   **Introduction to Structured Prediction**
    S. Nowozin, P.V. Gehler, J. Jancsary, and C. H. Lampert   **1**
    1.1   Structured Prediction   2
    1.2   Recent Developments   7
    1.3   Summary of the Chapters   10
    1.4   Conclusion   14
    1.5   References   15

2   **The Power of LP Relaxation for MAP Inference**
    S. Živný, T. Werner, and D. Průša   **19**
    2.1   Valued Constraint Satisfaction Problem   20
    2.2   Basic LP Relaxation   22
    2.3   Languages Solved by the BLP   22
    2.4   Universality of the BLP   31
    2.5   Conclusions   36
    2.6   References   38

3   **AD^3: A Fast Decoder for Structured Prediction**
    A. Martins   **43**
    3.1   Introduction   43
    3.2   Factor Graphs and MAP Decoding   45
    3.3   Factor Graphs for NLP   48
    3.4   LP-MAP Decoding   52
    3.5   Alternating Directions Dual Decomposition (AD^3)   55
    3.6   Local Subproblems in AD^3   61
    3.7   Experiments   65
    3.8   Related Work   68
    3.9   Conclusions   69

3.10 References 70

4 **Generalized Sequential Tree-Reweighted Message Passing**
   T. Schoenemann and V. Kolmogorov   **75**
   4.1 Introduction 75
   4.2 Background and Notation 77
   4.3 TRW-S Algorithm 80
   4.4 Algorithm's Analysis 86
   4.5 Experimental Results 89
   4.6 Conclusions 91
   4.7 Appendices 94
   4.8 References 100

5 **Smoothed Coordinate Descent for MAP Inference**
   O. Meshi, T. Jaakkola, and A. Globerson   **103**
   5.1 Introduction 104
   5.2 MAP and LP Relaxations 106
   5.3 Coordinate Minimization Algorithms 111
   5.4 Dual Convergence Rate Analysis 113
   5.5 Primal Convergence 116
   5.6 The Augmented Dual LP Algorithm 118
   5.7 Experiments 120
   5.8 Discussion 123
   5.9 Appendix: Primal Convergence Rate 125
   5.10 References 129

6 **Getting Feasible Variable Estimates from Infeasible Ones:
   MRF Local Polytope Study**
   B. Savchynskyy and S. Schmidt   **133**
   6.1 Introduction 133
   6.2 Optimizing Projection 138
   6.3 MRF Inference and Optimizing Projections 141
   6.4 Optimizing Projection in Algorithmic Schemes 146
   6.5 Experimental Analysis and Evaluation 150
   6.6 Conclusions 153
   6.7 References 155

7 **Perturb-and-MAP Random Fields: Reducing Random
   Sampling to Optimization, with Applications in Computer
   Vision**
   G. Papandreou and A. Yuille   **159**
   7.1 Introduction 160

7.2 Energy-Based Modeling: Standard Deterministic and Probabilistic Approaches 162

7.3 Perturb-and-MAP for Gaussian and Sparse Continuous MRFs 166

7.4 Perturb-and-MAP for MRFs with Discrete Labels 171

7.5 Related Work and Recent Developments 180

7.6 Discussion 182

7.7 References 182

8 **Herding for Structured Prediction**
   Y. Chen, A.E. Gelfand, and M. Welling **187**

8.1 Introduction 188

8.2 Integrating Local Models Using Herding 194

8.3 Application: Image Segmentation 199

8.4 Application: Go Game Prediction 205

8.5 Conclusion 209

8.6 References 211

9 **Training Structured Predictors Through Iterated Logistic Regression**
   J. Domke **213**

9.1 Introduction 213

9.2 Linear vs. Nonlinear Learning 215

9.3 Overview 216

9.4 Loss Functions 216

9.5 Message-Passing Inference 220

9.6 Joint Learning and Inference 222

9.7 Logistic Regression 223

9.8 Reducing Structured Learning to Logistic Regression 224

9.9 Function Classes 225

9.10 Example 230

9.11 Conclusions 231

9.12 Appendix: Proofs 232

9.13 References 237

10 **PAC-Bayesian Risk Bounds and Learning Algorithms for the Regression Approach to Structured Output Prediction**
   S. Giguère, F. Laviolette, M. Marchand, and A. Rolland **239**

10.1 Introduction 240

10.2 From Structured Output Prediction to Vector-Valued Regression 241

10.3 A PAC-Bayesian Bound with Isotropic Gaussians 244

10.4 A Sample Compressed PAC-Bayesian Bound 247

10.5 Empirical Results 252

10.6 Conclusion 255

10.7 Appendix 255

10.8 References 264

11 Optimizing the Measure of Performance
J. Keshet   **267**

11.1 Introduction 267

11.2 Structured Perceptron 269

11.3 Large Margin Structured Predictors 270

11.4 Conditional Random Fields 273

11.5 Direct Loss Minimization 274

11.6 Structured Ramp Loss 275

11.7 Structured Probit Loss 276

11.8 Risk Minimization Under Gibbs Distribution 278

11.9 Conclusions 279

11.10 References 279

12 Structured Learning from Cheap Data
X. Lou, M. Kloft, G. Rätsch and F. A. Hamprecht   **281**

12.1 Introduction 282

12.2 Running Example: Structured Learning for Cell Tracking . . 284

12.3 Strategy I: Structured Learning from Partial Annotations . . 287

12.4 Strategy II: Structured Data Retrieval via Active Learning . 294

12.5 Strategy III: Structured Transfer Learning 299

12.6 Discussion and Conclusions 303

12.7 References 303

13 Dynamic Structured Model Selection
D. Weiss and B. Taskar   **307**

13.1 Introduction 307

13.2 Meta-Learning a Myopic Value-Based Selector 310

13.3 Applications to Sequential Prediction 312

13.4 Meta-Learning a Feature Extraction Policy 318

13.5 Applications to Sequential Prediction Revisited 325

13.6 Conclusion 329

13.7 References 331

14 Structured Prediction for Event Detection
M. Hoai and F. de la Torre   **333**

14.1 Introduction 333

14.2 Structured Prediction for Event Detection 336
14.3 Early Event Detection 339
14.4 Sequence Labeling 345
14.5 Experiments 349
14.6 Summary 357
14.7 References 358

15 Structured Prediction for Object Boundary Detection in Images
S. Todorovic **363**

15.1 Introduction 363
15.2 Related Work 365
15.3 Edge Extraction and Properties 367
15.4 Sequential Labeling of Edges 369
15.5 HC-Search 372
15.6 Results 375
15.7 Conclusion 385
15.8 References 386

16 Genome Annotation with Structured Output Learning
J. Behr, G. Schweikert and G. Rätsch **389**

16.1 Introduction: The Genome Annotation Problem 390
16.2 Inference 397
16.3 Learning 400
16.4 Experiments 406
16.5 Conclusions 410
16.6 References 412

Series Foreword

The yearly Neural Information Processing Systems (NIPS) workshops bring together scientists with broadly varying backgrounds in statistics, mathematics, computer science, physics, electrical engineering, neuroscience, and cognitive science, unified by a common desire to develop novel computational and statistical strategies for information processing and to understand the mechanisms for information processing in the brain. In contrast to conferences, these workshops maintain a flexible format that both allows and encourages the presentation and discussion of work in progress. They thus serve as an incubator for the development of important new ideas in this rapidly evolving field. The series editors, in consultation with workshop organizers and members of the NIPS Foundation Board, select specific workshop topics on the basis of scientific excellence, intellectual breadth, and technical impact. Collections of papers chosen and edited by the organizers of specific workshops are built around pedagogical introductory chapters, while research monographs provide comprehensive descriptions of workshop-related topics, to create a series of books that provides a timely, authoritative account of the latest developments in the exciting field of neural computation.

Michael I. Jordan and Thomas G. Dieterich

Preface

Machine learning is one of the fastest growing areas of computer science, and with good reason: predictive machine learning models trained on ever growing data sets provide relevant information to scientists and business decision makers alike, as well as enabling intelligent consumer applications.

Structured prediction refers to machine learning models that predict relational information that has structure such as being composed of multiple interrelated parts. For example, these models are used to predict a natural language sentence or segment an image into meaningful components. Structured prediction models are important in many application domains and have been used with great success in biology, computer vision, and natural language processing.

This volume is not the first on the topic of structured prediction; seven years ago, in 2007, MIT Press released the edited volume *Predicting Structured Data*. Since then structured prediction has blossomed into many application areas, but it has not settled down yet; there continues to be a stream of interesting and original work. In an introduction chapter, we summarize the state-of-the-art and recent developments. The remainder of the volume is a careful selection of contributed chapters.

We would like to thank all chapter contributors for their high-quality work, Marie Lufkin Lee from MIT Press for her support and patience, Suvrit Sra for help in preparing a LaTeX template for this volume, and Jasmin Pielorz for help with proofreading and copy-editing.

We dedicate this volume to the memory of Ben Taskar, a pioneer of the field.

Sebastian Nowozin, Peter V. Gehler,
Jeremy Jancsary, Christoph H. Lampert

Cambridge, Tübingen, Vienna, Klosterneuburg
January 2014

1 Introduction to Structured Prediction

Sebastian Nowozin   Sebastian.Nowozin@Microsoft.com
Microsoft Research
Cambridge, United Kingdom

Peter V. Gehler   Peter.Gehler@tuebingen.mpg.de
Max Planck Insitute for Intelligent Systems
72076 Tübingen, Germany

Jeremy Jancsary   Jeremy.Jancsary@Nuance.com
Nuance Communications
Vienna, Austria

Christoph H. Lampert   chl@ist.ac.at
IST Austria
A-3400 Klosterneuburg, Austria

Structured prediction refers to machine learning models that predict multiple interrelated and dependent quantities. These models are commonly used in computer vision, speech recognition, natural language processing, and computational biology to accurately reflect prior knowledge, task-specific relations, and constraints. A wide variety of types of models is used, and they are expressive and powerful, but exact computation in these models is often intractable. This difficulty, paired with the practical significance, has resulted in a broad research effort in recent years to design structured prediction models and approximate inference and learning procedures that are computationally efficient. This chapter gives an introduction to structured prediction and summarizes the main approaches. It includes a discussion of the research trends in the field since 2007 and provides further references for the interested reader.

1.1   Structured Prediction

The general structured prediction problem is defined as follows. Given an observation $x \in \mathcal{X}$, make a prediction $y \in \mathcal{Y}(x)$ as

$$y = f(x). \tag{1.1}$$

The set $\mathcal{Y}(x)$ is typically finite but exponentially large, and its size may depend on the input x. A popular choice is to use an index set $I = \{1, 2, \ldots, m\}$ and define both input x and prediction y as

$$x = (x_1, \ldots, x_m), \qquad \text{and} \qquad y = (y_1, \ldots, y_m).$$

For example, I can index all words in a sentence or all pixels in an image.

Researchers working in structured prediction are concerned with the *representation* of the function f, procedures for *evaluating* $f(x)$ for a given input x, and *learning* f from a class of functions $\mathcal{F}$ given annotated training data consisting of pairs (x, y) of data instances.

We describe these three aspects below, but first we would like to define how to measure the quality of a structured prediction model (1.1) by means of loss functions.

Loss Functions and Decision Rules.   A generally accepted criterion for assessing the quality of our model is that of the *expected loss* of our model as a function of the true generating probability distribution $q(x, y)$ and a *loss function*[1] $\ell : \mathcal{Y}(x) \times \mathcal{Y}(x) \rightarrow \mathbb{R}$. The distribution $q(x, y)$ is the sampling distribution we encounter when our model (1.1) is used; for example, it could be the joint distribution of emails x and spam/no-spam decisions y that are sent to a particular email address. We do not know q, but a standard assumption is that we are able to obtain independent and identically distributed (iid) samples from it. The loss function $\ell(z, y)$ quantifies—on an arbitrary but fixed scale—the loss suffered if z happens to be the truth and we decide for y. The quality of a structured prediction model can now be quantified as the *risk*,

$$\mathcal{R}(f, q, \ell) = \mathbb{E}_{(x,y) \sim q} \left[\ell(y, f(x)) \right]. \tag{1.2}$$

---

1. Alternatively, an equivalent definition can be made using *utility functions*; we want to maximize utility or minimize loss, but except for a change in sign, both definitions are identical. The loss function can be more generally defined as $\ell : \mathcal{Y} \times \mathcal{D} \rightarrow \mathbb{R}$, where $\mathcal{D}$ is the *decision domain*, which can differ from $\mathcal{Y}$.

Because $\mathcal{R}$ depends on the unknown distribution q, the expectation is approximated using a data set $D = \{(x^{(i)}, y^{(i)})\}_{i=1,\ldots,N}$ sampled iid from q, yielding the *empirical risk*,

$$\mathcal{R}_{\mathrm{emp}}(f, D, \ell) = \frac{1}{N} \sum_{i=1}^{N} \ell(y^{(i)}, f(x^{(i)})). \tag{1.3}$$

While there are different philosophies with respect to how to best build structured prediction models and which loss functions are relevant to an application, the criterion (1.3) is widely accepted.

The best possible risk, which is the lowest possible, is known as the *Bayes risk*. It is defined by making the optimal decisions with the knowledge of q, that is, $\mathcal{R}_{\mathrm{Bayes}}(q, \ell) = \mathcal{R}(f_{\mathrm{Bayes}}, q, \ell)$, where f_{Bayes} is the Bayes-optimal predictor,

$$f_{\mathrm{Bayes}}(x) = \operatorname*{argmin}_{y \in \mathcal{Y}(x)} \mathbb{E}_{z \sim q(z|x)} \left[\ell(z, y) \right]. \tag{1.4}$$

Representation.   For representing the function f, different choices exist; one popular branch of the literature defines $f(x)$ as the maximizer of an auxiliary optimization problem,

$$f(x) = \operatorname*{argmax}_{y \in \mathcal{Y}(x)} F(x, y, \theta), \tag{1.5}$$

where $\theta \in \Theta$ are model parameters. In many applications, solving (1.5) corresponds to solving a combinatorial optimization problem. The function $F(x, y, \theta)$ to be maximized is commonly parametrized as a linear form,

$$F(x, y, \theta) = \langle \phi(x, y), \theta \rangle, \tag{1.6}$$

where $\Theta = \mathbb{R}^d$ and $\phi(x, y)$ is a *joint feature map*, transforming x and y into a large but fixed size feature vector. The class of functions is now indexed by θ, and we have

$$\mathcal{F} = \{F(\cdot, \cdot, \theta) \mid \theta \in \mathbb{R}^d\}. \tag{1.7}$$

Another approach to construct structured prediction functions is by starting with a probabilistic model and applying Bayesian decision theory (Berger, 1985). For this we assume that we have a model for the conditional distribution $p(y|x; \theta)$ over $\mathcal{Y}(x)$. Together with a loss function ℓ, we can then use the *Bayes decision rule*,

$$f(x) = \operatorname*{argmin}_{y \in \mathcal{Y}(x)} \mathbb{E}_{z \sim p(z|x)} \left[\ell(z, y) \right]. \tag{1.8}$$

This rule is identical to (1.4), except we replaced the unknown distribution q with our model p. Intuitively (1.8) selects our prediction so that we minimize our expected loss under every possibility z, weighted by our beliefs about the state of the world as encoded in $p(z|x)$. The similarity between (1.8) and (1.4) implies that if p equals the true distribution q, then our decisions made using the Bayes decision rule will be optimal, that is, they will achieve the *Bayes risk*.

Evaluation.   Using either definition (1.5) or (1.8), in order to make predictions, we need to solve an optimization problem, an instance of an *inference problem*. Depending on the structure of F and $\mathcal{Y}(x)$, problem (1.5) may be intractable to solve exactly, and we need to develop *approximate inference* methods. When using (1.5), such methods are often called *energy minimization methods*, and a large part of the structured perdiction literature is concerned with their properties. In case (1.8) is used, the tractability depends on the distribution p, the loss function ℓ, and the set $\mathcal{Y}(x)$. For example, if the so-called 0/1-loss $\ell_{0/1}(z, y) = 1_{\{y \neq z\}}$ is used, the problem reduces to the *maximum-aposteriori* (MAP) decision rule,

$$f(x) = \underset{y \in \mathcal{Y}(x)}{\operatorname{argmax}} \ p(y|x). \tag{1.9}$$

If the loss function decomposes additively over individual dimensions of its arguments, then we can solve (1.8) in two steps, where first a set of low-dimensional marginal distributions $p(y_i|x)$ is inferred, and then decisions are independently made by minimizing $\mathbb{E}_{z_i \sim p(z_i|x)}[\ell_i(z_i, y_i)]$ (Marroquin et al., 1987). Inferring the marginal distributions $p(y_i|x)$, also known as *marginal beliefs*, requires probabilistic inference methods for the model. In the last fifteen years, a large number of approximate inference methods have been developed to this end.

One important class of methods, the linear programming relaxations, apply to discrete graphical models (Wainwright and Jordan, 2008). For these models (1.5) can be reformulated as an integer linear program, which can be relaxed to a polynomial-time solvable linear program for which specialized message-passing algorithms have been developed. These algorithms are now popularly used and provide robust inference for otherwise challenging models, but until recently, understanding the structure and limitations of the linear programming relaxation approach has been an open question.

Learning.   Structured prediction models can be learned in different ways from a given data set of iid samples. If the direct form of the predictor (1.5) is adopted, then the most popular choice is *regularized risk minimization*

(Vapnik and Chervonenkis, 1974), in which we minimize the regularized empirical risk,

$$\hat{f} = \underset{f \in \mathcal{F}}{\operatorname{argmin}} \ \Omega(f) + \frac{1}{N}\sum_{i=1}^{N} \ell(y^{(i)}, f(x^{(i)})). \tag{1.10}$$

Here $\Omega(f)$ is a regularizer that controls the capacity of the learned model $\hat{f}$. While (1.10) has served as motivation for a large number of general machine learning methods, the application to structured prediction problems was only enabled through the work of Tsochantaridis et al. (2004), who showed how (1.10) can be implemented in the structured case when the linear form (1.6) for the definition of f is used.

They propose the *structured support vector machine*, which learns the parameters θ of the predictor f by solving the problem

$$\underset{\theta \in \mathbb{R}^d}{\operatorname{argmin}} \ \frac{1}{2}\|\theta\|^2 + \frac{\lambda}{N}\sum_{i=1}^{N} L(y^{(i)}, x^{(i)}, \theta), \tag{1.11}$$

where $\lambda > 0$ is a regularization parameter, and we define

$$L(y^{(i)}, x^{(i)}, \theta) = \max_{y \in \mathcal{Y}(x^{(i)})} \left[\ell(y^{(i)}, y) - F(x^{(i)}, y^{(i)}, \theta) + F(x^{(i)}, y, \theta) \right]. \tag{1.12}$$

It can be shown that $L(y^{(i)}, x^{(i)}, \theta) \geq \ell(y^{(i)}, f(x^{(i)}))$, that is, L is an upper bound of ℓ for any θ. Therefore, (1.11) is an upper bound of the empirical risk (1.3), and by minimization of the upper bound, we can find model parameters with low empirical risk. Given enough training data, the empirical risk will be close to the true risk (1.2). While it is not trivial to solve (1.11), it is a convex optimization problem, and the tractability of the formulation has enabled a large number of structured prediction applications.

When the probabilistic perspective is adopted, learning of the model is performed using the model likelihood, using either maximum likelihod estimation (MLE) or Bayesian inference (Koller and Friedman, 2009). The model can either be generative $p(x, y|\theta)$ or discriminative $p(y|x, \theta)$ as in conditional random fields (Lafferty et al., 2001). The generative model provides an explicit model for the inputs x, whereas the discriminative model always conditions on an observed x. For the following example, let us use a discriminative model. We specify a *prior distribution* $p(\theta)$ for the model parameters and then solve

$$\hat{\theta} = \underset{\theta \in \Theta}{\operatorname{argmax}} \ p(\theta) \prod_{i=1}^{N} p(y^{(i)}|x^{(i)}, \theta), \tag{1.13}$$

for the maximum likelihood estimate $\hat{\theta}$ or use Bayes rule to define a posterior belief over θ given the data set D as

$$p(\theta|D) \;\; = \;\; \frac{p(\theta)\,p(D|\theta)}{p(D)} \tag{1.14}$$

$$= \;\; \frac{p(\theta)\prod_{i=1}^{N} p(y^{(i)}|x^{(i)},\theta)}{\int_{\Theta} p(\theta)\prod_{i=1}^{N} p(y^{(i)}|x^{(i)},\theta)\,\mathrm{d}\theta} \tag{1.15}$$

$$\propto \;\; p(\theta)\prod_{i=1}^{N} p(y^{(i)}|x^{(i)},\theta). \tag{1.16}$$

At test time, given a new observation x, we proceed as follows. In case the MLE is used, the predictive distribution is derived from the point estimate $\hat{\theta}$ simply as $p(y|x,\hat{\theta})$. In case the posterior $p(\theta|D)$ is used, the predictive distribution marginalizes over all parameter uncertainty as

$$p(y|x) = \int_{\Theta} p(y|x,\theta)\,p(\theta|D)\,\mathrm{d}\theta. \tag{1.17}$$

Learning structured prediction models is challenging because it is usually intractable to perform exact computation of the required quantities, with few exceptions—for example, in so-called linear chain models. In both (1.13) and (1.16), we use $p(y^{(i)}|x^{(i)},\theta)$, but this important distribution typically cannot be exactly computed. Likelihood-based learning of structured models has therefore required approximations; a large variety of approximate inference and estimation methods have been proposed. A rough grouping of these methods is into stochastic and deterministic approximations.

Stochastic approximations perform Monte Carlo simulations to approximate expectations and integrals in the learning objective. Examples are MCMC-MLE (Descombes et al., 1999) and stochastic maximum likelihood approaches such as contrastive divergence (Hinton, 2002; Carreira-Perpiñán and Hinton, 2005).

Deterministic approximations typically optimize an auxiliary objective function; the class of *variational approximations* such as *mean field* methods (Saul and Jordan, 1995; Xing et al., 2003), *loopy belief propagation* (Yedidia et al., 2004), or more generally methods derived from the minimization of statistical divergence measures (Minka, 2005) are commonly used for otherwise intractable models. Another class of deterministic approximations instead modify the likelihood function itself to obtain tractable estimators; these include the *pseudolikelihood* (Besag, 1972, 1977), more general *composite likelihoods* (Lindsay, 1988; Varin et al., 2010), and *score matching* (Hyvärinen, 2005).

All these approximations have different trade-offs with respect to computational effort, the robustness and accuracy of the inference results, as well as the theory that is known about them. It is fair to say that while great progress has been made, for most models, there is not yet a clear favorite among the above approximate methods.

1.2   Recent Developments

We now briefly summarize the most significant developments in the field of structured prediction since around 2007, when the previous volume in this series was published (Bakır et al., 2007).

Joint Optimization over Parameters and Inference.   Meshi et al. (2010) introduced a clever method to approximately solve (1.10) for discrete graphical models. In their method they rewrite ℓ as a maximization problem over vectors μ in the *local polytope* so that (1.10) is of a min-max structure with multiple inner maximization problems. The inner problems corresponding to ℓ are then dualized using convex duality to obtain a joint min-min problem over parameters θ as well as dual message vectors. The advantage of this is that one can now interleave message passing updates and parameter updates, whereas previously every parameter update required a message passing scheme to run to convergence. The result is an efficient learning method. A similar but more general method has been proposed by Hazan and Urtasun (2010). In this volume, Chapter 9 by Justin Domke continues this line of work to learn more expressive non-linear model potentials in which the parameter update step is replaced by a non-linear logistic regression subproblem.

Integrated Estimation and Inference.   A recent take on how to deal with the intractability of structured prediction models is due to Domke (2011), Ross et al. (2011b), and Stoyanov et al. (2011). The idea is to take a model and an iterative approximate inference procedure, such as loopy belief propagation, and to view them as one computational unit that iteratively transforms some initial state into an inference result. As such, when using a fixed number of inference iterations, it is just a non-linear differentiable mapping from parameters and observations to inference results. This mapping is parametrized by the original model parameters, and as long as we can compute the gradient with respect to these parameters, a gradient-based optimizer can be used to minimize the empirical risk (Domke, 2013; Ross et al., 2011b). The combination of model and approximate inference procedure into a more or less black box non-linear map breaks the conceptual separation between model and inference (Murphy, 2012). As a result, we can no longer easily exchange the inference procedure for another because the inference procedure is now part of the model. The resulting model is tractable by construction and seems to work well empirically.

Sequential Prediction.   A promising way to overcome the intractabilities associated with structured prediction models is to treat the problem as a sequential prediction problem. The *SEARN* algorithm (Daumé et al., 2009) was the first practical method in this respect, followed by *Dagger* (Ross et al., 2011a). In case the original problem has a sequential structure—for example, this is the case in many models operating on natural language sentences—this approach is natural and in effect learns a *policy* that makes one decision at a time, given a context of the observed input and the previous policy decisions. The difficulty in this approach is that the policy decisions are a function of the previous policy decisions; this violates the common iid assumption and makes it important to provide realistic and non-perfect inputs to the policy. In effect this precludes the naive approach of simply replacing previous decisions with ground truth annotations. SEARN and Dagger overcome this difficulty but still make the strong assumption that a natural sequential order of decisions exists.

In this volume, the *SLEDGE* method in Chapter 15 by Todorovic is an application of sequential prediction to edge labeling in natural images. Chapter 13 by Weiss and Taskar also uses a sequential policy but not in order to make predictions but instead to select models with different runtime-accuracy tradeoffs to provide the best possible predictions for a given computational budget; here the context is provided by the predictions made by computationally cheaper models. This goal is also pursued in the recent work of Grubb et al. (2013), who propose to learn an iterative decoding policy, iteratively improving parts of the prediction while minimizing computational expenditure.

Stacking, Auto-context, and Cascade Architectures.   A natural method to enlarge model capacity is to use multiple models in a sequential cascade, where each model receives as input the original input as well as the output of the previous model. This idea was introduced in machine learning as *stacking* (Cohen and de Carvalho, 2005; Wolpert, 1992) and in computer vision as *auto-context* (Tu, 2008; Tu and Bai, 2010), and it has proven successful in improving predictive performance in structured prediction models. It is generally applicable, provides nested model classes of increasing capacity, and can tractably overcome limiting model assumptions.

Munoz et al. (2010) use this idea in a hierarchical image segmentation model and, in addition, prevent overfitting of the cascade by training on separate subsets of the data. Kontschieder et al. (2013) build on the cascade idea for semantic image segmentation; their model proceeds by filtering intermediate posterior distributions in the image plane using a geodesic filter, and subsequent evaluations of decision tree nodes are allowed to condition on these filtered posteriors. Schmidt et al. (2013) use a cascade of tractable random field models to perform deblurring; each cascade stage improves the performance of the reconstructed image.

Perturb-and-MAP Models and Inference. For discrete probabilistic graphical models, sometimes the maximum-aposteriori problem (MAP) can be solved for exactly in polynomial time, whereas exact marginalization is NP-hard. This is the case for example in models defined by a submodular Gibbs energy functions. Papandreou and Yuille (2011) introduced an approach named *Perturb-and-MAP*, in which samples from the approximate distribution defined by the model are obtained by carefully constructing perturbations to model parameters. They then run MAP inference in the perturbed model to obtain a single sample. In Chapter 7, they discuss this method in more detail.

Tarlow et al. (2012) recognized that the Perturb-and-MAP construction is not limited to graphical models but can be applied whenever a combinatorial optimization problem defined on the predictions is tractable, for example, in bipartite matching and network optimization problems. They name this more general class of models the *randomized optimum models*, and this view allows the construction of probabilistic models that no longer correspond to known graphical models. The Perturb-and-MAP ideas have also been used to derive novel approximation techniques for the partition function in discrete graphical models (Hazan and Jaakkola, 2012).

Multiple Predictions and Diverse Predictions. The structured prediction framework (1.1) makes a single prediction that achieves small loss. Recently, some works have considered the possibility of making multiple predictions. The motivation for doing so is to present these solutions to a decision maker or larger system as a summary. The decision maker may then select one solution, or an automated system may perform a more complicated inference on the small set of candidates. This setting is distinct from sampling from the posterior distribution of a model $p(y|x)$ because the choice of solutions returned should still be optimal under a modified risk function.

Fromer and Globerson (2009) consider the problem of restricting the linear programming relaxation to produce the second best and k-best MAP solution. This is revealing about the structure of the LP relaxation but suffers from solutions that are too similar to be useful. Batra et al. (2012) consider instead the problem of diverse predictions and use a greedy procedure that restricts the next solution to be dissimilar to all previous solutions. Guzmán-Rivera et al. (2012) define a loss function on sets of predictions as the minimum of the original loss applied to all elements of the predicted set.

While multiple predictions are useful in an interactive scenario, it is less clear how they may help to solve the original structured prediction problem.

1.3   Summary of the Chapters

Linear Programming Relaxation.   An important recent development is the emergence of an efficient linear programming approach to structured prediction. This is reflected by the large number of chapters in this volume that deal with the linear programming approach; we now give a brief summary of these chapters.

In Chapter 2, Stanislav Živný, Tomáš Werner, and Daniel Průša give a comprehensive overview of the linear programming (LP) relaxation approach to minimize functions of discrete variables. They provide a characterization of the family of functions that are exactly solvable by the LP approach and establish that the LP arising from the relaxation approach is as hard to solve as an arbitrary linear program. Both results are important but for different reasons: the characterization result establishes the limits of the relaxation approach in general, and the LP hardness result demonstrates that there is little hope for finding a special purpose algorithm to solve LP relaxations arising from discrete function minimization problems.

Chapter 3 by André Martins introduces a practical algorithm for solving such linear programming relaxations arising from discrete factor graph models. The algorithm is based on the alternating direction method of multipliers (ADMM) (Boyd et al., 2011) and comes with convergence guarantees and good practical performance. One consequence of applying ADMM to the linear programming relaxation is that the subproblems that need to be solved become quadratic programs. This is fine for low-order factors but complicates inference when higher order factors are used. For these, Martins introduces an active set strategy that enables ADMM even for cases where the quadratic subproblem is difficult to solve.

In Chapter 4, Schoenemann and Kolmogorov also introduce a general and efficient algorithm for solving the LP relaxation. Their algorithm generalizes the original *TRW-S* method (Kolmogorov, 2006), which is among the most efficient practical methods for solving maximum-a-posteriori problems in random fields with arbitrary *pairwise* potentials and has been used extensively in computer vision. TRW-S achieves monotonic descent in its objective function via updates along monotonic chains. Unlike more recent developments, such as the ADMM-based approach by André Martins, however, TRW-S is not guaranteed to establish a global optimum of the LP relaxation. Nonetheless, its solutions can be shown to satisfy an intuitive property called *weak tree agreement*. Here, Schoenemann and Kolmogorov generalize this property, as well as the concept of monotonic chains, to factors involving an arbitrary number of variables by moving from trees to the more general concept of *junction trees*.

In Chapter 5, Meshi, Jaakkola, and Globerson propose an efficient and a globally convergent solver for the MAP LP relaxation. Their approach starts from the dual linear program, which is structurally simpler than the primal and can be rewritten as a convex optimization problem. Although convex, it is not differentiable and, as a result, has to be solved using either inefficient subgradient methods or methods that are efficient but cannot guarantee optimality. The proposed method instead smoothes the dual problem so it becomes differentiable and efficient coordinate descent approaches become globally convergent. The authors provide a precise convergence rate analysis for both primal and dual iterates and demonstrate the usefulness experimentally.

In Chapter 6, Savchynskyy and Schmidt consider a particular sub-problem that occurs in many approaches to solving the LP relaxation of MAP inference but also in numerous other linear programming problems with certain separability properties. Specifically, many algorithms yield iterates that do not satisfy the primal constraint set (e.g., are infeasible with respect to the local polytope, in the special case of the LP relaxation for graphical models). This is true, for instance, for the many approaches based on a convex dual of the LP relaxation: Although it is known that primal-feasible solutions can be recovered from the dual iterates via *dual averaging* in many cases (e.g., Anstreicher and Wolsey, 2009), this property only holds in the limit, and convergence may be too slow in practice. To counter this problem, Savchynyskyy and Schmidt propose an elegant explicit approach to attaining primal feasibility—based on *optimizing projections*—that has useful applications in primal-dual optimization schemes, adaptive step size selection in subgradient methods, as well as stopping criteria.

Modeling.   While graphical models took center stage in the last few years, a number of original approaches show how to define a probabilistic model and use non-linear model components to enhance model capacity. The following three chapters describe such innovations.

George Papandreou and Alan Yuille describe a new technique in Chapter 7 for drawing samples from a probability distribution, given by a probabilistic graphical model, that only requires repeated calls to a routine for MAP prediction. The main idea is to use extreme value theory to study the distribution of MAP states when the energy function of the underlying graphical model is perturbed. The analysis shows that choosing the perturbations from a Gumbel distribution causes the MAP states to be distributed approximately like samples from the original distribution. For Gaussian graphical models, this relation is even exact.

In Chapter 8, Yutian Chen, Andrew E. Gelfand, and Max Welling present *Herding*, a different approach to structured models that implements a dynamical system for structured prediction. Herding works by producing a sequence of parameters, thus resulting in a sequence of predictions instead of a single one. This stands in contrast to the common training and test phase divide. The authors derive this approach as the zero temperature limit of the classical log-likelihood estimator and relate it to the Structured Perceptron algorithm. As an practically interesting application, Chen and co-authors then derive Herding update equations that can be used to combine multiple piece-wise trained local models into a global consistent one.

In Chapter 9, Justin Domke introduces an integrated learning and inference approach to learning structured prediction models. He shows that parameter estimation and message passing inference can be written as a joint differentiable objective function. Fixing the parameters, the objective can be optimized by ordinary message passing updates. When fixing the messages, the objective becomes a logistic regression objective that can be optimized by any procedure typically used for logistic regression. In particular, this viewpoint enables the use of non-linear parametrizations, and Domke demonstrates this possibility by using decision trees and multi-layer perceptrons to parametrize his potential functions. The resulting algorithm is general and flexible but also simple to implement and applicable to cyclic models.

Theory.   The theoretical understanding of structured prediction has made significant progress over the last years. This finding is reflected in this volume by two chapters that concentrate on this aspect.

In Chapter 10, Sebastièn Giguère, Francois Laviolette, Mario Marchand, and Amèlie Rolland provide a PAC-Bayesian analysis of the quadratic regression approach to structured prediction, which had been proposed by Cortes et al. (2007). The use of a quadratic loss function induced by a kernel in label space allows the training of structured predictors without the need to compute expectations over exponentially sized state spaces, as Conditional

Random Fields do, or to solve potentially NP-hard loss-augmented inference problems. One particular result of their analysis is the observation that the training algorithm proposed in Cortes et al. (2007) can be interpreted as the minimization of a probabilistic bound on the generalization error.

Chapter 11 by Joseph Keshet focuses on theoretical properties of the different learning objective functions that have been proposed for training structured prediction systems. Keshet illustrates how most of this formulating results from different techniques for bounding the empirical risk in Equation (1.10), and he studies in particular which learning problems are consistent in the limit case infinite data case.

Resource-Aware Learning.   In Chapter 12, Xinghua Lou, Marius Kloft, Gunnar Rätsch, and Fred A. Hamprecht address the problem of learning structured models from partial annotations only. This scenario is commonplace in many applications; this chapter reports on the application of multiple cell tracking. For this problem, training data are abundant, but full annotation is unfeasible. Three strategies of how partial annotations can be used are described throughout the chapter. The first approach modifies the loss function of the structured SVM to also include partial annotations. Further, an active learning scenario is developed that selects, during a training phase, examples to be passed for annotation to a human expert. Finally, a structured transfer learning approach is presented, which implements regularization of multiple related tasks by introducing parameter tying. All approaches are validated with extensive algorithmic and empirical experiments.

In Chapter 13, Weiss and Taskar show how to consider the runtime of evaluating the structured predictor during test-time explicitly. They propose to use reinforcement learning to learn a policy that decides adaptively on how to allocate a global computational budget to feature computation optimally, as measured by expected improved accuracy of the predictions. Thus, for any fixed budget, an optimal tradeoff between runtime and accuracy can be achieved.

In Chapter 14, Minh Hoai and Fernando de la Torre introduce structured prediction methods for event detection problems, such as facial action unit detection and hand gesture recognition. The proposed *SegSVM* method takes into account the temporal ordering and consistency of events and moreover is efficient at test time in that its complexity is linear in the sequence length. The model parameters can be estimated by solving a convex optimization problem. Together with the reported good empirical performance, these properties make the method a practical choice for event detection problems.

In Chapter 15 Sinisa Todorovic describes a method for unsupervised boundary detection. This is an important pre-processing task for many applications in computer vision, while at the same time it touches fundamental problems of computer vision: organization and grouping of image content. Boundary detection is posed as a structured prediction problem, namely, a binary segmentation task over the image domain. The difficulty is that its structure, for example, relation between contour lines, cannot be easily encoded in simple factor graphs. This chapter proposes two algorithms that circumvent this problem by formulating the search for a segmentation as a sequential decision process. Sequential decisions allow for adaption of inference based on intermediate decisions, and this takes more complex structured dependencies into account. The decision process is then optimized based on a benchmark data set of images with boundary annotations.

In Chapter 16, Behr, Schweikert, and Rätsch consider the problem of genome annotation, an area of computational biology in which machine learning has become increasingly prevalent. One important aspect of genome annotation is to detect and define functionally important parts of the genome. Formally, this task can be approached as a segmentation problem, where, in addition to the hidden location of genes, their *exon-intron* structures have to be predicted from the DNA sequence. Toward this end, Behr et al. present an approach based on learning Hidden Semi-Markov Models in a structural SVM framework. For the case when multiple different transcripts are being generated from the same gene and multiple segmentations hence have to be predicted simultaneously, the authors propose a Mixed Integer Programming formulation leading to sparse solutions. The effectiveness of their approach is supported by experiments in two international competitions that demonstrate state-of-the-art performance.

1.4   Conclusion

In this chapter, we have given an overview of the field of structured prediction, with its main approaches, difficulties, and current trends. We conclude with a description of the intended target audience and a list of recent textbook references the reader may be interested in.

Audience.   This book is targeted at a broad audience of researchers and students working in machine learning, as well as related areas such as natural language processing, computer vision, or robotics. Some chapters are didactic and summarize the current state of the art in structured prediction, whereas others present novel results. The variety of applications considered in this volume is broad: the chapters cover predicting outcomes in the game of Go, natural language parsing, genome analysis, biological image analysis, and natural image understanding. By including different applications, we hope the reader will appreciate that the same underlying principles and techniques are working successfully in diverse application domains, and we hope to inspire the reader to apply these techniques in his or her own application.

Textbooks. There is now a considerable selection of excellent textbook introductions to building sophisticated machine learning models. We suggest the following books mostly covering graphical models to the interested reader.

Bishop (2006) provides an excellent introduction to Bayesian models and machine learning, as does Barber (2011). The textbook of Koller and Friedman (2009) comprehensively covers discrete probabilistic graphical models and approximate inference, and the tutorial-style book of Wainwright and Jordan (2008) is an excellent introduction to variational inference in graphical models. Murphy (2012) broadly covers machine learning from a largely Bayesian viewpoint.

The edited volume of Bakır et al. (2007) in the same series as this volume summarizes the work on structured prediction until 2007; there are two tutorials covering much of this work, the first with a computer vision focus (Nowozin and Lampert, 2011), and the second with a natural language processing focus in (Smith, 2011).

1.5 References

K. M. Anstreicher and L. A. Wolsey. Two "well-known" properties of subgradient optimization. *Mathematical Programming*, 120(1):213–220, 2009.

G. H. Bakır, B. Taskar, T. Hofmann, B. Schölkopf, A. Smola, and S. V. N. Vishwanathan. *Predicting Structured Data.* MIT Press, 2007.

D. Barber. *Bayesian Reasoning and Machine Learning.* Cambridge University Press, 2011.

D. Batra, P. Yadollahpour, A. Guzmán-Rivera, and G. Shakhnarovich. Diverse M-best solutions in markov random fields. In *Computer Vision - ECCV 2012 - 12th European Conference on Computer Vision, Florence, Italy, October 7-13, 2012, Proceedings, Part V*, volume 7576 of *Lecture Notes in Computer Science*, pages 1–16. Springer, 2012.

J. O. Berger. *Statistical Decision Theory and Bayesian Analysis.* Springer, 1985.

J. Besag. Efficiency of pseudolikelihood estimation for simple Gaussian fields. *Biometrica*, (64):616–618, 1977.

J. E. Besag. Nearest-neighbour systems and the auto-logistic model for binary data. *Journal of the Royal Statistical Society. Series B (Methodological)*, pages 75–83, 1972.

C. M. Bishop. *Pattern Recognition and Machine Learning*. Springer, 2006.

S. P. Boyd, N. Parikh, E. Chu, B. Peleato, and J. Eckstein. Distributed optimization and statistical learning via the alternating direction method of multipliers. *Foundations and Trends in Machine Learning*, 3(1):1–122, 2011.

M. Á. Carreira-Perpiñán and G. E. Hinton. On contrastive divergence learning. In *Proceedings of the Tenth International Workshop on Artificial Intelligence and Statistics*. Society for Artificial Intelligence and Statistics NP, 2005.

W. W. Cohen and V. R. de Carvalho. Stacked sequential learning. In L. P. Kaelbling and A. Saffiotti, editors, *IJCAI-05, Proceedings of the Nineteenth International Joint Conference on Artificial Intelligence, Edinburgh, Scotland, UK, July 30-August 5, 2005*, pages 671–676. Professional Book Center, 2005.

C. Cortes, M. Mohri, and J. Weston. A general regression framework for learning string-to-string mappings. In G. Bakır, T. Hofmann, B. Schölkopf, A. J. Smola, B. Taskar, and S. V. N. Vishwanathan, editors, *Predicting Structured Data*, chapter 8, pages 143–168. MIT Press, 2007.

H. Daumé, J. Langford, and D. Marcu. Search-based structured prediction. *Machine Learning*, 75(3):297–325, 2009.

X. Descombes, R. D. Morris, J. Zerubia, and M. Berthod. Estimation of Markov random field prior parameters using Markov chain Monte Carlo maximum likelihood. *IEEE Transactions on Image Processing*, 8(7):954–963, 1999.

J. Domke. Parameter learning with truncated message-passing. In *CVPR*, pages 2937–2943. IEEE, 2011.

J. Domke. Learning graphical model parameters with approximate marginal inference. *IEEE Trans. Pattern Anal. Mach. Intell*, 35(10):2454–2467, 2013.

M. Fromer and A. Globerson. An LP view of the M-best MAP problem. In Y. Bengio, D. Schuurmans, J. D. Lafferty, C. K. I. Williams, and A. Culotta, editors, *Advances in Neural Information Processing Systems 22: 23rd Annual Conference on Neural Information Processing Systems 2009. Proceedings of a meeting held 7-10 December 2009, Vancouver, British Columbia, Canada*, pages 567–575. Curran Associates, Inc, 2009.

A. Grubb, D. Munoz, A. J. Bagnell, and M. Hebert. Speedmachines: Anytime structured prediction. *arXiv preprint arXiv:1312.0579*, 2013.

A. Guzmán-Rivera, D. Batra, and P. Kohli. Multiple choice learning: Learning to produce multiple structured outputs. In P. L. Bartlett, F. C. N. Pereira, C. J. C. Burges, L. Bottou, and K. Q. Weinberger, editors, *Advances in Neural Information Processing Systems 25: 26th Annual Conference on Neural Information Processing Systems 2012. Proceedings of a meeting held December 3-6, 2012, Lake Tahoe, Nevada, United States*, pages 1808–1816, 2012.

T. Hazan and T. Jaakkola. On the partition function and random maximum A-posteriori perturbations. In *ICML*, 2012.

T. Hazan and R. Urtasun. A primal-dual message-passing algorithm for approximated large scale structured prediction. In *Advances in Neural Information Processing Systems*, pages 838–846, 2010.

G. E. Hinton. Training products of experts by minimizing contrastive divergence. *Neural Computation*, 14(8):1771–1800, 2002.

A. Hyvärinen. Estimation of non-normalized statistical models by score matching. *JMLR*, 6:695–709, 2005. URL `http://www.jmlr.org/papers/v6/hyvarinen05a.html`.

D. Koller and N. Friedman. *Probabilistic Graphical Models - Principles and Techniques*. MIT Press, 2009.

V. Kolmogorov. Convergent tree-reweighted message passing for energy minimization. *IEEE Transactions on Pattern Analysis and Machine Intelligence*, 28(10): 1568–1583, 2006.

P. Kontschieder, P. Kohli, J. Shotton, and A. Criminisi. GeoF: Geodesic forests for learning coupled predictors. In *CVPR*, pages 65–72. IEEE, 2013.

J. D. Lafferty, A. McCallum, and F. C. N. Pereira. Conditional random fields: Probabilistic models for segmenting and labeling sequence data. In C. E. Brodley and A. P. Danyluk, editors, *Proceedings of the Eighteenth International Conference on Machine Learning (ICML 2001)*, pages 282–289. Morgan Kaufmann, 2001.

B. G. Lindsay. Composite likelihood methods. *Contemporary Mathematics*, 80, 1988.

J. L. Marroquin, S. K. Mitter, and T. A. Poggio. Probabilistic solutions of ill-posed problems in computational vision. *American Statistical Association Journal*, 82 (397):293, 1987.

O. Meshi, D. Sontag, T. Jaakkola, and A. Globerson. Learning efficiently with approximate inference via dual losses. In *Proceedings of the 27th International Conference on Machine Learning (ICML-10)*, pages 783–790. Omnipress, 2010.

T. Minka. Divergence measures and message passing. Microsoft Research Technical Report, MSR-TR-2005-173, 2005.

D. Munoz, J. A. Bagnell, and M. Hebert. Stacked hierarchical labeling. In *Computer Vision - ECCV 2010 - 11th European Conference on Computer Vision, Heraklion, Crete, Greece, September 5-11, 2010, Proceedings, Part VI*, volume 6316 of *Lecture Notes in Computer Science*, pages 57–70. Springer, 2010.

K. P. Murphy. *Machine Learning: A Probabilistic Perspective*. MIT Press, 2012.

S. Nowozin and C. H. Lampert. Structured learning and prediction in computer vision. *Foundations and Trends in Computer Graphics and Vision*, 6(3-4):185–365, 2011.

G. Papandreou and A. L. Yuille. Perturb-and-MAP random fields: Using discrete optimization to learn and sample from energy models. In *IEEE International Conference on Computer Vision, ICCV 2011, Barcelona, Spain, November 6-13, 2011*, pages 193–200. IEEE, 2011.

S. Ross, G. J. Gordon, and D. Bagnell. A reduction of imitation learning and structured prediction to no-regret online learning. In G. J. Gordon, D. B. Dunson, and M. Dudík, editors, *Proceedings of the Fourteenth International Conference on Artificial Intelligence and Statistics, AISTATS 2011, Fort Lauderdale, USA, April 11-13, 2011*, volume 15 of *JMLR Proceedings*, pages 627–635. Microtome, 2011a.

S. Ross, D. Munoz, M. Hebert, and A. J. Bagnell. Learning message-passing inference machines for structured prediction. In *Computer Vision and Pattern Recognition (CVPR)*, pages 2737–2744. IEEE, 2011b.

L. K. Saul and M. I. Jordan. Exploiting tractable substructures in intractable networks. In *NIPS*, 1995.

U. Schmidt, C. Rother, S. Nowozin, J. Jancsary, and S. Roth. Discriminative non-blind deblurring. In *CVPR*, pages 604–611. IEEE, 2013.

N. A. Smith. *Linguistic Structure Prediction.* Synthesis Lectures on Human Language Technologies. Morgan & Claypool Publishers, 2011.

V. Stoyanov, A. Ropson, and J. Eisner. Empirical risk minimization of graphical model parameters given approximate inference, decoding, and model structure. In G. J. Gordon, D. B. Dunson, and M. Dudík, editors, *AISTATS*, volume 15 of *JMLR Proceedings*, pages 725–733. Microtome, 2011.

D. Tarlow, R. P. Adams, and R. S. Zemel. Randomized optimum models for structured prediction. In N. D. Lawrence and M. Girolami, editors, *Proceedings of the Fifteenth International Conference on Artificial Intelligence and Statistics, AISTATS 2012, La Palma, Canary Islands, April 21-23, 2012*, volume 22 of *JMLR Proceedings*, pages 1221–1229. Microtome, 2012.

I. Tsochantaridis, T. Hofmann, T. Joachims, and Y. Altun. Support vector machine learning for interdependent and structured output spaces. In *Machine Learning, Proceedings of the Twenty-first International Conference (ICML 2004), Banff, Alberta, Canada, July 4-8, 2004*, volume 69. ACM, 2004.

Z. Tu. Auto-context and its application to high-level vision tasks. In *CVPR*. IEEE Computer Society, 2008.

Z. Tu and X. Bai. Auto-context and its application to high-level vision tasks and 3D brain image segmentation. *IEEE Trans. Pattern Anal. Mach. Intell*, 32(10): 1744–1757, 2010.

V. Vapnik and A. Chervonenkis. *Theory of pattern recognition (in Russian)*. Nauka, Moscow, 1974.

C. Varin, N. Reid, and D. Firth. An overview of composite likelihood methods. *Statistica Sinica*, 2010.

M. J. Wainwright and M. I. Jordan. Graphical models, exponential families, and variational inference. *Foundations and Trends in Machine Learning*, 1(1-2).1–305, 2008.

D. H. Wolpert. Stacked generalization. *Neural Networks*, 5:241–259, 1992.

E. P. Xing, M. I. Jordan, and S. J. Russell. A generalized mean field algorithm for variational inference in exponential families. In *UAI '03, Proceedings of the 19th Conference in Uncertainty in Artificial Intelligence, Acapulco, Mexico*, pages 583–591. Morgan Kaufmann, 2003.

J. S. Yedidia, W. T. Freeman, and Y. Weiss. Constructing free energy approximations and generalized belief propagation algorithms. MERL Technical Report, 2004-040, 2004. http://www.merl.com/papers/docs/TR2004-040.pdf.

2   The Power of LP Relaxation for MAP Inference

Stanislav Živný   `standa@cs.ox.ac.uk`
Department of Computer Science
University of Oxford
Oxford, UK

Tomáš Werner   `werner@cmp.felk.cvut.cz`
Daniel Průša   `prusapa1@cmp.felk.cvut.cz`
Center for Machine Perception
Faculty of Electrical Engineering
Czech Technical University
Prague, Czech Republic

Minimization of a partially separable function of many discrete variables is ubiquitous in machine learning and computer vision, in tasks like maximum a posteriori (MAP) inference in graphical models or structured prediction. Among successful approaches to this problem is linear programming (LP) relaxation. We discuss LP relaxation from two aspects. First, we review recent results that characterize languages (classes of functions permitted to form the objective function) for which the problem is solved by the relaxation exactly. Second, we show that solving the LP relaxation is not easier than solving any linear program, which makes a discovery of an efficient algorithm for the LP relaxation unlikely.

The topic of this chapter is the problem of minimizing a partially separable function of many discrete variables. That is, given a set of variables, we minimize the sum of functions each depending only on a subset of the variables. This NP-hard combinatorial optimization problem frequently arises in machine learning and computer vision, in tasks like MAP inference in graphical models (Lauritzen, 1996; Koller and Friedman, 2009; Wainwright and

Jordan, 2008) and structured prediction (Nowozin and Lampert, 2011). It is also known as discrete energy minimization or valued constraint satisfaction. The problem is formally defined in Section 2.1.

The problem has a natural linear programming (LP) relaxation, proposed independently by a number of authors (Shlezinger, 1976; Koster et al., 1998; Chekuri et al., 2005), that is defined in Section 2.2. Algorithms based on LP relaxation are among the most successful ones for tackling the problem in practice (Szeliski et al., 2008).

In this chapter, we discuss the power of the relaxation from two aspects. In the first part of the chapter, Section 2.3, we focus on the question of what languages are exactly solved by the LP relaxation. This means we consider subclasses of the problem in which the structure (hypergraph) is arbitrary but the functions belong to a given subset (language) of all possible functions. For instance, it is well known that if all the functions are submodular, then the problem is tractable, no matter what its structure is. In this case, the LP relaxation is tight. We review the recent results by Thapper and Živný (2013), Thapper and Živný (2012), Kolmogorov et al. (2013), and Kolmogorov and Živný (2013), which characterize all languages solved by the LP relaxation. This is accompanied by a number of concrete examples of such languages.

Given the (widely accepted) usefulness of the LP relaxation, many authors have proposed algorithms to solve this linear program efficiently. In the second part of the chapter, Section 2.4, we review the result by Průša and Werner (2013), which states that solving the LP relaxation is not easier than solving any linear program. This result is negative, showing that finding a very efficient algorithm for the LP relaxation is as hard as improving the complexity of the best known algorithm for general LP.

In the sequel, we denote sets by $\{\cdots\}$ and ordered tuples by $\langle\cdots\rangle$. The set of all subsets of a set A is denoted by 2^A and the set of all k-element subsets of A by $\binom{A}{k}$. For a tuple $\mathbf{x}$, we denote by x_i its ith component.

2.1   Valued Constraint Satisfaction Problem

Let V be a finite set of *variables*. Each variable $i \in V$ can take states $x_i \in D$, where the *domain* D is the same for each variable. Let $\overline{\mathbb{Q}} = \mathbb{Q} \cup \{\infty\}$ denote the set of extended rational numbers. A function $\Phi: D^V \to \overline{\mathbb{Q}}$ is *partially separable* if it can be written as

$$\Phi(\mathbf{x}) = \sum_{S \in H} \phi_S(\mathbf{x}_S) \tag{2.1}$$

where $H \subseteq 2^V$ is a collection of subsets of V (so that $\langle V, H \rangle$ is a hypergraph) and each variable subset $S \in H$ is assigned a function $\phi_S \colon D^{|S|} \to \overline{\mathbb{Q}}$. Here, $\mathbf{x}_S = \langle x_i \mid i \in S \rangle \in D^S$ denotes the restriction of the assignment $\mathbf{x} = \langle x_i \mid i \in V \rangle \in D^V$ to variables S, where the order of elements of the tuple $\mathbf{x}_S$ is given by some fixed total order on V.

Example 2.1. For $V = \{1, 2, 3, 4\}$ and $H = \{\{2, 3, 4\}, \{1, 2\}, \{2, 3\}, \{1\}\}$, we have (where we abbreviated $\phi_{\{2,3,4\}}$ by ϕ_{234}, etc.)

$$\Phi(x_1, x_2, x_3, x_4) = \phi_{234}(x_2, x_3, x_4) + \phi_{12}(x_1, x_2) + \phi_{23}(x_2, x_3) + \phi_1(x_1).$$

Our aim is to minimize function (2.1) over all assignments $\mathbf{x} \in D^V$. In this chapter, we assume that the domain D has a finite size (i.e., the variables are discrete). This problem is known under many names, such as MAP inference in graphical models (or Markov random fields), discrete energy minimization, or min-sum problem. In constraint programming (Rossi et al., 2006), it has been studied under the name *valued* (or *weighted*) *constraint satisfaction problem* (VCSP) (Schiex et al., 1995; Cohen et al., 2006b). We will follow this terminology. Here, each function ϕ_S is called a *constraint*[1] with *scope* S and *arity* $|S|$. The arity of the problem is $\max_{S \in H} |S|$. The values of the functions ϕ_S are called *costs*.

Problems involving only functions with costs from $\{0, \infty\}$ (so-called *hard* or *crisp* constraints) are known as *constraint satisfaction problems* (CSPs) (Cohen and Jeavons, 2006); these are decision problems asking for the existence of a zero-cost labeling. This type of problem has the longest history, started by the pioneering work of Montanari (1974). Problems involving functions with arbitrary costs from $\overline{\mathbb{Q}}$ are known as *valued* CSPs (VCSPs). VCSPs are sometimes called *general-valued* to emphasize the fact that the costs can be both finite (from $\mathbb{Q}$) and infinite. The following two subclasses of valued CPSs have been studied intensively in the literature. Problems involving only functions with costs from $\{0, 1\}$ are known as *maximum constraint satisfaction problems* (Max-CSPs). Problems involving only functions with costs from $\mathbb{Q}$ (so-called *soft* constraints) are known as *finite-valued* CSPs.[2]

---

1. For historical reasons, costs are often required to be non-negative in the constraint community.
2. In the approximation community, Max-CSPs are referred to as CSPs and finite-valued CSPs are referred to as generalized CSPs.

2.2   Basic LP Relaxation

The LP relaxation of VCSP reads

$$\sum_{S \in H} \sum_{\mathbf{x} \in D^S} \phi_S(\mathbf{x})\, \mu_S(\mathbf{x}) \to \min \tag{2.2a}$$

$$\sum_{\mathbf{y} \in D^S \,|\, y_i = x} \mu_S(\mathbf{y}) = \mu_i(x), \qquad i \in S \in H,\ x \in D \tag{2.2b}$$

$$\sum_{x \in D} \mu_i(x) = 1, \qquad i \in V \tag{2.2c}$$

$$\mu_S(\mathbf{x}) \geq 0, \qquad S \in H,\ \mathbf{x} \in D^S \tag{2.2d}$$

$$\mu_i(x) \geq 0, \qquad i \in V,\ x \in D \tag{2.2e}$$

We minimize over functions $\mu_S \colon D^{|S|} \to \mathbb{R}$, $S \in H$, and $\mu_i \colon D \to \mathbb{R}$, $i \in V$. These functions can be seen as probability distributions on D^S and D, respectively. The marginalization constraint (2.2b) imposes that μ_i is the marginal of μ_S for every $i \in S \in H$. In (2.2a) we define that $\infty \cdot 0 = 0$. Thus, if the LP is feasible, then $\phi_S(\mathbf{x}_S) = \infty$ implies $\mu_S(\mathbf{x}_S) = 0$.

An LP relaxation of VCSP, similar or closely related to (2.2), has been proposed independently by many authors (Shlezinger, 1976; Koster et al., 1998; Chekuri et al., 2005; Wainwright et al., 2005; Kingsford et al., 2005; Cooper, 2008; Cooper et al., 2010a; Kun et al., 2012). Equivalently, it can be understood as dual decomposition (or Lagrangian relaxation) of VCSP (Johnson et al., 2007; Komodakis et al., 2011; Sontag et al., 2011).

We refer to (2.2) as the *basic* LP relaxation (BLP) of VCSP. It is the first level in the hierarchy of Sherali and Adams (1990), which provides successively tighter LP relaxations of an integer LP. Several authors proposed finer-grained hierarchies of LP relaxations of VCSP (Wainwright and Jordan, 2008; Johnson et al., 2007; Werner, 2010; Franc et al., 2012).

2.3   Languages Solved by the BLP

In this section, we will be interested in the question of which VCSPs are exactly (as opposed to, for instance, approximately) solved by BLP. Prior to this, we focus on a more general question of which classes of VCSPs can be solved in polynomial time. Such classes are called *tractable*.

Tractability of CSPs.   Because CSPs are NP-hard in general, it is natural to study restrictions on the general framework that guarantee tractability.

The most studied are so-called *language* restrictions that impose restrictions on the types of constraints allowed in the instance. The computational complexity of language-restricted CSPs is known for problems over two-element domains (Schaefer, 1978), three-element domains (Bulatov, 2006), conservative CSPs (class of CSPs containing all unary functions) (Bulatov, 2011), and a few others (Barto et al., 2009). Most results rely heavily on algebraic methods (Jeavons et al., 1997; Bulatov et al., 2005).

Structural restrictions on CSPs do not impose any condition on the type of constraints (functions) but restrict how the constraints interact, that is, the hypergraph (Gottlob et al., 2000). Complete complexity classifications are known for structurally restricted bounded-arity CSPs (Dalmau et al., 2002; Grohe, 2007) and unbounded-arity CSPs (Marx, 2010). Some results are also known for so-called *hybrid* CSPs, which combine structural and language restrictions (see, e.g., Cooper et al. (2010b)).

Tractability of VCSPs.   The study of structural restrictions for VCSPs has not led to essentially new results as hardness results for CSPs immediately apply to (more general) VCSPs, and all known tractable (bounded-arity) structural classes for CSPs extend easily to VCSPs, see (Dechter, 2003). There are not many results on hybrid restrictions for VCSPs (Cooper and Živný, 2011, 2012), including the permuted submodular VCSPs (Schlesinger, 2007) and planar max-cut (Hadlock, 1975).

The main topic of Section 2.3 is the tractability of language-restricted VCSPs. By a *language*, we mean a set Γ of functions $\phi \colon D^r \to \overline{\mathbb{Q}}$, possibly of different arities r. For a language Γ, we denote by VCSP(Γ) the set of all VCSP instances with constraints from Γ (i.e., $\phi_S \in \Gamma$ for every $S \in H$) and an arbitrary hypergraph $\langle V, H \rangle$. We call a language Γ *tractable* if for every finite subset $\Gamma' \subseteq \Gamma$, any instance from VCSP(Γ') can be solved in polynomial time. A language Γ is called *intractable* if for some finite subset $\Gamma' \subseteq \Gamma$, the class VCSP(Γ') is NP-hard.

2.3.1   Examples of Languages

In this section, we give examples of languages and review tractability results for them that were obtained in the past.

As a motivation, we start with the well-known concept of submodularity (Schrijver, 2003; Fujishige, 2005). Let the set D be totally ordered. An r-ary function $\phi \colon D^r \to \overline{\mathbb{Q}}$ is *submodular* if and only if, for every $\mathbf{x}, \mathbf{y} \in D^r$,

$$\phi(\mathbf{x}) + \phi(\mathbf{y}) \;\geq\; \phi(\min(\mathbf{x}, \mathbf{y})) + \phi(\max(\mathbf{x}, \mathbf{y})). \tag{2.3}$$

Here, min and max returns the component-wise minimum and maximum, respectively, of its two arguments, with respect to the total order on D.

The definition of submodularity can be straightforwardly generalized as follows. A binary *operation* is a mapping $f\colon D^2 \to D$. For r-tuples $\mathbf{x}, \mathbf{y} \in D^r$, we denote by $f(\mathbf{x}, \mathbf{y})$ the result of applying f on $\mathbf{x}$ and $\mathbf{y}$ component-wise, that is, $f(\mathbf{x}, \mathbf{y}) = (f(x_1, y_1), \ldots, f(x_r, y_r)) \in D^r$.

Definition 2.1 (Binary multimorphism (Cohen et al., 2006b)). *Let $f, g\colon D^2 \to D$ be binary operations. We say that an r-ary function $\phi\colon D^r \to \overline{\mathbb{Q}}$ admits $\langle f, g \rangle$ as a* multimorphism *if for all $\mathbf{x}, \mathbf{y} \in D^r$ it holds that*

$$\phi(\mathbf{x}) + \phi(\mathbf{y}) \;\geq\; \phi(f(\mathbf{x}, \mathbf{y})) + \phi(g(\mathbf{x}, \mathbf{y})). \tag{2.4}$$

We say that a language Γ admits $\langle f, g \rangle$ as a multimorphism if every function $\phi \in \Gamma$ admits $\langle f, g \rangle$ as a multimorphism.

Example 2.2 (Submodularity). Let Γ be the set of functions $\phi\colon D^r \to \overline{\mathbb{Q}}$ (with D totally ordered and $r \geq 1$) that admit $\langle \min, \max \rangle$ as a multimorphism. Using a polynomial-time algorithm for minimizing submodular set functions (Schrijver, 2000; Iwata et al., 2001), Cohen et al. (2006b) have shown that the language Γ is tractable. For $\mathbb{Q}$-valued functions, this also immediately follows from the result by Schlesinger and Flach (2006).

Example 2.3 (Bisubmodularity). Let $D = \{0, 1, 2\}$. We define two binary operations $\min_0$ and $\max_0$ by

$$\min_0(x, y) \;=\; \begin{cases} 0 & \text{if } 0 \neq x \neq y \neq 0 \\ \min(x, y) & \text{otherwise} \end{cases},$$

$$\max_0(x, y) \;=\; \begin{cases} 0 & \text{if } 0 \neq x \neq y \neq 0 \\ \max(x, y) & \text{otherwise} \end{cases}.$$

Let Γ be the set of functions admitting $\langle \min_0, \max_0 \rangle$ as a multimorphism. These functions are known as *bisubmodular* functions. The language Γ has been shown tractable for $\mathbb{Q}$-valued functions (even if given by oracles) by Fujishige and Iwata (2005).

Example 2.4 (k-submodularity). Let Γ be the set of functions called *k-submodular*, with $D = \{0, 1, \ldots, d\}$ for some $d \geq 2$ and admitting $\langle \min_0, \max_0 \rangle$, defined in Example 2.3, as a multimorphism. The tractability of this language for $d \geq 3$ was left open in the work of Huber and Kolmogorov (2012).

Example 2.5 ((Symmetric) tournament pair). A *tournament* operation is a binary operation $f\colon D^2 \to D$ such that (i) f is commutative (i.e., $f(x, y) = $

$f(y, x)$ for all $x, y \in D$), and (ii) f is conservative (i.e., $f(x, y) \in \{x, y\}$ for all $x, y \in D$). The *dual* of a tournament operation is the unique tournament operation g satisfying $x \neq y \Rightarrow f(x, y) \neq g(x, y)$. A *tournament pair* is a pair $\langle f, g \rangle$ where f and g are tournament operations. A tournament pair $\langle f, g \rangle$ is *symmetric* if g is the dual of f.

Let Γ be a $\overline{\mathbb{Q}}$-valued language that admits a symmetric tournament pair (STP) multimorphism. Cohen et al. (2008) have shown, by a reduction to the minimization problem for submodular functions (see Example 2.2), that any such Γ is tractable.

Let Γ be an arbitrary $\overline{\mathbb{Q}}$-valued language that admits any tournament pair multimorphism. Cohen et al. (2008) have shown, by a reduction to the symmetric tournament pair case, that any such Γ is also tractable.

Example 2.6 (Strong tree-submodularity). Let the elements of D be arranged into a tree, T. Given $a, b \in T$, let P_{ab} denote the unique path in T between a and b of length (number of edges) $d(a, b)$, and let $P_{ab}[i]$ denote the ith vertex on P_{ab}, where $0 \leq i \leq d(a, b)$ and $P_{ab}[0] = a$. Define the binary operations $f(a, b) = P_{ab}[\lfloor d(a, b)/2 \rfloor]$ and $g(a, b) = P_{ab}[\lceil d(a, b)/2 \rceil]$.

A function (or language) admitting $\langle f, g \rangle$ as a multimorphism has been called *strongly tree-submodular*. The tractability of $\mathbb{Q}$-valued strongly tree-submodular languages on binary trees has been shown by Kolmogorov (2011), but the tractability of strongly tree-submodular languages on non-binary trees was left open.

Example 2.7 (Weak tree-submodularity). Assume that the elements of D form a rooted tree T. For $a, b \in T$, let $f(a, b)$ be defined as the highest common ancestor of a and b in T, that is, the unique node on the path P_{ab} that is an ancestor of both a and b. Let $g(a, b)$ be the unique node on the path P_{ab} such that the distance between a and $g(a, b)$ is the same as the distance between b and $f(a, b)$.

A function (or language) admitting $\langle f, g \rangle$ as a multimorphism has been called *weakly tree-submodular*, because it can be shown that tree-submodularity implies weak tree-submodularity. The tractability of $\mathbb{Q}$-valued weakly tree-submodular languages on chains[3] and forks[4] has been shown by Kolmogorov (2011) and left open for all other trees.

Note that k-submodular functions are a special case of weakly tree-submodular functions, obtained for $D = \{0, 1, \ldots, d\}$ and T consisting of the root node 0 and d children.

---

3. A chain is a binary tree in which all nodes except leaves have exactly one child.
4. A fork is a binary tree in which all nodes except leaves and one special node have exactly one child. The special node has exactly two children.

Example 2.8 (1-defect). Let b and c be two distinct elements of D and let $\preceq$ be a partial order on D, which relates all pairs of elements except for b and c. We call $\langle f, g \rangle$, where $f, g \colon D^2 \to D$ are binary operations, a *1-defect* if f and g are both commutative and satisfy the following conditions:

- If $\{x, y\} \neq \{b, c\}$ then $f(x, y) = \min(x, y)$ and $g(x, y) = \max(x, y)$.
- If $\{x, y\} = \{b, c\}$ then $\{f(x, y), g(x, y)\} \cap \{x, y\} = \emptyset$ and $f(x, y) \preceq g(x, y)$.

The tractability of $\mathbb{Q}$-valued languages that admit a 1-defect multimorphism has been shown by Jonsson et al. (2011). This result generalizes the tractability result for weakly tree-submodular languages on chains and forks but is incomparable with the tractability result for strongly tree-submodular languages on binary trees.

Example 2.9 (Submodularity on lattices). Let the set D, endowed with a partial order, form a lattice with the meet operation $\wedge$ and the join operation $\vee$. Let Γ be the language admitting $\langle \wedge, \vee \rangle$ as a multimorphism.

If the lattice is a chain (i.e., the order on D is total), we obtain the language of submodular functions (Example 2.2). For distributive lattices, the tractability of Γ has been established by Schrijver (2000). Until recently, the tractability of Γ for non-distributive lattices was widely open, and only partial results were known (Krokhin and Larose, 2008; Kuivinen, 2011), but the work of Thapper and Živný (2012), which we will discuss in Sections 2.3.2 and 2.3.3, settled this question.

Example 2.10 (Conservative languages). A language that contains all unary functions (and possibly some other functions) is called *conservative*. Kolmogorov and Živný (2013) have shown that a $\mathbb{Q}$-valued conservative language can be only tractable if it admits an STP multimorphism (see Example 2.5). Kolmogorov and Živný (2013), in Theorem 3.5, have given a precise condition under which a $\overline{\mathbb{Q}}$-valued conservative language is tractable. This condition is somewhat technical so we will not state it here, but we mention that it involves a pair of complementary multimorphisms: one is an STP multimorphism and the other one is a ternary[5] multimorphism involving two majority and one minority operations. The algorithm involves a preprocessing step, after which the resulting instance admits an STP multimorphism.

---

5. In order to state the property precisely, one needs to generalize Definition 2.1 to a triple of ternary operations, see (Kolmogorov and Živný, 2013) for more details.

Example 2.11 (Potts model). Let Γ contain all unary functions and a single binary function $\phi_{\mathsf{Potts}}\colon D^2 \to \mathbb{Q}$ defined by

$$\phi_{\mathsf{Potts}}(x, y) = \begin{cases} 0 & \text{if } x = y \\ 1 & \text{if } x \neq y \end{cases}.$$

This conservative language is known in statistical mechanics as the Potts model with external field (Mezard and Montanari, 2009) and is frequently used for image segmentation (Rother et al., 2004). For $|D| = 2$, ϕ_{Potts} is submodular and hence Γ is tractable. For $|D| > 2$, Γ is intractable.

Example 2.12 (Max-Cut). Let Γ contain a single function $\phi_{\mathsf{mc}}\colon D^2 \to \mathbb{Q}$ defined by

$$\phi_{\mathsf{mc}}(x, y) = \begin{cases} 1 & \text{if } x = y \\ 0 & \text{if } x \neq y \end{cases}.$$

This language models the well-known Max-Cut problem (Garey and Johnson, 1979) and thus Γ is intractable for any $|D| \geq 2$.

2.3.2 Power of BLP for Finite-Valued Languages

Given the long list of examples from Section 2.3.1, one might expect that perhaps multimorphism could define *all* tractable languages. It turns out that this is not the case, and in order to capture more tractable languages, one needs to consider a more general notion. We start with an example.

Example 2.13 (Skew bisubmodularity). We extend the notion of bisubmodularity (Example 2.3) to *skew bisubmodularity* introduced by Huber et al. (2013). Let $D = \{0, 1, 2\}$. Recall the definition of operations $\min_0$ and $\max_0$ from Example 2.3. We define

$$\max_1(x, y) = \begin{cases} 1 & \text{if } 0 \neq x \neq y \neq 0 \\ \max(x, y) & \text{otherwise} \end{cases}.$$

A function $\phi\colon D^r \to \overline{\mathbb{Q}}$ is called α-bisubmodular, for some real $0 < \alpha \leq 1$, if for every $\mathbf{x}, \mathbf{y} \in D^r$,

$$\phi(\mathbf{x}) + \phi(\mathbf{y}) \geq \phi(\min_0(\mathbf{x}, \mathbf{y})) + \alpha\phi(\max_0(\mathbf{x}, \mathbf{y})) + (1 - \alpha)f(\max_1(\mathbf{x}, \mathbf{y})).$$

Note that 1-bisubmodular functions are (ordinary) bisubmodular functions.

The previous example suggests that it is not enough to consider only two operations with equal weight. In fact it is necessary to consider *probability distributions* over *all* binary operations. We denote by $\Omega_D^{(2)}$ the set of all binary operations $f\colon D^2 \to D$.

Definition 2.2 (Binary fractional polymorphism (Cohen et al., 2006a)). *Let ω be a probability distribution on $\Omega_D^{(2)}$. We say that ω is a* binary fractional polymorphism *of an r-ary function $\phi\colon D^r \to \mathbb{Q}$ if, for every $\mathbf{x}, \mathbf{y} \in D^r$,*

$$\frac{1}{2}(\phi(\mathbf{x}) + \phi(\mathbf{y})) \geq \sum_{f \in \Omega_D^{(2)}} \omega(f)\,\phi(f(\mathbf{x}, \mathbf{y})). \tag{2.5}$$

One can see the LHS of (2.5) as the average of $\phi(\mathbf{x})$ and $\phi(\mathbf{y})$ and the RHS as the expectation of $\phi(f(\mathbf{x}, \mathbf{y}))$ with respect to the probability distribution ω. We define the *support* of ω to be the set

$$\operatorname{supp}(\omega) = \{\, f \mid \omega(f) \neq 0 \,\} \tag{2.6}$$

of operations that get non-zero probability.

Note that a binary multimorphism $\langle f, g \rangle$ is a fractional polymorphism ω defined by $\omega(f) = \omega(g) = \frac{1}{2}$ and $\omega(h) = 0$ for all $h \notin \{f, g\}$. In this case, we have $\operatorname{supp}(\omega) = \{f, g\}$ and inequality (2.5) simplifies to (2.4).

A binary fractional polymorphism ω defined on D is called *symmetric* if every function from the support of ω is symmetric, that is, every $f \in \operatorname{supp}(\omega)$ satisfies $f(x, y) = f(y, x)$ for every $x, y \in D$. The following result is a consequence of the work of Thapper and Živný (2012) and Kolmogorov (2013), see also (Kolmogorov et al., 2013).

Theorem 2.1. *Let Γ be a $\mathbb{Q}$-valued language with a finite domain D. BLP solves all instance from $\mathrm{VCSP}(\Gamma)$ if and only if Γ admits a binary symmetric fractional polymorphism.*

Note that Theorem 2.1 proves tractability of all $\mathbb{Q}$-valued languages defined in Examples 2.2–2.10 as well as the skew bisubmodular languages defined in Example 2.13.

The following surprising result, due to Thapper and Živný (2013), shows that languages defined by binary symmetric fractional polymorphisms are the *only* tractable languages.

Theorem 2.2. *Let Γ be a $\mathbb{Q}$-valued language with a finite domain D. Either Γ admits a binary symmetric fractional polymorphism or $\mathrm{VCSP}(\Gamma)$ can be reduced to Max-Cut and thus is NP-hard.*

We remark that the reduction to Max-Cut mentioned in Theorem 2.2 is not just a polynomial-time reduction but a so-called *expressibility* reduction (Živný, 2012). Moreover, for a finite language Γ, one can test for the existence of a binary symmetric fractional polymorphism of Γ via a linear program that has polynomial size in $|\Gamma|$ and double-exponential size in $|D|$. More details can be found in Thapper and Živný (2013).

2.3.3   Power of BLP for General-Valued Languages

In Section 2.3.2, we have given a complete characterization of tractable $\mathbb{Q}$-valued languages and have shown that BLP solves them all. In this section, we will deal with $\overline{\mathbb{Q}}$-valued languages.

First, we will be interested in the question of which $\overline{\mathbb{Q}}$-valued languages are solvable by BLP. In order to do so, we need to extend the definition of binary fractional polymorphisms in two ways: to $\overline{\mathbb{Q}}$-valued functions and to fractional polymorphisms of arbitrary arities.

A k-ary *operation* is a mapping $f\colon D^k \to D$. We denote by $\Omega_D^{(k)}$ the set of all k-ary operations on D.

Definition 2.3 (Fractional polymorphism (Cohen et al., 2006a))**.** *Let ω be a probability distribution on $\Omega_D^{(k)}$. We say that ω is a k-ary fractional polymorphism of an r-ary function $\phi\colon D^r \to \overline{\mathbb{Q}}$ if, for every $\mathbf{x}^1, \ldots, \mathbf{x}^k \in D^r$,*

$$\frac{1}{k} \sum_{i=1}^{k} \phi(\mathbf{x}^i) \;\geq\; \sum_{f \in \Omega_D^{(k)}} \omega(f)\, \phi(f(\mathbf{x}^1, \ldots, \mathbf{x}^k)), \tag{2.7}$$

where we define $0 \cdot \infty = 0$ on the RHS of (2.7).

The support of ω is defined by (2.6). A k-ary fractional polymorphism ω is *symmetric* if every $f \in \mathrm{supp}(\omega)$ satisfies $f(x_1, \ldots, x_k) = f(x_{\pi(1)}, \ldots, x_{\pi(k)})$ for every $x_1, \ldots, x_k \in D$ and every permutation π on $\{1, \ldots, k\}$.

The following characterization of the power of BLP for general-valued languages is due to Thapper and Živný (2012), see also (Kolmogorov et al., 2013).

Theorem 2.3. *Let Γ be a $\overline{\mathbb{Q}}$-valued language with a finite domain D. BLP solves all instances from* $\mathrm{VCSP}(\Gamma)$ *if and only if Γ admits a k-ary symmetric fractional polymorphism of every arity $k \geq 2$.*

Note that, unlike in the $\mathbb{Q}$-valued case (Theorem 2.1), it is not clear whether the characterization given in Theorem 2.3 is decidable. Nevertheless, Thapper and Živný (2012) have also given a sufficient condition on Γ for BLP to solve all instances from $\mathrm{VCSP}(\Gamma)$. We state this condition in Theorem 2.4.

A k-ary projection (on the ith coordinate) is the operation $e_i^{(k)}\colon D^k \to D$ defined by $e_i^{(k)}(x_1, \ldots, x_k) = x_i$. A set $\mathcal{O}$ of operations defined on D *generates* an operation f if f can be obtained by composition from projections (of arbitrary arities) and operations from O.

Theorem 2.4. *Let Γ be a $\overline{\mathbb{Q}}$-valued language with a finite domain D. Suppose that Γ admits a k-ary fractional polymorphism ω such that $\operatorname{supp}(\omega)$ generates an m-ary symmetric operation. Then Γ admits an m-ary symmetric fractional polymorphism.*

Corollary 2.5. *Let Γ be a $\overline{\mathbb{Q}}$-valued language with a finite domain D. Suppose that for every $k \geq 2$, Γ admits a (not necessarily k-ary) fractional polymorphisms ω so that $\operatorname{supp}(\omega)$ generates a k-ary symmetric operation. Then BLP solves any instance from $\operatorname{VCSP}(\Gamma)$.*

Note that the condition (of admitting symmetric fractional polymorphisms of all arities) from Theorem 2.3 trivially implies the condition from Corollary 2.5, thus showing that the condition from Corollary 2.5 is a characterization of the power of BLP.

A binary operation $f\colon D^2 \to D$ is called a *semi-lattice operation* if f is associative, commutative, and idempotent. Because any semi-lattice operation trivially generates symmetric operations of all arities, Corollary 2.5 shows that most $\overline{\mathbb{Q}}$-valued languages defined in Examples 2.2–2.10 as well as the skew bisubmodular languages from Example 2.13 are tractable. In the case of 1-defect languages from Example 2.8, a bit more work is needed to show the existence of symmetric operations of all arities, see (Thapper and Živný, 2012) for details. The $\overline{\mathbb{Q}}$-valued languages defined in Example 2.5 can be reduced, via a preprocessing described by Cohen et al. (2008), to an instance that is submodular and thus solvable by BLP as described in Example 2.2. The $\overline{\mathbb{Q}}$-valued languages defined in Example 2.10 can be reduced, via a preprocessing described by Kolmogorov and Živný (2013), to an instance that is submodular and thus solvable by BLP (see Example 2.2).

We finish this section with mentioning that obtaining a full complexity classification of all general-valued languages is extremely challenging. Indeed, even a classification of $\{0, \infty\}$-valued languages is not known. The so-called *Feder-Vardi Conjecture* (Feder and Vardi, 1998) states that every $\{0, \infty\}$-valued language is either tractable or intractable (note that assuming $P \neq NP$, Ladner (1975) showed that there are problems of intermediate complexity). However, there are some interesting results in this area. First, general-valued languages on two-element domains have been classified by Cohen et al. (2006b). Second, an algebraic theory providing a powerful tool for analyzing the complexity of general-valued languages has been established by Cohen et al. (2011, 2013) and already used for simplifying the hardness part of the classification of general-valued languages on two-element domains (Creed and Živný, 2011). Finally, conservative general-valued languages (see Example 2.10) have been completely classified by Kolmogorov and Živný (2013).

2.4 Universality of the BLP

We have seen that the BLP relaxation solves many VCSP languages. Moreover, it has been empirically observed (Wainwright et al., 2005; Kolmogorov, 2006; Werner, 2007; Szeliski et al., 2008; Kappes et al., 2013) that it is tight for many VCSP instances that do not belong to any known tractable class. For other instances, it yields lower bounds, which can be used, for instance, in exact search algorithms. For all these reasons, solving the BLP is of great practical interest.

The popular simplex and interior point methods are, due to their quadratic space complexity, applicable in practice only to small BLP instances. For larger instances, BLP can be solved efficiently for binary VCSPs with domain size $|D| = 2$ because in this case, BLP can be reduced in linear time to the max-flow problem (Boros and Hammer, 2002; Rother et al., 2007). A lot of effort has been invested to develop efficient algorithms to exactly solve the BLP of more general VCSPs. Among the proposed algorithms are those based on subgradient methods (Schlesinger and Giginjak, 2007; Komodakis et al., 2011), smoothing methods (Weiss et al., 2007; Johnson et al., 2007; Ravikumar et al., 2008; Savchynskyy et al., 2011), and augmented Lagrangian methods (Martins et al., 2011; Schmidt et al., 2011; Meshi and Globerson, 2011).

In this section, we show that solving linear program (2.2) is not easier than solving an arbitrary linear program, in the following sense.

Theorem 2.6 (Průša and Werner (2013)). *Every linear program can be reduced in linear time to the BLP relaxation (2.2) of a binary $\overline{\mathbb{Q}}$-valued VCSP with domain size $|D| = 3$.*

This result suggests that trying to find an efficient algorithm to exactly solve the BLP may be futile because it might mean improving the complexity of the best known algorithm for general LP, which is unlikely.

In the rest of this section, we prove Theorem 2.6 by giving an algorithm that, for an arbitrary input LP, constructs a binary $\overline{\mathbb{Q}}$-valued VCSP with $|D| = 3$ whose basic LP relaxation solves the input LP.

2.4.1   The Input Linear Program

The input linear program minimizes $\mathbf{c} \cdot \mathbf{x}$ over the polyhedron

$$P = \{\, \mathbf{x} = \langle x_1, \ldots, x_n \rangle \in \mathbb{R}^n \mid \mathbf{A}\mathbf{x} = \mathbf{b}, \ \mathbf{x} \geq \mathbf{0} \,\}, \tag{2.8}$$

where $\mathbf{A} = [a_{ij}] \in \mathbb{Z}^{m \times n}$, $\mathbf{b} = \langle b_1, \ldots, b_m \rangle \in \mathbb{Z}^m$, $\mathbf{c} = \langle c_1, \ldots, c_n \rangle \in \mathbb{Z}^n$, and $m \leq n$. Any LP representable by a finite number of bits can be described this way.

Before encoding, the system $\mathbf{A}\mathbf{x} = \mathbf{b}$ is rewritten as follows. Each equation

$$a_{i1}x_1 + \cdots + a_{in}x_n = b_i \tag{2.9}$$

is rewritten as

$$a_{i1}^+ x_1 + \cdots + a_{in}^+ x_n = a_{i1}^- x_1 + \cdots + a_{in}^- x_n + b_i \tag{2.10}$$

where $b_i \geq 0$, $a_{ij}^+ \geq 0$, $a_{ij}^- \geq 0$, and $a_{ij} = a_{ij}^+ - a_{ij}^-$. Moreover, it is assumed without loss of generality that neither side of (2.10) vanishes for any feasible $\mathbf{x}$.

The following lemmas are not surprising. Their proofs can be found in Průša and Werner (2013).

Lemma 2.7. *Let* $\mathbf{x} = \langle x_1, \ldots, x_n \rangle$ *be a vertex of the polyhedron* P. *Each component* x_j *of* $\mathbf{x}$ *satisfies either* $x_j = 0$ *or* $M^{-1} \leq x_j \leq M$, *where*

$$M = m^{m/2}(B_1 \times \cdots \times B_{n+1})$$
$$B_j = \max(1, |a_{1j}|, \ldots, |a_{mj}|), \quad j = 1, \ldots, n$$
$$B_{n+1} = \max(1, |b_1|, \ldots |b_m|).$$

Lemma 2.8. *Let* P *be bounded. Then for any* $\mathbf{x} \in P$, *each component of* $\mathbf{A}^+ \mathbf{x}$ *and* $\mathbf{A}^- \mathbf{x} + \mathbf{b}$ *is not greater than* $N = M(B_1 + \cdots + B_{n+1})$.

The last lemma shows that we can restrict ourselves to input LPs with a bounded polyhedron P.

Lemma 2.9. *Every linear program can be reduced in linear time to a linear program over a bounded polyhedron.*

2.4.2   Elementary Constructions

The output of the reduction will be a VCSP with domain size $|D| = 3$ and hypergraph $H = \binom{V}{1} \cup E$ where $E \subseteq \binom{V}{2}$ (i.e., there is a unary constraint for each variable and binary constraints for a subset of variable pairs). We

Figure 2.1: A pair of variables $\{i, j\} \in E$ with $|D| = 3$. Each variable is depicted as a box, its state $x \in D$ as a circle, and each state pair $\langle x, y \rangle \in D^2$ of two variables as an edge. Each circle is assigned a unary pseudomarginal $\mu_i(x)$ and each edge is assigned a binary pseudomarginal $\mu_{ij}(x, y)$. One normalization condition (2.2c) imposes for unary pseudomarginals a, b, c that $a + b + c = 1$. One marginalization condition (2.2b) imposes for pairwise pseudomarginals p, q, r that $a = p + q + r$.

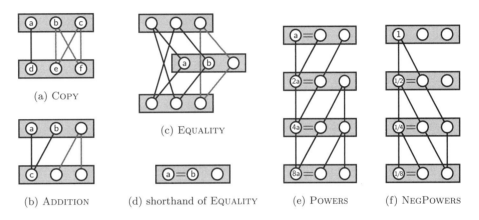

(a) COPY

(c) EQUALITY

(b) ADDITION

(d) shorthand of EQUALITY

(e) POWERS

(f) NEGPOWERS

Figure 2.2: Elementary constructions. The visible edges have costs $\phi_{ij}(x, y) = 0$ and the invisible edges have costs $\phi_{ij}(x, y) = \infty$. Different line styles of the visible edges distinguish different elementary constructions.

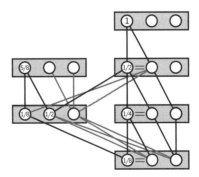

Figure 2.3: Construction of a unary pseudomarginal with value $\frac{5}{8}$. The example can be generalized in an obvious way to construct the value $2^{-d}k$ for any $d, k \in \mathbb{N}$ such that $2^{-d}k \leq 1$. If more than two values are added, intermediate results are stored in auxiliary variables using COPY.

denote the binary constraints ϕ_S for $S = \{i, j\} \in E$ by ϕ_{ij}. Following Wainwright and Jordan (2008), we refer to the values of the functions μ_i and μ_{ij} as unary and binary *pseudomarginals*, respectively.

We will depict binary VCSPs by diagrams, commonly used in the constraint programming literature. Figure 2.1 illustrates the meaning of conditions (2.2b) and (2.2c) of the BLP in these diagrams.

The encoding algorithm uses several elementary constructions as its building blocks. Each construction is a stand-alone VCSP with crisp binary constraints, $\phi_{ij}: D^2 \to \{0, \infty\}$, that imposes a certain simple constraint on feasible unary pseudomarginals. Note that for any feasible pseudomarginals, $\phi_{ij}(x, y) = \infty$ implies $\mu_{ij}(x, y) = 0$. Each construction is defined by a diagram, in which visible edges have cost $\phi_{ij}(x, y) = 0$ and invisible edges have cost $\phi_{ij}(x, y) = \infty$. The elementary constructions are as follows:

COPY, Figure 2.2(a), enforces equality of two unary pseudomarginals a, d in two variables $\{i, j\} \in E$ while imposing no other constraints on b, c, e, f. Precisely, if $a, b, c, d, e, f \geq 0$ and $a + b + c = 1 = d + e + f$, then there exist pairwise pseudomarginals feasible to (2.2) if and only if $a = d$.

ADDITION, Figure 2.2(b), adds two unary pseudomarginals a, b in one variable and represents the result as a unary pseudomarginal $c = a + b$ in another variable. No other constraints are imposed on the remaining unary pseudomarginals.

EQUALITY, Figure 2.2(c), enforces equality of two unary pseudomarginals a, b in a single variable, introducing two auxiliary variables. No other constraints are imposed on the remaining unary pseudomarginals. In the sequel, this construction will be abbreviated by omitting the two auxiliary variables and writing the equality sign between the two circles, as in Figure 2.2(d).

POWERS, Figure 2.2(e), creates the sequence of unary pseudomarginals with values $2^i a$ for $i = 0, \dots, d$, each in a separate variable. We will call d the *depth* of the pyramid.

NEGPOWERS, Figure 2.2(f), is similar to POWERS but constructs values 2^{-i} for $i = 0, \dots, d$.

Figure 2.3 shows an example of how the elementary constructions can be combined.

2.4.3   Encoding

Now we will formulate the encoding algorithm. The variables of the output VCSP and their states will be numbered by integers, $D = \{1, 2, 3\}$ and $V = \{1, \dots, |V|\}$.

The algorithm is initialized as follows:

1.1. For each variable x_j in the input LP, introduce a new variable j into V and set $\phi_j(1) = c_j$. Pseudomarginal $\mu_j(1)$ will represent variable x_j. After this step, we have $V = \{1, \ldots, n\}$.

1.2. For each variable $j \in V$, build POWERS with the depth $d_j = \lfloor \log_2 B_j \rfloor$ based on state 1. This yields the sequence of numbers $2^i \mu_j(1)$, $i = 0, \ldots, d_j$.

1.3. Build NEGPOWERS with the depth $d = \lceil \log_2 N \rceil$. By Lemma 2.8, the choice of d ensures that all values represented by pseudomarginals will be bounded by 1.

After initialization, the algorithm proceeds by encoding each equation (2.10) in turn. The ith equation (2.10) is encoded as follows:

2.1. Construct pseudomarginals with values $a_{ij}^+ x_j$, $a_{ij}^- x_j$, $j = 1, \ldots, n$, by summing selected values from POWERS built in Step 1.2, similarly as in Figure 2.3.

2.2. Construct a pseudomarginal with value $2^{-d} b_i$ by summing selected values from the NEGPOWERS built in Step 1.3, similarly as in Figure 2.3. The value $2^{-d} b_i$ represents b_i, which sets the scale between the input and output polyhedron to 2^{-d}.

2.3. Represent each side of the equation by summing all its terms by repetitively applying ADDITION and COPY.

2.4. Apply COPY to enforce equality of the two sides of the equation.

Finally, set $\phi_i(x) = 0$ for all $i > n$ or $x \in \{2, 3\}$.

Figure 2.4 shows the output VCSP for an example input LP.

2.4.4   The Length of the Encoding

Here we finalize the proof of Theorem 2.6 by showing that the encoding time is linear. Since the encoding of vector $\mathbf{c}$ is clearly done in linear time, it suffices to show that the encoding time is linear in the length L of the binary representation of matrix $\mathbf{A}$ and vector $\mathbf{b}$. Because this time is obviously linear[6] in $|E|$, it suffices to show that $|E| = \mathcal{O}(L)$.

---

6. The only thing that may not be obvious is how to multiply large integers a, b in linear time. But this issue can be avoided by instead computing $p(a, b) = 2^{\lceil \log_2 a \rceil + \lceil \log_2 b \rceil}$, which can be done in linear time using bitwise operations. Because $ab \leq p(a, b) \leq (2a)(2b)$, the bounds like M become larger, but this does not affect the overall complexity.

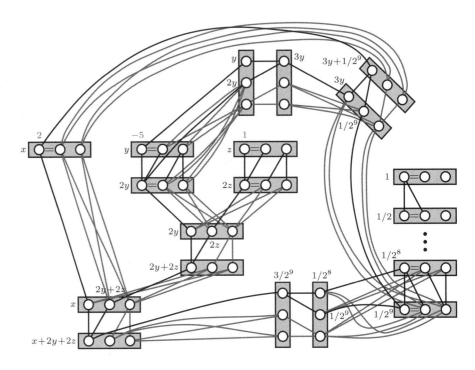

Figure 2.4: The VCSP whose BLP relaxation solves the linear program $\min\{\,2x - 5y + z \mid x + 2y + 2z = 3;\ x = 3y + 1;\ x, y, z \ge 0\,\}$.

Variable pairs are created only when a variable is created and the number of variable pairs added with one variable is always bounded by a constant. Therefore, $|E| = \mathcal{O}(|V|)$.

We clearly have the inequality $L \ge \max(mn, \log_2 B_1 + \cdots + \log_2 B_{n+1})$. The algorithm creates $\sum_{j=1}^{n}(d_j + 1)$ variables in Step 1.2 and $d+1$ variables in Step 1.3. By comparison with the above inequality, both of these numbers are $\mathcal{O}(L)$.

Finally, encoding one equality (2.10) adds at most as many variables as there are bits in the binary representation of all its coefficients. The cumulative sum is thus $\mathcal{O}(L)$.

2.5   Conclusions

LP relaxation is a successful approach to the problem of minimizing a partially separable function of many discrete variables, which is also known as the VCSP. In this chapter, we have presented two types of theoretial results on the BLP relaxation of VCSP: in Section 2.3, we characterized languages solves exactly by BLP, and in Section 2.4, we showed that solving BLP is as hard as solving an arbitrary LP.

These results suggest a number of questions. The first class of questions concerns the fact that rather than finding a global optimum of the LP relaxation, it is easier to find its local dual optimum with respect to block-coordinate moves. The latter in fact means reparameterizing the problem such that the locally minimal tuples are arc consistent (Shlezinger, 1976; Werner, 2007), which has been called *virtual arc consistency* by Cooper et al. (2010a). Virtual arc consistency is enforced by the popular message-passing algorithms such as min-sum diffusion (Kovalevsky and Koval, approx. 1975; Werner, 2007, 2010), TRW-S (Kolmogorov, 2006) (see its generalization to VCSPs of any arity in Chapter 4), and MPLP (Globerson and Jaakkola, 2008; Sontag et al., 2011), as well as by the algorithms (Koval and Schlesinger, 1976; Cooper et al., 2010a). Regarding Section 2.3, one can ask which languages are solved by enforcing virtual arc consistency. For instance, it is known that enforcing virtual arc consistency solves submodular languages of any arity (Werner, 2010; Cooper et al., 2010a), but for other languages, the question is open. Regarding Section 2.4, one can ask whether enforcing virtual arc consistency is easier than solving the BLP exactly.

Recall that one can construct, in a number of ways, a hierarchy of increasingly tighter LP relaxations of VCSP (Sherali and Adams, 1990; Wainwright and Jordan, 2008; Johnson et al., 2007; Werner, 2010; Franc et al., 2012). BLP (2.2) is only one level of this hierarchy. As the second question, one can ask how much power these higher-order relaxations add to BLP. Theorems 2.1 and 2.2 imply the surprising fact that *all* tractable finite-valued languages are solved by BLP; hence, higher-order relaxations do not allow us to solve any more languages. However, could BLP and more generally higher-order relaxations be useful for interesting, not necessarily language-restricted, classes of VCSPs?

Acknowledgments

D. Průša and T. Werner have been supported by the Grant Agency of the Czech Republic project P202/12/2071. D. Průša has been supported by the EC project FP7-ICT-247525 and T. Werner by the EC project FP7-ICT-270138.

2.6   References

L. Barto, M. Kozik, and T. Niven. The CSP dichotomy holds for digraphs with no sources and no sinks (a positive answer to a conjecture of Bang-Jensen and Hell). *SIAM Journal on Computing*, 38(5):1782–1802, 2009.

E. Boros and P. L. Hammer. Pseudo-Boolean optimization. *Discrete Applied Mathematics*, 123(1-3):155–225, 2002.

A. Bulatov. A dichotomy theorem for constraint satisfaction problems on a 3-element set. *Journal of the ACM*, 53(1):66–120, 2006.

A. Bulatov. Complexity of conservative constraint satisfaction problems. *ACM Transactions on Computational Logic*, 12(4), 2011. Article 24.

A. Bulatov, A. Krokhin, and P. Jeavons. Classifying the complexity of constraints using finite algebras. *SIAM Journal on Computing*, 34(3):720–742, 2005.

C. Chekuri, S. Khanna, J. Naor, and L. Zosin. A linear programming formulation and approximation algorithms for the metric labeling problem. *SIAM Journal on Discrete Mathematics*, 18(3):608–625, 2005.

D. Cohen and P. Jeavons. The complexity of constraint languages. In F. Rossi, P. van Beek, and T. Walsh, editors, *The Handbook of Constraint Programming*. Elsevier, 2006.

D. A. Cohen, M. C. Cooper, and P. G. Jeavons. An algebraic characterisation of complexity for valued constraints. In *Intl. Conf. on Principles and Practice of Constraint Programming (CP)*, pages 107–121. Springer, 2006a.

D. A. Cohen, M. C. Cooper, P. G. Jeavons, and A. A. Krokhin. The complexity of soft constraint satisfaction. *Artificial Intelligence*, 170(11):983–1016, 2006b.

D. A. Cohen, M. C. Cooper, and P. G. Jeavons. Generalising submodularity and Horn clauses: Tractable optimization problems defined by tournament pair multimorphisms. *Theoretical Computer Science*, 401(1-3):36–51, 2008.

D. A. Cohen, P. Creed, P. G. Jeavons, and S. Živný. An algebraic theory of complexity for valued constraints: Establishing a Galois connection. In *Intl. Symp. on Mathematical Foundations of Computer Science (MFCS)*, pages 231–242. Springer, 2011.

D. A. Cohen, M. C. Cooper, P. Creed, P. Jeavons, and S. Živný. An algebraic theory of complexity for discrete optimisation. *SIAM Journal on Computing*, 2013. To appear.

M. C. Cooper. Minimization of locally defined submodular functions by optimal soft arc consistency. *Constraints*, 13(4):437–458, 2008.

M. C. Cooper, S. de Givry, M. Sánchez, T. Schiex, M. Zytnicki, and T. Werner. Soft arc consistency revisited. *Artificial Intelligence*, 174(7–8):449–478, 2010a.

M. C. Cooper, P. G. Jeavons, and A. Z. Salamon. Generalizing constraint satisfaction on trees: Hybrid tractability and variable elimination. *Artificial Intelligence*, 174(9–10):570–584, 2010b.

M. C. Cooper and S. Živný. Hybrid tractability of valued constraint problems. *Artificial Intelligence*, 175(9-10):1555–1569, 2011.

M. C. Cooper and S. Živný. Tractable triangles and cross-free convexity in discrete optimisation. *Journal of Artificial Intelligence Research*, 44:455–490, 2012.

P. Creed and S. Živný. On minimal weighted clones. In *Intl. Conf. on Principles and Practice of Constraint Programming (CP)*, pages 210–224. Springer, 2011.

V. Dalmau, P. G. Kolaitis, and M. Y. Vardi. Constraint satisfaction, bounded treewidth, and finite-variable logics. In *Intl. Conf. on Principles and Practice of Constraint Programming (CP)*, pages 310–326. Springer, 2002.

R. Dechter. *Constraint Processing*. Morgan Kaufmann, 2003.

T. Feder and M. Y. Vardi. The computational structure of monotone monadic SNP and constraint satisfaction: A study through datalog and group theory. *SIAM Journal on Computing*, 28(1):57–104, 1998.

V. Franc, S. Sonnenburg, and T. Werner. Cutting plane methods in machine learning. In S. Sra, S. Nowozin, and S. J. Wright, editors, *Optimization for Machine Learning*. MIT Press, 2012.

S. Fujishige. *Submodular Functions and Optimization*. North-Holland, 2005.

S. Fujishige and S. Iwata. Bisubmodular function minimization. *SIAM Journal on Discrete Mathematics*, 19(4):1065–1073, 2005.

M. R. Garey and D. S. Johnson. *Computers and Intractability: A Guide to the Theory of NP-Completeness*. W.H. Freeman, 1979.

A. Globerson and T. Jaakkola. Fixing max-product: Convergent message passing algorithms for MAP LP-relaxations. In *Conf. on Neural Information Processing Systems (NIPS)*, pages 553–560, 2008.

G. Gottlob, N. Leone, and F. Scarcello. A comparison of structural CSP decomposition methods. *Artificial Intelligence*, 124(2):243–282, 2000.

M. Grohe. The complexity of homomorphism and constraint satisfaction problems seen from the other side. *Journal of the ACM*, 54(1):1–24, 2007.

F. Hadlock. Finding a maximum cut of a planar graph in polynomial time. *SIAM Journal on Computing*, 4(3):221–225, 1975.

A. Huber and V. Kolmogorov. Towards minimizing k-submodular functions. In *Intl. Symp. on Combinatorial Optimization (ISCO)*, pages 451–462. Springer, 2012.

A. Huber, A. Krokhin, and R. Powell. Skew bisubmodularity and valued CSPs. In *ACM-SIAM Symp. on Discrete Algorithms (SODA)*, pages 1296–1305. SIAM, 2013.

S. Iwata, L. Fleischer, and S. Fujishige. A combinatorial strongly polynomial algorithm for minimizing submodular functions. *Journal of the ACM*, 48(4): 761–777, 2001.

P. G. Jeavons, D. A. Cohen, and M. Gyssens. Closure properties of constraints. *Journal of the ACM*, 44(4):527–548, 1997.

J. K. Johnson, D. M. Malioutov, and A. S. Willsky. Lagrangian relaxation for MAP estimation in graphical models. In *Allerton Conf. on Communication, Control and Computing*, pages 64–73. Curran Associates, Inc., 2007.

P. Jonsson, F. Kuivinen, and J. Thapper. Min CSP on four elements: Moving beyond submodularity. In *Intl. Conf. on Principles and Practice of Constraint Programming (CP)*, pages 438–453. Springer, 2011.

J. H. Kappes, B. Andres, F. A. Hamprecht, C. Schnörr, S. Nowozin, D. Batra, S. Kim, B. X. Kausler, J. Lellmann, N. Komodakis, and C. Rother. A comparative study of modern inference techniques for discrete energy minimization problem. In *Conf. on Computer Vision and Pattern Recognition (CVPR)*. IEEE, 2013.

C. L. Kingsford, B. Chazelle, and M. Singh. Solving and analyzing side-chain positioning problems using linear and integer programming. *Bioinformatics*, 21 (7):1028–1039, 2005.

D. Koller and N. Friedman. *Probabilistic Graphical Models: Principles and Techniques*. MIT Press, 2009.

V. Kolmogorov. Convergent tree-reweighted message passing for energy minimization. *IEEE Transactions on Pattern Analysis and Machine Intelligence*, 28(10): 1568–1583, 2006.

V. Kolmogorov. Submodularity on a tree: Unifying $L^\sharp$-convex and bisubmodular functions. In *Intl. Symp. on Mathematical Foundations of Computer Science (MFCS)*, pages 400–411. Springer, 2011.

V. Kolmogorov. The power of linear programming for finite-valued CSPs: A constructive characterization. In *Intl. Coll. on Automata, Languages and Programming (ICALP)*, pages 625–636. Springer, 2013.

V. Kolmogorov, J. Thapper, and S. Živný. The power of linear programming for general-valued CSPs. 2013. Submitted for publication.

V. Kolmogorov and S. Živný. The complexity of conservative valued CSPs. *Journal of the ACM*, 60(2), 2013.

N. Komodakis, N. Paragios, and G. Tziritas. MRF energy minimization and beyond via dual decomposition. *IEEE Transactions on Pattern Analysis and Machine Intelligence*, 33(3):531–552, 2011.

A. Koster, S. van Hoesel, and A. Kolen. The partial constraint satisfaction problem: Facets and lifting theorems. *Operations Research Letters*, 23(3–5):89–97, 1998.

V. K. Koval and M. I. Schlesinger. Dvumernoe programmirovanie v zadachakh analiza izobrazheniy (Two-dimensional programming in image analysis problems). *Automatics and Telemechanics*, 8:149–168, 1976. In Russian.

V. A. Kovalevsky and V. K. Koval. A diffusion algorithm for decreasing the energy of the max-sum labeling problem. Glushkov Institute of Cybernetics, Kiev, USSR. Unpublished, approx. 1975.

A. Krokhin and B. Larose. Maximizing supermodular functions on product lattices, with application to maximum constraint satisfaction. *SIAM Journal on Discrete Mathematics*, 22(1):312–328, 2008.

F. Kuivinen. On the complexity of submodular function minimisation on diamonds. *Discrete Optimization*, 8(3):459–477, 2011.

G. Kun, R. O'Donnell, S. Tamaki, Y. Yoshida, and Y. Zhou. Linear programming, width-1 CSPs, and robust satisfaction. In *Innovations in Theoretical Computer Science (ITCS) Conf.*, pages 484–495. ACM, 2012.

R. Ladner. On the structure of polynomial time reducibility. *Journal of the ACM*, 22:155–171, 1975.

S. Lauritzen. *Graphical Models*. Oxford University Press, 1996.

A. L. Martins, M. A. T. Figueiredo, P. M. Q. Aguiar, N. A. Smith, and E. P. Xing. An augmented Lagrangian approach to constrained MAP inference. In *Intl. Conf. on Machine Learning (ICML)*, pages 169–176. Omnipress, 2011.

D. Marx. Tractable hypergraph properties for constraint satisfaction and conjunctive queries. In *ACM Symp. on Theory of Computing (STOC)*, pages 735–744. ACM, 2010.

O. Meshi and A. Globerson. An alternating direction method for dual MAP LP relaxation. In *Conf. on Machine Learning and Knowledge Discovery in Databases (ECML PKDD)*, 2011.

M. Mezard and A. Montanari. *Information, Physics, and Computation*. Oxford University Press, 2009.

U. Montanari. Networks of Constraints: Fundamental properties and applications to picture processing. *Information Sciences*, 7:95–132, 1974.

S. Nowozin and C. H. Lampert. Structured learning and prediction in computer vision. *Foundations and Trends in Computer Graphics and Vision*, 6(3-4):185–365, 2011.

D. Průša and T. Werner. Universality of the local marginal polytope. In *Conf. on Computer Vision and Pattern Recognition (CVPR)*. IEEE, 2013.

P. Ravikumar, A. Agarwal, and M. J. Wainwright. Message-passing for graph-structured linear programs: proximal projections, convergence and rounding schemes. In *Intl. Conf. on Machine Learning (ICML)*, pages 800–807. ACM, 2008.

F. Rossi, P. van Beek, and T. Walsh, editors. *Handbook of Constraint Programming*. Elsevier, 2006.

C. Rother, V. Kolmogorov, and A. Blake. "GrabCut": Interactive foreground extraction using iterated graph cuts. In *SIGGRAPH*, pages 309–314. ACM Press, 2004.

C. Rother, V. Kolmogorov, V. S. Lempitsky, and M. Szummer. Optimizing binary MRFs via extended roof duality. In *Conf. on Computer Vision and Pattern Recognition (CVPR)*. IEEE, 2007.

B. Savchynskyy, J. Kappes, S. Schmidt, and C. Schnörr. A study of Nesterov's scheme for Lagrangian decomposition and MAP labeling. In *Conf. on Computer Vision and Pattern Recognition (CVPR)*, pages 1817–1823. IEEE, 2011.

T. J. Schaefer. The complexity of satisfiability problems. In *ACM Symp. on Theory of Computing (STOC)*, pages 216–226. ACM, 1978.

T. Schiex, H. Fargier, and G. Verfaillie. Valued constraint satisfaction problems: Hard and easy problems. In *Intl. Joint Conf. on Artificial Intelligence (IJCAI)*, pages 631–637. Morgan Kaufmann, 1995.

D. Schlesinger. Exact solution of permuted submodular MinSum problems. In *Conf. on Energy Minimization Methods in Computer Vision and Pattern Recognition (EMMCVPR)*, pages 28–38. Springer, 2007.

D. Schlesinger and B. Flach. Transforming an arbitrary MinSum problem into a binary one. Technical Report TUD-FI06-01, Dresden University of Technology, Germany, 2006.

M. I. Schlesinger and V. V. Giginjak. Solving (max,+) problems of structural pattern recognition using equivalent transformations. *Upravlyayushchie Sistemy i Mashiny (Control Systems and Machines), Kiev, Naukova Dumka*, 1 and 2, 2007. ISSN 0130-5395. In Russian, English translation available on www.

S. Schmidt, B. Savchynskyy, J. H. Kappes, and C. Schnörr. Evaluation of a first-order primal-dual algorithm for MRF energy minimization. In *Conf. on Energy Minimization Methods in Computer Vision and Pattern Recognition*, pages 89–103. Springer, 2011.

A. Schrijver. A combinatorial algorithm minimizing submodular functions in strongly polynomial time. *Journal of Combinatorial Theory, Series B*, 80(2): 346–355, 2000.

A. Schrijver. *Combinatorial Optimization: Polyhedra and Efficiency*, volume 24 of *Algorithms and Combinatorics*. Springer, 2003.

H. D. Sherali and W. P. Adams. A hierarchy of relaxations between the continuous and convex hull representations for zero-one programming problems. *SIAM Journal of Discrete Mathematics*, 3(3):411–430, 1990.

M. I. Shlezinger. Syntactic analysis of two-dimensional visual signals in noisy conditions. *Cybernetics and Systems Analysis*, 12(4):612–628, 1976. Translation from Russian.

D. Sontag, A. Globerson, and T. Jaakkola. Introduction to dual decomposition for inference. In S. Sra, S. Nowozin, and S. J. Wright, editors, *Optimization for Machine Learning*. MIT Press, 2011.

R. Szeliski, R. Zabih, D. Scharstein, O. Veksler, V. Kolmogorov, A. Agarwala, M. Tappen, and C. Rother. A comparative study of energy minimization methods for markov random fields with smoothness-based priors. *IEEE Transactions on Pattern Analysis and Machine Intelligence*, 30(6):1068–1080, 2008.

J. Thapper and S. Živný. The power of linear programming for valued CSPs. In *IEEE Symp. on Foundations of Computer Science (FOCS)*, pages 669–678. IEEE, 2012.

J. Thapper and S. Živný. The complexity of finite-valued CSPs. In *ACM Symp. on the Theory of Computing (STOC)*, pages 695–704. ACM, 2013.

M. Wainwright, T. Jaakkola, and A. Willsky. MAP estimation via agreement on trees: Message passing and linear programming. *IEEE Transactions on Information Theory*, 51(11):3697–3717, 2005.

M. J. Wainwright and M. I. Jordan. Graphical models, exponential families, and variational inference. *Foundations and Trends in Machine Learning*, 1(1-2):1–305, 2008.

Y. Weiss, C. Yanover, and T. Meltzer. MAP estimation, linear programming and belief propagation with convex free energies. In *Conf. on Uncertainty in Artificial Intelligence (UAI)*, 2007.

T. Werner. A linear programming approach to max-sum problem: A review. *IEEE Transactions on Pattern Analysis and Machine Intelligence*, 29(7):1165–1179, 2007.

T. Werner. Revisiting the linear programming relaxation approach to Gibbs energy minimization and weighted constraint satisfaction. *IEEE Transactions on Pattern Analysis and Machine Intelligence*, 32(8):1474–1488, 2010.

S. Živný. *The complexity of valued constraint satisfaction problems*. Cognitive Technologies. Springer, 2012.

3   AD^3: A Fast Decoder for Structured Prediction

André F. T. Martins   atm@priberam.pt
Priberam Labs & Instituto de Telecomunicações
Lisbon, Portugal

In this chapter, we present AD^3, a new algorithm for approximate maximum a posteriori (MAP) decoding on factor graphs, based on the alternating directions method of multipliers. AD^3 can handle many models often encountered in natural language processing (NLP) and information retrieval (IR), such as models with first-order logic constraints, budget and knapsack constraints, and combinations of structured models that are hard to decode jointly. Like other dual decomposition algorithms, AD^3 has a modular architecture, where local subproblems are solved independently, and their solutions are gathered to compute a global update. The key characteristic of AD^3 is that each local subproblem has a quadratic regularizer, leading to faster convergence, both theoretically and in practice. To solve these AD^3 subproblems, we present an active set method that requires only a local MAP decoder (the same requirement as subgradient-based dual decomposition), making AD^3 applicable to a wide range of problems. We discuss two recent applications of AD^3 in NLP problems: dependency parsing and compressive summarization.

3.1   Introduction

Graphical models enable compact representations of probability distributions, being widely used in natural language processing (NLP), computer vision, signal processing, and computational biology (Pearl, 1988; Lauritzen, 1996; Koller and Friedman, 2009). Given a graphical model, a central problem is that of decoding the most probable (a.k.a. *maximum a posteriori* (MAP)) configuration. Unfortunately, exact MAP decoding is intractable for many graphical models of interest in applications, such as those involving non-local features or structural constraints. This fact has motivated a significant research effort on approximate techniques.

In this chapter, we turn our attention to *LP-MAP decoding* (Schlesinger, 1976), a linear relaxation that underlies recent message-passing and dual decomposition algorithms (Wainwright et al., 2005; Kolmogorov, 2006; Werner, 2007; Komodakis et al., 2007; Globerson and Jaakkola, 2008; Jojic et al., 2010).[1] All these algorithms have a similar consensus-based architecture: they repeatedly perform certain "local" operations in the graph (as outlined in Table 3.1) until some form of local agreement is achieved. The simplest example is the *projected subgradient dual decomposition* (PSDD) algorithm of Komodakis et al. (2007), which has recently enjoyed great success in NLP applications (see Rush and Collins (2012) and references therein). The major drawback of PSDD is that it is too slow to achieve consensus in large problems, requiring $O(1/\epsilon^2)$ iterations for an ϵ-accurate solution.

Here, we introduce an algorithm called AD^3 (*alternating directions dual decomposition*), which allies the modularity of dual decomposition with the effectiveness of augmented Lagrangian optimization via the *alternating directions method of multipliers* (Glowinski and Marroco, 1975; Gabay and Mercier, 1976). AD^3 has an iteration bound of $O(1/\epsilon)$, an order of magnitude better than the PSDD algorithm. Like PSDD, AD^3 alternates between a *broadcast* operation, where subproblems are assigned to local workers, and a *gather* operation, where the local solutions are assembled by a controller, which produces an estimate of the global solution. The key difference is that AD^3 regularizes their local subproblems toward these global estimate, which has the effect of speeding up consensus. In many cases of interest, there are closed-form solutions or efficient procedures for solving the AD^3 local subproblems (which are quadratic). For factors lacking such a solution, we introduce an *active set method* that requires only a local MAP decoder (the same requirement as in PSDD). This paves the way for using AD^3 with dense or structured factors. AD^3 was originally proposed in Martins et al. (2011a) and has been successfully applied to several NLP problems (Martins et al., 2011b, 2013; Das et al., 2012; Almeida and Martins, 2013). An open-source implementation is available at `http://www.ark.cs.cmu.edu/AD3`.

---

1. See Chapter 4 of this volume for further details about LP-MAP decoding, along with a generalization of the TRW-S algorithm of Wainwright et al. (2005) and Kolmogorov (2006).

Algorithm	Local Operation
Loopy BP (Pearl, 1988)	max-marginals
TRW-S (Wainwright et al., 2005; Kolmogorov, 2006)	max-marginals
MPLP (Globerson and Jaakkola, 2008)	max-marginals
PSDD (Komodakis et al., 2007)	MAP
ADD (Jojic et al., 2010)	marginals
AD^3 (Martins et al., 2011a)	QP/MAP

Table 3.1: Several approximate MAP decoders and the kind of the local operations they need to perform at the factors to pass messages and compute beliefs. With the exception of loopy BP, all algorithms in this table are instances of LP-MAP decoders. In Section 3.6, we will see that the quadratic problems (QPs) required by AD^3 can be solved as a sequence of local MAP problems.

This chapter is organized as follows. We provide background on factor graphs and the MAP decoding problem in Section 3.2. In Section 3.3, we discuss two important NLP applications—dependency parsing and summarization—along with factor graph representations. In Section 3.4, we discuss the LP-MAP relaxation and the PSDD algorithm. In Section 3.5, we derive AD^3 and analyze its convergence properties. The AD^3 subproblems are addressed in Section 3.6, where we present the active set method. Section 3.7 reports experiments using AD^3 for the two NLP applications above. Finally, related work is discussed in Section 3.8, and Section 3.9 concludes.

3.2 Factor Graphs and MAP Decoding

3.2.1 Factor Graphs

Let $Y_1, \ldots, Y_M$ be random variables describing a structured output, with each Y_i taking values in a finite set $\mathcal{Y}_i$. We follow the common assumption in structured prediction that some of these variables have strong statistical dependencies. In this chapter, we use *factor graphs* (Tanner, 1981; Kschischang et al., 2001), a convenient way of representing such dependencies that captures directly the factorization assumptions in a model.

Definition 3.1 (Factor graph). *A factor graph is a bipartite graph $G := (V, F, E)$, comprised of:*

- variable nodes $V := \{1, \ldots, M\}$, *corresponding to the variables $Y_1, \ldots, Y_M$;*
- factor nodes F *(disjoint from V);*

■ edges $E \subseteq V \times F$ *linking variable nodes to factor nodes.*

We denote by $F(i) := \{\alpha \in F \mid (i,\alpha) \in E\}$ the set of factors linked to the ith variable and, conversely, by $V(\alpha) := \{i \in V \mid (i,\alpha) \in E\}$ the set of variables appearing in factor α. We use the short notation $\boldsymbol{Y}_\alpha := (Y_i)_{i \in V(\alpha)}$ to refer to tuples of random variables, which take values on the product set $\mathcal{Y}_\alpha := \prod_{i \in V(\alpha)} \mathcal{Y}_i$. We say that the joint probability distribution of $Y_1, \ldots, Y_M$ factors according to $G = (V, F, E)$ if it can be written as

$$\mathbb{P}(Y_1 = y_1, \ldots, Y_M = y_M) \;\propto\; \exp\left(\sum_{i \in V} \boldsymbol{\theta}_i(y_i) + \sum_{\alpha \in F} \boldsymbol{\theta}_\alpha(\boldsymbol{y}_\alpha)\right), \qquad (3.1)$$

where $\boldsymbol{\theta}_i(\cdot)$ and $\boldsymbol{\theta}_\alpha(\cdot)$ are, respectively, *unary* and *higher-order* log-potential functions. These functions define "local" scores for the variable nodes and for configurations of variables within the factor nodes. To accommodate hard constraints (discussed in Section 3.2.3), we allow these functions to take values in $\bar{\mathbb{R}} := \mathbb{R} \cup \{-\infty\}$.

3.2.2 MAP Decoding

Given a probability distribution specified as in (3.1), an important task is that of finding an assignment with maximal probability (the so-called *MAP assignment/configuration*):

$$\widehat{\boldsymbol{y}}_1, \ldots, \widehat{\boldsymbol{y}}_M \;\in\; \operatorname*{argmax}_{y_1, \ldots, y_M} \sum_{i \in V} \boldsymbol{\theta}_i(y_i) + \sum_{\alpha \in F} \boldsymbol{\theta}_\alpha(\boldsymbol{y}_\alpha). \qquad (3.2)$$

A solver for problem (3.2) is called a *MAP decoder*. In fact, this problem is not specific to probabilistic models: other models (*e.g.*, trained to maximize margin) also lead to maximizations of the form above. Unfortunately, for a general factor graph G, this combinatorial problem is NP-hard (Koller and Friedman, 2009), so one must resort to approximations.

In this chapter, we will address a class of approximations based on linear programming relaxations, which will be described formally in Section 3.4.

3.2.3 Dense, Hard, and Structured Factors

Along this chapter, we will consider factors of three kinds: *dense factors*, *hard constraint factors*, and *structured factors*.

A dense factor is one whose log-potential function satisfies $\boldsymbol{\theta}_\alpha(\boldsymbol{y}_\alpha) > -\infty$ for every $\boldsymbol{y}_\alpha \in \mathcal{Y}_\alpha$. To represent a dense factor computationally, we need to store $O(|\mathcal{Y}_\alpha|)$ real numbers (one per factor configuration). Because $|\mathcal{Y}_\alpha|$

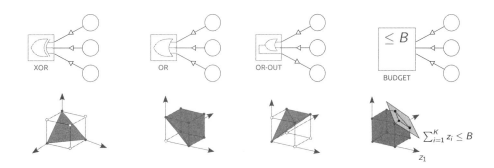

Figure 3.1: Hard constraint factors and their marginal polytopes; the AD^3 subproblems (3.20) are projections onto these polytopes. The three factors on the left represent one-hot XOR, OR, and OR-with-output logical constraints. The rightmost one is a budget factor, requiring at most B variables to be active.

grows exponentially with the number of variables linked to the factor, dense factors are only tractable for small values of $|V(\alpha)|$.

Hard constraint factors have special log-potential functions that are indicators of an *acceptance set* $S_\alpha \subseteq \mathcal{Y}_\alpha$. In other words, $\boldsymbol{\theta}_\alpha(.)$ is of the form:

$$\boldsymbol{\theta}_\alpha(\boldsymbol{y}_\alpha) := \begin{cases} 0, & \text{if } \boldsymbol{y}_\alpha \in S_\alpha, \\ -\infty, & \text{otherwise.} \end{cases} \tag{3.3}$$

These factors ensure that any configuration not in the acceptance set will have zero probability. This has applications in error-correcting decoding (Richardson and Urbanke, 2008), bipartite graph matching (Duchi et al., 2007), computer vision (Nowozin and Lampert, 2009), and various problems in NLP (Sutton, 2004; Smith and Eisner, 2008; Das et al., 2012). An example is *logic factors* (Martins et al., 2011b), which compute logic functions over binary variables, serving as building blocks for expressing declarative constraints in *first-order logic*. Such constraints are useful to inject domain knowledge into a problem (Richardson and Domingos, 2006; Chang et al., 2008). Figure 3.1 shows examples of logic factors (see Martins (2012) for how to perform computations with those factors).

Finally, structured factors have log-potential functions with an additional layer of structure, which allows them to be represented in a compact way. For example, they can form a chain model or a tree or can even have an

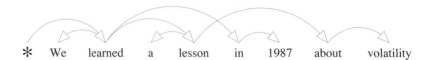

Figure 3.2: Example of a sentence (input) and its dependency parse tree (output to be predicted); this is a directed spanning tree where each arc (h, m) represents a syntactic relationships between a *head* word h and a *modifier* word m.

internal factor graph representation[2] themselves, such as

$$\boldsymbol{\theta}_\alpha(\boldsymbol{y}_\alpha) := \sum_{i \in V(\alpha)} \xi_i(y_i) + \sum_{\beta \in F_\alpha} \xi_\beta(\boldsymbol{y}_\beta), \tag{3.4}$$

where $F_\alpha \subseteq 2^{V(\alpha)}$. Because they have compact representations, structured factors are able to scale to large values of $|V(\alpha)|$.

3.3   Factor Graphs for NLP

Many problems in NLP can be cast as structured prediction (Smith, 2011). In this section, we describe factor graph representations for two concrete NLP problems: *dependency parsing* and *compressive summarization*. Later, in Section 3.7, we will show experimental results for these two tasks.

3.3.1   "Turbo" Parsing

Dependency parsing is an important problem in NLP (Kübler et al., 2009). Given a sentence with L words, to which a special root symbol $*$ is prepended, the goal is to find a directed spanning tree, where each arc represents a syntactic function, linking a *head word* to a *modifier word*.[3] For example, in Figure 3.2, three arcs depart from the head word "learned": one pointing to the modifier "We" (the subject), another to "lesson" (the object), and another to "in" (which introduces a prepositional phrase).

---

2. In the literature, structured factors are often not considered as factors on their own, but instead as subgraphs of a larger graph that includes their internal factorization. Here, we consider structured factors explicitly, abstracting away their internal structure. This allows us to deal with combinatorial structures that are not directly represented as a graphical model, such as probabilistic context-free grammars.
3. This is the definition of *non-projective* dependency parsing, the one used throughout this chapter. A formalism is *projective* parsing, which in addition constrains the arcs to be nested. See Kübler et al. (2009) for more details.

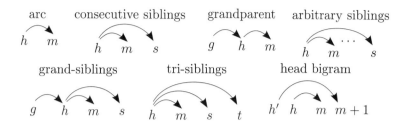

Figure 3.3: The parts used in our model. First-order models factor over arcs (Eisner, 1996; McDonald et al., 2005), and second-order models include also consecutive siblings and grandparents (Carreras, 2007). Our parsers add also *arbitrary* siblings (not necessarily consecutive) and head bigrams, as in Martins et al. (2011b), in addition to third-order features for grand- and tri-siblings (Koo and Collins, 2010).

The simplest dependency parsing models are *arc-factored*. In these models, one has $O(L^2)$ scores—one score for every possible arc linking two words—and the goal is to pick the spanning tree maximizing the sum of the scores in its arcs. This problem can be solved efficiently with an algorithm for finding maximal spanning trees (Chu and Liu, 1965; Edmonds, 1967; McDonald et al., 2005). Unfortunately, arc-factored parsers perform poorly because they do not capture enough interactions among the dependency arcs, and extending the model to include larger substructures (*e.g.*, pairs of arcs) renders the decoding problem NP-hard (McDonald and Satta, 2007).

In Martins et al. (2010b), we introduced the concept of "turbo parser," which encapsulates several top-performing approximate dependency parsers (Smith and Eisner, 2008; Martins et al., 2009; Koo et al., 2010). The name designates parsers that decode factor graphs by ignoring the effects caused by the cycles of the graph.[4] These parsers trade off exact decoding by the ability to include scores for more complex substructures, resulting in more expressive models and higher accuracies. Figure 3.3 shows an example of such substructures (or *parts*) that constitute a recent third-order parser (Martins et al., 2013). These parts can be represented by a factor graph that mixes dense, hard constraint, and structured factors, which we define next.

The variable nodes of the factor graph stand for the $O(L^2)$ possible dependency arcs linking each pair of words, each associated with a binary variable. The factors are the following:

- A hard-constraint factor, linked to all the variables, imposing that they jointly define a well-formed tree.

---

4. The name stems from "turbo codes," a class of high-performance error-correcting codes introduced by Berrou et al. (1993) for which decoding algorithms are equivalent to running belief propagation in a graph with loops (McEliece et al., 1998).

- Head automata factors modeling the left and right sequences of consecutive siblings, grandparents, grand-siblings, and tri-siblings. Each of these structured factors is a chain model that, for a given head word, assigns a score for the sequence of modifiers and (eventually) the grandparent. These factors have internal structure relying on horizontal and vertical Markov assumptions.

- Binary pairwise factors (also called Ising factors) for every possible pair of siblings. These are simple dense factors.

- A structured factor modeling the sequence of heads, with scores depending on the heads of consecutive words. This is also a chain model.

We will see in the sequel that a crucial operation to be performed at each factor is computing local MAP configurations. For all factors listed above, this can be done efficiently, as described in Martins et al. (2013).

3.3.2 Compressive Summarization

Our second NLP application is compressive summarization (Almeida and Martins, 2013). We are given a collection of documents about a given topic, and the goal is to generate a summary with less than B words, where B is a budget. Let N be the total number of sentences in the collection, where the nth sentence has L_n words. We constrain our summary's sentences to be *compressions* of the original sentences obtained by deleting some words.[5]

We define one binary variable for every word of every sentence, yielding vectors $\boldsymbol{z}_n := (z_{n,\ell})_{\ell=1}^{L_n}$. A good summary is typically a trade-off among three important qualities: *conciseness*, *informativeness*, and *grammaticality*. This can be made formal by defining the following optimization problem:

$$
\begin{aligned}
\text{maximize} \quad & g(\boldsymbol{z}) + \sum_{n=1}^{N} h_n(\boldsymbol{z}_n) \\
\text{w.r.t.} \quad & \boldsymbol{z}_n \in \{0,1\}^{L_n}, \ n = 1, \ldots, N \\
\text{s.t.} \quad & \sum_{n=1}^{N} \sum_{\ell=1}^{L_n} z_{n,\ell} \leq B,
\end{aligned}
\tag{3.5}
$$

---

5. This constraint is substantially weaker than that of *extractive summarizers*, which form a summary by picking full sentences. Our motivation is to make better use of the budget using shorter snippets to accommodate more information.

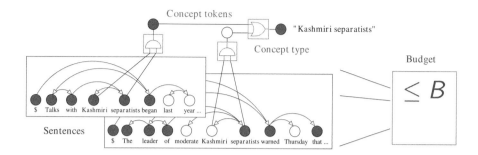

Figure 3.4: Components of our compressive summarizer. The sentence-level factors at the bottom left belong to the compression model and promote grammaticality. The logic factors at the top form the coverage component. Finally, the budget factor at the right side, is connected to the word nodes; it ensures that the summary fits the word limit.

where $g(\boldsymbol{z})$ is a *global informativeness score* based on how many "concepts"[6] are covered by the summary $\boldsymbol{z}$, and the $h_n(\boldsymbol{z}_n)$ are *local grammaticality scores*, computed at the sentence level.

Figure 3.4 shows a factor graph representation for this task, where circles represent variables and rectangles represent factors. We introduce a binary variable for each word in the original sentences; to handle concepts, we distinguish between *concept types* (a list of word bigram types that appear frequently in the collection) and *concept tokens* (occurrences of those bigrams in the text), and we also introduce binary variables for those. Note that types and tokens are logically related: a concept type is present in the summary if at least one concept token is present. This is captured by the logic factors in Figure 3.4; this part of the graph takes care of the *informativeness score* $g(\boldsymbol{z})$. Then, for each sentence in the collection, we introduce a structured factor that computes a *grammaticality score* $h_n(\boldsymbol{z}_n)$ inspired by prior work in sentence compression (Knight and Marcu, 2000). The sentence is first parsed, yielding a dependency tree like in Figure 3.2; $h_n(\boldsymbol{z}_n)$ is then defined as a sum of penalties for the arcs deleted in the compression (see Almeida and Martins 2013). The internal structure of this factor is given by a tractable tree-shaped model. Finally, we have a *budget factor* imposing that at most B words can be selected, which takes care of conciseness.

---

6. For simplicity, we assume concepts are *word bigrams* (as in Gillick et al. (2008)), but other representations would be possible, such as phrases or predicate-argument structures.

3.4 LP-MAP Decoding

We now describe a class of methods for approximate MAP decoding based on a *linear programming relaxation* of the problem (3.2), known in the literature as Schlesinger's linear relaxation (Schlesinger, 1976; Werner, 2007).[7]

Let us start by representing the log-potential functions in (3.1) in vector notation, $\boldsymbol{\theta}_i := (\boldsymbol{\theta}_i(y_i))_{y_i \in \mathcal{Y}_i} \in \bar{\mathbb{R}}^{|\mathcal{Y}_i|}$ and $\boldsymbol{\theta}_\alpha := (\boldsymbol{\theta}_\alpha(\boldsymbol{y}_\alpha))_{\boldsymbol{y}_\alpha \in \mathcal{Y}_\alpha} \in \bar{\mathbb{R}}^{|\mathcal{Y}_\alpha|}$. We introduce "local" probability distributions over the variables and factors, which we represent as vectors of the same size as $\boldsymbol{\theta}_i$ and $\boldsymbol{\theta}_\alpha$:

$$\boldsymbol{p}_i \in \Delta^{|\mathcal{Y}_i|}, \ \forall i \in V \quad \text{and} \quad \boldsymbol{q}_\alpha \in \Delta^{|\mathcal{Y}_\alpha|}, \ \forall \alpha \in F, \tag{3.6}$$

where $\Delta^K := \{\boldsymbol{u} \in \mathbb{R}^K \mid \boldsymbol{u} \geq \mathbf{0}, \ \mathbf{1} \cdot \boldsymbol{u} = 1\}$ denotes the K-dimensional probability simplex. We stack these distributions into vectors $\boldsymbol{p}$ and $\boldsymbol{q}$, with dimensions $P := \sum_{i \in V} |\mathcal{Y}_i|$ and $Q := \sum_{\alpha \in F} |\mathcal{Y}_\alpha|$, respectively. If these local probability distributions are "valid" marginal probabilities (*i.e.*, marginals realizable by some global probability distribution $\mathbb{P}(Y_1, \ldots, Y_M)$), then a necessary (but not sufficient) condition is that they are *locally consistent*. In other words, they must satisfy the following *calibration equations*:

$$\sum_{\boldsymbol{y}_\alpha \sim y_i} q_\alpha(\boldsymbol{y}_\alpha) = p_i(y_i), \qquad \forall y_i \in \mathcal{Y}_i, \ \forall (i, \alpha) \in E, \tag{3.7}$$

where the notation $\sim$ means that the summation is over all configurations $\boldsymbol{y}_\alpha$ whose ith element equals y_i. Equation (3.7) can be written in vector notation as $\mathbf{M}_{i\alpha}\boldsymbol{q}_\alpha = \boldsymbol{p}_i, \ \forall (i, \alpha) \in E$, where we define *consistency matrices*

$$\mathbf{M}_{i\alpha}(y_i, \boldsymbol{y}_\alpha) = \begin{cases} 1, & \text{if } \boldsymbol{y}_\alpha \sim y_i \\ 0, & \text{otherwise.} \end{cases} \tag{3.8}$$

The set of locally consistent distributions forms the *local polytope*:

$$\mathcal{L}(G) = \left\{ (\boldsymbol{p}, \boldsymbol{q}) \in \mathbb{R}^{P+Q} \ \middle| \ \begin{array}{ll} \boldsymbol{q}_\alpha \in \Delta^{|\mathcal{Y}_\alpha|}, & \forall \alpha \in F \\ \mathbf{M}_{i\alpha}\boldsymbol{q}_\alpha = \boldsymbol{p}_i, & \forall (i, \alpha) \in E \end{array} \right\}. \tag{3.9}$$

We consider the following linear program (the *LP-MAP decoding problem*):

LP-MAP: maximize $\displaystyle\sum_{\alpha \in F} \boldsymbol{\theta}_\alpha \cdot \boldsymbol{q}_\alpha + \sum_{i \in V} \boldsymbol{\theta}_i \cdot \boldsymbol{p}_i$
with respect to $(\boldsymbol{p}, \boldsymbol{q}) \in \mathcal{L}(G).$ $\tag{3.10}$

---

7. Chapter 2 of the current volume gives a detailed overview of what is known about this linear programming relaxation, including some hardness results.

If the solution $(\boldsymbol{p}^*, \boldsymbol{q}^*)$ of (3.10) happens to be integral, then each $\boldsymbol{p}_i^*$ and $\boldsymbol{q}_\alpha^*$ will be at corners of the simplex (*i.e.*, they will be indicator vectors of local configurations y_i^* and $\boldsymbol{y}_\alpha^*$), in which case the output $(y_i^*)_{i \in V}$ is guaranteed to be a solution of the MAP decoding problem (3.2). Under certain conditions—for example, when the factor graph G does not have cycles—(3.10) is guaranteed to have integral solutions. In general, however, the LP-MAP decoding problem (3.10) is a relaxation of (3.2). Geometrically, $\mathcal{L}(G)$ is an outer approximation of the *marginal polytope*, defined as the set of valid marginals (Wainwright and Jordan, 2008).

3.4.1   Dual Decomposition

While any off-the-shelf LP solver can be used for solving (3.10), specialized algorithms have been designed to exploit the graph structure, achieving superior performance on several benchmarks (Yanover et al., 2006). An example is the *projected subgradient dual decomposition* (PSDD) algorithm, proposed by Komodakis et al. (2007), which has old roots in optimization (Dantzig and Wolfe, 1960; Everett, 1963; Guignard and Kim, 1987). As we will see in Section 3.5, there is a strong affinity between PSDD and the main focus of this chapter, AD^3.

Let us first express (3.10) as a consensus problem. For each edge $(i, \alpha) \in E$, we define a potential function $\boldsymbol{\theta}_{i\alpha} := (\boldsymbol{\theta}_{i\alpha}(y_i))_{y_i \in \mathcal{Y}_i}$ that satisfies $\sum_{\alpha \in F(i)} \boldsymbol{\theta}_{i\alpha} = \boldsymbol{\theta}_i$; a trivial choice is $\boldsymbol{\theta}_{i\alpha} = |F(i)|^{-1}\boldsymbol{\theta}_i$, which spreads the unary potentials evenly across the factors. Because we have an equality constraint $\boldsymbol{p}_i = \mathbf{M}_{i\alpha}\boldsymbol{q}_\alpha$, (3.10) is equivalent to the following *primal formulation*:

$$
\textbf{LP-MAP-P:} \quad \text{maximize} \quad \sum_{\alpha \in F} \left(\boldsymbol{\theta}_\alpha + \sum_{i \in V(\alpha)} \mathbf{M}_{i\alpha}^\top \boldsymbol{\theta}_{i\alpha} \right) \cdot \boldsymbol{q}_\alpha
$$

$$
\text{with respect to} \quad \boldsymbol{p} \in \mathbb{R}^P, \quad \boldsymbol{q}_\alpha \in \Delta^{|\mathcal{Y}_\alpha|}, \forall \alpha \in F, \tag{3.11}
$$

$$
\text{subject to} \quad \mathbf{M}_{i\alpha}\boldsymbol{q}_\alpha = \boldsymbol{p}_i, \ \forall (i, \alpha) \in E.
$$

Note that, although the $\boldsymbol{p}$-variables do not appear in the objective of (3.11), they play a fundamental role through the constraints in the last line. Indeed, this set of constraints complicates the optimization problem, which would otherwise be separable into independent subproblems, one per factor. Introducing Lagrange multipliers $\boldsymbol{\lambda}_{i\alpha} := (\lambda_{i\alpha}(y_i))_{y_i \in \mathcal{Y}_i}$ for these equality constraints, we arrive at the following *dual formulation*:

$$\textbf{LP-MAP-D:} \qquad \text{minimize} \qquad g(\boldsymbol{\lambda}) := \sum_{\alpha \in F} g_\alpha(\boldsymbol{\lambda}) \tag{3.12}$$

$$\text{with respect to} \quad \boldsymbol{\lambda} \in \Lambda,$$

where $\Lambda := \left\{ \boldsymbol{\lambda} \mid \sum_{\alpha \in F(i)} \boldsymbol{\lambda}_{i\alpha} = \mathbf{0}, \ \forall i \in V \right\}$ is a linear subspace, and each $g_\alpha(\boldsymbol{\lambda})$ is the solution of a *local subproblem*:

$$g_\alpha(\boldsymbol{\lambda}) := \max_{\boldsymbol{q}_\alpha \in \Delta^{|\mathcal{Y}_\alpha|}} \left(\boldsymbol{\theta}_\alpha + \sum_{i \in V(\alpha)} \mathbf{M}_{i\alpha}^\top (\boldsymbol{\theta}_{i\alpha} + \boldsymbol{\lambda}_{i\alpha}) \right) \cdot \boldsymbol{q}_\alpha \tag{3.13}$$

$$= \max_{\boldsymbol{y}_\alpha \in \mathcal{Y}_\alpha} \left(\boldsymbol{\theta}_\alpha(\boldsymbol{y}_\alpha) + \sum_{i \in V(\alpha)} (\boldsymbol{\theta}_{i\alpha}(y_i) + \lambda_{i\alpha}(y_i)) \right). \tag{3.14}$$

The last equality is justified by the fact that maximizing a linear objective over the probability simplex gives the largest component of the score vector.

Note that the local subproblem (3.14) can be solved by a COMPUTEMAP procedure, which receives unary potentials $\xi_{i\alpha}(y_i) := \boldsymbol{\theta}_{i\alpha}(y_i) + \lambda_{i\alpha}(y_i)$ and factor potentials $\boldsymbol{\theta}_\alpha(\boldsymbol{y}_\alpha)$ (eventually structured) and returns the MAP $\widehat{\boldsymbol{y}}_\alpha$.

Problem (3.12) is often referred to as the *master* or *controller* and each local subproblem (3.14) as a *slave* or *worker*. The master problem (3.12) can be solved with a *projected subgradient algorithm*.[8] By Danskin's rule (Bertsekas, 1999), a subgradient of g_α is readily given by

$$\frac{\partial g_\alpha(\boldsymbol{\lambda})}{\partial \boldsymbol{\lambda}_{i\alpha}} = \mathbf{M}_{i\alpha} \widehat{\boldsymbol{q}}_\alpha, \quad \forall (i, \alpha) \in E; \tag{3.15}$$

and the projection onto Λ amounts to a centering operation. Putting these pieces together yields Algorithm 3.1. At each iteration, the algorithm broadcasts the current Lagrange multipliers to all the factors. Each factor adjusts its internal unary log-potentials (line 6) and invokes the COMPUTEMAP procedure (line 7). The solutions achieved by each factor are then gathered and averaged (line 10), and the Lagrange multipliers are updated with step size η_t (line 11).

The two following propositions, proved in Rush and Collins (2012), establish the convergence properties of Algorithm 3.1.

Proposition 3.1 (Convergence rate). *If the non-negative step size sequence* $(\eta_t)_{t \in \mathbb{N}}$ *is diminishing and non-summable* $(\lim \eta_t = 0$ *and* $\sum_{t=1}^\infty \eta_t = \infty)$,

---

8. A slightly different formulation is presented by Sontag et al. (2011), which yields a subgradient algorithm with no projection.

Algorithm 3.1 PSDD Algorithm (Komodakis et al., 2007)

1: **input:** graph G, parameters $\boldsymbol{\theta}$, maximum number of iterations T, stepsizes $(\eta_t)_{t=1}^T$
2: for each $(i, \alpha) \in E$, choose $\boldsymbol{\theta}_{i\alpha}$ such that $\sum_{\alpha \in F(i)} \boldsymbol{\theta}_{i\alpha} = \boldsymbol{\theta}_i$
3: initialize $\boldsymbol{\lambda} = \mathbf{0}$
4: **for** $t = 1$ **to** T **do**
5:      **for each** factor $\alpha \in F$ **do**
6:          set unary log-potentials $\boldsymbol{\xi}_{i\alpha} := \boldsymbol{\theta}_{i\alpha} + \boldsymbol{\lambda}_{i\alpha}$, for $i \in V(\alpha)$
7:          set $\widehat{\boldsymbol{q}}_\alpha := \text{COMPUTEMAP}(\boldsymbol{\theta}_\alpha + \sum_{i \in V(\alpha)} \mathbf{M}_{i\alpha}^\top \boldsymbol{\xi}_{i\alpha})$
8:          set $\widehat{\boldsymbol{q}}_{i\alpha} := \mathbf{M}_{i\alpha} \widehat{\boldsymbol{q}}_\alpha$, for $i \in V(\alpha)$
9:      **end for**
10:      compute average $\boldsymbol{p}_i := |F(i)|^{-1} \sum_{\alpha \in F(i)} \widehat{\boldsymbol{q}}_{i\alpha}$ for each $i \in V$
11:      update $\boldsymbol{\lambda}_{i\alpha} := \boldsymbol{\lambda}_{i\alpha} - \eta_t (\widehat{\boldsymbol{q}}_{i\alpha} - \boldsymbol{p}_i)$ for each $(i, \alpha) \in E$
12: **end for**
13: **output:** dual variable $\boldsymbol{\lambda}$ and upper bound $g(\boldsymbol{\lambda})$

---

then Algorithm 3.1 converges to the solution $\boldsymbol{\lambda}^*$ of LP-MAP-D (3.12). Furthermore, after $T = O(1/\epsilon^2)$ iterations, we have $g(\boldsymbol{\lambda}^{(T)}) - g(\boldsymbol{\lambda}^*) \leq \epsilon$.

Proposition 3.2 (Certificate of optimality)**.** *If, at some iteration of Algorithm 3.1, all the local subproblems are in agreement (i.e., if $\widehat{\boldsymbol{q}}_{i\alpha} = \boldsymbol{p}_i$ after line 10, for all $i \in V$), then (i) $\boldsymbol{\lambda}$ is a solution of LP-MAP-D (3.12), and (ii) $\boldsymbol{p}$ is binary-valued and a solution of both LP-MAP-P and MAP.*

Propositions 3.1–3.2 imply that, if the LP-MAP relaxation is tight, then Algorithm 3.1 will eventually yield the exact MAP configuration along with a certificate of optimality. Unfortunately, in large graphs with many overlapping factors, it has been observed that convergence can be quite slow in practice (Martins et al., 2011b). This is not surprising given that it attempts to reach a consensus among all overlapping components; the larger this number is, the harder it is to achieve consensus. We describe in the next section another LP-MAP decoder (AD³) with a faster convergence rate.

3.5 Alternating Directions Dual Decomposition (AD³)

AD³ obviates some of the weaknesses of PSDD by replacing the subgradient method with the *alternating directions method of multipliers* (ADMM).[9]

Before going into a formal derivation, let us go back to the PSDD algorithm to pinpoint the crux of its weaknesses. It resides in two aspects:

---

9. See Boyd et al. (2011, Section 3.1) for a historical perspective on ADMM as a faster alternative to subgradient methods.

1. *The dual objective function $g(\boldsymbol{\lambda})$ is non-smooth.* This is circumvented by using "subgradients" rather than "gradients." Yet non-smooth optimization lacks some of the good properties of its smooth counterpart. Ensuring convergence requires diminishing step sizes, leading to slow convergence rates, such as the $O(1/\epsilon^2)$ iteration bound stated in Proposition 3.1.

2. *Consensus is promoted solely by the Lagrange multipliers* (see line 6 in Algorithm 3.1). These can be regarded as "price adjustments" that are made at each iteration and lead to a reallocation of resources. However, no "memory" exists about past allocations or adjustments, so the workers never know how far they are from consensus. One may suspect that a smarter use of these quantities may accelerate convergence.

The first of these aspects has been addressed by the accelerated dual decomposition method of Jojic et al. (2010), which improves the iteration bound to $O(1/\epsilon)$; we discuss that work further in Section 3.8. We will see that AD^3 also yields a $O(1/\epsilon)$ iteration bound with some additional advantages. The second aspect is addressed by AD^3 by broadcasting *the current global solution* in addition to the Lagrange multipliers, allowing the workers to regularize their subproblems toward that solution.

3.5.1   Augmented Lagrangians, ADMM, and AD^3

Augmented Lagrangian methods have a rich and long-standing history in optimization (Hestenes, 1969; Powell, 1969; Bertsekas, 1999, Section 4.2). Given an optimization problem with equality constraints (such as the one in (3.11)), the *augmented Lagrangian function* is the sum of the Lagrangian with a quadratic constraint violation penalty. For (3.11), it is

$$
\begin{aligned}
L_\eta(\boldsymbol{q},\boldsymbol{p},\boldsymbol{\lambda}) \;=\; & \sum_{\alpha\in F}\left(\boldsymbol{\theta}_\alpha+\sum_{i\in V(\alpha)}\mathbf{M}_{i\alpha}^\top(\boldsymbol{\theta}_{i\alpha}+\boldsymbol{\lambda}_{i\alpha})\right)\cdot\boldsymbol{q}_\alpha-\sum_{(i,\alpha)\in E}\boldsymbol{\lambda}_{i\alpha}\cdot\boldsymbol{p}_i \\
& -\frac{\eta}{2}\sum_{(i,\alpha)\in E}\|\mathbf{M}_{i\alpha}\boldsymbol{q}_\alpha-\boldsymbol{p}_i\|^2,
\end{aligned}
\tag{3.16}
$$

where the scalar $\eta > 0$ controls the weight of the penalty.

The most famous augmented Lagrangian method is the *method of multipliers*, which alternates between maximizing the augmented Lagrangian function with respect to the primal variables (in our problem, a joint maximization of $L_\eta(\boldsymbol{q},\boldsymbol{p},\boldsymbol{\lambda})$ w.r.t. $\boldsymbol{q}$ and $\boldsymbol{p}$), followed by an update of the Lagrange multipliers. Unfortunately, the quadratic term in (3.16) couples together the variables $\boldsymbol{q}$ and $\boldsymbol{p}$, making their joint maximization unappealing. ADMM (Glowinski and Marroco, 1975; Gabay and Mercier, 1976) avoids this shortcoming by replacing this joint maximization by a single block Gauss-Seidel-type step. This yields the following updates (where we have defined the product of simplices $\Delta_F^\times := \prod_{\alpha \in F} \Delta^{|\mathcal{Y}_\alpha|}$):

$$\textbf{Broadcast:} \quad \boldsymbol{q}^{(t+1)} := \operatorname*{argmax}_{\boldsymbol{q} \in \Delta_F^\times} L_\eta(\boldsymbol{q}, \boldsymbol{p}^{(t)}, \boldsymbol{\lambda}^{(t)}), \tag{3.17}$$

$$\textbf{Gather:} \quad \boldsymbol{p}^{(t+1)} := \operatorname*{argmax}_{\boldsymbol{p} \in \mathbb{R}^P} L_\eta(\boldsymbol{q}^{(t+1)}, \boldsymbol{p}, \boldsymbol{\lambda}^{(t)}), \tag{3.18}$$

$$\textbf{Multiplier update:} \quad \boldsymbol{\lambda}_{i\alpha}^{(t+1)} := \boldsymbol{\lambda}_{i\alpha}^{(t)} - \eta \left(\mathbf{M}_{i\alpha} \boldsymbol{q}_\alpha^{(t)} - \boldsymbol{p}_i^{(t)} \right), \forall (i, \alpha) \in E. \tag{3.19}$$

We next analyze the broadcast and gather steps and prove a proposition about the multiplier update.

Broadcast Step.   The maximization (3.17) can be carried out in parallel at the factors, as in PSDD. The only difference is that, instead of a local MAP computation, each worker needs to solve a *quadratic program* of the form:

$$\max_{\boldsymbol{q}_\alpha \in \Delta^{|\mathcal{Y}_\alpha|}} \left(\boldsymbol{\theta}_\alpha + \sum_{i \in V(\alpha)} \mathbf{M}_{i\alpha}^\top (\boldsymbol{\theta}_{i\alpha} + \boldsymbol{\lambda}_{i\alpha}) \right) \cdot \boldsymbol{q}_\alpha - \frac{\eta}{2} \sum_{i \in V(\alpha)} \| \mathbf{M}_{i\alpha} \boldsymbol{q}_\alpha - \boldsymbol{p}_i \|^2. \tag{3.20}$$

The subproblem (3.20) differs from the linear subproblem (3.13)–(3.14) in the PSDD algorithm by including an Euclidean penalty term, which penalizes deviations from the global consensus. In Section 3.6, we will give efficient procedures to solve these local subproblems.

Gather Step.   The solution of (3.18) has a closed form; (3.18) is separable into independent optimizations for each $i \in V$; defining $\boldsymbol{q}_{i\alpha} := \mathbf{M}_{i\alpha} \boldsymbol{q}_\alpha$,

$$\begin{aligned} \boldsymbol{p}_i^{(t+1)} \quad &:= \quad \operatorname*{argmin}_{\boldsymbol{p}_i \in \mathbb{R}^{|\mathcal{Y}_i|}} \sum_{\alpha \in F(i)} \left(\boldsymbol{\lambda}_{i\alpha} \cdot \boldsymbol{p}_i + \frac{\eta}{2} \| \boldsymbol{q}_{i\alpha} - \boldsymbol{p}_i \|^2 \right) \\ &= \quad |F(i)|^{-1} \sum_{\alpha \in F(i)} \left(\boldsymbol{q}_{i\alpha} - \eta^{-1} \boldsymbol{\lambda}_{i\alpha} \right) \\ &= \quad |F(i)|^{-1} \sum_{\alpha \in F(i)} \boldsymbol{q}_{i\alpha}. \end{aligned} \tag{3.21}$$

The equality in the last line is due to the following proposition:

Proposition 3.3. *The sequence* $\boldsymbol{\lambda}^{(1)}, \boldsymbol{\lambda}^{(2)}, \ldots$ *produced by* (3.17)–(3.19) *is dual feasible, i.e., we have* $\boldsymbol{\lambda}^{(t)} \in \Lambda$ *for every t, with* Λ *as in* (3.12).

Algorithm 3.2 Alternating Directions Dual Decomposition (AD³)

1:    **input:** graph G, parameters $\boldsymbol{\theta}$, penalty constant η
2:    initialize $\boldsymbol{p}$ uniformly (*i.e.*, $p_i(y_i) = 1/|\mathcal{Y}_i|, \forall i \in V, y_i \in \mathcal{Y}_i$)
3:    initialize $\boldsymbol{\lambda} = \mathbf{0}$
4:    **repeat**
5:      **for each** factor $\alpha \in F$ **do**
6:        set unary log-potentials $\boldsymbol{\xi}_{i\alpha} := \boldsymbol{\theta}_{i\alpha} + \boldsymbol{\lambda}_{i\alpha}$, for $i \in V(\alpha)$
7:        set $\widehat{\boldsymbol{q}}_\alpha := \text{SOLVEQP}\left(\boldsymbol{\theta}_\alpha + \sum_{i \in V(\alpha)} \mathbf{M}_{i\alpha}^\top \boldsymbol{\xi}_{i\alpha}, (\boldsymbol{p}_i)_{i \in V(\alpha)}\right)$, the problem (3.20)
8:        set $\widehat{\boldsymbol{q}}_{i\alpha} := \mathbf{M}_{i\alpha}\widehat{\boldsymbol{q}}_\alpha$, for $i \in V(\alpha)$
9:      **end for**
10:     compute average $\boldsymbol{p}_i := |F(i)|^{-1} \sum_{\alpha \in F(i)} \widehat{\boldsymbol{q}}_{i\alpha}$ for each $i \in V$
11:     update $\boldsymbol{\lambda}_{i\alpha} := \boldsymbol{\lambda}_{i\alpha} - \eta\left(\widehat{\boldsymbol{q}}_{i\alpha} - \boldsymbol{p}_i\right)$ for each $(i, \alpha) \in E$
12:    **until** convergence
13:    **output:** primal variables $\boldsymbol{p}$ and $\boldsymbol{q}$, dual variable $\boldsymbol{\lambda}$, upper bound $g(\boldsymbol{\lambda})$

Proof. We have

$$
\begin{aligned}
\sum_{\alpha \in F(i)} \boldsymbol{\lambda}_{i\alpha}^{(t+1)} &= \sum_{\alpha \in F(i)} \boldsymbol{\lambda}_{i\alpha}^{(t)} - \eta\left(\sum_{\alpha \in F(i)} \boldsymbol{q}_{i\alpha}^{(t+1)} - |F(i)|\boldsymbol{p}_i^{(t+1)}\right) \\
&= \sum_{\alpha \in F(i)} \boldsymbol{\lambda}_{i\alpha}^{(t)} - \eta\left(\sum_{\alpha \in F(i)} \boldsymbol{q}_{i\alpha}^{(t+1)} - \sum_{\alpha \in F(i)}\left(\boldsymbol{q}_{i\alpha}^{(t+1)} - \eta^{-1}\boldsymbol{\lambda}_{i\alpha}^{(t)}\right)\right) \\
&= \mathbf{0}.
\end{aligned}
$$

$\square$

Assembling all these pieces together leads to AD³ (Algorithm 3.2). Notice that AD³ retains the modular structure of PSDD (Algorithm 3.1). The key difference is that AD³ also broadcasts the current global solution to the workers, allowing them to regularize their subproblems toward that solution, thus speeding up the consensus. This is embodied in the procedure SOLVEQP (line 7), which replaces COMPUTEMAP of Algorithm 3.1.

3.5.2   Convergence Analysis

Convergence of AD³ follows directly from the general convergence properties of ADMM. Unlike PSDD (Algorithm 3.1), convergence is ensured with a fixed step size η; therefore, no annealing is required.

Proposition 3.4 (Convergence). *Let $(\boldsymbol{q}^{(t)}, \boldsymbol{p}^{(t)}, \boldsymbol{\lambda}^{(t)})_t$ be the sequence of iterates produced by Algorithm 3.2. Then the following holds:*

1. The primal sequence $(\boldsymbol{p}^{(t)}, \boldsymbol{q}^{(t)})_{t \in \mathbb{N}}$ converges to a solution of the LP-MAP-P (3.11); as a consequence, primal feasibility of LP-MAP-P is achieved in the limit, i.e., $\|\mathbf{M}_{i\alpha}\boldsymbol{q}_\alpha^{(t)} - \boldsymbol{p}_i^{(t)}\| \to 0, \quad \forall(i, \alpha) \in E$;

2. *The dual sequence* $(\boldsymbol{\lambda}^{(t)})_{t\in\mathbb{N}}$ *converges to a solution of LP-MAP-D (3.12); moreover, this sequence is always dual feasible, i.e., it is contained in* Λ.

Proof. 1 and the first part of 2 are general properties of ADMM (Glowinski and Le Tallec, 1989, Theorem 4.2). The second part of statement 2 stems from Proposition 3.3.   □

The next proposition states the $O(1/\epsilon)$ iteration bound of AD³, which is better than the $O(1/\epsilon^2)$ bound of PSDD.

Proposition 3.5 (Convergence rate)*. Let* $\boldsymbol{\lambda}^*$ *be a solution of LP-MAP-D (3.12),* $\bar{\boldsymbol{\lambda}}_T := \frac{1}{T}\sum_{t=1}^{T}\boldsymbol{\lambda}^{(t)}$ *be the "averaged" Lagrange multipliers after* T *iterations of AD³, and* $g(\bar{\boldsymbol{\lambda}}_T)$ *the corresponding estimate of the dual objective (an upper bound). Then,* $g(\bar{\boldsymbol{\lambda}}_T) - g(\boldsymbol{\lambda}^*) \le \epsilon$ *after* $T \le C/\epsilon$ *iterations, where*

$$C \;\le\; \frac{5\eta}{2}|E| + \frac{5}{2\eta}\|\boldsymbol{\lambda}^*\|^2. \tag{3.22}$$

Proof. A detailed proof is presented in Martins et al. (2012), adapting a recent result of Wang and Banerjee (2012) concerning convergence of ADMM in a variational inequality setting.   □

As expected, the bound (3.22) increases with the number of overlapping variables, quantified by the number of edges $|E|$ and the magnitude of the optimal dual vector $\boldsymbol{\lambda}^*$. Note that if there is a good estimate of $\|\boldsymbol{\lambda}^*\|$, then (3.22) can be used to choose a step size η that minimizes the bound.[10] The optimal stepsize is $\eta = \|\boldsymbol{\lambda}^*\| \times |E|^{-1/2}$, which would lead to $T \le 5\epsilon^{-1}|E|^{1/2}$.

3.5.3 Other Details and Extensions

Primal and Dual Residuals. Because the AD³ iterates are dual feasible, it is also possible to check the conditions in Proposition 3.2 to obtain optimality certificates, as in PSDD. Moreover, even when the LP-MAP relaxation is not tight, AD³ can provide stopping conditions by keeping track of primal and dual residuals (an important advantage over PSDD), as described in Boyd et al. (2011). The *primal residual* $r_P^{(t)}$ is the amount by which the agreement constraints are violated,

$$r_P^{(t)} = \frac{\sum_{(i,\alpha)\in E}\|\mathbf{M}_{i\alpha}\boldsymbol{q}_\alpha^{(t)} - \boldsymbol{p}_i^{(t)}\|^2}{\sum_{(i,\alpha)\in E}|\mathcal{Y}_i|} \in [0,1]. \tag{3.23}$$

---

10. Although Proposition 3.4 guarantees convergence for any choice of η, this parameter may strongly impact the behavior of the algorithm. In our experiments, we dynamically adjust η in earlier iterations using the heuristic described in Boyd et al. (2011, Section 3.4.1).

The *dual residual* $r_D^{(t)}$ is the amount by which a dual optimality condition is violated,

$$r_D^{(t)} = \frac{\sum_{(i,\alpha)\in E} \|\boldsymbol{p}_i^{(t)} - \boldsymbol{p}_i^{(t-1)}\|^2}{\sum_{(i,\alpha)\in E} |\mathcal{Y}_i|} \in [0, 1]. \tag{3.24}$$

We adopt as stopping criterion that these two residuals fall below 10^{-6}.

Approximate Solutions of the Local Subproblems. The next proposition states that convergence may still hold even if the local subproblems are only solved approximately. The importance of this result will be clear in Section 3.6.1, where we describe a general iterative algorithm for solving the local quadratic subproblems. Essentially, Proposition 3.6 allows these subproblems to be solved numerically up to some accuracy without compromising global convergence, as long as the accuracy of the solutions improves sufficiently fast over AD^3 iterations.

Proposition 3.6 (Eckstein and Bertsekas, 1992)**.** *For every iteration t, let $\widehat{\boldsymbol{q}}^{(t)}$ contain the exact solutions of (3.20) and $\tilde{\boldsymbol{q}}^{(t)}$ those produced by an approximate algorithm. Then Proposition 3.4 still holds, provided that the sequence of errors is summable, i.e., $\sum_{t=1}^{\infty} \|\widehat{\boldsymbol{q}}^{(t)} - \tilde{\boldsymbol{q}}^{(t)}\| < \infty$.*

Caching the Subproblems. In practice, considerable speed-ups can be achieved by *caching* the subproblems, following a strategy proposed for PSDD by Koo et al. (2010). After a few iterations, many variables $\boldsymbol{p}_i$ reach a consensus (*i.e.*, $\boldsymbol{p}_i^{(t)} = \boldsymbol{q}_{i\alpha}^{(t+1)}, \forall \alpha \in F(i)$) and enter an idle state: they are left unchanged by the $\boldsymbol{p}$-update (line 10), and so do the Lagrange variables $\boldsymbol{\lambda}_{i\alpha}^{(t+1)}$ (line 11). If at iteration t all variables in a subproblem at factor α are idle, then $\boldsymbol{q}_\alpha^{(t+1)} = \boldsymbol{q}_\alpha^{(t)}$; hence, the corresponding subproblem does not need to be solved. Typically, many variables and subproblems enter this idle state after the first few rounds. We will show the practical benefits of caching in the experimental section (Section 3.7.1, Figure 3.5).

Exact Decoding with Branch-and-Bound. Recall that AD^3, as just described, solves the LP-MAP relaxation, which is not only always tight. Das et al. (2012) propose to wrap AD^3 into a *branch-and-bound* search procedure to find the *exact MAP*, using the property that the optimal objective value of LP-MAP is an *upper bound* of MAP, and that AD^3, along its execution, keeps track of a sequence of feasible dual points (as guaranteed by Proposition 3.4, item 2), building tighter and tighter upper bounds. Although this procedure has worst-case exponential runtime, it was found empirically quite effective in problems for which the relaxations are near exact.

3.6   Local Subproblems in AD³

We now turn our attention to the AD³ local subproblems (3.20). In many important cases, these QPs can be solved efficiently. Some examples are:

- Ising factors (Martins et al., 2011a), which can be solved in constant time.

- The logic constraint factors in Section 3.2.3, useful as building blocks for expressing soft and hard constraints in first-order logic (Martins et al., 2011a); these can be solved in linear time with respect to the number of variables linked to the factor.[11]

- Budget and knapsack factors, which are important for dealing with cardinality-based potentials or to promote diversity (Tarlow et al., 2010; Almeida and Martins, 2013). Runtime is again linear in the size of the factor.

- Parity-check factors (Barman et al., 2011), used in low-density parity check decoding. Runtime is $O(L \log L)$, where L is the number of parity check bits.

In fact, for hard-constraint factors, the AD³ subproblems have a nice geometric interpretation as Euclidean projection onto the marginal polytope of the factor (as illustrated in Figure 3.1). In this section, we complement these results with a general *active-set procedure* for solving the AD³ subproblems for *arbitrary* factors, the only requirement being a black-box MAP solver—the same as the PSDD algorithm. This makes AD³ applicable to a wide range of problems. In particular, it makes possible to handle *structured factors* (Section 3.2.3) by invoking specialized MAP decoders.[12]

3.6.1   Active Set Method

Our active set method is based on Nocedal and Wright (1999, Section 16.4); it is an iterative algorithm that addresses the AD³ subproblems (3.20) by solving a sequence of linear problems. By subtracting a constant, re-scaling,

---

11. This is also the asymptotic complexity for computing the MAP for those factors. While the complexities reported by Martins et al. (2011a) have an extra logarithmic term, in all cases the runtime can drop to linear by using linear-time selection algorithms. We refer the interested reader to Almeida and Martins (2013) for details.

12. Past work (Martins et al., 2011a) suggested another strategy (*graph binarization*) to deal with dense and structured factors. However, this is outperformed, in practice, by the active set method we next present (see Martins 2012, Figure 6.3, for a comparison).

and flipping signs, (3.20) can be written more compactly as

$$\text{minimize} \quad \frac{1}{2}\|\mathbf{M}\boldsymbol{q}_\alpha - \boldsymbol{a}\|^2 - \boldsymbol{b} \cdot \boldsymbol{q}_\alpha \qquad (3.25)$$

$$\text{with respect to} \quad \boldsymbol{q}_\alpha \in \mathbb{R}^{|\mathcal{Y}_\alpha|}$$

$$\text{subject to} \quad \mathbf{1} \cdot \boldsymbol{q}_\alpha = 1, \quad \boldsymbol{q}_\alpha \geq \mathbf{0},$$

where $\boldsymbol{a} := (\boldsymbol{a}_i)_{i \in V(\alpha)}$, with $\boldsymbol{a}_i := \boldsymbol{p}_i + \eta^{-1}(\boldsymbol{\theta}_{i\alpha} + \boldsymbol{\lambda}_{i\alpha})$; $\boldsymbol{b} := \eta^{-1}\boldsymbol{\theta}_\alpha$; and $\mathbf{M} := (\mathbf{M}_{i\alpha})_{i \in V(\alpha)}$ denotes a matrix with $\sum_i |\mathcal{Y}_i|$ rows and $|\mathcal{Y}_\alpha|$ columns.

The next crucial proposition (proved in Martins et al. (2012)) states that problem (3.25) always admits a *sparse solution*.

Proposition 3.7. *Problem* (3.25) *admits a solution* $\boldsymbol{q}_\alpha^* \in \mathbb{R}^{|\mathcal{Y}_\alpha|}$ *with at most* $\sum_{i \in V(\alpha)} |\mathcal{Y}_i| - V(\alpha) + 1$ *non-zero components.*

The fact that the solution lies in a low-dimensional subspace makes active set methods appealing, because they only keep track of an *active set* of variables, that is, the non-zero components of $\boldsymbol{q}_\alpha$. Proposition 3.7 tells us that such an algorithm only needs to maintain at most $O(\sum_i |\mathcal{Y}_i|)$ elements in the active set—note the *additive*, rather than multiplicative, dependency on the number of values of the variables. Our active set method seeks to identify the low-dimensional support of the solution $\boldsymbol{q}_\alpha^*$ by generating sparse iterates $\boldsymbol{q}_\alpha^{(1)}, \boldsymbol{q}_\alpha^{(2)}, \ldots$, while it maintains a working set $W \subseteq \mathcal{Y}_\alpha$ with the inequality constraints of (3.25) that are *inactive* along the way (*i.e.*, those $\boldsymbol{y}_\alpha$ for which $q_\alpha(\boldsymbol{y}_\alpha) > 0$ holds strictly). Each iteration adds or removes elements from the working set while it monotonically decreases the objective of Equation (3.25).[13]

Lagrangian and KKT Conditions. Let τ and $\boldsymbol{\mu}$ be dual variables associated with the equality and inequality constraints of (3.25), respectively. The Lagrangian function is

$$L(\boldsymbol{q}_\alpha, \tau, \boldsymbol{\mu}) = \frac{1}{2}\|\mathbf{M}\boldsymbol{q}_\alpha - \boldsymbol{a}\|^2 - \boldsymbol{b} \cdot \boldsymbol{q}_\alpha - \tau(1 - \mathbf{1} \cdot \boldsymbol{q}_\alpha) - \boldsymbol{\mu} \cdot \boldsymbol{q}_\alpha. \qquad (3.26)$$

---

13. Our description differs from Nocedal and Wright (1999) in which their working set contains *active* rather than inactive constraints. In our case, most constraints are active for the optimal $\boldsymbol{q}_\alpha^*$; therefore, it is appealing to store the ones that are not.

This gives rise to the following Karush-Kuhn-Tucker (KKT) conditions:

$$\mathbf{M}^\top (\boldsymbol{a} - \mathbf{M}\boldsymbol{q}_\alpha) + \boldsymbol{b} = \tau \mathbf{1} - \boldsymbol{\mu} \quad (\nabla_{\boldsymbol{q}_\alpha} L = \mathbf{0}) \tag{3.27}$$

$$\mathbf{1} \cdot \boldsymbol{q}_\alpha = 1, \ \boldsymbol{q}_\alpha \geq \mathbf{0}, \ \boldsymbol{\mu} \geq \mathbf{0} \quad \text{(Primal/dual feasibility)} \tag{3.28}$$

$$\boldsymbol{\mu} \cdot \boldsymbol{q}_\alpha = \mathbf{0} \quad \text{(Complementary slackness).} \tag{3.29}$$

The method works as follows. At each iteration s, it first checks whether the current iterate $\boldsymbol{q}_\alpha^{(s)}$ is a *subspace minimizer*, *i.e.*, if it optimizes the objective of (3.25) in the sparse subspace defined by the working set W, $\{\boldsymbol{q}_\alpha \in \Delta^{|\mathcal{Y}_\alpha|} \mid q_\alpha(\boldsymbol{y}_\alpha) = 0, \forall \boldsymbol{y}_\alpha \notin W\}$. This check can be made by first solving a relaxation where the inequality constraints are ignored. Because in this subspace the components of $\boldsymbol{q}_\alpha$ not in W will be zeros, one can simply delete those entries from $\boldsymbol{q}_\alpha$ and $\boldsymbol{b}$ and the corresponding columns in $\mathbf{M}$; we use a horizontal bar to denote these truncated $\mathbb{R}^{|W|}$-vectors. The problem can be written as:

$$\begin{aligned} \text{minimize} \quad & \frac{1}{2}\|\bar{\mathbf{M}}\bar{\boldsymbol{q}}_\alpha - \boldsymbol{a}\|^2 - \bar{\boldsymbol{b}} \cdot \bar{\boldsymbol{q}}_\alpha \\ \text{with respect to} \quad & \bar{\boldsymbol{q}}_\alpha \in \mathbb{R}^{|W|} \\ \text{subject to} \quad & \mathbf{1} \cdot \bar{\boldsymbol{q}}_\alpha = 1. \end{aligned} \tag{3.30}$$

The solution of this equality-constrained QP can be found by solving a system of KKT equations:[14]

$$\begin{bmatrix} \bar{\mathbf{M}}^\top \bar{\mathbf{M}} & \mathbf{1} \\ \mathbf{1}^\top & 0 \end{bmatrix} \begin{bmatrix} \bar{\boldsymbol{q}}_\alpha \\ \tau \end{bmatrix} = \begin{bmatrix} \bar{\mathbf{M}}^\top \boldsymbol{a} + \bar{\boldsymbol{b}} \\ 1 \end{bmatrix}. \tag{3.31}$$

The solution of (3.31) will give $(\hat{\boldsymbol{q}}_\alpha, \hat{\tau})$, where $\hat{\boldsymbol{q}}_\alpha \in \mathbb{R}^{|\mathcal{Y}_\alpha|}$ is padded back with zeros. If it happens that $\hat{\boldsymbol{q}}_\alpha = \boldsymbol{q}_\alpha^{(s)}$, then the current iterate $\boldsymbol{q}_\alpha^{(s)}$ is a subspace minimizer; otherwise, a new iterate $\boldsymbol{q}_\alpha^{(s+1)}$ will be computed. We discuss these two events next.

Case 1: $\boldsymbol{q}_\alpha^{(s)}$ is a subspace minimizer. If this happens, then it may be that $\boldsymbol{q}_\alpha^{(s)}$ is the optimal solution of (3.25). By looking at the KKT conditions (3.27)–(3.29), we have that this will happen if and only if $\mathbf{M}^\top(\boldsymbol{a} - \mathbf{M}\boldsymbol{q}_\alpha^{(s)}) +$

---

14. Note that this is a low-dimensional problem, because we are working in a sparse working set. By caching the inverse of the matrix in the left-hand side, this system can be solved in time $O(|W|^2)$ at each iteration. See Martins et al. (2012) for further details.

$\boldsymbol{b} \leq \tau^{(s)} \mathbf{1}$. Define $\boldsymbol{w} := \boldsymbol{a} - \mathbf{M}\boldsymbol{q}_\alpha$. The condition above is equivalent to

$$\max_{\boldsymbol{y}_\alpha \in \mathcal{Y}_\alpha} \left(b(\boldsymbol{y}_\alpha) + \sum_{i \in V(\alpha)} w_i(y_i) \right) \leq \tau^{(s)}. \tag{3.32}$$

It turns out that this maximization is precisely a *local MAP decoding problem*, given a vector of unary potentials $\boldsymbol{w}$ and factor potentials $\boldsymbol{b}$. Thus, the maximizer $\widehat{\boldsymbol{y}}_\alpha$ can be computed via the COMPUTEMAP procedure, which we assume available. If $b(\widehat{\boldsymbol{y}}_\alpha) + \sum_{i \in V(\alpha)} w_i(\widehat{y}_i) \leq \tau^{(s)}$, then the KKT conditions are satisfied and we are done. Otherwise, $\widehat{\boldsymbol{y}}_\alpha$ indicates the most violated condition; we will add it to the active set W and proceed.

Case 2: $q_\alpha^{(s)}$ is not a subspace minimizer.   If this happens, then we compute a new iterate $\boldsymbol{q}_\alpha^{(s+1)}$ by keeping searching in the same subspace. We have already solved a relaxation in (3.30). If we have $\widehat{q}_\alpha(\boldsymbol{y}_\alpha) \geq 0$ for all $\boldsymbol{y}_\alpha \in W$, then the relaxation is tight, so we just set $\boldsymbol{q}_\alpha^{(s+1)} := \widehat{\boldsymbol{q}}_\alpha$ and proceed. Otherwise, we move as much as possible in the direction of $\widehat{\boldsymbol{q}}_\alpha$ while keeping feasibility by defining $\boldsymbol{q}_\alpha^{(s+1)} := (1 - \beta)\boldsymbol{q}_\alpha^{(s)} + \beta\widehat{\boldsymbol{q}}_\alpha$—as described in Nocedal and Wright (1999), the value of $\beta \in [0, 1]$ can be computed in closed form:

$$\beta = \min \left\{ 1, \min_{\boldsymbol{y}_\alpha \in W \,:\, q_\alpha^{(s)}(\boldsymbol{y}_\alpha) > \widehat{q}_\alpha(\boldsymbol{y}_\alpha)} \frac{q_\alpha^{(s)}(\boldsymbol{y}_\alpha)}{q_\alpha^{(s)}(\boldsymbol{y}_\alpha) - \widehat{q}_\alpha(\boldsymbol{y}_\alpha)} \right\}. \tag{3.33}$$

If $\beta < 1$, then this update will have the effect of making one of the constraints active by zeroing out $q_\alpha^{(s+1)}(\boldsymbol{y}_\alpha)$ for the minimizing $\boldsymbol{y}_\alpha$ above. This so-called "blocking constraint" is thus removed from the working set W.

Algorithm 3.3 describes the complete procedure. The active set W is initialized arbitrarily: a strategy that works well in practice is, in the first AD³ iteration, initialize $W := \{\widehat{\boldsymbol{y}}_\alpha\}$, where $\widehat{\boldsymbol{y}}_\alpha$ is the MAP configuration given log-potentials $\boldsymbol{a}$ and $\boldsymbol{b}$; and in subsequent AD³ iterations, warm-start W with the support of the solution obtained in the previous iteration.

Each iteration of Algorithm 3.3 improves the objective of (3.25), and the algorithm is guaranteed to stop after a finite number of steps (Nocedal and Wright, 1999, Theorem 16.5). In practice, because it is run as a subroutine of AD³, Algorithm 3.3 does not need to be run to optimality, which is convenient in early iterations of AD³ (this is supported by Proposition 3.6). The ability to warm-start with the solution from the previous round is useful in practice: we have observed that, thanks to this warm-starting strategy, few inner iterations are typically necessary for the correct active set to be identified. We will see some empirical evidence in Section 3.7.1.

Algorithm 3.3 Active Set Algorithm for Solving a General AD^3 Subproblem

---

1: **input:** Parameters $\boldsymbol{a}, \boldsymbol{b}, \mathbf{M}$, starting point $\boldsymbol{q}_\alpha^{(0)}$
2: initialize $W^{(0)}$ as the support of $\boldsymbol{q}_\alpha^{(0)}$
3: **for** $s = 0, 1, 2, \ldots$ **do**
4:      solve the KKT system and obtain $\widehat{\boldsymbol{q}}_\alpha$ and $\widehat{\tau}$ (Eq. 3.31)
5:      **if** $\widehat{\boldsymbol{q}}_\alpha = \boldsymbol{q}_\alpha^{(s)}$ **then**
6:          compute $\boldsymbol{w} := \boldsymbol{a} - \mathbf{M}\widehat{\boldsymbol{q}}_\alpha$
7:          obtain the tighter constraint $\widehat{\boldsymbol{y}}_\alpha$ via $\boldsymbol{e}_{\widehat{\boldsymbol{y}}_\alpha} = \textsc{ComputeMAP}(\boldsymbol{b} + \mathbf{M}^\top \boldsymbol{w})$
8:          **if** $b(\widehat{\boldsymbol{y}}_\alpha) + \sum_{i \in V(\alpha)} w_i(\widehat{y}_i) \leq \widehat{\tau}$ **then**
9:              return solution $\widehat{\boldsymbol{q}}_\alpha$
10:         **else**
11:             add the most violated constraint to the active set: $W^{(s+1)} := W^{(s)} \cup \{\widehat{\boldsymbol{y}}_\alpha\}$
12:         **end if**
13:     **else**
14:         compute the interpolation constant β as in (3.33)
15:         set $\boldsymbol{q}_\alpha^{(s+1)} := (1 - \beta)\boldsymbol{q}_\alpha^{(s)} + \beta\widehat{\boldsymbol{q}}_\alpha$
16:         **if** if $\beta < 1$ **then**
17:             pick the blocking constraint $\widehat{\boldsymbol{y}}_\alpha$ in (3.33)
18:             remove $\widehat{\boldsymbol{y}}_\alpha$ from the active set: $W^{(s+1)} := W^{(s)} \setminus \{\widehat{\boldsymbol{y}}_\alpha\}$
19:         **end if**
20:     **end if**
21: **end for**
22: **output:** $\widehat{\boldsymbol{q}}_\alpha$

3.7   Experiments

We next provide empirical results using AD^3 for the NLP applications described in Section 3.3. We refer the interested reader to Martins et al. (2012) for a broader empirical evaluation in other tasks and datasets.

3.7.1   Turbo Parsing

We applied AD^3 to multilingual dependency parsing using third-order models and the factor graph representation described in Section 3.3.1.[15]

For English, we used two data sets: English-I was derived from the Penn Treebank (Marcus et al., 1993), converted to a dependency treebank by applying the head rules of Yamada and Matsumoto (2003). For this data set, the resulting dependencies are all *projective* (i.e., all the dependency arcs are nested, see footnote 3). English-II contains non-projective dependencies and is the data set used in the CoNLL 2008 shared task (Surdeanu et al., 2008). Non-projective dependencies are particularly appropriate for languages with

---

15. The resulting parser is released as free software under the name `TurboParser` `2.1` and available for download at `http://www.ark.cs.cmu.edu/TurboParser`.

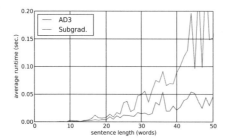 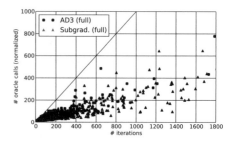

Figure 3.5: Left: averaged runtimes in the English-I dev-set as a function of the sentence length. For PSDD, we chose for each sentence the most favorable stepsize in $\{0.001, 0.01, 0.1, 1\}$. Right: number of calls to COMPUTEMAP for AD^3 and PSDD as a function of the number of iterations (the number of calls is normalized by dividing by the number of factors). In PSDD, this number would equal the number of iterations if there was no caching (black line); in AD^3, it would be even higher because COMPUTEMAP is called multiple times in the active set algorithm. Yet both algorithms make significantly fewer calls. Remarkably, after just a few iterations, the number of calls made by AD^3 and PSDD is comparable, as the number of active set iterations is quickly amortized during the execution of AD^3.

a more flexible word order, such as Czech, Dutch, and German; we report here results for those languages using the CoNLL-X data sets (Buchholz and Marsi, 2006) with the standard splits.[16]

For each language, we trained linear models using various features decomposing over the parts in Figure 3.3 depending on words, part-of-speech tags, and arc direction and length. To ensure valid parse trees at test time, we rounded fractional solutions as in Martins et al. (2009), yet solutions were integral $\approx 95\%$ of the time. Figure 3.5 shows average runtimes of AD^3 and PSDD on this task as a function of the sentence length. Clearly, AD^3 scales better, even though it needs to solve more involved local subproblems. It turns out that the caching and warm-starting procedures are crucial in achieving these runtimes, as illustrated in the right part of the figure.

Table 3.2 shows results for several languages, comparing accuracies and speeds with those of state-of-the-art parsers, including projective parsers such as Rush and Petrov (2012) and Zhang and McDonald (2012). For English-I, these parsers are in advantage, because they constrain their predicted trees to be projective and therefore easier to decode. Yet even in this data set, our parser's accuracy does not lag behind these strong competitors, being faster than the system of Zhang and McDonald (2012) based on beam search but considerable slower than the highly optimized vine cascade approach of Rush and Petrov (2012), which permits exact decoding with

---

16. Experiments with more languages and baselines are reported in Martins et al. (2013).

	AD^3	K^+10	M^+11	RP12	ZM12
English-I	**93.07**/735	92.46/112	92.53/66	92.7–/4,460*	93.06/220
English-II	**93.22**/785	92.57/131	92.68/–		
Dutch	**86.19**/599	85.81/121	85.53/–		
German	**92.41**/965		91.89/–	90.8–/2,880	91.35/–
Czech	**90.32**/501		89.46/–		

Table 3.2: Dependency parsing results for different data sets. Reported are unlabeled attachment scores ignoring punctuation (left) and parsing speeds in tokens per second (right). K^+10 is Koo et al. (2010); M^+11 is Martins et al. (2011b); RP12 is Rush and Petrov (2012); ZM12 is Zhang and McDonald (2012). Our speeds include the time necessary for pruning, evaluating features, and decoding as measured on an Intel Core i7 processor @3.4 GHz. The others are speeds reported in the cited papers, converted to tokens per second. The RP12 results on English I, marked with an asterisk, are not directly comparable, because a different dependency conversion scheme was used (see Martins et al. (2013) for details).

dynamic programming. For the other four data sets, `TurboParser` achieved the best reported scores, with speeds that are the highest reported among higher-order non-projective parsers. More details about these experiments are presented in Martins et al. (2013).

3.7.2 Summarization

Our second task is compressive summarization, where we applied AD^3 to the factor graph in Section 3.3.2. The model was trained in a multi-task setting, as described in Almeida and Martins (2013), leveraging data sets for compressive summarization (Berg-Kirkpatrick et al., 2011), manual abstracts from DUC/TAC tasks, and a data set collected by Woodsend and Lapata (2011) containing 4,481 sentence pairs from the English and Simple English Wikipedias. Evaluation is on the non-update portion of the TAC-2008 data set, containing 48 multi-document summarization problems; each provides 10 related news articles as input and asks for a summary with up to 100 words, which is evaluated against four manually written abstracts. We applied a simple rounding procedure to obtain valid summaries from fractional LP-MAP solutions (see Almeida and Martins (2013) for details).

Table 3.3 summarizes the results. The three leftmost columns refer to strong baselines: ICSI-1, the best performing system in the TAC-2008 evaluation (which is extractive), and two recent compressive summarizers (Berg-Kirkpatrick et al., 2011; Woodsend and Lapata, 2012). All these systems use off-the-shelf ILP solvers. The remaining columns show the results achieved by our implementation of a pure extractive system and a compressive sum-

ICSI-1	BGK'11	WL'12	Extr., ILP	Comp., ILP	Comp., AD^3
11.03/–	11.71/–	11.37/–	11.16/0.265	**12.40**/10.394	**12.30**/0.406

Table 3.3: Results for compressive summarization. Shown are ROUGE-2 recall scores (Lin, 2004) and averaged runtimes (in seconds) to solve a summarization problem in TAC-2008. The three leftmost baselines are Gillick et al. (2008), Berg-Kirkpatrick et al. (2011), and Woodsend and Lapata (2012). The remaining columns are our implementation of ILP-based extractive and compressive systems (decoded with GLPK) and our compressive system decoded with AD^3.

Japan dispatched four military ships to help Russia rescue seven crew members aboard a small submarine trapped on the seabed in the Far East. The Russian Pacific Fleet said the crew had 120 hours of oxygen reserves *on board when the submarine submerged at midday Thursday (2300 GMT Wednesday) off the Kamchatka peninsula, the stretch of Far Eastern Russia facing the Bering Sea.* The submarine, *used in rescue, research and intelligence-gathering missions,* became stuck at the bottom of the Bay of Berezovaya off Russia's Far East coast when its propeller was caught *in a fishing net.* The Russian submarine had been tending an underwater antenna mounted to the sea floor *when it became snagged on a wire helping to stabilize a ventilation cable attached to the antenna.* Rescue crews lowered a British remote-controlled underwater vehicle to a Russian mini-submarine trapped *deep* under the Pacific Ocean, hoping to free the vessel and its seven trapped crewmen *before their air supply ran out.*

Figure 3.6: Example summary from our system. Removed text is *grayed out.*

marizer, decoded with GLPK (the ILP solver used by Berg-Kirkpatrick et al. (2011)) and AD^3. The ROUGE scores show that the compressive summarizers yield considerable benefits in content coverage over extractive systems, confirming previous findings (Berg-Kirkpatrick et al., 2011). Our gains with respect to the compressive baselines come from our multi-task training procedure. Regarding the runtimes, we see that AD^3 is orders of magnitude faster than the (exact) ILP solver, with a similar accuracy level; and it is competitive with the speed of an extractive summarizer. To our knowledge, this is the first time a compressive summarizer achieves such a favorable accuracy/speed tradeoff. Figure 3.6 shows an example summary.

3.8   Related Work

A few related methods have appeared in the literature after our earlier work in AD^3 (Martins et al., 2010a, 2011a).

Meshi and Globerson (2011) also applied ADMM to LP-MAP decoding, although addressing the *dual* rather than the primal. Yedidia et al. (2011) proposed a *divide-and-concur algorithm* for low-density parity check

(LDPC) decoding, which resembles a non-convex version of AD^3. Barman et al. (2011) proposed an algorithm analogous to AD^3 for the same LDPC decoding problem; their subproblems correspond to projections onto the parity polytope, for which they have derived an efficient algorithm. More recently, Fu et al. (2013) proposed a Bethe-ADMM procedure resembling AD^3 but with a variant of ADMM that makes the subproblems become local marginal computations.

A different strategy was proposed by Jojic et al. (2010) to overcome the limitations of the PSDD algorithm pointed out in Section 3.5. They also achieve a $O(1/\epsilon)$ iteration bound by smoothening the objective of (3.12) with an "entropic" perturbation (controlled by a "temperature" parameter) and applying an accelerated gradient method (Nesterov, 2005). An advantage is that the local subproblems become marginal computations, which are formally simpler than our QPs (3.25). However, there are two drawbacks: first, they need to operate at near-zero temperatures, which leads to numerical instabilities in some structured factors (the $O(1/\epsilon)$ bound requires setting the temperature to $O(\epsilon)$); second, the solution of the local subproblems is always *dense*, which precludes the benefits of caching.

3.9 Conclusions

We introduced AD^3, an LP-MAP decoder based on ADMM. AD^3 enjoys the modularity of dual decomposition methods and achieves faster consensus than subgradient algorithms, both theoretically (with its $O(1/\epsilon)$ iteration bound) and in practice.

AD^3 can handle hard constraint factors, such as those arising from statements in first-order logic and budget constraints, which are typical in NLP and IR applications. For dense and structured factors, we introduced an *active set method* for solving the AD^3 subproblems, which requires only a local MAP decoder as a black-box. We have shown the effectiveness of AD^3 in two important NLP applications; dependency parsing and summarization.

Acknowledgments

I would like to thank Noah Smith, Mário Figueiredo, Eric Xing, Pedro Aguiar, and Miguel Almeida. This work was partially supported by the EU/FEDER programme, QREN/POR Lisboa (Portugal), under the Intelligo project (contract 2012/24803), and by a FCT grant PTDC/EEI-SII/2312/2012.

3.10   References

M. B. Almeida and A. F. T. Martins. Fast and robust compressive summarization with dual decomposition and multi-task learning. In *Proc. of the Annual Meeting of the Association for Computational Linguistics*, 2013.

S. Barman, X. Liu, S. Draper, and B. Recht. Decomposition methods for large scale LP decoding. In *49th Annual Allerton Conference on Communication, Control, and Computing*, pages 253–260. IEEE, 2011.

T. Berg-Kirkpatrick, D. Gillick, and D. Klein. Jointly learning to extract and compress. In *Proc. of Annual Meeting of the Association for Computational Linguistics*, 2011.

C. Berrou, A. Glavieux, and P. Thitimajshima. Near Shannon limit error-correcting coding and decoding. In *Proc. of International Conference on Communications*, volume 93, pages 1064–1070, 1993.

D. Bertsekas. *Nonlinear Programming*. Athena Scientific, 2nd edition, 1999.

S. Boyd, N. Parikh, E. Chu, B. Peleato, and J. Eckstein. *Distributed Optimization and Statistical Learning via the Alternating Direction Method of Multipliers*. Now Publishers, 2011.

S. Buchholz and E. Marsi. CoNLL-X shared task on multilingual dependency parsing. In *International Conference on Natural Language Learning*, 2006.

X. Carreras. Experiments with a higher-order projective dependency parser. In *International Conference on Natural Language Learning*, 2007.

M. Chang, L. Ratinov, and D. Roth. Constraints as prior knowledge. In *International Conference of Machine Learning: Workshop on Prior Knowledge for Text and Language Processing*, July 2008.

Y. J. Chu and T. H. Liu. On the shortest arborescence of a directed graph. *Science Sinica*, 14:1396–1400, 1965.

G. Dantzig and P. Wolfe. Decomposition principle for linear programs. *Operations Research*, 8(1):101–111, 1960.

D. Das, A. Martins, and N. Smith. An exact dual decomposition algorithm for shallow semantic parsing with constraints. In *Proc. of First Joint Conference on Lexical and Computational Semantics (*SEM)*, 2012.

J. Duchi, D. Tarlow, G. Elidan, and D. Koller. Using combinatorial optimization within max-product belief propagation. *Advances in Neural Information Processing Systems*, 19, 2007.

J. Eckstein and D. Bertsekas. On the Douglas-Rachford splitting method and the proximal point algorithm for maximal monotone operators. *Mathematical Programming*, 55(1):293–318, 1992.

J. Edmonds. Optimum branchings. *Journal of Research of the National Bureau of Standards*, 71B:233–240, 1967.

J. Eisner. Three new probabilistic models for dependency parsing: An exploration. In *Proc. of International Conference on Computational Linguistics*, pages 340–345, 1996.

H. Everett. Generalized Lagrange multiplier method for solving problems of optimum allocation of resources. *Operations Research*, 11(3):399–417, 1963.

Q. Fu, H. Wang, and A. Banerjee. Bethe-ADMM for tree decomposition based parallel MAP inference. In *Proc. of Uncertainty in Artificial Intelligence*, 2013.

D. Gabay and B. Mercier. A dual algorithm for the solution of nonlinear variational problems via finite element approximation. *Computers and Mathematics with Applications*, 2(1):17–40, 1976.

D. Gillick, B. Favre, and D. Hakkani-Tur. The ICSI summarization system at TAC 2008. In *Proc. of Text Understanding Conference*, 2008.

A. Globerson and T. Jaakkola. Fixing max-product: Convergent message passing algorithms for MAP LP-relaxations. *Neural Information Processing Systems*, 20, 2008.

R. Glowinski and P. Le Tallec. *Augmented Lagrangian and Operator-Splitting Methods in Nonlinear Mechanics*. Society for Industrial Mathematics, 1989.

R. Glowinski and A. Marroco. Sur l'approximation, par éléments finis d'ordre un, et la résolution, par penalisation-dualité, d'une classe de problèmes de Dirichlet non linéaires. *Rev. Franc. Automat. Inform. Rech. Operat.*, 9:41–76, 1975.

M. Guignard and S. Kim. Lagrangean decomposition: A model yielding stronger Lagrangean bounds. *Mathematical Programming*, 39(2):215–228, 1987.

M. Hestenes. Multiplier and gradient methods. *Journal of Optimization Theory and Applications*, 4:302–320, 1969.

V. Jojic, S. Gould, and D. Koller. Accelerated dual decomposition for MAP inference. In *International Conference of Machine Learning*, 2010.

K. Knight and D. Marcu. Statistics-based summarization—step one: Sentence compression. In *Prof. of National Conference on Artificial Intelligence*, 2000.

D. Koller and N. Friedman. *Probabilistic Graphical Models: Principles and Techniques*. The MIT Press, 2009.

V. Kolmogorov. Convergent tree-reweighted message passing for energy minimization. *IEEE Transactions on Pattern Analysis and Machine Intelligence*, 28:1568–1583, 2006.

N. Komodakis, N. Paragios, and G. Tziritas. MRF optimization via dual decomposition: Message-passing revisited. In *Proc. of International Conference on Computer Vision*, 2007.

T. Koo and M. Collins. Efficient third-order dependency parsers. In *Proc. of Annual Meeting of the Association for Computational Linguistics*, pages 1–11, 2010.

T. Koo, A. M. Rush, M. Collins, T. Jaakkola, and D. Sontag. Dual decomposition for parsing with non-projective head automata. In *Proc. of Empirical Methods for Natural Language Processing*, 2010.

F. R. Kschischang, B. J. Frey, and H. A. Loeliger. Factor graphs and the sum-product algorithm. *IEEE Transactions on Information Theory*, 47, 2001.

S. Kübler, R. McDonald, and J. Nivre. *Dependency parsing*. Morgan & Claypool Publishers, 2009.

S. Lauritzen. *Graphical Models*. Clarendon Press, 1996.

C.-Y. Lin. Rouge: A package for automatic evaluation of summaries. In S. S. Marie-Francine Moens, editor, *Text Summarization Branches Out: Proceedings of the ACL-04 Workshop*, pages 74–81, Barcelona, Spain, July 2004.

M. Marcus, M. Marcinkiewicz, and B. Santorini. Building a large annotated corpus of English: The Penn Treebank. *Computational linguistics*, 19(2):313–330, 1993.

A. F. T. Martins. *The Geometry of Constrained Structured Prediction: Applications to Inference and Learning of Natural Language Syntax.* PhD thesis, Carnegie Mellon University and Instituto Superior Técnico, 2012.

A. F. T. Martins, N. A. Smith, and E. P. Xing. Concise Integer Linear Programming Formulations for Dependency Parsing. In *Proc. of Annual Meeting of the Association for Computational Linguistics*, 2009.

A. F. T. Martins, N. A. Smith, E. P. Xing, P. M. Q. Aguiar, and M. A. T. Figueiredo. Augmented Dual Decomposition for MAP Inference. In *Neural Information Processing Systems: Workshop in Optimization for Machine Learning*, 2010a.

A. F. T. Martins, N. A. Smith, E. P. Xing, M. A. T. Figueiredo, and P. M. Q. Aguiar. Turbo parsers: Dependency parsing by approximate variational inference. In *Proc. of Empirical Methods for Natural Language Processing*, 2010b.

A. F. T. Martins, M. A. T. Figueiredo, P. M. Q. Aguiar, N. A. Smith, and E. P. Xing. An augmented Lagrangian approach to constrained MAP inference. In *Proc. of International Conference on Machine Learning*, 2011a.

A. F. T. Martins, N. A. Smith, P. M. Q. Aguiar, and M. A. T. Figueiredo. Dual decomposition with many overlapping components. In *Proc. of Empirical Methods for Natural Language Processing*, 2011b.

A. F. T. Martins, M. A. T. Figueiredo, P. M. Q. Aguiar, N. A. Smith, and E. P. Xing. Alternating directions dual decomposition, 2012. Arxiv preprint arXiv:1212.6550.

A. F. T. Martins, M. B. Almeida, and N. A. Smith. Turning on the turbo: Fast third-order non-projective turbo parsers. In *Proc. of the Annual Meeting of the Association for Computational Linguistics*, 2013.

R. McDonald and G. Satta. On the complexity of non-projective data-driven dependency parsing. In *International Conference on Parsing Technologies*, 2007.

R. T. McDonald, F. Pereira, K. Ribarov, and J. Hajic. Non-projective dependency parsing using spanning tree algorithms. In *Proc. of Empirical Methods for Natural Language Processing*, 2005.

R. J. McEliece, D. J. C. MacKay, and J. F. Cheng. Turbo decoding as an instance of Pearl's "belief propagation" algorithm. *IEEE Journal on Selected Areas in Communications*, 16(2), 1998.

O. Meshi and A. Globerson. An alternating direction method for dual MAP LP relaxation. In *European Conference on Machine Learning and Principles and Practice of Knowledge Discovery in Databases*, 2011.

Y. Nesterov. Smooth minimization of non-smooth functions. *Mathematical Programming*, 103(1):127–152, 2005.

J. Nocedal and S. Wright. *Numerical Optimization.* Springer, 1st edition, 1999.

S. Nowozin and C. Lampert. Global connectivity potentials for random field models. In *IEEE Conference on Computer Vision and Pattern Recognition*, pages 818–825. IEEE, 2009.

J. Pearl. *Probabilistic Reasoning in Intelligent Systems: Networks of Plausible Inference.* Morgan Kaufmann, 1988.

M. Powell. A method for nonlinear constraints in minimization problems. In R. Fletcher, editor, *Optimization*, pages 283–298. Academic Press, 1969.

M. Richardson and P. Domingos. Markov logic networks. *Machine Learning*, 62 (1):107–136, 2006.

T. Richardson and R. Urbanke. *Modern Coding Theory*. Cambridge University Press, 2008.

A. Rush and M. Collins. A tutorial on dual decomposition and Lagrangian relaxation for inference in natural language processing. *Journal of Artificial Intelligence Research*, 45:305–362, 2012.

A. M. Rush and S. Petrov. Vine pruning for efficient multi-pass dependency parsing. In *Proc. of Conference of the North American Chapter of the Association for Computational Linguistics*, 2012.

M. Schlesinger. Syntactic analysis of two-dimensional visual signals in noisy conditions. *Kibernetika*, 4:113–130, 1976.

D. Smith and J. Eisner. Dependency parsing by belief propagation. In *Proc. of Empirical Methods for Natural Language Processing*, 2008.

N. A. Smith. *Linguistic Structure Prediction*, volume 13 of *Synthesis Lectures on Human Language Technologies*. Morgan and Claypool, May 2011.

D. Sontag, A. Globerson, and T. Jaakkola. Introduction to dual decomposition for inference. In *Optimization for Machine Learning*. MIT Press, 2011.

M. Surdeanu, R. Johansson, A. Meyers, L. Màrquez, and J. Nivre. The CoNLL-2008 Shared Task on Joint Parsing of Syntactic and Semantic Dependencies. *Proc. of International Conference on Natural Language Learning*, 2008.

C. Sutton. Collective segmentation and labeling of distant entities in information extraction. Technical report, DTIC Document, 2004.

R. Tanner. A recursive approach to low complexity codes. *IEEE Transactions on Information Theory*, 27(5):533–547, 1981.

D. Tarlow, I. E. Givoni, and R. S. Zemel. HOP-MAP: Efficient message passing with high order potentials. In *AISTATS*, 2010.

M. Wainwright and M. Jordan. *Graphical Models, Exponential Families, and Variational Inference*. Now Publishers, 2008.

M. Wainwright, T. Jaakkola, and A. Willsky. MAP estimation via agreement on trees: Message-passing and linear programming. *IEEE Transactions on Information Theory*, 51(11):3697–3717, 2005.

H. Wang and A. Banerjee. Online alternating direction method. In *Proc. of International Conference on Machine Learning*, 2012.

T. Werner. A linear programming approach to max-sum problem: A review. *IEEE Transactions on Pattern Analysis and Machine Intelligence*, 29:1165–1179, 2007.

K. Woodsend and M. Lapata. Wikisimple: Automatic simplification of wikipedia articles. In *Proc. of AAAI Conference on Artificial Intelligence*, pages 927–932, 2011.

K. Woodsend and M. Lapata. Multiple aspect summarization using integer linear programming. In *Proc. of Empirical Methods in Natural Language Processing*, 2012.

H. Yamada and Y. Matsumoto. Statistical dependency analysis with support vector machines. In *Proc. of International Conference on Parsing Technologies*, 2003.

C. Yanover, T. Meltzer, and Y. Weiss. Linear programming relaxations and belief propagation–an empirical study. *Journal of Machine Learning Research*, 7:1887–1907, 2006.

J. Yedidia, Y. Wang, and S. Draper. Divide and concur and difference-map BP decoders for LDPC codes. *IEEE Transactions on Information Theory*, 57(2): 786–802, 2011.

H. Zhang and R. McDonald. Generalized higher-order dependency parsing with cube pruning. In *Proc. of Empirical Methods in Natural Language Processing*, 2012.

4   Generalized Sequential Tree-Reweighted Message Passing

Thomas Schoenemann　　　　　　thomasschoenemann@yahoo.de

Vladimir Kolmogorov　　　　　　vnk@ist.ac.at
IST Austria
Klosterneuburg, Austria

This chapter addresses the problem of approximate MAP-MRF inference in general graphical models. Following Werner (2010), we consider a family of linear programming relaxations of the problem where each relaxation is specified by a set of nested pairs of factors for which the marginalization constraint needs to be enforced. We develop a generalization of the tree-reweighted message passing (TRW-S) algorithm (Kolmogorov, 2006) for this problem, where we use a decomposition into junction *chains, monotonic w.r.t. some ordering on the nodes. This generalizes the* monotonic *chains in (Kolmogorov, 2006) in a natural way. We also show how to deal with nested factors in an efficient way. Experiments show an improvement over min-sum diffusion, MPLP, and subgradient algorithms on a number of computer vision problems.*

4.1   Introduction

This chapter is devoted to the problem of minimizing a function of discrete variables represented as a sum of *factors*, where a factor is a term depending on a certain subset of variables. The problem is also known as MAP-MRF inference in a graphical model. Due to the generality of the definition, it has applications in many areas. Probably the most well-studied case is when each factor depends on at most two variables (*pairwise MRFs*). Many inference algorithms have been proposed. One prominent approach is to try to solve a natural linear programming (LP) relaxation of the problem, sometimes called *Schlesinger LP* (Werner, 2007). A lot of research went into developing efficient solvers for this special LP as detailed below.

A similar LP can also be formulated for higher-order MRFs. In fact, this can be done in many ways. We follow the formalism of Werner (2010) who describes a family of LP relaxations specified by a set of pairs of nested factors for which the marginalization constraint needs to be enforced. This approach can also be used for pairwise MRFs: we can obtain a hierarchy of progressively tighter relaxations by (i) grouping some pairwise factors into larger factors (or introducing higher-order factors with zero cost functions), and (ii) formulating an LP for the resulting higher-order MRF. This hierarchy covers the *Sherali-Adams hierarchy* but gives a finer control over the relaxation (see Sontag, 2010).

Contributions.   We present a new algorithm for solving the relaxation discussed above. It builds on the *sequential tree-reweighted message passing* (TRW-S) algorithm of Kolmogorov (2006), which in turn builds on Wainwright et al. (2005). TRW-S showed a good performance for pairwise MRFs (Szeliski et al., 2008; Tarlow et al., 2011; Savchynskyy et al., 2012), so generalizing it to higher-order MRFs is a natural direction. While developing such a generalization, we had to overcome some technical difficulties, such as finding the right definition for *monotonic junction chains* and deciding how to deal with nested factors.

Related Work.   First, we discuss techniques that perform a block-coordinate ascent on the objective function. Note, they may get stuck in a suboptimal point (Kolmogorov, 2006; Werner, 2007).

Besides Kolmogorov (2006), the most related methods are *min-sum diffusion* (MSD) (Werner, 2010) and *tree-consistency bound optimization* (TBCO) (Meltzer et al., 2009). The latter proposed a general framework for obtaining convergent algorithms. It covers many existing techniques (e.g., MSD and *MPLP*), as well as ours. However, Meltzer et al. (2009) did not propose any specific choices for the case of higher-order factors, restricting experiments to four-connected grids. The efficiency of computing min-marginals was also not considered. In contrast, the focus of our chapter is on investigating which choices lead to more efficient techniques in practice. Note, monotonicity for the higher-order case was not mentioned in (Meltzer et al., 2009). The same applies to Zheng et al. (2012); again, they did not propose specific choices for graphs other than regular grids.

Other coordinate ascent techniques (formulated for restricted cases) include MPLP (Globerson and Jaakkola, 2007; Sontag et al., 2008, 2011) and the method in Kumar and Torr (2008); they address the problem of tightening Schlesinger LP for pairwise MRFs. Hazan and Shashua (2010) considered the case of *factor graphs* or relaxations with *singleton separators*.

A lot of research also went into developing algorithms that are guaranteed to converge to an optimal solution of the LP. This topic is covered in more details in Chapters 5 and 3. Examples include subgradient techniques (Storvik and Dahl, 2000; Schlesinger and Giginyak, 2007; Komodakis and Paragios, 2008, 2009), smoothing the objective with a temperature parameter that gradually goes to zero (Johnson et al., 2007), proximal projections (Ravikumar et al., 2010), Nesterov schemes (Jojic et al., 2010; Savchynskyy et al., 2011), an augmented Lagrangian method (Martins et al., 2011; Meshi and Globerson, 2011), a proximal gradient method (Schmidt et al., 2011) (formulated for the general LP in Werner, 2010), a bundle method (Kappes et al., 2012), a mirror descent method (Luong et al., 2012), and the "smoothed version of TRW-S" (Savchynskyy et al., 2012).

Our results in Section 5.7 indicate that TRW-S generally outperforms other popular techniques that we tested, namely MSD, MPLP, and a subgradient method.

4.2 Background and Notation

We closely follow the notation of Werner (2010). Let V be the set of nodes. For node $v \in V$, let $\mathcal{X}_v$ be the finite set of possible labels for v. For a subset $A \subseteq V$, let $\mathcal{X}_A = \times_{v \in A} \mathcal{X}_v$ be the set of labelings of A, and let $\mathcal{X} = \mathcal{X}_V$ be the set of labelings of V. Our goal is to minimize the function

$$f(\boldsymbol{x} \mid \bar{\theta}) = \sum_{A \in \mathcal{F}} \bar{\theta}_A(\boldsymbol{x}_A), \quad \boldsymbol{x} \in \mathcal{X} \tag{4.1}$$

where $\mathcal{F} \subset 2^V$ is a set of non-empty subsets of V (also called *factors*), $\boldsymbol{x}_A$ is the restriction of $\boldsymbol{x}$ to $A \subseteq V$, and $\bar{\theta}$ is a vector with components $(\bar{\theta}_A(\boldsymbol{x}_A) \mid A \in \mathcal{F}, \boldsymbol{x}_A \in \mathcal{X}_A)$.

Let J be a fixed set of pairs of the form (A, B), where $A, B \in \mathcal{F}$ and $B \subset A$. Note that $(\mathcal{F}, J)$ is a directed acyclic graph. We will be interested in solving the following relaxation of the problem:

$$\min_{\mu \in \mathcal{L}(J)} \sum_{A \in \mathcal{F}} \sum_{\boldsymbol{x}_A} \bar{\theta}_A(\boldsymbol{x}_A) \mu_A(\boldsymbol{x}_A) \tag{4.2}$$

where $\mu_A(\boldsymbol{x}_A) \in \mathbb{R}$ for $A \in \mathcal{F}, \boldsymbol{x}_A \in \mathcal{X}_A$ are the variables and $\mathcal{L}(J)$ is the J-based *local polytope* of $(V, \mathcal{F})$:

$$\mathcal{L}(J) = \left\{ \mu \geq 0 \;\middle|\; \begin{array}{ll} \displaystyle\sum_{\boldsymbol{x}_A} \mu_A(\boldsymbol{x}_A) = 1 & \forall A \in \mathcal{F} \\ \displaystyle\sum_{\boldsymbol{x}_A : \boldsymbol{x}_A \sim \boldsymbol{x}_B} \mu_A(\boldsymbol{x}_A) = \mu_B(\boldsymbol{x}_B) & \forall (A, B) \in J, \boldsymbol{x}_B \end{array} \right\}. \tag{4.3}$$

We use the following implicit restriction convention: for $B \subseteq A$, whenever symbols $\boldsymbol{x}_A$ and $\boldsymbol{x}_B$ appear in a single expression, they do not denote independent joint states, but $\boldsymbol{x}_B$ denotes the restriction of $\boldsymbol{x}_A$ to nodes in B. Sometimes we will emphasize this fact by writing $\boldsymbol{x}_A \sim \boldsymbol{x}_B$, as in (4.3).

One simple choice it to set $J = \{(A, \{i\}) \,|\, i \in A \in \mathcal{F}, |A| \geq 2\}$. Graph $(\mathcal{F}, J)$ is then known as a *factor graph*, and the resulting relaxation is sometimes called the *basic LP relaxation* (BLP). It is known that this relaxation is tight if each term $\bar{\theta}_A$ is a submodular function (Werner, 2010). A larger class of functions that can be solved with BLP has been recently identified in Thapper and Živný (2012) and Kolmogorov (2013), who in fact completely characterized classes of *Valued Constraint Satisfaction Problems* for which the BLP relaxation is always tight; we refer to Chapter 2 for details.

For many practical problems, however, the BLP relaxation is not tight; then we can add extra edges to J to tighten the relaxation. Note, in general conditions $A, B \in \mathcal{F}, B \subseteq A$ do not imply that $(A, B) \in J$. Requiring the latter would be unreasonable; if, for example, $|A|, |B| \gg 1$, then adding edge (A, B) to J would lead to a relaxation that is computationally infeasible to solve.

Proposition 4.1. *The following two operations do not affect the set $\mathcal{L}(J)$, and thus relaxation (4.2):*

- *pick edges $(A, B), (B, C) \in J$, add (A, C) to J.*   (4.4a)
- *pick edges $(A, B), (A, C) \in J$ with $C \subset B$, add (B, C) to J.*   (4.4b)

A proof is given in Appendix A. We denote $\bar{J}$ the closure of J with respect to these operations; in other words, $\bar{J}$ is obtained from J by applying operations (4.4) while possible. We have $\mathcal{L}(\bar{J}) = \mathcal{L}(J)$.

Remark 1. Taking the closure will not cost us anything: each pass of our final Algorithm 4.3 uses at most one message operation per factor in $\mathcal{F}$.

Using $\bar{J}$ will be quite important; for example, it will allow us to extend an ordering on nodes to an ordering on factors in a consistent way.

Reparameterization and Dual Problem.   For each $(A, B) \in J$, let $m_{AB} = (m_{AB}(\boldsymbol{x}_B) \mid \boldsymbol{x}_B \in \mathcal{X}_B)$ be a *message* from A to B. Each message vector $m = (m_{AB} \mid (A, B) \in J)$ defines a new vector $\theta = \bar{\theta}[m]$ according to

$$\theta_B(\boldsymbol{x}_B) = \bar{\theta}_B(\boldsymbol{x}_B) + \sum_{A:(A,B)\in J} m_{AB}(\boldsymbol{x}_B) - \sum_{C:(B,C)\in J} m_{BC}(\boldsymbol{x}_C) \, . \qquad (4.5)$$

It is easy to check that $\bar{\theta}$ and θ define the same objective function (i.e., $f(\boldsymbol{x} \mid \bar{\theta}) = f(\boldsymbol{x} \mid \theta)$ for all labelings $\boldsymbol{x} \in \mathcal{X}$). Thus, θ is a *reparameterization* of $\bar{\theta}$ (Wainwright et al., 2005). If $\theta = \bar{\theta}[m]$ for some vector m, then we will write this as $\theta \equiv \bar{\theta}$.

Using the notion of reparameterization, we can write the dual of (4.2) as follows (Werner, 2010):

$$\max_{\theta \equiv \bar{\theta}} \sum_{A \in \mathcal{F}} \min_{\boldsymbol{x}_A} \theta_A(\boldsymbol{x}_A) \, . \qquad (4.6)$$

Convex Combination of Subproblems.   Let $\mathcal{T}$ be a set of subproblem indexes and $\rho : \mathcal{T} \to (0, 1]$ be a probability distribution on $\mathcal{T}$ with $\sum_T \rho^T = 1$. Each subproblem $T \in \mathcal{T}$ is characterized by the set of factors $\mathcal{F}_T \subseteq \mathcal{F}$. For factor $A \in \mathcal{F}$, let $\mathcal{T}_A = \{T \in \mathcal{T} \mid A \in \mathcal{F}_T\}$ be the set of subproblems containing A. For each $T \in \mathcal{T}$, we will have vector θ^T of the same dimension as $\bar{\theta}$. The collection of vectors θ^T will be denoted as $\boldsymbol{\theta} = (\theta^T \mid T \in \mathcal{T})$. Let Ω be the following constraint set for $\boldsymbol{\theta}$:

$$\Omega = \left\{ \boldsymbol{\theta} \; \middle| \; \begin{array}{l} \theta_A^T(\boldsymbol{x}_A) = 0 \quad \forall T, A \in \mathcal{F} - \mathcal{F}_T, \boldsymbol{x}_A \\ \sum_T \rho^T \theta^T \equiv \bar{\theta} \end{array} \right\} . \qquad (4.7)$$

The first condition says that θ^T must respect the structure of subproblem T, while the second condition means that $\boldsymbol{\theta}$ is a *ρ-reparameterization* of $\bar{\theta}$ (Wainwright et al., 2005).

For a vector $\boldsymbol{\theta} = (\theta^T \mid T \in \mathcal{T})$, let us define

$$\Phi(\boldsymbol{\theta}) = \sum_T \rho^T \min_{\boldsymbol{x}} f(\boldsymbol{x} \mid \theta^T) \, . \qquad (4.8)$$

Clearly, if $\boldsymbol{\theta} \in \Omega$, then $\Phi(\boldsymbol{\theta})$ is a lower bound on the minimum of function $f(\boldsymbol{x} \mid \bar{\theta})$. Our goal will be to compute vector $\boldsymbol{\theta} \in \Omega$ that maximizes this bound, i.e. solve the problem

$$\max_{\boldsymbol{\theta} \in \Omega} \Phi(\boldsymbol{\theta}) \, . \qquad (4.9)$$

Decomposition into Junction Trees. For a factor $A \in \mathcal{F}$, we denote $\mathcal{F}_A = \{B \in \mathcal{F} \mid (A, B) \in \bar{J}\} \cup \{A\}$. We say that factor $A \in \mathcal{F}$ is *outer* if it has no incoming edges in $(\mathcal{F}, J)$ (or equivalently in $(\mathcal{F}, \bar{J})$). The set of outer factors will be denoted as $\mathcal{O} \subseteq \mathcal{F}$. Non-outer factors will be called *separators*, and their set will be denoted as $\mathcal{S} = \mathcal{F} - \mathcal{O}$. Finally, for subproblem $T \in \mathcal{T}$, we denote $\mathcal{O}_T = \mathcal{O} \cap \mathcal{F}_T$.

In this chapter, we will be interested in decompositions satisfying the following properties:

1. *There holds $\mathcal{F}_T = \bigcup_{A \in \mathcal{O}_T} \mathcal{F}_A$. Thus, subproblem T is completely specified by its set of outer factors $\mathcal{O}_T$.*

2. *There exists a junction tree $(\mathcal{O}_T, \mathcal{E}_T)$, i.e., a tree-structured graph $(\mathcal{O}_T, \mathcal{E}_T)$ with the running intersection property (Cowell et al., 1999): for any $A, B \in \mathcal{O}_T$, all factors $C \in \mathcal{O}_T$ on the unique path connecting A and B satisfy $A \cap B \subseteq C$.*

3. *For each $(A, B) \in \mathcal{E}_T$, there holds $A \cap B \in \mathcal{F}_A$ and $A \cap B \in \mathcal{F}_B$.*

In general, conditions $A, B \in \mathcal{F}$, $B \subseteq A$ do not imply $B \in \mathcal{F}_A$. However, the following holds (see Appendix B):

Proposition 4.2. *If $A, B \in \mathcal{F}_T$ and $B \subseteq A$, then $B \in \mathcal{F}_A$.*

We will slightly restrict the allowed sets J by assuming

4. *If $v \in A \in \mathcal{F}$, then $\{v\} \in \mathcal{F}_A$.*

and also allow only one tree per outer factor:

5. *There holds $|\mathcal{T}_A| = 1$ for each $A \in \mathcal{O}$.*

The last condition is not really an inherent limitation,[1] but it will help to simplify the presentation of the algorithm. Furthermore, in practice, there is no clear reason to cover outer factors more than once.

4.3   TRW-S Algorithm

We will start with a general version of the algorithm for an arbitrary decomposition into junction trees, and then we present a specialized version for *monotonic junction chains*. We will need the following notation. For tree

---

1. If we have a decomposition in which factor $A \in \mathcal{O}$ belongs to several trees, then we can do the following transformation: add to V new "dummy" nodes v_T for each $T \in \mathcal{T}_A$, add to $\mathcal{F}$ new outer factors $A \cup \{v_T\}$ with zero cost functions, add to J edges $(A \cup \{v_T\}, A)$, and finally assign $A \cup \{v_T\}$ to tree T.

T and factor $A \in \mathcal{F}_T$, we denote

$$\nu_A^T(\boldsymbol{x}_A) = \sum_{B \in \mathcal{F}_A} \theta_B^T(\boldsymbol{x}_B) \, . \tag{4.10}$$

We say that ν_A^T gives *correct min-marginals for* T if

$$\nu_A^T(\boldsymbol{x}_A) = \min_{\boldsymbol{x}:\boldsymbol{x} \sim \boldsymbol{x}_A} f(\boldsymbol{x} \mid \theta_A^T) \qquad \forall \boldsymbol{x}_A \, . \tag{4.11}$$

4.3.1   General Version of TRW-S

The algorithm will rely on two operations:

---

1. Average factor $B \in \mathcal{S}$:

- compute $\nu_B = \left(\sum_{T \in \mathcal{T}_B} \rho^T \nu_B^T \right) / \left(\sum_{T \in \mathcal{T}_B} \rho^T \right)$ (4.12a)
- update parameters θ_B^T for $T \in \mathcal{T}_B$ to get $\nu_B^T = \nu_B$ for all $T \in \mathcal{T}_B$ (4.12b)

---

2. Send message $A \to B$ in T, where $A, B \in \mathcal{F}_T, (A, B) \in \bar{J}$:

- compute $\delta^T(\boldsymbol{x}_B) = \min_{\boldsymbol{x}_A : \boldsymbol{x}_A \sim \boldsymbol{x}_B} \nu_A^T(\boldsymbol{x}_A) - \nu_B^T(\boldsymbol{x}_B)$ (4.13a)

- update $\theta_A^T(\boldsymbol{x}_A) := \theta_A^T(\boldsymbol{x}_A) - \delta^T(\boldsymbol{x}_B)$ $\forall \boldsymbol{x}_A$ (4.13b)

          $\theta_B^T(\boldsymbol{x}_B) := \theta_B^T(\boldsymbol{x}_B) + \delta^T(\boldsymbol{x}_B)$ $\forall \boldsymbol{x}_B$ (4.13c)

Note that after update (4.13), message $A \to B$ becomes *valid* in T, i.e., there holds $\min_{\boldsymbol{x}_A : \boldsymbol{x}_A \sim \boldsymbol{x}_B} \nu_A^T(\boldsymbol{x}_A) = \nu_B^T(\boldsymbol{x}_B)$ for all $\boldsymbol{x}_B$. This is equivalent to

$$\min_{\boldsymbol{x}_A : \boldsymbol{x}_A \sim \boldsymbol{x}_B} \sum_{C \in \mathcal{F}_A - \mathcal{F}_B} \theta_C^T(\boldsymbol{x}_C) = 0 \qquad \forall \boldsymbol{x}_B \, . \tag{4.14}$$

The TRW-S algorithm given below simply performs min-marginal averaging operations for factors $B \in \mathcal{S}$.

Algorithm 4.1 TRW-S

1:   initialize $\boldsymbol{\theta}$ with some vector in Ω
2:   **repeat** until some stopping criterion
3:      **for** factors $B \in \mathcal{S}$ **do** in some fixed order that visits each factor in $\mathcal{S}$ at least once
4:         for each $T \in \mathcal{T}_B$ reparameterize θ^T so that ν_B^T gives correct min-marginals for B (4.11)
5:         average B using (4.12)
6:      **end for**
7:   **end repeat**

Note, Algorithm 4.1 is a special case of TBCO from Meltzer et al. (2009). We postpone its analysis until Section 4.4. One of the properties is the monotonicity of the lower bound: $\Phi(\boldsymbol{\theta})$ never goes down. We also formally prove that the algorithm is characterized by the same stopping condition as the MSD algorithm (Werner, 2010) (up to reparameterization).

Step 4 of the algorithm requires computing min-marginals for factor B in tree $T \in \mathcal{T}_B$. This can be done via a junction tree algorithm (Cowell et al., 1999) in two steps as follows. (i) Choose a factor $A \in \mathcal{O}_T$ that contains B; make A the root of tree $(\mathcal{O}_T, \mathcal{E}_T)$. For each directed edge $(C, D) \in \mathcal{E}_T$ oriented toward A, send a message $C \rightarrow S$ using eq. (4.13) where $S = C \cap D$. Do it in the "inward order" that starts from the leaves. (ii) If $A \neq B$ send a message $A \rightarrow B$ using (4.13).

It is not difficult to see that after step (i), ν_A^T gives correct min-marginals for T. A sketch of the proof is as follows. After sending message $C \rightarrow S$ from a leaf C, this message becomes valid, i.e., (4.14) holds. This means that removing factors $\{E \mid E \cap (C - S) \neq \varnothing\}$ from $\mathcal{F}_T$ will not affect min-marginals for the remaining factors. Applying this argument inductively gives the claim.

4.3.2   TRW-S with Monotonic Chains

Running the junction tree algorithm from scratch every time would be inefficient if trees are large. Fortunately, we can speed up computations by reusing previously passed messages. The general idea of not recomputing messages when they would not change has appeared several times in the literature in different contexts (e.g., Huang and Darwiche, 1996; Minka and Qi, 2003; Kolmogorov, 2006). To make most of this idea, we now impose the following assumption on the decomposition; it will allow computing min-marginals by sending messages only from immediate neighbors.

6. *Each tree $(\mathcal{O}_T, \mathcal{E}_T)$ is a monotonic chain w.r.t. some fixed total order $\leq$ on V, i.e., it is an ordered sequence of factors $A_1, \ldots, A_k$ such that for each pair of consecutive factors $(A_i, A_{i+1}) \in \mathcal{E}_T$ intersecting at $S = A_i \cap A_{i+1} \in \mathcal{S}$ there holds*

$$u < v < w \qquad \forall u \in A_i - S, v \in S, w \in A_{i+1} - S \,. \tag{4.15}$$

The total order on factors in $\mathcal{O}_T$ corresponding to chain T will be denoted as $\preceq^T$. From now on we will treat $\mathcal{E}_T$ as a *directed* set of edges that contains pairs (A, A') with $A \prec^T A'$. It is convenient to define for factor $A \in \mathcal{O}_T$ "left"

Figure 4.1: Example of a chain with three outer factors $X = abc$, $Y = bcd$, $Z = de$. (For brevity, factors $\{x, y, \ldots, z\}$ are written as $xy \ldots z$.) The order of factors in $\mathcal{S}$ is reflected by their x-coordinates.

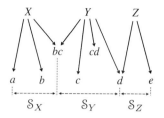

and "right" separators as

$$\mathtt{sep}^- A = \begin{cases} A' \cap A & \text{if } \exists (A', A) \in \mathcal{E}_T \\ \{\min A\} & \text{if } A \text{ is the first factor in } T \end{cases}, \tag{4.16a}$$

$$\mathtt{sep}^+ A = \begin{cases} A \cap A' & \text{if } \exists (A, A') \in \mathcal{E}_T \\ \{\max A\} & \text{if } A \text{ is the last factor in } T \end{cases}. \tag{4.16b}$$

Here min and max are taken w.r.t. to $\leq$; therefore, $\{\min A\}$ and $\{\max A\}$ are singleton separators in $\mathcal{F}_A$. Note, we dropped the dependence of $\mathtt{sep}^- A, \mathtt{sep}^+ A$ on T due to Assumption 5.

Algorithm. First, we select an ordering $\preceq$ on $\mathcal{S}$ that *extends* ordering $\leq$, i.e., the following holds:
- *if* $\min A < \min B$ *and* $\max A \leq \max B$, *then* $A \prec B$;
- *if* $\max A > \max B$ *and* $\min A \geq \min B$, *then* $A \succ B$.

This can be done in several ways, e.g., by choosing a unique sequence $\sigma_A = (\min A, \max A, \ldots)$ for each $A \in \mathcal{S}$ and then setting $\preceq$ as the lexicographical order on σ_A (using $\leq$ for comparing components of σ_A).

The choice of $\preceq$ will determine the order of averaging operations: the algorithm will alternate between a forward pass (processing factors in $\mathcal{S}$ in the order $\preceq$) and a backward pass (using the reverse order). For a factor $A \in \mathcal{O}$, we define (see Figure 4.1)

$$\mathcal{S}_A = \{B \in \mathcal{F}_A \cap \mathcal{S} \mid \mathtt{sep}^- A \preceq B \preceq \mathtt{sep}^+ A\}. \tag{4.17}$$

It is possible to prove the following (see Appendix C):

Proposition 4.3. *If ordering $\preceq$ extends $\leq$ and T is a monotonic chain w.r.t. $\leq$, then $\mathcal{F}_T \cap \mathcal{S} = \bigcup_{A \in \mathcal{O}_T} \mathcal{S}_A$.*

We now formulate the TRW-S algorithm.

Remark 2. It follows from Proposition 4.3 and (4.17) that in step 4 there exists exactly one factor A with stated properties, with one exception: if B is

---

Algorithm 4.2 TRW-S with monotonic chains

1: initialize $\boldsymbol{\theta} \in \Omega$
2: **for each** $B \in \mathcal{S}$ **do** in the order $\preceq$
3: $\quad$ **for each** $T \in \mathcal{T}_B$ **do**
4: $\quad$ $\quad$ find $A \in \mathcal{O}_T$ with $B \in \mathcal{S}_A$, $B \neq \mathtt{sep}^- A$; if it exists, send message $A \to B$ in T (4.13)
5: $\quad$ **end for**
6: $\quad$ average B using (4.12)
7: **end for**
8: if a stopping criterion is satisfied, terminate; otherwise reverse the ordering and go to step 2

---

the first factor in $\mathcal{F}_T \cap \mathcal{S}$ (i.e., $B = \mathtt{sep}^- A_1$ where $A_1 \in \mathcal{O}_T$ is the first factor of chain T), then no such A exists. Note, we do not send messages $A \to \mathtt{sep}^- A$ for $A \in \mathcal{O}$ because these messages remain valid from the previous reverse pass (see the analysis in Section 4.4).

Remark 3. As we will show later, sometimes we may speed up message passing operations. Consider the example in Figure 4.1. When passing message $Y \to c$ in the forward pass, we know that message $Y \to bc$ is valid (from the previous reverse pass); therefore, we can compute increment $\delta^T(\boldsymbol{x}_c)$ in (4.13a) by going through labelings $\boldsymbol{x}_{bc}$ rather than through labelings $\boldsymbol{x}_Y$.

Now consider message $X \to b$ in the forward pass. Message $X \to bc$ is invalid at this point, so we cannot use the trick above. However, we can instead "preemptively" compute message $X \to bc$ (without reparameterizing anything) and then use it for both b and bc. Details are given in the next section.

4.3.3   Implementation via Messages

It is easy to see that each step of Algorithm 4.2 preserves property $\theta_C^T = \theta_C^{T'}$ for $T, T' \in \mathcal{T}_C$, $C \in \mathcal{F}$ (assuming that it holds after initialization). Therefore, it suffices to store the *cumulative* vector $\theta = \sum_T \rho^T \theta^T$; components of vector $\boldsymbol{\theta} = (\theta^T)$ are then given by

$$\theta_C^T = \frac{1}{\rho_C} \theta_C \qquad \forall C \in \mathcal{F}, T \in \mathcal{T}_C \tag{4.18}$$

where $\rho_C = \sum_{T \in \mathcal{T}_C} \rho^T$ is the *factor appearance probability*. By construction, vector θ is a reparameterization of $\bar{\theta}$ (4.5), so we can store it via messages $m = (m_{AB} \mid (A, B) \in J)$, where $J = \{(A, B) \mid A \in \mathcal{O}, B \in \mathcal{S}_A\}$. We thus have

$$\theta_A(\boldsymbol{x}_A) \;=\; \bar\theta_A(\boldsymbol{x}_A) - \sum_{B:(A,B)\in J} m_{AB}(\boldsymbol{x}_B) \quad \forall A \in \mathcal{O}\,, \tag{4.19a}$$

$$\theta_B(\boldsymbol{x}_B) \;=\; \bar\theta_B(\boldsymbol{x}_B) + \sum_{A:(A,B)\in J} m_{AB}(\boldsymbol{x}_B) \quad \forall B \in \mathcal{S}\,. \tag{4.19b}$$

For efficiency reasons we will also store vectors θ_B for $B \in \mathcal{S}$ explicitly so that we don't need to recompute them from m every time. The resulting algorithm is given below.

Algorithm 4.3 TRW-S with monotonic chains

1:   set $m_{AB} := \mathbf{0}$ $\forall (A,B) \in J$ and $\theta_B := \bar\theta_B$ $\forall B \in \mathcal{S}$
2:   **for each** $B \in \mathcal{S}$ **do** in the order $\preceq$
3:   $\quad$ set $\theta_B := \bar\theta_B$
4:   $\quad$ **for each** $(A,B) \in J$ **do**
5:   $\quad\quad$ **if** $B \neq \mathbf{sep}^- A$ **then**
6:   $\quad\quad\quad$ update

$$m_{AB}(\boldsymbol{x}_B) := \min_{\boldsymbol{x}_A:\boldsymbol{x}_A\sim\boldsymbol{x}_B}\left[\bar\theta_A(\boldsymbol{x}_A) - \sum_{(A,C)\in J, C\neq B} m_{AC}(\boldsymbol{x}_C) + \sum_{C\in[\mathcal{F}_A\cap\mathcal{S}]-\mathcal{F}_B} \frac{\rho_A}{\rho_C}\theta_C(\boldsymbol{x}_C) \right]$$

7:   $\quad\quad\quad$ */* optional: for numerical stability */*
$\quad\quad\quad$ set $\gamma := \min_{\boldsymbol{x}_B} m_{AB}(\boldsymbol{x}_B)$, update $m_{AB}(\boldsymbol{x}_B) \mathrel{-}= \gamma$
8:   $\quad\quad$ **end if**
9:   $\quad\quad$ update $\theta_B \mathrel{+}= m_{AB}$
10: $\quad$ **end for**
11: **end for**
12: if a stopping criterion is satisfied, terminate; otherwise reverse the ordering and go to step 2

Reusing Messages in Nested Factors.   Suppose that we have two factors $P, B \in \mathcal{S}_A$, $A \in \mathcal{O}$ with $B \subset P$ such that B is processed immediately **after** P in chain $T \in \mathcal{T}_A$ (i.e., there are no other factors in $\mathcal{S}_A$ between P and B). When processing edge (A,B), we know that (A,P) contains a valid message. This allows us to speed up the computation of a message from A to B. Namely, we need to perform the update $m_{AB} \mathrel{+}= \rho_A \delta^T$, where
$\delta^T(\boldsymbol{x}_B) = \min_{\boldsymbol{x}_A:\boldsymbol{x}_A\sim\boldsymbol{x}_B} \nu_A^T(\boldsymbol{x}_A) - \nu_B^T(\boldsymbol{x}_B) = \min_{\boldsymbol{x}_P:\boldsymbol{x}_P\sim\boldsymbol{x}_B} \nu_P^T(\boldsymbol{x}_P) - \nu_B^T(\boldsymbol{x}_B)$. Thus, the update in step 6 can be replaced by the equivalent update

$$m_{AB}(\boldsymbol{x}_B) \mathrel{+}= \min_{\boldsymbol{x}_P:\boldsymbol{x}_P\sim\boldsymbol{x}_B} \sum_{C\in\mathcal{F}_P-\mathcal{F}_B} \frac{\rho_A}{\rho_C}\theta_C(\boldsymbol{x}_C)\,.$$

Now suppose that $P, B \in \mathcal{S}_A$, $A \in \mathcal{O}$, $B \subset P$ and B is processed immediately **before** P (i.e., there are no other factors in $\mathcal{S}_A$ between B and P). In that case, we can replace step 6 for factor B with the following:

(a) set $m_{AP}^\circ := m_{AP}$, update m_{AP} as in step 6 (where B is replaced with P), set $\delta_{AP} := m_{AP} - m_{AP}^\circ$;

(b) compute

$$\delta(\boldsymbol{x}_B) := \min_{\boldsymbol{x}_P : \boldsymbol{x}_P \sim \boldsymbol{x}_B} \left[\delta_{AP}(\boldsymbol{x}_P) + \sum_{C \in \mathcal{F}_P - \mathcal{F}_B} \frac{\rho_A}{\rho_C} \theta_C(\boldsymbol{x}_P) \right] ;$$

(c) update $m_{AB} \mathrel{+}= \delta$ and $m_{AP}(\boldsymbol{x}_P) \mathrel{-}= \delta(\boldsymbol{x}_B)$.

It can be checked that (i) the resulting message m_{AB} is the same as the one that would be computed in step 6; and (ii) when passing message $A \to P$ (during the averaging step for P), the update in step 6 would not change m_{AP}. Thus, the latter update can be skipped (although the normalization step 6 still needs to be applied). Note, in operations (a)-(c), we modify m_{AP} but do not change θ_P; therefore, equality (4.19b) for factor P temporarily becomes violated (but gets restored after processing P).

4.4　Algorithm's Analysis

We will first analyze the general version of TRW-S (Algorithm 4.1). Then we show that after the first forward pass, Algorithm 4.2 is a special case of Algorithm 4.1. During the averaging step 6, vectors ν_B^T give correct min-marginals for trees $T \in \mathcal{T}_B$.

4.4.1　Analysis of Algorithm 4.1

We will need a few definitions. Consider subset $A \subseteq V$ and a vector φ_A with components $\varphi_A(\boldsymbol{x}_A)$. We define relation $\langle \varphi_A \rangle \subseteq \times_{v \in A} \mathcal{X}_v$ as

$$\langle \varphi_A \rangle = \{ \boldsymbol{x}_A \mid \varphi_A(\boldsymbol{x}_A) = \min_{\boldsymbol{x}_A'} \varphi_A(\boldsymbol{x}_A') \} . \tag{4.20}$$

For a tree $T \in \mathcal{T}$, we define vector ν^T with components $(\nu^T(\boldsymbol{x}) \mid \boldsymbol{x} \in \mathcal{X})$ via

$$\nu^T(\boldsymbol{x}) = f(\boldsymbol{x} \mid \theta^T) = \sum_{B \in \mathcal{F}_T} \theta_B^T(\boldsymbol{x}_B) . \tag{4.21}$$

This can be viewed as a generalization of (4.10). We emphasize that vectors ν^T and ν_A^T for $A \in \mathcal{F}_T$ are uniquely determined by vector θ^T via a linear transformation.

A *projection* of relation $\mathcal{R} \subseteq \times_{v \in A} \mathcal{X}_v$ to subset $B \subseteq A$ is defined as

$$\pi_B(\mathcal{R}) = \{ \boldsymbol{x}_B \mid \boldsymbol{x}_A \in \mathcal{R} \} . \tag{4.22}$$

(Recall that $\boldsymbol{x}_B$ is the restriction of labeling $\boldsymbol{x}_A$ to B.)

Weak Tree Agreement. We now define a condition characterizing a stopping criterion for TRW-S.

Definition 4.1. *Vector $\boldsymbol{\theta} = (\theta^T \mid T \in \mathcal{T})$ is said to satisfy the* enhanced weak tree agreement *(EWTA) condition for factor $B \in \mathcal{F}$ if $\pi_B(\langle \nu^T \rangle) = \pi_B(\langle \nu^{T'} \rangle)$ for $T, T' \in \mathcal{T}_B$.*

It satisfies the WTA for $B \in \mathcal{F}$ if there exist non-empty relations $(\mathcal{R}^T \subseteq \langle \nu^T \rangle \mid T \in \mathcal{T})$ s.t. $\pi_B(\mathcal{R}^T) = \pi_B(\mathcal{R}^{T'})$ for $T, T' \in \mathcal{T}_B$.

Vector $\boldsymbol{\theta}$ is said to satisfy EWTA (WTA) if it satisfies EWTA (WTA) for all $B \in \mathcal{F}$.

Clearly, EWTA implies WTA (but not the other way around).

Theorem 4.4. *Let $\boldsymbol{\theta}$, $\tilde{\boldsymbol{\theta}}$ be, respectively, the vectors before and after averaging step 4 for factor B.*
(a) The lower bound does not decrease: $\Phi(\tilde{\boldsymbol{\theta}}) \geq \Phi(\boldsymbol{\theta})$.
(b) If $\boldsymbol{\theta}$ satisfies WTA for B with relations $(\mathcal{R}^T \mid T \in \mathcal{T})$, then $\tilde{\boldsymbol{\theta}}$ also satisfies WTA with the same set of relations. Furthermore, $\Phi(\tilde{\boldsymbol{\theta}}) = \Phi(\boldsymbol{\theta})$.
(c) If $\Phi(\tilde{\boldsymbol{\theta}}) = \Phi(\boldsymbol{\theta})$, then $\langle \tilde{\nu}^T \rangle \subseteq \langle \nu^T \rangle$ for each $T \in \mathcal{T}$.
(d) If $\Phi(\tilde{\boldsymbol{\theta}}) = \Phi(\boldsymbol{\theta})$ and $\boldsymbol{\theta}$ does not satisfy EWTA for B, then $\langle \tilde{\nu}^T \rangle \subset \langle \nu^T \rangle$ for at least one tree $T \in \mathcal{T}_B$.

A proof is given in Appendix D.

Corollary 4.5.
• *If $\boldsymbol{\theta}$ satisfies WTA, then Algorithm 4.1 will not increase the lower bound $\Phi(\boldsymbol{\theta})$ and furthermore after a finite number of steps, $\boldsymbol{\theta}$ will satisfy EWTA.*
• *If $\boldsymbol{\theta}$ does not satisfy WTA, then bound $\Phi(\boldsymbol{\theta})$ will increase after a finite number of steps.*

Proof. The first claim follows from parts (b,d) of theorem 4.4. To prove the second claim, assume that $\Phi(\boldsymbol{\theta})$ stays constant after an arbitrary number of steps. From parts (c,d), we conclude that after a finite number of steps, we get vector $\tilde{\boldsymbol{\theta}}$ satisfying EWTA such that $\langle \tilde{\nu}^T \rangle \subseteq \langle \nu^T \rangle$ for all T. This means that $\boldsymbol{\theta}$ satisfies WTA with relations $\mathcal{R}^T = \langle \tilde{\nu}^T \rangle$. $\qquad\square$

Relation to Min-Sum Diffusion. We now show that WTA condition is closely related to the stopping criterion of the MSD algorithm (Werner,

2010). Recall that MSD tries to maximize lower bound

$$\Psi(\theta) = \sum_{A \in \mathcal{F}} \min_{\boldsymbol{x}_A} \theta_A(\boldsymbol{x}_A) \tag{4.23}$$

over vectors $\theta \equiv \bar{\theta}$. Its stopping criterion is described in the following definition.

Definition 4.2. *Vector $\theta \equiv \bar{\theta}$ is said to satisfy the enhanced J-consistency condition if $\pi_B(\langle \theta_A \rangle) = \langle \theta_B \rangle$ for each $(A, B) \in J$. It is said to satisfy the J-consistency condition if there exist non-empty relations $(\mathcal{R}_B \subseteq \langle \theta_B \rangle \,|\, B \in \mathcal{F})$, such that $\pi_B(\mathcal{R}_A) = \mathcal{R}_B$ for each $(A, B) \in J$.*

We denote Ω^* to be the set of vectors $\boldsymbol{\theta} \in \Omega$ that satisfy the WTA condition, and Λ^* to be the set of vectors $\theta \equiv \bar{\theta}$ that satisfy the J-consistency condition.

Theorem 4.6. *There exist mappings $\phi : \Omega^* \to \Lambda^*$ and $\psi : \Lambda^* \to \Omega^*$ that preserve the value of the lower bound, i.e., $\Psi(\phi(\boldsymbol{\theta})) = \Phi(\boldsymbol{\theta})$ and $\Phi(\psi(\theta)) = \Psi(\theta)$.*

A proof is given in Appendix E.

4.4.2 Analysis of Algorithm 4.2

We now analyze the TRW-S algorithm with monotonic chains. In order to do this, we will reformulate it slightly. Namely, we will maintain factor $\text{CUR}_T \in \mathcal{O}_T$ for each $T \in \mathcal{T}$ ("current outer factor of chain T") and factor $\text{CHILD}_A \in \mathcal{S}_A$ for each $A \in \mathcal{O}$:

1: initialize $\boldsymbol{\theta} \in \Omega$
    for each $T \in \mathcal{T}$ set $\text{CUR}_T =$ first factor of chain T
    for each $A \in \mathcal{O}$ set $\text{CHILD}_A = \textsf{sep}^- A$
2: **for each** $B \in \mathcal{S}$ **do** in the order $\preceq$
3:    | **for each** $T \in \mathcal{T}_B$ **do**
4:    | | let $A = \text{CUR}_T$
5:    | | if $\text{CHILD}_A \neq B$ then send message $A \to B$ in T (eq. 4.13) and update $\text{CHILD}_A := B$
6:    | | if $B = \textsf{sep}^+ A$ and $\exists (A, A') \in \mathcal{E}_T$ set $\text{CUR}_T := A'$
7:    | **end for**
8:    | average B using (4.12)
9: **end for**
10: if a stopping criterion is satisfied, terminate; otherwise reverse the ordering and go to step 2

It should be clear that this algorithm is equivalent to Algorithm 4.2. In particular, the following is maintained:

Proposition 4.7. *(a) In step 5, there holds $B \in \mathcal{S}_A$.*
(b) If $A' \in \mathcal{O}_T$, $A' \prec^T \mathrm{CUR}_T$, then $\mathrm{CHILD}_{A'} = \mathrm{sep}^+ A'$.
(c) If $A' \in \mathcal{O}_T$, $A' \succ^T \mathrm{CUR}_T$, then $\mathrm{CHILD}_{A'} = \mathrm{sep}^- A'$.

The algorithm's correctness will follow from:

Theorem 4.8. *(a) Each step of the algorithm preserves the validity of edges (A, CHILD_A), $A \in \mathcal{O}_T$ in T: if the edge contained a valid message in T before the step (eq. 4.14), then this message remains valid afterwards.*
(b) After the first forward pass, all edges (A, CHILD_A), $A \in \mathcal{O}_T$ are valid in T. Consequently, in step 6, vector ν_B^T gives correct min-marginals in T for each $T \in \mathcal{T}_B$.

Proof. Consider loop 2-9 for factor B, and let us fix tree $T \in \mathcal{T}_B$. Let A be the factor defined in step 4: $A = \mathrm{CUR}_T$. It is clear that sending message $A \to B$ in T makes edge (A, B) valid and averaging B in step 8 preserves the validity of this edge (see 4.14).

Now consider factor $A' \in \mathcal{O}_T$, $A' \prec A$, and define $S = \mathrm{CHILD}_{A'} = \mathrm{sep}^+ A'$. Let us show that an update of vectors θ_C^T for $C \in \mathcal{F}_A$ preserves the validity of edge (A', S) in T. We need to prove that $C \notin \mathcal{F}_{A'} - \mathcal{F}_S$ (because the definition of a valid edge involves only vectors θ_D^T for $D \in \mathcal{F}_{A'} - \mathcal{F}_S$). Suppose that $C \in \mathcal{F}_{A'}$. By the running intersection property we have $C \subseteq A$, where A'' is the right neighbor of A', i.e., $(A', A'') \in \mathcal{E}_T$. Therefore, $C \subseteq A' \cap A'' = \mathrm{sep}^+ A' = S$, and so $C \in \mathcal{F}_S$ and $C \notin \mathcal{F}_{A'} - \mathcal{F}_S$, as claimed.

A similar argument can be used for factors $A' \in \mathcal{O}_T$, $A' \succ A$. Part (a) is proved. Part (b) easily follows from part (a) and the fact that step 5 makes edge $A \to B$ valid in T. $\qquad\square$

4.5 Experimental Results

We compare the proposed TRW-S to our own implementations (available at `https://github.com/Thomas1205/Optimization-Toolbox`) of MSD (Werner, 2010), MPLP (Sontag et al., 2011) and subgradient methods (SG) (Komodakis and Paragios, 2009), the latter with (non-monotonic) chains where each outer factor belongs to exactly one chain.[2] Our current imple-

---

2. We used a step size-rule that resembles the one in Koo et al. (2010), namely $\lambda/(K+1)$ where K is the number of times an iteration produced an inferior bound. We tried several λs and chose the one that performs best after 500 iterations (for a given instance). We also tested the step-size rule from Komodakis et al. (2007) for problems in the top row of Table 4.1, but it was inferior to our rule. A potential reason is that this rule depends on

mentation of TRW-S does not support the second "reuse" scheme described at the end of Section 4.3.3. Because timings are implementation-dependent, we also report a "message effort measure, where each minimization computation over a factor of size n contributes n. All experiments were run on a Core i5 machine with 2.5 GHz.

We evaluate the methods on problems from the fields of computer vision and natural language processing, where the inputs and results for the computer vision problems are shown in Figure 4.2. We consider **(1)** image segmentation with a generalized Potts model with 2x2 blocks and 4 labels; **(2+3)** factor and constraint-based curvature (Schoenemann et al., 2012; El-Zehiry and Grady, 2010; Strandmark and Kahl, 2011) with 2 labels and an 8-connectivity based on RegionCurv (`https://github.com/PetterS/regioncurv`); **(4)** histogram-based image segmentation with two labels (Vicente et al., 2009); **(5)** stereo disparity estimation with second order differences and 8 disparities; and **(6)** word alignment (Schoenemann, 2011), where we use 100 sentence pairs from the Europarl Italian-English corpus and all variables are binary.

Problems 1, 2, and 5 use low-order factors only, the remaining problems are of high order (16, 9600 and 5281, respectively). Constraint-based curvature requires handling integer linear constraints, where we use the method of Potetz and Lee (2008) for the message computations. Histogram image segmentation and word alignment require cardinality potentials; the latter also uses 1-of-N potentials. We handle this as in Tarlow et al. (2010). Here, MPLP has an advantage over TRW-S: with the specialized computations, it effectively only needs to visit each factor once per iteration (as is always the case for the subgradient method). TRW-S needs to visit each factor multiple times per iteration, so it is much slower. However, we show below that immense speed-ups are possible by reusing previous computations: for factors with n variables, a minimization of a 1-of-N potential then takes $\mathcal{O}(1)$ rather than $\mathcal{O}(n)$ (in most cases[3]), for a BILP factor $\mathcal{O}(k)$ rather than

---

the primal integral solution, so if the relaxation is not tight, the gap will always remain large. (Note, in this case, the step size doesn't go to zero, so convergence to the optimum is not guaranteed.) Note that for stereo TRW-S was pretty close to the optimum after 250 iters while the primal solution of SG was still far away after 500 iters.

We also informally tested the step-size rule from Torresani et al. (2012) but found it to be inferior as well.

3. We keep track of the two lowest values. If one of them increases beyond the second best, we need to revisit all values.

$\mathcal{O}(n \cdot k)$, where k can[4] be $\mathcal{O}(n)$, and for a cardinality factor $\mathcal{O}(n)$ rather than $\mathcal{O}(n \log(n))$. The downside is that we need more memory.

Singleton Separators.   Table 4.1 compares the four methods with singleton separators on all problems. For problems of low order TRW-S performs always best, using less message effort than MSD and MPLP. SG has a lower message effort, but higher running times: handling and projecting the gradients takes time, and one also has to compute minimizers along with the minimal values. Figure 4.3 plots how the energies evolve w.r.t. message effort on stereo for the different methods. For the high-order terms, TRW-S is beaten once, for histogram segmentation and by SG. With reuse, the running times of TRW-S are competitive for the high-order problems, although for constraint curvature the memory increases twofold.

Pairwise Separators.   Experiments with pair separators are evaluated in Table 4.2, as mentioned only for low-order problems. A plot for stereo is provided in Figure 4.3. Again, TRW-S is beaten once by the subgradient method, this time for factor-based curvature. Possibly a different variable order might boost TRW-S here. Otherwise, TRW-S performs best. It always outperforms MSD, and due to the reuse scheme, each iteration is also faster. For problems with a large number of pair separators, SG finally profits from its reduced message effort: for the Potts model, it is clearly fastest after a comparable number of iterations.

4.6   Conclusions

We showed how to generalize the TRW-S algorithm from pairwise MRFs to arbitrary graphical models. To improve efficiency, we had to overcome several challenges: (i) Find a suitable definition of monotonic junction chains that depends only on the order on nodes and then extend this order to other factors in a consistent way. (ii) Make sure that parameters for the same factor in different chains stay the same (thus allowing an implementation via messages); we achieved this by passing messages only from outer factors. (iii) Find a way to reuse message computations in nested factors.

TRW-S has shown a good performance for pairwise graphical models (Szeliski et al., 2008; Tarlow et al., 2011), where it is among state-

---

4. For a constraint $l \leq \sum_{k=1}^{K} x_k - \sum_{l=1}^{L} y_l \leq u : k = \min\{K, u+L\} - \max\{-L, l-K\} + 1$. If $K = L$ and $l = u = 0$, then this gives $n + 1$. For curvature always $K \leq 4$.

	Gen. Potts				Factor Curvature				2nd-Order Stereo			
	Bound	Time	MEff	Mem	Bound	Time	MEff	Mem	Bound	Time	MEff	Mem
MPLP	7734036	38	115M	42M	22858924	310	734M	51M	121841.2	150	246M	27M
MSD	7731966	38	115M	42M	22884886	304	734M	51M	121862.7	140	246M	27M
TRW-S	7737053*	25	86M	45M	22893060	79	532M	71M	123421.2	35	163M	37M
SG	7737435	22	29M	46M	22835838	106	202M	86M	117835.8	55	81M	44M

	Constraint Curvature				Histogram Segm.				Word Alignment			
	Bound	Time	MEff	Mem	Bound	Time	MEff	Mem	Bound	Time	MEff	Mem
MPLP	22953894	467	9.7G	123M	40881	37	47G	11M	7650	67	50G	52M
MSD	24216403	470	9.7G	124M	41714	178	47G	11M	8435	212	50G	52M
TRW-S	24233506	1528	8.9G	183M	41756	8990	47G	14M	8127	11170	50G	62M
TRW-S/ru	"	200	"	278M	"	171	"	14M	"	187	"	66M
SG	24082000	341	759M	203M	42039	62	28M	17M	9774	138	129M	66M

Table 4.1: Singleton separators: relaxation values, timings (in seconds), message effort and memory for the compared schemes. Timings *exclude* any time spent on computing the intermediate bounds. We ran 250 iterations of TRW-S (forward+backward passes) and 500 of all other methods. MPLP and MSD can probably be sped up at the cost of extra memory. TRW-S/ru means that we employ reuse for high-order factors. A "*" indicates that the method converged before the set number of iterations was used up.

	Gen. Potts				Factor Curvature				2nd-Order Stereo			
	Bound	Time	MEff	Mem	Bound	Time	MEff	Mem	Bound	Time	MEff	Mem
MSD	7736742	514	463M	49M	22904652	202	1.8G	110M	124183.7	951	682M	230M
TRW-S	7737053*	379	202M	59M	22903356	171	724M	162M	125725.9	248	273M	265M
SG	7736938	114	58M	47M	23410902	136	202M	117M	125722.0	423	136M	227M

Table 4.2: Pair separators: experiments with low order factors. We give relaxation values, timings, message effort, and memory consumption. The comments for the above table apply here as well.

of-the-art techniques for problems such as stereo[5] (Savchynskyy et al., 2012). We have shown that the proposed generalization to higher-order terms performs similarly well: it usually beats MSD and MPLP, with the exception of word alignment, and while it is sometimes beaten by

---

5. This holds for a CPU implementation because the "oracle call" of smoothed TRW-S in Savchynskyy et al. (2012) was 5-10 times slower than that of the simple TRW-S. On GPU, the "oracle calls" took similar times, and so smoothed TRW-S outperformed simple TRW-S.

(a) stereo   (c) segmentation with gen. Potts model

(b) segmentation with curvature   (d) segmentation with histograms

Figure 4.2: Input data and results for the tested computer vision problems:
(a) stereo disparity estimation: two input images (half-scale), and the computed
disparity map; **(b)** from left to right: input for curvature segmentation (64×64
pixels), result with constraint curvature, result with factor curvature and singleton
separators, result with factor curvature and pair separators. The curvature weight
was 10000; **(c)** input for image segmentation with 2x2 Potts prior, results with
singleton (middle) and pairwise separators (right). The smoothness weight is 5000;
(d) input and output for histogram image segmentation with seeds, smoothness
weight 2.

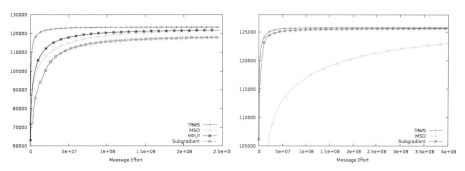

Figure 4.3: Plots of energy versus message effort for singleton (left) and pair
separators (right) for stereo.

subgradient methods, these are also often heavily inferior and require
the tuning of the step-size parameter. When reusing previous computations, the proposed method has amenable running times even for high-
order problems. Hence, we hope that it will become one of the standard tools for MAP-MRF inference. The implementation is available
at `https://github.com/Thomas1205/Optimization-Toolbox`.

It has been shown (Sontag et al., 2008; Batra et al., 2011) that tightening
the relaxation by adding higher-order constraints (e.g., short cycles) is an
effective strategy for solving challenging instances. Our work allows us to
combine the tightening strategy and the TRW-S technique. Given results
in Savchynskyy et al. (2012), Sontag et al. (2008), and Batra et al. (2011),

it is reasonable to assume that this would yield a state-of-the-art method for some applications.

One of the disadvantages of TRW-S is that it is not guaranteed to solve the LP: like MSD and MPLP, it can get stuck in a suboptimal point. We see two ways to address this issue: (1) Interleave TRW-S and another technique that is guaranteed to solve the LP (e.g., a subgradient method), or (2) a smoothed version of TRW-S (Savchynskyy et al., 2012). At the moment, such a solution has been presented only for the standard (pairwise) TRW-S, but we believe that generalizing it using our scheme should not be too difficult (we need to replace the max-product BP with the sum-product version).

Note that for some applications, suboptimality of message passing techniques does not seem to be an issue: TRW either yields a global optimum or gets close (Yanover et al., 2006; Szeliski et al., 2008). Also, solving the LP to optimality may not be necessary: instead of squeezing the last bit from the current LP relaxation, one can try to tighten the relaxation by adding higher-order constraints as in Sontag et al. (2008), Batra et al. (2011), and Sontag et al. (2012), and run TRW-S again.

4.7 Appendices

Appendix A: Proof of Proposition 4.1

Part (a) For each $\boldsymbol{x}_C$, we can write

$$
\sum_{\boldsymbol{x}_A:\boldsymbol{x}_A\sim\boldsymbol{x}_C} \mu_A(\boldsymbol{x}_A) = \sum_{\boldsymbol{x}_B:\boldsymbol{x}_B\sim\boldsymbol{x}_C} \sum_{\boldsymbol{x}_A:\boldsymbol{x}_A\sim\boldsymbol{x}_B} \mu_A(\boldsymbol{x}_A)
$$
$$
\overset{(1)}{=} \sum_{\boldsymbol{x}_B:\boldsymbol{x}_B\sim\boldsymbol{x}_C} \mu_B(\boldsymbol{x}_B)
$$
$$
\overset{(2)}{=} \mu_C(\boldsymbol{x}_C),
$$

where (1) holds because $(A, B) \in J$ and (2) holds because $(B, C) \in J$. Thus, the constraint for (A, C) follows from constraints for $(A, B), (B, C)$.

Part (b) For each $\boldsymbol{x}_C$, we can write

$$
\sum_{\boldsymbol{x}_B:\boldsymbol{x}_B\sim\boldsymbol{x}_C} \mu_B(\boldsymbol{x}_B) \overset{(1)}{=} \sum_{\boldsymbol{x}_B:\boldsymbol{x}_B\sim\boldsymbol{x}_C} \sum_{\boldsymbol{x}_A:\boldsymbol{x}_A\sim\boldsymbol{x}_B} \mu_A(\boldsymbol{x}_A)
$$
$$
= \sum_{\boldsymbol{x}_A:\boldsymbol{x}_A\sim\boldsymbol{x}_C} \mu_A(\boldsymbol{x}_A)
$$
$$
\overset{(2)}{=} \mu_C(\boldsymbol{x}_C),
$$

where (1) holds because $(A, B) \in J$ and (2) holds because $(A, C) \in J$. Thus, the constraint for (B, C) follows from constraints for $(A, B), (A, C)$.

Appendix B: Proof of Proposition 4.2

Because set $\bar{J}$ is closed under operations (4.4a)-(4.4b), we get

- If $B \in \mathcal{F}_A$, $C \in \mathcal{F}_B$, then $C \in \mathcal{F}_A$.   (4.24a)
- If $B, C \in \mathcal{F}_A$, $B \supseteq C$, then $C \in \mathcal{F}_B$.   (4.24b)

First, let us prove the proposition assuming that $A \in \mathcal{O}_T$. Consider $B \in \mathcal{F}_T$, $B \subset A$. Pick a factor $A' \in \mathcal{O}_T$ with $B \in \mathcal{F}_{A'}$ (it exists by Assumption 1); if there are several such factors, pick one for which the distance from A to A' in the tree $(\mathcal{O}_T, \mathcal{E}_T)$ is minimal. We need to show that this distance is zero (i.e., $A = A$). Suppose not; let $A'' \in \mathcal{O}_T$ be the neighbor of A' (i.e., $(A', A'') \in \mathcal{E}_T$), which is closer to A than A'. By the running intersection property, $A' \cap A \subseteq A''$, and so $B \subseteq A''$. Denote $S = A' \cap A''$; as we showed, $B \subseteq S$. By Assumption 3, $S \in \mathcal{F}_{A'}$ and $S \in \mathcal{F}_{A''}$. Because $B \in \mathcal{F}_{A'}$, we have $B \in \mathcal{F}_S$ by property (4.24b). Property (4.24a) and the fact $S \in \mathcal{F}_{A''}$ then gives $B \in \mathcal{F}_{A''}$. This contradicts to the choice of A'.

It remains to prove the proposition in the case when $A \in \mathcal{F}_T - \mathcal{O}_T$. Pick a factor $A' \in \mathcal{O}_T$ with $A \in \mathcal{F}_{A'}$. As we showed above, we have $B \in \mathcal{F}_A$; therefore, property (4.24b) gives $B \in \mathcal{F}_A$.

Appendix C: Proof of Proposition 4.3

We need to show that for each $B \in \mathcal{F}_T \cap \mathcal{S}$ there exists $A \in \mathcal{O}_T$ with $B \in \mathcal{S}_A$. Assume that $|\mathcal{O}_T| \geq 2$ and thus $|A| \geq 2$ for all $A \in \mathcal{O}_T$; otherwise the claim is trivial.

Let $A_1, \ldots, A_k$ be the sequence of factors in $\mathcal{O}_T$. Denote $u_i = \min A_i$, $v_i = \max A_i$ (w.r.t. $\leq$). We have $u_i = \min \mathsf{sep}^- A_i < \min \mathsf{sep}^+ A_i$ and $\max \mathsf{sep}^- A_i < \max \mathsf{sep}^+ A_i = v_i$; because $\preceq$ extends $\leq$, we get $\mathsf{sep}^- A_i \prec \mathsf{sep}^+ A_i$. Therefore,

$$\{u_1\} = \mathsf{sep}^- A_1 \prec \mathsf{sep}^+ A_1 = \mathsf{sep}^- A_2 \prec \ldots \tag{4.25}$$
$$\ldots \prec \mathsf{sep}^+ A_{k-1} = \mathsf{sep}^- A_k \prec \mathsf{sep}^+ A_k = \{v_k\} \,.$$

We also have

$$\{u_1\} = \min \mathcal{F}_T \cap \mathcal{S} \qquad \{v_k\} = \max \mathcal{F}_T \cap \mathcal{S} \tag{4.26}$$

where $\min, \max$ are taken w.r.t. $\preceq$. Indeed, for each $B \in \mathcal{F}_T \cap \mathcal{S}$, there exists $A_i \in \mathcal{O}_T$ with $B \in \mathcal{F}_{A_i}$ (by Assumption 1); using Assumption 6 and the fact that $\preceq$ extends $\leq$, we get $\{u_1\} \prec \{u_2\} \prec \ldots \preceq \{u_i\} \preceq B$. The second equation in (4.26) is proved in a similar way.

Consider $B \in \mathcal{F}_T \cap \mathcal{S}$. Equations (4.25), (4.26) imply that there exists at least one factor $A_i \in \mathcal{O}_T$ with $\mathsf{sep}^- A_i \preceq B \preceq \mathsf{sep}^+ A_i$. It remains to show that $B \subseteq A_i$; then we will have $B \in \mathcal{F}_{A_i}$ by proposition 4.2, implying $B \in \mathcal{S}_{A_i}$.

Consider node $v \in B$. There holds $\{u_i\} \preceq \mathsf{sep}^- A \preceq B$, and therefore $u_i \leq v$. Similarly, $v \leq v_i$. Monotonicity assumption 4.3.2 then implies that $v \in A$. The claim is proved.

Appendix D: Proof of Theorem 4.4

Averaging B does not affect parameters in trees $T \in \mathcal{T}_B$, so for the purpose of the proof, we can assume w.l.o.g. that $\mathcal{T} = \mathcal{T}_B$. Furthermore, we can assume that $\min_{\boldsymbol{x}} \nu^T(\boldsymbol{x}) = 0$ for each $T \in \mathcal{T}_B$ (this can be achieved by adding a constant to $\nu^T(\boldsymbol{x})$; clearly, this does not affect theorem's claims). We thus have

$$\Phi(\boldsymbol{\theta}) = \sum_{T \in \mathcal{T}_B} \rho^T \min_{\boldsymbol{x}} \nu^T(\boldsymbol{x}) = 0 \, . \tag{4.27}$$

By construction, before the averaging, ν_B^T gives correct min-marginals for T in B (4.11). It is easy to see that the same holds after the averaging, i.e., $\tilde{\nu}_B^T$ gives correct min-marginals for function $f(\cdot \,|\, \tilde{\theta}^T)$. (This is because in the definition of min-marginals we fix labeling $\boldsymbol{x}_B$, and vectors $\theta^T, \tilde{\theta}^T$ differ only in components $\theta_B^T(\boldsymbol{x}_B)$.)

We thus have $\min_{\boldsymbol{x}_B} \nu_B^T(\boldsymbol{x}_B) = \min_{\boldsymbol{x}} \nu^T(\boldsymbol{x}) = 0$. Inspecting (4.12), we conclude that $\tilde{\nu}_B^T(\boldsymbol{x}_B) \geq 0$ for each $\boldsymbol{x}_B$. This gives part (a):

$$\Phi(\tilde{\boldsymbol{\theta}}) = \sum_{T \in \mathcal{T}_B} \rho^T \min_{\boldsymbol{x}} \tilde{\nu}^T(\boldsymbol{x}) = \sum_{T \in \mathcal{T}_B} \rho_B^T \min_{\boldsymbol{x}_B} \tilde{\nu}_B^T(\boldsymbol{x}_B) \geq 0 \, .$$

To prove part (b), suppose that $\boldsymbol{\theta}$ satisfies RWTA for B with relations $(\mathcal{R}^T \,|\, T \in \mathcal{T})$. We need to show that $\mathcal{R}^T \subseteq \langle \tilde{\nu}^T \rangle$ for each $T \in \mathcal{T}_B$. Consider labeling $\boldsymbol{x} \in \mathcal{R}^T$. For each $T' \in \mathcal{T}_B$ we have $\boldsymbol{x}_B \in \pi_B(\mathcal{R}^T) = \pi_B(\mathcal{R}^{T'})$; therefore, $\exists \boldsymbol{x}^{T'} \in \langle \nu^{T'} \rangle$ with $\boldsymbol{x}_B^{T'} = \boldsymbol{x}_B$. Because $\nu_B^{T'}$ gives correct min-marginals for B in tree T', we conclude that $\nu_B^{T'}(\boldsymbol{x}_B) = 0$. This implies that $\tilde{\nu}_B^T(\boldsymbol{x}_B) = 0$ (see 4.12). This implies that $\boldsymbol{x}_B \in \langle \tilde{\nu}_B^T \rangle$ and thus $\boldsymbol{x} \in \langle \tilde{\nu}^T \rangle$.

It remains to prove parts (c,d). We assume from now on that the bound does not change: $\Phi(\tilde{\boldsymbol{\theta}}) = \Phi(\boldsymbol{\theta})$; thus, $\min_{\boldsymbol{x}_B} \tilde{\nu}_B^T(\boldsymbol{x}_B) = 0$ for $T \in \mathcal{T}$.

Let as fix tree $T \in \mathcal{T}_B$, and let $\boldsymbol{x}$ be a labeling in $\langle \tilde{\nu}^T \rangle$, so $\boldsymbol{x}_B \in \langle \tilde{\nu}_B^T \rangle$. We have $\tilde{\nu}_B^T(\boldsymbol{x}_B) = 0$; inspecting (4.12), we conclude that $\nu_B^{T'}(\boldsymbol{x}_B) = 0$ for all $T' \in \mathcal{T}_B$, and so $\boldsymbol{x}_B \in \langle \nu_B^T \rangle$ and $\boldsymbol{x} \in \langle \nu^T \rangle$. This proves that $\langle \tilde{\nu}^T \rangle \subseteq \langle \nu^T \rangle$.

Now assume that WTA for B does not hold. This means that there exist trees $T, T' \in \mathcal{T}_B$ and labeling $\boldsymbol{x} \in \langle \nu^T \rangle$ such that $\boldsymbol{x}_B \notin \langle \nu_B^{T'} \rangle$. The latter condition means that $\nu_B^{T'}(\boldsymbol{x}_B) > 0$, and therefore $\tilde{\nu}_B^T(\boldsymbol{x}_B) > 0$, $\boldsymbol{x}_B \notin \langle \tilde{\nu}_B^T \rangle$ and $\boldsymbol{x} \notin \langle \tilde{\nu}^T \rangle$. Thus, $\langle \tilde{\nu}^T \rangle$ is a strict subset of $\langle \nu^T \rangle$.

Appendix E: Proof of Theorem 4.6

Constructing Mapping $\phi : \Omega^* \to \Lambda^*$. The construction will be based on the following lemma.

Lemma 4.9. *Consider tree $T \in \mathcal{T}$ and non-empty relation $\mathcal{R} \subseteq \langle \theta^T \rangle$. Vector θ^T can be reparameterized in such a way that it satisfies*
(a) $\theta_B^T(\boldsymbol{x}_B) = 0$ for each $B \in \mathcal{F}_T \cap \mathcal{S}$ and each $\boldsymbol{x}_B$;
(b) $\pi_A(\mathcal{R}) \subseteq \langle \theta_A^T \rangle$ for each $A \in \mathcal{O}_T$;
(c) $\min_{\boldsymbol{x}} f(\boldsymbol{x} \mid \theta^T) = \sum_{A \in \mathcal{O}_T} \min_{\boldsymbol{x}_A} \theta_A^T(\boldsymbol{x}_A)$.

Proof. We use induction on the size of the tree. If $\mathcal{O}_T = \{A\}$, then the claim is straightforward: for each $B \in \mathcal{F}_A$ we just need to "move" parameter θ_B^T to the outer factor $A \in \mathcal{O}_T$, i.e., update $\theta_A^T(\boldsymbol{x}_A) \mathrel{+}= \theta_B^T(\boldsymbol{x}_B)$, $\theta_B^T(\boldsymbol{x}_B) := 0$.

Now consider the induction step. Suppose that $|\mathcal{O}_T| \geq 2$. Let us pick a leaf factor $A \in \mathcal{O}_T$ and do the following. First, reparameterize θ^T so that ν_A^T gives correct min-marginals for A in T (4.11). Second, for each $B \in \mathcal{F}_A$, "move" all parameters θ_B^T to A, as above. Now consider tree T' obtained from T by removing factor A. Vector $\theta^{T'}$ is obtained from θ^T by setting $\theta_A^{T'} := 0$. Using the fact that ν_A^T gives correct min-marginals for A, we conclude that $\mathcal{R}^{T'} \subseteq \langle \theta^{T'} \rangle$, where we defined $\mathcal{R}^{T'} = \mathcal{R}^T$. Let us now reparameterize $\theta^{T'}$ (together with θ^T) using the induction hypothesis.

By construction, the obtained reparameterization θ satisfies (a). Because $\theta_A^T = \nu_A^T$ gives correct min-marginals for factor A, we have $\pi_A(\langle \theta^T \rangle) = \langle \theta_A^T \rangle$, so property (b) holds for factor A. For other factors in $\mathcal{O}_T - \{A\}$, property (b) holds by the induction hypothesis.

To prove (c), we first observe that

$$\sum_{A' \subset \mathcal{O}_{T'}} \min_{\boldsymbol{x}_{A'}} \theta_{A'}^{T'}(\boldsymbol{x}_{A'}) \stackrel{(1)}{=} \min_{\boldsymbol{x}} f(\boldsymbol{x} \mid \theta^{T'}) = f(\boldsymbol{x}^* \mid \theta^{T'})$$

$$= f(\boldsymbol{x}^* \mid \theta^T) - \theta_A^T(\boldsymbol{x}^*) \stackrel{(2)}{=} \nu_A^T(\boldsymbol{x}^*) - \theta_A^T(\boldsymbol{x}^*) = 0$$

where $\boldsymbol{x}^*$ is a labeling in $\mathcal{R}^T = \mathcal{R}^{T'}$; (1) holds by the induction hypothesis and (2) holds because by construction ν_A^T gives correct min-marginals in T. We can now write

$$\min_{\boldsymbol{x}} f(\boldsymbol{x} \mid \theta^T) = \min_{\boldsymbol{x}_A} \nu_A^T(\boldsymbol{x}_A) = \min_{\boldsymbol{x}_A} \theta_A^T(\boldsymbol{x}_A) = \sum_{A' \in \mathcal{O}_T} \min_{\boldsymbol{x}_{A'}} \theta_{A'}^T(\boldsymbol{x}_{A'}) .$$

☐

We can now construct mapping $\phi : \Omega^* \to \Lambda^*$. Consider vector $\boldsymbol{\theta} \in \Omega^*$ that satisfies WTA with relations $(\mathcal{R}^T \,|\, T \in \mathcal{T})$. Let us reparameterize each vector θ^T as described in lemma 4.9. Clearly, this operation does not affect $\Phi(\boldsymbol{\theta})$, and $\boldsymbol{\theta}$ still satisfies WTA with relations $(\mathcal{R}^T \,|\, T \in \mathcal{T})$. The result of mapping ϕ is now defined as $\theta_A = \sum_{T \in \mathcal{T}} \rho^T \theta^T$. For each $B \in \mathcal{F}$ define $\mathcal{R}_B = \pi_B(\mathcal{R}^T)$ where $T \in \mathcal{T}_B$. (Note, $\mathcal{R}_B$ does not depend on which T is chosen because WTA holds; see 4.1.) It is easy to see that θ satisfies relaxed J-consistency condition with relations $(\mathcal{R}_B \,|\, B \in \mathcal{F})$. We also have

$$
\begin{aligned}
\Phi(\boldsymbol{\theta}) &= \sum_{T \in \mathcal{T}} \rho^T \min_{\boldsymbol{x}} f(\boldsymbol{x} \,|\, \theta^T) = \sum_{T \in \mathcal{T}} \sum_{A \in \mathcal{O}_T} \rho^T \min_{\boldsymbol{x}_A} \theta_A^T(\boldsymbol{x}_A) \\
&= \sum_{A \in \mathcal{O}} \min_{\boldsymbol{x}_A} \theta_A(\boldsymbol{x}_A) = \sum_{A \in \mathcal{F}} \min_{\boldsymbol{x}_A} \theta_A(\boldsymbol{x}_A) = \Psi(\theta) \ .
\end{aligned}
$$

Constructing Mapping $\psi : \Lambda^* \to \Omega^*$.   Consider vector $\theta \equiv \bar{\theta}$ that satisfies the J-consistency condition with relations $(\mathcal{R}_B \,|\, B \in \mathcal{F})$. The argument used in the proof of proposition 4.1 implies that the $\bar{J}$-consistency also holds.

First, let us do the following: for each $B \in \mathcal{S}$, pick outer factor $A \in \mathcal{O}$ with $B \in \mathcal{F}_A$ and "move" vector θ_B to A, i.e., update $\theta_A(\boldsymbol{x}_A) \mathrel{+}= \theta_B(\boldsymbol{x}_B)$, $\theta_B(\boldsymbol{x}_B) := 0$.

Lemma 4.10. *The update above does not affect* $\Psi(\theta)$, *and* θ *still satisfies the relaxed J-consistency condition with relations* $(\mathcal{R}_B \,|\, B \in \mathcal{F})$.

Proof. Let θ and $\tilde{\theta}$ be the vectors before and after the update for factors $A \in \mathcal{O}$, $B \in \mathcal{F}_A - \{A\}$, respectively. Consider labeling $\boldsymbol{x}_A \in \mathcal{R}_A \subseteq \langle \theta_A \rangle$. Note that $\boldsymbol{x}_B \in \pi_B(\mathcal{R}_A) = \mathcal{R}_B \subseteq \langle \theta_B \rangle$. To prove the second claim, we need to show that $\boldsymbol{x}_A \in \langle \tilde{\theta}_A \rangle$. This holds because for any other labelings $\boldsymbol{x}_A'$

$$
\tilde{\theta}_A(\boldsymbol{x}_A) = \theta_A(\boldsymbol{x}_A) + \theta_B(\boldsymbol{x}_B) \le \theta_A(\boldsymbol{x}_A') + \theta_B(\boldsymbol{x}_B') = \tilde{\theta}_A(\boldsymbol{x}_A') \ .
$$

The first part holds because

$$
\begin{aligned}
\min_{\boldsymbol{x}_A'} \tilde{\theta}_A(\boldsymbol{x}_A) + \min_{\boldsymbol{x}_B'} \tilde{\theta}_B(\boldsymbol{x}_B) &= \tilde{\theta}_A(\boldsymbol{x}_A) + \tilde{\theta}_B(\boldsymbol{x}_B) \\
&= \theta_A(\boldsymbol{x}_A) + \theta_B(\boldsymbol{x}_B) = \min_{\boldsymbol{x}_A'} \theta_A(\boldsymbol{x}_A) + \min_{\boldsymbol{x}_B'} \theta_B(\boldsymbol{x}_B) \ .
\end{aligned}
$$

☐

We now have vector θ with $\theta_B(\boldsymbol{x}_B) = 0$ for all $B \in \mathcal{S}$.

Lemma 4.11. *Consider tree* $T = (\mathcal{O}_T, \mathcal{E}_T)$. *Define vector* θ^T *as follows:*
$\theta^T_A = \frac{1}{\rho^T} \theta_A$ *for* $A \in \mathcal{O}_T$ *and* $\theta^T_B(\boldsymbol{x}_B) = 0$ *for* $B \in \mathcal{S}, T \in \mathcal{T}_B$. *Define relation*

$$\mathcal{R}^T = \{\boldsymbol{x} \mid \boldsymbol{x}_A \in \mathcal{R}_A \quad \forall A \in \mathcal{O}_T\} \tag{4.28}$$

(a) $\pi_B(\mathcal{R}^T) = \mathcal{R}_B$ *for each* $B \in \mathcal{F}_T$.
(b) $f(\boldsymbol{x}^T \mid \theta^T) = \sum_{A \in \mathcal{O}_T} \min_{\boldsymbol{x}_A} \theta^T_A(\boldsymbol{x}_A)$ *for each* $\boldsymbol{x}^T \in \mathcal{R}^T$.
(c) $\mathcal{R}^T \subseteq \langle \nu^T \rangle$.

Proof. It suffices to show that $\pi_A(\mathcal{R}^T) = \mathcal{R}_A$ for each $A \in \mathcal{O}_T$; for $B \in \mathcal{F}_A - \{A\}$, we will then have $\pi_B(\mathcal{R}^T) = \pi_B(\mathcal{R}_A) = \mathcal{R}_B$, where the last equality holds because $(A, B) \in \bar{J}$ and θ satisfies the $\bar{J}$-consistency condition with relations $(\mathcal{R}_B \mid B \in \mathcal{F})$.

We use induction on the size of the tree. For $\mathcal{O}_T = \{A\}$ the claim is obvious; suppose that $|\mathcal{O}_T| \geq 2$. Pick a leaf factor $A \in \mathcal{O}_T$, with $(A, \hat{A}) \in \mathcal{E}_T$. Let T' be the tree obtained from T by removing factor A and $S = A \cap \hat{A} \in \mathcal{F}_{T'}$. We assume that $\rho^{T'} = \rho^T$. By the running intersection property, $(A - S) \cap A' = \varnothing$ for $A' \in \mathcal{O}_T - \{A\}$.

Let $\boldsymbol{x}'$ be a labeling in $\mathcal{R}^{T'}$. By the induction hypothesis, $\boldsymbol{x}'_S \in \mathcal{R}_S$. Let $\boldsymbol{x}_A$ be labeling in $\mathcal{R}_A$ with $\boldsymbol{x}_S = \boldsymbol{x}'_S$ (it exists because $(A, S) \in \bar{J}$ and $\bar{J}$-consistency holds). Let $\boldsymbol{x}$ be the labeling obtained from $\boldsymbol{x}'$ by changing the labeling of $A - S$ from $\boldsymbol{x}'_{A-S}$ to $\boldsymbol{x}_{A-S}$. Clearly, $\boldsymbol{x} \in \mathcal{R}^T$.

The argument above and the induction hypothesis show that $\mathcal{R}_{A'} \subseteq \pi_{A'}(\mathcal{R}^T)$ for each $A' \in \mathcal{O}_T - \{A\}$. The fact that $\mathcal{R}_A \subseteq \pi_A(\mathcal{R}^T)$ is also clear (in the argument above we can first choose $\boldsymbol{x}_A \in \mathcal{R}_A$, and then $\boldsymbol{x}' \in \mathcal{R}^{T'}$ which is consistent with $\boldsymbol{x}$ on S). The inclusion $\pi_{A'}(\mathcal{R}^T) \subseteq \mathcal{R}_{A'}$ for $A' \in \mathcal{O}_T$ follows from the definition of $\mathcal{R}^T$. This proves part (a). Part (b) is also easy to prove: for each $\boldsymbol{x}^T \in \mathcal{R}^T$, we have

$$f(\boldsymbol{x}^T \mid \theta^T) = \sum_{A' \in \mathcal{O}_T} \theta^T_{A'}(\boldsymbol{x}^T_{A'}) \overset{(1)}{=} \sum_{A' \in \mathcal{O}_T} \min_{\boldsymbol{x}_{A'}} \theta^T_{A'}(\boldsymbol{x}_{A'}),$$

where (1) holds by the induction hypothesis and the fact that $\boldsymbol{x}^T_A \in \mathcal{R}_A$. Finally, part (c) follows from (b) and the fact that $\sum_{A \in \mathcal{O}_T} \min_{\boldsymbol{x}_A} \theta^T_A(\boldsymbol{x}_A)$ is a lower bound on $\min_{\boldsymbol{x}} f(\boldsymbol{x} \mid \theta^T)$. $\qquad\square$

The result of mapping ψ is now defined as described in the lemma. It is easy to see that the obtained vector $\boldsymbol{\theta}$ satisfies WTA with relations $(\mathcal{R}^T \mid T \in \mathcal{T})$ from the lemma. We also have

$$\Phi(\boldsymbol{\theta}) = \sum_{T \in \mathcal{T}} \rho^T \min_{\boldsymbol{x}^T} \nu^T(\boldsymbol{x}^T) \overset{(1)}{=} \sum_{T \in \mathcal{T}} \sum_{A \in \mathcal{O}_T} \rho^T \min_{\boldsymbol{x}_A} \theta^T_A(\boldsymbol{x}_A) = \Psi(\boldsymbol{\theta}),$$

where (1) follows from lemma 4.11(b,c).

4.8   References

D. Batra, S. Nowozin, and P. Kohli. Tighter relaxations for MAP-MRF inference: A local primal-dual gap based separation algorithm. In *Intl. Conf. on Artificial Intelligence and Statistics*, 2011.

R. Cowell, A. Dawid, S. Lauritzen, and D. Spiegelhalter. *Probabilistic Networks and Expert Systems. Statistics for Eng. and Information Science.* Springer-Verlag, 1999.

N. El-Zehiry and L. Grady. Fast global optimization of curvature. In *Conf. on Computer Vision and Pattern Recognition*, 2010.

A. Globerson and T. Jaakkola. Fixing max-product: Convergent message passing algorithms for MAP LP-relaxations. In *Neural Information Processing Systems*, 2007.

T. Hazan and A. Shashua. Norm-product belief propagation: Primal-dual message-passing for approximate inference. *IEEE Trans. on Information Theory*, 56(12): 6294–6316, 2010.

C. Huang and A. Darwiche. Inference in belief networks: A procedural guide. *International Journal of Approximate Reasoning*, 15:225–263, 1996.

J. Johnson, D. M. Malioutov, and A. S. Willsky. Lagrangian relaxation for MAP estimation in graphical models. In *45th Annual Allerton Conference on Communication, Control and Computing*, 2007.

V. Jojic, S. Gould, and D. Koller. Accelerated dual decomposition for MAP inference. In *Intl. Conf. on Machine Learning*, 2010.

J. H. Kappes, B. Savchynskyy, and C. Schnörr. A bundle approach to efficient MAP-inference by Lagrangian relaxation. In *Conf. on Computer Vision and Pattern Recognition*, 2012.

V. Kolmogorov. Convergent tree-reweighted message passing for energy minimization. *IEEE Trans. on Pattern Analysis and Machine Intelligence*, 28(10):1568–1583, 2006.

V. Kolmogorov. The power of linear programming for finite-valued CSPs: A constructive characterization. In *Intl. Colloquium on Automata, Languages and Programming*, 2013.

N. Komodakis and N. Paragios. Beyond loose LP-relaxations: Optimizing MRFs by repairing cycles. In *European Conf. on Computer Vision*, 2008.

N. Komodakis and N. Paragios. Beyond pairwise energies: Efficient optimization for higher-order MRFs. In *Conf. on Computer Vision and Pattern Recognition*, 2009.

N. Komodakis, N. Paragios, and G. Tziritas. MRF optimization via dual decomposition: Message-passing revisited. In *Intl. Conf. on Computer Vision*, 2007.

T. Koo, A. M. Rush, M. Collins, T. Jaakkola, and D. Sontag. Dual decomposition for parsing with non-projective head automata. In *Empirical Methods in Natural Language Processing*, pages 1288–1298, 2010.

M. P. Kumar and P. Torr. Efficiently solving convex relaxations for MAP estimation. In *Intl. Conf. on Machine Learning*, 2008.

D. V. N. Luong, P. Parpas, D. Rueckert, and B. Rustem. Solving MRF minimization by mirror descent. In *Advances in Visual Computing*, pages 587–598, 2012.

A. F. T. Martins, M. A. T. Figueiredo, P. M. Q. Aguiar, N. A. Smith, and E. P. Xing. An augmented Lagrangian approach to constrained MAP inference. In *Intl. Conf. on Machine Learning*, 2011.

T. Meltzer, A. Globerson, and Y. Weiss. Convergent message passing algorithms: A unifying view. In *Uncertainty in Artificial Intelligence*, 2009.

O. Meshi and A. Globerson. An alternating direction method for dual MAP LP relaxation. In *European Conf. on Machine Learning (ECML PKDD)*, pages 470–483, 2011.

T. Minka and Y. Qi. Tree-structured approximations by expectation propagation. In *Neural Information Processing Systems*, 2003.

B. Potetz and T. Lee. Efficient belief propagation for higher-order cliques using linear constraint nodes. *Computer Vision and Image Understanding*, 112(1):39–54, 2008.

P. Ravikumar, A. Agarwal, and M. J. Wainwright. Message-passing for graph-structured linear programs: Proximal projections, convergence, and rounding schemes. *Journal of Machine Learning Research*, 11:1043–1080, 2010.

B. Savchynskyy, J. H. Kappes, S. Schmidt, and C. Schnörr. A study of Nesterov's scheme for Lagrangian decomposition and MAP labeling. In *Conf. on Computer Vision and Pattern Recognition*, 2011.

B. Savchynskyy, S. Schmidt, J. H. Kappes, and C. Schnörr. Efficient MRF energy minimization via adaptive diminishing smoothing. In *Uncertainty in Artificial Intelligence*, pages 746–755, 2012. Additional comparisons are in the poster available from http://hci.iwr.uni-heidelberg.de/Staff/bsavchyn/papers/savchynskyyUAI2012poster.pdf.

M. I. Schlesinger and V. V. Giginyak. Solution to structural recognition (MAX,+)-problems by their equivalent transformations. *Control Systems and Computers*, (1,2), 2007.

S. Schmidt, B. Savchynskyy, J. H. Kappes, and C. Schnörr. Evaluation of a first-order primal-dual algorithm for MRF energy minimization. In *EMMCVPR*, 2011.

T. Schoenemann. Probabilistic word alignment under the l_0 norm. In *Conf. on Computational Natural Language Learning*, 2011.

T. Schoenemann, F. Kahl, S. Masnou, and D. Cremers. A linear framework for region-based image segmentation and inpainting involving curvature penalization. *International Journal of Computer Vision*, 99(1):53–68, May 2012.

D. Sontag. *Approximate Inference in Graphical Models using LP Relaxations*. PhD thesis, MIT, Dept. of Electrical Engineering and Computer Science, 2010.

D. Sontag, T. Meltzer, A. Globerson, Y. Weiss, and T. Jaakkola. Tightening LP relaxations for MAP using message passing. In *Uncertainty in Artificial Intelligence*, 2008.

D. Sontag, A. Globerson, and T. Jaakkola. Introduction to dual decomposition for inference. In S. Sra, S. Nowozin, and S. Wright, editors, *Optimization for Machine Learning*. MIT Press, 2011.

D. Sontag, D. K. Choe, and Y. Li. Efficiently searching for frustrated cycles in MAP inference. In *Uncertainty in Artificial Intelligence*, 2012.

G. Storvik and G. Dahl. Lagrangian-based methods for finding MAP. *IEEE Trans. on Image Processing*, 9(3):469–479, March 2000.

P. Strandmark and F. Kahl. Curvature regularization for curves and surfaces in a global optimization framework. In *Intl. Conf. on Energy Minimization Methods in Computer Vision and Pattern Recognition*, 2011.

R. Szeliski, R. Zabih, D. Scharstein, O. Veskler, V. Kolmogorov, A. Agarwala, M. Tappen, and C. Rother. A comparative study of energy minimization methods for Markov Random Fields with smoothness-based priors. *IEEE Trans. on Pattern Analysis and Machine Intelligence*, 30(6):1068–1080, June 2008.

D. Tarlow, I. Givoni, and R. Zemel. HOP-MAP: Efficient message passing with higher order potentials. In *Intl. Conf. on Artificial Intelligence and Statistics*, Sardinia, Italy, 2010.

D. Tarlow, D. Batra, P. Kohli, and V. Kolmogorov. Dynamic tree block coordinate ascent. In *Intl. Conf. on Machine Learning*, 2011.

J. Thapper and S. Živný. The power of linear programming for valued CSPs. In *Symposium on Foundations of Computer Science*, 2012.

L. Torresani, V. Kolmogorov, and C. Rother. A dual decomposition approach to feature correspondence. *IEEE Trans. on Pattern Analysis and Machine Intelligence*, 99, 2012.

S. Vicente, V. Kolmogorov, and C. Rother. Joint optimization of segmentation and appearance models. In *Intl. Conf. on Computer Vision*, 2009.

M. Wainwright, T. Jaakkola, and A. Willsky. MAP estimation via agreement on (hyper)trees: Message-passing and linear-programming approaches. *IEEE Trans. on Information Theory*, 51(11):3697–3717, November 2005.

T. Werner. A linear programming approach to max-sum problem: A review. *IEEE Trans. on Pattern Analysis and Machine Intelligence*, 29(7):1165–1179, 2007.

T. Werner. Revisiting the linear programming relaxation approach to Gibbs energy minimization and weighted constraint satisfaction. *IEEE Trans. on Pattern Analysis and Machine Intelligence*, 32(8):1474–1488, 2010.

C. Yanover, T. Meltzer, and Y. Weiss. Linear programming relaxations and belief propagation: An empirical study. *Journal of Machine Learning Research*, 7:1887–1907, September 2006.

Y. Zheng, P. Chen, and J.-Z. Cao. MAP-MRF inference based on extended junction tree representation. In *Conf. on Computer Vision and Pattern Recognition*, 2012.

5   Smoothed Coordinate Descent for MAP Inference

Ofer Meshi   meshi@ttic.edu
TTIC
Chicago, IL

Tommi Jaakkola   tommi@csail.mit.edu
CSAIL, MIT
Cambridge, MA

Amir Globerson   gamir@cs.huji.ac.il
The Hebrew University
Jerusalem, Israel

Finding maximum a posteriori (MAP) assignments in graphical models is an important task in many applications. Because the problem is generally hard, linear programming (LP) relaxations are often used. Solving these relaxations efficiently is thus an important practical problem. In recent years, several authors have proposed message passing updates corresponding to coordinate descent in the dual LP. However, these are generally not guaranteed to converge to a global optimum. One approach to remedy this is to smooth the LP and perform coordinate descent on the smoothed dual. Here we provide a tutorial introduction to such algorithms, followed by an analysis of their convergence rate. We analyze the rate of convergence to both the primal and dual optima of the problems under different coordinate update schedules. Empirical evaluation supports our theoretical claims and shows that the method is highly competitive with state-of-the-art approaches that yield global optima.

5.1   Introduction

Many applications involve simultaneous prediction of multiple variables. For example, we may seek to label pixels in an image with their semantic classes or find the semantic role of words in a sentence. These problems can be cast as maximizing a function over a set of labels (or minimizing an energy function). The function typically decomposes into a sum of local functions over overlapping subsets of variables.

Such maximization problems are nevertheless typically hard (Koller and Friedman, 2009). Even for simple decompositions (e.g., subsets correspond to pairs of variables), maximizing over the set of labels is often provably NP-hard. One approach would be to reduce the problem to a tractable one (e.g., by constraining the model to a low tree-width graph). However, empirically, using more complex interactions together with approximate inference methods is often advantageous. One popular family of approximate methods is the linear programming (LP) relaxation approach (e.g., see Chapter 8 in Wainwright and Jordan, 2008). Although these LPs are tractable, general purpose LP solvers typically do not exploit the problem structure (Yanover et al., 2006). Therefore, a great deal of effort has gone into designing solvers that are specifically tailored to typical MAP-LP relaxations. These include, for example, cut-based algorithms (Boykov et al., 1999; Kolmogorov and Rother, 2007), accelerated gradient methods (Jojic et al., 2010; Savchynskyy et al., 2011), and augmented Lagrangian methods (Martins et al., 2011; Meshi and Globerson, 2011).

One class of particularly simple algorithms, which we will focus on here, are coordinate minimization-based approaches. Examples include max-sum-diffusion (Werner, 2007), MPLP (Globerson and Jaakkola, 2008), and TRW-S (Kolmogorov, 2006).[1] These work by first taking the dual of the LP and then optimizing the dual in a block coordinate fashion (see Sontag et al., 2011, for a review). In many cases, the coordinate block operations can be performed in closed form, resulting in updates quite similar to the max-product message passing algorithm. By coordinate minimization, we mean that at each step a set of coordinates is chosen, all other coordinates are fixed, and the chosen coordinates are set to their optimal value given the rest. This is different from a coordinate descent strategy, where instead a gradient step is performed on the chosen coordinates (rather than full optimization).

---

1. See Chapter 4 for a generalized version of TRW-S.

A main caveat of the coordinate minimization approach is that it will not necessarily find the global optimum of the LP (although in practice it often does). This is a direct result of the LP objective not being strictly convex. Several authors have proposed to smooth the LP with entropy terms and employ variants of coordinate minimization (Hazan and Shashua, 2010; Werner, 2009). However, the convergence rate of these methods has not been analyzed. Moreover, because the algorithms work in the dual, there is no simple procedure to map the result back into primal feasible variables. In this chapter, we provide a tutorial introduction to the smoothing approach to MAP LP relaxations and analyze its convergence rate.

Convergence rates for coordinate minimization are typically hard to obtain. As mentioned above, convergence to the global optimum is in fact not always achieved, and in these cases, the rate of convergence (e.g., to a local optimum) is not of much interest. However, there are many cases where global convergence is guaranteed asymptotically (e.g., Tseng, 2001), but the number of iterations needed to reach a given accuracy ϵ is not known.

The rate of convergence and its analysis depend on the update schedule used by the algorithm—namely, the choice of which coordinate (or block of coordinates) to update at each step. The simplest schedule is to decide on a given fixed permutation of the coordinates and update those in a cyclic manner. However, this seems to be the hardest case to analyze, and only recently have results been obtained for convergence rate in specific problem settings (Saha and Tewari, 2013).

Choosing non-cyclic update schedules seems to considerably simplify the analysis. One variant is to randomly choose the next coordinate block. The convergence rate of this stochastic schedule has been analyzed recently in Nesterov (2010) and Shalev-Shwartz and Tewari (2011). However, this was done not for coordinate minimization (which we study here) but rather for gradient descent steps along each coordinate. Another non-cyclic update is a greedy schedule, where at each step one chooses the coordinate that has the most "potential" for improving the objective.[2] Such greedy schemes have been studied, for example, in the context of coreset optimization and the Frank Wolfe method (Clarkson, 2010), but the resulting algorithms are different from coordinate minimization.[3]

In what follows, we review the smoothing approach to MAP LP relaxations and analyze its convergence rate. We study both greedy and stochastic schedules and analyze their rate of convergence to the dual optimum. We also introduce a simple mapping to primal variables and analyze the rate

---

2. This can be measured in various ways.
3. For example, they do not fully optimize each coordinate.

of convergence of these to the primal optimum.[4] Finally, we provide a brief review of the ADMM method, which illustrates a different way of using smoothing and coordinate descent to globally solve the MAP LP problem.

5.2   MAP and LP Relaxations

Consider a set of n discrete variables $X_1, \ldots, X_n$, and a set C of subsets of these variables (i.e., $c \in C$ is a subset of $\{1, \ldots, n\}$). We use x_i to denote particular assignments to these variables. Next, consider functions that decompose according to these subsets. In particular, each subset c is associated with a local function or factor $\theta_c(x_c)$, and we also include factors $\theta_i(x_i)$ for each individual variable.[5] These can be used to define the following "score" function, which returns a real value for any assignment to the n variables:

$$f(x_1, \ldots, x_n; \theta) = \sum_{c \in C} \theta_c(x_c) + \sum_{i=1}^{n} \theta_i(x_i). \tag{5.1}$$

We will often write $f(x; \theta)$, where x corresponds to the assignment to the n variables.

The MAP problem is to find an assignment x to all the variables, which maximizes $f(x; \theta)$. Namely:

$$\mathrm{MAP}(\theta) = \max_{x_1, \ldots, x_n} f(x_1, \ldots, x_n; \theta). \tag{5.2}$$

The above is a combinatorial optimization problem whose naive solution requires searching over 2^n possible assignments (for binary variables). This is indeed the worst-case complexity of such problems.[6] Linear programming relaxations are a popular approach to approximating combinatorial optimization problems. In what follows, we review the most common LP relaxation for the MAP problem (Wainwright and Jordan, 2008; Wainwright et al., 2005; Werner, 2007). See also Chapters 2 and 4 in this volume.

To obtain an LP relaxation for (5.2), we first write it as an integer linear program and then relax the integrality constraints. Consider a set of boolean variables $\mu_i(x_i) \in \{0, 1\}$ (one for each $i \in \{1, \ldots, n\}$ and value of x_i), that

---

4. A related analysis of MAP LP using smoothing appeared in Burshtein (2009). However, their approach is specific to LDPC codes and does not apply to general MAP problems as we analyze here.
5. Although singleton factors are not needed for generality, we keep them for notational convenience.
6. For example, max-cut can be easily seen as an instance of (5.2).

are constrained to be either zero or one. A setting $\mu_i(x_i) = 1$ will reflect the fact that the ith variable has the value x_i. Similarly, consider variables $\mu_c(x_c)$ (one for each $c \in C$ and value of x_c). A setting $\mu_c(x_c) = 1$ will reflect the fact that the variables in c are set to the value x_c. We denote an assignment to all the μ_i's and μ_c's by a vector μ.

We can now cast the MAP problem as an integer linear program as follows:[7]

$$
\begin{aligned}
\max \quad & \sum_c \sum_{x_c} \theta_c(x_c)\mu_c(x_c) + \sum_i \sum_{x_i} \theta_i(x_i)\mu_i(x_i) \\
s.t. \quad & \sum_{x_{c\setminus i}} \mu_c(x_c) = \mu_i(x_i) \quad , \quad \forall c, i \in c, x_i \\
& \sum_{x_i} \mu_i(x_i) = 1 \quad , \quad \forall i \\
& \sum_{x_c} \mu_c(x_c) = 1 \quad , \quad \forall c \\
& \mu_i(x_i) \in \{0,1\} \quad , \quad \forall i, x_i \\
& \mu_c(x_c) \in \{0,1\} \quad , \quad \forall c, x_c,
\end{aligned}
\tag{5.3}
$$

where in $\sum_{x_{c\setminus i}} \mu_c(x_c)$, we sum out all variables in c except i. To see that this is equivalent to the MAP problem, note that any feasible μ corresponds to an assignment $x_1, \ldots, x_n$.[8] The mapping is obtained by setting $X_i = x_i$, where x_i is the value such that $\mu_i(x_i) = 1$ (there is only one such value because of the constraints). Denote the assignment corresponding to μ by $x(\mu)$. Then the objective in (5.3) is $f(x(\mu); \theta)$. Finally, because each assignment x has a corresponding μ, we have the equivalence to MAP.

The above ILP can be naturally converted into an LP by relaxing the integrality constraint $\mu_\alpha(x_\alpha) \in \{0,1\}$ to $\mu_\alpha(x_\alpha) \in [0,1]$ (where α is either a variable i or a factor c). The resulting LP is:

$$
\begin{aligned}
PMAP : \max_{\mu \in \mathcal{M}_L} P(\mu) \quad &= \quad \max_{\mu \in \mathcal{M}_L} \left\{ \sum_c \sum_{x_c} \theta_c(x_c)\mu_c(x_c) + \sum_i \sum_{x_i} \theta_i(x_i)\mu_i(x_i) \right\} \\
&= \quad \max_{\mu \in \mathcal{M}_L} \mu \cdot \theta,
\end{aligned}
\tag{5.4}
$$

where $P(\mu)$ is the primal (linear) objective and $\mathcal{M}_L$ is given by[9]:

$$
\mathcal{M}_L = \left\{ \mu \geq 0 : \begin{array}{ll} \sum_{x_{c\setminus i}} \mu_c(x_c) = \mu_i(x_i) & \forall c, i \in c, x_i \\ \sum_{x_i} \mu_i(x_i) = 1 & \forall i \end{array} \right\}.
\tag{5.5}
$$

The set $\mathcal{M}_L$ is often referred to as the *local marginal polytope* (Wainwright and Jordan, 2008).

---

7. Note that the normalization constraint on μ_c is redundant but is usually included.
8. Our derivation here is similar to Weiss et al. (2007).
9. We can neglect the upper bound on μ because it is enforced by the normalization constraint.

If the maximizer of $PMAP$ has only integral values, then it solves the ILP, and $x(\mu)$ is the MAP solution. However, in the general case, the solution may be fractional (Wainwright and Jordan, 2008) and the maximum of $PMAP$ is an upper bound on $MAP(\theta)$.

5.2.1   The Dual LP

The linear program in (5.4) can be solved in polynomial time using generic LP solvers. However, these do not use the special structure of the problem and can often result in impractical running times (Yanover et al., 2006). Thus, in recent years, considerable research effort has gone into designing specific algorithms for solving (5.4). Many of these are based on the notion of dual coordinate descent. Namely, they take the convex dual of (5.4) and perform block coordinate descent on its variables. Because our algorithms will be closely related to this approach, we briefly introduce the dual objective.

The dual variables will be denoted by $\delta_{ci}(x_i)$, where there is one such variable for each i, c, x_i. These can be intuitively understood as messages from subset c to node i, reflecting a belief that the ith variable has value x_i. The convex dual of (5.4) is then:

$$\min_\delta \sum_c \max_{x_c} \left(\theta_c(x_c) - \sum_{i:i \in c} \delta_{ci}(x_i) \right) + \sum_i \max_{x_i} \left(\theta_i(x_i) + \sum_{c:i \in c} \delta_{ci}(x_i) \right). \quad (5.6)$$

This objective may also be derived using the dual decomposition framework (e.g., see Sontag et al., 2011; Komodakis et al., 2011).

The advantage of the optimization problem in (5.6) is that it is unconstrained, and thus can be optimized using simple convex optimization approaches. One example is subgradient descent and its accelerated variants (e.g., see Komodakis et al., 2011; Savchynskyy et al., 2011; Jojic et al., 2010).

Another nice property of (5.6) is that minimizing over some blocks of coordinates can be done in closed form given a fixed value of the other coordinates. This is the basis of the dual coordinate descent algorithms mentioned earlier. However, as also mentioned earlier, these algorithms are generally not guaranteed to converge to a global optimum. In what follows, we review a smoothing approach that preserves that nice structure of coordinate descent algorithms but results in global convergence.

5.2.2   Smoothing the LP

Because global convergence is desirable, several authors have considered a smoothed version of the LP in (5.4). As we shall see, this offers several advantages over solving the LP directly. The basic idea is as follows. Given a parameter $\tau > 0$, we construct a new primal problem $PMAP_\tau$ that is $O(\frac{1}{\tau})$ *close* to the original $PMAP$ (see below for a precise definition). The dual of $PMAP$ is denoted by $DMAP_\tau$. It is similar in structure to (5.6), but with one key difference: the global optimum of $DMAP_\tau$ can be found using coordinate descent and with guarantees on convergence rate.

Define the following primal objective:

$$P_\tau(\mu) = \mu \cdot \theta + \frac{1}{\tau} \sum_c H(\mu_c) + \frac{1}{\tau} \sum_i H(\mu_i), \tag{5.7}$$

where $H(\mu_c)$ and $H(\mu_i)$ are the entropies of the corresponding distributions.[10] Now define the following smoothed primal optimization problem:

$$PMAP_\tau : \quad \max_{\mu \in \mathcal{M}_L} P_\tau(\mu). \tag{5.8}$$

Note that as $\tau \to \infty$ we obtain the original primal problem. In fact, a stronger result can be shown. Specifically, the optimal value of $PMAP$ is $O(\frac{1}{\tau})$ close to the optimal value of $PMAP_\tau$. This justifies using the smoothed objective P_τ as a proxy to P in (5.4). We express this in the following lemma (which appears in similar forms in Hazan and Shashua (2010) and Nesterov (2005)).

Lemma 5.1. *Denote by μ^* the optimum of problem $PMAP$ in (5.4) and by $\hat{\mu}^*$ the optimum of problem $PMAP_\tau$ in (5.8). Then:*

$$\hat{\mu}^* \cdot \theta \le \mu^* \cdot \theta \le \hat{\mu}^* \cdot \theta + \frac{H_{\max}}{\tau}, \tag{5.9}$$

where $H_{\max} = \sum_c \log |x_c| + \sum_i \log |x_i|$ (here $|x_\alpha|$ is the number of possible configurations of variables or factors). In other words, the smoothed optimum is an $O(\frac{1}{\tau})$-optimal solution of the original non-smoothed problem.

5.2.3   The Dual of the Smoothed LP

As mentioned above, we shall be particularly interested in the dual of $PMAP_\tau$ because it facilitates simple coordinate minimization updates. As in the non-smooth case (see Section 5.2.1), our dual variables will be denoted by $\delta_{ci}(x_i)$. Before introducing the dual objective, we define the *soft-max* function, which plays a key role in this dual. Given a function $v(x)$ over

---

10. Namely, $H(\mu_i) = -\sum_{x_i} \mu_i(x_i) \log \mu_i(x_i)$, and $H(\mu_c) = -\sum_{x_c} \mu_c(x_c) \log \mu_c(x_c)$.

some variable x and a parameter τ, we define the soft-max of v by:

$$\operatorname*{smax}_{x}\left(v(x);\tau\right)=\frac{1}{\tau}\log\sum_{x}\exp\left(\tau v(x)\right). \tag{5.10}$$

The soft-max is closely related to the max function in several ways:

- It upper bounds the max, namely: $\operatorname{smax}_{x}(v(x);\tau)\geq\max_{x}v(x)$ for all τ values.

- As $\tau\to\infty$, the soft-max approaches the max, namely:

$$\lim_{\tau\to\infty}\operatorname*{smax}_{x}\left(v(x);\tau\right)=\max_{x}v(x). \tag{5.11}$$

We now turn to the dual of $PMAP_\tau$. Standard duality transformation shows that the dual objective is (e.g., see Boyd and Vandenberghe, 2004)[11]:

$$F(\delta)=\sum_{c}\operatorname*{smax}_{x_c}\left(\theta_c(x_c)-\sum_{i:i\in c}\delta_{ci}(x_i);\tau\right)+\sum_{i}\operatorname*{smax}_{x_i}\left(\theta_i(x_i)+\sum_{c:i\in c}\delta_{ci}(x_i);\tau\right). \tag{5.12}$$

The dual is an unconstrained smooth minimization problem:

$$DMAP_\tau : \min_{\delta} F(\delta). \tag{5.13}$$

Convex duality implies that the optima of $DMAP_\tau$ and $PMAP_\tau$ coincide. Comparing (5.6) to (5.12), we see that the original and smooth duals are identical with the exception that max in the original is replaced with soft-max in the smoothed version. This is rather convenient as most of the structure that facilitated simple coordinate descent algorithms in the original dual can still be exploited.

Finally, we shall be interested in transformations between dual variables δ and primal variables μ (see Section 5.5). The following are the transformations obtained from the Lagrangian derivation (i.e., they can be used to switch from *optimal* dual variables to *optimal* primal variables).

$$\mu_c(x_c;\delta)\quad\propto\quad\exp\left(\tau\theta_c(x_c)-\tau\sum_{i:i\in c}\delta_{ci}(x_i)\right)$$

$$\mu_i(x_i;\delta)\quad\propto\quad\exp\left(\tau\theta_i(x_i)+\tau\sum_{c:i\in c}\delta_{ci}(x_i)\right)$$

---

11. This results from the fact that the conjugate of the entropy function is the $\log\sum\exp$ function.

We denote the vector of all such marginals by $\mu(\delta)$. For the dual variables δ that minimize $F(\delta)$, it holds that $\mu(\delta)$ are feasible (i.e., $\mu(\delta) \in \mathcal{M}_L$). However, we will also consider $\mu(\delta)$ for non-optimal δ and show how to obtain primal feasible approximations from $\mu(\delta)$. These will be helpful in obtaining primal convergence rates.

It is easy to see that $\left(\nabla F(\delta^t)\right)_{c,i,x_i} = \mu_i(x_i; \delta^t) - \mu_c(x_i; \delta^t)$, where (with some abuse of notation) we denote $\mu_c(x_i) = \sum_{x_{c\setminus i}} \mu_c(x_{c\setminus i}, x_i)$. The elements of the gradient thus correspond to inconsistency between the marginals $\mu(\delta^t)$ (i.e., the degree to which they violate the constraints in (5.5)). We shall make repeated use of this fact to link primal and dual variables.

5.3 Coordinate Minimization Algorithms

In this section, we propose several coordinate minimization procedures for solving $DMAP_\tau$ (5.13). We first set some notation to define block coordinate minimization algorithms. Denote the objective we want to minimize by $F(\delta)$, where δ corresponds to a set of N variables. Now define $\mathcal{S} = \{S_1, \ldots, S_M\}$ as a set of subsets, where each subset $S_i \subseteq \{1, \ldots, N\}$ describes a coordinate block. We will assume that $S_i \cap S_j = \emptyset$ for all i, j and that $\cup_i S_i = \{1, \ldots, N\}$.

Block coordinate minimization algorithms work as follows: at each iteration, first set $\delta^{t+1} = \delta^t$. Next choose a block S_i and set:

$$\delta_{S_i}^{t+1} = \underset{\delta_{S_i}}{\text{argmin}}\, F_i(\delta_{S_i}; \delta^t), \tag{5.14}$$

where we use $F_i(\delta_{S_i}; \delta^t)$ to denote the function F restricted to the variables δ_{S_i} and where all other variables are set to their value in δ^t. In other words, at each iteration, we fully optimize only over the variables δ_{S_i} while fixing all other variables. We assume that the minimization step in (5.14) can be solved in closed form, which is indeed the case for the updates we consider below.

Regarding the choice of an update schedule, several options are available:

- **Cyclic**: Decide on a fixed order (e.g., $S_1, \ldots, S_M$) and cycle through it.

- **Stochastic**: Draw an index i uniformly at random[12] at each iteration and use the block S_i.

- **Greedy**: Denote by $\nabla_{S_i} F(\delta^t)$ the gradient $\nabla F(\delta^t)$ evaluated at coordinates S_i only. The greedy scheme is to choose S_i that maximizes

---

12. Non-uniform schedules are also possible. We consider the uniform for simplicity.

$\|\nabla_{S_i} F(\delta^t)\|_\infty$. In other words, choose the set of coordinates that corresponds to maximum gradient of the function F. Intuitively this corresponds to choosing the block that promises the maximal (local) decrease in objective. Note that to find the best coordinate, we presumably must process all sets S_i to find the best one. We will show later that this can be done rather efficiently in our case.

In our analysis, we shall focus on the Stochastic and Greedy cases and analyze their rate of convergence. The cyclic case is typically hard to analyze, with results only under multiple conditions that do not hold here (see e.g., Saha and Tewari, 2013).

Another consideration when designing coordinate minimization algorithms is the choice of block size. One possible choice is all variables $\delta_{ci}(\cdot)$ (for a specific pair c, i). This is the block chosen in the max-sum-diffusion (MSD) algorithm (see Werner, 2007, 2009, for non-smooth and smooth MSD). A larger block that also facilitates closed form updates is the set of variables $\delta_{\cdot i}(\cdot)$, namely, all messages into a variable i from factors c such that $i \in c$. We call this a *star* update. The update is used in Meshi et al. (2010) for the non-smoothed dual (but the possibility of applying it to the smoothed version is mentioned).

To derive the block updates, one needs to fix all variables except those in the block and then set the latter to minimize $F(\delta)$. Because $F(\delta)$ is differentiable, this is pretty straightforward. The MSD update turns out to be:

$$\delta_{ci}^{t+1}(x_i) = \delta_{ci}^t(x_i) + \frac{1}{2\tau} \log \frac{\mu_c^t(x_i)}{\mu_i^t(x_i)}$$

for all x_i. Here we use $\mu_i^t(x_i), \mu_c^t(x_c)$ to denote the marginal obtained from (5.14) when using δ^t. Similarly, the star update is given by:

$$\delta_{ci}^{t+1}(x_i) = \delta_{ci}^t(x_i) + \frac{1}{\tau} \log \mu_c^t(x_i) - \frac{1}{N_i + 1} \cdot \frac{1}{\tau} \log \left(\mu_i^t(x_i) \cdot \prod_{c' : i \in c'} \mu_{c'}^t(x_i) \right)$$

for all $c : i \in c$ and all x_i, where $N_i = |\{c : i \in c\}|$.

It is interesting to consider the improvement in $F(\delta)$ as a result of an update. For the MSD update, it can be shown to be exactly:

$$F(\delta^t) - F(\delta^{t+1}) = -\frac{1}{\tau} \log \left(\sum_{x_i} \sqrt{\mu_i^t(x_i) \cdot \mu_c^t(x_i)} \right)^2 .$$

This is known as the *Bhattacharyya divergence measure* between the pair of distributions $\mu_i^t(x_i)$ and $\mu_c^t(x_i)$ (Bhattacharyya, 1946). Similarly, for the star update, the improvement in objective is exactly:

$$F(\delta^t) - F(\delta^{t+1}) = -\frac{1}{\tau} \log \left(\sum_{x_i} \left(\mu_i^t(x_i) \cdot \prod_{c:i \in c} \mu_c^t(x_i) \right)^{\frac{1}{N_i+1}} \right)^{N_i+1},$$

which is known as *Matusita's divergence measure* (Matusita, 1967) and is a generalization of the Bhattacharyya divergence to several distributions. Thus, in both cases, the improvement can be easily computed before actually applying the update and is directly related to how consistent the distributions $\mu_c^t(x_i), \mu_i^t(x_i)$ are. Recall that at the optimum, they all agree because $\mu \in \mathcal{M}_L$, and thus the anticipated improvement is zero.

5.4   Dual Convergence Rate Analysis

We begin with the convergence rates of the dual F using greedy and random schemes described in Section 5.3. In Section 5.5, we subsequently show how to obtain a primal feasible solution and how the dual rates give rise to primal rates. Our analysis builds on the fact that we can lower bound the improvement at each step as a function of some norm of the block gradient.

5.4.1   Greedy Block Minimization

Theorem 5.2. *Define B_1 to be a constant such that $\|\delta^t - \delta^*\|_1 \le B_1$ for all t. If there exists $k > 0$ so that* coordinate minimization *of each block S_i satisfies:*

$$F(\delta^t) - F(\delta^{t+1}) \ge \frac{1}{k} \|\nabla_{S_i} F(\delta^t)\|_\infty^2 \tag{5.15}$$

for all t, then for any $\epsilon > 0$ after $T = \frac{kB_1^2}{\epsilon}$ iterations of the greedy algorithm, $F(\delta^T) - F(\delta^*) \le \epsilon$.

Proof. Using Hölder's inequality, we obtain the bound:

$$F(\delta^t) - F(\delta^*) \le \nabla F(\delta^t)^\top (\delta^t - \delta^*) \le \|\nabla F(\delta^t)\|_\infty \cdot \|\delta^t - \delta^*\|_1.$$

This implies: $\|\nabla F(\delta^t)\|_\infty \ge \frac{1}{B_1} \left(F(\delta^t) - F(\delta^*) \right)$. Now, using the condition on the improvement and the greedy nature of the update, we obtain a bound on the improvement:

$$
\begin{aligned}
F(\delta^t) - F(\delta^{t+1}) \;\geq\; & \frac{1}{k}\|\nabla_{S_i}F(\delta^t)\|_\infty^2 = \frac{1}{k}\|\nabla F(\delta^t)\|_\infty^2 \\
\geq\; & \frac{1}{kB_1^2}\left(F(\delta^t) - F(\delta^*)\right)^2 \\
\geq\; & \frac{1}{kB_1^2}\left(F(\delta^t) - F(\delta^*)\right)\left(F(\delta^{t+1}) - F(\delta^*)\right).
\end{aligned}
$$

Hence,

$$
\begin{aligned}
\frac{1}{kB_1^2} \;\leq\; & \frac{F(\delta^t) - F(\delta^*) - \left(F(\delta^{t+1}) - F(\delta^*)\right)}{\left(F(\delta^t) - F(\delta^*)\right)\left(F(\delta^{t+1}) - F(\delta^*)\right)} \\
=\; & \frac{1}{F(\delta^{t+1}) - F(\delta^*)} - \frac{1}{F(\delta^t) - F(\delta^*)}.
\end{aligned}
$$

Summing over t we obtain:

$$
\frac{T}{kB_1^2} \leq \frac{1}{F(\delta^T) - F(\delta^*)} - \frac{1}{F(\delta^0) - F(\delta^*)} \leq \frac{1}{F(\delta^T) - F(\delta^*)},
$$

and the desired result follows.   □

5.4.2   Stochastic Block Minimization

Theorem 5.3. *Define B_2 to be a constant such that $\|\delta^t - \delta^*\|_2 \leq B_2$ for all t. If there exists $k > 0$ so that coordinate minimization of each block S_i satisfies:*

$$
F(\delta^t) - F(\delta^{t+1}) \geq \frac{1}{k}\|\nabla_{S_i}F(\delta^t)\|_2^2 \tag{5.16}
$$

for all t, then for any $\epsilon > 0$ after $T = \frac{k|\mathcal{S}|B_2^2}{\epsilon}$ iterations of the stochastic algorithm we have that $\mathbb{E}[F(\delta^T)] - F(\delta^*) \leq \epsilon$, where the expectation is taken with respect to the randomization of blocks.

   The proof is similar to Nesterov's analysis (see Theorem 1 in Nesterov (2010)). The proof in Nesterov (2010) relies on the improvement condition in (5.16) and not on the precise nature of the update. Note that because the cost of the update is roughly linear in the size of the block, this bound does not tell us which block size is better (the cost of an update times the number of blocks is roughly constant).

5.4.3   Analysis of $DMAP_\tau$ Block Minimization

We can now obtain rates for our coordinate minimization scheme for optimizing $DMAP_\tau$ by finding the k to be used in the conditions of (5.15) and (5.16). The results for the MSD and star updates are given below.

Proposition 5.4. *The MSD update satisfies the conditions in (5.15) and (5.16) with $k = 4\tau$.*

Proposition 5.5. *The star update for variable i satisfies the conditions in (5.15) and (5.16) with $k = 4\tau N_i$.*

This can be shown using Equation 2.4 in Nesterov (2004), which states that if $F_i(\delta_{S_i}; \delta)$, (5.14), has Lipschitz constant L_i, then (5.16) is satisfied with $k = 2L_i$. We can then use known bounds on the Lipschitz constant of the blocks (this can be calculated as in Savchynskyy et al. (2011)) to obtain the result.[13] To complete the analysis, it turns out that B_1 and B_2 can be bounded via a function of θ by bounding $\|\delta\|_1$ (see Appendix). We proceed to discuss the implications of these bounds.

5.4.4   Comparing the Different Schemes

The results we derived have several implications. First, we see that both stochastic and greedy schemes achieve a rate of $O(\frac{\tau}{\epsilon})$. This matches the known rates for regular (non-accelerated) gradient descent on functions with Lipschitz continuous gradient (see e.g., Nesterov (2004)), although in practice coordinate minimization is often much faster.

The main difference between the greedy and stochastic rates is that the factor $|\mathcal{S}|$ (the number of blocks) does not appear in the greedy rate and does appear in the stochastic one. This can have a considerable effect because $|\mathcal{S}|$ is either the number of variables n (in the star update) or the sum of factor sizes $\sum_c |\{i : i \in c\}|$ (in MSD). Both can be significant (e.g., the number of edges in a pairwise MRF model). The greedy algorithm does pay a price for this advantage, because it has to find the optimal block to update at each iteration. However, for the problem we study here, this can be done efficiently using a priority queue. To see this, consider the star update. A change in the variables $\delta_{\cdot i}(\cdot)$ will only affect the blocks that correspond to variables j that are in factors c such that $i \in c$. In many cases, this is small (e.g., low degree pairwise MRFs), and thus we will only have to change the

---

13. This can be also shown directly. For the MSD block see Kailath (1967), and for the star block, we provide a direct proof in Meshi et al. (2012).

priority queue a small number of times, and this cost would be negligible when using a Fibonacci heap for example.[14] Indeed, our empirical results show that the greedy algorithm consistently outperforms the stochastic one (see Section 5.7).

As mentioned before, our analysis does not provide insight on which block size should be preferred; however, in practice, larger blocks usually perform better (see Section 5.7).

5.5 Primal Convergence

Thus far we have considered only dual variables. However, it is often important to recover the primal variables. We therefore focus on extracting primal feasible solutions from current δ and characterize the degree of primal optimality and associated rates. The primal variables $\mu(\delta)$, (5.14), need not be feasible in the sense that the consistency constraints in (5.5) are not necessarily satisfied. This is true also for other approaches to recovering primal variables from the dual, such as averaging subgradients when using subgradient descent (see e.g., Sontag et al., 2011).

We propose a simple two-step algorithm for transforming any dual variables δ into primal feasible variables $\tilde{\mu}(\delta) \in \mathcal{M}_L$. The resulting $\tilde{\mu}(\delta)$ will also be shown to converge to the optimal primal solution in Section 5.5.1. The procedure is described in Algorithm 5.1 below.

---

14. This was also used in the residual belief propagation approach (Elidan et al., 2006), which, however, is less theoretically justified than what we propose here.

Algorithm 5.1 Mapping to a Feasible Primal Point

Step 1: Make marginals consistent.

For all i do: $\bar{\mu}_i(x_i) = \frac{1}{1+\sum_{c:i \in c} \frac{1}{|X_{c \setminus i}|}} \left(\mu_i(x_i) + \sum_{c:i \in c} \frac{1}{|X_{c \setminus i}|} \mu_c(x_i) \right)$

For all c do: $\bar{\mu}_c(x_c) = \mu_c(x_c) - \sum_{i:i \in c} \frac{1}{|X_{c \setminus i}|} \left(\mu_c(x_i) - \bar{\mu}_i(x_i) \right)$

Step 2: Make marginals non-negative.

$\lambda = 0$

for $c \in C, x_c$ **do**

    if $\bar{\mu}_c(x_c) < 0$ **then**

        $\lambda = \max \left\{ \lambda, \frac{-\bar{\mu}_c(x_c)}{-\bar{\mu}_c(x_c) + \frac{1}{|X_c|}} \right\}$

    else if $\bar{\mu}_c(x_c) > 1$ **then**

        $\lambda = \max \left\{ \lambda, \frac{\bar{\mu}_c(x_c) - 1}{\bar{\mu}_c(x_c) - \frac{1}{|X_c|}} \right\}$

    end if

end for

for $\ell = 1, \ldots, n; c \in C$ **do**

    $\tilde{\mu}_\ell(x_\ell) = (1 - \lambda)\bar{\mu}_\ell(x_\ell) + \lambda \frac{1}{|X_\ell|}$

end for

Importantly, all steps consist of cheap elementary local calculations in contrast to other methods previously proposed for this task (compare to Savchynskyy et al., 2011; Werner, 2011). The first step performs a Euclidian projection of $\mu(\delta)$ to consistent marginals $\bar{\mu}$. Specifically, it solves:

$$\begin{aligned}
\min_{\bar{\mu}} \quad & \tfrac{1}{2} \|\mu(\delta) - \bar{\mu}\|^2 \\
\text{s.t.} \quad & \bar{\mu}_c(x_i) = \bar{\mu}_i(x_i) \ , \quad \forall \, c, i \in c, x_i \\
& \textstyle\sum_i \bar{\mu}_i(x_i) = 1 \ , \quad \forall i.
\end{aligned} \qquad (5.17)$$

Note that we did not include non-negativity constraints above, so the projection might result in negative $\bar{\mu}$. In the second step, we "pull" $\bar{\mu}$ back into the feasible regime by taking a convex combination with the uniform distribution u (see Burshtein (2009), for a related approach). In particular, this step solves the simple problem of finding the smallest $\lambda \in [0, 1]$ such that $0 \leq \tilde{\mu} \leq 1$ (where $\tilde{\mu} = (1-\lambda)\bar{\mu} + \lambda u$). Because this step interpolates between two distributions that satisfy consistency and normalization constraints, $\tilde{\mu}$ will be in the local polytope $\mathcal{M}_L$.

5.5.1 Primal Convergence Rate

Now that we have a procedure for obtaining a primal solution, we analyze the corresponding convergence rate. First, we show that if we have δ for which $\|\nabla F(\delta)\|_\infty \leq \epsilon$, then $\tilde{\mu}(\delta)$ (after Algorithm 1) is an $O(\epsilon)$ primal optimal solution.

Theorem 5.6. *Denote by P_τ^* the optimum of the smoothed primal $PMAP_\tau$. For any set of dual variables δ, and any $\epsilon \in R(\tau)$ (see Appendix for definition of $R(\tau)$), it holds that if $\|\nabla F(\delta)\|_\infty \leq \epsilon$, then $P_\tau^* - P_\tau(\tilde{\mu}(\delta)) \leq C_0\epsilon$. The constant C_0 depends only on the parameters θ and is independent of τ.*

The proof is given in the Appendix. The key idea is to break $F(\delta) - P_\tau(\tilde{\mu}(\delta))$ into components and show that each component is upper bounded by $O(\epsilon)$. The range $R(\tau)$ consists of $\epsilon \geq O(\frac{1}{\tau})$ and $\epsilon \leq O(e^{-\tau})$. As we show in the Appendix, this range is large enough to guarantee any desired accuracy in the non-smoothed primal. We can now translate dual rates into primal rates. This can be done via the following well-known lemma:

Lemma 5.7. *Any convex function F with Lipschitz continuous gradient and Lipschitz constant L satisfies $\|\nabla F(\delta)\|_2^2 \leq 2L\left(F(\delta) - F(\delta^*)\right)$.*

These results lead to the following theorem.

Theorem 5.8. *Given any algorithm for optimizing $DMAP_\tau$ and $\epsilon \in R(\tau)$, if the algorithm is guaranteed to achieve $F(\delta^t) - F(\delta^*) \leq \epsilon$ after $O(g(\epsilon))$ iterations, then it is guaranteed to be ϵ primal optimal, i.e., $P_\tau^* - P_\tau(\tilde{\mu}(\delta^t)) \leq \epsilon$ after $O(g(\frac{\epsilon^2}{\tau}))$ iterations.*[15]

Proof. Using $F(\delta^t) - F(\delta^*) \leq \epsilon$ and Lemma 5.7, we have that $\|\nabla F(\delta)\|_2^2 \leq 2L\epsilon$. Because the Lipschitz constant of $F(\delta)$ is $O(\tau)$, this implies $\|\nabla F(\delta)\|_2^2 \leq O(\tau\epsilon)$. We then use the fact that $\|\nabla F(\delta)\|_\infty^2 \leq \|\nabla F(\delta)\|_2^2$ to get $\|\nabla F(\delta)\|_\infty \leq O(\sqrt{\tau\epsilon})$. Finally, using Theorem 5.6, we obtain $P_\tau^* - P_\tau(\tilde{\mu}(\delta)) \leq O(\sqrt{\tau\epsilon})$, which completes the proof. $\square$

The theorem lets us directly translate dual convergence rates into primal ones. Note that it applies to any algorithm for $DMAP_\tau$ (not only coordinate minimization), and the only property of the algorithm used in the proof is $F(\delta^t) \leq F(0)$ for all t. Put in the context of our previous results, any algorithm that achieves $F(\delta^t) - F(\delta^*) \leq \epsilon$ in $t = O(\tau/\epsilon)$ iterations is guaranteed to achieve $P_\tau^* - P_\tau(\tilde{\mu}(\delta^{t'})) \leq \epsilon$ in $t' = O(\tau^2/\epsilon^2)$ iterations.

5.6   The Augmented Dual LP Algorithm

An alternative approach to deal with the non-smoothness of the dual MAP LP objective in (5.6) is based on an augmented Lagrangian method known as the Alternating Direction Method of Multipliers (ADMM) (Glowinski

---

15. We omit constants not depending on τ and ϵ.

and Marrocco, 1975; Gabay and Mercier, 1976; Boyd et al., 2011). Here we provide a short review of this approach and its application to MAP LP relaxations.

The ADMM framework is designed to handle convex optimization problems with the following constrained form:

$$\text{minimize } f(x) + g(z) \quad \text{s.t. } Ax = z, \tag{5.18}$$

where f and g are general convex functions.

The ADMM approach begins by adding the function $\frac{\rho}{2} \|Ax - z\|^2$ to the above objective, where $\rho > 0$ is a penalty parameter. This results in the optimization problem:

$$\text{minimize } f(x) + g(z) + \frac{\rho}{2} \|Ax - z\|^2 \quad \text{s.t. } Ax = z. \tag{5.19}$$

The augmenting quadratic term can be seen as smoothing the objective function. Clearly, the above has the same optimum as (5.18) because when the constraints $Ax = z$ are satisfied, the added quadratic term equals zero.

The Lagrangian of the augmented problem (5.19) is given by:

$$\mathcal{L}_\rho(x, z, \nu) = f(x) + g(z) + \nu^\top (Ax - z) + \frac{\rho}{2} \|Ax - z\|^2, \tag{5.20}$$

where ν is a vector of Lagrange multipliers. The solution to the problem of (5.19) is given by $\max_\nu \min_{x,z} \mathcal{L}_\rho(x, z, \nu)$. The ADMM method provides an elegant algorithm for finding this saddle point. The idea is to combine subgradient ascent over ν with coordinate descent over the x and z variables. The method applies the following iterations:

$$
\begin{aligned}
x^{t+1} &= \underset{x}{\operatorname{argmin}} \, \mathcal{L}_\rho(x, z^t, \nu^t) \\
z^{t+1} &= \underset{z}{\operatorname{argmin}} \, \mathcal{L}_\rho(x^{t+1}, z, \nu^t) \\
\nu^{t+1} &= \nu^t + \rho \left(Ax^{t+1} - z^{t+1} \right).
\end{aligned}
\tag{5.21}
$$

The algorithm consists of primal and dual updates, where the primal update is executed sequentially, minimizing first over x and then over z. This split retains the decomposition of the objective that has been lost due to the introduction of the quadratic term. Furthermore, it can be viewed as a coordinate descent algorithm with x and z blocks on $\mathcal{L}(x, z, \nu^t)$ for some fixed ν^t.

The ADMM algorithm is guaranteed to converge to the global optimum of (5.18) under rather mild conditions (Boyd et al., 2011). Moreover, it was recently shown that it has a convergence rate of $O(1/\epsilon)$ (He and Yuan, 2012; Wang and Banerjee, 2012), which is similar to accelerated gradient

(Nesterov, 2005; Jojic et al., 2010) but does not require pre-smoothing of the objective.

There are various ways to apply ADMM to the dual LP (5.6). The challenge is to design the constraints in a way that facilitates efficient closed-form solutions for all updates. To this end, we duplicate the variables δ and denote the second copy by $\bar{\delta}$. We then introduce additional variables λ_c corresponding to the summation of δs pertaining to factor c. To enforce overall agreement, we introduce the constraints $\delta_{ci}(x_i) = \bar{\delta}_{ci}(x_i)$ for all $c, i : i \in c, x_i$, and $\lambda_c(x_c) = \sum_{i:i\in c} \bar{\delta}_{ci}(x_i)$ for all c, x_c.

Following the ADMM framework, we add quadratic terms and obtain the augmented Lagrangian for the dual MAP-LP problem of (5.6):

$$
\mathcal{L}_\rho(\delta, \lambda, \bar{\delta}, \gamma, \mu) =
$$

$$
\sum_i \max_{x_i} \left(\theta_i(x_i) + \sum_{c:i\in c} \delta_{ci}(x_i) \right) + \sum_c \max_{x_c} \left(\theta_c(x_c) - \lambda_c(x_c) \right)
$$

$$
+ \sum_c \sum_{i:i\in c} \sum_{x_i} \gamma_{ci}(x_i) \left(\delta_{ci}(x_i) - \bar{\delta}_{ci}(x_i) \right) + \frac{\rho}{2} \sum_c \sum_{i:i\in c} \sum_{x_i} \left(\delta_{ci}(x_i) - \bar{\delta}_{ci}(x_i) \right)^2
$$

$$
+ \sum_c \sum_{x_c} \mu_c(x_c) \left(\lambda_c(x_c) - \sum_{i:i\in c} \bar{\delta}_{ci}(x_i) \right) + \frac{\rho}{2} \sum_c \sum_{x_c} \left(\lambda_c(x_c) - \sum_{i:i\in c} \bar{\delta}_{ci}(x_i) \right)^2 .
$$

To see the relation of this formulation to (5.20), notice that the variables (δ, λ) correspond to x, the variables $\bar{\delta}$ correspond to z (with $g(z) = 0$), and the multipliers (γ, μ) correspond to ν. The nice property of this decomposition is that all algorithmic steps in (5.21) can be done in simple closed-form updates. These updates as well as a detailed derivation can be found in Meshi and Globerson (2011).

Finally, we note that ADMM can also be applied to the primal (see e.g., Martins et al. (2011); Chapter 3 in this volume).

5.7   Experiments

In this section, we evaluate the performance of coordinate minimization algorithms on toy and real-world MAP problems. We begin with a toy problem to demonstrate the effect of smoothing on the convergence of coordinate minimization. This toy problem was given in Kolmogorov (2006), Appendix D, to illustrate that coordinate descent for the non-smooth dual LP can get stuck at non-optimal points. In Figure 5.1, we compare the

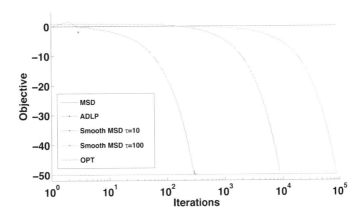

Figure 5.1: Comparison of smooth and non-smooth coordinate minimization algorithms on a toy MAP problem. The figure shows for each algorithm the dual objective as a function of the number of iterations. The optimal value of the non-smooth LP is marked with a thin dashed line.

convergence behavior of non-smooth MSD, smooth MSD, and ADLP.[16] We first see that non-smooth coordinate minimization (MSD) is caught in a suboptimal fixed point. In contrast, the smooth MSD algorithm is able to converge to the optimum of the smoothed dual objective of (5.12). Figure 5.1 also shows the effect of the smoothing parameter τ. As τ increases, the smoothed optimum gets closer to the LP optimum, but convergence time grows linearly with τ, as our analysis suggests. Finally, we observe that ADLP quickly converges to the optimum of the non-smooth LP.

We next compare coordinate minimization algorithms to state-of-the-art baselines on a real-world MAP problem. Because the MSD block has similar or slightly inferior performance compared with the star block, we show here results only for the latter. We compare the running time of greedy coordinate minimization, stochastic coordinate minimization, full gradient descent, and FISTA—an accelerated gradient method (Beck and Teboulle, 2009). For completeness, we provide here the updates of both gradient-based algorithms:

16. We run both MSD algorithms in stochastic schedule. Results are reported per iteration. Runtime is not identical to those, because the ADLP update is more costly.

Algorithm 5.2 Gradient Descent

1: **for** $t = 1, \ldots$ **do**
2:          $\delta^{t+1} = \delta^t - \frac{1}{L}\nabla F(\delta^t)$
3: **end for**

Algorithm 5.3 FISTA

1: $\bar{\delta}^1 = \delta^0, \quad \alpha^1 = 1$
2: **for** $t = 1, \ldots$ **do**
3:          $\delta^t = \bar{\delta}^t - \frac{1}{L}\nabla F(\bar{\delta}^t)$
4:          $\alpha^{t+1} = \frac{1+\sqrt{1+4(\alpha^t)^2}}{2}$
5:          $\bar{\delta}^{t+1} = \delta^t + \left(\frac{\alpha^t - 1}{\alpha^{t+1}}\right)\left(\delta^t - \delta^{t-1}\right)$
6: **end for**

Gradient descent is known to converge in $O\left(\frac{1}{\epsilon}\right)$ iterations while FISTA converges in $O\left(\frac{1}{\sqrt{\epsilon}}\right)$ iterations (Beck and Teboulle, 2009). We compare the performance of the algorithms on protein side-chain prediction problems from the data set of Yanover et al. (2006). These problems involve finding the 3D configuration of rotamers given the backbone structure of a protein. The problems are modeled by singleton and pairwise factors and can be posed as finding an MAP assignment for the given model.

Figure 5.2(a) shows the objective value for each algorithm over time. We first notice that the greedy algorithm converges faster than the stochastic one. This is in agreement with our theoretical analysis. Second, we observe that the coordinate minimization algorithms are competitive with the accelerated gradient method FISTA and are much faster than the gradient method. Third, as Theorem 5.8 predicts, primal convergence is slower than dual convergence (notice the logarithmic timescale). Finally, we can see that better convergence of the dual objective corresponds to better convergence of the primal objective, in both fractional and integral domains. In our experiments, the quality of the decoded integral solution (dashed lines) significantly exceeds that of the fractional solution. Although sometimes a fractional solution can be useful, if only an integral solution is sought, then it could be enough to decode directly from the dual variables.

Figure 5.2(b) shows overall statistics for the proteins in the data set. Here we run each algorithm until the duality gap drops below a fixed desired precision ($\epsilon = 0.1$) and compare the total runtime. The table presents the ratio of runtime of each algorithm w.r.t. the greedy algorithm (t_{alg}/t_{greedy}). These results are consistent with the example in Figure 5.2(a).

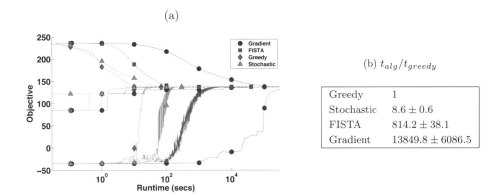

Figure 5.2: Comparison of coordinate minimization, gradient descent, and the accelerated gradient algorithms on protein side-chain prediction task. Figure (a) shows a typical run of the algorithms. For each algorithm, the dual objective of (5.12) is plotted as a function of execution time (upper solid line). The value (5.8) of the feasible primal solution of Algorithm 5.1 is also shown (lower solid line), as well as the objective (5.3) of the best decoded integer solution (dashed line; those are decoded directly from the dual variables δ). Table (b) shows the ratio of runtime of each algorithm w.r.t. the greedy algorithm. The mean ratio over the proteins in the data set is shown followed by standard error.

5.8   Discussion

This chapter provided a tutorial introduction to the smoothing approach to MAP LP relaxations. It was shown that coordinate descent on the smoothed dual results in simple updates, and the rate of convergence can be analyzed for different coordinate update schedules.

We also showed how such dual iterates can be turned into primal feasible iterates and analyzed the rate with which these primal iterates converge to the primal optimum. The primal mapping is of considerable practical value, as it allows us to monitor the distance between the upper (dual) and lower (primal) bounds on the optimum and use this as a stopping criterion. Note that this cannot be done without a primal feasible solution. An alternative, commonly used progress criterion is to decode an integral solution from the dual variables and see whether its value is close to the dual upper bound. However, this will only work if $PMAP$ has an integral solution and we have managed to decode it.

The overall rates we obtain are of the order $O(\frac{\tau}{\epsilon})$ for the $DMAP_\tau$ problem. If one requires an ϵ accurate solution for $PMAP$, then τ needs to be set to $O(\frac{1}{\epsilon})$ (5.9) and the overall rate is $O(\frac{1}{\epsilon^2})$ in the dual. As noted in Jojic et al. (2010) and Savchynskyy et al. (2011), a faster rate of $O(\frac{1}{\epsilon})$ may be obtained using accelerated methods such as with the method of Nesterov (2005) or FISTA (Beck and Teboulle, 2009). However, these also have an extra factor of N, which does not appear in the greedy rate. This could partially explain the excellent performance of the greedy scheme when compared with FISTA (see Section 5.7).

As mentioned earlier, there are various ways of choosing the block of coordinates to update. Here we focused mainly on the *star* update, where a variable i is chosen and $\delta_{ci}(x_i)$ are updated for all values of c, x_i. An alternative choice is to choose c, i and update $\delta_{ci}(x_i)$ for all x_i values. This corresponds to the MSD update of Werner (2007). While we have provided some of the results for the MSD case (e.g., see Proposition 5.4), we did not analyze the overall runtime expected for the two variants (e.g., for the greedy scheme, different queue maintenance costs will be incurred). Empirically, we observed that the star update is typically faster, as may intuitively be expected due to more coordinates being updated. Understanding the effect of block length and the resulting tradeoffs is an interesting problem for further study.

Another block update strategy is the so-called MPLP update, where for a given c, the variables $\delta_{ci}(x_i)$ are updated for all $i \in c, x_i$. Interestingly, we were unable to obtain these in closed form for the particular entropy smoothing we use here (i.e., for the dual in (5.12)). It would be interesting to seek primal regularization schemes where such coordinate blocks have closed-form updates.

The main goal of smoothing was to obtain a dual that is differentiable and where coordinate descent globally converges. The way this is achieved here is by introducing entropy regularization into the primal. It would be interesting to study other forms of primal regularization and the resulting smooth duals. For example, one may consider ℓ_2 regularization on μ. It is not clear, however, that closed form updates are available in this case for dual coordinate minimization. An additional regularization form to consider is ℓ_2 regularization on δ in the dual.

Both our empirical and theoretical results highlight the advantage of greedy update schedules. The advantage comes from the fact that the choice of block to update is quite efficient because its cost is of the order of the other computations required by the algorithm. This can be viewed as a theoretical reinforcement of selective scheduling algorithms such as Residual Belief Propagation (Elidan et al., 2006).

The convergence rates we provided were for obtaining an accuracy ϵ with respect to the primal or dual objective optima. However, in analyzing combinatorial optimization problems with polynomial time algorithms, one typically obtains the number of iterations required to find the optimal (discrete) solution without reference to accuracy. To obtain such runtimes in our case, we can focus on problems where the LP is integral (e.g., mincut; proof in Taskar et al., 2006). If the LP solution is close enough to optimal, this can be shown to imply that it can be rounded to the optimal integral assignment.[17] Such an analysis was performed in Ravikumar et al. (2010) and can be done in our case as well.

Finally, our analysis relates to sequential updates of coordinates. Thus, it is not immediately applicable to distributed asynchronous implementations. It would be interesting to extend the results to the distributed setting (e.g., Bradley et al., 2011).

Acknowledgments

This work was supported by BSF grant 2008303. Ofer Meshi is a recipient of the Google Europe Fellowship in Machine Learning, and this research was supported in part by this Google Fellowship.

5.9   Appendix: Primal Convergence Rate

In this section, we prove Theorem 5.6.

Proof. $\|\nabla F(\delta)\|_\infty \leq \epsilon$ guarantees that $\mu = \mu(\delta)$ are ϵ-consistent in the sense that $|\mu_i(x_i) - \mu_c(x_i)| \leq \epsilon$ for all $c, i \in c$ and x_i. Algorithm 5.1 maps any such ϵ-consistent μ to locally consistent marginals $\tilde{\mu}$ such that

$$|\mu_i(x_i) - \tilde{\mu}_i(x_i)| \leq 3\epsilon N_{\max}, \quad |\mu_c(x_c) - \tilde{\mu}_c(x_c)| \leq 2\epsilon N_{\max}^2, \qquad (5.22)$$

for all i, x_i, c, and x_c, where $N_{\max} = \max\{\max_i N_i, \max_c N_c\}$. In other words, $\|\mu - \tilde{\mu}\|_\infty \leq K\epsilon$. This can be easily derived from the update in Algorithm 5.1 and the fact that $|\mu_i(x_i) - \mu_c(x_i)| \leq \epsilon$.

Next, it can be shown that $F(\delta) = P_\tau(\mu(\delta))$. It follows that $P_\tau^* \leq F(\delta) \leq P_\tau(\mu)$, where the first inequality follows from weak duality.

For clarity, we define

$$\mu \cdot \theta = \sum_i \sum_{x_i} \mu_i(x_i)\theta_i(x_i) + \sum_c \sum_{x_c} \mu_c(x_c)\theta_c(x_c) \qquad (5.23)$$

$$H(\mu) = \sum_i H(\mu_i(\cdot)) + \sum_c H(\mu_c(\cdot)) \qquad (5.24)$$

---

17. Assuming a unique integral optimum.

Thus, we have:

$$
\begin{aligned}
P_\tau^* \leq P_\tau(\mu) &= \mu \cdot \theta + \frac{1}{\tau} H(\mu) \\
&= (\tilde{\mu} + \mu - \tilde{\mu}) \cdot \theta + \frac{1}{\tau} H(\tilde{\mu}) + \frac{1}{\tau}(H(\mu) - H(\tilde{\mu})) \\
&\leq P_\tau(\tilde{\mu}) + \|\mu - \tilde{\mu}\|_\infty \|\theta\|_1 + \frac{1}{\tau}(H(\mu) - H(\tilde{\mu})) \\
&\leq P_\tau(\tilde{\mu}) + K\epsilon \|\theta\|_1 + \frac{1}{\tau}(H(\mu) - H(\tilde{\mu})) \qquad (5.25)
\end{aligned}
$$

Here we have used Hölder's inequality for the first inequality and (5.22) for the second inequality.

It remains to bound $\frac{1}{\tau}(H(\mu) - H(\tilde{\mu}))$ by a linear function of ϵ. We note that it is impossible to achieve such a bound in general (e.g., see Berend and Kontorovich (2012)). However, because the entropy is bounded, the difference is also bounded. Now, if we also restrict ϵ to be large enough $\epsilon \geq \frac{1}{\tau}$, then we obtain the bound:

$$
\frac{1}{\tau}(H(\mu) - H(\tilde{\mu})) \leq \frac{1}{\tau} H_{\max} \leq \epsilon H_{\max} \qquad (5.26)
$$

We thus obtain that (5.25) is of the form $P_\tau(\tilde{\mu}) + O(\epsilon)$, and the result follows.

For the high-accuracy regime (small ϵ), we provide a similar bound for the case $\epsilon \leq O(e^{-\tau})$. Let $v = \mu - \tilde{\mu}$, so we have:

$$
\begin{aligned}
H(\mu) - H(\tilde{\mu}) &= H(\tilde{\mu} + v) - H(\tilde{\mu}) \\
&\leq H(\tilde{\mu}) + \nabla H(\tilde{\mu})^\top v - H(\tilde{\mu}) \\
&= -\sum_i \sum_{x_i} v_i(x_i) \log \tilde{\mu}_i(x_i) - \sum_c \sum_{x_c} v_c(x_c) \log \tilde{\mu}_c(x_c)
\end{aligned}
$$

where the inequality follows from the concavity of entropy, and the second equality is true because $\sum_{x_i} v_i(x_i) = 0$ and similarly for $v_c(x_c)$. Now, from the definition of $\mu_i(x_i; \delta)$, we obtain the following bound:

$$
\mu_i(x_i; \delta) = \frac{1}{Z_i} e^{\tau(\theta_i(x_i) + \sum_{c:i \in c} \delta_{ci}(x_i))} \geq \frac{1}{|X_i|} e^{-2\tau(\|\theta_i\|_\infty + \|\delta_i\|_1)}
$$

We will show below (Lemma 5.9) that $\|\delta_i\|_1$ remains bounded by a constant A independent of τ. Thus, we can write:

$$
\mu_i(x_i; \delta) \geq \frac{1}{|X_{\max}|} e^{-2\tau(\|\theta_i\|_\infty + A)}
$$

where $|X_{\max}| = \max\{\max_i |X_i|, \max_c |X_c|\}$. We define

$$
\gamma_0 = \frac{1}{(2|X_{\max}|)^\tau} e^{-2\tau(\|\theta_i\|_\infty + A)},
$$

and thus for any $\tau \geq 1$, we have that $\mu_i(x_i; \delta)$ is bounded away from zero by $2^\tau \gamma_0$. Because we assume that $\epsilon \leq \gamma_0$, we can bound $\tilde{\mu}$ from below by γ_0. As a result, because $\|v_i\|_\infty \leq K\epsilon$,

$$
\begin{aligned}
-\frac{1}{\tau} \sum_i \sum_{x_i} v_i(x_i) \log \tilde{\mu}_i(x_i) &\leq -\frac{1}{\tau}(\log \gamma_0)|X_i|K\epsilon \\
&= (2(\|\theta_i\|_\infty + A) + \log(2|X_{\max}|))|X_i|K\epsilon
\end{aligned}
$$

and similarly for the other entropy terms.

Again, we obtain that (5.25) is of the form $P_\tau(\tilde{\mu}) + O(\epsilon)$, and the result holds.

In conclusion, we have shown that if $\|\nabla F(\delta)\|_\infty \leq \epsilon$, then for large values $\epsilon \geq \frac{1}{\tau}$ and small values $\epsilon \leq \frac{1}{(2|X_{\max}|)^\tau}e^{-2\tau(\|\theta_i\|_\infty + A)}$, we have that $P_\tau^* - P_\tau(\tilde{\mu}) \leq O(\epsilon)$. Our analysis does not cover values in the middle range, but next we argue that the covered range is useful. $\qquad\square$

The allowed range of ϵ (namely, $\epsilon \in R(\tau)$) seems like a restriction. However, as we argue next, taking $\epsilon \geq \frac{1}{\tau}$ (i.e., $\epsilon \in R(\tau)$) is all we need to obtain a desired accuracy in the non-smoothed primal.

Suppose one wants to solve the original problem $PMAP$ to within accuracy ϵ'. There are two sources of inaccuracy, namely, the smoothing and suboptimality. To ensure the desired accuracy, we require that $P_\tau^* - P^* \leq \alpha\epsilon'$ and likewise $P_\tau(\tilde{\mu}) - P_\tau^* \leq (1-\alpha)\epsilon'$. In other words, we allow $\alpha\epsilon'$ suboptimality due to smoothing and $(1-\alpha)\epsilon'$ due to suboptimality.

For the first condition, it is enough to set the smoothing constant as: $\tau \geq \frac{H_{\max}}{\alpha\epsilon'}$. The second condition will be satisfied as long as we use an ϵ such that $\epsilon \leq \frac{(1-\alpha)\epsilon'}{(K\|\theta\|_1 + H_{\max})}$ (see (5.25) and (5.26)). If we choose $\alpha = \frac{H_{\max}}{K\|\theta\|_1 + 2H_{\max}}$, then we obtain that this ϵ satisfies $\epsilon \geq \frac{1}{\tau}$ and therefore $\epsilon \in R(\tau)$.

Lemma 5.9. *Assume δ is a set of dual variables satisfying $F(\delta) \leq F(0)$, where $F(0)$ is the dual value corresponding to $\delta = 0$. We can require $\sum_{c:i\in c} \delta_{ci}(x_i) = 0$ because $F(\delta)$ is invariant to constant shifts. Then it holds that:*

$$
\sum_{c,i,x_i} |\delta_{ci}(x_i)| = \|\delta\|_1 \leq A, \tag{5.27}
$$

where

$$
A = 2 \max_i |X_i| \left(F(0) + \sum_i \max_{x_i} |\theta_i(x_i)| + \sum_c \max_{x_c} |\theta_c(x_c)| \right). \tag{5.28}
$$

Proof. To show this, we bound

$$\max_{\delta} \sum_{c,i,x_i} r_{ci}(x_i)\delta_{ci}(x_i)$$

$$\text{s.t. } F(\delta) \leq F(0) \tag{5.29}$$

$$\sum_{c:i \in c} \delta_{ci}(x_i) = 0$$

For any $r_{ci}(x_i) \in [-1, 1]$. The dual problem turns out to be:

$$\min_{\mu,\gamma,\alpha} \quad \alpha(F(0) - \sum_{c,x_c} \mu_c(x_c)\theta_c(x_c) - \sum_{i,x_i} \mu_i(x_i)\theta_i(x_i) - \sum_i H(\mu_i(x_i)) - \sum_c H(\mu_c(x_c))$$

$$\text{s.t.} \quad \mu_i(x_i) - \mu_c(x_i) = \frac{r_{ci}(x_i) - \gamma_{ci}}{\alpha}$$

$$\mu_i(x_i) \geq 0, \mu_c(x_c) \geq 0 \tag{5.30}$$

$$\sum_{x_i} \mu_i(x_i) = 1, \sum_{x_c} \mu_c(x_c) = 1$$

$$\alpha \geq 0$$

We will next upper bound this minimum with a constant independent of r and thus obtain an upper bound that holds for all r. To do this, we will present a feasible assignment to the variables α, μ, γ above and use the value they attain. First, we set $\alpha = \hat{\alpha} = 2 \max_i |X_i|$. Next, we note that for this $\hat{\alpha}$, the objective of (5.30) is upper bounded by A (as defined in (5.28)). Thus, we only need to show that $\hat{\alpha} = 2 \max_i |X_i|$ is indeed a feasible value, and this will be done by showing feasible values for the other variables denoted by $\hat{\mu}, \hat{\gamma}$. First, we set

$$\hat{\mu}_i(x_i) \quad = \quad \frac{1}{|X_i|}$$

and

$$\hat{\gamma}_{ci} = \frac{1}{|X_i|} \sum_{x_i} r_{ci}(x_i) \tag{5.31}$$

Next, we define $\nu_{ci}(x_i)$ (for all c, i, x_i) as follows:

$$\nu_{ci}(x_i) = \hat{\mu}_i(x_i) - \frac{r_{ci}(x_i) - \hat{\gamma}_{ci}}{\hat{\alpha}} \tag{5.32}$$

It can easily be shown that $\nu_{ci}(x_i)$ is a valid distribution over x_i (i.e., non negative and sums to one). Thus, we can define:

$$\hat{\mu}_c(x_c) = \prod_{i \in c} \nu_{ci}(x_i) \tag{5.33}$$

Because $\hat{\mu}_c(x_c)$ is a product of distributions over the variables in c, it is also a valid distribution. Thus, it follows that all constraints in (5.30) are satisfied by $\hat{\alpha}, \hat{\gamma}, \hat{\mu}$, and the desired bound holds.

☐

5.10   References

A. Beck and M. Teboulle. A fast iterative shrinkage-thresholding algorithm for linear inverse problems. *SIAM J. Img. Sci.*, 2(1):183–202, March 2009.

D. Berend and A. Kontorovich. A reverse Pinsker inequality. *CoRR*, abs/1206.6544, 2012.

A. Bhattacharyya. On a measure of divergence between two multinomial populations. *Sankhyā: The Indian Journal of Statistics (1933-1960)*, 7(4):401–406, 1946.

S. Boyd and L. Vandenberghe. *Convex Optimization*. Cambridge University Press, 2004.

S. Boyd, N. Parikh, and E. Chu. *Distributed Optimization and Statistical Learning Via the Alternating Direction Method of Multipliers*. Now Publishers, 2011.

Y. Boykov, O. Veksler, and R. Zabih. Fast approximate energy minimization via graph cuts. In *Proc. IEEE Conf. Comput. Vision Pattern Recog.*, 1999.

J. K. Bradley, A. Kyrola, D. Bickson, and C. Guestrin. Parallel coordinate descent for l1-regularized loss minimization. In *International Conference on Machine Learning (ICML 2011)*, Bellevue, Washington, June 2011.

D. Burshtein. Iterative approximate linear programming decoding of LDPC codes with linear complexity. *IEEE Transactions on Information Theory*, 55(11):4835–4859, 2009.

K. L. Clarkson. Coresets, sparse greedy approximation, and the Frank-Wolfe algorithm. *ACM Trans. Algorithms*, 6(4):63:1–63:30, September 2010.

G. Elidan, I. Mcgraw, and D. Koller. Residual belief propagation: Informed scheduling for asynchronous message passing. In *Proceedings of the Twenty-second Conference on Uncertainty in AI (UAI)*, 2006.

D. Gabay and B. Mercier. A dual algorithm for the solution of nonlinear variational problems via finite-element approximations. *Computers and Mathematics with Applications*, 2:17–40, 1976.

A. Globerson and T. Jaakkola. Fixing max-product: Convergent message passing algorithms for MAP LP-relaxations. In J. Platt, D. Koller, Y. Singer, and S. Roweis, editors, *NIPS 20*. MIT Press, 2008.

R. Glowinski and A. Marrocco. Sur lapproximation, par elements finis dordre un, et la resolution, par penalisation-dualité, dune classe de problems de dirichlet non lineares. *Revue Française d'Automatique, Informatique, et Recherche Opérationelle*, 9:4176, 1975.

T. Hazan and A. Shashua. Norm-product belief propagation: Primal-dual message-passing for approximate inference. *IEEE Transactions on Information Theory*, 56(12):6294–6316, 2010.

B. He and X. Yuan. On the $O(1/n)$ convergence rate of the Douglas-Rachford alternating direction method. *SIAM J. Numer. Anal.*, 50(2):700–709, April 2012.

V. Jojic, S. Gould, and D. Koller. Fast and smooth: Accelerated dual decomposition for MAP inference. In *Proceedings of International Conference on Machine Learning (ICML)*, 2010.

T. Kailath. The divergence and Bhattacharyya distance measures in signal selection. *IEEE Transactions on Communication Technology*, 15(1):52–60, February 1967.

D. Koller and N. Friedman. *Probabilistic Graphical Models: Principles and Techniques.* MIT Press, 2009.

V. Kolmogorov. Convergent tree-reweighted message passing for energy minimization. *IEEE Transactions on Pattern Analysis and Machine Intelligence*, 28(10): 1568–1583, 2006.

V. Kolmogorov and C. Rother. Minimizing nonsubmodular functions with graph cuts-a review. *IEEE Trans. Pattern Anal. Mach. Intell.*, 29(7):1274–1279, July 2007.

N. Komodakis, N. Paragios, and G. Tziritas. MRF energy minimization and beyond via dual decomposition. *Pattern Analysis and Machine Intelligence, IEEE Transactions on*, 33:531–552, March 2011.

A. L. Martins, M. A. T. Figueiredo, P. M. Q. Aguiar, N. A. Smith, and E. P. Xing. An augmented Lagrangian approach to constrained MAP inference. In *Proceedings of International Conference on Machine Learning (ICML)*, pages 169–176, 2011.

K. Matusita. On the notion of affinity of several distributions and some of its applications. *Annals of the Institute of Statistical Mathematics*, 19:181–192, 1967.

O. Meshi and A. Globerson. An alternating direction method for dual MAP LP relaxation. In *ECML PKDD*, pages 470–483. Springer-Verlag, 2011.

O. Meshi, D. Sontag, T. Jaakkola, and A. Globerson. Learning efficiently with approximate inference via dual losses. In *Proceedings of the 27th International Conference on Machine Learning*, pages 783–790, New York, 2010. ACM.

O. Meshi, T. Jaakkola, and A. Globerson. Convergence rate analysis of MAP coordinate minimization algorithms. In P. Bartlett, F. Pereira, C. Burges, L. Bottou, and K. Weinberger, editors, *Advances in Neural Information Processing Systems 25*, pages 3023–3031. 2012.

Y. Nesterov. *Introductory Lectures on Convex Optimization: A Basic Course*, volume 87. Kluwer Academic Publishers, 2004.

Y. Nesterov. Smooth minimization of non-smooth functions. *Math. Prog.*, 103(1): 127–152, May 2005.

Y. Nesterov. Efficiency of coordinate descent methods on huge-scale optimization problems. Core discussion papers, Universit Catholique de Louvain, 2010.

P. Ravikumar, A. Agarwal, and M. J. Wainwright. Message-passing for graph-structured linear programs: Proximal methods and rounding schemes. *Journal of Machine Learning Research*, 11:1043–1080, March 2010.

A. Saha and A. Tewari. On the nonasymptotic convergence of cyclic coordinate descent methods. *SIAM Journal on Optimization*, 23(1):576–601, 2013.

B. Savchynskyy, S. Schmidt, J. Kappes, and C. Schnörr. A study of Nesterov's scheme for lagrangian decomposition and MAP labeling. *IEEE Conference on Computer Vision and Pattern Recognition (CVPR)*, 2011.

S. Shalev-Shwartz and A. Tewari. Stochastic methods for ℓ_1-regularized loss minimization. *Journal of Machine Learning Research*, 12:1865–1892, July 2011.

D. Sontag, A. Globerson, and T. Jaakkola. Introduction to dual decomposition for inference. In *Optimization for Machine Learning*, pages 219–254. MIT Press, 2011.

B. Taskar, S. Lacoste-Julien, and M. Jordan. Structured prediction, dual extragradient and Bregman projections. *Journal of Machine Learning Research*, pages 1627–1653, 2006.

P. Tseng. Convergence of a block coordinate descent method for nondifferentiable minimization 1. *Journal of Optimization Theory and Applications*, 109(3):475–494, 2001.

M. Wainwright and M. I. Jordan. *Graphical Models, Exponential Families, and Variational Inference*. Now Publishers Inc., Hanover, MA, USA, 2008.

M. Wainwright, T. Jaakkola, and A. Willsky. MAP estimation via agreement on trees: Message-passing and linear programming. *IEEE Transactions on Information Theory*, 51(11):3697–3717, 2005.

H. Wang and A. Banerjee. Online alternating direction method. In *ICML*, 2012.

Y. Weiss, C. Yanover, and T. Meltzer. MAP estimation, linear programming and belief propagation with convex free energies. In *Proceedings of the 23rd Conference on Uncertainty in Artificial Intelligence*, pages 416–425. AUAI Press, 2007.

T. Werner. A linear programming approach to max-sum problem: A review. *IEEE Transactions on Pattern Analysis and Machine Intelligence*, 29(7):1165–1179, 2007.

T. Werner. Revisiting the decomposition approach to inference in exponential families and graphical models. Technical Report CTU-CMP-2009-06, Czech Technical University, 2009.

T. Werner. How to compute primal solution from dual one in MAP inference in MRF? In *Control Systems and Computers (special issue on Optimal Labeling Problems in Structual Pattern Recognition)*, 2011.

C. Yanover, T. Meltzer, and Y. Weiss. Linear programming relaxations and belief propagation: An empirical study. *Journal of Machine Learning Research*, 7:1887–1907, 2006.

6 Getting Feasible Variable Estimates from Infeasible Ones: MRF Local Polytope Study

Bogdan Savchynskyy bogdan.savchynskyy@iwr.uni-heidelberg.de
University of Heidelberg
Heidelberg, Germany

Stefan Schmidt schmidtsstefan@googlemail.com
Heidelberg Engineering GmbH
Heidelberg, Germany

This chapter proposes a method for the construction of approximate feasible primal solutions from infeasible ones for large-scale optimization problems possessing certain separability properties. Whereas the infeasible primal estimates can typically be produced from (sub-)gradients of the dual function, it is often not easy to project them to the primal feasible set, because the projection itself has a complexity comparable to the complexity of the initial problem. We propose an alternative efficient method to obtain feasibility and show that its properties influencing the convergence to the optimum are similar to the properties of the Euclidean projection. We apply our method to the local polytope relaxation of inference problems for Markov Random Fields and discuss its advantages compared to existing methods.

6.1 Introduction

Convex relaxations of combinatorial problems, as appearing in computer vision, processing of medical data, or analysis of transport networks, often contain millions of variables and hundreds of thousands of constraints.

It is also quite common to employ their dual formulations to allow for more efficient optimization, which due to strong duality also delivers primal solutions. Indeed, approximate primal solutions can usually be reconstructed from (sub-)gradients of the dual objective. However, these are typically infeasible. Because of the problem size, only first-order methods (based on the function and its [sub-]gradient evaluation only) can be applied. Because feasibility is not guaranteed up to the optimum, it is hardly attainable for such methods because of their slow convergence. The classical trick— (Euclidean) projection to the feasible set—cannot be used efficiently because of the problem size.

A striking example of such a situation, which we explore in this chapter, is the reconstruction of feasible primal estimates for local polytope relaxations of Markov random field (MRF) inference problems (Schlesinger, 1976; Werner, 2007; Wainwright and Jordan, 2008), studied in Chapter 2.

Motivation: Why Feasible Relaxed Primal Estimates Are Needed. It is often the case for convex relaxations of combinatorial problems that not a relaxed solution but an integer approximation thereof is used in applications. Such integer primal estimates can be obtained from the dual ones due to the complementary slackness condition and using heuristic local search or rounding procedures (Werner, 2007; Kolmogorov, 2006; Ravikumar et al., 2010). However, such integer estimates do not converge to the optimum of the relaxed problem in general.

In contrast, a sequence of *feasible* solution estimates of the *relaxed problem* converging to the optimum guarantees vanishing of the corresponding duality gap and, hence, (i) determines a theoretically sound stopping condition (Boyd and Vandenberghe, 2004); (ii) provides a basis for the comparison of different optimization schemes for a given problem; and (iii) enables the construction of adaptive optimization schemes depending on the duality gap, for example, adaptive step-size selection in subgradient-based schemes (Komodakis et al., 2011; Kappes et al., 2012) or adaptive smoothing selection procedures for non-smooth problems (Savchynskyy et al., 2012). Another example is the tightening of relaxations with cutting plane-based approaches (Sontag et al., 2008).

Contribution. We propose an efficient and well-scalable method for constructing feasible points from infeasible ones for a certain class of separable convex problems. The method guarantees convergence of the constructed feasible point sequence to the optimum of the problem if only this convergence holds for their infeasible counterparts. We theoretically and empirically show how this method works in a local polytope relaxation framework for MRF inference problems. We formulate and prove our results in a general way, which allows us to apply them to arbitrary convex optimization problems having a similar separable structure.

6.1.1   Formulation of the Main Result

We start by stating the main result of the chapter for a separable linear programming problem. The result has a special form, which appears in the MRF energy minimization problem. This example illustrates the idea of the method and avoids shading it with numerous technical details. We refer to Sections 6.2 and 6.3 for all proofs, special cases, and generalizations.

Let $\langle \cdot, \cdot \rangle$ denote an inner product of two vectors in a Euclidean space. Let $\mathbb{R}^n_+$ denote the non-negative cone of the n-dimensional Euclidean space $\mathbb{R}^n$. Let $I = \{1, \ldots, N\}$, $J = \{1, \ldots, M\}$ be sets of integer indexes and $\mathcal{N}(j)$, $j \in J$ be a collection of subsets of I. Let further $x \in \mathbb{R}^{nI}_+$ be a collection of $(x_i \in \mathbb{R}^n_+, \ i \in I)$ and $y \in \mathbb{R}^{mJ}_+$ denote $(y_j \in \mathbb{R}^m_+, \ j \in J)$. Let A_{ij}, $i \in I$, $j \in J$, and B_i, $i \in I$ be full-rank matrices of dimensions $m \times n$ and $n \times k$ for some $k < n$ and let $c_i \in \mathbb{R}^k$. Consider the following separable linear programming problem in the standard form:

$$\min_{\substack{x \in \mathbb{R}^{nI}_+ \\ y \in \mathbb{R}^{mJ}_+}} \sum_{i=1}^{N} \langle a_i, x_i \rangle + \sum_{j=1}^{M} \langle b_j, y_j \rangle \tag{6.1}$$

$$A_{ij} y_j = x_i, \ i \in \mathcal{N}(j), \ j \in J,$$
$$B_i x_i = c_i, \ i \in I.$$

Let C be the feasible set of (6.1) and the mapping $\mathcal{P} \colon \mathbb{R}^{nI}_+ \times \mathbb{R}^{mJ}_+ \to C$ be defined such that $\mathcal{P}(x, y) = (x', y')$, where

$$x'_i = \operatorname*{argmin}_{\tilde{x}_i \in \mathbb{R}^n_+} (x_i - \tilde{x}_i)^2 \text{ s.t. } B_i \tilde{x}_i = c_i, \ i \in I; \tag{6.2}$$

$$y'_j := \operatorname*{argmin}_{y_j \in \mathbb{R}^m_+} \langle b_j, y_j \rangle \text{ s.t. } A_{ij} y_j = x'_i, \ i \in \mathcal{N}(j). \tag{6.3}$$

The main result of this chapter is that *from the convergence of $(x^t, y^t) \in \mathbb{R}^{nI} \times \mathbb{R}^{mJ}$, $t = 1, 2, \ldots \infty$, to the set of optimal solutions of (6.1), it follows that $\mathcal{P}(x^t, y^t)$ converges to the set of optimal solutions as well.*

Please note that

- $\mathcal{P}(x^t, y^t)$ is always feasible due to its construction;

- in contrast to the Euclidean projection onto the set C, which constitutes a problem of size comparable to that of the initial one in (6.1), to compute $\mathcal{P}(x^t, y^t)$, one has to solve many, but *small* quadratic and linear optimization problems (6.2)–(6.3), assuming that $n \ll I$, $m \ll J$ and $N(J) \ll I$. To this end, such powerful, but not very well scalable tools as simplex or interior point methods can be used due to the small size of these problems.

In Section 6.2, we additionally show how the convergence speed of $\mathcal{P}(x^t, y^t)$ depends on coefficients a_i and b_i.

Assuming that the set C corresponds to the local polytope, variables x_i and y_i to unary and binary "max-marginals" and weights a_i and b_j to unary and pairwise potentials, respectively, this result allows for an efficient estimation of feasible primal points from infeasible ones for MRF energy minimization algorithms, which has been considered as a non-trivial problem in the past (Werner, 2007).

6.1.2   Related Work on MRF Inference

The two most important inference problems for MRFs are maximum a posteriori (MAP) inference and marginalization (Wainwright and Jordan, 2008). Both are intractable in general, and thus both require some relaxation. The simplest convex relaxation for both is based on exchanging the underlying convex hull of the feasible set, the marginal polytope, by an approximation called the local polytope, studied in Chapter 2. However, even with this approximation, the problems remain non-trivial, although solvable, at least theoretically. A series of algorithmic schemes were proposed to this end for the local polytope relaxations of both MAP (see Chapter 5 and works of Storvik and Dahl, 2000; Komodakis et al., 2011; Schlesinger and Giginyak, 2007; Ravikumar et al., 2010; Savchynskyy et al., 2011; Schmidt et al., 2011; Kappes et al., 2012; Savchynskyy et al., 2012; Martins et al., 2011) and marginalization (Wainwright et al., 2005; Jancsary and Matz, 2011; Hazan and Shashua, 2010). It turns out that the corresponding dual problems have dramatically fewer variables and contain simple constraints (Werner, 2007, 2009); hence, they can even be formulated as unconstrained problems, as done by Schlesinger and Giginyak (2007) and Kappes et al. (2012). Therefore, most of the approaches address optimization of the dual objectives. A common difficulty for such approaches is the computation of a *feasible* relaxed primal estimate from the current dual one. *Infeasible* estimates can typically be obtained from the subgradients of the dual function, as shown by Komodakis et al. (2011), or from the gradients of the smoothed dual, as done by Johnson et al. (2007), Werner (2009), and Savchynskyy et al. (2011).

Even some approaches working in the primal domain (see Section 5.6 and works of Hazan and Shashua, 2010; Martins et al., 2011; Schmidt et al.,

2011) maintain infeasible primal estimates, whilst feasibility is guaranteed only in the limit.

Quite efficient primal schemes based on graph cuts, as proposed by Boykov et al. (2001), do not solve the problem in general, and optimality guarantees provided by them are typically too weak. Hence, we discuss neither of these here, nor the widespread message passing and belief propagation (Kolmogorov, 2006; Weiss and Freeman, 2001) methods (discussed also in Chapter 4), which also do not guarantee the attainment of the optimum of the relaxed problem.

Feasible Primal Estimates. The literature on obtaining feasible primal solutions for MRF inference problems from infeasible ones is not very vast. Apart from our conference papers (Savchynskyy et al., 2011; Schmidt et al., 2011; Savchynskyy et al., 2012) describing special cases of our method in application to the MRF local polytope, we are aware of only three recent works contributing to this topic (Schlesinger et al., 2011; Werner, 2011). The most recent and practical method is described in Chapter 5.

The method proposed by Schlesinger et al. (2011) is formulated in the form of an algorithm able to determine whether a given solution accuracy ε is attained. To this end, it restricts the set of possible primal candidate solutions and solves an auxiliary quadratic programming (QP) problem. However, this approach is unsuited to compute *the actually attained ε* directly, and the auxiliary QP in the worst case grows linearly with the size of the initial linear programming problem. Hence, obtaining a feasible primal solution becomes prohibitively slow as the size of the problem gets larger.

Another closely related method was proposed by Werner (2011). It is, however, only suited to determine whether a given solution of the dual problem is an optimal one. This makes it non-practical because the state-of-the-art methods achieve the exact solution of the considered problem only in the limit, after a potentially infinite number of iterations.

The recent method described in Chapter 5 is simple, yet efficient. However, as we show in Section 6.2 (Theorem 6.4), our method applied on top of *any* other, including the one described in Chapter 5, delivers better primal estimates, except for the cases when the estimates of the other method coincide with ours.

6.1.3   Content and Organization of the Chapter

In Section 6.2, we describe a general formulation and mathematical properties of the *optimizing projection* $\mathcal{P}(x, y)$, as already introduced for a special case in (6.2) and (6.3). We do this without relating it to inference in MRFs. This shows the generality of the method and keeps the exposition simple. Section 6.3 is devoted to local polytope relaxations of the MAP and marginalization inference problems for MRFs, and it specifies how the feasible estimates can be constructed for these. In Section 6.4, we discuss different optimization schemes for the local polytope relaxation for which the primal estimates can be reconstructed from the dual ones. Finally, Sections 6.5 and 6.6 contain the experimental evaluation and the conclusions, respectively.

6.2   Optimizing Projection

Let us denote by $\Pi_C \colon \mathbb{R}^n \to C$ a Euclidean projection to a set $C \subset \mathbb{R}^n$. Let $X \subseteq \mathbb{R}^n$ and $Y \subseteq \mathbb{R}^m$ be two subsets of Euclidean spaces and $C \subset X \times Y$ be a closed convex set. We will denote as C_X the set $\{x \in X \mid \exists y \in Y \colon (x,y) \in C\}$, that is, the projection of C to X.

The main definition of the chapter introduces the notion of *the optimizing projection* in its general form. A possible simplification and the corresponding discussion follow the definition.

Definition 6.1. *Let* $f \colon X \times Y \to \mathbb{R}$ *be a continuous convex function of two variables. The mapping* $\mathcal{P}_{f,C} \colon X \times Y \to C$ *such that* $\mathcal{P}_{f,C}(x,y) = (x',y')$ *defined as*

$$x' = \Pi_{C_X}(x)\,, \tag{6.4}$$

$$y' = \operatorname{argmin}_{y\,:\,(x',y)\in C} f(x',y)\,, \tag{6.5}$$

is called optimizing projection *onto the set* C *w.r.t. the function* f.

This definition provides the way to get *the feasible* point $(x',y') \in C$ from an arbitrary infeasible one (x,y). Of course, getting just any feasible point is not a big issue in many cases. However, as we will soon see, the introduced optimizing projection possesses properties similar to the properties of a standard Euclidean projection, which makes it a useful tool in cases when its computation is easier than the one needed for the Euclidean projection. To this end, both the partial projection (6.4) and the partial minimization (6.5) should be efficiently computable.

The role of projection (6.4) is to make x "feasible" (i.e., to guarantee for x' that there is at least one $y \in \mathcal{Y}$ such that $(x',y) \in C$, which guarantees the definition to be well defined). If this condition holds already for x, then it is easy to see that $x' = x$ and hence computing (6.4) is trivial. We will call such *x feasible* w.r.t. C. Indeed, in (6.4), one can apply an arbitrary projection because they all satisfy the mentioned property. However, we provide our analysis for Euclidean projections only.

Example 6.1. *Consider the linear programming problem (6.1) from the introduction. It is reasonable to construct an optimizing projection $\mathcal{P}_{f,C}(x,y)$ for it as in (6.2)–(6.3), denoting with f and C the objective function and the feasible set of the problem (6.1).*

We will deal with objective functions that fulfill the following definition:

Definition 6.2. *A function $f\colon X \times Y \to \mathbb{R}$ is called Lipschitz-continuous w.r.t. its first argument x, if there exists a finite constant $L_X(f) \geq 0$, such that $\forall y \in Y,\ x, x' \in X$,*

$$|f(x,y) - f(x',y)| \leq L_X(f)\|x - x'\| \tag{6.6}$$

holds. Similarly, f is Lipschitz-continuous w.r.t.

- y if $|f(x,y) - f(x,y')| \leq L_Y(f)\|y - y'\|$ for all $x \in X,\ y, y' \in Y$ and some constant $L_Y(f) \geq 0$;
- $z = (x,y)$ if $|f(x,y) - f(x',y')| \leq L_{XY}(f)\|z - z'\|$ for all $z, z' \in X \times Y$ and some constant $L_{XY}(f) \geq 0$.

The following theorem specifies the main property of the optimizing projection, namely, its continuity with respect to the optimal value of f.

Theorem 6.1. *Let $f\colon X \times Y \to \mathbb{R}$ be a continuous convex function and let f_C^* be its minimum on the convex set C. Then*

- *for any $z^t = (x^t, y^t) \in X \times Y$, $t = 0, \ldots, \infty$, from $|f(x^t, y^t) - f_C^*| \xrightarrow{t \to \infty} 0$ and $\|z^t - \Pi_C(z^t)\| \xrightarrow{t \to \infty} 0$ follows*

$$|f(\mathcal{P}_{f,C}(x^t, y^t)) - f_C^*| \xrightarrow{t \to \infty} 0. \tag{6.7}$$

- *for any $z = (x,y) \in X \times Y$, from Lipschitz-continuity of f w.r.t. its second argument y and feasibility of x w.r.t. C follows:*

$$|f(\mathcal{P}_{f,C}(x,y)) - f_C^*| \leq |f(x,y) - f_C^*| + L_Y(f)\|z - \Pi_C(z)\|. \tag{6.8}$$

- *for any $z = (x,y) \in X \times Y$, from Lipschitz-continuity of f w.r.t. both its arguments x and y follows*

$$|f(\mathcal{P}_{f,C}(x,y)) - f_C^*| \leq |f(x,y) - f_C^*| + (L_X(f) + L_Y(f))\|z - \Pi_C(z)\|. \tag{6.9}$$

Theorem 6.1 basically states that if the sequence $z^t = (x^t, y^t) \in X \times Y$, $t = 1, \ldots, \infty$, weakly converges to the optimum of f, then the same also holds for $\mathcal{P}_{f,C}(x^t, y^t)$. Moreover, for Lipschitz-continuous functions the rate of convergence is preserved up to a multiplicative constant. Note that $\mathcal{P}_{f,C}(x, y)$ *does not actually depend on y*; the argument y is needed only for convergence estimates (6.8)–(6.9), but not for the optimizing projection itself.

Remark 6.1. *Let us provide a bound similar to (6.8) for the Euclidean projection to get an idea how good the estimate (6.8) is:*

$$|f(\Pi_C(z)) - f_C^*| \leq |f(\Pi_C(z)) - f(z)| + |f(z) - f_C^*|$$
$$\leq |f(z) - f_C^*| + L_{XY}(f)\|z - \Pi_C(z)\|. \quad (6.10)$$

We see that bounds (6.9) and (6.10) for the optimizing mapping and Euclidean projection differ only by a constant factor: in the optimizing mapping, the Lipschitz continuity of the objective f is considered w.r.t. to each variable x and y separately, whereas the Euclidean projection is based on the Lipschitz continuity w.r.t. the pair of variables (x, y).

The following technical lemma shows the difference between these two Lipschitz constants. Together with the next one, it will be used in Section 6.3:

Lemma 6.2. *The linear function $f(x, y) = \langle a, x \rangle + \langle b, y \rangle$ is Lipschitz-continuous with Lipschitz constants $L_X(f) \leq \|a\|$, $L_Y(f) \leq \|b\|$ and $L_{XY}(f) \leq \sqrt{L_X(f)^2 + L_Y(f)^2}$.*

Lemma 6.3. *The function $f(z) = \langle a, z \rangle + \sum_{i=1}^N z_i \log z_i$, where $\log$ denotes the natural logarithm, is*

- *continuous on $[0, 1]^N \ni z$ and*
- *Lipschitz-continuous on $[\varepsilon, 1]^N \ni z$, $\varepsilon > 0$, with Lipschitz-constant*

$$L_{XY}(f) \leq \|a\| + N|1 + \log \varepsilon|. \quad (6.11)$$

An important property of the optimizing projection is its *optimality*. Contrary to the Euclidean projection, it can deliver better estimates even when applied to an already *feasible* point $(x, y) \in C$, which is stated by the following theorem.

Theorem 6.4 (Optimality of optimizing projection). *Let $(x, y) \in C$; then $f(\mathcal{P}_{f,C}(x, y)) \leq f(x, y)$, and the inequality holds strictly if $y \notin \arg\min_{y': (x,y') \in C} f(x, y')$.*

The proof of the theorem is straightforward and follows from Definition 6.1 and the fact that $x' = x$.

6.3   MRF Inference and Optimizing Projections

In this section, we consider optimization problems related to inference in MRFs and construct corresponding optimizing projections. We switch from the general mathematical notation used in the previous sections to the one specific for the considered field; in particular, we mostly follow the book of Wainwright and Jordan (2008).

6.3.1   MAP-Inference Problem

Let $\mathcal{G} = (\mathcal{V}, \mathcal{E})$ be an undirected graph, where $\mathcal{V}$ is a finite set of nodes and $\mathcal{E} \subset \mathcal{V} \times \mathcal{V}$ is a set of edges. Further, let $\mathcal{X}_v$, $v \in \mathcal{V}$, be finite *sets of labels*. The set $\mathcal{X} = \otimes_{v \in \mathcal{V}} \mathcal{X}_v$, where $\otimes$ denotes the Cartesian product, will be called *labeling set*, and its elements $x \in \mathcal{X}$ are *labelings*. Thus, each labeling is a collection $(x_v \colon v \in \mathcal{V})$ of labels. To shorten notation, we will use x_{uv} for a pair of labels (x_u, x_v) and $\mathcal{X}_{uv}$ for $\mathcal{X}_u \times \mathcal{X}_v$. The collections of numbers θ_{v,x_v}, $v \in \mathcal{V}$, $x_v \in \mathcal{X}_v$ and $\theta_{uv,x_{uv}}$, $uv \in \mathcal{E}$, $x_{uv} \in \mathcal{X}_{uv}$, will be called *unary* and *pairwise potentials*, respectively. The collection of all potentials will be denoted by θ. The MAP inference problem reads

$$\min_{x \in \mathcal{X}} E(x) := \sum_{v \in \mathcal{V}} \theta_v(x_v) + \sum_{uv \in \mathcal{E}} \theta_{uv}(x_u, x_v), \tag{6.12}$$

and consists of finding a labeling with the smallest total potential (energy).

An alternative way of writing problem (6.12) is to express it in the form of a scalar product of the vector θ with a suitably constructed binary vector $\delta(x)$, $x \in \mathcal{X}$: $\min_{x \in \mathcal{X}} \langle \theta, \delta(x) \rangle$.

The problem is NP-hard in general; hence it is commonly accepted to consider its convex relaxations. The one most widely used is its *local polytope* relaxation, defined in the following subsection.

6.3.2   Primal Relaxed MAP Problem

Denoting $\mathbb{R}^{\sum_{v \in \mathcal{V}} |\mathcal{X}_v| + \sum_{uv \in \mathcal{E}} |\mathcal{X}_{uv}|}$ as $\mathbb{R}(\mathbb{M})$ and the corresponding non-negative cone $\mathbb{R}_+^{\sum_{v \in \mathcal{V}} |\mathcal{X}_v| + \sum_{uv \in \mathcal{E}} |\mathcal{X}_{uv}|}$ as $\mathbb{R}_+(\mathbb{M})$, one writes (Schlesinger, 1976; Werner, 2007) the local polytope (linear programming) relaxation of an MAP inference problem as

$$\min_{\mu \in \mathbb{R}_+(\mathbb{M})} \sum_{v \in \mathcal{V}} \sum_{x_v \in \mathcal{X}_v} \theta_{v,x_v} \mu_{v,x_v} + \sum_{uv \in \mathcal{E}} \sum_{x_{uv} \in \mathcal{X}_{uv}} \theta_{uv,x_{uv}} \mu_{uv,x_{uv}}$$

$$\text{s.t.} \quad \begin{array}{l} \sum_{x_v \in \mathcal{X}_v} \mu_{v,x_v} = 1, \; v \in \mathcal{V}, \\ \sum_{x_v \in \mathcal{X}_v} \mu_{uv,x_{uv}} = \mu_{u,x_u}, \; x_u \in \mathcal{X}_u, \; uv \in \mathcal{E}, \\ \sum_{x_u \in \mathcal{X}_u} \mu_{uv,x_{uv}} = \mu_{v,x_v}, \; x_v \in \mathcal{X}_v, \; uv \in \mathcal{E}. \end{array} \tag{6.13}$$

The constraints in (6.13) form the *local polytope*, later on denoted as $\mathcal{L}$. Slightly abusing notation, we will briefly write problem (6.13) as $\min_{\mu \in \mathcal{L}} E(\mu) := \min_{\mu \in \mathcal{L}} \langle \theta, \mu \rangle$.

Optimizing Projection. We will denote as θ_w and μ_w, $w \in \mathcal{V} \cup \mathcal{E}$, the collections of θ_{w,x_w} and μ_{w,x_w}, $x_w \in \mathcal{X}_w$, respectively. Hence, the vectors θ and μ become collections of θ_w and μ_w, $w \in \mathcal{V} \cup \mathcal{E}$. The n-dimensional simplex $\{x \in \mathbb{R}_+^n : \sum_{i=1}^n x_i = 1\}$ will be denoted as $\Delta(n)$.

Problem (6.13) has a separable structure, that is, for suitably selected matrices A_{uv}, it can be written as

$$\min_{\mu \in \mathbb{R}(\mathbb{M})} \sum_{v \in \mathcal{V}} \langle \theta_v, \mu_v \rangle + \sum_{uv \in \mathcal{E}} \langle \theta_{uv}, \mu_{uv} \rangle$$

$$\text{s.t.} \quad \begin{array}{l} \mu_v \in \Delta(|\mathcal{X}_v|), \qquad v \in \mathcal{V}, \\ A_{uv}\mu_{uv} = \mu_v, \; \mu_{uv} \geq 0, \quad uv \in \mathcal{E}. \end{array} \tag{6.14}$$

Note that under fixed μ_v, the optimization of (6.14) splits into small independent subproblems, one for each $uv \in \mathcal{E}$. We will use this fact to compute the optimizing projection onto the local polytope $\mathcal{L}$ as follows.

Let $\mu_{\mathcal{V}}$ and $\mu_{\mathcal{E}}$ be collections of primal variables corresponding to graph nodes and edges, respectively (i.e., $\mu_{\mathcal{V}} = (\mu_v, \; v \in \mathcal{V})$, $\mu_{\mathcal{E}} = (\mu_{uv}, \; uv \in \mathcal{E})$ and $\mu = (\mu_{\mathcal{V}}, \mu_{\mathcal{E}})$). The corresponding subspaces will be denoted by $\mathbb{R}(\mathbb{M}_{\mathcal{V}})$ and $\mathbb{R}(\mathbb{M}_{\mathcal{E}})$. Then according to (6.14) and Definition 6.1, the optimizing projection $\mathcal{P}_{E,\mathcal{L}} : \mathbb{R}(\mathbb{M}_{\mathcal{V}}) \times \mathbb{R}(\mathbb{M}_{\mathcal{E}}) \to \mathcal{L}$ maps $(\mu_{\mathcal{V}}, \mu_{\mathcal{E}})$ to $(\mu'_{\mathcal{V}}, \mu'_{\mathcal{E}})$ defined as

$$\mu'_v = \Pi_{\Delta(|\mathcal{X}_v|)}(\mu_v), \; v \in \mathcal{V}, \tag{6.15}$$

$$\mu'_{uv} = \arg \min_{\substack{\mu_{uv} \geq 0 \\ \text{s.t.} \; A_{uv}\mu_{uv} = \mu'_v}} \langle \theta_{uv}, \mu_{uv} \rangle, \; uv \in \mathcal{E}. \tag{6.16}$$

Note that both (6.15) and (6.16) can be computed efficiently. Projection to a simplex in (6.15) can be done by the method proposed by Michelot (1986). The optimization problem in (6.16) constitutes a small-sized *trans-*

portation problem well studied in linear programming (see e.g., the textbook of Bazaraa and Jarvis, 1977).

Let us apply Theorem 6.1 and Lemma 6.2 to the optimizing projection $\mathcal{P}_{E,\mathcal{L}}$ introduced by (6.15)–(6.16). According to these, the convergence rate of a given sequence $\mu^t \in \mathbb{R}(\mathbb{M})$ in the worst case slows down by a factor $L_{\mathbb{M}_\mathcal{V}}(E) + L_{\mathbb{M}_\mathcal{E}}(E) \leq \|\theta_\mathcal{V}\| + \|\theta_\mathcal{E}\|$. This factor can be quite large, but because the optimum E^* grows together with the value $\|\theta_\mathcal{V}\| + \|\theta_\mathcal{E}\|$, its influence on the obtained *relative* accuracy is typically much lower than the value itself.

Remark 6.2. *However, if θ contains "infinite" numbers, typically assigned to pairwise factors $\theta_\mathcal{E}$ to model "hard" constraints, both optimizing and Euclidean projections can be quite bad, which is demonstrated by the following simple example: $\mathcal{V} = \{v, u\}$, $\mathcal{E} = \{uv\}$, $\mathcal{X}_v = \mathcal{X}_u = \{0, 1\}$, $\theta_{00} = \theta_{11} = \theta_{01} = 0$, $\theta_{10} = \infty$. If now $\mu_{v,1} > \mu_{u,1}$, optimizing w.r.t. μ_{uv} leads to $\theta_{10} \cdot \mu_{vu,10} = \infty \cdot (\mu_{v,1} - \mu_{u,1})$, whose value can be arbitrary large, depending on the actual numerical value approximating ∞. Because neither the optimizing projection nor the Euclidean one take into account the actual values of pairwise factors when assigning values to $\mu_\mathcal{V}$, the relation $\mu_{v,1} > \mu_{u,1}$ is not controlled.*

We provide a numerical simulation related to infinite values of pairwise potentials in Section 6.5.

Remark 6.3 (Higher-order models and relaxations). *The generalization of the optimizing projection (6.15)–(6.16) for both higher-order models and higher-order local polytopes (Wainwright and Jordan, 2008, Section 8.5) is quite straightforward. The underlying idea remains the same: one has to fix a subset of variables such that the resulting optimization problem splits into a number of small ones.*

Remark 6.4 (Efficient representation of the relaxed primal solution). *Note that because the pairwise primal variables $\mu_\mathcal{E}$ can be easily recomputed from the unary ones $\mu_\mathcal{V}$, it is sufficient to store only the latter if one is not interested in specific values of pairwise variables $\mu_\mathcal{E}$. Because of possible degeneracy, there may exist multiple vectors $\mu_\mathcal{E}$ optimizing the energy E for a given $\mu_\mathcal{V}$.*

6.3.3 Relaxed Dual MAP Problem

In this section, we consider the Lagrange dual to the problem (6.13). Let us denote as $\mathcal{N}(v) = \{u \in \mathcal{V} : uv \in \mathcal{E}\}$ the set of neighboring nodes of a node $v \in \mathcal{V}$. We consider the dual variable $\nu \in \mathbb{R}(\mathbb{D})$ to consist of the following groups of coordinates: ν_v, $v \in \mathcal{V}$; ν_{uv}, $uv \in \mathcal{E}$; and $\nu_{v \to u, x_v}$,

$v \in \mathcal{V}$, $u \in \mathcal{N}(v)$, $x_v \in \mathcal{X}_v$. In this notation, the dual to (6.13) reads

$$\max_{\nu \in \mathbb{R}(\mathbb{D})} \sum_{v \in \mathcal{V}} \nu_v + \sum_{uv \in \mathcal{E}} \nu_{uv} \tag{6.17}$$

$$\text{s.t.} \quad \begin{aligned} \theta_{v,x_v} - \sum_{u \in \mathcal{N}(v)} \nu_{v \to u, x_v} &\geq \nu_v, \ v \in \mathcal{V}, \ x_v \in \mathcal{X}_v, \\ \theta_{uv,x_{uv}} + \nu_{u \to v, x_u} + \nu_{v \to u, x_v} &\geq \nu_{uv}, \ uv \in \mathcal{E}, x_{uv} \in \mathcal{X}_{uv}. \end{aligned}$$

We will use the notation $\mathcal{U}(\nu) := \sum_{v \in \mathcal{V}} \nu_v + \sum_{uv \in \mathcal{E}} \nu_{uv}$ for the objective function of (6.17).

Optimizing Projection. The dual (6.17) possesses clear separability as well: after fixing all variables except ν_v, $v \in \mathcal{V}$, and ν_{uv}, $uv \in \mathcal{E}$, the optimization splits into a series of small and straightforward minimizations over a small set of values

$$\nu_v = \min_{x_v \in \mathcal{X}_v} \theta_{v,x_v} - \sum_{u \in \mathcal{N}(v)} \nu_{v \to u, x_v}, \ v \in \mathcal{V}, \tag{6.18}$$

$$\nu_{uv} = \min_{x_{uv} \in \mathcal{X}_{uv}} \theta_{uv,x_{uv}} + \nu_{u \to v, x_u} + \nu_{v \to u, x_v}, \ uv \in \mathcal{E}. \tag{6.19}$$

The formula (6.18) can be applied directly for each $v \in \mathcal{V}$ and (6.19) accordingly for each $uv \in \mathcal{E}$.

We denote by $\mathbb{D}$ the dual feasible set defined by the constraints of (6.17). We split all dual variables into two groups. The first one will contain "messages" $\nu_\to = (\nu_{v \to u}, \ v \in \mathcal{V}, \ u \in \mathcal{N}(v))$, that are variables, which reweight unary and pairwise potentials leading to an improvement in the objective. The vector space containing all possible values of these variables will be denoted as $\mathbb{R}(\mathbb{D}_\to)$. The second group will contain lower bounds on optimal reweighted unary and pairwise potentials $\nu_0 = (\nu_w, \ w \in \mathcal{V} \cup \mathcal{E})$. The total sum of their values constitutes the dual objective. All possible values of these variables will form the vector space $\mathbb{R}(\mathbb{D}_0)$. Hence, the optimizing projection $\mathcal{P}_{\mathcal{U},\mathbb{D}} \colon \mathbb{R}(\mathbb{D}_\to) \times \mathbb{R}(\mathbb{D}_0) \to \mathbb{R}(\mathbb{D})$ maps $(\nu_\to, \nu_0)$ to $(\nu'_\to, \nu'_0)$ as

$$\nu'_{v \to u} = \nu_{v \to u}, \ v \in \mathcal{V}, \ u \in \mathcal{N}(v), \tag{6.20}$$

$$\nu'_v = \min_{x_v \in \mathcal{X}_v} \theta_{v,x_v} - \sum_{u \in \mathcal{N}(v)} \nu'_{v \to u, x_v}, \ v \in \mathcal{V}, \tag{6.21}$$

$$\nu'_{uv} = \min_{x_{uv} \in \mathcal{X}_{uv}} \theta_{uv,x_{uv}} + \nu_{u \to v, x_u} + \nu'_{v \to u, x_v}, \ uv \in \mathcal{E}. \tag{6.22}$$

Note that (6.20) corresponds to the projection (6.4), which has the form $\Pi_{\mathbb{R}(\mathbb{D}_\to)}(\nu_\to) = \nu_{\to 0}$ and is thus trivial.

Applying Theorem 6.1 and Lemma 6.2 to the optimizing projection $\mathcal{P}_{\mathcal{U},\mathbb{D}}$ yields that the convergence of the projected ν^t slows down no more than by a factor $L_{\mathbb{D}_0} \leq |\sqrt{\mathcal{V}}| + |\sqrt{\mathcal{E}}|$ and does not depend on the potentials θ. However, because the optimal energy value often grows proportionally to

$|\mathcal{V}| + |\mathcal{E}|$, the influence of the factor on the estimated related precision is typically insignificant.

6.3.4   Entropy-Smoothed Primal Problem

Let $H: \mathbb{R}_+^n \to \mathbb{R}$ be *an entropy* function defined as $H(z) = -\sum_{i=1}^n z_i \log z_i$ and the dimensionality n defined by the dimensionality of the input. The problem

$$\min_{\mu \in \mathbb{R}_+(\mathbb{M})} \hat{E} := \min_{\mu \in \mathbb{R}_+(\mathbb{M})} \langle \theta, \mu \rangle - \sum_{w \in \mathcal{V} \cup \mathcal{E}} c_w H(\mu_w)$$

$$\text{s.t.} \quad \begin{aligned} &\sum_{x_v \in \mathcal{X}_v} \mu_{v,x_v} = 1, \ v \in \mathcal{V}, \\ &\sum_{x_v \in \mathcal{X}_v} \mu_{uv,x_{uv}} = \mu_{u,x_u}, \ x_u \in \mathcal{X}_u, \ uv \in \mathcal{E}, \\ &\sum_{x_u \in \mathcal{X}_u} \mu_{uv,x_{uv}} = \mu_{v,x_v}, \ x_v \in \mathcal{X}_v, \ uv \in \mathcal{E}, \end{aligned} \tag{6.23}$$

is closely related to the primal relaxed one in (6.13) and arises when one applies the smoothing technique (Nesterov, 2004; Jojic et al., 2010; Savchynskyy et al., 2011, 2012; Hazan and Shashua, 2010) or considers approximations for marginalization inference (Wainwright and Jordan, 2008; Wainwright et al., 2005; Jancsary and Matz, 2011). We refer to the works of Heskes (2004), Weiss et al. (2007) and Hazan and Shashua (2010) for a description of the sufficient conditions for convexity of (6.23). Assuming a precision $\varepsilon = 10^{-16}$ to be sufficient for practical needs, we equip (6.23) with an additional set of box constraints $\mu \in [\varepsilon, 1]^{|\mathbb{M}|}$, where $|\mathbb{M}|$ is the dimensionality of the vector μ. This is done to obtain a finitely large Lipschitz constant according to Lemma 6.3.

Optimizing Projection.   Denoting the local polytope $\mathcal{L}$ augmented with the additional box-constraints $\mu \in [\varepsilon, 1]^{|\mathbb{M}|}$ as $\hat{\mathcal{L}}$, we define the corresponding optimizing projection $\mathcal{P}_{\hat{E}, \hat{L}}(\mu)$ as

$$\mu'_v = \Pi_{\Delta(|\mathcal{X}_v|) \cap [\varepsilon, 1]^{|\mathcal{X}_v|}}(\mu_v), \ v \in \mathcal{V}, \tag{6.24}$$

for $uv \in \mathcal{E}$:

$$\begin{aligned} \mu'_{uv} = \arg \min_{\mu_{uv} \in [\varepsilon, 1]^{|\mathcal{X}_{uv}|}} \ & \langle \theta_{uv} - c_{uv} \log(\mu_{uv}), \mu_{uv} \rangle \\ \text{s.t.} \ & A_{uv} \mu_{uv} = \mu'_v, \end{aligned} \tag{6.25}$$

where $\log z$, $z \in \mathbb{R}^n$, is defined coordinate-wise. By applying Theorem 6.1 and Lemma 6.3, one obtains that the convergence rate of a given sequence $\mu^t \in \mathbb{R}(\mathbb{M})$ slows down by a factor $\|\theta_\mathcal{V}\| + \|\theta_\mathcal{E}\| + \sum_{w \in \mathcal{V} \cup \mathcal{E}} |\mathcal{X}_w| |1 + \log \varepsilon|$ in the worst case, where the last term constitutes a difference to the optimizing projection $\mathcal{P}_{E, \mathcal{L}}$ for the primal MAP-inference problem (6.13).

Remark 6.5. *Indeed, the additional constraints $\mu \in [\varepsilon, 1]^{|\mathbb{M}|}$ are needed only for the theoretical analysis of the projected estimate $\mathcal{P}_{\hat{E}, \hat{\mathcal{L}}}(\mu)$, to show that when the true marginals μ become close to 0, the optimizing projection (and in fact the Euclidean one also) behaves worse.*

However, there is no reason to use these constraints in practice. According to Theorem 6.1, the projected feasible estimates will converge to the optimum of the problem together with the non-projected infeasible ones even without the box constraints, due to continuity of the entropy H. Only the speed of convergence of the projected estimates will decrease logarithmically. Moreover, omitting the box constraints $\mu \in [\varepsilon, 1]^{|\mathbb{M}|}$ simplifies the computations in (6.24) and (6.25). The first one then corresponds to the projection onto the simplex and the second one to a small-sized entropy minimization, *efficiently solvable by the Newton method after resorting to its corresponding* smooth and *unconstrained* dual problem.

Moreover, we suggest to threshold μ_v by setting μ_{v,x_v} to zero if it is less than the precision ε. That decreases the size of the subproblem (6.25) and allows us to avoid numerical problems.

6.4   Optimizing Projection in Algorithmic Schemes

In the previous sections, we concentrated on the way to compute the optimizing projection, assuming that a weakly converging (but infeasible) sequence is given. In this section, we briefly discuss how these infeasible sequences can be generated.

6.4.1   Prox-Point Primal-Dual Algorithms

In the simplest case, the (infeasible) estimates μ^t for the primal (6.13) and ν^t for the dual (6.17) problems are generated by an algorithm on each iteration t, as is typical for primal-dual algorithms. These algorithms address the relaxed problem (6.13) in its saddle-point formulation

$$\max_{\mu \geq 0} \min_{\nu} \quad \{ \langle -b, \nu \rangle + \langle \mu, A^\top \nu \rangle - \langle \theta, \mu \rangle \}. \tag{6.26}$$

The matrix A corresponds to equality constraints in (6.13). Some of the methods (described in Section 5.6 and works of Martins et al., 2011; Fu and Banerjee, 2013) additionally approach (6.26) with prox-terms of the form $\|A\mu - b\|^2$ or $\|A^\top \nu - \theta\|^2$. Some of these algorithms maintain feasible dual estimates ν^t as in Section 5.6 and in works of Martins et al. (2011) and Fu and Banerjee (2013), whereas others do not, as done by Schmidt et al. (2011).

However, to the best of our knowledge, none of these algorithms maintains feasibility of the primal estimates μ^t with respect to the problem (6.13). One can obtain the feasible estimates, as well as the duality gap estimation, by applying the optimizing projection $\mathcal{P}_{E,\mathcal{L}}(\mu^t)$ defined by (6.15)–(6.16) and—if needed—$\mathcal{P}_{\mathcal{U},\mathbb{D}}(\nu^t)$ defined by (6.20)–(6.22), respectively.

6.4.2   Dual Decomposition-Based Algorithms

There is an alternative way to formulate a dual problem to (6.13) based on the Lagrangian or dual decomposition. This technique allows us to construct particularly efficient inference algorithms. We will review the reconstruction of primal estimates for these algorithms in this section.

For the sake of brevity, we consider the case where the master graph $\mathcal{G} = (\mathcal{V}, \mathcal{E})$ can be covered by two *acyclic* subgraphs $\mathcal{G}^i = (\mathcal{V}^i, \mathcal{E}^i)$, $i = 1, 2$, such that each edge of $\mathcal{G}$ is covered only once, and each vertex twice (i.e., by either subgraph: $\mathcal{V}^1 = \mathcal{V}^2 = \mathcal{V}$, $\mathcal{E}^i \cup \mathcal{E}^2 = \mathcal{E}$ and $\mathcal{E}^1 \cap \mathcal{E}^2 = \emptyset$). An example is a grid graph, which allows such a decomposition into two subgraphs corresponding to its rows and columns.

Introducing

$$\theta^i_{uv} = \begin{cases} \theta_{uv}, & uv \in \mathcal{E}^i \\ 0, & uv \notin \mathcal{E}^i \end{cases} , \; i = 1, 2, \tag{6.27}$$

and assuming $\theta^1_{v,x_v} + \theta^2_{v,x_v} = \theta_{v,x_v}$, $\forall v \in \mathcal{V}, x_v \in \mathcal{X}_v$, which can be rewritten in a parametric way as $\theta^1_{v,x_v} = \frac{\theta_{v,x_v}}{2} + \lambda_{v,x_v}$ and $\theta^2_{v,x_v} = \frac{\theta_{v,x_v}}{2} - \lambda_{v,x_v}$, $\lambda_{v,x_v} \in \mathbb{R}$, one obtains a lower bound

$$\min_{x \in \mathcal{X}} E(\theta, x) = \min_{x \in \mathcal{X}} \langle \theta, \delta(x) \rangle \geq \max_{\lambda \in \mathbb{R}(\Lambda)} \sum_{i=1}^{2} \min_{x \in \mathcal{X}} \langle \theta^i, \delta(x) \rangle = \min_{\mu \in \mathcal{L}} \langle \theta, \mu \rangle . \tag{6.28}$$

Here $\mathbb{R}(\Lambda) := \mathbb{R}^{\sum_{v \in \mathcal{V}} |\mathcal{X}_v|}$. The last equality is not straightforward and holds for a decomposition of $\mathcal{G}$ to *arbitrary* acyclic subgraphs. We refer to the work of Komodakis et al. (2011) for its proof.

The unconstrained concave, but non-smooth problem

$$\max_{\lambda \in \mathbb{R}(\Lambda)} U(\lambda) := \max_{\lambda \in \mathbb{R}(\Lambda)} \sum_{i=1}^{2} \min_{x \in \mathcal{X}} \langle \theta^i, \delta(x) \rangle \tag{6.29}$$

is dual to the relaxed problem (6.13).

In the following two paragraphs, we will provide several different expressions for computing μ^{it}_w, $w \in \mathcal{V}^i \cup \mathcal{E}^i$, $i = 1, 2$, which will serve as coordinates of the *infeasible* primal sequences converging to the optimum of the problems (6.13) or (6.23), respectively. Although multiple ways of constructing such a sequence out of these coordinates are possible, we will use the following scheme in our experiments:

$$\bar{\mu}_v^t = \frac{1}{2}(\mu_v^{1t} + \mu_v^{2t}), \quad \bar{\mu}_{uv}^t = \begin{cases} \mu_{uv}^{1t}, & uv \in \mathcal{E}^1 \\ \mu_{uv}^{2t}, & uv \in \mathcal{E}^2 \end{cases}, \quad uv \in \mathcal{E}. \tag{6.30}$$

To transform the sequences into feasible ones, we will apply corresponding $(\mathcal{P}_{E,\mathcal{L}}$ or $\mathcal{P}_{\hat{E},\hat{L}})$ optimizing projections to $\bar{\mu}^t$.

Subgradient and Bundle Methods.   The subgradient method

$$\lambda^{t+1} = \lambda^t + \tau^t \frac{\partial U}{\partial \lambda}(\lambda^t), \text{ where } \tau^t \to 0 \text{ and } \sum_{t=1}^{\infty} \tau^t = \infty, \tag{6.31}$$

of Shor et al. (1985) was one of the first optimization algorithms with convergence guarantees, independently applied by Storvik and Dahl (2000) and later by Schlesinger and Giginyak (2007) and Komodakis et al. (2007) to tackle (6.29). It is based on the fact that the subgradient $\frac{\partial U}{\partial \lambda} = \delta_V(x^{*1}) - \delta_V(x^{*2})$, where $x^{*i} = \arg\min_{x \in \mathcal{X}} \langle \theta^i(\lambda), \delta(x) \rangle$, is efficiently computable by dynamic programming when graphs $\mathcal{G}^i$ are acyclic.

It is shown by Larsson et al. (1999) and later applied by Komodakis et al. (2011) (see also Sontag et al., 2011, Section 1.7.1) that both *time-averaged*

$$\mu_w^{it} := \frac{\sum_{k=1}^t \delta_w(x^{*i,k})}{t}, \quad w \in \mathcal{V}^i \cup \mathcal{E}^i \tag{6.32}$$

and *step-size averaged* labelings

$$\mu_w^{it} := \frac{\sum_{k=1}^t \tau^k \delta_w(x^{*i,k})}{\sum_{k=1}^t \tau^k}, \quad w \in \mathcal{V}^i \cup \mathcal{E}^i, \tag{6.33}$$

where $x^{*i} = \arg\min_{x \in \mathcal{X}} \langle \theta^i(\lambda^t), \delta(x) \rangle$ and t denotes the iteration counter of the algorithm (6.31), can be used to construct a primal sequence converging to the optimum of the primal relaxed problem (6.13). Sequences $\bar{\mu}^t$, constructed as in (6.30) out of μ_w^{it} defined by either (6.32) or (6.33), are infeasible, however (i.e., they do not fulfill constraints of (6.13) up to the optimum). They can be turned into feasible ones with the optimizing projection $\mathcal{P}_{E,\mathcal{L}}$ defined by (6.15)–(6.16).

The coordinates of a converging infeasible primal sequence for the bundle method can be constructed as $\mu_w^{it} := \frac{\sum_{k=1}^t \xi^k \delta_w(x^{*i,k})}{\sum_{k=1}^t \xi^k}$, $w \in \mathcal{V}^i \cup \mathcal{E}^i$, where coefficients ξ^k are the weights of the k-th subgradient in the bundle (Kappes et al., 2012, Equation 23).

Smoothing/Marginalization Inference. Another group of optimization algorithms (Savchynskyy et al., 2011, 2012; Hazan and Shashua, 2010; Ravikumar et al., 2010; Johnson et al., 2007) overcomes the non-smoothness of the dual problem (6.29) by smoothing it prior to optimization. To this end, the "min" operation in (6.29) is replaced by the well-known "log-sum-exp" (or negative soft-max) function (Rockafellar and Wets, 2004; Nesterov, 2004), yielding

$$\hat{U}_\rho(\lambda) := -\sum_{i=1}^{2} \rho \log \sum_{x \in \mathfrak{X}} \exp \left\langle -\theta^i(\lambda)/\rho, \delta(x) \right\rangle, \quad \rho > 0. \tag{6.34}$$

This approximation becomes tighter as ρ decreases, as stated by the well-known inequality $\hat{U}_\rho(\lambda) + 2\rho \log |\mathfrak{X}| \geq U(\lambda) \geq \hat{U}_\rho(\lambda)$. Maximization of $\hat{U}_\rho$ over $\mathbb{R}(\Lambda)$ is dual to minimization of the entropy-smoothed energy $\hat{E}$ over $\mathcal{L}$ (for certain coefficients c_w) defined in (6.23) and hence is used also for approximate marginalization inference (Wainwright et al., 2005; Jancsary and Matz, 2011).

Let us define the coordinates of the primal sequence as

$$\mu_{w,x_w}^{it} := \frac{\sum\limits_{x' \in \mathfrak{X}, x'_w = x_w} \exp \left\langle -\theta^i(\lambda^t)/\rho, \delta(x') \right\rangle}{\exp(-\hat{U}_\rho^i(\lambda^t)/\rho)}, \quad w \in \mathcal{V}^i \cup \mathcal{E}^i, \tag{6.35}$$

where λ^t converges to the optimum of $\hat{U}_\rho$ as $t \to \infty$. Note that the μ^{it} correspond to sum-prod marginals of the subgraphs $\mathcal{G}^i$, and are efficiently computable by dynamic programming when $\mathcal{G}^i$ are acyclic. It is known (Savchynskyy et al., 2011) that the sequence $\overline{\mu}^t$ constructed from μ_{w,x_w}^{it} as in (6.30) converges to the optimum of (6.23) as $t \to \infty$. Application of the optimizing projection $\mathcal{P}_{\hat{E},\hat{L}}(\mu)$ defined in Section 6.3.4 turns the *infeasible* sequence $\overline{\mu}^t$ into a feasible one.

Remark 6.6. *If the final objective of the optimization is not the entropy-smoothed primal problem (6.23), but the primal MAP inference (6.13), and the smoothing is used as an optimization tool to speed up or guarantee convergence (Savchynskyy et al., 2011, 2012; Hazan and Shashua, 2010; Johnson et al., 2007), one can obtain even better primal bounds at a lower computational cost. Namely, the optimizing projection $\mathcal{P}_{E,\mathcal{L}}$ can be applied to approximate the optimal solution of the primal MAP-inference problem (6.13). Denote $\hat{\mu}' = (\hat{\mu}'_\mathcal{V}, \hat{\mu}'_\mathcal{E}) = \mathcal{P}_{\hat{E},\hat{\mathcal{L}}}(\mu_\mathcal{V}, \mu_\mathcal{E})$ and $\mu' = (\mu'_\mathcal{V}, \mu'_\mathcal{E}) = \mathcal{P}_{E,\mathcal{L}}(\mu_\mathcal{V}, \mu_\mathcal{E})$.*

Ignoring the box constraints according to the recommendations of Remark 6.5, from the definitions (6.15) and (6.24), it follows that $\hat{\mu}'_\mathcal{V} = \mu'_\mathcal{V}$, and thus due to (6.16) and (6.25), $E(\mu') \leq E(\hat{\mu}')$. This means that the projection $\mathcal{P}_{E,\mathcal{L}}$ is preferable for approximating the minimum of E over $\mathcal{L}$

even in the case when the smoothed problem (6.23) *was optimized rather than the original non-smooth* (6.13). *As an additional benefit, one obtains faster convergence of the projection even from the worst-case analysis due to a better estimate of the Lipschitz constant for the function E compared to the function $\hat{E}$, as provided by Lemmas 6.2 and 6.3.*

6.4.3   Non-smooth Coordinate Descent: TRWS, MPLP, and Others

We are not aware of methods for reconstructing primal solutions of the relaxed MAP inference problem (6.13) from dual estimates for non-smooth coordinate descent-based schemes like TRW-S of Kolmogorov (2006) and MPLP of Globerson and Jaakkola (2007). Indeed, these schemes do not solve the relaxed MAP problem in general; hence, even if one had such a method at hand, it would not guarantee convergence of the primal estimates to the optimum.

6.5   Experimental Analysis and Evaluation

The main goal of this section is to show how Theorem 6.1 works in practice. To this end, we provide three different experiments. All three address the relaxed MAP inference problem (6.13) and include reconstruction of *feasible* primal estimates for it. Additionally, we refer to the works of Savchynskyy et al. (2011), Schmidt et al. (2011), and Savchynskyy et al. (2012) for experiments with an extended set of benchmark data.

In the first experiment, we show convergence of the feasible primal estimates for three different algorithms. In the second one, we show advantages of the feasible relaxed primal estimates over integral primal estimates for efficient adaptive algorithms. Finally, the third experiment shows that the bounds (6.8)–(6.9) allow a qualitative prediction of the objective value in the (feasible) projected point.

For the experiments, we used our own implementations of the First Order Primal-Dual Algorithm (FPD) of Chambolle and Pock (2010) (originally proposed by Pock et al., 2009) as described by Schmidt et al. (2011); the adaptive diminishing smoothing algorithm ADSAL proposed by Savchynskyy et al. (2012); the dual decomposition-based subgradient ascent SG with an adaptive step-size rule (Kappes et al., 2012, Equation 17) and primal estimates based on time-averaged subgradients (see Section 6.4.2); and finally Nesterov's accelerated gradient ascent method NEST applied to the smoothed dual decomposition-based objective studied by Savchynskyy et al.

(2011). All implementations are based on data structures of the OpenGM library by Andres et al. (2012).

The optimizing projection to the local polytope w.r.t. to the MAP energy (6.15)–(6.16) is computed using our implementation of a specialization of the simplex algorithm for transportation problems (Bazaraa and Jarvis, 1977). We adopted an elegant method by Bland (1977), also discussed in the textbook of Papadimitriou and Steiglitz (1998), to avoid cycling. The source code of the solver is available as part of the OpenGM library.

Feasible Primal Bound Estimation. In the first experiment, we demonstrate that for all three groups of methods discussed in Section 6.4, our method efficiently provides feasible primal estimates for the MAP inference problem (6.13). To this end, we generated a 256×256 grid model with four variable states ($|\mathcal{X}_v| = 4$) and potentials θ randomly distributed in the interval $[0, 1]$. We solved the LP relaxation of the MAP inference problem (6.13) with `FPD` as a representative of methods dealing with infeasible primal estimates, `ADSAL` as the fastest representative of smoothing-based algorithms and the subgradient method `SG`. The corresponding plot is presented in Figure 6.1 (left). We note that for *all* algorithms, the time needed to compute the optimizing projection $\mathcal{P}_{E,\mathcal{L}}$ did not exceed the time needed to compute the subgradient/gradient of the respective dual function and typically required 0.01-0.02 s on a 3GHz machine. The generated data set is not LP tight; hence, the obtained relaxed primal solution has a significantly lower energy than the integer one. In contrast to the situation when only non-relaxed integer primal estimates would be computed, the primal and dual bounds of the relaxed problem converge to the same limit value. Due to the feasibility of both primal and dual estimates, the primal and dual objective functions' values bound the optimal value of the relaxed problem from above and below, respectively.

Relaxed Primal Estimates for Adaptive Algorithms We demonstrate the practical usefulness of feasible relaxed primal estimates with the diminishing smoothing `ADSAL` algorithm of Savchynskyy et al. (2012). It optimizes the smooth dual (6.34) with a degree of smoothing ρ, which decreases with the estimated duality gap. In the original work of Savchynskyy et al. (2012), the primal bound is computed with the optimizing projection as described in Remark 6.6. To demonstrate its importance, we substituted this computation with an estimation of an integer solution by rounding (as done by Kolmogorov, 2006, in the TRW-S algorithm). Figure 6.1 (right) shows the difference between convergence of the original `ADSAL` algorithm and its modification on the randomly generated 25×25 grid model with

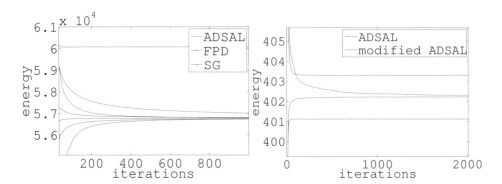

Figure 6.1: Left: Convergence of the primal (upper curves) and dual (lower curves) bounds to the same optimal limit value for `ADSAL`, `FPD`, and `SG` algorithms. The obtained integer bound is plotted as a dotted line.
Right: Convergence of the original `ADSAL` algorithm and its modification. In the modified algorithm, an integral labeling provides a primal bound for the smoothing update, whereas in the original algorithm a feasible *relaxed* primal estimate is used.

four labels. Since the gap between the integer and the dual bounds does not vanish, the smoothing does not vanish either, and the overall algorithm gets stuck in a suboptimal point, whereas the original algorithm based on the relaxed primal estimate converges to the optimum.

Evaluation of Convergence Estimates.   The third experiment is devoted to the evaluation of the convergence estimates (6.8)–(6.9) provided by Theorem 6.1. To this end, we generated four LP-tight grid-structured data sets with known optimal labeling. We refer to the work of Schmidt et al. (2011) for a description of the generation process. The resulting unary and pairwise potentials were distributed in the interval $[-10, 10]$. We picked a random subset of edges not belonging to the optimal labeling and assigned them "infinite" values. We created four data sets with "infinities" equal to $10\,000$, $100\,000$, $1\,000\,000$, and $10\,000\,000$ and ran `NEST` for inference. According to Theorem 6.1, the energy E evaluated on projected feasible estimates $\mathcal{P}_{E,\mathcal{L}}(\overline{\mu}_{\mathcal{V}}^t, \overline{\mu}_{\mathcal{E}}^t)$, $t = 1, \ldots, \infty$, where the *infeasible* estimates $\overline{\mu}^t$ were constructed as in Section 6.4.2, can be represented as

$$E(\mathcal{P}_{E,\mathcal{L}}(\overline{\mu}_{\mathcal{V}}^t, \overline{\mu}_{\mathcal{E}}^t)) = F(\overline{\mu}^t) + L_Y(E)\|\overline{\mu}^t - \Pi_{\mathcal{L}}\overline{\mu}^t\| \tag{6.36}$$

for a suitably selected function F. Because `NEST` is a purely dual method and "infinite" pairwise potentials did not contribute significantly to the values and gradients of the (smoothed) dual objective, the infeasible primal estimates $\overline{\mu}^t$ (with t denoting an iteration counter) were the same for all four different approximations of the infinity value. Because according to Lemma 6.2 the Lipschitz constant $L_Y(E)$ is asymptotically proportional to the norm of

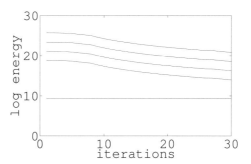

Figure 6.2: Convergence of the obtained primal feasible solution for four data sets that differ only by the values used as "infinity." The energy values are plotted in logarithmic scale. From bottom to top: optimal log-energy, primal bounds corresponding to infinity values equal to 10 000, 100 000, 1 000 000 and 10 000 000.

the pairwise potentials $\|\theta_{\mathcal{E}}\|$, we plotted the values $\log E(\mathcal{P}_{E,\mathcal{L}}(\overline{\mu}_{\mathcal{V}}^{t}, \overline{\mu}_{\mathcal{E}}^{t}))$ as a function of t for all four data sets in Figure 6.2. As predicted by Theorem 6.1, the corresponding energy values differ by approximately a factor of 10, as the "infinite" values do. Due to the logarithmic energy scale, this difference corresponds to equal log-energy distances between the curves in Figure 6.2.

6.6   Conclusions

We presented an efficient and quite general optimizing projection method for computing feasible primal estimates for dual and primal-dual optimization schemes. The method provides convergence guarantees similar to those of the Euclidean projection but, contrary to the latter, allows for efficient computations if the feasible set and the objective function possess certain separability properties. Like any optimization tool, it has certain limitations related to the Lipschitz continuity of the primal objective; however, exactly the same limitations are also characteristic for the Euclidean projection. Hence, they cannot be considered as particular disadvantages of this method but must rather be considered as disadvantages of projection methods in general. These limitations can only be overcome by constructing algorithms that intrinsically maintain feasible primal estimates during iterations. The construction of such algorithms has to be addressed in future work.

Acknowledgements

This work has been supported by the German Research Foundation (DFG) within the program "Spatio-/Temporal Graphical Models and Applications in Image Analysis," grant GRK 1653.

Proofs

Theorem 6.1.

Proof. We will denote $(x^p, y^p) = z^p = \Pi_C(z)$ and $(x', y') = \mathcal{P}_{f,C}(x, y)$. Note that

- from $f_C^* \leq f(x', y') \leq f(x', y'')$ for any $y'' \in Y$ such that $(x', y'') \in C$ it follows that

$$f_C^* \leq f(x', y') \leq f(x', y^p), \tag{6.37}$$

- from $\|z - z^p\| = \sqrt{\|x - x^p\|^2 + \|y - y^p\|^2}$ it follows that

$$\|y - y^p\| \leq \|z - z^p\| \text{ and } \|x - x^p\| \leq \|z - z^p\|. \tag{6.38}$$

- according to (6.4) $x' = \Pi_{C_X}(x) = \operatorname{argmin}_{\tilde{x} \in C_X} \|x - \tilde{x}\|$ and hence

$$\|x - x'\| \leq \|x - x^p\| \tag{6.39}$$

since $x^p \in C_X$. Combining this with (6.38), we obtain

$$\|x - x'\| \leq \|z - z^p\|. \tag{6.40}$$

- The triangle inequality $\|x' - x^p\| \leq \|x' - x\| + \|x - x^p\|$ and (6.39) applied to $x^{t'} := \Pi_{C_X}(x^t)$ and $(x^{tp}, y^{tp}) := \Pi_C(x^t, y^t)$ in place of x' and (x^p, y^p), respectively, suggest that from $\|(x^t, y^t) - \Pi_C(x^t, y^t)\| \xrightarrow{t \to \infty} 0$ follows that

$$\|x^{t'} - x^{tp}\| \xrightarrow{t \to \infty} 0 \text{ and } \|x - x^{t'}\| \xrightarrow{t \to \infty} 0. \tag{6.41}$$

Implication (6.7) follows from (6.41), continuity of f and inequality

$$|f(\mathcal{P}_{f,C}(x^t, y^t)) - f_C^*| = |f(x^{t'}, y^{t'}) - f_C^*| \overset{(6.37)}{\leq} |f(x^{t'}, y^{tp}) - f_C^*|$$
$$\leq |f(x^{t'}, y^{tp}) - f(x^{t'}, y^t)| + |f(x^{t'}, y^t) - f_C^*|. \tag{6.42}$$

Implication (6.8) follows from

$$|f(\mathcal{P}_{f,C}(x,y)) - f_C^*| = |f(x',y') - f_C^*| \overset{(6.37)}{\leq} |f(x',y^p) - f_C^*|$$
$$\leq |f(x',y^p) - f(x',y)| + |f(x',y) - f_C^*| \leq L_Y(f)\|y-y^p\| + |f(x',y) - f_C^*|$$
$$\overset{(6.38)}{\leq} L_Y(f)\|z - z^p\| + |f(x',y) - f_C^*|. \quad (6.43)$$

assuming that $x' = x$.

Implication (6.9) follows from (6.43) and Lipschitz-continuity of f w.r.t. x:

$$|f(\mathcal{P}_{f,C}(x,y)) - f_C^*| \overset{(6.43)}{\leq} L_Y(f)\|z - z^p\| + |f(x',y) - f_C^*|$$
$$\leq L_Y(f)\|z - z^p\| + |f(x',y) - f(x,y)| + |f(x,y) - f_C^*|$$
$$\leq L_Y(f)\|z - z^p\| + L_X(f)\|x' - x\| + |f(x,y) - f_C^*|$$
$$\overset{(6.40)}{\leq} L_Y(f)\|z - z^p\| + L_X(f)\|z - z^p\| + |f(x,y) - f_C^*|$$
$$= (L_Y(f) + L_X(f))\|z - z^p\| + |f(x,y) - f_C^*|. \quad (6.44)$$

$\square$

Lemma 6.2.

Proof. All three Lipschitz-constants are derived from the Cauchy-Bunyakovsky-Schwarz inequality $\langle c, \nu \rangle \leq \|c\| \cdot \|\nu\|$, $c, \nu \in \mathbb{R}^N$, applied, respectively, to x, y, and $z = (x,y)$ in place of ν. $\square$

Lemma 6.3.

Proof. The function $f_i(z_i) = z_i \log z_i$ of a single variable is differentiable on $[\varepsilon, M]$ and its derivative $f_i'(z_i) = 1 + \log z_i$ is monotone increasing, hence $f_i(z_i)$ is convex. This implies $f_i(z_i) - f_i(z_i') \leq f_i'(z_i)(z_i - z_i')$ and $|f_i(z_i) - f_i(z_i')| \leq |f_i'(z_i)||(z_i - z_i')|$. Taking into account that due to monotonicity $|f_i'(z_i)| \leq \max\{|1 + \log \varepsilon|, |1 + \log M|\}$ for $z_i \in [\varepsilon, M]$, and using the fact that $L(f_1 + f_2) \leq L(f_1) + L_f(f_2)$ together with Lemma 6.2, one obtains (6.11). $\square$

6.7 References

B. Andres, T. Beier, and J. H. Kappes. OpenGM: A C++ library for discrete graphical models. Technical report, arXiv:1206.0111, 2012.

M. S. Bazaraa and J. J. Jarvis. *Linear Programming and Network Flows*. Wiley, 1977.

R. G. Bland. New finite pivoting rules for the simplex method. *Mathematics of Operations Research*, pages 103–107, 1977.

S. Boyd and L. Vandenberghe. *Convex Optimization*. Cambridge University Press, 2004.

Y. Boykov, O. Veksler, and R. Zabih. Fast approximate energy minimization via graph cuts. *IEEE Transactions on Pattern Analysis and Machine Intelligence*, 23:1222–1239, 2001.

A. Chambolle and T. Pock. A first-order primal-dual algorithm for convex problems with applications to imaging. *Journal of Mathematical Imaging and Vision*, pages 1–26, 2010.

Q. Fu and H. W. A. Banerjee. Bethe-ADMM for tree decomposition based parallel MAP inference. In *Proceedings of the Conference on Uncertainty in Artificial Intelligence*, 2013.

A. Globerson and T. Jaakkola. Fixing max-product: Convergent message passing algorithms for MAP LP-relaxations. In *Proceedings of the Conference on Neural Information Processing Systems*, 2007.

T. Hazan and A. Shashua. Norm-product belief propagation: Primal-dual message-passing for approximate inference. *IEEE Transactions on Information Theory*, 56(12):6294 –6316, December 2010.

T. Heskes. On the uniqueness of loopy belief propagation fixed points. *Neural Computation*, 16(11):2379–2413, 2004.

J. Jancsary and G. Matz. Convergent decomposition solvers for tree-reweighted free energies. In *Proceedings of the Conference on Artificial Intelligence and Statistics*, 2011.

J. K. Johnson, D. Malioutov, and A. S. Willsky. Lagrangian relaxation for MAP estimation in graphical models. In *Proceedings of the Allerton Conference on Communication, Control and Computation*, 2007.

V. Jojic, S. Gould, and D. Koller. Accelerated dual decomposition for MAP inference. In *Proceedings of the International Conference on Machine Learning*, pages 503–510, 2010.

J. H. Kappes, B. Savchynskyy, and C. Schnörr. A bundle approach to efficient MAP-inference by Lagrangian relaxation. In *Proceedings of the Conference on Computer Vision and Pattern Recognition*, 2012.

V. Kolmogorov. Convergent tree-reweighted message passing for energy minimization. *IEEE Transactions on Pattern Analysis and Machine Intelligence*, 28(10): 1568–1583, 2006.

N. Komodakis, N. Paragios, and G. Tziritas. MRF optimization via dual decomposition: Message-passing revisited. In *Proceedings of the International Conference on Computer Vision*, 2007.

N. Komodakis, N. Paragios, and G. Tziritas. MRF energy minimization and beyond via dual decomposition. *IEEE Transactions on Pattern Analysis and Machine Intelligence*, 33:531–552, March 2011.

T. Larsson, M. Patriksson, and A.-B. Strömberg. Ergodic, primal convergence in dual subgradient schemes for convex programming. *Mathematical Programming*, 86:283–312, 1999.

A. F. T. Martins, M. A. T. Figueiredo, P. M. Q. Aguiar, N. A. Smith, and E. P. Xing. An augmented Lagrangian approach to constrained MAP inference. In *Proceedings of the International Conference on Machine Learning*, 2011.

C. Michelot. A finite algorithm for finding the projection of a point onto the canonical simplex of Rn. *Journal of Optimization Theory and Applications*, 50 (1):195–200, 1986.

Y. Nesterov. Smooth minimization of non-smooth functions. *Mathematical Programming*, Ser. A(103):127–152, 2004.

C. H. Papadimitriou and K. Steiglitz. *Combinatorial Optimization: Algorithms and Complexity.* Dover Publications, 2nd edition, 1998.

T. Pock, D. Cremers, H. Bischof, and A. Chambolle. An algorithm for minimizing the piecewise smooth Mumford-Shah functional. In *Proceedings of the International Conference on Computer Vision*, 2009.

P. Ravikumar, A. Agarwal, and M. Wainwright. Message-passing for graph-structured linear programs: Proximal methods and rounding schemes. *Journal of Machine Learning Research*, 11:1043–1080, 2010.

R. Rockafellar and R. J.-B. Wets. *Variational Analysis.* Springer, 2nd edition, 2004.

B. Savchynskyy, J. Kappes, S. Schmidt, and C. Schnörr. A study of Nesterov's scheme for Lagrangian decomposition and MAP labeling. In *Proceedings of the Conference on Computer Vision and Pattern Recognition*, 2011.

B. Savchynskyy, S. Schmidt, J. Kappes, and C. Schnörr. Efficient MRF energy minimization via adaptive diminishing smoothing. In *Proceedings of the Conference on Uncertainty in Artificial Intelligence*, pages 746–755, 2012.

M. Schlesinger and V. Giginyak. Solution to structural recognition (max,+)-problems by their equivalent transformations. in 2 parts. *Control Systems and Computers*, (1-2), 2007.

M. Schlesinger, E. Vodolazskiy, and N. Lopatka. Stop condition for subgradient minimization in dual relaxed (max,+) problem. In *Proceedings of the Conference on Energy Minimization Methods in Computer Vision and Pattern Recognition*, 2011.

M. I. Schlesinger. Syntactic analysis of two-dimensional visual signals in the presence of noise. *Kibernetika*, (4):113–130, July-August 1976.

S. Schmidt, B. Savchynskyy, J. Kappes, and C. Schnörr. Evaluation of a first-order primal-dual algorithm for MRF energy minimization. In *Proceedings of the Conference on Energy Minimization Methods in Computer Vision and Pattern Recognition*, 2011.

N. Z. Shor, K. C. Kiwiel, and A. Ruszcayski. *Minimization methods for non-differentiable functions.* Springer-Verlag New York, Inc., 1985.

D. Sontag, T. Meltzer, A. Globerson, Y. Weiss, and T. Jaakkola. Tightening LP relaxations for MAP using message-passing. In *Proceedings of the Conference on Uncertainty in Artificial Intelligence*, pages 503–510, 2008.

D. Sontag, A. Globerson, and T. Jaakkola. Introduction to dual decomposition for inference. *Optimization for Machine Learning*, 1, 2011.

G. Storvik and G. Dahl. Lagrangian-based methods for finding MAP solutions for MRF models. *IEEE Transactions on Image Processing*, 9(3):469–479, 2000.

M. Wainwright, T. Jaakkola, and A. Willsky. A new class of upper bounds on the log partition function. *IEEE Transactions on Information Theory*, 51:2313–2335, 2005.

M. J. Wainwright and M. I. Jordan. Graphical models, exponential families, and variational inference. *Foundations and Trends in Machine Learning*, 1(1-2):1–305, 2008.

Y. Weiss and W. T. Freeman. On the optimality of solutions of the max-product belief-propagation algorithm in arbitrary graphs. *IEEE Transactions on Information Theory*, 47(2):736–744, 2001.

Y. Weiss, C. Yanover, and T. Meltzer. MAP estimation, linear programming and belief propagation with convex free energies. In *Proceedings of the Conference on Uncertainty in Artificial Intelligence*, 2007.

T. Werner. A linear programming approach to max-sum problem: A review. *IEEE Transactions on Pattern Analysis and Machine Intelligence*, 29(7), July 2007.

T. Werner. Revisiting the decomposition approach to inference in exponential families and graphical models. Technical report, CMP, Czech TU, 2009.

T. Werner. How to compute primal solution from dual one in MAP inference in MRF? *Control Systems and Computers*, (2), March-April 2011.

7   Perturb-and-MAP Random Fields: Reducing Random Sampling to Optimization, with Applications in Computer Vision

George Papandreou   gpapan@ttic.edu
Toyota Technological Institute at Chicago
Chicago, USA

Alan Yuille   yuille@stat.ucla.edu
University of California, Los Angeles
Los Angeles, USA

Probabilistic Bayesian methods such as Markov random fields are well suited for modeling structured data, providing a natural conceptual framework for capturing the uncertainty in interpreting them and automatically learning model parameters from training examples. However, Bayesian methods are often computationally too expensive for large-scale applications compared with deterministic energy minimization techniques.

This chapter presents an overview of a recently introduced "Perturb-and-MAP" generative probabilistic random field model, which produces in a single shot a random sample from the whole field by first injecting noise into the energy function, then solving an optimization problem to find the least energy configuration of the perturbed system. Perturb-and-MAP random fields thus turn fast deterministic energy minimization methods into computationally efficient probabilistic inference machines and make Bayesian inference practically tractable for large-scale problems, as illustrated in challenging computer vision applications such as image inpainting and deblurring, image segmentation, and scene labeling.

7.1 Introduction

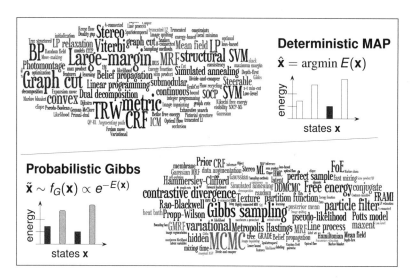

Figure 7.1: Deterministic energy minimization vs. probabilistic Gibbs modeling. Perturb-and-MAP attempts to bridge the gap between these two approaches.

Structured prediction models are typically built around an energy function, which assigns to each possible configuration vector $\boldsymbol{x} = (x_1, \ldots, x_N)$ a real-valued energy $E(\boldsymbol{x})$, with more preferable configurations getting lower energies.

As illustrated in Figure 7.1, there are two quite distinct ways to work with energy-based models. The first is entirely deterministic and amounts to finding a single most probable (MAP) configuration of minimum energy, $\hat{\boldsymbol{x}} = \operatorname{argmin}_{\boldsymbol{x}} E(\boldsymbol{x})$. Such deterministic methods are computationally appealing thanks to fast energy minimization algorithms that can efficiently optimize large-scale problems for important families of energy functions involving both continuous and discrete-valued variables. Parameter learning in this setting is typically performed with large-margin methods.

The second class of methods is probabilistic, assigning to each state a Gibbs probability $f_G(\boldsymbol{x}) \propto e^{-E(\boldsymbol{x})}$. Their key advantage over MAP inference is that they also allow uncertainty quantification in interpreting ambiguous data. The probabilistic framework also enables learning model parameters from training examples using maximum likelihood. However, probabilistic inference is in general considerably more difficult than optimization, because it requires capturing multiple solutions plausible under the posterior distribution instead of just a single MAP configuration.

This chapter presents an overview of the recently introduced Perturb-and-MAP method, which attempts to reduce probabilistic inference to an energy minimization problem, thus establishing a link between the optimization and probabilistic inference approaches to energy-based modeling. As illustrated in Figure 7.2, Perturb-and-MAP is a two-step generative process: (1) In a Perturb step, we inject additive random noise $N(\boldsymbol{x})$ into the system's energy function, followed by (2) a MAP step, in which we find the minimum energy configuration of the perturbed system. By properly designing the noise injection process we can generate exact Gibbs samples from Gaussian Markov random fields (MRFs) and good approximate samples from discrete-label MRFs.

Of course, studying the output sensitivity to input perturbations is omnipresent under many different guises, not only in machine learning but also in optimization, signal processing, control, computer science, and theoretical psychology, among others. However, Perturb-and-MAP is unique in using random perturbations as the defining building block of a structured probabilistic model and setting the ambitious goal of replicating the Gibbs distribution using this approach.

```
function PERTURB-AND-MAP
    Ẽ(x) = E(x) + N(x)    ▷ Perturb
    x̃ = argminₓ Ẽ(x)        ▷ MAP
    return x̃              ▷ Random sample
end function
```

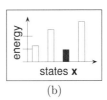 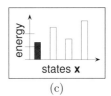

(a)   (b)   (c)

Figure 7.2: (a) The generic Perturb-and-MAP random sampling algorithm. (b) Original energies $E(\boldsymbol{x})$. (c) Perturbed energies $\tilde{E}(\boldsymbol{x})$. The MAP state $\hat{\boldsymbol{x}}$ and the Perturb-and-MAP sample $\tilde{\boldsymbol{x}}$ are shown shaded in (b) and (c), respectively.

While deterministic MAP inference summarizes the solution space into a single most probable estimate, Perturb-and-MAP gives other low-energy states the chance to arise as random samples for some instantiations of the perturbation noise and is thus able to represent the whole probability landscape. Perturb-and-MAP follows a fundamentally different approach compared with other approximate probabilistic inference methods such as Markov Chain Monte-Carlo (MCMC) and Variational Bayes (VB), which are contrasted with Perturb-and-MAP in Figure 7.3. MCMC is broadly applicable and can provide accurate results but is typically computationally expensive for large-scale problems. When the distribution has multiple modes, MCMC mixes slowly and becomes particularly ineffective because it moves in small steps through the state space. Crucially, Perturb-and-MAP generates samples in a single shot, completely bypassing the Markov Chain slow mixing problem and thus has no difficulty in dealing with multimodal distributions. Variational Bayesian methods such as mean field or variational bounding approximate a complicated probability landscape with a simpler parametric distribution. VB is typically faster yet less accurate than MCMC and also faces difficulties in the presence of multiple modes.

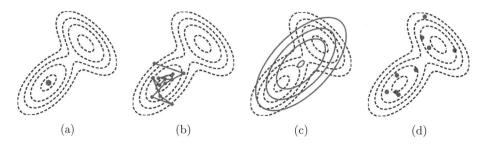

(a)　　　　　(b)　　　　　(c)　　　　　(d)

Figure 7.3: Capturing a complicated probability landscape (in dashed lines) with standard approximate inference methods vs. Perturb-and-MAP. (a) Deterministic MAP. (b) Markov Chain Monte-Carlo. (c) Variational Bayes. (d) Perturb-and-MAP.

Perturb-and-MAP was initially developed for drawing exact random samples from Gaussian MRFs. This efficient Gaussian sampling algorithm can also be used as a sub-routine and considerably accellerate both MCMC and VB in applications involving continuous sparse potentials. We discuss these in Section 7.3. This line of research led to the development of Perturb-and-MAP for discrete MRFs, which we discuss in Section 7.4. We present a summary of recent related work in Section 7.5.

7.2 Energy-Based Modeling: Standard Deterministic and Probabilistic Approaches

7.2.1 Energies and Gibbs MRFs for Modeling Inverse Problems

Structured prediction for solving inverse problems is typically formulated in terms of energy functions. Given an input vector of noisy measurements y, our goal is to estimate the latent state output vector $x = (x_1, \ldots, x_N)$. The elements of the state vector $x_i \in \mathcal{L}$ can take either continuous or discrete values from the label set $\mathcal{L}$. As shown in Figure 7.4, in image processing applications such as image inpainting or deblurring, the state vector x corresponds to a real-valued clean image that we wish to recover from its partial or degraded version y. In computer vision applications such as image segmentation or labeling, the state vector x corresponds to an assignment of image areas to different image segments or semantic object classes. Probabilistic Bayesian techniques offer a natural framework for combining the measurements with prior information in tackling such inverse problems.

(a)   (b)   (c)   (d)

Figure 7.4: In inverse modeling, we use observations $\boldsymbol{y}$ (top row) to infer a latent interpretation $\boldsymbol{x}$ (bottom row). Image processing examples: (a) Inpainting. (b) Deblurring. Computer vision examples: (c) Figure-ground segmentation. (d) Scene labeling.

Given a specific measurement $\boldsymbol{y}$, we quantify a particular interpretation $\boldsymbol{x}$ by means of a *deterministic* energy function $E(\boldsymbol{x})$, where for notational convenience we are suppressing its dependence on the measurements $\boldsymbol{y}$. We will be working with energy functions of the general form

$$E(\boldsymbol{x};\boldsymbol{\theta}) = \langle \boldsymbol{\theta},\, \boldsymbol{\phi}(\boldsymbol{x}) \rangle = \sum_{j=1}^{M} \theta_j \phi_j(\boldsymbol{x})\,, \tag{7.1}$$

where $\boldsymbol{\theta} \in \mathbb{R}^M$ is a real-valued parameter vector of length M and $\boldsymbol{\phi}(\boldsymbol{x}) = (\phi_1(\boldsymbol{x}),\ldots,\phi_M(\boldsymbol{x}))^T$ is a vector of potentials or *sufficient statistics*. We can interpret θ_j as the weight assigned to the feature $\phi_j(\boldsymbol{x})$: we have many different design goals or sources of information (e.g., smoothness prior, measurements), each giving rise to some features whose weighted linear combination constitutes the overall energy function. Each potential often depends on a small subset of the latent variables, which is made explicit in a factor graph representation of the energy function shown in Figure 7.5.

The Gibbs distribution is the standard way to induce a *probabilistic* model from the energy function. It defines a Markov random field whose probability density/mass function has the exponential family form

$$f_G(\boldsymbol{x};\boldsymbol{\theta}) = Z^{-1}(\boldsymbol{\theta}) \exp\left(-E(\boldsymbol{x};\boldsymbol{\theta})\right)\,, \tag{7.2}$$

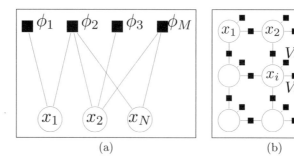

Figure 7.5: (a) The factor graph representation of the energy makes explicit which variables affect each potential. (b) A standard nearest neighbor 2-D grid MRF with unary and pairwise potentials, $\boldsymbol{\phi} = (\{V_i\}, \{V_{ij}\})$.

where $Z(\boldsymbol{\theta}) = \sum_{\boldsymbol{x}} \exp(-E(\boldsymbol{x}; \boldsymbol{\theta}))$ is the partition function and summation over $\boldsymbol{x}$ should be interpreted as integration in the case of a continuous label space $\mathcal{L}$.

MAP inference in the Gibbs model (i.e., computing the most probable configuration, $\hat{\boldsymbol{x}} = \operatorname{argmax}_{\boldsymbol{x}} f_G(\boldsymbol{x})$) is equivalent to solving the energy minimization problem $\hat{\boldsymbol{x}} = \operatorname{argmin}_{\boldsymbol{x}} E(\boldsymbol{x})$. Thanks to powerful modern energy minimization algorithms, exact or high-quality approximate MAP inference can be performed efficiently for several important energy models. However, other key queries on the Gibbs model, such as computing the marginals $f_G(x_i) = \sum_{\boldsymbol{x} \setminus x_i} f_G(\boldsymbol{x})$ or random sampling, are computationally hard.

7.2.2   Probabilistic Parameter Learning From Training Examples

While we typically select the feature set $\boldsymbol{\phi}$ by hand, we can exercise much control on the behavior of the energy-based model by setting the parameters $\boldsymbol{\theta}$ to appropriate values. The high-level goal is to select the weight vector $\boldsymbol{\theta}$ in a way that the model assigns low energies to desirable configurations and high energies to everything else.

When the number of parameters M is small, we can set them to reasonable values by hand. However, a more principled way is to automatically learn the parameters from a training set of K structured labeled examples $\{\boldsymbol{x}_k\}_{k=1}^K$. Discriminative learning criteria such as structured max-margin (Taskar et al., 2003; LeCun et al., 2007; Szummer et al., 2008; Koller and Friedman, 2009) are powerful and described in detail in other chapters of this volume. Computationally, they are iterative and typically require modified MAP inference at each parameter update step, which is computationally efficient for many energy models often used in practice.

In the probabilistic setting that is the focus of this chapter, maximum (penalized) likelihood (ML) is the natural criterion for learning the weights. Given the labeled training set $\{\boldsymbol{x}_k\}_{k=1}^K$, we fit the parameters $\boldsymbol{\theta}$ by maximizing the Gibbs log-likelihood function $L_G(\boldsymbol{\theta}) = -\log Z(\boldsymbol{\theta}) - (1/K)\sum_{k=1}^K E(\boldsymbol{x}_k;\boldsymbol{\theta})$, possibly also including an extra penalty term regularizing the weights. For fully observed models and energies of the form (7.1), the log-likelihood is a concave function of the weights $\boldsymbol{\theta}$, and thus the global maximum can be found by gradient ascent (Hinton and Sejnowski, 1983; Zhu et al., 1998; Koller and Friedman, 2009). The gradient is $\partial L_G/\partial\theta_j = E_{\boldsymbol{\theta}}^G\{\phi_j(\boldsymbol{x})\} - E_D\{\phi_j(\boldsymbol{x})\}$. Here $E_{\boldsymbol{\theta}}^G\{\phi_j(\boldsymbol{x})\} \triangleq \sum_{\boldsymbol{x}} f_G(\boldsymbol{x};\boldsymbol{\theta})\phi_j(\boldsymbol{x}) = -\partial(\log Z)/\partial\theta_j$ and $E_D\{\phi_j(\boldsymbol{x})\} \triangleq (1/K)\sum_{k=1}^K \phi_j(\boldsymbol{x}_k)$ are, respectively, the expected sufficient statistics under the Gibbs model and the data distribution. Upon convergence, $E_{\boldsymbol{\theta}}^G\{\phi_j(\boldsymbol{x})\} = E_D\{\phi_j(\boldsymbol{x})\}$. Thus, ML estimation of the Gibbs model can be thought of as moment matching: random samples drawn from the trained model reproduce the sufficient statistics observed in the training data.

The chief computational challenge in ML parameter learning of the Gibbs model lies in estimating the model sufficient statistics $E_{\boldsymbol{\theta}}^G\{\phi_j(\boldsymbol{x})\}$. Note that this inference step needs to be repeated at each parameter update step. The model sufficient statistics can be computed exactly in tree-structured (and low tree-width) graphs, but in general graphs, one needs to resort to MCMC techniques for approximating them (Hinton and Sejnowski, 1983; Zhu et al., 1998; Hinton, 2002), an avenue considered too costly for many computer vision applications. Deterministic approximations such as variational techniques or loopy sum-product belief propagation do exist, but often they are not accurate enough. Simplified criteria such as pseudo-likelihood (Besag, 1975) have been applied as substitutes to ML, but they can sometimes give results grossly different than ML.

Beyond model training, random sampling is useful in itself; it reveals what are typical instances of the model—what the model has in its "mind"—and in applications such as texture synthesis (Zhu et al., 1998). Further, we might be interested not only in the global minimum energy configuration but in the marginal densities or posterior means as well (Schmidt et al., 2010). In loopy graphs, these quantities are typically intractable to compute, the only viable way being through sampling. Our Perturb-and-MAP random field model is designed specifically so as to be amenable to rapid sampling.

7.3   Perturb-and-MAP for Gaussian and Sparse Continuous MRFs

Gaussian Markov random fields (GMRFs) are an important MRF class describing continuous variables linked by quadratic potentials (Besag, 1974; Szeliski, 1990; Weiss and Freeman, 2001; Rue and Held, 2005). They are useful for modeling inherently Gaussian data and as building blocks for constructing more complex models.

7.3.1   Exact GMRF Sampling by Local Perturbations

We will be working with a GMRF defined by the energy function

$$E(\boldsymbol{x};\boldsymbol{\theta}) = \frac{1}{2}(\boldsymbol{F}\boldsymbol{x} - \boldsymbol{\mu}_0)^T \boldsymbol{\Sigma}_0^{-1}(\boldsymbol{F}\boldsymbol{x} - \boldsymbol{\mu}_0) = \frac{1}{2}\boldsymbol{x}^T \boldsymbol{J}\boldsymbol{x} - \boldsymbol{k}^T\boldsymbol{x} + (\text{const})\,, \quad (7.3)$$

where $\boldsymbol{J} = \boldsymbol{F}^T\boldsymbol{\Sigma}_0^{-1}\boldsymbol{F}$, $\boldsymbol{k} = \boldsymbol{F}^T\boldsymbol{\Sigma}_0^{-1}\boldsymbol{\mu}_0$. The energy can be cast in the generic inner product form of (7.1) by defining the parameters $\boldsymbol{\theta} = (\boldsymbol{k}, \text{vec}(\boldsymbol{J}))$ and features $\boldsymbol{\phi}(\boldsymbol{x}) = (-\boldsymbol{x}, \frac{1}{2}\text{vec}(\boldsymbol{x}\boldsymbol{x}^T))$. We assume a diagonal matrix $\boldsymbol{\Sigma}_0 = \text{Diag}(\Sigma_1, \dots, \Sigma_M)$, implying that the energy can be decomposed as a sum of M independent terms $E(\boldsymbol{x};\boldsymbol{\theta}) = \sum_{j=1}^{M} \frac{1}{2\Sigma_j}(\boldsymbol{f}_j^T\boldsymbol{x} - \mu_j)^2$, where $\boldsymbol{f}_j^T$ is the j-th row of the measurement matrix $\boldsymbol{F}$ and μ_j is the j-th entry of the vector $\boldsymbol{\mu}_0$.

The corresponding Gibbs distribution $f_G(\boldsymbol{x})$ is a multivariate Gaussian $\mathcal{N}(\boldsymbol{\mu}, \boldsymbol{\Sigma})$ with covariance matrix $\boldsymbol{\Sigma} = \boldsymbol{J}^{-1}$ and mean vector $\boldsymbol{\mu} = \boldsymbol{J}^{-1}\boldsymbol{k}$. The MAP estimate $\hat{\boldsymbol{x}} = \text{argmin}_{\boldsymbol{x}} \frac{1}{2}\boldsymbol{x}^T\boldsymbol{J}\boldsymbol{x} - \boldsymbol{k}^T\boldsymbol{x}$ under this Gaussian model coincides with the mean and amounts to solving the $N \times N$ linear system $\boldsymbol{J}\boldsymbol{\mu} = \boldsymbol{k}$. Solving this linear system with direct exact methods requires a Cholesky factorization of $\boldsymbol{J}$ whose complexity is $\mathcal{O}(N^2)$ for banded system matrices with tree-width $\mathcal{O}(\sqrt{N})$ arising in typical image analysis problems on 2-D grids. We can perform approximate MAP inference much faster using iterative techniques such as preconditioned conjugate gradients (Golub and Van Loan, 1996) or multigrid (Terzopoulos, 1988), whose complexity for many computer vision models is $\mathcal{O}(N^{3/2})$ or even $\mathcal{O}(N)$.

Standard algorithms for sampling from the GMRF also require a Cholesky factorization of $\boldsymbol{J}$ and thus have the same large time and memory complexity of direct system solvers. However, the following result shows that we can draw *exact* GMRF samples by Perturb-and-MAP:

Proposition 7.1. *Assume that we replace the quadratic potential mean $\boldsymbol{\mu}_0$ by its perturbed version $\tilde{\boldsymbol{\mu}}_0 \sim \mathcal{N}(\boldsymbol{\mu}_0, \boldsymbol{\Sigma}_0)$, followed by finding the MAP of the perturbed model $\tilde{\boldsymbol{x}} = \boldsymbol{F}^T\boldsymbol{\Sigma}_0^{-1}\tilde{\boldsymbol{\mu}}_0$. Then $\tilde{\boldsymbol{x}}$ is an exact sample from the original GMRF $\mathcal{N}(\boldsymbol{\mu}, \boldsymbol{\Sigma})$.*

Proof. Because $\tilde{\boldsymbol{\mu}}_0$ is Gaussian, $\tilde{\boldsymbol{x}} = \boldsymbol{J}^{-1}\boldsymbol{F}^T\boldsymbol{\Sigma}_0^{-1}\tilde{\boldsymbol{\mu}}_0$ also follows a multivariate Gaussian distribution. It has mean $E\{\tilde{\boldsymbol{x}}\} = \boldsymbol{\mu}$ and covariance matrix $E\{(\tilde{\boldsymbol{x}} - \boldsymbol{\mu})(\tilde{\boldsymbol{x}} - \boldsymbol{\mu})^T\} = \boldsymbol{J}^{-1}\boldsymbol{F}^T\boldsymbol{\Sigma}_0^{-1}\boldsymbol{F}\boldsymbol{J}^{-1} = \boldsymbol{\Sigma}$. $\square$

It is noteworthy that the algorithm only involves locally perturbing each potential separately, $\tilde{\mu}_j \sim \mathcal{N}(\mu_j, \Sigma_j)$, and turns any existing GMRF MAP algorithm into an effective random sampler.

As an example, we show in Figure 7.6 an image inpainting application in which we fill in the flat areas of an image given the values at its edges under a 2-D thin-membrane prior GMRF model (Terzopoulos, 1988; Szeliski, 1990; Malioutov et al., 2008), which involves pairwise quadratic potentials $V_{ij} = \frac{1}{2\Sigma}(x_i - x_j)^2$ between nearest neighbors connected as in Figure 7.5(b). We show both the posterior mean/MAP estimate and a random sample under the model, both computed in a fraction of a second by solving a Poisson equation by a $\mathcal{O}(N)$ multigrid solver originally developed for solving PDE problems (Terzopoulos, 1988).

Figure 7.6: Reconstructing an image from its value on edges under a nearest-neighbor GMRF model. (a) Masked image. (b) Posterior mean/MAP estimate $\hat{\boldsymbol{x}}$. (c) Random sample $\tilde{\boldsymbol{x}}$.

7.3.2   Efficient MCMC Inference in Conditionally Gaussian Models

Gaussian models have proven inadequate for image modeling as they fail to capture important aspects of natural image statistics, such as the heavy tails in marginal histograms of linear filter responses. Nevertheless, much richer statistical image tools can be built if we also incorporate into our models latent variables or allow nonlinear interactions between multiple Gaussian fields, and thus the GMRF sampling technique we describe here is useful within this wider setting (Weiss and Freeman, 2007; Roth and Black, 2009; Papandreou et al., 2008).

In Papandreou and Yuille (2010), we discuss the integration of our GMRF sampling algorithm in a block-Gibbs sampling context, where the conditionally Gaussian continuous variables and the conditionally independent latent variables are sampled alternately. The most straightforward way to capture the heavy tailed histograms of natural images is to model each filter response with a Gaussian mixture expert, thus using a single discrete assignment variable at each factor (Papandreou et al., 2008; Schmidt et al., 2010). We show in Figure 7.7 an image inpainting example following this approach, in which a wavelet domain hidden Markov tree model is used (Papandreou et al., 2008).

Figure 7.7: Filling in missing image parts from the ancient wall paintings of Thera (Papandreou, 2009). Image inpainting with a wavelet domain model and block Gibbs sampling inference (Papandreou et al., 2008).

Efficient GMRF Perturb-and-MAP sampling can also be used in conjunction with Gaussian scale mixture (GSM) models for which the latent scale variable is continuous (Andrews and Mallows, 1974). We demonstrate this in the context of Bayesian signal restoration by sampling from the posterior distribution under a total variation (TV) prior, employing the GSM characterization of the Laplacian density. We show in Figure 7.8 an example of 1-D signal restoration under a TV signal model. The standard MAP estimator features characteristic staircasing artifacts (Nikolova, 2007). Block Gibbs sampling from the posterior distribution allows us to efficiently approximate the posterior mean estimator, which outperforms the MAP estimator in terms of mean square error or peak signal-to-noise (PSNR). Although individual posterior random samples are worse in terms of PSNR, they accurately capture the micro-texture of the original clean signal.

7.3.3 Variational Inference for Bayesian Compressed Sensing

Variational inference is increasingly popular for probabilistic inference in sparse models, providing the basis for many modern Bayesian compressed sensing methods. At a high level, variational techniques in this setting typi-

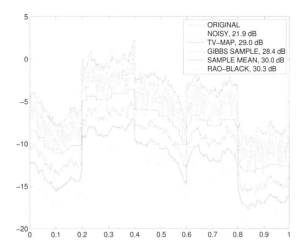

Figure 7.8: Signal denoising under a total variation prior model and alternative estimation criteria. From top to bottom, the graphs show: (a) Original latent clean signal, synthesized by adding Laplacian noise increments to a piece-wise constant signal. (b) Noisy version of the signal, corrupted by Gaussian i.i.d. noise. (c) MAP estimator under a TV prior model. (d) A single sample from the TV posterior Gibbs distribution. (e) Posterior mean estimator obtained by averaging multiple samples. (f) Rao-Blackwellized posterior mean estimator (Papandreou and Yuille, 2010).

cally approximate the true posterior distribution with a parameterized Gaussian, which allows closed-form computations. Inference amounts to adjusting the variational parameters to make the fit as tight as possible (Wainwright and Jordan, 2008). Mostly related to our work are Attias (1999), Lewicki and Sejnowski (2000), Girolami (2001), Chantas et al. (2010), Seeger and Nickisch (2011a). Multiple alternative criteria exist to quantify the fit quality, giving rise to approximations such as variational bounding (Jordan et al., 1999), mean field or ensemble learning, and expectation propagation (EP) (Minka, 2001), as well as different iterative algorithms for optimizing each specific criterion (see Bishop (2006), Palmer et al. (2005), for further discussions about the relations among these variational approaches).

All variational algorithms we study in this chapter are of a double-loop nature, requiring Gaussian variance estimation in the outer loop and sparse point estimation in the inner loop (Seeger and Nickisch, 2011a, 2011b; van Gerven et al., 2010). The ubiquity of the Gaussian variance computation routine is not coincidental. Variational approximations try to capture uncertainty in the intractable posterior distribution along the directions of sparsity. These are naturally encoded in the covariance matrix of the proxy Gaussian variational approximation. Marginal Gaussian variance computation is also required in automatic relevance determination algorithms for sparse Bayesian learning (MacKay, 1992) and relevance vector machine training

(Tipping, 2001); the methods we review here could also be applied in that context.

It turns out that variance computation in large-scale Gaussian models is computationally challenging, and a host of sophisticated techniques have been developed for this purpose, which often only apply to restricted classes of models (Schneider and Willsky, 2001; Sudderth et al., 2004; Malioutov et al., 2008).

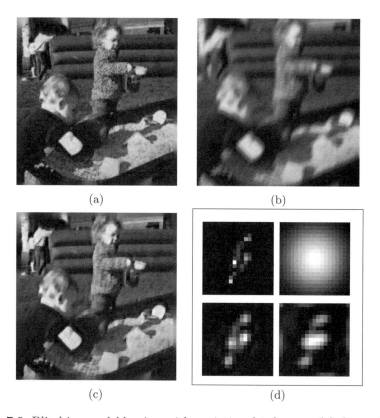

(a)

(b)

(c)

(d)

Figure 7.9: Blind image deblurring with variational inference. (a) Ground truth. (b) Blurred input image. (c) Estimated clean image. (d) Ground truth (top-left) and iteratively estimated blur kernel (clock-wise, starting from a diffuse Gaussian profile at top-right).

Perturb-and-MAP allows us to efficiently sample from the GMRF model and thus makes it practical to employ the generic sample-based estimator for computing Gaussian variances. More specifically, we repeatedly draw K independent GMRF samples $\{\tilde{x}_k\}_{k=1}^{K}$ from which we can estimate the covariance matrix

$$\hat{\boldsymbol{\Sigma}} = \frac{1}{K} \sum_{k=1}^{K} (\tilde{\boldsymbol{x}}_k - \boldsymbol{\mu})(\tilde{\boldsymbol{x}}_k - \boldsymbol{\mu})^T .$$ (7.4)

This Monte-Carlo estimator, whose accuracy is independent of the problem size, is particularly attractive if only relatively rough variance estimates suffice, as is often the case in practice. We show in Figure 7.9 an example of applying this variational Bayesian estimation methodology in the problem of blind image deblurring (Papandreou and Yuille, 2011b).

7.4 Perturb-and-MAP for MRFs with Discrete Labels

7.4.1 Introduction

We now turn our attention to MRFs on discrete labels, which go back to the classic Ising and Potts models in statistical physics. Discrete-valued MRFs offer a natural and sound probabilistic modeling framework for a host of image analysis and computer vision problems involving discrete labels, such as image segmentation and labeling, texture synthesis, and deep learning (Besag, 1974; Geman and Geman, 1984; Zhu et al., 1998; Hinton, 2002; Koller and Friedman, 2009). Exact probabilistic inference and maximum likelihood model parameter fitting is intractable in general MRFs defined on 2-D domains, and one has to employ random sampling schemes to perform these tasks (Geman and Geman, 1984; Hinton, 2002).

Recent powerful discrete energy minimization algorithms such as graph cuts, linear programming relaxations, or loopy belief propagation (Boykov et al., 2001; Kolmogorov and Zabih, 2004; Kolmogorov and Rother, 2007; Koller and Friedman, 2009) can efficiently find or well approximate the most probable (MAP) configuration for certain important classes of MRFs. They have had a particularly big impact on computer vision; for a recent overview, see the volume edited by Blake et al. (2011).

Our work on the Perturb-and-MAP discrete random field model has been motivated by the exact GMRF sampling algorithm described in Section 7.3. While the underlying mathematics and methods are completely different in the discrete setup, we have shown in Papandreou and Yuille (2011a) that the intuition of local perturbations followed by global optimization can also lead to powerful sampling algorithms for discrete label MRFs. Subsequent work by other groups, summarized in Section 7.5, has extended our results and explored related directions.

A surprising finding of our study has been the identification of a perturbation process from extreme value statistics, which turns the Perturb-and-MAP model identical to its Gibbs counterpart even in the discrete setting. Although this perturbation is too expensive to be applicable in large-scale models, it nevertheless suggests low-order perturbations that result in perturbed energies that are effectively as easy to minimize as the original unperturbed one while producing high-quality random samples.

Perturb-and-MAP endows discrete energy minimization algorithms such as graph cuts with probabilistic capabilities that allow them to support qualitatively new computer vision applications. We illustrate some of them in image segmentation and scene labeling experiments experiments. First, drawing several posterior samples from the model allows us to compute posterior marginal probabilities and quantify our confidence in the MAP solution. Second, efficient random sampling allows learning of MRF or CRF parameters using the moment matching rule, in which the model parameters are updated until the generated samples reproduce the (weighted) sufficient statistics of the observed data.

7.4.2   Model Definition and Weight Space Geometry

We assume a deterministic energy function that takes the inner product form of (7.1) (i.e., $E(\boldsymbol{x}; \boldsymbol{\theta}) = \langle \boldsymbol{\theta}, \boldsymbol{\phi}(\boldsymbol{x}) \rangle$) with x_i taking values in a discrete label set $\mathcal{L}$. A Perturb-and-MAP random sample is obtained by $\tilde{\boldsymbol{x}} = \operatorname{argmin}_{\boldsymbol{x}} E(\boldsymbol{x}; \boldsymbol{\theta} + \boldsymbol{\epsilon})$, where $\boldsymbol{\epsilon}$ is a real-valued random additive parameter perturbation vector. By construction, we can efficiently draw exact one-shot samples from the Perturb-and-MAP model by solving an energy minimization problem.

Thanks to the inner product form of the energy function, the Perturb-and-MAP model has a simple geometric interpretation in the parameter space. In particular, a state $\boldsymbol{x} \in \mathcal{L}^N$ will be minimizing the deterministic energy if, and only if, $E(\boldsymbol{x}; \boldsymbol{\theta}) \leq E(\boldsymbol{q}; \boldsymbol{\theta}), \forall \boldsymbol{q} \in \mathcal{L}^N$. This set of $|\mathcal{L}|^N$ linear inequalities defines a polyhedron $\mathcal{P}_{\boldsymbol{x}}$ in the weight space

$$\mathcal{P}_{\boldsymbol{x}} = \{\boldsymbol{\theta} \in \mathbb{R}^M : \langle \boldsymbol{\theta}, \boldsymbol{\phi}(\boldsymbol{x}) - \boldsymbol{\phi}(\boldsymbol{q}) \rangle \leq 0, \forall \boldsymbol{q} \in \mathcal{L}^N \} . \tag{7.5}$$

Actually, $\mathcal{P}_{\boldsymbol{x}}$ is a polyhedral cone (Boyd and Vandenberghe, 2004) because $\boldsymbol{\theta} \in \mathcal{P}_{\boldsymbol{x}}$ implies $\alpha \boldsymbol{\theta} \in \mathcal{P}_{\boldsymbol{x}}$, for all $\alpha \geq 0$. These polyhedral cones are dually related to the marginal polytope $\mathcal{M} = \operatorname{conv}(\{\boldsymbol{\phi}(\boldsymbol{x})\}, \boldsymbol{x} \in \mathcal{L}^N)$, as illustrated in Figure 7.10 (see Wainwright and Jordan (2008), for background on the marginal polytope). The polyhedra $\mathcal{P}_{\boldsymbol{x}}$ partition the weight space $\mathbb{R}^M$ into regions of influence of each discrete state $\boldsymbol{x} \in \mathcal{L}^N$. Under the Perturb-and-MAP model, $\boldsymbol{x}$ will be assigned to a particular state $\boldsymbol{x}$ if, and only

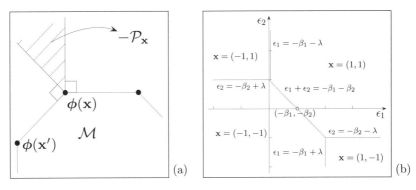

Figure 7.10: Perturb-and-MAP geometry. (a) The polyhedral cones $\mathcal{P}_{\boldsymbol{x}}$ are dual to the corner cones of the marginal polytope $\mathcal{M}$. (b) The Ising P-M model with $N = 2$ nodes and perturbations only in the unary terms, $\tilde{\beta}_i = \beta_i + \epsilon_i$, for parameter values $\beta_1 = -1$, $\beta_2 = 0$, and $\lambda = 1$. The $\boldsymbol{\epsilon}$-space is split into four polyhedra, with $\boldsymbol{x}(\boldsymbol{\epsilon}) = \boldsymbol{x}$ iff $\boldsymbol{\epsilon} \in \mathcal{P}_{\boldsymbol{x}} - \boldsymbol{\theta}$.

if, $\boldsymbol{\theta} + \boldsymbol{\epsilon} \in \mathcal{P}_{\boldsymbol{x}}$ or, equivalently, $\boldsymbol{\epsilon} \in \mathcal{P}_{\boldsymbol{x}} - \boldsymbol{\theta} \triangleq \{\boldsymbol{\epsilon} \in \mathbb{R}^M : \boldsymbol{\theta} + \boldsymbol{\epsilon} \in \mathcal{P}_{\boldsymbol{x}}\}$. In other words, if a specific instantiation of the perturbation $\boldsymbol{\epsilon}$ falls in the shifted polyhedron $\mathcal{P}_{\boldsymbol{x}} - \boldsymbol{\theta}$, then the Perturb-and-MAP model generates $\boldsymbol{x}$ as a sample.

We assume that perturbations are drawn from a density $f_{\boldsymbol{\epsilon}}(\boldsymbol{\epsilon})$, which does not depend on the parameters $\boldsymbol{\theta}$. The probability mass of a state $\boldsymbol{x}$ under the Perturb-and-MAP model is then the weighted volume of the corresponding shifted polyhedron under the perturbation measure

$$f_{PM}(\boldsymbol{x}; \boldsymbol{\theta}) = \int_{\mathcal{P}_{\boldsymbol{x}} - \boldsymbol{\theta}} f_{\boldsymbol{\epsilon}}(\boldsymbol{\epsilon}) d\boldsymbol{\epsilon}, \tag{7.6}$$

which is the counterpart of the Gibbs density in (7.2). It is intractable (NP-hard) to compute the volume of general polyhedra in a high-dimensional space (see e.g., Ben-Tal et al., 2009, Chapter 2.2). However, for the class of perturbed energy functions that can be globally minimized efficiently, we can readily draw exact samples from the Perturb-and-MAP model without ever explicitly evaluating the integrals in (7.6).

7.4.3 Example: The Perturb-and-MAP Ising model

Let us illustrate these ideas by considering the Perturb-and-MAP version of the classic Ising model. The Ising energy over the discrete "spins" $x_i \in \{-1, 1\}$ is defined as

$$E(\boldsymbol{x}; \boldsymbol{\theta}) = \frac{-1}{2} \sum_{i=1}^{N} \left(\beta_i x_i + \sum_{i'=i+1}^{N} \lambda_{ii'} x_i x_{i'} \right), \tag{7.7}$$

where β_i is the external field strength ($\beta_i > 0$ favors $x_i = 1$) and $\lambda_{ii'}$ is the coupling strength, with attractive coupling $\lambda_{ii'} > 0$ favoring the same spin for x_i and $x_{i'}$. This energy function can be written in the standard inner product form of (7.1) with $\boldsymbol{\theta} = (\{\beta_i\}, \{\lambda_{ii'}\})^T$ and $\boldsymbol{\phi}(\boldsymbol{x}) = \frac{-1}{2}(\{x_i\}, \{x_i x_{i'}\})^T$. The MRF defined by (7.2) is the Ising Gibbs random field.

Defining a Perturb-and-MAP Ising random field requires specifying the parameter perturbation density. In this example, we leave the binary term parameters $\lambda_{ii'}$ intact and only perturb the unary term parameters β_i. In particular, for each unary factor, we set $\tilde{\beta}_i = \beta_i + \epsilon_i$, with ϵ_i i.i.d. samples from the logistic distribution with density $l(z) = \frac{1}{4}\operatorname{sech}^2(\frac{z}{2})$. This corresponds to the order-1 Gumbel perturbation we discuss in Section 7.4.5 and ensures that if a particular node x_i is completely isolated, then it will follow the same Bernoulli distribution $\Pr\{x_i = 1\} = 1/(1 + e^{-\beta_i})$ as in the Gibbs case. The ϵ-space geometry in the case of two labels ($N = 2$) under the Ising energy $E(\boldsymbol{x}; \boldsymbol{\theta}) = -0.5(\beta_1 x_1 + \beta_2 x_2 + \lambda x_1 x_2)$ for a specific value of the parameters $\boldsymbol{\theta}$ and perturbations only to unary terms is depicted in Figure 7.10.

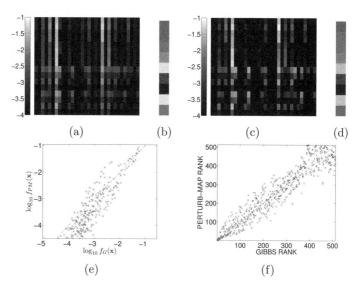

(a)   (b)   (c)   (d)

(e)   (f)

Figure 7.11: We compare the Gibbs (exact computation) and the Perturb-and-MAP (10^6 Monte-Carlo runs) models induced from an Ising energy on 3×3 grid, with β_i and $\lambda_{ii'}$ i.i.d. from $\mathcal{N}(0, 1)$. (a) Gibbs log-probabilities $\log_{10} f_G(\boldsymbol{x})$ for each of the 2^9 states, arranged as a $2^5 \times 2^4$ matrix. (b) Gibbs marginal probabilities $f_G(x_i = 1)$ for each of the nine nodes. (c) Perturb-and-MAP log-probabilities $\log_{10} f_{PM}(\boldsymbol{x})$. (d) Perturb-and-MAP marginal probabilities $f_{PM}(x_i = 1)$. (e) Scatter-plot of state log probabilities under the two models. (f) Scatter-plot of states ranked by their probabilities under the two models.

We compare in Figure 7.11 the Gibbs and Perturb-and-MAP models for a small-scale Ising energy involving nine variables on a 3×3 grid with 4-nearest neighbors connectivity and randomly generated parameters. The probability landscape (i.e., the probabilities of each of the 2^9 states) looks quite similar under the two models (see Figure 7.11(a) and (c)). The same holds for the corresponding marginal probabilities, shown in Figure 7.11(b) and (d). To further compare the probability landscape under the two models, we show a scatter plot of their log probabilities in Figure 7.11(e), as well as a scatter plot of the states ranked by their probability in Figure 7.11(f). Perturb-and-MAP in this example is particularly close to Gibbs for the leading (most probable) states but tends to underestimate the least probable states.

7.4.4   Parameter Estimation by Moment Matching

We would like to estimate the parameters $\boldsymbol{\theta}$ of the Perturb-and-MAP model from a labeled training set $\{\boldsymbol{x}_k\}_{k=1}^K$ by maximizing the log-likelihood

$$L_{PM}(\boldsymbol{\theta}) = (1/K) \sum_{k=1}^{K} \log f_{PM}(\boldsymbol{x}_k; \boldsymbol{\theta}) . \tag{7.8}$$

We can design the perturbations so the Perturb-and-MAP log-likelihood L_{PM} is a concave function of $\boldsymbol{\theta}$. This ensures that the likelihood landscape is well behaved and allows the use of local search techniques for parameter estimation, exactly as in the Gibbs case. Specifically, the following result is shown in Papandreou and Yuille (2011a):

Proposition 7.2. *If the perturbations $\boldsymbol{\epsilon}$ are drawn from a log-concave density $f_{\boldsymbol{\epsilon}}(\boldsymbol{\epsilon})$, then the log-likelihood $L_{PM}(\boldsymbol{\theta})$ is a concave function of the energy parameters $\boldsymbol{\theta}$.*

The family of log-concave distributions (Boyd and Vandenberghe, 2004) (i.e., $\log f_{\boldsymbol{\epsilon}}(\boldsymbol{\epsilon})$ is a concave function of $\boldsymbol{\epsilon}$) includes the Gaussian, the logistic, and other commonly used distributions.

The gradient of $L_{PM}(\boldsymbol{\theta})$ is in general hard to compute. Motivated by the parameter update formula in the Gibbs case from Section 7.2.2, we opt for the moment matching learning rule, $\theta_j(t+1) = \theta_j(t) + r(t)\Delta\theta_j$, where

$$\Delta\theta_j = E_{\boldsymbol{\theta}}^{PM}\{\phi_j(\boldsymbol{x})\} - E_D\{\phi_j(\boldsymbol{x})\} . \tag{7.9}$$

Here $E_{\boldsymbol{\theta}}^{PM}\{\phi_j(\boldsymbol{x})\} \triangleq \sum_{\boldsymbol{x}} f_{PM}(\boldsymbol{x}; \boldsymbol{\theta})\phi_j(\boldsymbol{x})$ is the expected sufficient statistic under the Perturb-and-MAP model for the current parameter values $\boldsymbol{\theta}$, which we can efficiently estimate by drawing exact samples from it. We typically adjust the learning rate by a Robbins-Monro type schedule (e.g.,

$r(t) = r_1/(r_2 + t)$). Figure 7.12 illustrates parameter learning by moment matching in a spatially homogenous Ising energy model.

While the above moment matching rule was originally motivated by analogy to the Gibbs case (Papandreou and Yuille, 2011a), its fixed points do not need to be exact minima of the Perturb-and-MAP log-likelihood (7.8). Subsequent work has shown that moment matching performs gradient ascent for an objective function that lower bounds the Gibbs likelihood function (Hazan and Jaakkola, 2012). Moreover, this lower bound turns out to be concave even for perturbation densities $f_\epsilon(\epsilon)$ that are not log-concave.

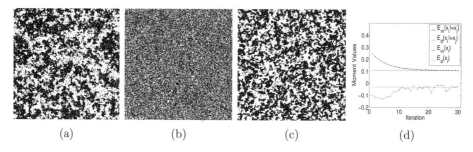

(a)   (b)   (c)   (d)

Figure 7.12: Perturb-and-MAP Ising random field parameter learning. The two model parameters, the global coupling strength λ and field strength β, are fitted by moment matching. (a) Gibbs Ising model sample used as training image. (b) Perturb-and-MAP Ising sample at initial parameter values. (c) Perturb-and-MAP Ising sample at final parameter values. (d) Model moments as they converge to training data moments.

7.4.5   Perturb-and-MAP Perturbation Design

Although any perturbation density induces a legitimate Perturb-and-MAP model, it is desirable to carefully design it so the Perturb-and-MAP model approximates as closely as possible the corresponding Gibbs MRF. The Gibbs MRF has important structural properties that are not automatically satisfied by the Perturb-and-MAP model under arbitrary perturbations: (a) Unlike the Gibbs MRF, the Perturb-and-MAP model is not guaranteed to respect the state ranking induced by the energy (i.e., $E(\boldsymbol{x}) \leq E(\boldsymbol{x}')$ does not necessarily imply $f_{PM}(\boldsymbol{x}) \geq f_{PM}(\boldsymbol{x}')$; see Figure 7.11(f)). (b) The Markov dependence structure of the Gibbs MRF follows directly from the support of the potentials $\phi_j(\boldsymbol{x})$, while the Perturb-and-MAP might give rise to longer-range probabilistic dependencies. (c) The maximum entropy distribution under moment constraints $E\{\phi_j(\boldsymbol{x})\} = \bar{\phi}_j$ has the Gibbs form; the Perturb-and-MAP model trained by moment matching can reproduce these moments but will in general have smaller entropy than its Gibbs counterpart.

The *Gumbel* distribution arising in extreme value theory (Steutel and Van Harn, 2004) turns out to play an important role in our effort to design a perturbation mechanism that yields a Perturb-and-MAP model closely resembling the Gibbs MRF. It is a continuous univariate distribution with log-concave density $g(z) = \exp(-(-z + e^z))$. We can efficiently draw independent Gumbel variates by transforming standard uniform samples by $u \to \log(-\log(u))$. The Gumbel density naturally fits into the Perturb-and-MAP model, thanks to the following key Lemma (see also Kuzmin and Warmuth, 2005):

Lemma 7.3. *Let* $(\theta_1, \ldots, \theta_m)$, *with* $\theta_n \in \mathbb{R}$, $n = 1, \ldots, m$. *We additively perturb them by* $\tilde{\theta}_n = \theta_n + \epsilon_n$, *with* ϵ_n *i.i.d. zero-mode Gumbel samples. Then:*

(a) The minimum of the perturbed parameters $\tilde{\theta}_{min} \triangleq \min_{n=1:m}\{\tilde{\theta}_n\}$ *follows a Gumbel distribution with mode* θ_0, *where* $e^{-\theta_0} = \sum_{n=1}^{m} e^{-\theta_n}$.

(b) The probability that $\tilde{\theta}_n$ *is the minimum value is* $\Pr\{\mathrm{argmin}(\tilde{\theta}_1, \ldots, \tilde{\theta}_m) = n\} = e^{-\theta_n}/e^{-\theta_0}$.

Note that $\theta_0 = -\log(\sum_{n=1}^{m} e^{-\theta_n}) = -\log Z$. This connection is pursued in detail by Hazan and Jaakkola (2012), which develops a Perturb-and-MAP-based approximation to the partition function.

We can use this Lemma to construct a Perturb-and-MAP model that exactly replicates the Gibbs distribution as follows. The Gibbs random field on N sites x_i, $i = 1, \ldots, N$, each allowed to take a value from the discrete label set $\mathcal{L}$, can be considered as a discrete distribution with $|\mathcal{L}|^N$ states. This can be made explicit if we enumerate $\{\boldsymbol{x}_j, j = 1, \ldots, \bar{M} = |\mathcal{L}|^N\}$ all the states and consider the maximal equivalent re-parameterization of (7.1)

$$\bar{E}(\boldsymbol{x}; \bar{\boldsymbol{\theta}}) \triangleq \langle \bar{\boldsymbol{\theta}}, \bar{\boldsymbol{\phi}}(\boldsymbol{x}) \rangle = \langle \boldsymbol{\theta}, \boldsymbol{\phi}(\boldsymbol{x}) \rangle, \qquad (7.10)$$

where $\bar{\theta}_j = E(\boldsymbol{x}_j; \boldsymbol{\theta}) = \langle \boldsymbol{\theta}, \boldsymbol{\phi}(\boldsymbol{x}_j) \rangle$, $j = 1, \ldots, \bar{M}$, is the *fully expanded* potential table and $\bar{\phi}_j(\boldsymbol{x})$ is the indicator function of the state $\boldsymbol{x}_j$ (i.e., equals 1 if $\boldsymbol{x} = \boldsymbol{x}_j$ and 0 otherwise). Using Lemma 7.3, we can show:

Proposition 7.4. *If we perturb each entry of the fully expanded* $\mathcal{L}^N$ *potential table with i.i.d. Gumbel noise samples* $\epsilon_j, j = 1, \ldots, \bar{M}$, *then the Perturb-and-MAP and Gibbs models coincide (i.e.,* $f_{PM}(\boldsymbol{x}; \boldsymbol{\theta}) = f_G(\boldsymbol{x}; \boldsymbol{\theta})$*).*

This order-N perturbation is not practically applicable when N is large because it independently perturbs all $\bar{M} = |\mathcal{L}|^N$ entries of the fully expanded potential table and effectively destroys the local Markov structure of the energy function, rendering it too hard to minimize. Nevertheless, it shows that it is possible to design a Perturb-and-MAP model that exactly replicates the Gibbs MRF.

In practice, we employ low-order Gumbel perturbations. In our simplest order-1 design, we only add Gumbel noise to the unary potential tables. More specifically, for an energy function $E(\boldsymbol{x}) = \sum_{i=1}^{N} V_i(x_i) + \sum_j V_j(\boldsymbol{x}_j)$, which includes potentials $V_i(x_i)$ of order-1 and potentials $V_j(\boldsymbol{x}_j)$ of order-2 or higher, we add i.i.d. Gumbel noise to each of the $|\mathcal{L}|$ entries of each order-1 potential while leaving the higher-order potentials intact. This yields perturbed energies that are effectively as easy to minimize as the original unperturbed one while producing random samples closely resembling Gibbs MRF samples. We can improve the Perturb-and-MAP sample quality by Gumbel perturbations of order-2 or higher as described in Papandreou and Yuille (2011a). However, higher-order perturbations typically make the perturbed energy minimization problem harder to solve.

7.4.6   Applications and Experiments

We present experiments with the Perturb-and-MAP model applied to image segmentation and scene labeling.

Our *interactive image segmentation* experiments have been performed on the Grabcut data set, which includes human annotated ground truth segmentations (Rother et al., 2004). The task is to segment a foreground object given a relatively tight tri-map imitating user input obtained by a lasso or pen tool.

In our implementation, we closely follow the CRF formulation of Rother et al. (2011), using the same parameters for defining the image-based CRF terms and considering pixel interactions in an 8-neighborhood. We used our Perturb-and-MAP sampling algorithm with order-2 Gumbel perturbation and QPBO optimization (Kolmogorov and Rother, 2007) to learn the weights of the potentials—five weights in total, one for the unary and one for each of the four pairwise connections of the center pixel with its S, E, NE, SE neighbors. Using these parameters, we obtained a classification error rate of 5.6% with the global MAP decision rule. This is similar to the best results attainable with the particular CRF model and hand-tuned weights.

In Figure 7.13, we illustrate the ability of the Perturb-and-MAP model to produce soft segmentation maps. The soft segmentation map (average over 20 posterior samples) gives a qualitatively accurate estimate of the segmentation uncertainty, which could potentially be useful in guiding user interaction in an interactive segmentation application.

We next consider an application of Perturb-and-MAP random fields in *scene layout labeling* (Hoiem et al., 2007). We use the tiered layout model

Figure 7.13: Interactive image segmentation results on the Grabcut data set. Parameters learned by Perturb-and-MAP moment matching. (a) Original image. (b) Least energy MAP solution. (c) Soft Perturb-and-MAP segmentation. (d) The corresponding segmentation mask.

of Felzenszwalb and Veksler (2010), which allows exact global inference by efficient dynamic programming (Felzenszwalb and Veksler, 2010). The model has a relatively large number of parameters, making it difficult to hand tune. Training them with the proposed techniques illustrates our ability to effectively learn model parameters from labeled data.

We closely follow the evaluation approach of Felzenszwalb and Veksler (2010) in setting up the experiment. We use the data set of 300 outdoor images (and the standard cross-validation splits into training/test sets) with ground truth from Hoiem et al. (2007). Similarly to Felzenszwalb and Veksler (2010), we use five labels: T (sky), B (ground), L (facing left), R (facing right) and C (front facing), where the last three labels denote the middle region. We do not include the classes "porous" and "solid." The unary scores are produced using classifiers that we trained using the data set and software provided by Hoiem et al. (2007) following the standard five-fold cross-validation protocol.

We first fit the tiered scene model parameters (pairwise compatibility tables between the different classes) on the training data using Perturb-and-MAP moment matching (order-1 Gumbel perturbation). Weights are initialized as Potts CRF potentials and refined by moment matching rules. We separated the training set in batches of 10 images each and stopped after 50 epochs over the training set. We have measured the performance of the trained model in terms of average accuracy on the test set. We have tried two decision criteria-MAP (least energy configuration) and marginal MODE (i.e., assign each pixel to the label that appears most frequently in 20 random Perturb-And-Map conditional samples from the model)-obtaining accuracy

82.7% and 82.6%, respectively. Our results are better than the unary-only baseline mean accuracy of 82.1% (Hoiem et al., 2007), and the MAP and MODE results of 82.1% and 81.8%, respectively, that we obtained with the hand-set weights of Felzenszwalb and Veksler (2010).

In Figure 7.14, we show some indicative examples of different scene layout labelings obtained by the unary-only, the tiered MAP, and the Perturb-and-MAP models. The uncertainty of the solution is indicated by entropy maps. The marginal mode and entropies shown are Monte Carlo estimates using 20 Perturb-and-MAP samples.

Figure 7.14: Tiered scene labeling results with pairwise potentials learned by our Perturb-and-MAP moment matching algorithm. Left to right: image; unary-only MAP; tiered MAP; one tiered Perturb-and-MAP sample; tiered Perturb-and-MAP marginal mode; tiered Perturb-and-MAP marginal entropy.

7.5   Related Work and Recent Developments

To our knowledge, adding noise to the weighted edges of a graph so as to randomize the minimum energy configuration found by mincuts was first proposed by Blum et al. (2004) in the context of a submodular binary MRF energy arising in semi-supervised learning. Their goal was to break graph symmetries and allow the standard mincut algorithm to produce a different solution at each run. They interpret the relative frequency of each node, receiving one or the other label as a confidence score for binary classification. However, beyond randomizing the deterministic mincut algorithm, they do not study the implied probabilistic model as a stand-alone object or attempt to design the perturbation mechanism so as to approximate the corresponding Gibbs model. Indeed, the choice of perturbation distribution is not discussed at all in Blum et al. (2004).

Herding (Welling, 2009) builds a deterministic dynamical system on the model parameters designed so as to reproduce the data sufficient statistics, which is similar in spirit to the moment-matching algorithm we use for learning. However, herding is still not a probabilistic model and cannot summarize the data into a concise set of model parameters.

As pointed out to us by McAllester (2012), Perturb-and-MAP is closely related to PAC-Bayes (McAllester, 1998), and PAC-Bayesian theorems such as those in Germain et al. (2009) can be adapted to the Perturb-and-MAP setting. Model perturbations through the associated concept of stochastic Gibbs classifier play a key role to PAC-Bayesian theory, but PAC-Bayes typically aims at producing generalization guarantees for the deterministic classifier instead of capturing the uncertainty in the posterior distribution.

Averaging over multiple samples, Perturb-and-MAP allows efficiently estimating (sum-) marginal densities and thus quantifying the per-node solution uncertainty even in graphs with loops. Max-product belief propagation (Wainwright et al., 2005) and dynamic graph-cuts (Kohli and Torr, 2008) can compute max-marginals, which give some indication of the uncertainty in label assignments (Kohli and Torr, 2008) but cannot directly estimate marginal densities.

A number of different groups have followed up on our work (Papandreou and Yuille, 2011a) and further developed it in different directions. In their randomized optimum models, Tarlow et al. (2012) introduce variants of the Perturb-and-MAP model for discrete problems such as bi-partite matching and pursue maximum-likelihood learning of the model parameters using efficient MCMC algorithms.

The work in Hazan and Jaakkola (2012) has offered a better understanding of the Perturb-and-MAP moment-matching learning rule, showing that it optimizes a well-defined concave lower bound of the Gibbs likelihood function. Moreover, they have shown how Perturb-and-MAP can be used for computing approximations to the partition function. This connection relates Perturb-and-MAP more directly to the standard MRF inference problem.

Another related partition function estimation algorithm is proposed in Ermon et al. (2013). Interestingly, their method amounts to progressively introducing more random constraints, followed by energy minimization, in a randomized Constrain-and-MAP scheme.

While probabilistic random sampling allows one to explore alternative plausible solutions, Batra et al. (2012) propose to explicitly enforce diversity in generating a sequence of deterministic solutions.

The work in Roig et al. (2013) is an excellent demonstration of how uncertainty quantification can yield practical benefits in a semantic image labeling setting. They employ Perturb-and-MAP to identify on the fly image areas with ambiguous labeling and only compute expensive features when their addition is likely to considerably decrease labeling entropy.

7.6 Discussion

This chapter has presented an overview of the Perturb-and-MAP method, which turns established deterministic energy minimization algorithms into efficient probabilistic inference machines. This is a promising new direction with many important open questions for both theoretical and application-driven research: (1) An in-depth systematic comparison of Perturb-and-MAP and more established approximate inference techniques such as MCMC or Variational Bayes is still lacking. (2) So far, there is no clear characterization of the approximation quality of the Perturb-and-MAP model relative to its Gibbs counterpart and how perturbation design affects it. (3) Unlike MCMC, which allows trading off approximation quality with computation time by simply running the Markov chain for longer, there is currently no way to iteratively improve the quality of Perturb-and-MAP samples. (4) The modeling capacity of Perturb-and-MAP needs to be explored in several more computer vision and machine learning applications.

For further information and links to related works in this exciting emerging area, we point the reader to the NIPS Workshop on Perturbations, Optimization, and Statistics, organized in 2012 and 2013 by T. Hazan, D. Tarlow, A. Rakhlin, and the first author of this chapter.

Acknowledgments

Our work has been supported by the U.S. Office of Naval Research under MURI grant N000141010933; the NSF under award 0917141; the AFOSR under grant 9550-08-1-0489; and the Korean Ministry of Education, Science, and Technology under the Korean National Research Foundation WCU program R31-10008. We would like to thank M. Welling, M. Seeger, T. Hazan, D. Tarlow, D. McAllester, A. Montanari, S. Roth, I. Kokkinos, M. Raptis, M. Ranzato, and C. Lampert for their feedback at various stages of this work.

7.7 References

D. Andrews and C. Mallows. Scale mixtures of normal distributions. *J. of Royal Stat. Soc. (Series B)*, 36(1):99–102, 1974.

H. Attias. Independent factor analysis. *Neural Computation*, 11:803–851, 1999.

D. Batra, P. Yadollahpour, A. Guzman-Rivera, and G. Shakhnarovich. Diverse m-best solutions in Markov random fields. In *Proc. European Conf. on Computer Vision*, 2012.

A. Ben-Tal, L. El Ghaoui, and A. Nemirovski. *Robust Optimization*. Princeton University Press, 2009.

J. Besag. Spatial interaction and the statistical analysis of lattice systems. *J. of Royal Stat. Soc. (Series B)*, 36(2):192–236, 1974.

J. Besag. Statistical analysis of non-lattice data. *J. of Royal Stat. Soc. Series D (The Statistician)*, 24(3):179–195, 1975.

C. Bishop. *Pattern Recognition and Machine Learning*. Springer, 2006.

A. Blake, P. Kohli, and C. Rother, editors. *Markov Random Fields for Vision and Image Processing*. MIT Press, 2011.

A. Blum, J. Lafferty, M. Rwebangira, and R. Reddy. Semi-supervised learning using randomized mincuts. In *International Conference on Machine Learing (ICML)*, 2004.

S. Boyd and L. Vandenberghe. *Convex Optimization*. Cambridge University Press, 2004.

Y. Boykov, O. Veksler, and R. Zabih. Fast approximate energy minimization via graph cuts. *IEEE Trans. Pattern Anal. Mach. Intell.*, 23(11):1222–1239, 2001.

G. Chantas, N. Galatsanos, R. Molina, and A. Katsaggelos. Variational Bayesian image restoration with a product of spatially weighted total variation image priors. *IEEE Trans. Image Process.*, 19(2):351–362, 2010.

S. Ermon, C. Gomes, A. Sabharwal, and B. Selman. Taming the curse of dimensionality: Discrete integration by hashing and optimization. In *International Conference on Machine Learing (ICML)*, 2013.

P. Felzenszwalb and O. Veksler. Tiered scene labeling with dynamic programming. In *IEEE Computer Society Conference on Computer Vision and Pattern Recognition (CVPR)*, 2010.

S. Geman and D. Geman. Stochastic relaxation, Gibbs distributions, and the Bayesian restoration of images. *IEEE Trans. Pattern Anal. Mach. Intell.*, 6(6):721–741, 1984.

P. Germain, A. Lacasse, F. Laviolette, and M. Marchand. PAC-Bayesian learning of linear classifiers. In *International Conference on Machine Learing (ICML)*, 2009.

M. Girolami. A variational method for learning sparse and overcomplete representations. *Neural Computation*, 13:2517–2532, 2001.

G. Golub and C. Van Loan. *Matrix Computations*. John Hopkins University Press, 1996.

T. Hazan and T. Jaakkola. On the partition function and random maximum a-posteriori perturbations. In *International Conference on Machine Learing (ICML)*, 2012.

G. Hinton. Training products of experts by minimizing contrastive divergence. *Neural Computation*, 14(8):1771–1800, 2002.

G. Hinton and T. Sejnowski. Optimal perceptual inference. In *IEEE Computer Society Conference on Computer Vision and Pattern Recognition (CVPR)*, 1983.

D. Hoiem, A. Efros, and M. Hebert. Recovering surface layout from an image. *Int. J. of Comp. Vis.*, 75(1):151–172, 2007.

M. Jordan, J. Ghahramani, T. Jaakkola, and L. Saul. An introduction to variational methods for graphical models. *Machine Learning*, 37:183–233, 1999.

P. Kohli and P. Torr. Measuring uncertainty in graph cut solutions. *Computer Vision and Image Understanding*, 112(1):30–38, 2008.

D. Koller and N. Friedman. *Probabilistic Graphical Models*. MIT Press, 2009.

V. Kolmogorov and C. Rother. Minimizing non-submodular functions with graph cuts – a review. *IEEE Trans. Pattern Anal. Mach. Intell.*, 29(7):1274–1279, 2007.

V. Kolmogorov and R. Zabih. What energy functions can be minimized via graph cuts? *IEEE Trans. Pattern Anal. Mach. Intell.*, 26(2):147–159, 2004.

D. Kuzmin and M. K. Warmuth. Optimum follow the leader algorithm. In *Workshop on Computational Learning Theory (COLT)*, 2005.

Y. LeCun, S. Chopra, R. Hadsell, M. Ranzato, and F.-J. Huang. A tutorial on energy-based learning. In G. Bakir, T. Hofmann, B. Schölkopf, A. Smola, B. Taskar, and S. Vishwanathan, editors, *Predicting Structured Data*. MIT Press, 2007.

M. Lewicki and T. Sejnowski. Learning overcomplete representations. *Neural Computation*, 12:337–365, 2000.

D. MacKay. Bayesian interpolation. *Neural Computation*, 4(3):415–447, 1992.

D. Malioutov, J. Johnson, M. Choi, and A. Willsky. Low-rank variance approximation in GMRF models: Single and multiscale approaches. *IEEE Trans. Signal Process.*, 56(10):4621–4634, 2008.

D. McAllester. Some PAC-Bayesian theorems. In *Workshop on Computational Learning Theory (COLT)*, 1998.

D. McAllester. Connections between Perturb-and-MAP and PAC-Bayes. Personal communication, 2012.

T. Minka. Expectation propagation for approximate Bayesian inference. In *Uncertainty in Artificial Intelligence (UAI)*, 2001.

M. Nikolova. Model distortions in Bayesian MAP reconstruction. *Inv. Pr. and Imag.*, 1(2):399–422, 2007.

J. Palmer, D. Wipf, K. Kreutz-Delgado, and B. Rao. Variational EM algorithms for non-Gaussian latent variable models. In *Conference on Neural Information Processing Systems (NIPS)*, 2005.

G. Papandreou. *Image Analysis and Computer Vision: Theory and Applications in the Restoration of Ancient Wall Paintings*. PhD thesis, NTUA, School of ECE, 2009.

G. Papandreou and A. Yuille. Gaussian sampling by local perturbations. In *Conference on Neural Information Processing Systems (NIPS)*, 2010.

G. Papandreou and A. Yuille. Perturb-and-MAP random fields: Using discrete optimization to learn and sample from energy models. In *International Conference on Computer Vision (ICCV)*, 2011a.

G. Papandreou and A. Yuille. Efficient variational inference in large-scale Bayesian compressed sensing. In *Proc. IEEE Workshop on Information Theory in Computer Vision and Pattern Recognition (in conjunction with ICCV)*, 2011b.

G. Papandreou, P. Maragos, and A. Kokaram. Image inpainting with a wavelet domain hidden Markov tree model. In *Proc. IEEE Int. Conf. Acous., Speech, and Signal Processing*, 2008.

G. Roig, X. Boix, S. Ramos, R. de Nijs, and L. Van Gool. Active MAP inference in CRFs for efficient semantic segmentation. In *International Conference on Computer Vision (ICCV)*, 2013.

S. Roth and M. Black. Fields of experts. *Int. J. of Comp. Vis.*, 82(2):205–229, 2009.

C. Rother, V. Kolmogorov, and A. Blake. Grabcut: Interactive foreground extraction using iterated graph cuts. In *Proc. ACM Int. Conference on Computer Graphics and Interactive Techniques*, pages 309–314, 2004.

C. Rother, V. Kolmogorov, Y. Boykov, and A. Blake. Interactive foreground extraction using graph cut. In *Advances in Markov Random Fields for Vision and Image Processing*. MIT Press, 2011.

H. Rue and L. Held. *Gaussian Markov Random Fields. Theory and Applications*. Chapman & Hall, 2005.

U. Schmidt, Q. Gao, and S. Roth. A generative perspective on MRFs in low-level vision. In *IEEE Computer Society Conference on Computer Vision and Pattern Recognition (CVPR)*, 2010.

M. Schneider and A. Willsky. Krylov subspace estimation. *SIAM J. Sci. Comp.*, 22(5):1840–1864, 2001.

M. Seeger and H. Nickisch. Large scale Bayesian inference and experimental design for sparse linear models. *SIAM J. Imaging Sci.*, 4(1):166–199, 2011a.

M. Seeger and H. Nickisch. Fast convergent algorithms for expectation propagation approximate Bayesian inference. In *Proc. Int. Conf. on Artificial Intelligence and Statistics*, 2011b.

F. Steutel and K. Van Harn. *Infinite Divisibility of Probability Distributions on the Real Line*. Dekker, 2004.

E. Sudderth, M. Wainwright, and A. Willsky. Embedded trees: Estimation of Gaussian processes on graphs with cycles. *IEEE Trans. Signal Process.*, 52(11): 3136–3150, 2004.

R. Szeliski. Bayesian modeling of uncertainty in low-level vision. *Int. J. of Comp. Vis.*, 5(3):271–301, 1990.

M. Szummer, P. Kohli, and D. Hoiem. Learning CRFs using graph cuts. In *Proc. European Conf. on Computer Vision*, 2008.

D. Tarlow, R. Adams, and R. Zemel. Randomized optimum models for structured prediction. In *Proc. Int. Conf. on Artificial Intelligence and Statistics*, 2012.

B. Taskar, C. Guestrin, and D. Koller. Max-margin Markov networks. In *Conference on Neural Information Processing Systems (NIPS)*, 2003.

D. Terzopoulos. The computation of visible-surface representations. *IEEE Trans. Pattern Anal. Mach. Intell.*, 10(4):417–438, 1988.

M. Tipping. Sparse Bayesian learning and the relevance vector machine. *Journal of Machine Learning Research (JMLR)*, 1:211–244, 2001.

M. van Gerven, B. Cseke, F. de Lange, and T. Heskes. Efficient Bayesian multivariate fMRI analysis using a sparsifying spatio-temporal prior. *NeuroImage*, 50: 150–161, 2010.

M. Wainwright and M. Jordan. Graphical models, exponential families, and variational inference. *Found. and Trends in Machine Learning*, 1(1-2):1–305, 2008.

M. Wainwright, T. Jaakkola, and A. Willsky. MAP estimation via agreement on trees: Message-passing and linear programming. *IEEE Trans. Inf. Theory*, 51 (11):3697–3717, 2005.

Y. Weiss and W. Freeman. Correctness of belief propagation in Gaussian graphical models of arbitrary topology. *Neural Computation*, 13(10):2173–2200, 2001.

Y. Weiss and W. Freeman. What makes a good model of natural images? In *IEEE Computer Society Conference on Computer Vision and Pattern Recognition (CVPR)*, 2007.

M. Welling. Herding dynamical weights to learn. In *International Conference on Machine Learing (ICML)*, 2009.

S. Zhu, Y. Wu, and D. Mumford. Filters, random fields and maximum entropy (FRAME): Towards a unified theory for texture modeling. *Int. J. of Comp. Vis.*, 27(2):107–126, 1998.

8   Herding for Structured Prediction

Yutian Chen   yutian.chen@eng.cam.ac.uk
University of Cambridge
Cambridge, UK

Andrew E. Gelfand   agelfand@uci.edu
University of California, Irvine
Irvine, CA, USA

Max Welling   m.welling@uva.nl
University of Amsterdam
Amsterdam, the Netherlands

This chapter introduces a Herding-based approach to structured prediction tasks. Herding is a general class of learning algorithms originally introduced for learning Markov random fields (MRFs). We introduce Herding in the structured prediction setting and establish connections between Herding and other approaches to structured prediction, including Conditional Random Fields (CRFs), Structured Support Vector Machines (S-SVMs), Max-Margin Markov (M^3) Networks, and the Structured Perceptron (SP). We also demonstrate that Herding can be used to effectively combine piecewise, locally trained conditional models into a harmonious global model. Herding does not require training of a CRF to integrate locally trained classifiers but instead generates pseudo-samples by iterating forward a weakly chaotic dynamical system. We show that the distribution of pseudo-samples produced by Herding is well defined even when the locally trained classifiers are inconsistent and give class marginals that disagree. The Herding approach is illustrated on two different tasks: (1) image segmentation, where classifiers based on local appearance cues are combined with pairwise boundary cues; and (2) Go game prediction, where local predictors on overlapping patches are coordinated for a consistent output.

8.1 Introduction

In this chapter, we introduce a Herding-based approach to structured prediction. Herding is a general class of learning algorithms originally introduced for learning Markov random field (MRF) models (Welling, 2009) and subsequently generalized to the discriminative prediction settings (Gelfand et al., 2010). The theoretical contribution and its application on image segmentation in this chapter are mainly based on the recent work of Chen et al. (2011) that further generalized Herding to structured prediction problems. Unlike most traditional learning approaches, which try to learn a single parameter setting that minimize a suitable loss function (e.g., the negative log-likelihood), Herding produces a non-convergent sequence of parameters that can be used to make predictions. In other words, rather than separating the prediction problem into a training phase followed by a test phase, Herding can produce predictions on the test set while it iterates.

Herding bears resemblance to many of the more well-known approaches to structured prediction. The Herding update rules are derived from the zero-temperature limit of the log-likelihood, and in this way Herding resembles both Conditional Random Fields (CRFs) (Lafferty et al., 2001) and max-margin methods, such as Structured Support Vector Machines (S-SVMs) (Tsochantaridis et al., 2004) and Max-Margin Markov (M^3) Networks (Taskar et al., 2003). Herding can also be seen as a generalization of the Structured Perceptron (SP) (Collins, 2002). In the remainder of this section, we formalize the structured prediction task and introduce Herding by contrasting it with the more well-known approaches to structured prediction.

8.1.1 Structured Prediction

In structured prediction, we are given a data set $\mathcal{D} = \{(\boldsymbol{x}^{(n)}, \boldsymbol{y}^{(n)})\}_{n=1}^{N}$ drawn independently from an unknown joint probability distribution $P(\boldsymbol{x}, \boldsymbol{y})$. We seek to learn a function $f : \mathcal{X} \to \mathcal{Y}$, from input space $\mathcal{X}$ to output space $\mathcal{Y} = \mathcal{Y}_1 \times \cdots \times \mathcal{Y}_M$. Let $\boldsymbol{y} = (y_1, \ldots, y_M)$ and assume that each component of $\boldsymbol{y}$ is K-valued (i.e., $y_i \in \{1, \ldots, K\}$). Finally, let $\boldsymbol{y}_\alpha$ denote subsets of $\boldsymbol{y}$.

We consider learning a linear prediction rule of the following form:

$$\hat{\boldsymbol{y}} = f(\boldsymbol{x}, \boldsymbol{w}) = \operatorname*{argmax}_{\boldsymbol{y} \in \mathcal{Y}} \sum_\alpha w_\alpha \psi_\alpha(\boldsymbol{y}_\alpha, \boldsymbol{x}), \tag{8.1}$$

where $\boldsymbol{w} = \{w_\alpha\}$ is a vector comprised of real-valued parameters $w_\alpha \in \mathbb{R}$ and each $\psi_\alpha(\boldsymbol{y}_\alpha, \boldsymbol{x}) : \mathcal{X} \times \mathcal{Y}_\alpha \to \mathbb{R}$ are corresponding real-valued feature functions. Note that the prediction rule is linear in w_α, but the feature functions may be non-linear. Throughout this chapter, we will use $\hat{\boldsymbol{y}}$ to indicate predictions made under the current parameter setting. We will also use $\boldsymbol{\psi} = \{\psi_\alpha\}$ to represent the vector of features corresponding to $\boldsymbol{w}$.

In order to clarify our notation, consider the problem of segmenting an image. In that task, each y_i is a pixel taking one of K labels (e.g., $y_i =$ Airplane or $y_i =$ Boat). We construct a planar graph, $G = (V, E)$, over the image by associating each pixel with a vertex and adding an edge between adjacent pixels. We might then introduce unary features, $\psi_i(y_i, \boldsymbol{x})$, for each pixel $i \in V$ and pairwise features, $\psi_{ij}(y_i, y_j, \boldsymbol{x})$, for each edge $e = (i, j) \in E$. Doing so would give us a problem with a total of $|V| + |E|$ parameters.

In the standard learning scenario, our goal is to use the data set $\mathcal{D}$ to find the setting of parameters $\boldsymbol{w}$ that "best" predicts outputs given inputs. The quality of the parameter setting is assessed via a loss function that measures the error incurred by predicting $\hat{\boldsymbol{y}} = f(\boldsymbol{x}, \boldsymbol{w})$ when the true output is $\boldsymbol{y}$. Let $\ell(\boldsymbol{x}^{(n)}, \boldsymbol{y}^{(n)}, \boldsymbol{w})$ denote the loss incurred on training point n given the parameter setting $\boldsymbol{w}$. The goal is then to find the setting $\boldsymbol{w}^\star$ with minimal empirical loss,

$$\boldsymbol{w}^\star = \operatorname*{argmin}_{\boldsymbol{w}} \mathcal{L}(\mathcal{D}, \boldsymbol{w}) = \operatorname*{argmin}_{\boldsymbol{w}} \frac{1}{N} \sum_{n=1}^{N} \ell(\boldsymbol{x}^{(n)}, \boldsymbol{y}^{(n)}, \boldsymbol{w}). \tag{8.2}$$

Several methods for finding $\boldsymbol{w}^\star$ have been proposed, including CRFs (Lafferty et al., 2001), which minimize the negative log-likelihood (or log-loss); S-SVMs (Tsochantaridis et al., 2004) and M^3 networks (Taskar et al., 2003), which minimize differently scaled versions of the hinge loss, and SPs (Collins, 2002), which minimize the (generalized) perceptron loss. As previously mentioned, Herding does not seek a single setting $\boldsymbol{w}^\star$ but rather produces a sequence of parameters $\dots, \boldsymbol{w}^{t-1}, \boldsymbol{w}^t, \boldsymbol{w}^{t+1}, \dots$ that can be used to predict a sequence of outputs $\dots, \hat{\boldsymbol{y}}^{t-1}, \hat{\boldsymbol{y}}^t, \hat{\boldsymbol{y}}^{t+1}, \dots$ for each input. In this way, Herding closely resembles the SP. However, Herding's update rules can be derived from a zero-temperature variant of the log-loss. We introduce Herding from this latter perspective.

8.1.2   Herding and the Zero Temperature Log-Loss

Consider a conditional Gibbs distribution of the form

$$p_\tau(\boldsymbol{y}|\boldsymbol{x}, \boldsymbol{w}) = \frac{1}{Z_\tau(\boldsymbol{x}, \boldsymbol{w})} \exp\left(\frac{1}{\tau} \sum_\alpha w_\alpha \psi_\alpha(\boldsymbol{y}_\alpha, \boldsymbol{x})\right), \tag{8.3}$$

where τ is a temperature parameter and $Z_\tau(\boldsymbol{x}, \boldsymbol{w})$ is the partition function

$$Z_\tau(\boldsymbol{x}, \boldsymbol{w}) = \sum_{y' \in \mathcal{Y}} \exp\left(\frac{1}{\tau} \sum_\alpha w_\alpha \psi_\alpha(\boldsymbol{y}'_\alpha, \boldsymbol{x})\right). \tag{8.4}$$

This conditional distribution in (8.3) is referred to as a CRF when $\tau = 1$, each y_i of $\boldsymbol{y}$ is associated with a vertex in some graph $G = (V, E)$, and each y_i satisfies the Markov property with respect to the graph G.

A common objective of learning is to find the model $p_\tau(\boldsymbol{y}|\boldsymbol{x}, \boldsymbol{w})$ that maximizes the probability of observing the outputs $\{\boldsymbol{y}^{(n)}\}_{n=1}^N$ given the inputs $\{\boldsymbol{x}^{(n)}\}_{n=1}^N$. When formulated as a minimization problem, this gives rise to the negative log-likelihood objective

$$\boldsymbol{w}^\star_{\tau,LL} = \operatorname*{argmin}_{\boldsymbol{w}} \mathcal{L}_{\tau,\mathrm{LL}}(\mathcal{D}, \boldsymbol{w}) = \operatorname*{argmin}_{\boldsymbol{w}} \frac{1}{N} \sum_{n=1}^N \ell_{\tau,\mathrm{LL}}(\boldsymbol{x}^{(n)}, \boldsymbol{y}^{(n)}, \boldsymbol{w}), \tag{8.5}$$

where the log-loss function is defined as:

$$\ell_{\tau,\mathrm{LL}}(\boldsymbol{x}, \boldsymbol{y}, \boldsymbol{w}) = -\tau \log p_\tau(\boldsymbol{y}|\boldsymbol{x}, \boldsymbol{w}) = -\sum_\alpha w_\alpha \psi_\alpha(\boldsymbol{y}_\alpha, \boldsymbol{x}) + \tau \log Z_\tau(\boldsymbol{x}, \boldsymbol{w}).$$

$$\tag{8.6}$$

The subscript τ in $\ell_{\tau,\mathrm{LL}}$ makes the dependence on temperature explicit.

Because the log partition function, $\log Z_\tau(\boldsymbol{x}, \boldsymbol{w})$, is convex in $\boldsymbol{w}$, the negative log-likelihood is a convex function of $\boldsymbol{w}$. Finding its minimum is possible using standard numerical optimization methods (e.g., limited memory BFGS) when the log-loss and its gradients can be computed efficiently. The full gradient updates are

$$w^t_\alpha = w^{t-1}_\alpha + \eta_{\alpha,t}\left(\mathbb{E}_{\hat{P}}[\psi_\alpha] - \frac{1}{N}\sum_n \sum_{y'} p_\tau(\boldsymbol{y}'|\boldsymbol{x}^{(n)}, \boldsymbol{w}^{t-1})\psi_\alpha(\boldsymbol{y}'_\alpha, \boldsymbol{x}^{(n)})\right),$$

$$\tag{8.7}$$

where $\eta_{\alpha,t}$ is a decreasing step size and $\mathbb{E}_{\hat{P}}[\psi_\alpha]$ is the empirical average value of feature ψ_α in the training data computed as

$$\mathbb{E}_{\hat{P}}[\psi_\alpha] = \frac{1}{N}\sum_{n=1}^N \psi_\alpha(\boldsymbol{y}^{(n)}_\alpha, \boldsymbol{x}^{(n)}). \tag{8.8}$$

Note that the setting $\boldsymbol{w}^\star_{\tau,LL}$ that minimizes (8.5) has the appealing property that the empirical average feature, $\mathbb{E}_{\hat{P}}[\psi_\alpha]$, will equal the average of that feature under the model — the well-known moment-matching property of maximum likelihood estimation.

The Herding loss is revealed by taking the zero-temperature limit, $\tau \to 0$, of (8.6)(Welling, 2009):

$$\ell_{\text{Herd}}(\boldsymbol{x}, \boldsymbol{y}, \boldsymbol{w}) = -\sum_{\alpha} w_{\alpha} \psi_{\alpha}(\boldsymbol{y}_{\alpha}, \boldsymbol{x}) + \max_{\boldsymbol{y}'} \left[\sum_{\alpha} w_{\alpha} \psi_{\alpha}(\boldsymbol{y}'_{\alpha}, \boldsymbol{x}) \right]. \quad (8.9)$$

Several observations about this loss function are made in Welling (2009), including the fact that it has a unique minima at $\boldsymbol{w} = 0$. As a result, it would seem pointless to minimize $\mathcal{L}_{\text{Herd}}(\mathcal{D}, \boldsymbol{w})$ by applying subgradient updates. However, this is exactly what Herding does! In particular, Herding iteratively applies the following updates:

$$\hat{\boldsymbol{y}}^{(n),t} = \underset{\boldsymbol{y}'}{\operatorname{argmax}} \sum_{\alpha} w_{\alpha}^{t-1} \psi_{\alpha}(\boldsymbol{y}'_{\alpha}, \boldsymbol{x}^{(n)}) \ \text{ for } \ n = 1 \ldots N, \quad (8.10)$$

$$w_{\alpha}^{t} = w_{\alpha}^{t-1} + \eta_{\alpha} \left(\mathbb{E}_{\hat{P}} \left[\psi_{\alpha} \right] - \frac{1}{N} \sum_{n} \psi_{\alpha}(\hat{\boldsymbol{y}}_{\alpha}^{(n),t}, \boldsymbol{x}^{(n)}) \right). \quad (8.11)$$

In Herding, the step-size η_{α} is held fixed (note the lack of dependence on t). Given suitable initialization of $\boldsymbol{w}^0$, this prevents convergence of the sequence to the trivial minima at $\boldsymbol{w} = 0$. Moreover, the sequence will be non-convergent if at least one incorrect prediction is made in every iteration (i.e., $\hat{\boldsymbol{y}}^{(n),t} \neq \boldsymbol{y}^{(n)}$ for at least one data point n in every iteration t). The sequence $\ldots, \boldsymbol{w}^{t-1}, \boldsymbol{w}^t, \boldsymbol{w}^{t+1}, \ldots$ will also not diverge as long as an easy to check criteria is satisfied (see Section 8.1.4 for more on this criterion). Last, and most importantly, the average over the sequence of features produced by Herding will *match* the empirical average of features in the following sense (Gelfand et al., 2010):

$$\left| \mathbb{E}_{\hat{P}} \left[\psi_{\alpha} \right] - \frac{1}{T} \sum_{t=1}^{T} \frac{1}{N} \sum_{n} \psi_{\alpha}(\hat{\boldsymbol{y}}_{\alpha}^{(n),t}, \boldsymbol{x}^{(n)}) \right| = \mathcal{O} \left(\frac{1}{T} \right) \quad \forall \alpha. \quad (8.12)$$

Thus, Monte Carlo averages over the sequence of states produced by Herding will match the moments of the training data as if they were sampled directly from $\hat{P}$ — albeit at a faster rate than independent sampling from $\hat{P}$. We will refer to these states as *pseudo-samples* from now on, as the Herding algorithm is a deterministic procedure rather than a random sampling algorithm. This matching property will be discussed in more detail in Section 8.2, so we defer further discussion until that time.

8.1.3   Herding and Max-Margin Methods

The model, $p(\boldsymbol{y}|\boldsymbol{x}, \boldsymbol{w}^{\star})$, that is learned by minimizing the log-loss does not utilize the knowledge that it will be used to make predictions under the

MAP prediction rule in (8.1). Training in this agnostic manner is justified by Bayesian decision theory when the learned model, $p(\boldsymbol{y}|\boldsymbol{x},\boldsymbol{w}^\star)$, closely resembles the true (and unknown) distribution, $P(\boldsymbol{y}|\boldsymbol{x})$, that our data were drawn from. If $p(\boldsymbol{y}|\boldsymbol{x},\boldsymbol{w}^\star)$ differs greatly from $P(\boldsymbol{y}|\boldsymbol{x})$, then it may be beneficial to find parameters that directly optimize the MAP prediction rule. This is exactly the aim of max-margin methods, such as S-SVMs and M^3 networks.

We follow the approach of Pletscher et al. (2010) in introducing max-margin methods as it facilitates comparison with Herding. In max-margin methods, one tries to minimize the following loss:

$$\ell_{\mathrm{MM}}(\boldsymbol{x},\boldsymbol{y},\boldsymbol{w}) = -\sum_\alpha w_\alpha \psi_\alpha(\boldsymbol{y}_\alpha,\boldsymbol{x}) + \max_{y'}\left[\sum_\alpha w_\alpha \psi_\alpha(\boldsymbol{y}'_\alpha,\boldsymbol{x}) + \Delta(\boldsymbol{y}',\boldsymbol{y})\right],$$
(8.13)

where $\Delta(\boldsymbol{y}',\boldsymbol{y})$ is a function that provides a margin between incorrect predictions ($\boldsymbol{y}'$) and the ground truth output ($\boldsymbol{y}$). In S-SVMs, the margin function might take the form:

$$\Delta(\boldsymbol{y}',\boldsymbol{y}) = \begin{cases} 0, & \text{if } \boldsymbol{y}' = \boldsymbol{y}, \\ 1, & \text{otherwise.} \end{cases}$$

In M^3 networks, the margin function decomposes over the components of $\boldsymbol{y}$. In either case, we see that the max-margin loss is equivalent to the Herding loss in (8.9), when the margin function is $\Delta(\boldsymbol{y}',\boldsymbol{y}) = 0$.

S-SVMs are commonly trained via subgradient updates that closely resemble the Herding updates

$$\hat{\boldsymbol{y}}^{(n),t} = \operatorname*{argmax}_{y'} \sum_\alpha w_\alpha^{t-1} \psi_\alpha(\boldsymbol{y}'_\alpha,\boldsymbol{x}^{(n)}) + \Delta(\boldsymbol{y}',\boldsymbol{y}^{(n)}) \text{ for } n = 1\ldots N,$$

$$w_\alpha^t = w_\alpha^{t-1} + \eta_{\alpha,t}\left(\mathbb{E}_{\hat{P}}\left[\psi_\alpha\right] - \frac{1}{N}\sum_n \psi_\alpha(\hat{\boldsymbol{y}}_\alpha^{(n),t},\boldsymbol{x}^{(n)})\right).$$
(8.14)

There are two primary differences between these updates and the Herding updates in (8.10, 8.11). The first change is the presence of the margin function $\Delta(\boldsymbol{y}',\boldsymbol{y})$ in the S-SVM updates. The second change is the dependence of the S-SVM step-size on t. In S-SVMs, the step-size is steadily decreased so as to find a single parameter setting $\boldsymbol{w}^\star$. Herding holds the step-size fixed across all t, which prevents convergence of the sequence of parameters (so long as an incorrect prediction is made on the training data in every iteration).

8.1.4   Herding and the SP

The SP was introduced by Collins for sequence labeling problems, such as the aforementioned POS tagging task (Collins, 2002). As its name suggests, it extends Rosenblatt's classic perceptron learning algorithm (Rosenblatt, 1958). The SP is delightful because of its simplicity. At every iteration t, choose a data point n_t from our data set[1] and apply the following update rule:

$$\hat{\boldsymbol{y}}^{(n_t)} = \operatorname*{argmax}_{\boldsymbol{y}'} \sum_\alpha w_\alpha^{t-1} \psi_\alpha(\boldsymbol{y}'_\alpha, \boldsymbol{x}^{(n_t)}),$$

$$w_\alpha^t = w_\alpha^{t-1} + \left(\psi_\alpha(\boldsymbol{y}_\alpha^{(n_t)}, \boldsymbol{x}) - \psi_\alpha(\hat{\boldsymbol{y}}_\alpha^{(n_t)}, \boldsymbol{x}) \right). \tag{8.15}$$

Note that if $\hat{\boldsymbol{y}} = \boldsymbol{y}$, then $w_\alpha^t = w_\alpha^{t-1}$ and our parameters do not change.

Written in this form, the SP differs from Herding only in that it is an online algorithm — updating on the training data one by one rather than on the entire training set. However, Herding generalizes the SP in a few important ways not immediately clear from the current presentation. First, in many applications (e.g., image segmentation), it is not possible to exactly find the MAP state, and one is forced to find an approximation to the MAP configuration. Approximate inference, it turns out, is non-problematic, and Herding will still satisfy the moment matching property in (8.12) so long as a simple to check condition from the Perceptron Cycling Theorem (PCT) is satisfied (Gelfand et al., 2010). This PCT condition also justifies the use of mini-batch updates that use a subset of the training data (including online schemes with a batch size of one). We describe the PCT condition now as its introduction will aid understanding of forthcoming results.

The PCT is a classic result due to (Minsky and Papert, 1969; Block and Levin, 1970), which states:

Theorem 8.1. *The sequence of (parameter) vectors* $\ldots, \boldsymbol{w}^{t-1}, \boldsymbol{w}^t, \boldsymbol{w}^{t+1}, \ldots$ *generated using the iterative procedure* $\boldsymbol{w}^{t+1} = \boldsymbol{w}^t + \boldsymbol{v}^t$ *remains bounded (i.e.,* $\|\boldsymbol{w}^t\|_2 < \|\boldsymbol{w}^0\|_2 + M$ *for some constant* $M > 0$*) if:*

1. *The domain of* $\boldsymbol{v}^t$ *is a finite set* $\mathbf{V}$*;*

2. *The norm of* $\boldsymbol{v}^t$ *is bounded — i.e.,* $\max_{\boldsymbol{v}' \in \mathbf{V}} \|\boldsymbol{v}'\|_2 < \infty$*; and*

3. *In every iteration* t*,* $\langle \boldsymbol{w}^t, \boldsymbol{v}^t \rangle \leq 0$*.*

---

1. Note that a data point can be picked multiple times.

As a consequence, if the PCT holds, then it can be shown that

$$\left\| \frac{1}{T} \sum_{t=1}^{T} \boldsymbol{v}^t \right\|_2 = \mathcal{O}\left(\frac{1}{T}\right), \tag{8.16}$$

which perhaps unsurprisingly has the form of the Herding moment matching property in (8.12).

The PCT can be applied to Herding by identifying the update vectors as

$$\boldsymbol{v}^t = \left(\mathbb{E}_{\hat{P}}[\boldsymbol{\psi}] - \frac{1}{N} \sum_n \boldsymbol{\psi}(\hat{\boldsymbol{y}}_\alpha^{(n),t}, \boldsymbol{x}^{(n)}) \right), \tag{8.17}$$

where as usual $\hat{\boldsymbol{y}}^{(n),t} = \operatorname{argmax}_{\boldsymbol{y}' \in \mathcal{Y}} \sum_\alpha w_\alpha^{t-1} \psi_\alpha(\boldsymbol{y}'_\alpha, \boldsymbol{x}^{(n)})$. The domain of the update vectors is a finite set $\mathbf{V}$ because in every iteration, there are an exponential number of configurations $\hat{\boldsymbol{y}}^{(n),t} \in \mathcal{Y}$ for each of the N data points. The norm of $\boldsymbol{v}^t$ will also be bounded if the feature functions are appropriately specified. The easy-to-check criteria referred to throughout this chapter is the third condition of the PCT — namely, that the inner product of the parameter and update vectors are less than or equal to zero. As long as this condition is satisfied in every iteration, we can use approximate inference or mini-batches when applying the Herding updates and still satisfy the Herding moment matching property of (8.12).

Herding also generalizes the SP in another important way. Because the Herding updates are derived by taking the zero temperature limit of the log-loss on a CRF model, the entire derivation can be repeated for a CRF model with hidden (unobserved) variables. The resulting algorithm can be viewed as an SP with hidden units that, much like discriminative Restricted Boltzmann Machines (RBMs), can capture complex interactions among the observed variables (see Gelfand et al., 2010, for more detail).

8.2   Integrating Local Models Using Herding

8.2.1   Piecewise Trained CRFs

CRFs are a standard approach for combining local features into a global conditional distribution over labels for structured prediction. To specify a CRF model, one must first define feature functions $\psi_\alpha(\boldsymbol{y}_\alpha, \boldsymbol{x})$, where $\boldsymbol{y}_\alpha$ is a subset of the labels associated with ψ_α and $\boldsymbol{x}$ are inputs. For example, in the image segmentation task, one might define a feature of the form:

$$\psi_i(y_i, y_j, x_i) = \begin{cases} 1 & \text{if } y_i = y_j \text{ AND } x_i > 0.5, \\ 0 & \text{otherwise.} \end{cases} \tag{8.18}$$

This feature encodes a preference for the label of pixel i to agree with the label of adjacent pixel j when the intensity at pixel i is greater than 0.5. The label subsets indexed by α can overlap, forming a loopy graph over the labels $\boldsymbol{y}$. In this way, the CRF framework can utilize rich features.

As discussed in the previous section, such features can be incorporated into a probabilistic model by associating model parameters $\{w_\alpha\}$ with each feature function $\{\psi_\alpha\}$:

$$p_{\text{CRF-1}}(\boldsymbol{y}|\boldsymbol{x}, \boldsymbol{w}) = \frac{1}{Z(\boldsymbol{x}, \boldsymbol{w})} \exp\left(\sum_\alpha w_\alpha \psi_\alpha(\boldsymbol{y}_\alpha, \boldsymbol{x}_\alpha) \right). \tag{8.19}$$

The model parameters can be learned from data by, for example, minimizing the log-loss described in (8.5). While this is quite elegant, it poses a practical problem in that each feature function ψ_α has a distinct parameter w_α to be estimated. In typical image labeling problems, there may be thousands of parameters to learn (e.g., one for every pixel and pair of pixels in every image). In such cases, there may be less than one pixel of information per parameter, which may lead to extreme over-fitting.

A common remedy for the explosion of parameters is to train the CRF model in stages. In the first stage, we train a set of local discriminative models (i.e., classifiers), and then in the second stage, we integrate the information from the local classifiers to make a coherent prediction. For example, in the image segmentation task, we might train a *unary* probability model $p_i(y_i|x_i)$ that predicts the label at pixel i and a *pairwise* classifier that predicts the probability that two adjacent pixels i and j have different labels $p_{ij}(y_i \neq y_j|x_i, x_j)$ and form a boundary.

One of the main questions addressed in the remainder of this chapter is how to effectively integrate the information of local, piecewise trained (Sutton and McCallum, 2007), discriminative probability models, $p_\alpha(\boldsymbol{y}_\alpha|\boldsymbol{x}_\alpha)$. A common approach is to incorporate the local classifiers by taking their log probabilities as feature functions and combine them using a small number of parameters to balance their respective local information.

This is exactly the approach adopted in Fulkerson et al. (2010), where the unary and pairwise classifiers are incorporated using feature functions $\psi_i(y_i, \boldsymbol{x}) = -\log p_i(y_i|x_i)$ and $\psi_{ij}(y_i, y_j, \boldsymbol{x}) = -\log p_{ij}(y_i \neq y_j|x_i, x_j)$. A single parameter λ is introduced to trade the relative importance of the unary and pairwise classifiers. This yields the following CRF model:

$$p_{\text{CRF-2}}(\boldsymbol{y}|\boldsymbol{x}, \lambda) = \frac{1}{Z(\boldsymbol{x}, \lambda)} \exp \left(\sum_i \log(p_i(y_i|x_i)) + \lambda \sum_{i,j} \log(p_{ij}(y_i \neq y_j|x_i, x_j)) \right).$$

$$(8.20)$$

In Fulkerson et al. (2010), the unary $p_i(y_i|x_i)$ and pairwise classifiers $p_{ij}(y_i \neq y_j|x_i, x_j)$ are trained independently. As a result, there is no longer reason to expect that the learned model's moments, $\mathbb{E}_{p_{\text{CRF-2}}}[\psi_\alpha]$, will match the moments of the training data, $\mathbb{E}_{\hat{P}}[\psi_\alpha]$, in the following sense (see Section 8.1.2):

$$\mathbb{E}_{p_{\text{CRF-2}}}[\psi_\alpha] = \mathbb{E}_{\hat{P}}[\psi_\alpha].$$

$$(8.21)$$

This is simply because we have only a single parameter to tune but need to satisfy a large collection of moment constraints (number of pixels plus number of neighboring pairs of pixels).

Instead, we might insist that our global model at least approximately matches the moment constraints

$$\mathbb{E}_p[\psi_\alpha] = \mathbb{E}_{p_\alpha}[\psi_\alpha],$$

$$(8.22)$$

where the joint empirical distribution $\hat{P}$ has been replaced with the local discriminative model p_α. For features of the form $\psi_{\alpha, \boldsymbol{z}_\alpha}(\boldsymbol{y}_\alpha) = \mathbb{I}[\boldsymbol{y}_\alpha = \boldsymbol{z}_\alpha]$, this condition implies that the joint distribution has marginals consistent with each local probability model

$$\sum_{\boldsymbol{y} \backslash \boldsymbol{y}_\alpha} p(\boldsymbol{y}|\boldsymbol{x}) = p_\alpha(\boldsymbol{y}_\alpha|\boldsymbol{x}_\alpha).$$

$$(8.23)$$

In the ongoing image segmentation example, this consistency condition means that $p(y_i|\boldsymbol{x}) = p_i(y_i|x_i)$ and $p(y_i, y_j|\boldsymbol{x}) = p_{ij}(y_i, y_j|x_i, x_j)$. However, with independently trained local classifiers, no joint model can achieve this as the p_α will likely be mutually *inconsistent*.

The Herding approach we describe in the next section provides an elegant solution to this problem. Given piecewise trained discriminative models, it produces a sequence of states $\ldots \hat{\boldsymbol{y}}^t, \hat{\boldsymbol{y}}^{t+1} \ldots$ that on average satisfy the marginalization condition in (8.22) when the local models are consistent. And if the local models are *inconsistent*, we show that the same procedure produces a sequence whose average behavior matches that of the closest consistent model. We thus gain some of the flexibility of the general CRF formulation of (8.19) in matching moments while retaining the parsimony of piecewise training local discriminative models.

8.2.2 Herding Local Models

The Herding approach we advocate attempts to identify a joint probability distribution over features ψ_α that approximately marginalize to the average features under the local models $\mathbb{E}_{p_\alpha}[\psi_\alpha]$. Let us first assume that the set of p_α are in fact consistent. For example, in the image segmentation task, this means that the pairwise probability model marginalizes down to the unary model: $\sum_{y_j} p_{ij}(y_i, y_j | x_i, x_j) = p_i(y_i | x_i)$, for all settings of y_i and adjacent pixels (i, j).

Consider the following Herding updates:

$$\hat{\boldsymbol{y}}^t = \underset{\boldsymbol{y}'}{\text{argmax}} \sum_\alpha w_\alpha^{t-1} \psi_\alpha(\boldsymbol{y}_\alpha', \boldsymbol{x}_\alpha), \tag{8.24}$$

$$w_\alpha^t = w_\alpha^{t-1} + \eta_\alpha \left(\mathbb{E}_{p_\alpha}[\psi_\alpha] - \psi_\alpha(\hat{\boldsymbol{y}}_\alpha^t, \boldsymbol{x}_\alpha) \right). \tag{8.25}$$

These are the same as the update equations in (8.10, 8.11), except that the empirical distribution $\hat{P}$ is replaced by the local model p_α and every image is processed independently. In the applications that follow, we use $\psi_{\alpha, \boldsymbol{z}_\alpha} = \mathbb{I}[\boldsymbol{y}_\alpha = \boldsymbol{z}_\alpha]$ (i.e., a unique feature for every state $\boldsymbol{z}_\alpha$ in every region).

It can now be shown (Gelfand et al., 2010) that if in every iteration we satisfy the PCT condition (see 8.1.4)

$$C^t = \sum_\alpha w_\alpha^{t-1} \left(\mathbb{E}_{p_\alpha}[\psi_\alpha] - \psi_\alpha(\hat{\boldsymbol{y}}_\alpha^t, \boldsymbol{x}_\alpha)) \right) \leq 0, \tag{8.26}$$

then it follows that

$$\left| \mathbb{E}_{p_\alpha}[\psi_\alpha] - \frac{1}{T} \sum_{t=1}^T \psi_\alpha(\hat{\boldsymbol{y}}_\alpha^t, \boldsymbol{x}_\alpha) \right| = \mathcal{O}\left(\frac{1}{T}\right). \tag{8.27}$$

We note that this convergence rate is much faster than the Monte Carlo average computed by independently sampling from p_α, which would converge at a rate of $\mathcal{O}(\sqrt{1/T})$.

Herding's updates generate sequences $\ldots, (\boldsymbol{w}^t, \hat{\boldsymbol{y}}^t), (\boldsymbol{w}^{t+1}, \hat{\boldsymbol{y}}^{t+1}), \ldots$ of parameters and states in such a way that the states come from some joint distribution $P(\boldsymbol{y}|\boldsymbol{x})$, which has moments $\mathbb{E}_{p_\alpha}[\psi_\alpha]$. Unlike CRF models, the entropy of this joint model is not expected to be maximal, although empirically it is often close. Perhaps surprisingly, for many problems, local maximizations are often sufficient to satisfy condition (8.26), allowing us to side-step hard inference. It should be noted that this is not always the case, in particular when the constraints are hard or impossible to satisfy as may arise for image segmentation.

We also emphasize that the dynamical system defined by (8.24) and (8.25) do not return a parameterized model. The sequence $\ldots (\boldsymbol{w}^t, \hat{\boldsymbol{y}}^t), (\boldsymbol{w}^{t+1}, \hat{\boldsymbol{y}}^{t+1}), \ldots$ never converges to a fixed point, and one should rather think of this as a deterministic process to generate "representative points." In fact, it can be shown that the dynamical system is weakly chaotic (Welling and Chen, 2010), meaning that the sequence over $\hat{\boldsymbol{y}}^t$ is not periodic and is insensitive to the initial setting of $\boldsymbol{w}^0$.

Not having an explicit model is not a problem for the applications we have in mind. For instance, in image segmentation, the dynamical system will generate a sequence of segmentations of the input image. From this sequence, we can extract the final segmentation by averaging.

The difference between the Herding approach to integrating locally trained models and the CRF-based approach adopted in Fulkerson et al. (2010) should now be clear. In the Herding approach, one iterates the Herding updates for several iterations, where each iteration requires finding the approximate MAP configuration for a subset of training images and then verifying that the resulting parameter update satisfies the PCT condition. In every iteration, one also makes predictions on each image in the test set. In contrast, in the CRF-based approach, one invests up-front time to identify a setting of the λ parameters that best balance the information from each local classifier. After finding such a parameter setting, a prediction can be made once on each image in the test set. The Herding approach is thus best suited for situations where the test set is known in advance and where it is relatively *easy* to perform MAP inference.

8.2.3   Herding With Inconsistent Marginals

We now describe how to handle inconsistent marginals in Herding. When the vector $\mathbb{E}_{p_\alpha}[\psi_\alpha]$ does not reside inside the marginal polytope $\mathcal{M} \stackrel{\text{def}}{=} \{\mathbb{E}_p[\psi_\alpha] | \forall p\}$, then by definition there does not exist a joint distribution $p(\boldsymbol{y}|\boldsymbol{x})$ with moments $\{\mathbb{E}_{p_\alpha}[\psi_\alpha]\}$. If we want to train a CRF without regularization, then parameters will diverge. For Herding this means that the condition in (8.26) cannot always be satisfied, and the norm of parameters $\boldsymbol{w}^t$ will also linearly diverge. Nevertheless, we can still obtain a stationary joint distribution of states $\hat{\boldsymbol{y}}^t$ from the Herding sequence. The potential numerical problems caused by the divergence of $\boldsymbol{w}^t$ can be easily prevented by taking an additional normalization step, $\boldsymbol{w} \leftarrow \boldsymbol{w}/M, \eta_\alpha \leftarrow \eta_\alpha/M$, for some constant M. This global scaling will not affect the state sequence $\{\hat{\boldsymbol{y}}^t\}$ in any way. The most important consequence of inconsistent marginals is that the moments of the joint distribution do not converge to $\mathbb{E}_{p_\alpha}[\psi_\alpha]$ anymore.

Instead, we prove in this chapter that the moments orthogonally project onto the marginal polytope.

In the following, we will denote the collection of expectations $\mathbb{E}_{p_\alpha}[\psi_\alpha]$ as $\bar{\psi}$ and the sample average of the features generated by Herding up to time T as $\tilde{\psi}^T = \frac{1}{T} \sum_{t=1}^{T} \psi(\hat{y}^t, x)$. We now claim that the following property holds:

Proposition 8.2. *Assume $\bar{\psi}$ is outside the marginal polytope $\mathcal{M}$ and the stepsize η_α is constant. Let $\bar{\psi}_\mathcal{M}$ be the L_2 projection of $\bar{\psi}$ onto $\mathcal{M}$. Then the average features of Herding $\tilde{\psi}^T$ converge to $\bar{\psi}_\mathcal{M}$ at the rate of $1/T$.*

For a proof of this proposition and the following corollary, see the appendix of Chen et al. (2011).

When η_α depends on the feature index α, we can construct an equivalent Herding sequence with a constant step-size and new features $\{\sqrt{\eta_\alpha}\psi_\alpha\}$. Then Proposition 8.2 still applies except that the L_2 distance is weighted by $\sqrt{\eta_\alpha}$. In this way, the step sizes control the relative importance of features. When we consider features of the form $\psi_{\alpha, z_\alpha}(y_\alpha) = \mathbb{I}[y_\alpha = z_\alpha]$, the marginal probabilities of Herding pseudo-samples will converge to the closest consistent marginals in $\mathcal{M}$.

As an immediate consequence of Proposition 8.2, Herding always improves on an initial set of moments $\bar{\psi}$ in the following sense:

Corollary 8.3. *Given a feature vector $\bar{\psi}$ that is an approximation to the expected feature w.r.t. some unknown distribution, $\bar{\psi}_{true}$. When running Herding dynamics with $\bar{\psi}$, the limit of the empirical average of features will not increase the L_2 error. Specifically, $\|\bar{\psi}_\mathcal{M} - \bar{\psi}_{true}\|_2 < \|\bar{\psi} - \bar{\psi}_{true}\|_2$ when $\bar{\psi} \notin \mathcal{M}$, and $\tilde{\psi}^T \to \bar{\psi}$ otherwise.*

8.3 Application: Image Segmentation

Piecewise training approaches are fairly common in computer vision tasks, such as image segmentation, because the vision community has spent considerable time developing state-of-the-art, highly specialized classifiers (e.g., edge or human detectors). Such classifiers are trained independently, often on disparate data sets, and utilize different input features (e.g., color, texture, etc.). As a result, the marginals produced by such classifiers are likely to be inconsistent. This provides an ideal setting in which to demonstrate the approximate marginal consistency property of Herding.

In this section, we consider the image segmentation task, where our goal is to produce a labeling y for each pixel of an input image x. In the simplest case, the pixel labels y_i are binary and indicate whether a pixel is foreground or background. In a more complex setting, the y_i may take one of K different class labels (e.g., Boat, Airplane, Sky, etc.). Because a typical image contains tens of thousands of pixels, it is fairly common to pre-process an image and group neighboring pixels into super-pixels. The result of this pre-processing is a CRF model with a far more manageable number of variables, one for each super-pixel.

We consider incorporating the output of two local classifiers. One of the classifiers provides unary conditional probabilities $\{p_i(y_i|x_i)\}$ on each super-pixel; the other classifier provides pairwise conditional probabilities $\{p_{ij}(y_i \neq y_j|x_i, x_j)\}$ on neighboring super-pixels. The former gives the probability that super-pixel i is of a particular class (e.g., $y_i = $ "Boat"), whereas the latter suggests the existence of boundaries.

We adopt the approach of Fulkerson et al. (2010) and use the CRF defined in (8.20) with a single parameter λ. The best value of λ is estimated on a validation set using grid search, and segmentations are predicted by finding the $\hat{\boldsymbol{y}}$ that maximizes $p_{\text{CRF-2}}(\boldsymbol{y}|\boldsymbol{x}, \lambda^\star)$.

Our Herding algorithm follows (8.24) and (8.25) with two types of features: $\mathbb{I}(y_i = k)$ and $\mathbb{I}(y_i \neq y_j)$. The step size η_α is scale free in the sense that multiplying all η_α by the same factor doesn't change the output of label sequence $\boldsymbol{y}^t$, and so without loss of generality, we set the step size for unary features to 1 and the step size for pairwise features to λ. The value of λ is used to trade off the strength of these two sources of information. The segmentations predicted by Herding are obtained by taking the most frequently occurring class label for each super-pixel in the Herding sequence

$$y_i^* = \underset{k}{\arg\max} \sum_{t=1}^{T} \mathbb{I}[y_i^t = k] \quad \forall i. \tag{8.28}$$

Notice that the role of the parameter λ is different in the CRF and Herding approaches. In the CRF model, λ controls the strength of smoothness; increasing λ always increases smoothness. However, Herding tries the respect all the probabilities, and λ measures how much attention we pay to each of these two sources of information. Increasing λ not only increases the smoothness where $p_{ij}(y_i \neq y_j)$ is small but also forces an edge where $p_{ij}(y_i \neq y_j)$ is large. As a special case, for a system of N super-pixels with $\lambda \gg 1$ and $p_{ij}(y_i \neq y_j) = 0$ for all neighbors in the label graph, the pairwise term dominates the system, and all super-pixels will take on the same value.

We apply Herding to image segmentation on the data set of the PASCAL VOC 2007 segmentation competition. We compare Herding's predictions to those made by a multi-class classifier using local appearance cues only and to the traditional CRF approach of Fulkerson et al. (2010). Interested readers can refer to Chen et al. (2011) for a comparison on the GrabCut data set.

On the PASCAL VOC 2007 data set, we follow a similar experiment setting as that of Fulkerson et al. (2010) and perform segmentation on the level of super-pixels. Each image is first over-segmented by the global probability of boundary (gPb) method (Arbelaez et al., 2011). The threshold is set to 0 to make sure most boundaries are retained. SIFT features are then extracted and quantized in order to build a visual dictionary. A local multi-class SVM is trained to provide unary marginals $p_i(y_i|x_i)$ using histograms of the visual words in each super-pixel and its neighbors at a distance at most N. The larger N is, the more context information is available for the local classifier, less noise in the feature histogram but also the more blurred the boundaries between super-pixels become. By increasing N, the segmentations of the local classifier changes from inaccurate and noisy but with clear, sharp boundaries to more accurate and smooth but with blurred boundaries (see the results of the local method of $N = 0$ in Figure 8.3 and $N = 3$ in Figure 8.1). The gPb algorithm provides the probability of a boundary between two super-pixels (i.e., the pairwise marginals $p_{ij}(y_i \neq y_j|\boldsymbol{x})$). The VOC test set includes 210 images, and the "trainval" set is split randomly into a training set of 322 images and a validation set of 100 images. The local classifier is trained on the training set, and the (hyper-)parameters of the CRF and Herding are estimated on the validation set.

For the local models, we predict the super-pixel labels based on the output of SVMs. For the CRF models, the MAP label is inferred using the graphcut algorithm (Boykov and Kolmogorov, 2004; Boykov et al., 2001; Kolmogorov and Zabih, 2004) with an energy as in (8.20). The parameter λ is estimated by grid search on the validation set. For the Herding method, the maximization step in (8.24) is also executed using graphcut. Because the original gPb score is trained on the BSDS data set and a lot of boundaries belonging to irrelevant categories of objects in the VOC data set are not considered, gPb should be calibrated first. The calibrated pairwise probability is computed as $p_{VOC}(y_i \neq y_j|\boldsymbol{x}) - p_{BSDS}(y_i \neq y_j|\boldsymbol{x})^\alpha$, where α controls how sparse the boundaries in the VOC data set are. The parameters λ and α are estimated on the validation set by first fixing $\alpha = 1$, estimating λ by grid search and then fixing λ and estimating α. More iterations can be done for better performance. Notice that for CRF, the function of λ and α appears in the same position in the pairwise term $\lambda\alpha \log(p_{ij}(y_i \neq y_j|x_i, x_j))\mathbb{I}(y_i \neq y_j)$, and a second parameter is therefore redundant.

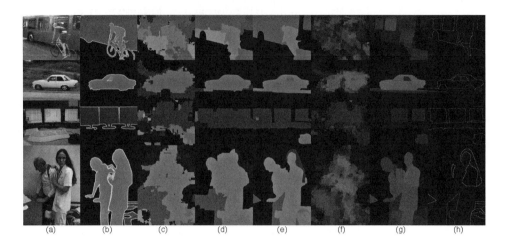

Figure 8.1: Examples of segmentation on Pascal VOC 2007 data set. Images on each line starting from left to right are, respectively: (a) the original image, (b) ground truth segmentation, results of (c) local classifier, (d) CRF and (e) Herding, results with intensity proportional to the posterior probability of the (f) local classifier and (g) Herding, and (h) the Herding estimate of the pairwise probability of the existence of a boundary (the corresponding posterior probability for CRF cannot be easily obtained). Neighboring superpixels of a distance up to three hops are used for training local SVM. Best viewed in color.

Figure 8.1 shows some examples of the test images, results of different algorithms, as well as their posterior probabilities. The local classifiers are trained on features from a neighborhood of $N = 3$. So the unary class distribution is already smoothed to some extent (compared to Figure 8.3 for the case of N=0). But Herding still leads to better smoothness and locates the boundaries more accurately. Most boundaries occur in the place with strong pairwise probabilities. CRF provides similar benefits as Herding for regularizing the local classifiers.

We evaluate the performance of these three models by two measurements. The first one is the average accuracy adopted by VOC 2007 Competition. It measures the average recall of pixels for each category. The second measurement is the one adopted by VOC competition after 2007. It measures the average of the intersection over union ratio for each category. The results of both evaluation methods are shown in Figure 8.2. The results show that both Herding and CRF increase the accuracy in most cases, and Herding always achieves the best accuracy except for $N = 2$ by the second measurement. The reduction of the advantage of Herding compared with CRF in the second measurement may be due to the fact that false-positive detections appear frequently in the background, which does not reduce the

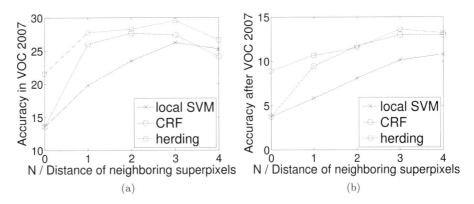

(a)   (b)

Figure 8.2: Average accuracy of segmentations by the local SVM classifier (cross), CRF (circle), and Herding (square) with different number of neighboring super-pixels used for extracting local features. N denotes the maximal distance of the neighboring super-pixel used. The left plot uses the 2007 segmentation benchmark criteria (average recall). The plot on the right uses the 2010 criteria on the 2007 data set (average overlap).

		background	aeroplane	bicycle	bird	boat	bottle	bus	car	cat	chair	cow	diningtable	dog	horse	motorbike	person	pottedplant	sheep	sofa	train	tvmonitor	Average
	Local	46	7	15	**10**	8	**10**	31	51	34	**17**	6	**16**	41	23	58	50	18	21	**15**	36	**39**	26
Recall	CRF	56	**20**	12	2	**15**	7	33	52	**59**	8	**10**	8	31	20	68	**55**	12	15	**15**	**49**	36	28
	Herd	**62**	3	**16**	3	7	7	**38**	58	50	15	2	11	**58**	**24**	**70**	54	**20**	**23**	14	47	**39**	**30**
	Local	50	**2**	6	**8**	2	0	13	21	14	2	**2**	4	8	10	24	20	6	**8**	**5**	12	10	11
Overlap	CRF	**65**	1	**8**	0	2	0	15	**30**	**17**	3	0	4	5	10	**37**	24	**9**	**8**	**5**	18	**13**	13
	Herd	60	**2**	4	4	**3**	**5**	**23**	28	15	**4**	0	**5**	**20**	**12**	31	22	6	**8**	3	18	12	**14**

Table 8.1: Accuracies per category and the average accuracy of PASCAL VOC 2007 data set. Each model uses the N value that maximizes the average test accuracy. The top table shows recall (PASCAL 2007 benchmark), and the bottom table shows overlap (PASCAL 2010 benchmark)

recall of the background category by much but will reduce the intersection over union ratio of the detected category.

Remarkably, Herding performs much better than the local method when $N = 0$. The accuracy is improved from 14% to 22% on the first measurement and 4% to 9% on the second measurement, whereas CRF does not help at all. The local classifier performs poorly because the histogram feature is computed from few pixels as discussed in Fulkerson et al. (2010). Thus, regularization on the pairwise term should improve the prediction. It turns out that the optimal value of λ for Herding is about 1.1×10^3, which

Figure 8.3: A typical example of segmentations when $N = 0$. The top two images are the original image (left) and the ground truth segmentation (right). The remaining four images (left to right, top to bottom) are, respectively, the segmentation of the local model, CRF, Herding, and a CRF with linear potential functions. The local model is noisy because the histogram of SIFT features is computed from few pixels.

means the importance of the pairwise feature is $\sqrt{\lambda} \approx 33$ times higher than the unary feature, matching our expectation. However, the best value for CRF is only about 1.1. The difference in the choice of λ leads to the significant difference in the segmentations as shown with a typical example in Figure 8.3. Herding outputs a highly smoothed result with clear boundaries whereas CRF does not noticeably change the decision of the local classifier.

Two properties of Herding previously stated in Section 8.3 would help explain the distinct choices of λ. Firstly, with a large λ, Herding tries to average the distribution of super-pixels in a smooth area. Although the local SVMs give noisy results, the average distributions still contain strong signals about the true category. In contrast, the CRF computes the product of distributions, which makes the noise in the final distribution even worse. So CRF has to choose a small λ. To verify this hypothesis, we train a CRF with energy as a linear function of features $p_i(y_i|x_i)$ and $p_{ij}(y_i \neq y_j|x_i, x_j)$

$$P_{\text{crf-linear}}(\boldsymbol{y}|\boldsymbol{x}) = \frac{1}{Z} \exp\left(\sum_i p_i(y_i|x_i) + \lambda \sum_{i,j} p_{ij}(y_i \neq y_j|x_i, x_j)\right), \quad (8.29)$$

which also computes the average of distributions when λ is large. The new CRF chooses a large λ (≈ 22) as expected, and the accuracy is improved to 16% and 7%, respectively. However, Figure 8.3 shows that the result is oversmoothed because of the high penalty of boundaries. Secondly, Herding not only increases smoothness in flat areas but also encourages boundaries at strong edges. That is why Herding still captures the shape of the object correctly even with a large value of λ.

8.4 Application: Go Game Prediction

In this section, we look at another application of the Herding algorithm to predicting the outcome of a Go game. A Go game is a board game where two players of different colors, black and white, place stones in turn on a 19×19 board. The player with the larger territory at the end of a game wins. The game of Go is known to be difficult for artificial intelligence approaches because it (1) has a large branch factor, 361, in the game tree; and (2) is hard to evaluate the *goodness* of an incomplete game because of long-distance correlations between stones. We tackle the second problem and propose to predict the outcome of a territory given an incomplete board as a structured prediction task. The predicted territory output can then be utilized as an evaluation function for the current board. Stern et al. (2004) proposed a CRF model for prediction with features based on pairs of neighboring stones. We treat this approach as a benchmark and compare it to the performance of Herding on the same problems.

In an incomplete game, every position has three possible values; *Black*, *White*, and *Empty*. At the end of a game, every position is occupied by either *Black* or *White*.[2] Denote by a vector $\boldsymbol{x} \in \{Black, White, Empty\}^N$ the stones of an incomplete game with $N = 19 \times 19$ and denote by a vector $\boldsymbol{y} \in \{0, 1\}^N$ the final territory, where 1 means *Black* and 0 means *White*. The task of this section is to model the conditional distribution $p(\boldsymbol{y}|\boldsymbol{x})$. While it can be quite difficult to directly compute the joint distribution of all the stones on the board, it is fairly easy to obtain a local conditional

---

2. We adopt the Chinese rule in scoring and ignore the stones shared by both players.

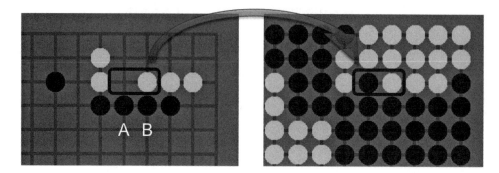

Figure 8.4: Part of a Go board of an incomplete game (left) and its final territory (right). A local model predicts the outcome of a patch (e.g., a pair of stones) based on its current values.

model for a small patch of stones $p_\alpha(\boldsymbol{y}_\alpha | \boldsymbol{x}_\alpha)$, where α denotes the position of the patch. Figure 8.4 illustrates a case where the local conditional model patch is a pair of neighboring stones. We also consider larger patches, such as a square patch or a cross-shaped patch consisting of a stone and its four immediate neighbors. Such patches are straightforward to introduce in Herding but difficult in the CRF model of Stern et al. (2004) because a larger patch introduces more parameters and makes inference more difficult.

The conditional probabilities for small patches can be estimated from a training set by counting the number of occurrences of each patch configuration at all patch locations. A uniform prior can be used to smooth this empirical estimate. These smoothed empirical estimates can be used as local predictions of the final territory of each patch $\mathbb{E}_{p_\alpha}[\mathbb{I}[\boldsymbol{y}_\alpha = \boldsymbol{z}_\alpha] | \boldsymbol{x}_\alpha], \forall \alpha, \boldsymbol{z}_\alpha$ given an incomplete game $\boldsymbol{x}$. We can use these estimates as the input feature moments, $\psi_{\alpha,\boldsymbol{z}}(\boldsymbol{y}) = \mathbb{I}[\boldsymbol{y}_\alpha = \boldsymbol{z}_\alpha]$, and run Herding in (8.24, 8.25) to produce pseudo-samples of the final territory of the whole board, $\{\boldsymbol{y}^t\}$. The average of these pseudo-samples are taken as our predicted final territory. Because the conditional probabilities are estimated independently at each location from a finite training set, we again have the problem of inconsistent moments. From the analysis in Section 8.2.3, the joint distribution of $\boldsymbol{y}$ from Herding will minimize its L_2 distance from the input local conditionals.

When the state of a patch in an incomplete game $\boldsymbol{x}_\alpha$ is all *Empty*, a local classifier cannot tell which player is more likely to win the patch. As an example, consider the empty patch "A-B" in Figure 8.4. The possession of this patch depends solely on the stones in its neighborhood. As a result, the local classifier p_{AB} will not provide any preference for y_A and y_B to be *Black* or *White*, and the four possible states of patch "A-B" will have equal probability: $p_{AB}(y_{AB} = BB) = p_{AB}(y_{AB} = WW)$ and $p_{AB}(y_{AB} = BW) = p_{AB}(y_{AB} = WB)$. Herding treats these probabilities as moments that the average over its pseudo-samples must match. These vague moments must be matched along with more informative moments from neighboring classifiers (e.g., from the black stones above patch "A-B"). Simultaneously satisfying all of these constraints will lead to the undesirable result that about half of the Herding pseudo-samples will be $y_A = Black$ and half $y_A = White$. We avoid this problem by reducing the four local moments into two input moments — namely, $p_{AB}(y_{AB} = BB \text{ or } WW)$ or $p_{AB}(y_{AB} = BW \text{ or } BW)$. This allows Herding to only check whether y_A and y_B have the same color and ignore the fact that y_A is more likely to be one color than the other. As a result, Herding is free to give high probability to either $y_A = Black$ or $y_A = White$ when neighboring patches have a strong preference for either player. In general, when the conditioning patch is all *Empty*, we reduce the inputs moments in this manner by combining states with opposing colors: $\mathbb{E}_{p_\alpha}[\mathbb{I}[\boldsymbol{y}_\alpha = \boldsymbol{z}_\alpha \text{ or } \neg \boldsymbol{z}_\alpha]|\boldsymbol{x}_\alpha$ is all *Empty*].

We compare the performance of Herding using a five-stone cross-shape patch with the *Boltzmann5* CRF model proposed by Stern et al. (2004). That CRF includes unary features for each single stone, $\psi_i(y_i) = y_i$, and pairwise features for neighboring stone pairs, $\psi_{ij}(y_i, y_j) = y_i y_j$. The MLE of the parameters is learned with two inference methods: a generalization of Swendsen-Wang sampler and loopy belief propagation (BP). Because the difference of the predictive performance w.r.t. cross-entropy is not significant between those two methods (see Figure 4 of Stern et al., 2004) and Swendsen-Wang is much slower than BP, we only compare Herding with a *Boltzmann5* model trained and tested with loopy BP.

We train and test our predictive models on a data set of $25,089$ games by professional players.[3] We prune the games that are not complete and use the GNU GO program[4] to obtain the final territory of the remaining games. The data set is then split into a training set of 5993 games and a test set of 2595 games. We follow the practice in Stern et al. (2004) and train Herding and CRF in three stages of 20, 80, and 150 moves. The predictive performance is evaluated at each of these stages using the metric of cross-entropy between actual territory outcomes, $\boldsymbol{y} \in \{0,1\}^N$, and the prediction, $\hat{\boldsymbol{y}} \in [0,1]^N$

$$\mathcal{H} = \frac{1}{N} \sum_{i=1}^{N} [y_i \log \hat{y}_i + (1 - y_i) \log(1 - \hat{y}_i)]. \tag{8.30}$$

Training each stage of the CRF model takes roughly three hours, whereas only 34 seconds were needed to compute the local conditional probabilities

---

3. Provided by `http://gokifu.com`.
4. Downloaded from `http://www.gnu.org/software/gnugo`.

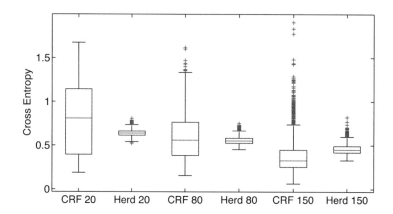

Figure 8.5: Cross-entropy of final territory prediction on the test set by the CRF model and Herding at moves 20, 80, and 150. Lower is better.

used by Herding. Prediction times are similar for the two methods: an average of 0.37 seconds per test game in the CRF and 0.5 seconds for Herding.

Figure 8.5 shows the cross-entropy on the test set with the CRF model and Herding. The mean of the cross-entropy for both the CRF model and Herding as well as the variance for the CRF decrease at later stages of games. This is reasonable because when a game is close to complete, it becomes easier to predict the final territory. Compared with the CRF, Herding has smaller variance across different games throughout all the stages. It also achieves better average prediction than the CRF at an early stage move 20) with both lower mean and smaller variance. But as the game progresses, the advantage diminishes, and it is eventually outperformed by the CRF at a later stage (move 150).

We compare the predictions of these two methods with a rule-based commercial software, "Many Faces of Go," using an example game in Figure 8.6. We can see the apparent difference between the predictions of Herding and the CRF. Herding tends to make conservative predictions especially in empty areas such as the middle of the board at move 20. It is confident only when one player has a clearly stronger influence, for instance, in the upper right corner. In contrast, the CRF tends to be overconfident about its predictions as shown in those empty areas at moves 20 and 80. This problem is also mentioned in Stern et al. (2004), where the Swendsen-Wang sampling algorithm gives more conservative predictions than loopy BP (Figure 2). However, it still appears to be overconfident, especially at the early stages when there are few stones nearby. As the game progresses, it becomes increasingly clear whose territory the remaining empty areas belong to. In that case, we should be able to make a confident prediction about those areas according to their surrounding stones' color, and the CRF method shows superior performance to Herding as observed at move 150. Also, we notice that the CRF is capable of detecting captured stones such as the two white stones in the lower middle part at moves 80 and 150, but it often makes false-positive mistakes at early stages of a game. In contrast, Herding usually has conservative predictions for captured stones.

8.5   Conclusion

In this chapter, we introduced the Herding approach to structured prediction problems and discussed its relationship to other prevailing methods including CRFs, S-SVMs, M^3 networks, and SPs. In particular, we present Herding as a new technique for combining local, discriminatively trained classifiers over subsets of labels into a harmonious joint model. The method is an alternative to piecewise trained CRFs and follows a markedly different philosophy, in that it never learns a joint model but rather generates representative points of some (unknown) joint distribution $p(\boldsymbol{y}|\boldsymbol{x})$.

An important theoretical contribution of this chapter relative to previous work (Gelfand et al., 2010) is that we prove that inconsistent marginals will be orthogonally projected onto the marginal polytope. This makes Herding a unique way to combine inconsistent local classifiers. Remarkably, the fast convergence rate of $\mathcal{O}(1/T)$ is preserved in this situation.

We demonstrated our algorithm on image segmentation and Go game prediction tasks, showing it is competitive in both tasks. Herding differs greatly from approaches that combine local predictions using CRFs. Predictions based on piecewise CRFs output the most likely assignment that maximizes the *product* of local beliefs (implicitly assuming independence), whereas Herding obtains a joint distribution over all labels that compromises among inconsistent local beliefs in terms of the L_2 distance. Herding's predictions often appear more coherent as a result (see Figures 8.1 and 8.6).

Because different local predictions may have varying confidence in their prediction, it is important to assign different weights during combination. In the image segmentation task, we optimize the relative step size λ on an evaluation set in order to balance the evidence from the local appearance cue and boundary information. In the Go prediction task, we ignore uninformative marginals from classifiers on empty patches. A more principled approach to weighting local classifiers is a direction of future research.

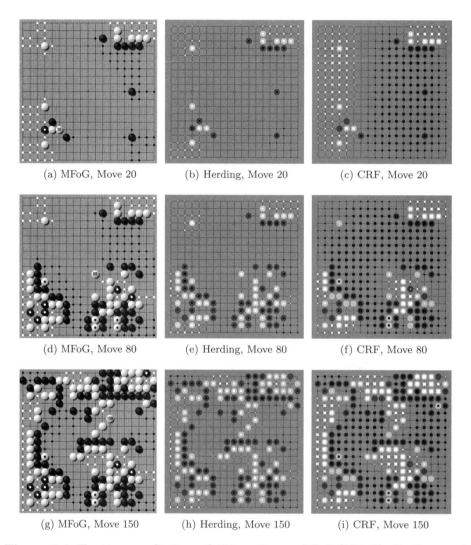

(a) MFoG, Move 20   (b) Herding, Move 20   (c) CRF, Move 20

(d) MFoG, Move 80   (e) Herding, Move 80   (f) CRF, Move 80

(g) MFoG, Move 150   (h) Herding, Move 150   (i) CRF, Move 150

Figure 8.6: Territory predictions of "Many Faces of Go" (MFoG), Herding, and the CRF model at three stages: moves 20, 80, and 150. The large circles represent current stones. MFoG outputs deterministic predictions (small dots). For the latter two methods, small squares represent final territory prediction from 0 (maximum white square) to 1 (maximum black square).

8.6   References

P. Arbelaez, M. Maire, C. Fowlkes, and J. Malik. Contour detection and hierarchical image segmentation. *IEEE Transactions on Pattern Analysis and Machine Intelligence*, 33(5), 2011. ISSN 0162-8828.

H. Block and S. Levin. On the boundedness of an iterative procedure for solving a system of linear inequalities. *Proceedings of the American Mathematical Society*, 26(2):229–235, 1970.

Y. Boykov and V. Kolmogorov. An experimental comparison of min-cut/max-flow algorithms for energy minimization in vision. *IEEE Transactions on Pattern Analysis and Machine Intelligence*, 26(9):1124–1137, September 2004.

Y. Boykov, O. Veksler, and R. Zabih. Efficient approximate energy minimization via graph cuts. *IEEE Transactions on Pattern Analysis and Machine Intelligence*, 20(12):1222–1239, November 2001.

Y. Chen, A. Gelfand, C. Fowlkes, and M. Welling. Integrating local classifiers through nonlinear dynamics on label graphs with an application to image segmentation. In *ICCV*, pages 2635–2642, 2011.

M. Collins. Discriminative training methods for hidden markov models: Theory and experiments with perceptron algorithms. In *Conference on Empirical Methods in Natural Language Processing (EMNLP)*, 2002.

B. Fulkerson, A. Vedaldi, and S. Soatto. Class segmentation and object localization with superpixel neighborhoods. In *Computer Vision, 2009 IEEE 12th International Conference on*, pages 670–677, 2010.

A. Gelfand, L. van der Maaten, Y. Chen, and M. Welling. On Herding and the cycling perceptron theorem. In *Advances in Neural Information Processing Systems 23*, pages 694–702, 2010.

V. Kolmogorov and R. Zabih. What energy functions can be minimized via graph cuts? *IEEE Transactions on Pattern Analysis and Machine Intelligence*, 26(2): 147–159, February 2004.

J. Lafferty, A. McCallum, and F. Pereira. Conditional random fields: Probabilistic models for segmenting and labeling sequence data. In *Proc. 18th International Conf. on Machine Learning*, pages 282–289, 2001.

M. Minsky and S. Papert. *Perceptrons — An Introduction to Computational Geometry*. MIT Press, 1969.

P. Pletscher, C. S. Ong, and J. M. Buhmann. Entropy and margin maximization for structured output learning. In *Proceedings of the 2010 European Conference on Machine Learning and Knowledge Discovery in Databases: Part III*, pages 83–98. Springer, 2010.

F. Rosenblatt. The perceptron — a probabilistic model for information storage and organization in the brain. *Psychological Review*, 65(6):386–408, 1958.

D. H. Stern, T. Graepel, and D. J. MacKay. Modelling uncertainty in the game of go. *Advances in Neural Information Processing Systems*, 17:1353–1360, 2004.

C. Sutton and A. McCallum. Piecewise pseudolikelihood for efficient training of conditional random fields. In *Proceedings of the 24th international conference on Machine learning*, pages 863–870. ACM, 2007.

B. Taskar, C. Guestrin, and D. Koller. Max-margin Markov networks. In *Neural Information Processing Systems (NIPS-03)*, Vancouver, Canada, 2003.

I. Tsochantaridis, T. Hofmann, T. Joachims, and Y. Altun. Support vector machine learning for interdependent and structured output spaces. In *Proceedings of the 21st International Conference on Machine Learning*, New York, 2004.

M. Welling. Herding dynamical weights to learn. In *Proceedings of the 21st International Conference on Machine Learning*, Montreal, Canada, 2009.

M. Welling and Y. Chen. Statistical inference using weak chaos and infinite memory. In *Proceedings of the Int'l Workshop on Statistical-Mechanical Informatics (IW-SMI 2010)*, pages 185–199, 2010.

9   Training Structured Predictors Through Iterated Logistic Regression

Justin Domke   justin.domke@nicta.com.au
NICTA & The Australian National University
Canberra, Australia

In a setting where approximate inference is necessary, structured learning can be formulated as a joint optimization of inference "messages" and local potentials. This chapter observes that, for fixed messages, the optimization problem with respect to potentials takes the form of a logistic regression problem biased by the current set of messages. This observation leads to an algorithm that alternates between message-passing inference updates and learning updates. It is possible to employ any set of potential functions where an algorithm exists to optimize a logistic loss, including linear functions, boosted decision trees, and multi-layer perceptrons.

9.1   Introduction

This chapter is concerned with the discrete structured prediction problem, in which some input vector x is used to predict an output vector y by maximizing an "energy" function F to find

$$y^* = \underset{y \in \mathcal{Y}}{\operatorname{argmax}} F(x, y). \tag{9.1}$$

Here, $x \in \mathcal{X}$ is the input space, typically a set of real vectors. The output space is a set of N dimensional vectors $y \in \mathcal{Y} = \mathcal{Y}_1 \times \mathcal{Y}_2 \times ... \times \mathcal{Y}_N$, where $\mathcal{Y}_i$ is a discrete set of the values y_i can obtain.

$$\{\alpha\} = \{\{1\}, ..., \{N\}, \{1, 2\}, ..., \{N-1, N\}\}$$

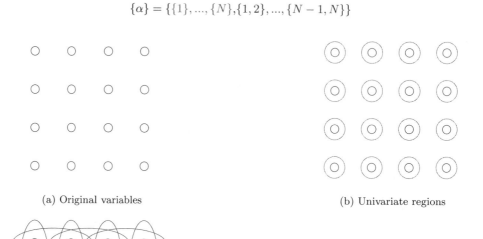

(a) Original variables   (b) Univariate regions

(c) Pair regions

Figure 9.1: In imaging problems, it is common to use a "grid" structure, where there is one region $\alpha = \{i\}$ corresponding to each pixel i and one region $\alpha = \{i, j\}$ corresponding to each neighboring pair in the four-connected grid.

Here, we assume that the function F decomposes as

$$F(x, y) = \sum_{\alpha} f_{\alpha}(x, y_{\alpha}). \tag{9.2}$$

This sum ranges over a set of *regions* α (Koller and Friedman, 2009, Sec 11.3.7.3), each of which is a subset of $\{1, 2, ..., N\}$. Each region is selected to capture a set of interdependent output variables (see Figure 9.1). The function f_{α} encourages the variables y_{α} to take on a value such that $f_{\alpha}(x, y_{\alpha})$ is high.

Given some annotated data set $(x^1, y^1), ..., (x^M, y^M)$, the structured learning problem is to pick the form of the function F. Intuitively speaking, one would like to select F such that

$$y^k \approx \underset{y \in \mathcal{Y}}{\text{argmax}} \; F(x^k, y) \qquad \forall k \in \{1, ..., M\}. \tag{9.3}$$

However, there are two complicating factors. First, it will typically be impossible to adjust F such that that (9.3) is exactly equal for all k. (More precisely, using a class of functions with sufficient power to accomplish, this would be undesirable due to overfitting.) Thus, a loss function must be specified to trade off between different types of errors on different examples. Secondly, when the function F changes, the maximizing argument of (9.3) changes discontinuously. Thus, the loss must be stated *implicitly* in terms of the result of a maximization, which presents computational difficulties in selecting the best function.

9.2   Linear vs. Nonlinear Learning

Most commonly, $F(x, y) = \sum_\alpha f_\alpha(x, y_\alpha)$ can be written in the linear form

$$F(x, y) = \sum_\alpha w^T \Phi_\alpha(x, y_\alpha).$$

The function Φ_α produces a set of features that reveal aspects of the interdependency of the variables y_α, possibly also taking into account the input x. The learning problem is then to select the vector of weights w so as to make the mapping in (9.1) accurate.

This chapter considers the more general case where each factor f_α is only assumed to be a member of some set of (possibly nonlinear) functions $\mathcal{F}_\alpha$. The learning problem is thus instead to select $f_\alpha \in \mathcal{F}_\alpha$ for all α.

A motivation for using more general function classes is the common existing practice to fit a nonlinear function class to predict each variable independently. These univariate potentials are then fixed, while linear weights are adjusted for interaction potentials (Section 9.9). There are two weaknesses to this approach. Firstly, only linear weights are learned for interaction potentials, rather than more powerful functions. Secondly, the nonlinear functions learned for the univariate potentials are suboptimal for joint prediction.

9.3 Overview

The algorithm presented in this chapter can be seen as building on two streams of research for fitting structured predictors in the setting where exact inference is intractable:

▪ Piecewise learning (Sutton and Mccallum, 2009) trains a structured predictor by splitting the model into a set of "pieces," which could be individual factors or other structures where exact inference can be performed. These pieces are then trained independently of the rest of the graph. This can be justified as a bound on the true likelihood. This has advantages of computational convenience and is fairly amenable to using nonlinear potential functions when learning but does not always lead to good performance for joint prediction, because the bound on the likelihood can be quite loose.

▪ Algorithms based on formulating a joint learning and inference objective (Hazan and Urtasun, 2012; Meshi et al., 2010) deal with approximate inference in a principled way by alternating between message-passing updates and gradient updates of parameters. However, these algorithms deal only with linear potential functions.

The algorithm presented in this chapter is similar to both of the above. As pictured in Figure 9.3, it begins by training all factors separately via logistic regression. This is similar to piecewise learning, and it is possible to use nonlinear factors. However, after this first step, message-passing inference proceeds, which creates a new set of logistic regression problems reflecting the biases from other factors. Iterating this process leads to an optimum of a learning objective reflecting both messages and potential functions.

Proofs of all the theorems stated in this chapter are given in the appendix.

9.4 Loss Functions

Structured learning usually follows the standard framework of empirical risk minimization, wherein given a data set $(x^1, y^1), ..., (x^N, y^N)$, the goal of learning is to select F to minimize the empirical risk

$$R(F) = \sum_k l(x^k, y^k; F), \tag{9.4}$$

for some loss function l. In early work on structured learning (Taskar et al., 2003), the loss takes the form

$$l_0(x^k, y^k; F) = -F(x^k, y^k) + \max_{y \in \mathcal{Y}} F(x^k, y) + \Delta(y^k, y), \qquad (9.5)$$

where $\Delta(y^k, y)$ is a discrepancy measure of how "different" y^k is from y. If $\Delta = 0$, notice that l_0 is a perceptron-type loss, which measures the energy of the top-scoring value $\max_{y \in \mathcal{Y}} F(x^k, y)$ minus the energy of the true value $F(x^k, y^k)$. The loss will be zero if y^k scores as well as any other value. When Δ is nonzero, it is necessary for the score of y^k to be at least $\Delta(y^k, y)$ better than y in order for the loss to be zero. Essentially, if some configuration y is extremely "bad," then y^k must score significantly higher than y in order to incur zero loss.

A common discrepancy function is the indicator $\Delta(y^k, y) = I[y^k \neq y]$, which is one if $y^k \neq y$ and zero if $y^k = y$. In this case, it is easy to show that the loss becomes the multiclass hinge loss (Crammer and Singer, 2002)

$$l_0(x^k, y^k; F) = \max\left(0, 1 + \max_{y \neq y^k \in \mathcal{Y}} F(x^k, y) - F(x^k, y^k)\right). \qquad (9.6)$$

Another common discrepancy (which will be used in the experiments later in this chapter) is the Hamming distance $\Delta(y^k, y) = \sum_i I[y_i^k \neq y_i]$, which measures the number of components in which y^k and y differ. The rest of this chapter will assume that the discrepancy decomposes over the set of regions, (i.e., it can be written as $\Delta(y^k, y) = \sum_\alpha \Delta_\alpha(y_\alpha^k, y_\alpha)$).

The maximization in (9.5) ranges over all discrete labelings, a set that is in general exponentially large. Thus, this loss is practical only when there exists a special structure that allows one to quickly find the maximum. For example, if the graph obeys a tree structure, then dynamic-programming algorithms can compute the maximum. If using a linear energy, learning can then proceed either through subgradient descent (Ratliff et al., 2007) or constraint generation methods (Tsochantaridis et al., 2005; Taskar et al., 2003).

To overcome these issues, a common approach is to use a relaxed version of the loss, where rather than optimizing over all discrete labelings, one optimizes over all sets of marginals. The relaxed loss is defined as

$$l_1(x^k, y^k; F) = -F(x^k, y^k) + \max_{\mu \in \mathcal{M}} F(x^k, \mu) + \Delta(y^k, \mu). \qquad (9.7)$$

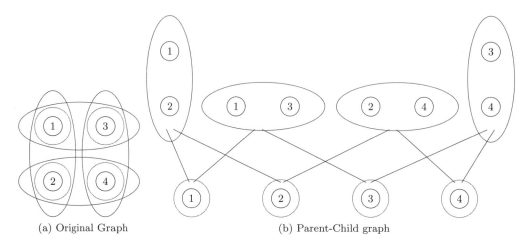

(a) Original Graph   (b) Parent-Child graph

Figure 9.2: An example graph with four nodes and eight regions, namely, $\{\alpha\} = \{\{1\}, \{2\}, \{3\}, \{4\}, \{1, 2\}, \{1, 3\}, \{2, 4\}, \{3, 4\}\}$. The parent child graph represents each region, with links between "parent" regions that contain all the nodes in "child" regions.

Here, $\mu = \{\mu_\alpha(y_\alpha)\}$ is a set of marginals, assigning some probability to each possible configuration of each region. As a slight abuse, the notation of F and Δ is overloaded to allow arguments of marginals.[1]

If the set $\mathcal{M}$ is defined appropriately, l_1 is equivalent to l_0. Specifically, suppose that each marginal μ_α is restricted to put all probability on one configuration, and that these assignments are consistent between regions that consider the same set of variables. Let $\mu_{\alpha\beta}(y_\beta) = \sum_{y_{\alpha\setminus\beta}} \mu_\alpha(y_\alpha)$ denote μ_α marginalized out over a subregion β. If $\mathcal{M}$ takes the form

$$
\begin{aligned}
\mathcal{M} = \{\mu | \mu_\alpha(y_\alpha) &\in \{0, 1\} && \forall \alpha, y_\alpha, \\
\sum_{y_\alpha} \mu_\alpha(y_\alpha) &= 1 && \forall \alpha, \\
\mu_{\alpha\beta}(y_\beta) &= \mu_\beta(y_\beta) && \forall \alpha \supset \beta, y_\beta\},
\end{aligned}
\tag{9.8}
$$

and it is not hard to show that l_0 and l_1 are equivalent. (See Chapter 2 for a detailed discussion of the marginal polytope and its relaxations.) Here, a "parent-child" representation of the graph is used, where each region α interacts with those regions that are subsets or supersets (Figure 9.2).

---

1. Specifically, F is defined as $F(x^k, \mu) = \sum_\alpha \sum_{y_\alpha} f_\alpha(x^k, y_\alpha)\mu_\alpha(y_\alpha)$, while Δ is defined as $\Delta(y^k, \mu) = \sum_\alpha \sum_{y_\alpha} \Delta_\alpha(y_\alpha^k, y_\alpha)\mu_\alpha(y_\alpha)$.

However, with this constraint set, l_1 is no easier to evaluate than l_0, as it takes the form of a difficult integer linear programming problem. However, as is commonly done to approximate integer programs (Vazirani, 2001), this can be approximated by replacing $\mathcal{M}$ with a set that makes the maximization in (9.7) easier. Specifically, it is common (Finley and Joachims, 2008) to use a linear programming relaxation like

$$
\begin{aligned}
\mathcal{M} = \{\mu | \mu_\alpha(y_\alpha) \in [0,1] \quad & \forall \alpha, y_\alpha, \\
\sum_{y_\alpha} \mu_\alpha(y_\alpha) = 1 \quad & \forall \alpha, \\
\mu_{\alpha\beta}(y_\beta) = \mu_\beta(y_\beta) \quad & \forall \alpha \supset \beta, y_\beta\},
\end{aligned}
\tag{9.9}
$$

which leads to a loss that can be evaluated through the solution of a linear programming problem. Moreover, because $\mathcal{M}$ has been replaced with a larger set, it is easy to see that $l_1 \geq l_0$, meaning good performance on this surrogate loss will guarantee good performance in the original one.

It is convenient to introduce the notation of

$$
\theta_F^k(y_\alpha) = f_\alpha(x^k, y_\alpha) + \Delta_\alpha(y_\alpha^k, y_\alpha),
\tag{9.10}
$$

in which case l_1 can be written in the equivalent form

$$
l_1(x^k, y^k; F) = -F(x^k, y^k) + \max_{\mu \in \mathcal{M}} \theta_F^k \cdot \mu,
\tag{9.11}
$$

where we define the inner product between θ and μ as

$$
\theta \cdot \mu = \sum_\alpha \sum_{y_\alpha} \theta(y_\alpha) \mu_\alpha(y_\alpha).
$$

Now, while it is tractable to compute l_1, it is not smooth as a function of F, which rules out the use of certain optimization methods for learning. A solution to this is to add "entropy" smoothing—that is, to replace the loss with

$$
l(x^k, y^k; F) = -F(x^k, y^k) + \max_{\mu \in \mathcal{M}} \left(\theta_F^k \cdot \mu + \epsilon \sum_\alpha H(\mu_\alpha) \right),
\tag{9.12}
$$

where $H(\mu_\alpha) = -\sum_{y_\alpha} \mu_\alpha(y_\alpha) \log \mu_\alpha(y_\alpha)$. Hazan and Urtasun (2012) consider a more general class of approximate entropies (where different factors α can have varying weights ϵ_α) and note that, depending on the entropy approximation and the divergence Δ, l_2 can encompass both surrogate likelihood (Wainwright, 2006) and structured prediction types of objectives.

Meshi et al. (2012) consider approximating the inference problem of $\max_{\mu \in \mathcal{M}} \theta \cdot \mu$ with the smoothed problem $\max_{\mu \in \mathcal{M}} \theta \cdot \mu + \epsilon \sum_\alpha H(\mu_\alpha)$. They show that message-passing algorithms for performing this maximization can have guaranteed convergence rates and the difference of the two objectives is linear in ϵ. A similar result can be shown that bounds the difference of the two losses as stated in the following theorem.

Theorem 9.1. *l and l_1 are bounded by (where $|y_\alpha| = \prod_{i \in \alpha} |\mathcal{Y}_i|$ is the number of configurations of y_α)*

$$l_1(x, y, F) \leq l(x, y, F) \leq l_1(x, y, F) + \epsilon H_{\max}, \quad H_{\max} = \sum_\alpha \log |y_\alpha|.$$

It is sometimes convenient to write l as

$$
\begin{aligned}
l(x^k, y^k; F) &= -F(x^k, y^k) + A(\theta_F^k), \\
A(\theta) &= \max_{\mu \in \mathcal{M}} \theta \cdot \mu + \sum_\alpha \epsilon H(\mu_\alpha).
\end{aligned}
$$

Intuitively speaking, here $F(x^k, y^k)$ measures the score of the correct output y^k. Meanwhile, $A(\theta_F^k)$ measures the score of the "worst" configuration, taking into account the discrepancy Δ and approximated using entropy smoothing and the relaxation of $\mathcal{M}$ from (9.9). Thus, one would like $F(x^k, y^k)$ to be large and $A(\theta_F^k)$ to be small, which is exactly what l measures.

9.5   Message-Passing Inference

Evaluating the loss defined in the previous section on a particular datum requires performing an optimization to evaluate $A(\theta_F^k)$ for that datum. As will be discussed in the following section, it is convenient to represent A in a dual form as a minimization.

Theorem 9.2. *$A(\theta)$ can be represented in the dual form $A(\theta) = \min_\lambda A(\lambda, \theta)$, where*

$$A(\lambda, \theta) = \max_{\mu \in \mathcal{N}} \theta \cdot \mu + \epsilon \sum_\alpha H(\mu_\alpha) + \sum_\alpha \sum_{\beta \subset \alpha} \sum_{x_\beta} \lambda_\alpha(x_\beta) \left(\mu_{\alpha\beta}(y_\beta) - \mu_\beta(y_\beta) \right),$$

$$(9.13)$$

and $\mathcal{N} = \{\mu | \sum_{y_\alpha} \mu_\alpha(y_\alpha) = 1 \, \forall \alpha, \mu_\alpha(y_\alpha) \geq 0 \, \forall \alpha, y_\alpha\}$ is the set of locally normalized pseudomarginals. Moreover, for a fixed λ, the maximizing μ is *given by*

$$\mu_\alpha(y_\alpha) = \frac{1}{Z_\alpha} \exp\left(\frac{1}{\epsilon}\left(\theta(y_\alpha) + \sum_{\beta \subset \alpha} \lambda_\alpha(y_\beta) - \sum_{\gamma \supset \alpha} \lambda_\gamma(y_\alpha)\right)\right), \quad (9.14)$$

where Z_α is a normalizing constant to ensure that $\sum_{y_\alpha} \mu_\alpha(y_\alpha) = 1$. Moreover, the actual value of $A(\lambda, \theta)$ is

$$A(\lambda, \theta) = \sum_\alpha \epsilon \log \sum_{y_\alpha} \exp\left(\frac{1}{\epsilon}\left(\theta(y_\alpha) + \sum_{\beta \subset \alpha} \lambda_\alpha(y_\beta) - \sum_{\gamma \supset \alpha} \lambda_\gamma(y_\alpha)\right)\right).$$
$$(9.15)$$

The problem remains of how to actually minimize $A(\lambda, \theta)$ with respect to λ. This is a smooth unconstrained optimization, which could in principle be performed by a variety of generic optimization methods, for example, gradient descent. However, there is now long precedent for optimizing objectives like this through "message-passing" algorithms that more closely mirror the structure of the graph (Wainwright and Jordan, 2008).

Consider doing coordinate descent. Danskin's theorem states that taking the derivative of $A(\lambda, \theta)$ with respect to an element $\lambda_\alpha(y_\beta)$ will recover the constraint that this multiplier enforces, namely, that

$$\frac{dA(\lambda, \theta)}{d\lambda_\alpha(y_\beta)} = \mu_{\alpha\beta}(y_\beta) - \mu_\beta(y_\beta),$$

where μ is as defined in (9.14).

Thus, if one can find a set of multipliers such that all marginalization constraints are satisfied, then the gradient of $A(\lambda, \theta)$ with respect to λ is zero, meaning the global optimum would have been found. In practice, such a solution cannot usually be found in closed form, and one resorts to iterative methods. Suppose, however, that one could adjust the values of a subset of multipliers $\lambda_\alpha(x_\beta)$ to enforce the corresponding set of constraints while leaving other multipliers fixed. This would mean $A(\lambda, \theta)$ is optimal in the adjusted multipliers for the fixed values of the nonadjusted multipliers. Thus, an iterative process that repeatedly adjusts blocks of multipliers like this constitutes a block coordinate descent scheme.

Different sizes of "blocks" are possible, ranging from a single set of multipliers from a region α to a subregion β, to subtrees of the original graph (Sontag and Jaakkola, 2009). Here, we consider an intermediate strategy, where, given some region ν, all multipliers $\lambda_\alpha(y_\nu)$, with $\alpha \supset \nu$ are adjusted simultaneously. This is essentially what is done in the parent-child algorithm (Heskes, 2006) and the "star" update of Meshi et al. (2012), albeit with slightly less general conditions on the graph structure than used here.

Theorem 9.3. *Suppose that, for all $\eta \supset \nu$ simultaneously, we set $\lambda'_\eta(y_\nu) = \lambda_\eta(y_\nu) + \delta_\eta(y_\nu)$, where*

$$\delta_\eta(y_\nu) = \frac{\epsilon}{1 + N_\nu} \left(\log \mu_\nu(y_\nu) + \sum_{\eta' \supset \nu} \log \mu_{\eta'\nu}(y_\nu) \right) - \epsilon \log \mu_{\eta\nu}(y_\nu) \quad (9.16)$$

and $N_\nu = |\{\eta | \eta \supset \nu\}|$. If μ' denotes the marginals after update, then the marginalization conditions $\mu'_{\eta\nu}(y_\nu) = \mu'_\nu(y_\nu)$ will hold. Moreover, each will be proportional to the geometric mean of all marginals considered, i.e.,

$$\mu'_{\eta\nu}(y_\nu) = \mu'_\nu(y_\nu) \propto \left(\mu_\nu(y_\nu) \prod_{\eta' \supset \nu} \mu_{\eta'\nu}(y_\nu) \right)^{1/(1+N_\nu)} . \quad (9.17)$$

9.6   Joint Learning and Inference

Explicitly writing the problem of minimizing the empirical risk (9.4) with respect to F using the final loss (9.12) gives the optimization of

$$
\begin{aligned}
\min_F R(F) &= \min_F \sum_k \left[-F(x^k, y^k) + A(\theta_F^k) \right] \\
&= \min_F \sum_k \left[-F(x^k, y^k) + \max_{\mu \in \mathcal{M}} \left(\theta_F^k \cdot \mu + \epsilon \sum_\alpha H(\mu_\alpha) \right) \right],
\end{aligned}
$$

which takes the form of a saddle-point problem, because one is minimizing with respect to F but maximizing with respect to all the inference variables. One could conceivably solve this through an algorithm for direct saddle-point optimization (Nedi and Ozdaglar, 2009), but this is less convenient than a joint minimiztion.

However, as shown in the previous section, $A(\theta)$ has a dual representation as $A(\theta) = \min_\lambda A(\lambda, \theta)$. Thus, one can instead write the problem of minimizing the empirical risk as

$$\min_F R(F) = \min_F \min_{\{\lambda^k\}} \sum_k \left[-F(x^k, y^k) + A\left(\lambda^k, \theta_F^k\right) \right], \quad (9.18)$$

where λ^k is the vector of messages corresponding to datum k. Meshi et al. (2010) pursue an optimization like (9.18), though without entropy smoothing. They learn linear weights through iteratively updating λ^k for a single datum k and then taking a stochastic gradient step with respect to weights. Similarly, but including entropy smoothing, Hazan and Urtasun (2012) learn linear weights, alternating between message-passing updates to $\{\lambda^k\}$ and gradient updates to weights.

This chapter builds on this previous work in two ways. As before, optimization alternates between updating the energy F and the messages λ. However, here it is observed that, given a fixed set of messages, the problem of optimizing F with respect to an individual factor f_α is equivalent to solving a logistic regression problem with "bias" terms determined by the current messages added to each datum. There are two possible reasons that such an observation might be useful. First, one can optimize the empirical risk "all the way" for fixed messages, rather than taking a single gradient step. This allows one to use a range of standard optimization methods, possibly speeding up convergence. Second, it is possible to use nonlinear functions f_α, provided only that some algorithm exists to minimize a logistic loss with respect to that function class. Thus, one can easily use decision trees in structured prediction, with no need to develop new specialized learning algorithms.

9.7   Logistic Regression

In traditional linear logistic regression, one is given a data set (x^1, y^1), ..., (x^N, y^N), where $x^k \in \mathcal{R}^N$, and $y^k \in \{1, 2, \ldots, L\}$. Then, the logistic regression optimization is to find

$$\max_W \sum_k \left[(Wx^k)_{y^k} - \log \sum_y \exp(Wx^k)_y \right].$$

Here, $(Wx)_y$ denotes the y-th component of the vector of "margins" Wx. One interpretation of this optimization is fitting a conditional likelihood with a probabilistic model of the form $p(y|x; W) \propto \exp(Wx)_y$ by maximum conditional likelihood. Alternatively, it can simply be seen as a convex surrogate for classification error.

To be used in structured prediction, two generalizations of this optimization are needed. First, this chapter generalizes this to the case where the mapping from the input x to margins is some arbitrary set of functions $\mathcal{F}$.

Then, the optimization is

$$\max_{f \in \mathcal{F}} \sum_k \left[f(x^k, y^k) - \log \sum_y \exp f(x^k, y) \right].$$

Note that this is equivalent to the previous optimization if $f(x, y) = (Wx)_y$ (i.e., that $\mathcal{F}$ is the set of linear functions).

The second generalization is to add a "bias" term b^k corresponding to each datum (x^k, y^k). This is simply a term given with the data set that biases the set of margins in a given direction. With these in place, the optimization becomes

$$\max_{f \in \mathcal{F}} \sum_k \left[f(x^k, y^k) + b^k(y^k) - \log \sum_y \exp \left(f(x^k, y) + b^k(y) \right) \right].$$

This loss can be solved under various function classes (albeit sometimes only to a local maximum).

9.8 Reducing Structured Learning to Logistic Regression

Algorithm 9.1 Structured Learning via Logistic Regression

---

1. For all k, α, initialize $\lambda^k(y_\alpha) \leftarrow 0$.

2. Repeat until convergence:

   (a) For all k, for all α, set the bias term to

   $$b_\alpha^k(y_\alpha) \leftarrow \frac{1}{\epsilon} \left(\Delta(y_\alpha^k, y_\alpha) + \sum_{\beta \subset \alpha} \lambda_\alpha^k(y_\beta) - \sum_{\gamma \supset \alpha} \lambda_\gamma^k(y_\alpha) \right).$$

   (b) For all α, solve the logistic regression problem

   $$f_\alpha \leftarrow \operatorname*{argmax}_{f_\alpha \in \mathcal{F}_\alpha} \sum_{k=1}^K \left[f_\alpha(x^k, y_\alpha^k) + b_\alpha^k(y_\alpha^k) - \log \sum_{y_\alpha} \exp \left(f_\alpha(x^k, y_\alpha) + b_\alpha^k(y_\alpha) \right) \right].$$

   (c) For all k, for all α, form updated parameters as

   $$\theta^k(y_\alpha) \leftarrow \epsilon f_\alpha(x^k, y_\alpha) + \Delta(y_\alpha^k, y_\alpha).$$

   (d) For all k, perform a fixed number of message-passing iterations to update λ^k using θ^k, (9.16).

This section presents the main technical result of the chapter, namely, that the problem of minimizing (9.18) with respect to f_α is equivalent to a logistic regression problem.

Theorem 9.4. *If f_α^* is the minimizer of (9.18) for fixed messages λ, then*

$$\frac{f_\alpha^*}{\epsilon} = \operatorname*{argmax}_{f_\alpha} \sum_k \left[f_\alpha(x^k, y_\alpha^k) + b_\alpha^k(y_\alpha^k) - \log \sum_{y_\alpha} \exp\left(f_\alpha(x^k, y_\alpha) + b_\alpha^k(y_\alpha) \right) \right],$$

(9.19)

where the set of biases are defined as

$$b_\alpha^k(y_\alpha) = \frac{1}{\epsilon}\left(\Delta(y_\alpha^k, y_\alpha) + \sum_{\beta \subset \alpha} \lambda_\alpha(y_\beta) - \sum_{\gamma \supset \alpha} \lambda_\gamma(y_\alpha) \right).$$

(9.20)

The proof of this theorem, which is given in the appendix, essentially consists of substituting the value of $A(\lambda, \theta)$ from (9.15) into $\sum_k \left[-F(x^k, y^k) + A\left(\lambda^k, \theta_F^k\right) \right]$ and performing some manipulations.

Using this result, learning can simply alternate between message-passing updates (which minimize (9.18) with respect to λ) and logistic regression updates to f_α (which minimize with respect to F). Algorithm 9.1 summarizes this approach.

9.9   Function Classes

All the function classes considered in this chapter assume that the input vector x has a subvector x_α corresponding to each factor α. Then the function f_α for factor α will depend on x only through x_α. Thus, through a slight abuse of notation, it is convenient to write $f_\alpha(x, y_\alpha)$ as $f_\alpha(x_\alpha, y_\alpha)$ to emphasize that it only depends on the subvector x_α.

9.9.1   Zero

For comparison purposes, the experiments will sometimes use the set $\mathcal{F}_\alpha$ of functions that consist of the "zero" function

$$f_\alpha(x_\alpha, y_\alpha) = 0.$$

Because there is only a single element f_α in $\mathcal{F}_\alpha$, optimizing a logistic loss is trivial.

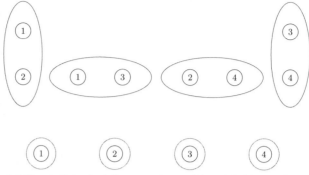

(a) Step 1: Solve logistic regression problems (similar to piecewise learning)

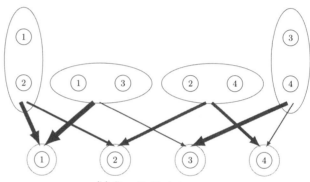

(b) Step 2: Update messages

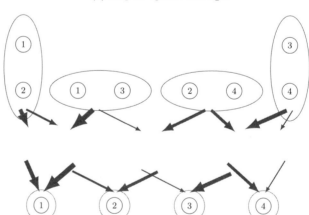

(c) Step 3: Solve biased logistic regression problems

Figure 9.3: An example of learning on the graph from Figure 9.2

9.9.2   Constant

Another simple class of functions is the set of "constant" functions

$$f_\alpha(x_\alpha, y_\alpha) = f_\alpha(y_\alpha)$$

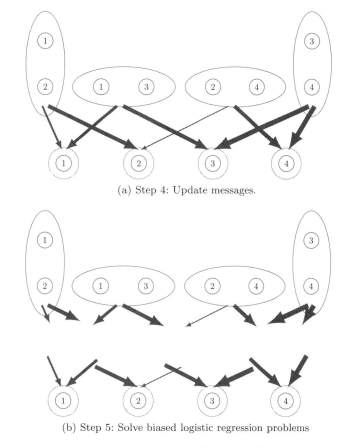

(a) Step 4: Update messages.

(b) Step 5: Solve biased logistic regression problems

Figure 9.4: An example of learning (continued).

that do not depend on x_α. These can be thought of simply as a table of values, one for each configuration y_α. Algorithmically, this class can be optimized over by fitting a linear function (as described in the following subsection) with single constant feature.

9.9.3   Linear

The most popular set of potential functions to be used in structured prediction is the linear functions. If $f_\alpha \in \mathcal{F}_\alpha$,

$$f_\alpha(x_\alpha, y_\alpha) = (W x_\alpha)_{y_\alpha}, \tag{9.21}$$

for some matrix W. Here, (9.21) should be understood as multiplying the vector x_α with the matrix W and then selecting the component corresponding to y_α.

Optimizing a logistic loss under this function class can be easily done by gradient-based methods that optimize over W. The following experiments use limited-memory BFGS to perform this optimization.

9.9.4   Boosted Decision Trees

Trees, or ensembles of trees, are another popular choice of potential function (Shotton et al., 2009; Gould et al., 2008; Xiao and Quan, 2009; Ladicky et al., 2009; Winn and Shotton, 2006; Nowozin et al., 2011; Schroff et al., 2008). Here, these are learned following the basic strategy of gradient boosting (Friedman, 1999). The basic idea is to repeatedly induce decision trees to reduce the logistic loss

$$L_k(f_\alpha) = f_\alpha(x_\alpha^k, y_\alpha^k) + b_\alpha^k(y_\alpha^k) - \log \sum_{y_\alpha} \exp\Big(f_\alpha(x_\alpha^k, y_\alpha) + b_\alpha^k(y_\alpha) \Big).$$

This is done by initializing $f_\alpha(x_\alpha, y_\alpha) = 0$ and then repeating the following steps:

1. For each datum, calculate the gradient of the loss $g^k(y_\alpha) = dL_k/df_\alpha(x_\alpha^k, y_\alpha^k)$
2. Induce a regression tree t to minimize $\sum_k \sum_{y_\alpha} \big(g^k(y_\alpha) - t(x_\alpha^k, y_\alpha^k) \big)^2$.
3. Leaving the split points of t fixed, adjust the values of the leaf nodes (via L-BFGS) to minimize the empirical risk $\sum_k L_k(f_\alpha + t)$.
4. Multiply t by a step length ν and add it to the ensemble as

$$f_\alpha(x_\alpha, y_\alpha) \leftarrow f_\alpha(x_\alpha, y_\alpha) + \nu \times t(x_\alpha, y_\alpha).$$

Several details are needed to fully describe the method.

First, note the a single regression tree t is induced for all classes, rather than inducing one tree for each class, as is more common. To do this, a tree needs to be induced to minimize a multivariate squared loss. This can be written as finding t to minimize $\sum_k \|g^k - t(x_\alpha^k)\|^2$, where g^k and $t(x_\alpha^k)$ are vectors of the values $g^k(y_\alpha)$ and $t(x_\alpha^k, y_\alpha)$, respectively. As is typical when fitting regression trees, this is done greedily: the algorithm repeatedly picks a dimension and split point to divide the data into two groups, such that the sum of squared distances of all points to the mean of g^k in the corresponding group is minimized. Implemented naively, this would require on the order of $D_{\text{in}} K^2 D_{\text{out}}$ operations,[2] where K is the number of data, D_{in} is the number of input dimensions, and D_{out} is the number of output dimensions. However,

---

2. There are K unique split points in each of the D_{in} dimensions, and checking the cost of each can be done with $K D_{\text{out}}$ operations.

exploiting a recursion in the structure of the costs can reduce this to the order of $D_{\text{in}}K(\log K + D_{\text{out}})$ operations.[3]

Second, when inducing the tree, splits are only considered that leave at least 1% of the original data in each leaf node. Nodes are not split at all if they contain less than 2.5% of the original data.

Finally, two heuristics are borrowed from stochastic gradient boosting. When inducing a tree in step 2 above and also when adjusting the values of the leaf nodes in step 3, only a random subset of 10,000 elements of the data is used (the same subset for both sets, but randomly selected for each iteration). This greatly speeds up computation and induces some randomness into the selected trees. Finally, a step size of $\nu = .25$ is used, which compensates for the randomness and improves test-set performance. A total of 200 boosting iterations are performed.

9.9.5   Multi-Layer Perceptrons

Multi-layer perceptrons are also sometimes used as potential functions (He et al., 2004; Silberman and Fergus, 2011). These experiments use a simple multi-layer perceptron with a single hidden layer, which can be written as

$$f_\alpha(x_\alpha, y_\alpha) = (W\sigma(Vx_\alpha))_{y_\alpha}.$$

This can be understood as multiplying the input x_α by a matrix V and passing it through the "sigmoid" function σ (that applies a tanh elementwise) to obtain a hidden representation $\sigma(Vx_\alpha)$. W maps this hidden representation to the ouput space. In all experiments, the hidden representation has 100 elements. To fit a logistic loss, stochastic gradient descent is used with mini-batches of size 100 and a step size of 0.25 for factors corresponding to single variables and 0.05 for pairs. A momentum constant of .9 is used, meaning each step taken is a combination of .9 of the last step and .1 of the current gradient.

Of course, gradient methods will only find a local optimum of the logistic loss. To at least guarantee improvement in each iteration, parameters are initialized to those from the previous iteration.

---

3. Here, $D_{\text{in}}K \log K$ is the cost of sorting each input dimension, and after sorting, all split points in each single input dimension can be evaluated in $K\text{D}_{\text{out}}$ time.

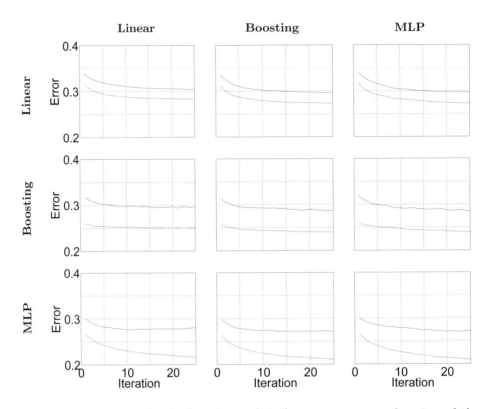

Figure 9.5: Training (dashed) and test (solid) error rates as a function of the number of learning iterations for each combination of univariate (rows) and pairwise (columns) potential functions.

9.10   Example

This section presents a simple example of learning using the Stanford Background data set (Gould et al., 2009), split into a training set of 572 and a test set of 143 images, each of resolution roughly 320 x 240. For each pixel, 41 univariate features were computed, including the RGB value, the x and y horizontal position normalized to [0,1], and a 36-component Histogram of Oriented Gradients (Dalal and Triggs, 2005). There are three pairwise features consisting of a constant of 1, the l_2 distance of the RGB components of the two pixels, and the output of a Sobel edge filter. Images were reduced to 20% resolution before computing features.

Learning proceeds through a set of iterations. In each learning iteration, the univariate potential function is updated, followed by 25 message-passing iterations (each of which passes over the entire image from top left to bottom right, then in the reverse order). This is followed by an update to the pairwise

	Zero	Constant	Linear	Boosting	MLP
Zero	.853 / .863	.641 / .673	.553 / .593	.470 / .483	.497 / .518
Constant	.769 / .793	.640 / .673	.553 / .593	.470 / .485	.497 / .518
Linear	.322 / .345	.304 / .329	.283 / .304	.272 / .296	.272 / .296
Boosting	.289 / .331	.259 / .304	.249 / .296	.239 / .287	.239 / .284
MLP	.262 / .310	.226 / .281	.216 / .280	.210 / .271	.209 / .272

Table 9.1: Train / Test Error rates for each combination of univariate (rows) and pairwise (columns) potential functions.

potentials and another 25 message-passing iterations. There were 25 total learning iterations.

The univariate training and test error rates are shown in Figure 9.5 and Table 9.1. It is easy to see that more powerful potential functions lead to lower training errors, but this is somewhat offset by more overfitting.

9.11   Conclusions

This chapter builds on two streams of previous work for structured learning. In the first, the likelihood is replaced with a piecewise (Sutton and Mccallum, 2009) or pseudolikelihood approximation. This decomposes the learning objective into a sum of local objectives. These can be optimized efficiently and make it possible to use nonlinear function classes, such as trees or multi-layer perceptrons. The downside of these training methods is that the approximation to the likelihood can sometimes be weak, leading to poor performance of the learned model in the face of joint prediction.

The second stream of related research is based on phrasing structured learning with linear predictors as a joint optimization of inference messages and model parameters (Hazan and Urtasun, 2012; Meshi et al., 2010), alternating between optimization of each. These optimize a loss that deals with approximate inference in a principled way but are fairly specific to linear energies.

The main result here is that, when pursing this latter strategy, optimizing model parameters with fixed inference messages leads to a set of logistic regression problems, each biased by the current messages. This yields an algorithm alternating between message passing updates and logistic regression problems. Given the high degree of similarity between logistic regression and piecewise training, one can view this as using message-passing to iteratively tighten a piecewise-style learning objective toward better joint prediction.

Additionally, it is easy to use any function class over which a logistic loss can be fit, such as ensembles of trees or multi-layer perceptrons.

Future work should understand the convergence rates of a procedure that alternates between message passing and logistic regression updates. Given the existing results on convergence rates for this style of message-passing inference (Meshi et al., 2012) and standard results for convex optimization, this could lead to joint convergence rates.

Another possible extension of this procedure would be to consider more general entropy approximations. That is, one might extend the approach described here to the case where the entropy smoothing takes the form of $\sum_\alpha \epsilon_\alpha H(\mu_\alpha)$, with different entropy weights ϵ_α for different regions α. This would allow the use of this style of algorithm for so-called "surrogate likelihood" (Wainwright, 2006) training, in which the likelihood is approximated using an algorithm like loopy belief propagation. Now, if $\epsilon_\alpha > 0$ for all α, then this extension is trivial. However, standard entropy approximations involve the use of negative weights, where $\epsilon_\alpha < 0$ for some α. These terms introduce non-convexity, which defeats obvious extensions of the method described here.

9.12   Appendix: Proofs

This appendix contains proofs of all the main results of the chapter.

Boundedness of Entropy Smoothing

Proof of Theorem 9.1. We can write

$$
\begin{aligned}
l(x, y; F) - l_1(x, y; F) &= -F(x, y) + \max_{\mu \in \mathcal{M}} \left(\theta \cdot \mu + \sum_\alpha \epsilon H(\mu_\alpha) \right) \\
&\quad + F(x, y) - \max_{\mu \in \mathcal{M}} \theta \cdot \mu \\
&= \max_{\mu \in \mathcal{M}} \left(\theta \cdot \mu + \sum_\alpha \epsilon H(\mu_\alpha) \right) - \max_{\mu \in \mathcal{M}} \theta \cdot \mu \\
&= \theta \cdot \mu' - \theta \cdot \mu^* + \sum_\alpha \epsilon H(\mu'_\alpha) \\
&\leq \epsilon \sum_\alpha \log |y_\alpha|,
\end{aligned}
$$

where we have defined $\mu^* = \operatorname{argmax}_{\mu \in \mathcal{M}} \theta \cdot \mu$ and $\mu' = \operatorname{argmax}_{\mu \in \mathcal{M}} \theta \cdot \mu + \epsilon \sum_\alpha H(\mu_\alpha)$. The last line follows from the fact that $\theta \cdot \mu^* \geq \theta \cdot \mu'$ and $H(\mu'_\alpha) \leq \log |y_\alpha|$.

□

Dual Representation of A

This section presents a proof that requires the following standard result.

Lemma 9.5. *The conjugate of the entropy is the "log-sum-exp" function. Formally,*

$$\max_{p:\sum_i p_i=1, p_i\geq 0} \theta \cdot p - \epsilon \sum_i p_i \log p_i = \epsilon \log \sum_i \exp \frac{\theta_i}{\epsilon}.$$

Moreover, the maximizing p is given by

$$p = \frac{\exp(\theta/\epsilon)}{\sum_i \exp(\theta_i/\epsilon)}$$

Proof of Theorem 9.2. Firstly, we transform the optimization of A into the following form, where we use a set $\mathcal{N}$ to denote the set of locally normalized distributions but explicitly enforce marginalization constraints.

$$A(\theta) \quad = \quad \max_{\mu \in \mathcal{N}} \theta \cdot \mu + \epsilon \sum_\alpha H(\mu_\alpha) \tag{9.22}$$

$$\text{s.t.} \quad \mu_{\alpha\beta}(y_\beta) = \mu_\beta(y_\beta) \, \forall \beta \subset \alpha, y_\beta \tag{9.23}$$

Next, if one introduces a set of Lagrange multipliers

$$\lambda = \{\lambda_\alpha(y_\beta), \forall \beta \subset \alpha, y_\alpha\},$$

then one can write A in the form

$$A(\theta) \quad = \quad \max_{\mu \in \mathcal{N}} \min_\lambda \theta \cdot \mu + \epsilon \sum_\alpha H(\mu_\alpha) \tag{9.24}$$

$$+ \sum_\alpha \sum_{\beta \subset \alpha} \lambda_\alpha(x_\beta)(\mu_{\alpha\beta}(y_\beta) - \mu_\beta(y_\beta)). \tag{9.25}$$

By Sion's theorem (Sion, 1958), it is possible to interchange the maximum and minimum. Thus, if we define

$$A(\lambda, \theta) \quad = \quad \max_{\mu \in \mathcal{N}} \theta \cdot \mu + \epsilon \sum_\alpha H(\mu_\alpha) \tag{9.26}$$

$$+ \sum_\alpha \sum_{\beta \subset \alpha} \lambda_\alpha(x_\beta)(\mu_{\alpha\beta}(y_\beta) - \mu_\beta(y_\beta)), \tag{9.27}$$

then we can represent $A(\theta)$ simply as $A(\theta) = \min_\lambda A(\lambda, \theta)$.

Now, we can re-write this objective as

$$\sum_\alpha \left(\sum_{y_\alpha} \theta(y_\alpha)\mu(y_\alpha) + \sum_\alpha \sum_{\beta \subset \alpha} \lambda_\alpha(x_\beta)(\mu_{\alpha\beta}(y_\beta) - \mu_\beta(y_\beta)) \right) + \epsilon \sum_\alpha H(\mu_\alpha)$$

$$= \sum_\alpha \left(\sum_{y_\alpha} \left(\theta(y_\alpha) + \sum_{\beta \subset \alpha} \lambda_\alpha(x_\beta) - \sum_{\gamma \supset \alpha} \lambda_\gamma(x_\alpha) \right) \mu_\alpha(y_\alpha) + \epsilon H(\mu_\alpha) \right).$$

It remains to actually calculate the μ that maximizes (9.27). The key observation here is that the variables $\mu(y_\alpha)$ corresponding to each factor can be optimized independently. If we consider an arbitrary factor α, then the problem is to maximize

$$\max_{\mu_\alpha} \quad \sum_{y_\alpha} \theta(y_\alpha)\mu_\alpha(y_\alpha) + \epsilon H(\mu_\alpha) \tag{9.28}$$

$$+ \sum_{\beta \subset \alpha} \lambda_\alpha(x_\beta)\mu_{\alpha\beta}(y_\beta) - \sum_{\gamma \supset \alpha} \lambda_\gamma(x_\alpha)\mu_\alpha(y_\alpha), \tag{9.29}$$

$$\text{s.t.} \quad \sum_{y_\alpha} \mu_\alpha(y_\alpha) = 1 \tag{9.30}$$

$$\mu_\alpha(y_\alpha) \geq 0. \tag{9.31}$$

We can re-write this as

$$\max_{\mu_\alpha} \sum_{y_\alpha} \left(\theta(y_\alpha) + \sum_{\beta \subset \alpha} \lambda_\alpha(x_\beta) - \sum_{\gamma \supset \alpha} \lambda_\gamma(x_\alpha) \right) \mu_\alpha(y_\alpha) + \epsilon H(\mu_\alpha) \tag{9.32}$$

$$\text{s.t.} \sum_{y_\alpha} \mu_\alpha(y_\alpha) = 1 \tag{9.33}$$

$$\mu_\alpha(y_\alpha) \geq 0. \tag{9.34}$$

Using the above lemma, we see that the solution is

$$\mu_\alpha(y_\alpha) \propto \exp\left(\frac{1}{\epsilon} \left(\theta(y_\alpha) + \sum_{\beta \subset \alpha} \lambda_\alpha(x_\beta) - \sum_{\gamma \supset \alpha} \lambda_\gamma(x_\alpha) \right) \right), \tag{9.35}$$

with a corresponding function value of

$$\epsilon \log \sum_{y_\alpha} \exp\left(\frac{1}{\epsilon}\left(\theta(y_\alpha) + \sum_{\beta \subset \alpha} \lambda_\alpha(x_\beta) - \sum_{\gamma \supset \alpha} \lambda_\gamma(x_\alpha)\right)\right). \tag{9.36}$$

$\square$

Message-Passing Update Equations

Proof of Theorem 9.3. It is not hard to see that, after update, the new marginals will obey the conditions

$$\mu'_\nu(y_\nu) \quad \propto \quad \mu_\nu(y_\nu) \exp\left(-\frac{1}{\epsilon}\sum_{\eta \supset \nu} \delta_\eta(y_\nu)\right) \tag{9.37}$$

$$\mu'_\eta(y_\eta) \quad \propto \quad \mu_\eta(y_\eta) \exp\left(\frac{1}{\epsilon}\delta_\eta(y_\nu)\right). \tag{9.38}$$

$$\mu'_{\eta\nu}(y_\nu) \quad \propto \quad \mu_{\eta\nu}(y_\nu) \exp\left(\frac{1}{\epsilon}\delta_\eta(y_\nu)\right). \tag{9.39}$$

Now, if the marginals are updated as above, then for all $\eta \supset \nu$,

$$\mu'_{\eta\nu}(y_\nu) \propto \mu_{\eta\nu}(y_\eta) \exp\left(\frac{\log\mu_\nu(y_\nu) + \sum_{\eta' \supset \nu} \log\mu_{\eta'\nu}(y_\nu)}{1 + N_\nu} - \log\mu_{\eta\nu}(y_\nu)\right) \tag{9.40}$$

$$= \exp\left(\log\mu_\nu(y_\nu) + \sum_{\eta' \supset \nu} \log\mu_{\eta'\nu}(y_\nu)\right)^{1/(1+N_\nu)}, \tag{9.41}$$

which can be seen to be equal to (9.17). Similarly, for ν itself,

$$\mu'_\nu(y_\nu) \propto \mu_\nu(y_\nu) \exp\left(-\frac{1}{\epsilon}\sum_{\eta \supset \nu} \delta_\eta(y_\nu)\right) \tag{9.42}$$

$$= \mu_\nu(y_\nu) \exp\left(-\frac{1}{1+N_\nu}\sum_{\eta \supset \nu}\left(\log\mu_\nu(y_\nu) + \sum_{\eta' \supset \nu}\log\mu_{\eta'\nu}(y_\nu)\right)\right.$$
$$+ \left. \sum_{\eta \supset \nu}\log\mu_\eta(y_\nu)\right) \tag{9.43}$$

$$= \mu_\nu(y_\nu) \exp\left(-\frac{N_\nu}{1+N_\nu}\left(\log\mu_\nu(y_\nu) + \sum_{\eta' \supset \nu}\log\mu_{\eta'\nu}(y_\nu)\right)\right.$$
$$+ \left. \sum_{\eta \supset \nu}\log\mu_\eta(y_\nu)\right) \tag{9.44}$$

$$= \mu_\nu(y_\nu)\mu_\nu(y_\nu)^{-N_\nu/(1+N_\nu)} \prod_{\eta' \supset \nu}\mu_{\eta'\nu}(y_\nu)^{-N_\nu/(1+N_\nu)} \prod_{\eta \supset \nu}\mu_{\eta\nu}(y_\nu), \tag{9.45}$$

which again is equal to (9.17).

$\square$

Logistic Regression Reduction

Proof of Theorem 9.4. If we consider minimizing $\sum_k\left[-F(x^k,y^k) + A\left(\lambda^k,\theta_F^k\right)\right]$ with respect to a single f_α, then it is easy to see from (9.2) and (9.15) that the problem is

$$\operatorname*{argmin}_{f_\alpha \in \mathcal{F}_\alpha} \sum_k \left[-f_\alpha(x^k,y^k) + \epsilon\log\sum_{y_\alpha}\exp\left(\frac{1}{\epsilon}\left(\theta_F^k(y_\alpha) + \sum_{\beta \subset \alpha}\lambda_\alpha(y_\beta) - \sum_{\gamma \supset \alpha}\lambda_\gamma(y_\alpha)\right)\right)\right],$$

substituting the definition of θ_F^k as $\theta_F^k(y_\alpha) = f_\alpha(x^k,y_\alpha) + \Delta_\alpha(y_\alpha^k,y_\alpha)$, and using the above set of biases, this is

$$\operatorname*{argmin}_{f_\alpha \in \mathcal{F}_\alpha} \sum_k \left[-f_\alpha(x^k,y^k) + \epsilon\log\sum_{y_\alpha}\exp\left(\frac{1}{\epsilon}f_\alpha(x^k,y_\alpha) + b_\alpha^k(y_\alpha)\right)\right].$$

Because adding or multiplying by a constant does not affect the minimizer, this is

$$\operatorname*{argmin}_{f_\alpha \in \mathcal{F}_\alpha} \sum_k \left[-\frac{1}{\epsilon}f_\alpha(x^k,y^k) - b_\alpha(x^k,y^k) + \log\sum_{y_\alpha}\exp\left(\frac{1}{\epsilon}f_\alpha(x^k,y_\alpha) + b_\alpha^k(y_\alpha)\right)\right].$$

Finally, observing that $\operatorname{argmin} g(\frac{1}{\epsilon}\cdot) = \epsilon\operatorname{argmin} g(\cdot)$ and that $\operatorname{argmin} -g(\cdot) = \operatorname{argmax} g(\cdot)$ gives the result.

☐

9.13 References

K. Crammer and Y. Singer. On the algorithmic implementation of multiclass kernel-based vector machines. *Journal of Machine Learning Research*, 2:265–292, 2002.

N. Dalal and B. Triggs. Histograms of oriented gradients for human detection. In *Proceedings of the Conference on Computer Vision and Pattern Recognition*, 2005.

T. Finley and T. Joachims. Training structural SVMs when exact inference is intractable. In *Proceedings of the International Conference on Machine Learning*, 2008.

J. H. Friedman. Stochastic gradient boosting. *Computational Statistics and Data Analysis*, 38:367–378, 1999.

S. Gould, J. Rodgers, D. Cohen, G. Elidan, and D. Koller. Multi-class segmentation with relative location prior. *International Journal of Computer Vision*, 80(3): 300–316, 2008.

S. Gould, R. Fulton, and D. Koller. Decomposing a scene into geometric and semantically consistent regions. In *Proceeding of International Conference on Computer Vision*, 2009.

T. Hazan and R. Urtasun. Efficient learning of structured predictors in general graphical models. *CoRR*, abs/1210.2346, 2012.

X. He, R. S. Zemel, and M. Á. Carreira-Perpiñán. Multiscale conditional random fields for image labeling. In *Proceedings of the Conference on Computer Vision and Pattern Recognition*, 2004.

T. Heskes. Convexity arguments for efficient minimization of the Bethe and Kikuchi free energies. *Journal of Artificial Intelligence Research*, 26:153–190, 2006.

D. Koller and N. Friedman. *Probabilistic Graphical Models: Principles and Techniques*. MIT Press, 2009.

L. Ladicky, C. Russell, P. Kohli, and P. H. S. Torr. Associative hierarchical CRFs for object class image segmentation. In *Proceedings of International Conference on Computer Vision*, 2009.

O. Meshi, D. Sontag, T. Jaakkola, and A. Globerson. Learning efficiently with approximate inference via dual losses. In *Proceedings of the International Conference on Machine Learning*, 2010.

O. Meshi, T. Jaakkola, and A. Globerson. Convergence rate analysis of MAP coordinate minimization algorithms. In *Proceedings of the Conference on Neural Information Processing Systems*, 2012.

A. Nedi and A. Ozdaglar. Subgradient methods for saddle-point problems. *Journal of Optimization Theory and Applications*, pages 205–228, 2009.

S. Nowozin, C. Rother, S. Bagon, T. Sharp, B. Yao, and P. Kohli. Decision tree fields. In *Proceedings of International Conference on Computer Vision*, 2011.

N. Ratliff, J. A. D. Bagnell, and M. Zinkevich. (Online) subgradient methods for structured prediction. In *Proceedings of the International Conference on Artificial Intelligence and Statistics*, 2007.

F. Schroff, A. Criminisi, and A. Zisserman. Object class segmentation using random forests. In *Proceedings of the British Machine Vision Conference*, 2008.

J. Shotton, J. M. Winn, C. Rother, and A. Criminisi. Textonboost for image understanding: Multi-class object recognition and segmentation by jointly modeling texture, layout, and context. *International Journal of Computer Vision*, 81(1): 2–23, 2009.

N. Silberman and R. Fergus. Indoor scene segmentation using a structured light sensor. In *Proceedings of International Conference on Computer Vision Workshops*, 2011.

M. Sion. On general minimax theorems. *Pacific Journal of Mathematics*, 8(1): 171–176, 1958.

D. Sontag and T. Jaakkola. Tree block coordinate descent for MAP in graphical models. In *Proceedings of the International Conference on Artificial Intelligence and Statistics*, 2009.

C. Sutton and A. Mccallum. Piecewise training for structured prediction. *Machine Learning*, 77:165–194, 2009.

B. Taskar, C. Guestrin, and D. Koller. Max-margin markov networks. In *Proceedings of the Conference on Neural Information Processing Systems*, 2003.

I. Tsochantaridis, T. Joachims, T. Hofmann, and Y. Altun. Large margin methods for structured and interdependent output variables. *J. Mach. Learn. Res.*, 6: 1453–1484, 2005.

V. V. Vazirani. *Approximation Algorithms*. Springer-Verlag, 2001.

M. Wainwright and M. Jordan. Graphical models, exponential families, and variational inference. *Foundations and Trends in Machine Learning*, 1(1-2):1–305, 2008.

M. J. Wainwright. Estimating the "wrong" graphical model: Benefits in the computation-limited setting. *Journal of Machine Learning Research*, 7:1829–1859, 2006.

J. M. Winn and J. Shotton. The layout consistent random field for recognizing and segmenting partially occluded objects. In *Proceedings of the Conference on Computer Vision and Pattern Recognition*, 2006.

J. Xiao and L. Quan. Multiple view semantic segmentation for street view images. In *Proceedings of International Conference on Computer Vision*, 2009.

10 PAC-Bayesian Risk Bounds and Learning Algorithms for the Regression Approach to Structured Output Prediction

Sébastien Giguère
Université Laval
Québec, Canada

sebastien.giguere.8@ulaval.ca

François Laviolette
Université Laval
Québec, Canada

francois.laviolette@ift.ulaval.ca

Mario Marchand
Université Laval
Québec, Canada

mario.marchand@ift.ulaval.ca

Amélie Rolland
Université Laval
Québec, Canada

amelie.rolland.1@ulaval.ca

Many structured output prediction algorithms, such as max-margin Markov networks and structural support vector machines, need to solve the (often NP-hard) pre-image problem during training and inference. The vector-valued regression approach has the computational advantage of avoiding this problem, at least, during training. In this chapter, we provide rigorous guarantees for this approach. More specifically, we show that the quadratic regression loss is a convex surrogate of the prediction loss when the output kernel satisfies some condition with respect to the prediction loss. We then present two upper bounds of the prediction risk that depend on the empirical quadratic risk of the predictor. The minimizer of the first bound is the predictor proposed by Cortes et al. (2007). The minimizer of the second bound was recently proposed by Giguère et al. (2013). Both predictors are compared on practical tasks, yielding similar but state-of-the-art accuracies.

10.1   Introduction

Structured output prediction is a supervised learning problem where the goal of the learner is to predict the correct output y associated to some given input x. Here, the output y can be a complex object, such as a sequence of symbols, a parse tree, or a graph. The predictor generally consists of a vector w of real-valued weights, and each input-output example (x, y) is mapped to a high-dimensional feature vector $\phi(x, y)$. The output predicted by w on input x is then the output y that maximizes the inner product $\langle w, \phi(x, y) \rangle$. However, as emphasized by Gärtner and Vembu (2009), this pre-image problem is often NP-hard. Consequently, any learning algorithm that needs to solve this pre-image problem, for several weight vectors and every training example, will often take a prohibitive running time. This is probably the most important problem facing several state-of-the-art structured output learning algorithms such as max-margin Markov networks (Taskar et al., 2004) and structural support vector machines (Tsochantaridis et al., 2005).

One of the first attempts to design a learning algorithm that avoids the pre-image problem is due to Cortes et al. (2007). They have proposed to find the predictor that minimizes an ℓ_2-regularized vector-valued regression objective (which does not depend on the predicted output for a given input). Also, they have obtained empirical results that compare favorably to those of structural SVM and max-margin Markov networks on the word-recognition data set used by Taskar et al. (2004). In this chapter, we present guarantees for such a regression approach by first showing that the quadratic loss function used by Cortes et al. (2007) provides a convex upper bound on the original prediction loss (that depends on the predicted output) provided that the output kernel satisfies some condition with respect to the prediction loss. We also present two PAC-Bayes upper bounds[1] for the prediction risk that depend on the quadratic empirical loss used by Cortes et al. (2007). These two bounds were first proposed by Giguère et al. (2013), the article on which this chapter is largely based. The minimizer of the first bound turns out to be the same as the one proposed by Cortes et al. (2007), whereas the minimizer of the second bound, valid for arbitrary reproducing kernel Hilbert spaces (RKHS), has been proposed by Giguère et al. (2013). Both predictors are compared on practical tasks.

PAC-Bayes theory has also been applied recently (McAllester, 2007) to structured output prediction for a stochastic predictor that aims at mini-

---

1. See McAllester (2003); Langford (2005) or Germain et al. (2009) for an introductory text about PAC-Bayesian theory

mizing the expected prediction risk. The resulting learning algorithms need to solve the pre-image problem on each example of the training set for each update of the predictor. In contrast, we present here risk bounds for learning algorithms that avoid solving the pre-image problem and produce a deterministic predictor instead of a stochastic one.

10.2 From Structured Output Prediction to Vector-Valued Regression

In the supervised learning setting, the learner has access to a set $S \stackrel{\text{def}}{=} \{(x_1, y_1), \ldots, (x_m, y_m)\}$ of m training examples, where each example consists of an input-output pair $(x, y) \in \mathcal{X} \times \mathcal{Y}$. The input space $\mathcal{X}$ and the output space $\mathcal{Y}$ are both arbitrary, but we assume the existence of both an input feature map $X : \mathcal{X} \to \mathcal{H}_\mathcal{X}$ and an output feature map $Y : \mathcal{Y} \to \mathcal{H}_\mathcal{y}$, where both $\mathcal{H}_\mathcal{X}$ and $\mathcal{H}_\mathcal{y}$ are high-dimensional vector spaces and, more generally, RKHS. In $\mathcal{H}_\mathcal{y}$, we use $\langle Y(y), Y(y') \rangle$ to denote the inner product and use $\|Y(y)\|^2 \stackrel{\text{def}}{=} \langle Y(y), Y(y) \rangle$ for the squared norm. The analogue notation is used in $\mathcal{H}_\mathcal{X}$.

Given access to a training set S, the task of the learner is to construct a structured predictor that is represented by a linear operator $\mathbf{W}$ that transforms vectors of $\mathcal{H}_\mathcal{X}$ into vectors of $\mathcal{H}_\mathcal{y}$. For any $x \in \mathcal{X}$ and any $\mathbf{W}$, the output $y_\mathbf{W}(x)$ predicted by $\mathbf{W}$ is given by

$$y_\mathbf{W}(x) \stackrel{\text{def}}{=} \operatorname*{argmin}_{y \in \mathcal{Y}} \|Y(y) - \mathbf{W}X(x)\| . \tag{10.1}$$

Note that $y_\mathbf{W}(x) = \operatorname{argmax}_{y \in \mathcal{Y}} \langle Y(y), \mathbf{W}X(x) \rangle$ whenever $\|Y(y)\|$ is the same for all $y \in \mathcal{Y}$. In this case, we recover the usual structured output prediction method when the joint feature vectors $\phi(x, y)$ are tensor products $X(x) \otimes Y(y)$. Because finding $y_\mathbf{W}(x)$ given x and $\mathbf{W}$ is generally NP-hard (Gärtner and Vembu, 2009), we want to avoid solving this pre-image problem.

We consider feature maps that are defined by kernels such that $K_\mathcal{y}(y, y') = \langle Y(y), Y(y') \rangle$ for all $(y, y') \in \mathcal{Y}^2$ and $K_\mathcal{X}(x, x') = \langle X(x), X(x') \rangle$ for all $(x, x') \in \mathcal{X}^2$. We will see that the proposed solutions for $\mathbf{W}$ will have the property that $\mathbf{W}X(x) = \sum_{i=1}^m \sum_{j=1}^m Y(y_i) A_{i,j} K_\mathcal{X}(x_j, x)$ for some $m \times m$ matrix $\mathbf{A}$. Consequently, the predicted output $y_\mathbf{W}(x)$ only requires the use of the kernels $K_\mathcal{X}$ and $K_\mathcal{y}$ (instead of the feature maps X and Y).

Note that this class of predictors $\mathbf{W} : \mathcal{H}_\mathcal{X} \to \mathcal{H}_\mathcal{y}$ is strictly included in the class of predictors studied by Brouard et al. (2011) and Kadri et al. (2013), where the input kernel has values $K_\mathcal{X}(x, x')$ that are operators : $\mathcal{H}_\mathcal{y} \to \mathcal{H}_\mathcal{y}$.

It is still unknown how the risk bounds developed in this chapter can be extended to this more general case.

We assume that each example (x, y) is generated independently according to some unknown distribution D. Given a function $L : \mathcal{Y} \times \mathcal{Y} \to \mathbb{R}$ that quantifies the loss incurred on (x, y) when the predicted output is $y_{\mathbf{w}}(x)$, the task of the learner is to find the predictor that minimizes the expected loss (or risk) $\mathbf{E}_{(x,y) \sim D} L(y_{\mathbf{w}}(x), y)$. We refer to L as the *prediction loss*.

Note that the output kernel $K_{\mathcal{Y}}$, being a similarity measure on $\mathcal{Y}^2$, induces a loss function $L_{K_{\mathcal{Y}}}$ defined as

$$L_{K_{\mathcal{Y}}}(y_{\mathbf{w}}(x), y) \;\overset{\text{def}}{=}\; \frac{1}{2} \|Y(y) - Y(y_{\mathbf{w}}(x))\|^2 \tag{10.2}$$
$$= \frac{K_{\mathcal{Y}}(y, y) + K_{\mathcal{Y}}(y_{\mathbf{w}}(x), y_{\mathbf{w}}(x))}{2} - K_{\mathcal{Y}}(y, y_{\mathbf{w}}(x)).$$

We refer to $L_{K_{\mathcal{Y}}}$ as the *output kernel loss*.

Both the prediction loss and the output kernel loss on (x, y) depend on the predicted output $y_{\mathbf{w}}(x)$. This is in sharp contrast with the *quadratic loss* $\|Y(y) - \mathbf{W}X(x)\|^2$, which does not depend on $y_{\mathbf{w}}(x)$. However, we can show that the quadratic loss provides an upper bound to the output kernel loss.

Lemma 10.1. *For any structured predictor* $\mathbf{W}$ *giving predictions as defined by (10.1), for any $(x, y) \in \mathcal{X} \times \mathcal{Y}$, we have*

$$L_{K_{\mathcal{Y}}}(y_{\mathbf{w}}(x), y) \;\leq\; 2 \|Y(y) - \mathbf{W}X(x)\|^2.$$

Proof. From the triangle inequality, we have, for all $\mathbf{W}$ and for all (x, y),

$$\|Y(y) - Y(y_{\mathbf{w}}(x))\| \leq \|Y(y) - \mathbf{W}X(x)\| + \|Y(y_{\mathbf{w}}(x)) - \mathbf{W}X(x)\|.$$

From (10.1), we have $\|Y(y_{\mathbf{w}}(x)) - \mathbf{W}X(x)\| \leq \|Y(y) - \mathbf{W}X(x)\|$ for all $\mathbf{W}$ and for all (x, y). Hence, from these two inequalities, we have $\|Y(y) - Y(y_{\mathbf{w}}(x))\| \leq 2\|Y(y) - \mathbf{W}X(x)\|$, which gives the lemma. $\qquad\square$

Lemma 10.1 has far-reaching consequences whenever we use an output kernel $K_{\mathcal{Y}}$ such that $L(y, y') \leq L_{K_{\mathcal{Y}}}(y, y')$ for all $(y, y') \in \mathcal{Y}^2$ because, in that case, we have

$$L(y_{\mathbf{w}}(x), y) \;\leq\; 2 \|Y(y) - \mathbf{W}X(x)\|^2,$$

for all predictors $\mathbf{W}$ and all $(x, y) \in \mathcal{X} \times \mathcal{Y}$.

Under these circumstances, a predictor $\mathbf{W}$ having a small quadratic risk $\mathbf{E}_{(x,y) \sim D} \|Y(y) - \mathbf{W}X(x)\|^2$ also has a small prediction risk

$$\mathbf{E}_{(x,y) \sim D} L(y_{\mathbf{w}}(x), y).$$

To minimize the prediction risk, we need to solve the (usually hard) pre-image problem of finding the predicted output $y_{\mathbf{w}}(x)$ for every example in the training set and for all predictors $\mathbf{W}$ tried by the learning algorithm. Thanks to Lemma 10.1, we can avoid this computational burden by performing the simpler regression task of minimizing the quadratic risk whenever we use an output kernel K_y for which the output kernel loss L_{K_y} upper bounds the prediction loss L.

Consider the case when the prediction loss L is the zero-one loss. In that case, any output kernel K_y for which there exists two different outputs y and y' having $K_y(y,y) = K_y(y',y') = K_y(y,y')$ will not give an output kernel loss L_{K_y} that upper bounds L. But the Dirac kernel for which $K_y(y,y') = 1$ if $y = y'$ and 0 otherwise gives an L_{K_y}, which is identical to L.

In the case where the prediction loss L is the Hamming distance, the Hamming kernel (given by the length of the largest string minus the Hamming distance between the two strings) provides an output structured loss L_{K_y} identical to L. One could also use any output kernel giving an L_{K_y} that upper bounds the Hamming distance at the expense of introducing an additional slackness between the quadratic risk and the prediction risk.

A predictor achieving a small quadratic risk also achieves a small prediction risk when the output kernel K_y gives an L_{K_y} that upper bounds L. However, there exist data-generating distributions where the predictor achieving the smallest possible quadratic risk has a substantially larger prediction risk than the predictor achieving the smallest possible prediction risk. In other words, there is no consistency guarantee for the regression approach to structured output prediction because no such guarantee exists for the particular case of binary classification.[2] However, the regression approach avoids the computational burden of dealing with the pre-image problem, and, under some distributions, there might be some kernels for which there exists predictors achieving a small quadratic risk.

Thanks to Lemma 10.1, any upper bound on the quadratic risk also provides a bound on the prediction risk (provided that there exists an output kernel loss that upper bounds the prediction loss). Consequently, the upper bounds proposed by Caponnetto and De Vito (2007) and Baldassarre et al. (2012) also provide bounds on the prediction risk for predictors minimizing the ℓ_2-regularized least-squares. However, instead of focusing explicitly on such predictors, we provide bounds that hold simultaneously for

---

2. Indeed, it is easy to find distributions for which the minimizer of the quadratic risk gives a classifier that achieves a much larger 0/1 risk than the optimal classifier. See the appendix for a simple example.

any predictor $\mathbf{W}$ and that depend on the empirical quadratic risk achieved by $\mathbf{W}$ on the training data.

10.3   A PAC-Bayesian Bound with Isotropic Gaussians

Values of the prediction loss $L(y_{\mathbf{w}}(x), y)$ are always between zero and one. However, this is clearly not the case for the quadratic loss $\|Y(y) - \mathbf{W}X(x)\|^2$. Theoretically attainable large loss values are well known to give loose concentration inequalities and, unavoidably, large risk bounds. Therefore, to obtain a tighter risk bound, we use the following lemma that upper bounds the prediction loss in terms of a bounded function of the quadratic loss.

Lemma 10.2. *For any prediction loss L upper-bounded by the output kernel loss L_{K_y}, for any (x, y), any $\mathbf{W}$, and any $a \geq 1$, we have*

$$L(y_{\mathbf{w}}(x), y) \;\leq\; \frac{ae}{e-1}\left(1 - e^{-\frac{2}{a}\|Y(y) - \mathbf{W}X(x)\|^2}\right).$$

Proof. For any $0 \leq x \leq 1$, we have $x \leq \frac{e}{e-1}\left(1 - e^{-x}\right)$. Therefore,

$$\frac{1}{a}L(y_{\mathbf{w}}(x), y) \leq \frac{e}{e-1}\left(1 - e^{-\frac{1}{a}L(y_{\mathbf{w}}(x), y)}\right)$$
$$\leq \frac{e}{e-1}\left(1 - e^{-\frac{2}{a}\|Y(y) - \mathbf{W}X(x)\|^2}\right),$$

where the last equality follows from Lemma 10.1 and the fact that L is upper bounded by L_{K_y}. □

10.3.1   The Risk Bound

We propose here an upper bound on the prediction risk that uses PAC-Bayes theory to upper bound $\mathbf{E}_{(x,y)\sim D}\left(1 - e^{-\frac{2}{a}\|Y(y) - \mathbf{W}X(x)\|^2}\right)$ for some $a \geq 0$. However, PAC-Bayes theory does not directly provide bounds on deterministic predictors such as $\mathbf{W}$. Instead, it provides guarantees for stochastic Gibbs predictors that are described in terms of a posterior distribution Q over deterministic predictors. More precisely, PAC-Bayes theory provides bounds for the Gibbs risk defined as the Q-average of the risk of deterministic predictors. The following theorem, due to Zhang (2006), provides an example of such a bound.[3]

---

3. Unfortunately, there is no dependence on the sample-size m in the theorem stated by Zhang (2006) because the one-example formulation was used. We obtain Theorem 10.3 if we use m examples instead of one.

Theorem 10.3. *(from Zhang, 2006) Let ζ be any loss function, and let P be any prior distribution on $\mathcal{W}$, the set of all the predictors $\mathbf{W} : \mathcal{H}_\mathfrak{X} \to \mathcal{H}_\mathcal{y}$. Then, for any D on $\mathfrak{X} \times \mathcal{y}$, with probability at least $1 - \delta$ over all training sets S sampled according to D^m, we have, simultaneously for all distributions Q on $\mathcal{W}$,*

$$- \mathop{\mathbf{E}}_{\boldsymbol{b} \sim Q} \ln \mathop{\mathbf{E}}_{(x,y) \sim D} e^{-\zeta(\boldsymbol{b}, x, y)} \leq$$

$$\frac{1}{m} \left(\mathop{\mathbf{E}}_{\boldsymbol{b} \sim Q} \sum_{i=1}^{m} \zeta(\boldsymbol{b}, x_i, y_i) + \mathrm{KL}(Q, P) + \ln \frac{1}{\delta} \right) ,$$

where $\mathrm{KL}(Q, P)$ denotes the Kullback-Leibler divergence between distributions Q and P.

To use Theorem 10.3, we restrict ourselves (in this section) to the case where both feature spaces $\mathcal{H}_\mathfrak{X}$ and $\mathcal{H}_\mathcal{y}$ are finite-dimensional vector spaces of dimensions $N_\mathfrak{X}$ and $N_\mathcal{y}$, respectively. The set of predictors thus coincides with the set of $N_\mathcal{y} \times N_\mathfrak{X}$ matrices. Each posterior is chosen to be an isotropic Gaussian of variance σ^2 and expectation $\mathbf{W}$. If $Q_{\mathbf{W},\sigma}(\mathbf{V})$ denotes the density at a matrix $\mathbf{V}$ of this posterior, we have

$$Q_{\mathbf{W},\sigma}(\mathbf{V}) = \left(\frac{1}{\sqrt{2\pi}\sigma} \right)^{N_\mathfrak{X} N_\mathcal{y}} e^{-\frac{1}{2\sigma^2} \|\mathbf{V} - \mathbf{W}\|^2} , \tag{10.3}$$

where, for any matrix $\mathbf{V}$, $\|\mathbf{V}\|^2 \stackrel{\text{def}}{=} \sum_{i=1}^{N_\mathcal{y}} \sum_{j=1}^{N_\mathfrak{X}} V_{i,j}^2$ (also called the Frobenius norm of $\mathbf{V}$).

For the prior P, we chose the (non-informative) isotropic Gaussian centered at the origin (*i.e.*, $P = Q_{\mathbf{0},\sigma}$). In that case, we have

$$\mathrm{KL}(Q_{\mathbf{W},\sigma}, P) = \frac{1}{2} \frac{\|\mathbf{W}\|^2}{\sigma^2} . \tag{10.4}$$

The next theorem provides an upper bound on the risk of the (deterministic) predictor $\mathbf{W}$ that depends on its empirical quadratic risk—not on the empirical risk of a stochastic (Gibbs) predictor. This new result was made possible by performing Gaussian integrals over functions of the quadratic loss and by observing that we can choose a value for σ such that the noise of the empirical quadratic risk is cancelled by the noise of the true quadratic risk whenever $K_\mathfrak{X}(x, x)$ is the same for all $x \in \mathfrak{X}$.

Theorem 10.4. *Consider any input kernel $K_\mathfrak{X}$ and any output kernel $K_\mathcal{y}$ inducing finite-dimensional feature spaces. Suppose that $K_\mathfrak{X}(x, x) = 1$ for all $x \in \mathfrak{X}$. Let D be any distribution on $\mathfrak{X} \times \mathcal{y}$. Then, for any prediction loss L upper bounded by the output kernel loss $L_{K_\mathcal{y}}$, with probability at least $1 - \delta$*

over all training sets S sampled according to D^m, we have, simultaneously for all predictors $\mathbf{W}$,

$$\mathop{\mathbf{E}}_{(x,y)\sim D} L(y_{\mathbf{w}}(x), y) \le \frac{5e}{e-1}\left[1 - e^{-\frac{1}{m}\left(2\sum_{i=1}^{m}\|Y(y_i)-\mathbf{W}X(x_i)\|^2 + \frac{9}{8}\|\mathbf{W}\|^2 + \ln\frac{1}{\delta}\right)}\right].$$

Proof. If we use Theorem 10.3 in the case of the quadratic loss with the proposed posterior $Q_{\mathbf{W},\sigma}$ and prior P, and if we use (10.4) and (10.5) and exploit the convexity of $-\ln x$, then we have that, with probability at least $1-\delta$,

$$-\ln\left(\mathop{\mathbf{E}}_{(x,y)\sim D}\mathop{\mathbf{E}}_{\mathbf{V}\sim Q_{\mathbf{W},\sigma}} e^{-2\|Y(y)-\mathbf{V}X(x)\|^2}\right) \le$$
$$\frac{1}{m}\left(\mathop{\mathbf{E}}_{\mathbf{V}\sim Q_{\mathbf{W},\sigma}} 2\sum_{i=1}^{m}\|Y(y_i) - \mathbf{V}X(x_i)\|^2 + \frac{\|\mathbf{W}\|^2}{2\sigma^2} + \ln\frac{1}{\delta}\right).$$

In the appendix, we provide proofs of the following Gaussian integrals:

$$\mathop{\mathbf{E}}_{\mathbf{V}\sim Q_{\mathbf{W},\sigma}} \|Y(y) - \mathbf{V}X(x)\|^2 = \|Y(y) - \mathbf{W}X(x)\|^2 + \sigma^2 N_y\|X(x)\|^2. \quad (10.5)$$

$$\mathop{\mathbf{E}}_{\mathbf{V}\sim Q_{\mathbf{W},\sigma}} e^{-2\|Y(y)-\mathbf{V}X(x)\|^2} = \left[\frac{\sigma^{N_x}}{\sqrt{1+4\sigma^2\|X(x)\|^2}}\right]^{N_y} e^{-\frac{2\|Y(y)-\mathbf{W}X(x)\|^2}{1+4\sigma^2\|X(x)\|^2}}. \quad (10.6)$$

Because, by hypothesis, $\|X(x)\|$ is a constant independent of x, with probability at least $1-\delta$,

$$\mathop{\mathbf{E}}_{(x,y)\sim D} 1 - e^{-2\frac{\|Y(y)-\mathbf{W}X(x)\|^2}{1+4\|X(x)\|^2\sigma^2}} \le 1 - e^{-\xi - \frac{1}{m}\left(2\sum_{i=1}^{m}\|Y(y_i)-\mathbf{W}X(x_i)\|^2 + \frac{\|\mathbf{W}\|^2}{2\sigma^2} + \ln\frac{1}{\delta}\right)},$$

$$(10.7)$$

where

$$\xi \stackrel{\text{def}}{=} N_y\left[2\|X(x)\|^2\sigma^2 + \ln\left(\frac{\sigma^{N_x}}{\sqrt{1+4\|X(x)\|^2\sigma^2}}\right)\right].$$

For $\|X(x)\| = 1$, the value of σ^2 satisfying $\xi = 0$ is monotonously increasing with N_x; going from $\sigma^2 = 0.6752...$ for $N_x = 1$ to $\sigma^2 = 1$ when $N_x \to \infty$. Consider inequality (10.7) when $\xi = 0$. In that case, $2/3 < \sigma^2 \le 1$. Then its right-hand side can be upper bounded by the same quantity but with σ^2 replaced by $2/3$, and its left-hand side can be lower bounded by the same quantity but with σ^2 replaced by 1. The theorem then follows by applying Lemma 10.2 for $a = 5$. $\square$

10.3.2 The Risk Bound Minimizer

The predictor $\mathbf{W}$ that minimizes the risk bound of Theorem 10.4 is the one that minimizes the multiple-output ridge regression objective F_{rr}, where

$$F_{rr}(\mathbf{W}) \stackrel{\text{def}}{=} C \sum_{i=1}^{m} \|Y(y_i) - \mathbf{W}X(x_i)\|^2 + \|\mathbf{W}\|^2,$$

for some value of $C > 0$. Note that F_{rr} is exactly the objective to minimize that was proposed by Cortes et al. (2007). At optimality, the gradient of F_{rr} must vanish. As shown by Cortes et al. (2007), the solution $\mathbf{W}^*$ is unique for finite C and is given by

$$\mathbf{W}^* = \sum_{i=1}^{m}\sum_{j=1}^{m} Y(y_i)(\mathbf{K}_{\mathcal{X}} + \frac{1}{C}\mathbf{I})_{i,j}^{-1} X^{\top}(x_j), \tag{10.8}$$

where $X^{\top}(x)$ denotes the transpose of vector $X(x)$, $\mathbf{K}_{\mathcal{X}}$ denotes the input kernel matrix, and $\mathbf{I}$ denotes the $m \times m$ identity matrix.

Because $\mathbf{W}^*$ is the minimizer of the ℓ_2-regularized least squares F_{rr}, the convergence rates established by Caponnetto and De Vito (2007) also apply to $\mathbf{W}^*$.

10.4 A Sample Compressed PAC-Bayesian Bound

Note that the predictor minimizing the ridge regression objective is a linear combination of simple predictors $Y(y_i)X^{\top}(x_j)$ that are identified by two training examples. Inspired by some recent work on PAC-Bayes sample compression (Laviolette and Marchand, 2007; Germain et al., 2011), we want to establish a guarantee on the true risk for arbitrary linear combinations of these simple structured output predictors. In contrast with Theorem 10.4, the obtained risk bound will be valid for feature spaces $\mathcal{H}_{\mathcal{X}}$ and $\mathcal{H}_{\mathcal{Y}}$ that are arbitrary RKHS (of possibly infinite dimensionality). For that purpose, let $X^{\dagger}(x)$ denote the dual of vector $X(x)$. The dual $X^{\dagger}(x)$ is a map from $\mathcal{H}_{\mathcal{X}}$ to $\mathbb{R}$, such that for all $(x, x') \in \mathcal{X}^2$, we have $X^{\dagger}(x)X(x') = \langle X(x), X(x') \rangle = K_{\mathcal{X}}(x, x')$. Thus, given a training set S of m examples, we consider predictors that can be written as

$$\mathbf{W} = \sum_{i=1}^{m}\sum_{j=1}^{m} Y(y_i) A_{i,j} X^{\dagger}(x_j), \tag{10.9}$$

where $A_{i,j} \in \mathbb{R}$ for all $(i,j) \in \{1,\ldots,m\}^2$. In this case, the quadratic loss $\|Y(y) - \mathbf{W}X(x)\|^2$ is now given by

$$\left\| Y(y) - \sum_{i=1}^{m}\sum_{j=1}^{m} A_{i,j} K_{\mathcal{X}}(x_j, x)Y(y_i) \right\|^2 \stackrel{\text{def}}{=} R(\mathbf{A}, x, y). \tag{10.10}$$

To connect with PAC-Bayes sample compression, let us write $\mathbf{A}$ in terms of a distribution $\mathbf{q}$ over $2m^2$ predictors. For this purpose, let $q_{i,j}^+ \geq 0$ be the weight on predictor $Y(y_i)X^{\dagger}(x_j)$ and let $q_{i,j}^- \geq 0$ be the weight on the opposite predictor $-Y(y_i)X^{\dagger}(x_j)$ such that

$$\sum_{i=1}^{m}\sum_{j=1}^{m}\sum_{s \in \{-1,+1\}} q_{i,j}^s = 1.$$

Now, without loss of generality, for all (i,j), let $A_{i,j} = \kappa \cdot (q_{i,j}^+ - q_{i,j}^-)$ for some $\kappa > 0$. For notational brevity, let $R(\mathbf{q}, x, y)$ be the quadratic loss obtained from $R(\mathbf{A}, x, y)$ when each $A_{i,j}$ is replaced by $\kappa \cdot (q_{i,j}^+ - q_{i,j}^-)$. In addition, let $\mathcal{I} \stackrel{\text{def}}{=} \{1,\ldots,m\}^2$ denote the set of all pairs of indices and let $\mathcal{B} \stackrel{\text{def}}{=} \{-1,+1\}$. We then have

$$R(\mathbf{q}, x, y) = \sum_{\mathbf{i} \in \mathcal{I}}\sum_{\mathbf{j} \in \mathcal{I}}\sum_{s \in \mathcal{B}}\sum_{t \in \mathcal{B}} q_{\mathbf{i}}^s q_{\mathbf{j}}^t \ell_{\mathbf{i},\mathbf{j}}^{s,t}(x, y),$$

where, for $\mathbf{i} = (i, i')$ and $\mathbf{j} = (j, j')$, we have

$$\ell_{\mathbf{i},\mathbf{j}}^{s,t}(x, y) \stackrel{\text{def}}{=} \langle Y(y) - \kappa s Y(y_i)K_{\mathcal{X}}(x_{i'}, x), Y(y) - \kappa t Y(y_j)K_{\mathcal{X}}(x_{j'}, x)\rangle. \tag{10.11}$$

An upper bound on $R(\mathbf{q}) \stackrel{\text{def}}{=} \mathbf{E}_{(x,y)\sim D} R(\mathbf{q}, x, y)$ also provides an upper bound on the prediction risk $\mathbf{E}_{(x,y)\sim D} L(y_{\mathbf{w}}(x), y)$ because, by Lemma 10.1, we have $L(y_{\mathbf{w}}(x), y) \leq 2R(\mathbf{q}, x, y)$ whenever $A_{i,j}$ is replaced by $\kappa \cdot (q_{i,j}^+ - q_{i,j}^-)$ in (10.9) and whenever the L is upper bounded by L_{K_y}. Our goal is thus to find a tight upper bound on $R(\mathbf{q})$ and then design an algorithm that finds $\mathbf{q}$ (hence, the predictor $\mathbf{W}$) that minimizes this upper bound.

10.4.1   The Risk Bound

The proposed risk bound follows from PAC-Bayes theory and depends on how far is the posterior distribution $\mathbf{q}$ from a prior $\mathbf{p}$. For $\mathbf{p}$, we choose the uniform distribution over $\mathcal{I} \stackrel{\text{def}}{=} \{1,\ldots,2m\}^2$ so that $p_{\mathbf{i}}^s = 1/(2m^2)$ for all $(\mathbf{i}, s) \in \mathcal{I} \times \mathcal{B}$, where $\mathcal{B} \stackrel{\text{def}}{=} \{-1,+1\}$. The posterior $\mathbf{q}$ is chosen to be *quasi-uniform*. By this we mean that for all $\mathbf{i} \in \mathcal{I}$, we have $q_{\mathbf{i}}^+ + q_{\mathbf{i}}^- = 1/m^2$. In that case, each $q_{\mathbf{i}}^s \in [0, 1/m^2]$ and, consequently, the KL-divergence $\mathrm{KL}(\mathbf{q}, \mathbf{p})$ is always at most $\ln 2$. Such a small upper bound on $\mathrm{KL}(\mathbf{q}, \mathbf{p})$

contributes significantly at reducing the risk bound closer to the empirical risk $R(\mathbf{q}, S) \stackrel{\text{def}}{=} (1/m) \sum_{i=1}^{m} R(\mathbf{q}, x_i, y_i)$. Moreover, restricting $\mathbf{q}$ to quasi-uniform distributions does not restrict the class of predictors considered by the learner. Indeed, for any predictor $\mathbf{W}$ described by some matrix $\mathbf{A}$ in (10.9), there exists $\kappa > 0$ and a quasi-uniform $\mathbf{q}$ such that $A_{i,j} = \kappa \cdot (q_{i,j}^+ - q_{i,j}^-)$.

Theorem 10.5. *Let $a \le \ell_{\mathbf{i},\mathbf{j}}^{s,t}(x, y) \le b$ for all $(x, y) \in \mathcal{X} \times \mathcal{Y}$, for all $(s, t) \in \mathcal{B}^2$, for all $(\mathbf{i}, \mathbf{j}) \in \mathcal{I}^2$, and for some interval $[a, b]$. Let D be any distribution on $\mathcal{X} \times \mathcal{Y}$. Let $m \ge 8$. Then, with probability at least $1 - \delta$ over all training sets S sampled according to D^m, we have, simultaneously for all quasi-uniform distributions $\mathbf{q}$ on $\mathcal{I}$,*

$$R(\mathbf{q}) \le R(\mathbf{q}, S) + \sqrt{\frac{b-a}{2(m-4)} \left[20 + \ln \left(\frac{8\sqrt{m}}{\delta} \right) \right]}.$$

Proof. Given the uniform prior $\mathbf{p}$, consider the Laplace transform

$$\mathcal{L}_{\mathbf{p}} \stackrel{\text{def}}{=} \sum_{\mathbf{i} \in \mathcal{I}} \sum_{\mathbf{j} \in \mathcal{I}} \sum_{s \in \mathcal{B}} \sum_{t \in \mathcal{B}} p_{\mathbf{i}}^s p_{\mathbf{j}}^t \exp \left(2(m-4) \left(\frac{\ell_{\mathbf{i},\mathbf{j}}^{s,t}(S) - a}{b - a} - \frac{\ell_{\mathbf{i},\mathbf{j}}^{s,t} - a}{b - a} \right)^2 \right),$$

where $\ell_{\mathbf{i},\mathbf{j}}^{s,t} \stackrel{\text{def}}{=} \mathbf{E}_{(x,y) \sim D} \ell_{\mathbf{i},\mathbf{j}}^{s,t}(x, y)$ and $\ell_{\mathbf{i},\mathbf{j}}^{s,t}(S) \stackrel{\text{def}}{=} (1/m) \sum_{i=1}^{m} \ell_{\mathbf{i},\mathbf{j}}^{s,t}(x_i, y_i)$. Note that $\ell_{\mathbf{i},\mathbf{j}}^{s,t}(S)$ is a biased estimate of $\ell_{\mathbf{i},\mathbf{j}}^{s,t}$ because it considers the loss on examples that are used for the predictors described by $(\mathbf{i}, s)$ and $(\mathbf{j}, t)$. To obtain an unbiased estimator, let $S_{\mathbf{i},\mathbf{j}} \stackrel{\text{def}}{=} \{(x_i, y_i) \in S : i \notin \mathbf{i} \cup \mathbf{j}\}$ and let $m_{\mathbf{i},\mathbf{j}} \stackrel{\text{def}}{=} |S_{\mathbf{i},\mathbf{j}}|$. Then, let[4] $\ell_{\mathbf{i},\mathbf{j}}^{s,t}(S_{\mathbf{i},\mathbf{j}}) \stackrel{\text{def}}{=} \frac{1}{m_{\mathbf{i},\mathbf{j}}} \sum_{k=1}^{m} I((x_k, y_k) \in S_{\mathbf{i},\mathbf{j}}) \ell_{\mathbf{i},\mathbf{j}}^{s,t}(x_k, y_k)$ be our unbiased estimator of $\ell_{\mathbf{i},\mathbf{j}}^{s,t}$. It is then straightforward to show that $\ell_{\mathbf{i},\mathbf{j}}^{s,t}(S_{\mathbf{i},\mathbf{j}}) - 4(b-a)/m \le \ell_{\mathbf{i},\mathbf{j}}^{s,t}(S) \le \ell_{\mathbf{i},\mathbf{j}}^{s,t}(S_{\mathbf{i},\mathbf{j}}) + 4(b-a)/m$ and, consequently, for $m \ge 8$

$$\left(\frac{\ell_{\mathbf{i},\mathbf{j}}^{s,t}(S) - a}{b - a} - \frac{\ell_{\mathbf{i},\mathbf{j}}^{s,t} - a}{b - a} \right)^2 \le \left(\frac{\ell_{\mathbf{i},\mathbf{j}}^{s,t}(S_{\mathbf{i},\mathbf{j}}) - a}{b - a} - \frac{\ell_{\mathbf{i},\mathbf{j}}^{s,t} - a}{b - a} \right)^2 + \frac{10}{m}. \qquad (10.12)$$

---

4. Here, $I(a) = 1$ if predicate a is true and $I(a) = 0$ otherwise.

Now, given $\mathrm{kl}(q,p) \stackrel{\text{def}}{=} q\ln(q/p) + (1-q)\ln[(1-q)/(1-p)]$, if we use $2(q-p)^2 \leq \mathrm{kl}(q,p)$, we obtain

$$\mathcal{L}_{\mathbf{p}} \leq \mathop{\mathbf{E}}_{S \sim D^m} \sum_{\mathbf{i} \in \mathcal{I}} \sum_{\mathbf{j} \in \mathcal{I}} \sum_{s \in \mathcal{B}} \sum_{t \in \mathcal{B}}$$

$$p_{\mathbf{i}}^s p_{\mathbf{j}}^t \, \exp\left(\frac{20}{m}(m-4) + m_{\mathbf{i},\mathbf{j}}\mathrm{kl}\left(\frac{\ell_{\mathbf{i},\mathbf{j}}^{s,t}(S_{\mathbf{i},\mathbf{j}}) - a}{b-a}, \frac{\ell_{\mathbf{i},\mathbf{j}}^{s,t} - a}{b-a}\right)\right)$$

$$= \exp\left(\frac{20}{m}(m-4)\right) \sum_{\mathbf{i} \in \mathcal{I}} \sum_{\mathbf{j} \in \mathcal{I}} \sum_{s \in \mathcal{B}} \sum_{t \in \mathcal{B}} p_{\mathbf{i}}^s p_{\mathbf{j}}^t \left(\prod_{i \in \mathbf{i} \cup \mathbf{j}} \mathop{\mathbf{E}}_{(x_i, y_i) \sim D}\right)$$

$$\mathop{\mathbf{E}}_{S_{\mathbf{i},\mathbf{j}} \sim D^{m_{\mathbf{i},\mathbf{j}}}} \exp\left(m_{\mathbf{i},\mathbf{j}}\mathrm{kl}\left(\frac{\ell_{\mathbf{i},\mathbf{j}}^{s,t}(S_{\mathbf{i},\mathbf{j}}) - a}{b-a}, \frac{\ell_{\mathbf{i},\mathbf{j}}^{s,t} - a}{b-a}\right)\right).$$

Because $S_{\mathbf{i},\mathbf{j}}$ is the arithmetic mean of $m_{\mathbf{i},\mathbf{j}}$ i.i.d. random variables, the lemma of Maurer (2004) tells us that the last expectation (over $S_{\mathbf{i},\mathbf{j}}$) is at most $2\sqrt{m_{\mathbf{i},\mathbf{j}}}$ and, consequently, $\mathcal{L}_{\mathbf{p}} \leq 2\sqrt{m}\exp(20(m-4)/m)$. Because $\mathcal{L}_{\mathbf{p}}$ is the expectation (over S) of a positive random variable, we can use Markov's inequality, which states that, with probability of at least $1 - \delta$ over the random draws of S, we have

$$\ln\left(\sum_{\mathbf{i} \in \mathcal{I}} \sum_{\mathbf{j} \in \mathcal{I}} \sum_{s \in \mathcal{B}} \sum_{t \in \mathcal{B}} p_{\mathbf{i}}^s p_{\mathbf{j}}^t \exp\left(2(m-4)\left(\frac{\ell_{\mathbf{i},\mathbf{j}}^{s,t}(S) - a}{b-a} - \frac{\ell_{\mathbf{i},\mathbf{j}}^{s,t} - a}{b-a}\right)^2\right)\right)$$

$$\leq \frac{20}{m}(m-4) + \ln\left(\frac{2\sqrt{m}}{\delta}\right).$$

By turning the expectation over $\mathbf{p}^2$ into an expectation over $\mathbf{q}^2$, and by using Jensen's inequality on the concavity of the logarithm, the last inequality implies that we have

$$\sum_{\mathbf{i} \in \mathcal{I}} \sum_{\mathbf{j} \in \mathcal{I}} \sum_{s \in \mathcal{B}} \sum_{t \in \mathcal{B}} q_{\mathbf{i}}^s q_{\mathbf{j}}^t \left(\frac{\ell_{\mathbf{i},\mathbf{j}}^{s,t}(S) - a}{b-a} - \frac{\ell_{\mathbf{i},\mathbf{j}}^{s,t} - a}{b-a}\right)^2$$

$$\leq \frac{1}{2(m-4)}\left(\mathrm{KL}(\mathbf{q}^2, \mathbf{p}^2) + 20 + \ln\frac{2\sqrt{m}}{\delta}\right)$$

for all $\mathbf{q}$. The theorem then follows by using Jensen's inequality on the convexity of $(q-p)^2$ and by using $\mathrm{KL}(\mathbf{q}^2, \mathbf{p}^2) = 2\mathrm{KL}(\mathbf{q}, \mathbf{p}) \leq 2\ln 2$ for quasi-uniform posteriors. $\qquad\square$

Hence, for quasi-uniform posteriors $\mathbf{q}$, the upper bound on $R(\mathbf{q})$ is close to $R(\mathbf{q}, S)$ whenever $(b-a) \ll m$. From (10.11), we can see that $(b-a)$

is at most $2B_y(1 + \kappa B_\mathcal{X})^2$ when $|K_\mathcal{X}(x, x')| \leq B_\mathcal{X}$ for all $(x, x') \in \mathcal{X}^2$ and $|K_y(y, y')| \leq B_y$ for all $(y, y') \in \mathcal{Y}^2$.

10.4.2   The Risk Bound Minimizer

The posterior $\mathbf{q}$ that minimizes the upper bound of Theorem 10.5 is the posterior minimizing $R(\mathbf{q}, S)$ under the constraint that $\mathbf{q}$ is quasi-uniform. In that case, each $q_{i,j}^s \in [0, 1/m^2]$. Because $A_{i,j} = \kappa \cdot (q_{i,j}^+ - q_{i,j}^-)$, the quasi-uniform constraint on $\mathbf{q}$ implies that $|A_{i,j}| \leq C$ for all $(i, j) \in \mathcal{I}$ and for some $C > 0$. Instead of handling these m^2 constraints, it is computationally much cheaper to replace them by the single ℓ_2 constraint $\sum_{(i,j) \in \mathcal{I}} A_{i,j}^2 \leq R^2$ for some $R > 0$. Note that, although this is an approximate solution, we have $|A_{i,j}| \leq R$ for all (i, j) whenever this ℓ_2 constraint is satisfied. Hence, given $R^2 \stackrel{\text{def}}{=} m^2 \rho^2$ and $R(\mathbf{A}, S) \stackrel{\text{def}}{=} \frac{1}{m} \sum_{i=1}^m R(\mathbf{A}, x_i, y_i)$, let us solve

$$
\begin{aligned}
\min_{\mathbf{A}} \quad & R(\mathbf{A}, S) \\
\text{s.t.} \quad & \sum_{i=1}^m \sum_{j=1}^m A_{i,j}^2 \leq R^2 \,.
\end{aligned}
\tag{10.13}
$$

Theorem 10.6. *Let $\mathcal{A}^*$ denote the set of solutions of (10.13). Let $\mathbf{K}_\mathcal{X}$ and $\mathbf{K}_y$ denote, respectively, the input and output kernel matrices. Let $v_1, \ldots, v_m$ and $\lambda_1, \ldots, \lambda_m$ denote, respectively, the eigenvectors and eigenvalues of $\mathbf{K}_\mathcal{X}$. Let $u_1, \ldots, u_m$ and $\delta_1, \ldots, \delta_m$ denote, respectively, the eigenvectors and eigenvalues of $\mathbf{K}_y$. Let $\mathcal{J} \stackrel{\text{def}}{=} \{(i, j) \in \mathcal{I} : \delta_i \lambda_j > 0\}$. Then*

$$
\sum_{i=1}^m \sum_{j=1}^m \gamma_{i,j} u_i v_j^\top \in \mathcal{A}^* \,,
$$

where $\gamma_{i,j}$ is given by

$$
\gamma_{i,j} =
\begin{cases}
0 & \text{if } \delta_i \lambda_j = 0 \\
\frac{u_i^\top v_j}{\lambda_j} & \text{if } \delta_i \lambda_j > 0
\end{cases}
\qquad \text{if } \sum_{(i,j) \in \mathcal{J}} \frac{(u_i^\top v_j)^2}{\lambda_j^2} \leq R^2 \,,
$$

$$
\gamma_{i,j} = \frac{\delta_i \lambda_j (u_i^\top v_j)}{\delta_i \lambda_j^2 + m\beta} \qquad \qquad \text{otherwise} \,,
$$

where $\beta > 0$ is the solution of

$$
\sum_{i=1}^m \sum_{j=1}^m \frac{\delta_i^2 \lambda_j^2 (u_i^\top v_j)^2}{(\delta_i \lambda_j^2 + m\beta)^2} = R^2 \,.
$$

Proof. Let $L(\mathbf{A}, \beta) \overset{\text{def}}{=} R(\mathbf{A}, S) + \beta \left(\|\mathbf{A}\|^2 - R^2 \right)$. Convex optimization theory tells us that if there exists $\beta \geq 0$ and $\mathbf{A}$ with $\|\mathbf{A}\|^2 \leq R^2$, which satisfies $\partial L / \partial \mathbf{A} = 0$ and $\beta \cdot \left(\|\mathbf{A}\|^2 - R^2 \right) = 0$, then $\mathbf{A} \in \mathcal{A}^*$. Here, we have

$$\frac{\partial L}{\partial \mathbf{A}} = \frac{2}{m} \mathbf{K}_y (\mathbf{A} \mathbf{K}_x - \mathbf{I}) \mathbf{K}_x + 2\beta \mathbf{A} = 0. \tag{10.14}$$

Because $\mathbf{K}_x$ and $\mathbf{K}_y$ are symmetric positive semi-definite $m \times m$ matrices, their eigenvalues are all non-negative and their eigenvectors constitute an orthonormal basis of $\mathbb{R}^m$. Thus, $\{u_i v_j^\top\}_{(i,j) \in \mathcal{J}}$ is an orthonormal basis of $\mathbb{R}^{m^2}$. Consequently, w.l.o.g., any $m \times m$ matrix $\mathbf{A}$ can be written as $\mathbf{A} = \sum_{i=1}^m \sum_{j=1}^m \gamma_{i,j} u_i v_j^\top$ for some values of $\gamma_{i,j}$. Hence, we have $\|\mathbf{A}\|^2 = \sum_{i=1}^m \sum_{j=1}^m \gamma_{i,j}^2$, and (10.14) becomes $\gamma_{i,j} (\delta_i \lambda_j^2 + m\beta) = \delta_i \lambda_j (u_i^\top v_j)$. When $\beta = 0$, that equation is solved for $\gamma_{i,j} = 0$ when $\delta_i \lambda_j = 0$ and $\gamma_{i,j} = (u_i^\top v_j)/\lambda_j$ when $\delta_i \lambda_j > 0$ (a solution where the ℓ_2 constraint is not active[5]). When $\beta > 0$, that equation is solved for $\gamma_{i,j} = (\delta_i \lambda_j (u_i^\top v_j))/(\delta_i \lambda_j^2 + m\beta)$, and in that case, we have $\|\mathbf{A}\|^2 = R^2$ with a unique non-zero solution for β. $\square$

Note that the eigenvectors and eigenvalues of $\mathbf{K}_x$ and $\mathbf{K}_y$ can be obtained from their singular value decompositions in $O(m^3)$ time. The solution for β can be obtained with Newton's method requiring $\Theta(m^2)$ time for each iteration. Finally, we can obtain $\mathbf{A}$ in $O(m^3)$ by using $\mathbf{A} = \mathbf{u} \boldsymbol{\gamma} \boldsymbol{b}^\top$ where $\mathbf{u}$ and $\boldsymbol{b}$ are matrices obtained by concatenating the column eigenvectors of $\mathbf{K}_y$ and $\mathbf{K}_x$, respectively, and where $\boldsymbol{\gamma}$ denotes the matrix of $\gamma_{i,j}$ values. Hence, the proposed solution of (10.13) is reached in $O(m^3)$ time whenever Newton's method requires at most $O(m)$ iterations.

10.5 Empirical Results

We have compared the solution given by (10.8) (Structured Output by Ridge Regression [SORR]) with the one given by Theorem 10.6 (Structured Output by Sample-Compression [SOSC]) on the word-recognition task studied by Taskar et al. (2004) and Cortes et al. (2007) and the enzyme classification task studied by Rousu et al. (2006). All hyper-parameters (C, ρ, and kernel parameters) were selected with 10-fold cross-validation (CV) on the training sets where we have relied on the pre-images (using Equation [10.1]) for that purpose only.

---

5. This is the smallest ℓ_2 norm solution of the unconstrained problem. The Moore-Penrose pseudo-inverse of $\mathbf{K}_x$ is also a solution of the unconstrained problem because, in that case, it suffices for $\mathbf{A}$ to satisfy $\mathbf{A} \mathbf{K}_x^2 = \mathbf{K}_x$.

Metric	Dirac Kernel		Hamming Kernel	
	SORR	**SOSC**	**SORR**	**SOSC**
0/1 risk	$0.0518_{\pm.0078}$	$0.0517_{\pm.0079}$	$0.0800_{\pm.0053}$	$0.0799_{\pm.0053}$
Letter risk	$0.0282_{\pm.0063}$	$0.0281_{\pm.0063}$	$0.0374_{\pm.0051}$	$0.0374_{\pm.0051}$

Table 10.1: Empirical results on the word-recognition task.

Metric	$H-M^3-\ell_\Delta$	$H-M^3-\ell_{\tilde{H}}$	SORR	SOSC
0/1 risk	0.957	0.855	0.640	0.684
Confidence intervals	$[0.949, 0.965]$	$[0.840, 0.869]$	$[0.621, 0.659]$	$[0.666, 0.702]$
Hierarchical risk	1.2	2.50	1.71	1.84
F1 score	0.6330	0.5340	0.5813	0.5569

Table 10.2: Empirical results on the enzyme hierarchical classification task.

The word-recognition task consists of predicting the correct word (a sequence of letters) associated with a manuscript picture of the same word. The metrics used for this data set are usually the 0/1-risk (the fraction of errors on words) and the letter risk (the fraction of errors on letters). Hence, following (10.2), we have used the Dirac kernel ($K_y(y, y') = I(y = y')$) and the Hamming kernel (which is given by the length of the largest string minus the Hamming distance between the two strings). The polynomial kernel of degree d was used for the input kernel. All experiments were done using the protocol described in Taskar et al. (2004) and Cortes et al. (2007). According to Cortes et al. (2007), SORR achieved better performance than structural SVM and max-margin Markov networks. Our empirical results are shown in Table 10.1. The error bars are the standard deviation of the corresponding risk over the different CV folds given by Taskar et al. (2004). Clearly, SORR and SOSC achieved similar generalization performance (with overlapping error bars) on both the 0/1 risk and the letter risk.

The enzymes hierarchical classification task consists of predicting a path in an enzyme classification scheme used by biologists to classify amino acid sequences of enzymatic proteins. As in Rousu et al. (2006), the four-gram kernel was used in the input space. Focusing on the hierarchical risk (the length of the incorrect sub-path from the root to the enzyme leaf) as the most natural metric for this data set, we have used the hierarchical kernel

	Dirac Kernel		Hamming Kernel	
Metric	**SORR**	**SOSC**	**SORR**	**SOSC**
0/1 risk	0.0517 ±.0079	0.0517 ±.0079	0.1328 ±.0128	0.1328 ±.0128
Letter risk	0.0281 ±.0063	0.0281 ±.0063	0.0387 ±.0057	0.0387 ±.0057

Table 10.3: Empirical results on the word-recognition task using the quadratic loss for the selection of hyper-parameters.

Metric	**SORR**	**SOSC**
0/1 risk	0.6774	0.7202
Confidence intervals	[0.659, 0.695]	[0.702, 0.737]
Hierarchical risk	1.77	1.87
F1 score	0.5616	0.5327

Table 10.4: Empirical results on the enzyme hierarchical classification task using the quadratic loss for the selection of hyper-parameters.

of Jacob et al. (2008) (given by the length of the common sub-path between two paths) on the output space. All experiments were done using the protocol described in Rousu et al. (2006), and our empirical results are shown in Table 10.2. We have also included the results obtained by Rousu et al. (2006) for $H-M^3-\ell_{\tilde{H}}$ and $H-M^3-\ell_\Delta$, which are variants of the max-margin Markov networks. In the case of the 0/1 risk (the fraction of misclassification errors), we have computed the 90% confidence intervals from the binomial tail inversion method of Langford (2005). From Table 10.2, we see that the 0/1 risk differences between all algorithms are significant (at 0.9 confidence level), with SORR being the best algorithm. For the hierarchical risk, note that from the central limit theorem, the standard deviation of this metric is given by $\sigma/\sqrt{n}$ for a testing set of $n = 1755$ examples when the hierarchical loss variance is σ^2. Because $\sigma \leq 3$ for the hierarchy of four levels, the hierarchical risk differences among all algorithms appear to be significant, with $H-M^3-\ell_\Delta$ being the best algorithm.

10.5.1   Avoiding the Pre-Image During Cross-Validation

As stated previously, the proposed learning algorithms do not require solving the pre-image problem during the training phase. To push this idea further, we also tried to avoid solving the pre-image problem for selecting hyper-parameters during cross-validation. In this second round of experiments, we choose hyper-parameters that minimize the quadratic loss of (10.10) instead of the prediction loss. This method is much faster when no efficient algorithm is known to solve the pre-image problem. Empirical results using the quadratic loss for hyper-parameter selection are shown in Tables 10.3 and 10.4 for the word-recognition task and enzymes hierarchical classification task, respectively. We can see that this approach yields competitive but slightly less accurate results for both algorithms on the word-recognition task with the Hamming kernel and the enzymes hierarchical classification task. Although solving the pre-image problem during cross-validation is essential to achieve optimal results, this approach could still be used to speed up the identification of favorable hyper-parameters and thus reduce the search space for optimal hyper-parameters.

10.6 Conclusion

In this chapter, we have shown that the quadratic regression loss is a convex surrogate of the prediction loss when the prediction loss is upper bounded by the output kernel loss. We have provided two PAC-Bayes upper bounds of the structured prediction risk that depend on the empirical quadratic risk of the deterministic predictor. The second bound, based on the PAC-Bayes sample-compression approach, is more general than the first bound as it holds for feature spaces that are arbitrary RKHS. The minimizer of the first bound, SORR, turns out to be the predictor proposed by Cortes et al. (2007), whereas the minimizer of the second bound, SOSC, is a predictor that was first presented in Giguère et al. (2013), the article on which this chapter is based. Both predictors have been compared on practical tasks, yielding similar but state-of-the-art accuracies. Finally, although it would be time-consuming, it would be interesting to see whether we can improve SOSC by using the full set of m^2 constraints instead of the single ℓ_2 constraint used in (10.13).

10.7 Appendix

In this appendix, we make use of the following notation: x_i denotes the ith entry of the (column) vector $X(x)$, y_j the jth entry of the (column) vector $Y(y)$, and $\mathbf{V}[i; j]$ the entry in position (i, j) of the matrix $\mathbf{V}$. Also, $\mathbf{V}[\,; j]$ denotes the jth column of the matrix $\mathbf{V}$. Finally, $\delta_{i,j}$ denotes the delta function, which gives 1 if $i = j$ and 0 otherwise.

10.7.1 Example of a Distribution Where the Minimizer of the Quadratic Risk has a Substantially Higher Error Rate Than the Optimal Classifier

We consider a simple one-dimensional binary classification problem where $\mathcal{X} = \mathbb{R}$ and $\mathcal{Y} = \{-1, +1\}$. We thus consider classifiers identified by a single scalar weight w, such that the output $h_w(x)$ on an input x is given by $h_w(x) = \mathrm{sgn}(wx)$. Now, consider a distribution D concentrated on four points $\{(x_1, y_1), (x_2, y_2), (x_3, y_3), (x_4, y_4)\}$. Let p_i denote the weight induced by D on x_i. Hence, $\sum_{i=1}^{4} p_i = 1$. The 0/1 risk is then given by $\sum_{i=1}^{4} p_i I(h_w(x_i) \neq y_i)$, and the quadratic risk is given by $\sum_{i=1}^{4} p_i (y_i - wx_i)^2$.

Let w_r denote the value of w minimizing the quadratic risk. Because the derivative (with respect to w) of the quadratic risk must vanish at w_r, we find that it is given by the solution of $w_r \sum_{i=1}^{4} p_i x_i^2 - \sum_{i=1}^{4} p_i y_i x_i = 0$ or equivalently by $w_r = \frac{\sum_{i=1}^{4} p_i y_i x_i}{\sum_{i=1}^{4} p_i x_i^2}$.

Now, let $x_1 = \epsilon$ with $p_1 = (1 - \epsilon)/2$ and $y_1 = +1$. Let $x_2 = -\epsilon$ with $p_2 = (1 - \epsilon)/2$ and $y_2 = -1$. Let $x_3 = 1/\epsilon$ with $p_3 = \epsilon/2$ and $y_3 = -1$. Let $x_4 = -1/\epsilon$ with $p_4 = \epsilon/2$ and $y_4 = +1$. Then note that, with this distribution, the 0/1 risk of a classifier with a positive weight w is equal to ϵ, and the 0/1 risk of a classifier with a negative weight w is equal to $1 - \epsilon$. The difference tends to the maximum value of 1 when ϵ goes to zero.

However, with this distribution, we have $w_r = \frac{-1 + \epsilon(1 - \epsilon)}{(1 - \epsilon)\epsilon^2 + (1/\epsilon)}$. Hence, w_r is negative for all ϵ between 0 and 1. Hence, the 0/1 risk of h_{w_r} is $(1 - \epsilon)$. However, there exists classifiers (those with positive w) having a 0/1 risk of ϵ.

10.7.2 Proof of (10.5)

$$\mathop{\mathbf{E}}_{\mathbf{V} \sim Q_{\mathbf{W},\sigma}} \|Y(y) - \mathbf{V}X(x)\|^2 = \|Y(y) - \mathbf{W}X(x)\|^2 + \sigma^2 N_y |X(x)\|^2. \quad (10.5)$$

Proof. Note that $\|Y(y) - \mathbf{V}X(x)\|^2 = \|Y(y)\|^2 - 2\langle Y(y), \mathbf{V}X(x)\rangle + \|\mathbf{V}X(x)\|^2$. Let us then compute the expectation according to $Q_{\mathbf{W},\sigma}$ of these three terms.

$$\mathop{\mathbf{E}}_{\mathbf{V} \sim Q_{\mathbf{W},\sigma}} \|Y(y)\|^2 = \|Y(y)\|^2$$

$$\mathop{\mathbf{E}}_{\mathbf{V} \sim Q_{\mathbf{W},\sigma}} 2\langle Y(y), \mathbf{V}X(x)\rangle = 2 \mathop{\mathbf{E}}_{\mathbf{V} \sim Q_{\mathbf{W},\sigma}} \langle Y(y), \sum_{l=1}^{N_x} x_l \mathbf{V}[\,;l]\rangle$$

$$= 2 \mathop{\mathbf{E}}_{\mathbf{V} \sim Q_{\mathbf{W},\sigma}} \sum_{l=1}^{N_x} \sum_{q=1}^{N_y} y_q \mathbf{V}[q;l] x_l$$

$$
= 2 \sum_{l=1}^{N_x} \sum_{q=1}^{N_y} y_q x_l \; \mathop{\mathbf{E}}_{\mathbf{V} \sim Q_{\mathbf{W},\sigma}} \mathbf{V}[q;l]
$$

$$
= 2 \sum_{l=1}^{N_x} \sum_{q=1}^{N_y} y_q x_l \; \mathbf{W}[q;l]
$$

$$
\vdots
$$

$$
= 2 \langle Y(y), \mathbf{W} X(x) \rangle
$$

For $\mathop{\mathbf{E}}_{\mathbf{V} \sim Q_{\mathbf{W},\sigma}} \|\mathbf{V} X(x)\|^2$, first note that, because $Q_{\mathbf{W},\sigma}$ is an *isotropic* Gaussian with mean $\mathbf{W}$ and variance σ^2, we have $\mathop{\mathbf{E}}_{\mathbf{V} \sim Q_{\mathbf{W},\sigma}} \mathbf{V}[q;l]\mathbf{V}[q;l] = \mathbf{W}[q;l] + \sigma^2$ and $\mathop{\mathbf{E}}_{\mathbf{V} \sim Q_{\mathbf{W},\sigma}} \mathbf{V}[q;l]\mathbf{V}[q;k] = \mathbf{W}[q;l]\mathbf{W}[q;k]$ if $l \neq k$. Thus, we have

$$
\mathop{\mathbf{E}}_{\mathbf{V} \sim Q_{\mathbf{W},\sigma}} \|\mathbf{V} X(x)\|^2 = \mathop{\mathbf{E}}_{\mathbf{V} \sim Q_{\mathbf{W},\sigma}} \sum_{l=1}^{N_x} \sum_{k=1}^{N_x} x_l x_k \langle \mathbf{V}[;l], \mathbf{V}[;k] \rangle
$$

$$
= \sum_{l=1}^{N_x} \sum_{k=1}^{N_x} x_l x_k \sum_{q=1}^{N_y} \mathop{\mathbf{E}}_{\mathbf{V} \sim Q_{\mathbf{W},\sigma}} \mathbf{V}[q;l]\mathbf{V}[q;k]
$$

$$
= \sum_{l=1}^{N_x} \sum_{\substack{k=1 \\ k \neq l}}^{N_x} x_l x_k \sum_{q=1}^{N_y} \mathbf{W}[q;l]\mathbf{W}[q;k]
$$

$$
+ \sum_{k=1}^{N_x} x_k x_k \sum_{q=1}^{N_y} (\mathbf{W}[q;l]\mathbf{W}[q;k] + \sigma^2)
$$

$$
= \left(\sum_{l=1}^{N_x} \sum_{k=1}^{N_x} x_l x_k \sum_{q=1}^{N_y} \mathbf{W}[q;l]\mathbf{W}[q;k] \right) + \sum_{k=1}^{N_x} x_k^2 \sum_{q=1}^{N_y} \sigma^2
$$

$$
= \|\mathbf{W} X(x)\|^2 + \sigma^2 N_y \|X(x)\|^2.
$$

From all that precedes, we then have

$$
\mathop{\mathbf{E}}_{\mathbf{V} \sim Q_{\mathbf{W},\sigma}} \|Y(y) - \mathbf{V} X(x)\|^2
$$

$$
= \|Y(y)\|^2 - 2\langle Y(y), \mathbf{W} X(x) \rangle + \|\mathbf{W} X(x)\|^2 + \sigma^2 N_y \|X(x)\|^2
$$

$$
= \|Y(y) - \mathbf{W} X(x)\|^2 + \sigma^2 N_y \|X(x)\|^2,
$$

and we are done. $\qquad\square$

10.7.3   Proof (10.6)

Proof. Let us prove that we have

$$\mathop{\mathbf{E}}_{\mathbf{V}\sim Q_{\mathbf{W},\sigma}} e^{-2\|Y(y)-\mathbf{V}X(x)\|^2} = \left[\frac{\sigma^{N_x}}{\sqrt{1+4\sigma^2\|X(x)\|^2}}\right]^{N_y} e^{-\frac{2\|Y(y)-\mathbf{W}X(x)\|^2}{1+4\sigma^2\|X(x)\|^2}}, \quad (10.6)$$

for the case where each component of vector X is non-zero. To see that the result will also hold for the case where X has some zero-valued components, note that the result will hold by replacing X with $X+\vec{\epsilon}$, where $\vec{\epsilon}$ is a vector whose entries are all equal to ϵ for an ϵ smaller than the smallest non-zero component of X. The result then comes out from the continuity with respect to X of the right-hand side of the above equation (taking the limit $\epsilon \to 0$). Now, let

$$I \stackrel{\text{def}}{=} \mathop{\mathbf{E}}_{\mathbf{V}\sim Q_{\mathbf{W},\sigma}} e^{-2\|Y(y)-\mathbf{V}X(x)\|^2} = \int \frac{d\mathbf{V}}{(\sigma\sqrt{2\pi})^{N_x N_y}} e^{-\frac{1}{2}\frac{\|\mathbf{V}-\mathbf{W}\|^2}{\sigma^2}} e^{-2\|Y(y)-\mathbf{V}X(x)\|^2}.$$

Performing the change of variables $\mathbf{U}=\mathbf{V}-\mathbf{W}$ gives

$$I = \int \frac{d\mathbf{U}}{(\sigma\sqrt{2\pi})^{N_x N_y}} e^{-\frac{1}{2}\frac{\|\mathbf{U}\|^2}{\sigma^2}} e^{-2\|Y(y)-(\mathbf{U}+\mathbf{W})X(x)\|^2}.$$

Now, let $\vec{A}$ be the vector of $\mathcal{H}_y$ defined as $\vec{A} \stackrel{\text{def}}{=} Y(y)-\mathbf{W}X(x)$, and let us denote by A_l the lth component of the vector $\vec{A}$. Then,

$$-2\|Y(y)-(\mathbf{U}+\mathbf{W})X(x)\|^2 = -2\|\vec{A}\|^2 + -2\|\mathbf{U}X(x)\|^2 + 4\langle\vec{A},\mathbf{U}X(x)\rangle.$$

This implies that

$$I = e^{-2\|\vec{A}\|^2} \int \frac{d\mathbf{U}}{(\sigma\sqrt{2\pi})^{N_x N_y}} e^{-\frac{1}{2}\left(\frac{\|\mathbf{U}\|^2}{\sigma^2}+4\|\mathbf{U}X(x)\|^2-8\langle\vec{A},\mathbf{U}X(x)\rangle\right)}. \quad (10.15)$$

An analysis of the argument of the exponential function of I
Let

$$Q \stackrel{\text{def}}{=} \left(\frac{\|\mathbf{U}\|^2}{\sigma^2} + 4\|\mathbf{U}X(x)\|^2 - 8\langle\vec{A},\mathbf{U}X(x)\rangle\right). \quad (10.16)$$

In the following, A_l denotes the lth component of the vector $\vec{A}$. Then,

$$\begin{aligned}
Q &= \sum_{i=1}^{N_x}\sum_{l=1}^{N_y}\frac{\mathbf{U}_{[l;i]}^2}{\sigma^2} + 4\|\sum_{i=1}^{N_x}\mathbf{U}_{[;i]}x_i\|^2 - 8\sum_{i=1}^{N_x}\langle\vec{A},\mathbf{U}_{[;i]}\rangle x_i \\
&= \sum_{i=1}^{N_x}\sum_{l=1}^{N_y}\frac{\mathbf{U}_{[l;i]}^2}{\sigma^2} + 4\sum_{i,j=1}^{N_x}\sum_{l=1}^{N_y}\mathbf{U}_{[l;i]}x_i\mathbf{U}_{[l;j]}x_j - 8\sum_{i,j=1}^{N_x}\sum_{l=1}^{N_y}\delta_{i,j}A_l\mathbf{U}_{[l;i]}x_i \\
&= \sum_{i,j=1}^{N_x}\sum_{l=1}^{N_y}\left(\frac{\delta_{i,j}}{\sigma^2}+4x_ix_j\right)\mathbf{U}_{[l;i]}\mathbf{U}_{[l;j]} - 8\sum_{i,j=1}^{N_x}\sum_{l=1}^{N_y}\delta_{i,j}A_l\mathbf{U}_{[l;i]}x_i. \quad (10.17)
\end{aligned}$$

Let us now define the matrices $\mathbf{N}$ and $\mathbf{Z}$, respectively of dimension $N_x \times N_y$ and $N_y \times N_x$, as follows, and let us rewrite (10.17) by using them:

$$\mathbf{N}_{[i;j]} \overset{\text{def}}{=} \frac{\delta_{i,j}}{\sigma^2} + 4x_i x_j \qquad \text{and} \qquad \mathbf{Z}_{[l;i]} \overset{\text{def}}{=} \frac{\mathbf{U}_{[l;i]}}{x_i} \ . \tag{10.18}$$

$$Q \ = \ \sum_{l=1}^{N_y} \left(\sum_{i,j=1}^{N_x} \mathbf{N}_{[i;j]} x_i x_j \mathbf{Z}_{[l;i]} \mathbf{Z}_{[l;j]} - 8 \sum_{i=1}^{N_x} A_l x_i^2 \mathbf{Z}_{[l;i]} \right) \ . \tag{10.19}$$

The following claim will transform Q in such a way that it will contain a single term including the integration variable $\mathbf{Z}$. This is a consequence of the Fermat's difference of square argument: $(A^2 - B^2) = (A - B)(A + B)$.

CLAIM 1: For any $l = 1, .., N_y$, *let* $B_l \overset{\text{def}}{=} \frac{4\sigma^2 A_l}{1 + 4\sigma^2 \|X(x)\|^2}$. *Then,*

$$Q \ = \ \sum_{l=1}^{N_y} \left(\sum_{i,j=1}^{N_x} \mathbf{N}_{[i;j]} x_i x_j (\mathbf{Z}_{[l;i]} - B_l)(\mathbf{Z}_{[l;j]} - B_l) \right) - \frac{16\|A\|^2 \sigma^2 \|X(x)\|^2}{1 + 4\sigma^2 \|X(x)\|^2} \ .$$

Proof of Claim 1. First note that $B_l \left(x_i^2 + 4x_i^2 \sigma^2 \|X(x)\|^2 \right) = 4A_l x_i^2 \sigma^2$. Then, because $x_i^2 = \sum_{j=1}^{N_x} \delta_{i,j} x_i x_j$ and $\|X(x)\|^2 \overset{\text{def}}{=} \sum_{j=1}^{N_x} x_j^2$, we have

$$\sum_{j=1}^{N_x} \mathbf{N}_{[i;j]} x_i x_j B_l \ = \ 4A_l x_i^2 \ . \tag{10.20}$$

Note also that

$$\begin{aligned}
\frac{16\sigma^4 A_l^2 \|X(x)\|^2}{1 + 4\sigma^2 \|X(x)\|^2} \ &= \ B_l^2 \left(\|X(x)\|^2 + 4\sigma^2 \|X(x)\|^4 \right) \\
&= \ B_l^2 \left(\sum_{i,j=1}^{N_x} \delta_{i,j} x_i x_j + \sum_{i,j=1}^{N_x} 4\sigma^2 x_i^2 x_j^2 \right) \\
&= \ \sum_{i,j=1}^{N_x} \mathbf{N}_{[i;j]} \sigma^2 x_i x_j B_l^2 \ .
\end{aligned}$$

Hence,

$$\begin{aligned}
&\sum_{l=1}^{N_y} \sum_{i,j=1}^{N_x} \left(\mathbf{N}_{[i;j]} x_i x_j (\mathbf{Z}_{[l;i]} - B_l)(\mathbf{Z}_{[l;j]} - B_l) \right) - \frac{16\|A\|^2 \sigma^2 \|X(x)\|^2}{1 + 4\sigma^2 \|X(x)\|^2} \\
&= \ \sum_{l=1}^{N_y} \left(\sum_{i,j=1}^{N_x} \left(\mathbf{N}_{[i;j]} x_i x_j (\mathbf{Z}_{[l;i]} - B_l)(\mathbf{Z}_{[l;j]} - B_l) \right) - \sum_{i,j=1}^{N_x} \mathbf{N}_{[i;j]} x_i x_j B_l^2 \right) \\
&= \ \sum_{l=1}^{N_y} \sum_{i,j=1}^{N_x} \left(\mathbf{N}_{[i;j]} x_i x_j \mathbf{Z}_{[l;i]} \mathbf{Z}_{[l;j]} - \mathbf{N}_{[i;j]} x_i x_j \mathbf{Z}_{[l;i]} B_l - \mathbf{N}_{[i;j]} x_i x_j B_l \mathbf{Z}_{[l;j]} \right. \\
&\qquad\qquad\qquad \left. + \mathbf{N}_{[i;j]} x_i x_j B_l^2 - \mathbf{N}_{[i;j]} x_i x_j B_l^2 \right) \\
&= \ \sum_{l=1}^{N_y} \left(\sum_{i,j=1}^{N_x} \mathbf{N}_{[i;j]} x_i x_j \mathbf{Z}_{[l;i]} \mathbf{Z}_{[l;j]} - 2 \sum_{i=1}^{N_x} \left(\sum_{j=1}^{N_x} \mathbf{N}_{[i;j]} x_i x_j \mathbf{Z}_{[l;i]} B_l \right) \right)
\end{aligned}$$

$$
= \sum_{l=1}^{N_y} \left(\sum_{i,j=1}^{N_x} \mathbf{N}_{[i;j]} x_i x_j \mathbf{Z}_{[l;i]} \mathbf{Z}_{[l;j]} - 2 \sum_{i=1}^{N_x} 4 A_l \mathbf{Z}_{[l;i]} x_i^2 \right) = Q.
$$

The penultimate equality comes from (10.20). Claim 1 is proved.

Transforming the integral I into a Gaussian integral

Let the operator $\star \colon \{1,..,N_y\} \times \{1,..,N_x\} \longrightarrow \{1,..,N_y N_x\}$ be defined as $l \star i \stackrel{\text{def}}{=} (l-1) \cdot N_x + i$. Note that for any $\tilde{l} \in \{1,..,N_y N_x\}$, there exists a unique two-tuple $(l,i) \in \{1,..,N_y\} \times \{1,..,N_x\}$, such that $\tilde{l} = l \star i$.

Let $\vec{z}$ be the vector of dimension $N_y N_x$ defined as $z_{l \star i} \stackrel{\text{def}}{=} \mathbf{Z}_{[l;i]}$ for any $l \in \{1,..,N_y\}$ and any $i \in \{1,..,N_x\}$.

Let $\vec{\mu}$ be the vector of dimension $N_y N_x$ defined as $\mu_{l \star i} \stackrel{\text{def}}{=} B_l$ for any $l \in \{1,..,N_y\}$ and any $i \in \{1,..,N_x\}$.

Let $\mathbf{M}$ be the matrix of dimension $(N_y N_x) \times (N_y N_x)$ defined as

$$
\mathbf{M}_{[l \star i \,;\, m \star j]} \stackrel{\text{def}}{=} \delta_{l,m} \mathbf{N}_{[i;j]} x_i x_j \quad \left(= \delta_{l,m} \left(\frac{\delta_{i,j}}{\sigma^2} + 4 x_i x_j x_i x_j \right) \right) \tag{10.21}
$$

for any $l, m \in \{1,..,N_y\}$ and any $i, j \in \{1,..,N_x\}$.

In what follows, the reader should interpret $\tilde{l}$ as $l \star i$ and $\tilde{m}$ as $m \star j$. Then,

$$
Q = \sum_{l=1}^{N_y} \left(\sum_{i,j=1}^{N_x} \mathbf{N}_{[i;j]} x_i x_j (\mathbf{Z}_{[l;i]} - B_l)(\mathbf{Z}_{[l;j]} - B_l) \right) - \frac{16 \|A\|^2 \sigma^2 \|X(x)\|^2}{1 + 4\sigma^2 \|X(x)\|^2}
$$

$$
= \sum_{m=1}^{N_y} \left(\sum_{l=1}^{N_y} \sum_{i,j=1}^{N_x} \left(\delta_{l,m} \mathbf{N}_{[i;j]} x_i x_j (\mathbf{Z}_{[l;i]} - B_l)(\mathbf{Z}_{[l;j]} - B_l) \right) \right) - \frac{16 \|A\|^2 \sigma^2 \|X(x)\|^2}{1 + 4\sigma^2 \|X(x)\|^2}
$$

$$
= \sum_{l=1}^{N_y} \sum_{i=1}^{N_x} \sum_{m=1}^{N_y} \sum_{j=1}^{N_x} \left(\delta_{l,m} \mathbf{N}_{[i;j]} x_i x_j (\mathbf{Z}_{[l;i]} - B_l)(\mathbf{Z}_{[l;j]} - B_l) \right) - \frac{16 \|A\|^2 \sigma^2 \|X(x)\|^2}{1 + 4\sigma^2 \|X(x)\|^2}
$$

$$
= \sum_{\tilde{l}=1}^{N_y N_x} \sum_{\tilde{m}=1}^{N_y N_x} \left((z_{\tilde{l}} - \mu_{\tilde{l}}) \, \mathbf{M}_{[\tilde{l};\tilde{m}]} \, (z_{\tilde{m}} - \mu_{\tilde{m}}) \right) - \frac{16 \|A\|^2 \sigma^2 \|X(x)\|^2}{1 + 4\sigma^2 \|X(x)\|^2} .
$$

Substituing this expression for Q into the integral I of (10.15) gives

$$
I = e^{-2\|\vec{A}\|^2} \int \frac{d\mathbf{U}}{(\sigma \sqrt{2\pi})^{N_x N_y}} e^{-\frac{1}{2} \left(\frac{\|\mathbf{U}\|^2}{\sigma^2} + 4\|\mathbf{U} X(x)\|^2 - 8 \langle \vec{A}, \mathbf{U} X(x) \rangle \right)} \tag{10.22}
$$

$$
= e^{-2\|\vec{A}\|^2} \prod_{i=1}^{N_x} |x_i|^{N_y} e^{\frac{8 \|\vec{A}\|^2 \sigma^2 \|X(x)\|^2}{1 + 4\sigma^2 \|X(x)\|^2}}
$$

$$
\int \frac{d\vec{z}}{(\sigma \sqrt{2\pi})^{N_x N_y}} e^{-\frac{1}{2} \sum_{\tilde{l}=1}^{N_y N_x} \sum_{\tilde{m}=1}^{N_y N_x} \left((z_{\tilde{l}} - \mu_{\tilde{l}}) \, \mathbf{M}_{[\tilde{l};\tilde{m}]} \, (z_{\tilde{m}} - \mu_{\tilde{m}}) \right)} \tag{10.23}
$$

$$= e^{-2\|\vec{A}\|^2} \prod_{i=1}^{N_x} |x_i|^{N_y} e^{\frac{8\|\vec{A}\|^2 \sigma^2 \|X(x)\|^2}{1+4\sigma^2\|X(x)\|^2}}$$

$$\int \frac{d\vec{z}}{\left(\sigma\sqrt{2\pi}\right)^{N_x N_y}} e^{-\frac{1}{2}\left((\vec{z}-\vec{\mu})^\top \mathbf{M}\,(\vec{z}-\vec{\mu})\right)} \qquad (10.24)$$

$$= e^{-2\|\vec{A}\|^2} \prod_{i=1}^{N_x} |x_i|^{N_y} e^{\frac{8\|\vec{A}\|^2 \sigma^2 \|X(x)\|^2}{1+4\sigma^2\|X(x)\|^2}} \frac{1}{\sqrt{\det(\mathbf{M})}}$$

$$\int \frac{d\vec{z}}{\left(\sigma\sqrt{2\pi}\right)^{N_x N_y}} \frac{1}{\sqrt{\det(\mathbf{M}^{-1})}} e^{-\frac{1}{2}\left((\vec{z}-\vec{\mu})^\top (\mathbf{M}^{-1})^{-1}\,(\vec{z}-\vec{\mu})\right)} \qquad (10.25)$$

$$= e^{-2\|\vec{A}\|^2} \prod_{i=1}^{N_x} |x_i|^{N_y} e^{\frac{8\|\vec{A}\|^2 \sigma^2 \|X(x)\|^2}{1+4\sigma^2\|X(x)\|^2}} \frac{1}{\sqrt{\det(\mathbf{M})}} \cdot 1 . \qquad (10.26)$$

Line (10.24) is a consequence of the fact that $\mathbf{U}_{[l;i]} = x_i \mathbf{Z}_{[l;i]}$ (see [10.18]) and of the fact that $\vec{z}_{\vec{l}} = \mathbf{Z}_{[l;i]}$. Line (10.26) comes from the fact that the integral of (10.25) is an integral of a Gaussian density that, therefore, equals 1. Lines (10.25) and (10.26) force $\mathbf{M}$ to be positive definite.

CLAIM 2: *The matrix* $\mathbf{M}$ *is positive definite and*

$$\det(\mathbf{M}) = \prod_{i=1}^{N_x} (x_i^2)^{N_y} \left(\frac{1}{\sigma^2}\right)^{N_x N_y} \left(1 + 4\sigma^2 \|X(x)\|^2\right)^{N_y} .$$

Before proving Claim 2, let us show that it implies the result.

$$I = e^{-2\|\vec{A}\|^2} \prod_{i=1}^{N_x} |x_i|^{N_y} e^{\frac{8\|\vec{A}\|^2 \sigma^2 \|X(x)\|^2}{1+4\sigma^2\|X(x)\|^2}} \frac{1}{\sqrt{\det(\mathbf{M})}}$$

$$= e^{-2\|\vec{A}\|^2} \prod_{i=1}^{N_x} |x_i|^{N_y} e^{\frac{8\|\vec{A}\|^2 \sigma^2 \|X(x)\|^2}{1+4\sigma^2\|X(x)\|^2}} \frac{1}{\sqrt{\prod_{i=1}^{N_x}(x_i^2)^{N_y} \left(\frac{1}{\sigma^2}\right)^{N_x N_y} (1+4\sigma^2\|X(x)\|^2)^{N_y}}}$$

$$= e^{-2\|\vec{A}\|^2} e^{\frac{8\|\vec{A}\|^2 \sigma^2 \|X(x)\|^2}{1+4\sigma^2\|X(x)\|^2}} \frac{1}{\sqrt{\left(\frac{1}{\sigma^2}\right)^{N_x N_y} (1+4\sigma^2\|X(x)\|^2)^{N_y}}}$$

$$= e^{\frac{-2\|\vec{A}\|^2}{1+4\sigma^2\|X(x)\|^2}} \frac{\sigma^{N_x N_y}}{\sqrt{(1+4\sigma^2\|X(x)\|^2)^{N_y}}} = e^{\frac{-2\|Y(y)-\mathbf{W}X(x)\|^2}{1+4\sigma^2\|X(x)\|^2}} \frac{\sigma^{N_x N_y}}{\sqrt{(1+4\sigma^2\|X(x)\|^2)^{N_y}}} .$$

To finish the proof, let us now prove Claim 2.

Proof of Claim 2. Let $\mathbf{X}$ be the diagonal matrix whose entries are the x_is, and note that the matrix $(\mathbf{N}_{[i;j]} x_i x_j)_{i;j}$ can be expressed as follows:

$$(\mathbf{N}_{[i;j]} x_i x_j)_{i;j} = \mathbf{X}\mathbf{N}\mathbf{X}. \qquad (10.27)$$

Now, from the definition of $\mathbf{M}$ and basic determinant's properties, we have

$$\det(\mathbf{M}) = \det\left((\delta_{l,m} \mathbf{N}_{[i;j]} x_i x_j)_{l\star i\,;\,m\star j}\right) \qquad (10.28)$$

$$= \left(\det \left((\mathbf{N}_{[i;j]} x_i x_j)_{i\,;\,j} \right) \right)^{N_y} \tag{10.29}$$

$$= \left(\det \left(\mathbf{X} \mathbf{N} \mathbf{X} \right) \right)^{N_y} \tag{10.30}$$

$$= \left(\left(\prod_{i=1}^{N_\mathcal{X}} x_i^2 \right) \det(\mathbf{N}) \right)^{N_y} . \tag{10.31}$$

Line (10.28) comes straightforwardly from the definition (see [10.21]). Line (10.29) comes from the fact that $\mathbf{M}$ is a matrix whose entries are all 0, except for N_y identical blocks of size $N_\mathcal{X} \times N_\mathcal{X}$ that are positioned in the diagonal of M, each one of these blocks being the matrix $(\mathbf{N}_{[i;j]} x_i x_j)_{i\,;\,j}$. Line (10.31) follows from the fact that $\det(\mathbf{X}) = \left(\prod_{i=1}^{N_\mathcal{X}} x_i \right)$.

Note also that the block structure of the matrix $\mathbf{M}$ implies that it has exactly the same eigenvalues as Matrix $(\mathbf{N}_{[i;j]} x_i x_j)_{i\,;\,j}$ (but with a multiplicity augmented by a factor of N_y).

Also, it follows from (10.27) that, for each eigenvalue λ of $(\mathbf{N}_{[i;j]} x_i x_j)_{i\,;\,j}$, there exists i such that $\frac{\lambda}{x_i^2}$ is an eigenvalue of $\mathbf{N}$. Indeed, because of (10.27), we have that

$$\det \left((\mathbf{N}_{[i;j]} x_i x_j)_{i\,;\,j} - \lambda \mathbf{X} \mathbf{X} \right) = \mathbf{0} \quad \Leftrightarrow \quad \det \left(\mathbf{N} - \lambda I \right) = \mathbf{0} .$$

This, in turn, implies that if $\mathbf{N}$ is positive definite, then so is $\mathbf{M}$. Hence, to prove Claim 2, we only have to show that $\mathbf{N}$ is positive definite and $\det(\mathbf{N}) = \left(\frac{1}{\sigma^2} \right)^{N_\mathcal{X}} \left(1 + 4\sigma^2 \|X(x)\|^2 \right)$.

Let us consider a matrix $\mathbf{O}$, defined as $\mathbf{O}_{[i;j]} = 4 x_i x_j$. Then, it is easy to see that $\lambda = 0$ is an eigenvalue of $\mathbf{O}$ of multiplicity $N_\mathcal{X} - 1$ because the rank of that matrix is 1. Note that line L_i of that matrix is always equal to $\frac{x_i}{x_1} L_1$. Moreover, we can easily see that $(x_1, \ldots, x_m)^\top$ is an eigenvector of $\mathbf{O}$ with eigenvalue $4\|X(x)\|^2$. Now, note that $\mathbf{N} = \mathbf{O} + \frac{1}{\sigma^2} \cdot I$. Thus, there is a one-to-one correspondence between the eigenvalues of $\mathbf{O}$ and those of $\mathbf{N}$: λ is an eigenvalue of the former if and only if $\lambda + \frac{1}{\sigma^2}$ is an eigenvalue of the latter. Thus, N is positive definite, and

$$\det(\mathbf{N}) = \left(\frac{1}{\sigma^2} \right)^{N_\mathcal{X}-1} \left(\frac{1}{\sigma^2} + 4\|X(x)\|^2 \right) = \left(\frac{1}{\sigma^2} \right)^{N_\mathcal{X}} \left(1 + 4\sigma^2 \|X(x)\|^2 \right) .$$

$\square$

10.7.4 Proof of $\frac{\partial}{\partial \mathbf{A}} R(\mathbf{A}, S)$ from (10.6)

Proof. From (10.9), we have $\quad \mathbf{W} = \sum_{i=1}^{m} \sum_{j=1}^{m} Y(y_i) A_{[i;j]} X^\dagger(x_j) = \mathbf{M}_y \mathbf{A} \mathbf{M}_\mathcal{X}^\dagger$, where M_y is a $N_y \times m$ matrix with $Y(y_i)$ in its i-th column. Similarly, $M_\mathcal{X}$ is a $N_\mathcal{X} \times m$ matrix with $X(x_j)$ in its j-th column.

$$
\begin{aligned}
R(\mathbf{A}, S) &= \frac{1}{m} \sum_{i=1}^{m} \| Y(y_i) - \mathbf{W} X(x_i) \|^2 &=& \frac{1}{m} \| \mathbf{M}_y - \mathbf{W} \mathbf{M}_x \|^2 \\
&= \frac{1}{m} \| \mathbf{M}_y - \mathbf{M}_y \mathbf{A} \mathbf{M}_x^\dagger \mathbf{M}_x \|^2 &=& \frac{1}{m} \| \mathbf{M}_y (\mathbf{I} - \mathbf{A} \mathbf{K}_x) \|^2 .
\end{aligned}
$$

$$
\begin{aligned}
\frac{\partial}{\partial A_{[i;j]}} R(\mathbf{A}, S) &= \frac{1}{m} \frac{\partial}{\partial A_{[i;j]}} \sum_{k,l=1}^{m} [\mathbf{M}_y (\mathbf{I} - \mathbf{A} \mathbf{K}_x)]_{[k;l]}^2 \\
&= \frac{2}{m} \sum_{k,l=1}^{m} [\mathbf{M}_y (\mathbf{I} - \mathbf{A} \mathbf{K}_x)]_{[k;l]} \frac{\partial}{\partial A_{[i;j]}} [\mathbf{M}_y (\mathbf{I} - \mathbf{A} \mathbf{K}_x)]_{[k;l]} \\
&= \frac{-2}{m} \sum_{k,l=1}^{m} [\mathbf{M}_y (\mathbf{I} - \mathbf{A} \mathbf{K}_x)]_{[k;l]} \\
&\qquad\qquad \frac{\partial}{\partial A_{[i;j]}} \left[\sum_{k',l'=1}^{m} \mathbf{M}_{y_{[k;k']}} \mathbf{A}_{[k';l']} \mathbf{K}_{x_{[l';l]}} \right] \\
&= \frac{-2}{m} \sum_{k,l=1}^{m} [\mathbf{M}_y (\mathbf{I} - \mathbf{A} \mathbf{K}_x)]_{[k;l]} \mathbf{M}_{y_{[k;i]}} \mathbf{K}_{x_{[j;l]}} \\
&= \frac{-2}{m} \sum_{k,l=1}^{m} (\mathbf{M}_y)_{[i;k]}^\dagger [\mathbf{M}_y (\mathbf{I} - \mathbf{A} \mathbf{K}_x)]_{[k;l]} \mathbf{K}_{x_{[j;l]}} \\
&= \frac{-2}{m} \sum_{l=1}^{m} \left[\mathbf{M}_y^\dagger \mathbf{M}_y (\mathbf{I} - \mathbf{A} \mathbf{K}_x) \right]_{[i;l]} \mathbf{K}_{x_{[j;l]}} \\
&= \frac{2}{m} [\mathbf{K}_y (\mathbf{A} \mathbf{K}_x - \mathbf{I}) \mathbf{K}_x]_{[i;j]} .
\end{aligned}
$$

$\square$

10.7.5 Details on how (10.14) becomes $\gamma_{i,j}(\delta_i \lambda_j^2 + m\beta) = \delta_i \lambda_j (u_i^\top v_j)$

Because $\{u_i v_j^\top\}_{(i,j) \in \mathcal{I}}$ constitutes an orthonormal basis of $\mathbb{R}^{m^2}$, we have

$$
\mathbf{A} = \sum_{i=1}^{m} \sum_{j=1}^{m} \gamma_{i,j} u_i v_j^\top , \tag{10.32}
$$

and because $\mathbf{K}_y = \sum_{k=1}^{m} \delta_k u_k u_k^\top$ and $\mathbf{K}_x = \sum_{l=1}^{m} \lambda_l v_l v_l^\top$, we also have

$$
\begin{aligned}
\mathbf{K}_y \mathbf{K}_x &= \sum_{k=1}^{m} \delta_k u_k u_k^\top \sum_{l=1}^{m} \lambda_l v_l v_l^\top &=& \sum_{k,l=1}^{m} \delta_k \lambda_l (u_k^\top v_l) u_k v_l^\top \\
\mathbf{K}_x^2 &= \sum_{l=1}^{m} \lambda_l v_l v_l^\top \sum_{l'=1}^{m} \lambda_{l'} v_{l'} v_{l'}^\top &=& \sum_{l=1}^{m} \lambda_l^2 v_l v_l^\top
\end{aligned}
$$

$$\mathbf{A}\mathbf{K}_{\mathcal{X}}^2 = \sum_{k=1}^{m}\sum_{l=1}^{m}\gamma_{k,l}u_k v_l^\top \sum_{l=1}^{m}\lambda_l^2 v_l v_l^\top = \sum_{k=1}^{m}\sum_{l=1}^{m}\gamma_{k,l}\lambda_l^2 u_k v_l^\top$$

$$\mathbf{K}_y\mathbf{A}\mathbf{K}_{\mathcal{X}}^2 = \sum_{k'=1}^{m}\delta_{k'}u_{k'}u_{k'}^\top \sum_{k=1}^{m}\sum_{l=1}^{m}\gamma_{k,l}\lambda_l^2 u_k v_l^\top = \sum_{k=1}^{m}\sum_{l=1}^{m}\gamma_{k,l}\delta_k\lambda_l^2 u_k v_l^\top .$$

Line (10.14) then becomes

$$\frac{2}{m}\mathbf{K}_y(\mathbf{A}\mathbf{K}_{\mathcal{X}} - \mathbf{I})\mathbf{K}_{\mathcal{X}} + 2\beta\mathbf{A} = 0$$

$$\frac{2}{m}\mathbf{K}_y\mathbf{A}\mathbf{K}_{\mathcal{X}}^2 - \frac{2}{m}\mathbf{K}_y\mathbf{K}_{\mathcal{X}} + 2\beta\mathbf{A} = 0$$

$$\sum_{k=1}^{m}\sum_{l=1}^{m}\left[\frac{2}{m}\gamma_{k,l}\delta_k\lambda_l^2 - \frac{2}{m}\lambda_l(u_k^\top v_l) + 2\beta\gamma_{k,l}\right]u_k v_l^\top = 0. \qquad (10.33)$$

Because $u_k v_l^\top$ are linearly independent vectors, (10.33) is satisfied when

$$\frac{2}{m}\gamma_{k,l}\delta_k\lambda_l^2 - \frac{2}{m}\lambda_l(u_k^\top v_l) + 2\beta\gamma_{k,l} = 0$$

$$\frac{2}{m}\gamma_{k,l}\delta_k\lambda_l^2 + 2\beta\gamma_{k,l} = \frac{2}{m}\lambda_l(u_k^\top v_l)$$

$$\gamma_{k,l}(\delta_k\lambda_l^2 + m\beta) = \delta_k\lambda_l(u_k^\top v_l).$$

10.8   References

L. Baldassarre, L. Rosasco, A. Barla, and A. Verri. Multi-output learning via spectral filtering. *Machine Learning*, 87:259–301, 2012.

C. Brouard, F. D'Alche-Buc, and M. Szafranski. Semi-supervised penalized output kernel regression for link prediction. In *International Conference on Machine Learning (ICML)*, 2011.

A. Caponnetto and E. De Vito. Optimal rates for the regularized least-squares algorithm. *Foundations of Computational Mathematics*, 7(3):331–368, 2007.

C. Cortes, M. Mohri, and J. Weston. A general regression framework for learning string-to-string mappings. In G. Bakır, T. Hofmann, B. Schölkopf, A. J. Smola, B. Taskar, and S. Vishwanathan, editors, *Predicting Structured Data*, chapter 8, pages 143–168. MIT Press, 2007.

T. Gärtner and S. Vembu. On structured output training: Hard cases and an efficient alternative. *Machine Learning*, 76(2-3):227–242, 2009.

P. Germain, A. Lacasse, F. Laviolette, and M. Marchand. PAC-Bayesian learning of linear classifiers. In *International Conference on Machine Learning (ICML)*, 2009.

P. Germain, A. Lacoste, F. Laviolette, M. Marchand, and S. Shanian. A PAC-Bayes sample-compression approach to kernel methods. In *International Conference on Machine Learning (ICML)*, 2011.

S. Giguère, F. Laviolette, M. Marchand, and K. Sylla. Risk bounds and learning algorithms for the regression approach to structured output prediction. In *International Conference on Machine Learning (ICML)*, 2013.

L. Jacob, B. Hoffmann, V. Stoven, and J.-P. Vert. Virtual screening of GPCRs: An in silico chemogenomics approach. *BMC Bioinformatics*, 9(1):363, 2008.

H. Kadri, M. Ghavamzadeh, and P. Preux. A generalized kernel approach to structured output learning. In *International Conference on Machine Learning (ICML)*, 2013.

J. Langford. Tutorial on practical prediction theory for classification. *Journal of Machine Learning Research*, 6:273–306, 2005.

F. Laviolette and M. Marchand. PAC-Bayes risk bounds for stochastic averages and majority votes of sample-compressed classifiers. *Journal of Machine Learning Research*, 8:1461–1487, 2007.

A. Maurer. A note on the PAC Bayesian theorem. *CoRR*, cs.LG/0411099, 2004.

D. McAllester. Generalization bounds and consistency for structured labeling. In G. Bakır, T. Hofmann, B. Schölkopf, A. J. Smola, B. Taskar, and S. Vishwanathan, editors, *Predicting Structured Data*, chapter 11, pages 247–261. MIT Press, 2007.

D. A. McAllester. PAC-Bayesian stochastic model selection. *Machine Learning*, 51 (1):5–21, 2003.

J. Rousu, C. Saunders, S. Szedmak, and J. Shawe-Taylor. Kernel-based learning of hierarchical multilabel classification models. *The Journal of Machine Learning Research*, 7:1601–1626, 2006.

B. Taskar, C. Guestrin, and D. Koller. Max-margin Markov networks. In S. Thrun, L. Saul, and B. Schölkopf, editors, *Advances in Neural Information Processing Systems 16*. MIT Press, 2004.

I. Tsochantaridis, T. Joachims, T. Hofmann, and Y. Altun. Large margin methods for structured and interdependent output variables. *Journal of Machine Learning Research*, 6:1453–1484, 2005.

T. Zhang. Information theoretical upper and lower bounds for statistical estimation. *IEEE Transaction on Information Theory*, 52:1307–1321, 2006.

11 Optimizing the Measure of Performance

Joseph Keshet
Bar-Ilan University
Ramat-Gan, Israel

joseph.keshet@biu.ac.il

The ultimate objective of discriminative learning is to train a system to optimize a desired measure of performance. In binary classification, we are interested in finding a function that assigns a binary label to a single object and minimizes the error rate (correct or incorrect) on unseen data. In structured prediction, we are interested in the prediction of a structured label, where the input is a complex object. Typically, each structured prediction task has its own measure of performance or evaluation metric, such as word error rate in speech recognition, the BLEU score in machine translation, or the intersection-over-union score in object segmentation. In this chapter, we review different objective functions for structured prediction and analyze them in the light of how they optimize the desired measure of performance.

11.1 Introduction

We begin by posing the structured learning setting. We consider a supervised learning setting with input objects $\boldsymbol{x} \subset \mathcal{X}$ and target labels $\boldsymbol{y} \in \mathcal{Y}$. The labels may be sequences, trees, grids, or other high-dimensional objects with internal structure. We assumed a fixed mapping $\boldsymbol{\phi} : \mathcal{X} \times \mathcal{Y} \to \mathbb{R}^d$ from the set of input objects and target labels to a real vector of length d. We call the elements of this mapping *feature maps* or *feature functions*.

Here, we consider a linear prediction rule with parameters $\boldsymbol{w} \in \mathbb{R}^d$, such that $\hat{\boldsymbol{y}}_{\boldsymbol{w}}$ is a good approximation to the true label of $\boldsymbol{x}$, as follows:

$$\hat{\boldsymbol{y}}_{\boldsymbol{w}}(\boldsymbol{x}) = \underset{\boldsymbol{y} \in \mathcal{Y}}{\operatorname{argmax}} \; \boldsymbol{w}^\top \boldsymbol{\phi}(\boldsymbol{x}, \boldsymbol{y}) \,. \tag{11.1}$$

Ideally, we would like to find $\boldsymbol{w}$ such that the prediction rule optimizes the expected desired *measure of preference* or *evaluation metric* on unseen data. For example, phone error rate or word error rate in automatic speech recognition, intersection-over-union (PASCAL VOC) in object segmentation, NDCG in search engines and BLEU score in machine translation. We define a *cost* function, $\ell(\boldsymbol{y}, \hat{\boldsymbol{y}}_{\boldsymbol{w}})$, to be a non-negative measure of error when predicting $\hat{\boldsymbol{y}}_{\boldsymbol{w}}$ instead of $\boldsymbol{y}$ as the label of $\boldsymbol{x}$. Our goal is to minimize this function. Often the desired evaluation metric is a utility function that needs to be maximized (like BLEU, NDCG), and then we define the cost to be 1 minus the evaluation metric.

We assume that there exists some unknown probability distribution ρ over pairs $(\boldsymbol{x}, \boldsymbol{y})$ where $\boldsymbol{y}$ is the desired output (or reference output) for input $\boldsymbol{x}$. We then want to set $\boldsymbol{w}$ so as to minimize the expected cost, or the *risk*, for predicting $\hat{\boldsymbol{y}}_{\boldsymbol{w}}$,

$$\boldsymbol{w}^* = \underset{\boldsymbol{w}}{\operatorname{argmin}} \ \mathbb{E}_{(\boldsymbol{x},\boldsymbol{y})\sim\rho}[\ell(\boldsymbol{y}, \hat{\boldsymbol{y}}_{\boldsymbol{w}}(\boldsymbol{x}))]. \tag{11.2}$$

This objective function is hard to minimize directly because the distribution ρ is unknown. We use a training set $\mathcal{S}$ of m examples that are drawn i.i.d. from ρ, $\mathcal{S} = \{(\boldsymbol{x}_1, \boldsymbol{y}_1), \ldots, (\boldsymbol{x}_m, \boldsymbol{y}_m)\}$. We replace the expectation in (11.2) with a mean over the training set. To avoid overfitting of the parameters $\boldsymbol{w}$ to the training set and to generalize over unseen test data, we add a normalization factor $\|\boldsymbol{w}\|_2^2$ that should reduce the capacity, or the Vapnik-Chervonenkis (VC) dimension, of the parameters $\boldsymbol{w}$ (Vapnik, 2000).

The cost is often a combinatorial non-convex quantity, which is hard to minimize. Hence, instead of minimizing the cost directly, we minimize a lightly different function called a *surrogate loss*, denoted $\bar{\ell}(\boldsymbol{w}, \boldsymbol{x}, \boldsymbol{y})$, and closely related to the cost. Overall, the objective function of (11.2) transforms into the following objective function:

$$\boldsymbol{w}^* = \underset{\boldsymbol{w}}{\operatorname{argmin}} \ \frac{1}{m} \sum_{i=1}^{m} \bar{\ell}(\boldsymbol{w}, \boldsymbol{x}_i, \boldsymbol{y}_i) + \frac{\lambda}{2}\|\boldsymbol{w}\|^2, \tag{11.3}$$

where λ is a trade-off parameter between the loss term and the regularization.

One way to formalize what is meant by saying that a learning algorithm is able to learn and optimize a cost function is the notion of *strong consistency*. This notion requires that for all distributions ρ on $(\boldsymbol{x}, \boldsymbol{y})$ and for any feature map (finite or infinite dimensional), the weight vectors $\boldsymbol{w}^*$ produced by

(11.3) satisfies

$$\lim_{m \to \infty} \frac{1}{m} \sum_{i=1}^{m} \bar{\ell}(\boldsymbol{w}^*, \boldsymbol{x}_i, \boldsymbol{y}_i) = \inf_{\boldsymbol{w}} \mathbb{E}_{(\boldsymbol{x}, \boldsymbol{y}) \sim \rho} [\ell(\boldsymbol{y}, \hat{\boldsymbol{y}}_{\boldsymbol{w}}(\boldsymbol{x}))], \qquad (11.4)$$

with probability one over the draw of the infinite sample.

We now review the different approaches to estimating the parameters $\boldsymbol{w}$, each with a different surrogate loss function.

11.2 Structured Perceptron

The seminal paper of Collins (2002) set the framework of structured prediction. It proposed an extension to the binary Perceptron algorithm to handle part-of-speech tagging. Perceptron is an online algorithm that works in rounds. At each round, the algorithm receives an instance $\boldsymbol{x}$ and predicts a label $\hat{\boldsymbol{y}}$. Then the target label is given, $\boldsymbol{y}$, and the algorithm updates the weight vector $\boldsymbol{w}$. Starting with $\boldsymbol{w}_0 = \boldsymbol{0}$, after each round, the algorithm outputs a weight vector $\boldsymbol{w}_t$. The weight vector after round t, $\boldsymbol{w}_{t+1}$, is defined as follows, where $(\boldsymbol{x}_t, \boldsymbol{y}_t)$ is drawn from the distribution ρ

$$\boldsymbol{w}_{t+1} = \boldsymbol{w}_t + \boldsymbol{\phi}(\boldsymbol{x}_t, \boldsymbol{y}_t) - \boldsymbol{\phi}(\boldsymbol{x}_t, \hat{\boldsymbol{y}}_{\boldsymbol{w}_t}). \qquad (11.5)$$

Note that whenever $\hat{\boldsymbol{y}}_{\boldsymbol{w}_t} = \boldsymbol{y}_t$, no update is made, and we have $\boldsymbol{w}_{t+1} = \boldsymbol{w}_t$. If $\hat{\boldsymbol{y}}_{\boldsymbol{w}_t} \neq \boldsymbol{y}_t$, then the update changes the parameter vector $\boldsymbol{w}_{t+1}$ in a way that favors $\boldsymbol{y}_t$ over $\hat{\boldsymbol{y}}_{\boldsymbol{w}_t}$.

In the *online* setting, only the weight vector of each round $\boldsymbol{w}_t$ and its performance on the next (unseen) object $\boldsymbol{x}_{t+1}$ are of interest (there is no "test set"). In this chapter, however, we are interested in the *batch* setting, that is, in a single weight vector $\boldsymbol{w}^*$ that performs well on unseen data sampled from ρ.

The Perceptron algorithm is often described as a technique to solve a linear feasibility problem that is aimed at satisfying a set of linear constraints (with no objective). Each constraint corresponds to a training example and asserts its correct prediction. If there is a weight vector $\boldsymbol{w}^*$ that satisfies all constraints, then it can be shown that the procedure of running iteratively over the data and updating the weight vector $\boldsymbol{w}_{t+1}$ using (11.5) converges, after a finite number of updates (Collins, 2002). In that case, we can use the weight vector of the last round $\boldsymbol{w}_T$ to serve as $\boldsymbol{w}^*$, and we say that the data are linearly *separable*. When no such $\boldsymbol{w}^*$ exists, we can convert the online Perceptron to a batch algorithm by setting $\boldsymbol{w}^*$ to the average of the weight vectors over all iterations (Dekel et al., 2004; Cesa-Bianchi et al., 2004).

We can think of the Perceptron algorithm as a stochastic sub gradient descent (SSGD) solution of the following optimization problem[1]

$$\boldsymbol{w}^* = \operatorname{argmin} \ \mathbb{E}_{(\boldsymbol{x}, \boldsymbol{y}) \sim \rho} \left[\boldsymbol{w}^\top \left(\boldsymbol{\phi}(\boldsymbol{x}, \hat{\boldsymbol{y}}_{\boldsymbol{w}}(\boldsymbol{x})) - \boldsymbol{\phi}(\boldsymbol{x}, \boldsymbol{y}) \right) \right]. \tag{11.6}$$

Using SSGD with a constant learning rate brings us to the update rule of (11.5). This optimization problem (11.6) is non-convex. From our perspective, however, a bigger problem is that the optimization problem defined by (11.6) is quite different from (11.2): the optimization problem (11.6) is defined independently of the cost function and therefore cannot be expected to yield good solutions to (11.2) when the data are not linearly separable.

11.3 Large Margin Structured Predictors

The idea is to generalize the hinge loss function used in binary support vector machines (SVMs) to the structured case. The first formulation was introduced by Taskar et al. (2003), and it is called *max-margin Markov networks* (M^3), where the generalized surrogate loss function is expressed in terms of the Hamming distance between the target label $\boldsymbol{y}$ and the predicted label $\hat{\boldsymbol{y}}_{\boldsymbol{w}}$. We denote the Hamming distance between $\boldsymbol{y}$ and $\hat{\boldsymbol{y}}_{\boldsymbol{w}}$ by $H(\boldsymbol{y}, \hat{\boldsymbol{y}}_{\boldsymbol{w}})$. The M^3 can be formulated by using the following *Hamming hinge loss* as a surrogate loss in the optimization function (11.3):

$$\bar{\ell}_{hamming}(\boldsymbol{w}, \boldsymbol{x}, \boldsymbol{y}) = \max_{\hat{\boldsymbol{y}} \in \mathcal{Y}} \left[H(\boldsymbol{y}, \hat{\boldsymbol{y}}) - \boldsymbol{w}^\top \boldsymbol{\phi}(\boldsymbol{x}, \boldsymbol{y}) + \boldsymbol{w}^\top \boldsymbol{\phi}(\boldsymbol{x}, \hat{\boldsymbol{y}}) \right] . \tag{11.7}$$

The use of the Hamming hinge loss function can be motivated as being a direct extension of the binary SVM. Consider the case where $\mathcal{Y} = \{-1, +1\}$, so $y \in \mathcal{Y}$ is a scalar, and $y = -\hat{y}_{\boldsymbol{w}}$. Set $\boldsymbol{\phi}(\boldsymbol{x}, \boldsymbol{y}) = \frac{1}{2} y \boldsymbol{\psi}(\boldsymbol{x})$, where $\boldsymbol{\psi} : \mathcal{X} \to \mathbb{R}^d$. In the binary case, the Hamming distance is reduced to the 0/1 error function, $H(y, \hat{y}_{\boldsymbol{w}}) = \mathbf{1}[y \neq \hat{y}_{\boldsymbol{w}}]$, therefore

$$\max_{\hat{\boldsymbol{y}} \in \mathcal{Y}} \left[H(\boldsymbol{y}, \hat{\boldsymbol{y}}_{\boldsymbol{w}}) - \boldsymbol{w}^\top \boldsymbol{\phi}(\boldsymbol{x}, \boldsymbol{y}) + \boldsymbol{w}^\top \boldsymbol{\phi}(\boldsymbol{x}, \hat{\boldsymbol{y}}) \right] = \max\{0, 1 - y \, \boldsymbol{w}^\top \boldsymbol{\psi}(\boldsymbol{x})\},$$

$$\tag{11.8}$$

which is the binary hinge loss function.

We can also justify the use of the Hamming hinge loss as a surrogate loss function from generalization bounds, which were given by Taskar et al.

---

1. Personal communication with David McAllester.

(2003) and McAllester (2006). In particular, consider the following generalization theorem stated in McAllester (2006, Theorem 62):

Theorem 11.1. *Assume that* $0 \leq \ell(\boldsymbol{y}, \hat{\boldsymbol{y}}) \leq 1$. *With probability at least* $1 - \delta$ *over the draw of the training set* $\mathcal{S}$ *of size* m, *the following holds simultaneously for all weight vectors* $\boldsymbol{w}$

$$\mathbb{E}_{(\boldsymbol{x}, \boldsymbol{y}) \sim \rho}[\ell(\boldsymbol{y}, \hat{\boldsymbol{y}}_{\boldsymbol{w}}(\boldsymbol{x}))]$$

$$\leq \frac{1}{m} \sum_{i=1}^{m} \max_{\hat{\boldsymbol{y}}} \mathbf{1} \left[\boldsymbol{w}^{\top} \boldsymbol{\phi}(\boldsymbol{x}_i, \boldsymbol{y}_i) - \boldsymbol{w}^{\top} \boldsymbol{\phi}(\boldsymbol{x}_i, \hat{\boldsymbol{y}}) \leq H(\boldsymbol{y}_i, \hat{\boldsymbol{y}}) \right] \ell(\boldsymbol{y}_i, \hat{\boldsymbol{y}})$$

$$+ \frac{\|\boldsymbol{w}\|^2}{m} + \sqrt{\frac{\|\boldsymbol{w}\|^2 \ln\left(\frac{2dm}{\|\boldsymbol{w}\|^2}\right) + \ln\left(\frac{m}{\delta}\right)}{2(m-1)}}, \quad (11.9)$$

where $\mathbf{1}[\pi]$ *denotes the indicator function:* $\mathbf{1}[\pi] = 1$ *if the predicate* π *is true and* 0 *otherwise.*

This generalization bound provides a rationalization of the use of Hamming hinge loss as a surrogate loss when the conditions $\boldsymbol{w}^{\top} \boldsymbol{\phi}(\boldsymbol{x}_i, \boldsymbol{y}_i) - \boldsymbol{w}^{\top} \boldsymbol{\phi}(\boldsymbol{x}_i, \hat{\boldsymbol{y}}) \leq H(\boldsymbol{y}_i, \hat{\boldsymbol{y}})$ hold for all $1 \leq i \leq m$. Similar rationalization can be derived from the bounds stated by Taskar et al. (2003).

Another formulation of large margin structured predictors is called *structural SVM* and was introduced by Tsochantaridis et al. (2005) with two variations. The first variation is called *margin-scaled* and is aimed at minimizing the following surrogate loss

$$\bar{\ell}_{margin}(\boldsymbol{w}, \boldsymbol{x}, \boldsymbol{y}) = \max_{\hat{\boldsymbol{y}} \in \mathcal{Y}} \left[\ell(\boldsymbol{y}, \hat{\boldsymbol{y}}) - \boldsymbol{w}^{\top} \boldsymbol{\phi}(\boldsymbol{x}, \boldsymbol{y}) + \boldsymbol{w}^{\top} \boldsymbol{\phi}(\boldsymbol{x}, \hat{\boldsymbol{y}}) \right]. \quad (11.10)$$

The second variation is called *slack-scaled* and is aimed at minimizing the following surrogate loss

$$\bar{\ell}_{slack}(\boldsymbol{w}, \boldsymbol{x}, \boldsymbol{y}) = \max_{\hat{\boldsymbol{y}} \in \mathcal{Y}} \ell(\boldsymbol{y}, \hat{\boldsymbol{y}}) \left[1 - \boldsymbol{w}^{\top} \boldsymbol{\phi}(\boldsymbol{x}, \boldsymbol{y}) + \boldsymbol{w}^{\top} \boldsymbol{\phi}(\boldsymbol{x}, \hat{\boldsymbol{y}}) \right]. \quad (11.11)$$

Both of those surrogate loss functions are justified as being convex upper bounds on the cost function. For the margin-scaled hinge loss, we have

$$\ell(\boldsymbol{y}, \hat{\boldsymbol{y}}_{\boldsymbol{w}}) = \ell(\boldsymbol{y}, \hat{\boldsymbol{y}}_{\boldsymbol{w}}) - \boldsymbol{w}^{\top} \boldsymbol{\phi}(\boldsymbol{x}, \boldsymbol{y}) + \boldsymbol{w}^{\top} \boldsymbol{\phi}(\boldsymbol{x}, \boldsymbol{y}) \quad (11.12)$$

$$\leq \ell(\boldsymbol{y}, \hat{\boldsymbol{y}}_{\boldsymbol{w}}) - \boldsymbol{w}^{\top} \boldsymbol{\phi}(\boldsymbol{x}, \boldsymbol{y}) + \boldsymbol{w}^{\top} \boldsymbol{\phi}(\boldsymbol{x}, \hat{\boldsymbol{y}}_{\boldsymbol{w}}) \quad (11.13)$$

$$\leq \max_{\hat{\boldsymbol{y}} \in \mathcal{Y}} \left(\ell(\boldsymbol{y}, \hat{\boldsymbol{y}}) - \boldsymbol{w}^{\top} \boldsymbol{\phi}(\boldsymbol{x}, \boldsymbol{y}) + \boldsymbol{w}^{\top} \boldsymbol{\phi}(\boldsymbol{x}, \hat{\boldsymbol{y}}) \right) \quad (11.14)$$

$$\leq \bar{\ell}_{margin}(\boldsymbol{w}, \boldsymbol{x}, \boldsymbol{y}), \quad (11.15)$$

where we used the definition of $\hat{\boldsymbol{y}}_{\boldsymbol{w}}$ in (11.1) for bounding (11.12) by (11.13). Likewise, a similar upper bound can be derived for the slack-scaled hinge loss. The upper bound converts the optimization problem (11.3) to a convex problem, which is of great technical and theoretical advantage. However, we are unaware of a guarantee that ensures that minimizing the convex upper bound $\bar{\ell}_{margin}$ or $\bar{\ell}_{slack}$ also minimizes the cost ℓ. This type of guarantee is often given in the analysis of approximation algorithms in terms of a multiplicative factor times the minimal objective, but we are unaware of any such result for the hinge loss.

The weight vector $\boldsymbol{w}$ can be found by several optimization techniques. The use of SSGD to solve (11.3) will help us to compare the update rule of $\boldsymbol{w}$ of different methods. In iteration t, we choose a random training example $(\boldsymbol{x}_{j_t}, \boldsymbol{y}_{j_t})$ by picking an index $j_t \in \{1, \ldots, m\}$ uniformly at random. Then we replace the objective in (11.3), where the surrogate loss is $\bar{\ell}_{margin}$ with an approximation based on the training example $(\boldsymbol{x}_{j_t}, \boldsymbol{y}_{j_t})$. The sub gradient of approximated objective is given by

$$\nabla_t = \boldsymbol{\phi}(\boldsymbol{x}_{j_t}, \hat{\boldsymbol{y}}_{\boldsymbol{w}_t}^{\ell}) - \boldsymbol{\phi}(\boldsymbol{x}_{j_t}, \boldsymbol{y}_{j_t}) + \lambda \boldsymbol{w}_t \,, \tag{11.16}$$

where

$$\hat{\boldsymbol{y}}_{\boldsymbol{w}_t}^{\ell} = \underset{\boldsymbol{y} \in \mathcal{Y}}{\operatorname{argmax}} \ \boldsymbol{w}_t^{\top} \boldsymbol{\phi}(\boldsymbol{x}_{j_t}, \boldsymbol{y}_{j_t}) + \ell(\boldsymbol{y}_{j_t}, \boldsymbol{y}) \,. \tag{11.17}$$

We call this type of inference *loss augmented inference*. Hence, we have the following update rule:

$$\boldsymbol{w}_{t+1} = (1 - \eta_t \lambda) \, \boldsymbol{w}_t + \eta_t \left(\boldsymbol{\phi}(\boldsymbol{x}_{j_t}, \boldsymbol{y}_{j_t}) - \boldsymbol{\phi}(\boldsymbol{x}_{j_t}, \hat{\boldsymbol{y}}_{\boldsymbol{w}_t}^{\ell}) \right) \,. \tag{11.18}$$

There are two main differences between the large margin algorithms and the "batch" Perceptron algorithm, namely, the regularization and the margin. Those differences can be seen by comparing the SVM update rule in (11.18) to the Perceptron update in (11.5). Note that a similar derivation can be used to find the update rule of the slack-scaled loss function and the Hamming loss function.

We would like to finish this section with a short discussion on consistency of the hinge loss functions. The large margin structured predictors are not consistent in the sense of (11.4), that is, they fail to converge on the optimal linear predictor even in the limit of infinite training data. It was shown (Lee et al., 2004) that the use of hinge loss in multiclass classification results in inconsistent algorithms. This claim can be extended to prove that the structural hinge losses are also inconsistent (McAllester, 2006).

11.4   Conditional Random Fields

Conditional random fields (CRFs) were proposed by Lafferty et al. (2001) as models that use the negative log-likelihood loss ("log loss") function as a surrogate loss function in (11.3), that is,

$$\bar{\ell}_{log}(\boldsymbol{w}, \boldsymbol{x}, \boldsymbol{y}) = -\ln P_{\boldsymbol{w}}(\boldsymbol{y} \,|\, \boldsymbol{x}) \,, \tag{11.19}$$

where

$$P_{\boldsymbol{w}}(\boldsymbol{y} \,|\, \boldsymbol{x}) = \frac{1}{Z_{\boldsymbol{w}}(\boldsymbol{x})} \exp\left\{ \boldsymbol{w}^\top \boldsymbol{\phi}(\boldsymbol{x}, \boldsymbol{y}) \right\} \tag{11.20}$$

and $Z_{\boldsymbol{w}}(\boldsymbol{x})$ is the partition function defined as

$$Z_{\boldsymbol{w}}(\boldsymbol{x}) = \sum_{\boldsymbol{y}' \in \mathcal{Y}} \exp\left\{ \boldsymbol{w}^\top \boldsymbol{\phi}(\boldsymbol{x}, \boldsymbol{y}') \right\}. \tag{11.21}$$

This defines a convex optimization problem. With SSGD, the update rule for an example j_t is

$$\boldsymbol{w}_{t+1} = (1 - \eta_t \lambda)\, \boldsymbol{w}_t + \eta_t \left(\boldsymbol{\phi}(\boldsymbol{x}_{j_t}, \boldsymbol{y}_{j_t}) - \mathbb{E}_{\boldsymbol{y}' \sim P_w(\boldsymbol{y}' \,|\, \boldsymbol{x})} \left[\boldsymbol{\phi}(\boldsymbol{x}_{j_t}, \boldsymbol{y}') \right] \right), \tag{11.22}$$

where

$$\mathbb{E}_{\boldsymbol{y}' \sim P_w(\boldsymbol{y}' \,|\, \boldsymbol{x})} \left[\boldsymbol{\phi}(\boldsymbol{x}_{j_t}, \boldsymbol{y}') \right] = \sum_{\boldsymbol{y}' \in \mathcal{Y}} P_{\boldsymbol{w}}(\boldsymbol{y}' \,|\, \boldsymbol{x})\, \boldsymbol{\phi}(\boldsymbol{x}_{j_t}, \boldsymbol{y}'). \tag{11.23}$$

Given a conditional probability model $P_{\boldsymbol{w}}(\boldsymbol{y} \,|\, \boldsymbol{x})$, when $\boldsymbol{w}$ is found according to (11.22), one could use the decision-theoretically optimal prediction rule that is defined as follows:

$$\hat{\boldsymbol{y}}_{\boldsymbol{w}}(\boldsymbol{x}) = \underset{\hat{\boldsymbol{y}}}{\operatorname{argmin}} \ \mathbb{E}_{\boldsymbol{y} \sim P_w(\boldsymbol{y} \,|\, \boldsymbol{x})} \left[\ell(\boldsymbol{y}, \hat{\boldsymbol{y}}) \right]. \tag{11.24}$$

If $P_{\boldsymbol{w}}(\boldsymbol{y} \,|\, \boldsymbol{x})$ equals $\rho(\boldsymbol{y}|\boldsymbol{x})$, then (11.24) gives an optimal decoding. For example, if the cost function is the 0/1 loss, $\ell(\boldsymbol{y}, \hat{\boldsymbol{y}}_{\boldsymbol{w}}) = \mathbf{1}[\boldsymbol{y} \neq \hat{\boldsymbol{y}}_{\boldsymbol{w}}]$, then from (11.24) we get the Bayes optimal decoder

$$\hat{\boldsymbol{y}}_{\boldsymbol{w}}(\boldsymbol{x}) = \underset{\hat{\boldsymbol{y}}}{\operatorname{argmin}} \mathbb{E}_{\boldsymbol{y} \sim P_w(\boldsymbol{y} \,|\, \boldsymbol{x})} \left[\mathbf{1}[\boldsymbol{y} \neq \hat{\boldsymbol{y}}] \right] = \underset{\hat{\boldsymbol{y}}}{\operatorname{argmax}} P(\boldsymbol{y} = \hat{\boldsymbol{y}}|\boldsymbol{x}). \tag{11.25}$$

However, because the log loss function (11.19) is defined independently of the cost function ℓ, the optimum of (11.3) with $\bar{\ell}_{log}$ is not expected to yield good solutions to (11.2).

11.5 Direct Loss Minimization

Direct loss minimization is a method focused at directly optimizing the measure of performance. As we have seen, the most common approaches to structured prediction, structural Perceptron, M^3, structural SVMs and CRFs, do not minimize the risk directly. Note that except for the structured Perceptron, all those approaches minimize a convex regularized surrogate loss function. An alternative to a convex relaxation is to perform SSGD directly on the objective in (11.2). This is conceptually puzzling in the case where the output space $\mathcal{Y}$ is discrete because the output $\hat{\boldsymbol{y}}_{\boldsymbol{w}}$ is not a differentiable function of $\boldsymbol{w}$. In that case, the gradient of the risk $\nabla_{\boldsymbol{w}}\mathbb{E}[\ell(\boldsymbol{y}, \hat{\boldsymbol{y}}_{\boldsymbol{w}}(\boldsymbol{x}))]$ does not equal the expected gradient of the cost $\mathbb{E}[\nabla_{\boldsymbol{w}}\ell(\boldsymbol{y}, \hat{\boldsymbol{y}}_{\boldsymbol{w}}(\boldsymbol{x}))]$. However, McAllester et al. (2010) showed that when the input space $\mathcal{X}$ is continuous, the gradient $\nabla_{\boldsymbol{w}}\mathbb{E}[\ell(\boldsymbol{y}, \boldsymbol{y}_{\boldsymbol{w}}(\boldsymbol{x}))]$ exists even when the output space $\mathcal{Y}$ is discrete.

Theorem 11.2. *For a finite set $\mathcal{Y}$ of possible output values, and for w in general position as defined in McAllester et al. (2010), we have*

$$\nabla_{\boldsymbol{w}}\mathbb{E}_{(\boldsymbol{x},\boldsymbol{y})\sim\rho}\Big[\ell(\boldsymbol{y}, \hat{\boldsymbol{y}}_{\boldsymbol{w}}(\boldsymbol{x}))\Big] = \lim_{\epsilon\to 0}\frac{\mathbb{E}_{(\boldsymbol{x},\boldsymbol{y})\sim\rho}\Big[\boldsymbol{\phi}(\boldsymbol{x}, \hat{\boldsymbol{y}}_{\boldsymbol{w}}^{\epsilon\ell}(\boldsymbol{x})) - \boldsymbol{\phi}(\boldsymbol{x}, \hat{\boldsymbol{y}}_{\boldsymbol{w}}(\boldsymbol{x}))\Big]}{\epsilon},$$

$$(11.26)$$

where

$$\hat{\boldsymbol{y}}_{\boldsymbol{w}}^{\epsilon\ell}(\boldsymbol{x}) = \operatorname*{argmax}_{\hat{\boldsymbol{y}}\in\mathcal{Y}}\ \boldsymbol{w}^{\top}\boldsymbol{\phi}(\boldsymbol{x}, \hat{\boldsymbol{y}}) + \epsilon\,\ell(\boldsymbol{y}, \hat{\boldsymbol{y}}) \qquad (11.27)$$

and $\hat{\boldsymbol{y}}_{\boldsymbol{w}}(\boldsymbol{x})$ is defined as in (11.1).

Consider the definition of the gradient of the risk using the Frèchet derivative

$$\Delta\boldsymbol{w}^{\top}\nabla_{\boldsymbol{w}}\mathbb{E}[\ell(\boldsymbol{y}, \hat{\boldsymbol{y}}_{\boldsymbol{w}}(\boldsymbol{x}))] = \lim_{\epsilon\to 0}\frac{\mathbb{E}\left[\ell(\boldsymbol{y}, \hat{\boldsymbol{y}}_{\boldsymbol{w}+\epsilon\Delta\boldsymbol{w}}(\boldsymbol{x})) - \ell(\boldsymbol{y}, \hat{\boldsymbol{y}}_{\boldsymbol{w}}(\boldsymbol{x}))\right]}{\epsilon}. \quad (11.28)$$

for any unit vector $\Delta\boldsymbol{w} \in \mathbb{R}^d$. The main idea of the proof is to show that the right-hand side of (11.28) equals the right-hand side of (11.26). This can be shown as follows. Express the expectation of the right-hand side of (11.26) as a surface integral over the decision boundary, when this boundary is with respect to the score of switching the label from $\hat{\boldsymbol{y}}_{\boldsymbol{w}}$ to $\hat{\boldsymbol{y}}_{\boldsymbol{w}}^{\epsilon\ell}$. Similarly, express the expectation of the right-hand side of (11.28) as a surface integral over the decision boundary when switching the label from $\hat{\boldsymbol{y}}_{\boldsymbol{w}}$ to $\hat{\boldsymbol{y}}_{\boldsymbol{w}+\epsilon\Delta\boldsymbol{w}}$. Then compare those two integrals analytically. The proof of the theorem is given in McAllester et al. (2010).

Using SSGD, an update rule can be written as

$$\boldsymbol{w}_{t+1} = \boldsymbol{w}_t + \frac{\eta_t}{\epsilon} \left(\boldsymbol{\phi}(\boldsymbol{x}_{j_t}, \boldsymbol{y}_{\boldsymbol{w}_t}(\boldsymbol{x}_{j_t})) - \boldsymbol{\phi}(\boldsymbol{x}_{j_t}, \hat{\boldsymbol{y}}_{\boldsymbol{w}_t}^{\epsilon\ell}(\boldsymbol{x}_{j_t})) \right) . \tag{11.29}$$

This type of update rule *moves away from worse labels*. In a similar fashion, we can derive an update rule that *moves toward better labels* and usually performs better in practice:

$$\boldsymbol{w}_{t+1} = \boldsymbol{w}_t + \frac{\eta_t}{\epsilon} \left(\boldsymbol{\phi}(\boldsymbol{x}_{j_t}, \hat{\boldsymbol{y}}_{\boldsymbol{w}_t}^{-\epsilon\ell}(\boldsymbol{x}_{j_t})) - \boldsymbol{\phi}(\boldsymbol{x}_{j_t}, \boldsymbol{y}_{\boldsymbol{w}_t}(\boldsymbol{x}_{j_t})) \right) . \tag{11.30}$$

This update was obtained by expressing the gradient in (11.28) with labels $\hat{\boldsymbol{y}}_{\boldsymbol{w}}$ and $\hat{\boldsymbol{y}}_{\boldsymbol{w}-\epsilon\Delta\boldsymbol{w}}$ rather than $\hat{\boldsymbol{y}}_{\boldsymbol{w}+\epsilon\Delta\boldsymbol{w}}$ and $\hat{\boldsymbol{y}}_{\boldsymbol{w}}$. In practice, ϵ can be chosen to be fixed on a held-out development set.

An open problem is how to properly incorporate regularization in the case where only a finite number of training examples is available. It should be noted that naive regularization with a norm of $\boldsymbol{w}$, such as regularizing with $\lambda\|\boldsymbol{w}\|^2$, is nonsensical as the risk $\mathbb{E}[\ell(\boldsymbol{y}, \hat{\boldsymbol{y}}_{\boldsymbol{w}}(\boldsymbol{x}))]$ is insensitive to the norm of $\boldsymbol{w}$. Early stopping may be a viable approach in practice.

11.6 Structured Ramp Loss

One approach to add a regularization term to the direct loss minimization update rule was proposed by McAllester and Keshet (2011). The idea is to use *structured ramp loss* (Do et al., 2008) as a surrogate loss function, which is defined as follows:

$$\bar{\ell}_{ramp}(\boldsymbol{w}, \boldsymbol{x}, \boldsymbol{y}) = \max_{\hat{\boldsymbol{y}} \in \mathcal{Y}} \left[\ell(\boldsymbol{y}, \hat{\boldsymbol{y}}) + \boldsymbol{w}^\top \boldsymbol{\phi}(\boldsymbol{x}, \hat{\boldsymbol{y}}) \right] - \max_{\tilde{\boldsymbol{y}} \in \mathcal{Y}} \left[\boldsymbol{w}^\top \boldsymbol{\phi}(\boldsymbol{x}, \tilde{\boldsymbol{y}}) \right] . \tag{11.31}$$

Using this surrogate loss in the optimization problem (11.3) results in a non-convex optimization problem. Finding the sub gradient of (11.3) with $\bar{\ell}_{ramp}$ and applying SSGD, we get the following update rule:

$$\boldsymbol{w}_{t+1} = (1 - \eta_t\lambda)\,\boldsymbol{w}_t + \eta_t \left(\boldsymbol{\phi}(\boldsymbol{x}_{j_t}, \boldsymbol{y}_{\boldsymbol{w}_t}(\boldsymbol{x}_{j_t})) - \boldsymbol{\phi}(\boldsymbol{x}_{j_t}, \hat{\boldsymbol{y}}_{\boldsymbol{w}_t}^{\ell}(\boldsymbol{x}_{j_t})) \right) . \tag{11.32}$$

This update is similar to the direct loss minimization update rule (11.29), except for the missing ϵ.

Conceptually, it seems that $\|\boldsymbol{w}\|$ in (11.32) serves as $1/\epsilon$ in the direct loss update rule: high value of $\|\boldsymbol{w}\|$ has the same effect as small ϵ in (11.29). According to Theorem 11.2, the sub gradient of the risk equals the expected difference in the feature maps when ϵ approaches zero. For the ramp loss, it can be shown (McAllester and Keshet, 2011) that when the norm of $\boldsymbol{w}$ goes to infinity, the ramp loss approaches the risk. The regularization of the structural ramp loss $\lambda\|\boldsymbol{w}\|^2$ prefers weight vectors $\boldsymbol{w}$ with small norms. Those conditions are somewhat contradicting, and it is an open problem to introduce a better regularization term with the structured ramp loss.

The structured ramp loss is consistent in the sense defined in (11.4). No convex surrogate loss function, such as log loss or hinge loss, can be consistent in this sense: for any nontrivial convex surrogate loss function one can give examples (a single feature suffices) where the learned weight vector is perturbed by outliers but where the outliers do not actually influence the optimal cost, see also Chapter 10 in this volume.

The structured ramp loss in (11.31) corresponds to the "away-from-bad" direct loss update version. Consider the following variant to the structured ramp loss:

$$\bar{\ell}'_{ramp}(\boldsymbol{w}, \boldsymbol{x}, \boldsymbol{y}) = \max_{\tilde{\boldsymbol{y}} \in \mathcal{Y}} \left[\boldsymbol{w}^\top \boldsymbol{\phi}(\boldsymbol{x}, \tilde{\boldsymbol{y}}) \right] - \max_{\hat{\boldsymbol{y}} \in \mathcal{Y}} \left[\boldsymbol{w}^\top \boldsymbol{\phi}(\boldsymbol{x}, \hat{\boldsymbol{y}}) - \ell(\boldsymbol{y}, \hat{\boldsymbol{y}}) \right] . \quad (11.33)$$

The sub gradient update equation for $\bar{\ell}'_{ramp}$ defines an update rule that corresponds to the "toward good" version of the direct loss minimization. However, we are unaware of a method for proving consistency for this surrogate loss function, and the method used in McAllester and Keshet (2011) is not suitable for this case.

11.7 Structured Probit Loss

We turn now to describe a different approach that is based on the concept of perturbations of the weight vector $\boldsymbol{w}$ (Keshet et al., 2011). We define the structured probit loss as

$$\bar{\ell}_{probit}(\boldsymbol{w}, \boldsymbol{x}, \boldsymbol{y}) = \mathbb{E}_{\boldsymbol{\epsilon} \sim \mathcal{N}(\boldsymbol{0}, \boldsymbol{I})} \left[\ell(\boldsymbol{y}, \hat{\boldsymbol{y}}_{\boldsymbol{w} + \boldsymbol{\epsilon}}(\boldsymbol{x})) \right] , \quad (11.34)$$

where $\boldsymbol{\epsilon} \in \mathbb{R}^d$ is a random vector drawn from the isotropic normal distribution. Note that the optimization problem (11.3), where the surrogate loss is the structured probit loss, is a non-convex optimization function. Plugging this loss into (11.3), we have:

$$\boldsymbol{w}^* = \operatorname*{argmin}_{\boldsymbol{w}} \frac{1}{m} \sum_{i=1}^{m} \bar{\ell}_{probit}(\boldsymbol{w}, \boldsymbol{x}_i, \boldsymbol{y}_i) + \frac{\lambda}{2} \|\boldsymbol{w}\|^2 . \quad (11.35)$$

The sub gradient of the objective (11.35), approximated with the training example $(\boldsymbol{x}_{j_t}, \boldsymbol{y}_{j_t})$ uniformly chosen at random, is given by

$$\nabla_{\boldsymbol{w}} \left[\bar{\ell}_{probit}(\boldsymbol{w}, \boldsymbol{x}_{j_t}, \boldsymbol{y}_{j_t}) + \frac{\lambda}{2} \|\boldsymbol{w}\|^2 \right] \tag{11.36}$$

$$= \nabla_{\boldsymbol{w}} \left[\mathbb{E}_{\boldsymbol{\epsilon} \sim \mathcal{N}(\boldsymbol{0}, \boldsymbol{I})} \left[\ell(\boldsymbol{y}_{j_t}, \hat{\boldsymbol{y}}_{\boldsymbol{w}+\boldsymbol{\epsilon}}(\boldsymbol{x}_{j_t})) \right] + \frac{\lambda}{2} \|\boldsymbol{w}\|^2 \right] \tag{11.37}$$

$$= \nabla_{\boldsymbol{w}} \left[\int (2\pi)^{-d/2} e^{-\frac{1}{2}\|\boldsymbol{\epsilon}\|^2} \ell(\boldsymbol{y}_{j_t}, \hat{\boldsymbol{y}}_{\boldsymbol{w}+\boldsymbol{\epsilon}}(\boldsymbol{x}_{j_t})) d\boldsymbol{\epsilon} + \frac{\lambda}{2} \|\boldsymbol{w}\|^2 \right] \tag{11.38}$$

$$= \nabla_{\boldsymbol{w}} \left[(2\pi)^{-d/2} \int e^{-\frac{1}{2}\|\boldsymbol{u}-\boldsymbol{w}\|^2} \ell(\boldsymbol{y}_{j_t}, \hat{\boldsymbol{y}}_{\boldsymbol{u}}(\boldsymbol{x}_{j_t})) d\boldsymbol{u} + \frac{\lambda}{2} \|\boldsymbol{w}\|^2 \right] \tag{11.39}$$

$$= (2\pi)^{-d/2} \int (\boldsymbol{u} - \boldsymbol{w}) e^{-\frac{1}{2}\|\boldsymbol{u}-\boldsymbol{w}\|^2} \ell(\boldsymbol{y}_{j_t}, \hat{\boldsymbol{y}}_{\boldsymbol{u}}(\boldsymbol{x}_{j_t})) d\boldsymbol{u} + \lambda \boldsymbol{w} \tag{11.40}$$

$$= (2\pi)^{-d/2} \int \boldsymbol{\epsilon} \, e^{-\frac{1}{2}\|\boldsymbol{\epsilon}\|^2} \ell(\boldsymbol{y}_{j_t}, \hat{\boldsymbol{y}}_{\boldsymbol{w}+\boldsymbol{\epsilon}}(\boldsymbol{x}_{j_t})) d\boldsymbol{\epsilon} + \lambda \boldsymbol{w} \tag{11.41}$$

$$= \mathbb{E}_{\boldsymbol{\epsilon}} \left[\boldsymbol{\epsilon} \, \ell(\boldsymbol{y}_{j_t}, \hat{\boldsymbol{y}}_{\boldsymbol{w}+\boldsymbol{\epsilon}}(\boldsymbol{x}_{j_t})) \right] + \lambda \boldsymbol{w} \,, \tag{11.42}$$

where we changed variables $\boldsymbol{\epsilon} = \boldsymbol{u} - \boldsymbol{w}$ in the transition from (11.38) to (11.39) and back to $\boldsymbol{u} = \boldsymbol{w} + \boldsymbol{\epsilon}$ in the transition from (11.40) to (11.41). The update rule is therefore

$$\boldsymbol{w}_{t+1} = (1 - \eta_t \lambda) \, \boldsymbol{w}_t + \eta_t \mathbb{E}_{\boldsymbol{\epsilon}} \left[\boldsymbol{\epsilon} \, \ell(\boldsymbol{y}_{j_t}, \hat{\boldsymbol{y}}_{\boldsymbol{w}+\boldsymbol{\epsilon}}(\boldsymbol{x}_{j_t})) \right] \,. \tag{11.43}$$

Practically, the expectation over the isotropic normal random noise $\boldsymbol{\epsilon}$ is replaced with an average of a vector of length d sampled from that distribution.

The following generalization bound was given in Keshet et al. (2011).

Theorem 11.3. *For fixed $\lambda > 1/2$, we have that with probability at least $1 - \delta$ over the draw of the training data the following inequality holds simultaneously for all $\boldsymbol{w}$*

$$\mathbb{E}_{(\boldsymbol{x}, \boldsymbol{y}) \sim \rho}[\bar{\ell}_{probit}(\boldsymbol{w}, \boldsymbol{x}, \boldsymbol{y})] \leq \frac{1}{1 - \frac{1}{2\lambda}} \left(\frac{1}{m} \sum_{i=1}^{m} \bar{\ell}_{probit}(\boldsymbol{w}, \boldsymbol{x}_i, \boldsymbol{y}_i) \right.$$
$$\left. + \frac{\lambda}{2m} \|\boldsymbol{w}\|^2 + \frac{\lambda \ln(1/\delta)}{m} \right). \tag{11.44}$$

It is interesting to note that minimizing the right-hand side of this bound with respect to $\boldsymbol{w}$, using SSGD, is identical to the derivation of the update rule above.

This loss function is found to be consistent in the strong sense as defined in (11.4) (McAllester and Keshet, 2011). Another advantage of this surrogate loss is that the cost function ℓ does not need to be decomposable as in structural SVM, direct loss minimization, and structural ramp loss. The decomposability is needed to solve loss-adjusted inference (11.17) using dynamic programming.[2] This, however, comes with a disadvantage: the need to infer $\hat{y}_{w+\epsilon}(x)$ many times in order to reliably estimate the expectation over ϵ.

An extension of the probit loss to more general distributions of ϵ was presented by Hazan et al. (2013), which might correspond to the noise of the problem. In that case, the regularization term in (11.3) is not necessarily $\|w\|^2$ but rather a function related to the distribution of ϵ.

11.8   Risk Minimization Under Gibbs Distribution

While CRFs aim to minimize the expected negative log likelihood, namely, the log loss, recall that we are interested in minimizing the risk. It was proposed by Smith and Eisner (2006) to minimize the risk under the Gibbs measure. Let us define the *structured logit* surrogate loss function as the conditional expectation of the cost, when the expectation is taken with respect to the *Gibbs distribution*, $P_w(y|x)$, as is defined in (11.19):

$$\bar{\ell}_{logit}(\boldsymbol{w}, \boldsymbol{x}, \boldsymbol{y}) = \mathbb{E}_{\boldsymbol{y}' \sim P_w(\boldsymbol{y}' \,|\, \boldsymbol{x})} \left[\ell(\boldsymbol{y}', \boldsymbol{y}) \right] = \sum_{\boldsymbol{y}' \in \mathcal{Y}} P_w(\boldsymbol{y}'|\boldsymbol{x}) \, \ell(\boldsymbol{y}', \boldsymbol{y}) \,. \quad (11.45)$$

An interesting property of the logit loss ℓ_{logit} is that when the norm of w approaches infinity, the logit loss converges to the risk.

Theorem 11.4.

$$\lim_{\alpha \to \infty} \bar{\ell}_{logit}(\alpha \boldsymbol{w}, \boldsymbol{x}, \boldsymbol{y}) = \ell(\boldsymbol{y}, \hat{\boldsymbol{y}}_w(\boldsymbol{x})) \,, \qquad\qquad (11.46)$$

where $\hat{y}_w(x)$ is defined in (11.1).

This theorem can be easily proven by explicitly expressing the logit loss as in (11.45). Then split the sum over the labels to the label $\hat{y}$ and the rest of the labels and apply the limit.

This theorem is only part of the whole consistency proof. What is missing is a generalization bound similar to (11.44), which makes the connection between the logit loss and the risk. This is still an open problem.

---

2. In principle, the decomposability is not always necessary in those methods as long as the loss augmented prediction still works (e.g., by branch-and-bound) (Blaschko and Lampert, 2008).

11.9 Conclusions

In this chapter, we compared different surrogate loss functions used by different algorithms for structured prediction. We presented the concept of consistency in the strong sense and showed that no convex surrogate loss function, such as log loss or hinge loss, can be consistent in this sense. We showed that some non-convex loss functions lead to consistency and maybe superior generalization. We have started to extend the ideas presented here to train models, such as graphical models and deep neural networks, so as to optimize the measure of performance on unseen data.

11.10 References

M. B. Blaschko and C. H. Lampert. Learning to localize objects with structured output regression. In *European Conference on Computer Vision (ECCV)*. Springer, 2008.

N. Cesa-Bianchi, A. Conconi, and C. Gentile. On the generalization ability of on-line learning algorithms. *IEEE Transactions on Information Theory*, 50(9): 2050–2057, 2004.

M. Collins. Discriminative training methods for hidden Markov models: Theory and experiments with perceptron algorithms. In *Conference on Empirical Methods in Natural Language Processing*, 2002.

O. Dekel, J. Keshet, and Y. Singer. Large margin hierarchical classification. In *International Conference on Machine Learing (ICML)*, 2004.

C. B. Do, Q. Le, C. H. Teo, O. Chapelle, and A. Smola. Tighter bounds for structured estimation. In *Conference on Neural Information Processing Systems (NIPS)*, pages 281–288, 2008.

T. Hazan, S. Maji, J. Keshet, and T. Jaakkola. On sampling from the Gibbs distribution with random maximum a-posteriori perturbations. In *Conference on Neural Information Processing Systems (NIPS)*, 2013.

J. Keshet, D. McAllester, and T. Hazan. PAC-Bayesian approach for minimization of phoneme error rate. In *International Conference on Acoustics, Speech, and Signal Processing (ICASSP)*, 2011.

J. Lafferty, A. McCallum, and F. Pereira. Conditional random fields: Probabilistic models for segmenting and labeling sequence data. In *International Conference on Machine Learing (ICML)*, pages 282–289, 2001.

Y. Lee, Y. Lin, and G. Wahba. Multicategory support vector machines: Theory and application to the classification of microarray data and satellite radiance data. *Journal of the American Statistical Association*, 99(465):67–81, 2004.

D. McAllester. Generalization bounds and consistency for structured labeling. In B. Schölkopf, A. J. Smola, B. Taskar, and S. Vishwanathan, editors, *Predicting Structured Data*, pages 247–262. MIT Press, 2006.

D. McAllester and J. Keshet. Generalization bounds and consistency for latent structural probit and ramp loss. In *Conference on Neural Information Processing Systems (NIPS)*, 2011.

D. McAllester, T. Hazan, and J. Keshet. Direct loss minimization for structured prediction. In *Conference on Neural Information Processing Systems (NIPS)*, 2010.

D. A. Smith and J. Eisner. Minimum risk annealing for training log-linear models. In *COLING/ACL*, pages 787–794, 2006.

B. Taskar, C. Guestrin, and D. Koller. Max-margin Markov networks. In *Conference on Neural Information Processing Systems (NIPS)*, 2003.

I. Tsochantaridis, T. Joachims, T. Hofmann, and Y. Altun. Large margin methods for structured and interdependent output variables. *Journal of Machine Learning Research (JMLR)*, 6:1453–1484, 2005.

V. Vapnik. *The Nature of Statistical Learning Theory*. Springer, 2000.

12   Structured Learning from Cheap Data

Xinghua Lou   xinghua.lou@gmail.com
Microsoft
1020 Enterprise Way, Sunnyvale, CA, USA

Marius Kloft   kloft@cbio.mskcc.org
Sloan-Kettering Institute and Courant Institute
415 E 68 St, New York, NY, USA

Gunnar Rätsch   raetsch@cbio.mskcc.org
Sloan-Kettering Institute
415 E 68 St, New York, NY, USA

Fred A. Hamprecht   fred.hamprecht@iwr.uni-heidelberg.de
Ruprecht-Karls-Universität Heidelberg
Speyerer Str 6, Heidelberg, Germany

Structured learning in its basic formulation requires fully annotated and accurate training data. Both requirements are often impractical, especially if training data need to be generated by human experts. This is because each training sample can consist of a large number of random variables whose state has to be specified, and also because annotators have to consider complex rules to yield valid output structure. This chapter presents several extensions of structured learning that seek to relieve the annotators' plight by enabling learning from "cheap data" and thus making the learning more "convenient." For the relevant problem of tracking an unknown number of divisible objects, this chapter highlights in a tutorial manner (i) structured learning from partial annotations, (ii) active structured learning, and (iii) structured transfer learning.

12.1 Introduction

Structured output predictions can typically be represented in terms of a graph with both vertex and edge attributes. For instance, each vertex may be associated with a semantic category, or each edge may have a connection strength. Such graphs are typically the minimizer of an optimization problem that combines unary terms — such as the propensity of a specific vertex to belong to a certain category — with constraints, or higher-order terms, that couple the predictions associated with each node or edge.

A relevant instance of structured output prediction is the object tracking problem. In a tracking-by-assignment approach, we have unary terms that seek to predict whether two targets in subsequent time steps are in fact identical. If such predictions were made independently, then the result may be paradoxical in that a single target at time t is simultaneously associated with two different predecessors at time $t - 1$. Clearly, if the merging of targets can be ruled out in the application at hand, then only one or the other association can be correct, but not both at the same time.

Such structured output prediction problems usually consist of energy terms whose parameters have to be estimated. This is made possible by supervised structured learning, which aims at *directly* optimizing the parameters such that the prediction model can reproduce the experts' annotation as accurately as possible. Structured learning has significantly broadened the applications of machine learning to many different fields (Figure 12.1). As with all supervised training, a sufficient and representative training data set is required, which, however, becomes a non-trivial issue for structured data. Firstly, unlike canonical classification or regression whose output is a single variable, a structured model consists of many more variables *per sample* (e.g., a DNA sequence can be as long as millions; Figure 12.1B). Secondly, those variables are interdependent, subject to some rules that have to be accounted for when annotating the sample (e.g., context-free grammars in parsing; Figure 12.1A).

This chapter is all about learning approaches that enable efficient learning with less human effort, which we refer to as *structured learning from cheap data*. We will use tracking-by-assignment as a running example in this chapter. Section 12.2 will show how it can be cast as a structured learning problem, opening the way to a principled parametrization of expressive models based on training data alone. However, in biological applications, we may easily observe thousands of targets in each frame of a video. A standard structured learning setup would consequently need training samples, each of

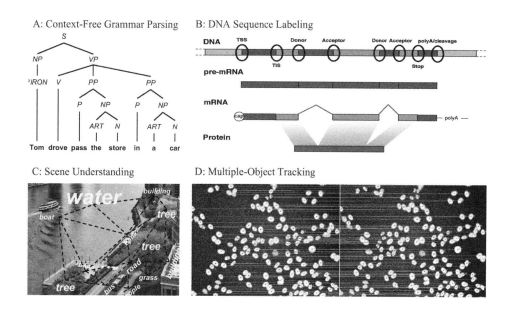

Figure 12.1: Typical structure prediction problems in natural language processing (A), computational biology (B), and computer vision (C and D).

which has a complex and large structure. Generating such expensive training data is tedious at best.

Section 12.3 shows how to *learn from partial annotations*. The unannotated parts of the data are treated as latent variables that also need to be optimized over. This often leads to hard, non-convex optimization problems that can only be solved approximately by expectation-maximization-type procedures. Computational efficiency is key in such iterative procedures, and we show how notable speed-ups can be achieved by the recycling of approximation bounds and an adjustment of convergence criteria over time. Given a good initialization (which is necessary given that these iterative schemes end up in a local optimum), such procedures reach competitive accuracy with only a fraction of full annotations. Theoretically, Section 12.3 also proves consistency of the loss functions used therein and offers a probabilistic bound on the generalization error of structured learning from partial annotations.

Section 12.4 presents an attractive alternative based on *active learning*, where one iteratively identifies part of a training set that is deemed most informative. The rationale is that judiciously choosing the training examples to be labeled should afford steeper learning curves (accuracy as a function of training set size) than randomly selecting a subset for labeling.

Finally, in Section 12.5, we illustrate *structured transfer learning*. The idea here is to regularize the training procedure by coupling the learning of the parameters to a related but different learning problems for which abundance training data are already available. This technique is an embodiment of the notion "extra data for better regularization."

The motivation, prior work, and necessary notation will be introduced at the beginning of each of the three main sections. In Section 12.6, we conclude with a brief discussion of the presented and future work.

12.2   Running Example: Structured Learning for Cell Tracking

Before diving into the technical details, we first introduce a structured prediction model for cell tracking that we will use throughout this chapter.

12.2.1   Background

Unlike conventional computer vision problems such as surveillance analysis, which contains a handful of (heterogeneous) objects, a bio-image sequence normally contains hundreds and even thousands of homogeneous objects that are divisible according to some biological process (e.g., cell division). The combination of such a vast amount and the complex underlying temporal events raises a new challenge to the vision community. As discussed in Meijering et al. (2009), conventional tracking techniques are not applicable because of either limited expressive power (e.g., level-set) or low scalability (e.g., particle filter). Alternatively, *tracking-by-assignment* methods have shown promising performance in capturing a complex mixture of events (Padfield et al., 2011) while also being scalable to even thousands of objects (Lou et al., 2011).

12.2.2   Generalized Pairwise Tracking Models

We assume a robust detection algorithm to detect objects (i.e., cells), but we accept errors such as over-segmentation and under-segmentation. We propose a *generalized pairwise tracking model* that encloses a mixture of events such as cell migration, cell division, as well as over- and under-segmentation (see Figure 12.2). Formally, given sets of detected objects $\{C, C'\}$ from two subsequent frames, the model assumes a multitude of possible assignment hypotheses (e.g., events) and seeks a subset that is most compatible with the observations and with the parameter learned from the

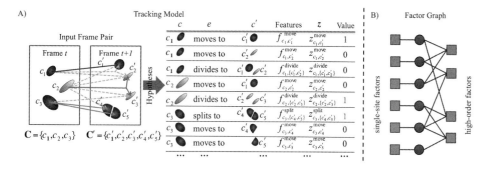

Figure 12.2: (A) Toy example: two sets of object candidates, and a small subset of the possible assignment hypotheses. One particular interpretation of the scene is indicated by solid arrows (left) or equivalently by a configuration of binary indicator variables y (rightmost column in table). Some rejected hypotheses are shown as light gray dash lines. (B) A factor graph representation of the proposed pairwise tracking model, which consists of unary potential as individual event scoring and high-order potential for guaranteeing consistency.

training data:

$$\underset{y\in\{0,1\}^M}{\operatorname{argmax}} \quad L(x,y;w) := \sum_{e\in\boldsymbol{E}}\sum_{c\in P(\boldsymbol{C})}\sum_{c'\in P(\boldsymbol{C}')}\langle f^e_{c,c'},w^e\rangle y^e_{cc'} \tag{12.1}$$

$$\text{s.t.}\quad \forall c'\in P(\boldsymbol{C}'),\sum_{e\in\boldsymbol{E}}\sum_{c\in P(\boldsymbol{C})} y^e_{c,c'}=1,\ (\text{consistency}) \tag{12.2}$$

$$\forall c\in P(\boldsymbol{C}),\sum_{e\in\boldsymbol{E}}\sum_{c'\in P(\boldsymbol{C}')} y^e_{c,c'}=1.\ (\text{consistency}) \tag{12.3}$$

Here, M is the total number of hypothetical events, $\boldsymbol{E}$ is a set of event types (migration, division, etc.), and $P(\boldsymbol{C})$ is a power set of $\boldsymbol{C}$ such that we can define events that express, for example, one-to-many matching as cell division is. Besides, $f^e_{c,c'}$ is a feature vector for the hypothetical event e between objects c and c' and, parametrized by w^e, $\langle f^e_{c,c'},w^e\rangle$, is the linear scoring of this hypothesis, which is counted if $y^e_{cc'}=1$ (i.e., selected).

However, y is subject to consistency constraints: each candidate in the first frame must have a single fate, and each candidate from the second frame has a unique past. That is, for hypotheses associated with the same candidate, only one of them can be accepted. To this end, as the corresponding factor graph representation (Kschischang et al., 2001) shows (Figure 12.2B), this model consists of unary factors that represent the scoring of individual hypothetical events and high-order factors that couple those events and guarantee consistency.

Obviously, 12.1 is a linear model, as $L(x,y;w) = \langle w, \Phi(x,y)\rangle$. Here, w is the concatenation of event-specific parameters, and $\Phi(x,y)$ is the concatenation of event-specific features summed up over all activated events, which is referred to as the *joint feature vector*.

For a given parameter w, we use integer linear programming (ILP) solvers to find the best assignments. Commercial solvers such as IBM's CPLEX, or Gurobi's tools can scale up to thousands of hypotheses (Lou et al., 2011).

12.2.3   Max-Margin Formulation and Optimization

Given N training frame pairs $\boldsymbol{X} = \{x_n\}$ and their correct assignments $\boldsymbol{Y}^* = \{y_n^*\}$, $n = 1, \ldots, N$, we attempt to find the decision boundary that maximizes the margin between the correct assignment y_n^* and the closest runner-up solution (i.e., the canonical max-margin learning paradigm) (Taskar et al., 2003; Tsochantaridis et al., 2006)

$$
\begin{aligned}
\underset{w, \boldsymbol{\xi} \geq \mathbf{0}}{\operatorname{argmin}} \quad & \lambda \Omega(w) + \sum_{n=1}^{N} \xi_n \\
\text{s. t.} \quad & \forall n, \forall y \in Y_n, L(x_n, y_n^*; w) - L(x_n, y; w) \geq \Delta(y_n^*, y) - \xi_n,
\end{aligned} \tag{12.4}
$$

where Y_n is the output space and using $\Delta(y_n^*, \hat{y}_n)$ instead of a fixed margin is known as *margin rescaling* (Tsochantaridis et al., 2006).

Because 12.4 involves an exponentially large number of constraints, the optimization problem cannot be written down explicitly, let alone be solved directly. We thus resort to the *bundle method* (Teo et al., 2010; Do and Artieres, 2012), which in turn is based on the *cutting plane* approach (see, e.g., (Tsochantaridis et al., 2006; Joachims et al., 2009; Rätsch et al., 2002)). Briefly, bundle methods iteratively construct piece-wise linear bounds for the empirical loss (i.e., "cutting" planes) until the bounds are sufficiently tight. The procedure terminates when the approximation gap ϵ (i.e., the difference between the true objective function and its linear bounds at current w) reaches a threshold (Teo et al., 2010).

12.2.4   Results: First Look

We compared the structured output learning algorithm above with L_1 and L_2 regularizer against several state-of-the-art cell tracking methods on the DCellIQ data set provided by Li et al. (2010). The results can be found in Table 12.1. Our structured learning-based method outperforms all of the other methods with a clear margin. Compared with Li et al. (2010), who first studied this data set, we obtained an improvement by more than one order of magnitude (0.30% vs. 6.18% loss), illustrating the power of structured output learning for this application.

12.2.5 Annotation Cost for Training Data Preparation

The encouraging performance boost by structured learning has a major requirement: a sufficiently large set of *representative training samples*. However, manually annotating hundreds of events per pair of frames is particularly labor-intensive and time-consuming. This severely limits the applicability of such advanced learning technique when deployed in real-world scenarios. For instance, annotating and validating a training data set like the DCellIQ data set takes **8 to 15 hours**.

12.3 Strategy I: Structured Learning from Partial Annotations

12.3.1 Motivation

Canonical structured learning always assumes fully annotated data (i.e., specifying the state of each and every random variable in the structured output). This is particularly expensive for complex and/or large structured outputs. For example, in natural language processing, manually constructing the entire parsing trees is labor-intensive. Also, in computational biology, as our running example is, even a single sample (i.e., a pair of frames) contains hundreds of events. This motivates us to investigate the possibility of learning structured prediction models using only *partial* annotations, namely, only a fraction of the complex structured output per training sample requires annotation. We consider this a viable approach because large, complex output structures are merely the compositional output of simple, local patterns. As per our examples above, the parsing tree is essentially constructed using rules from the context-free grammar, and for cell tracking,

Method	Description	Avg. Loss
Li et al. (2010)	Graph matching, no learning	6.18%
Padfield et al. (2011)	ILP as max-flow, no learning	1.64%
Manual tweaking	Tweaking via visual inspection on results	1.12%
Random forest	Learning local event classifiers	0.55%
Structured learning (L_1)	12.4 with L_1 regularization	0.45%
Structured learning (L_2)	12.4 with L_2 regularization	**0.30%**

Table 12.1: Comparison of average loss using six approaches on the DCellIQ data set. Compared with Li et al. (2010), who first studied this data set, structured learning obtained an improvement by a factor of 20 (0.30% vs. 6.18% loss).

the complete output assignment consists of local events such as cell migration and cell division.

We build on important previous work for multiclass classification with ambiguous labels. For example, Jin and Ghahramani (2002) proposed an EM-like algorithm that iteratively estimates the label distribution and classifies using this distribution as a prior. Recently, Cour et al. (2011) proposed convex loss for partial labels, which in turn resembles the one-versus-all loss (Zhang, 2004). We will extend this loss to structured data and discuss its properties. This work is also closely related to structured learning with latent variables (Yu and Joachims, 2009). The difference lies in the loss and the optimization strategy. Also, note that structured learning from partial annotations is different from semi-supervised or unsupervised structured learning (Zien et al., 2007). In those settings, training samples are either completely annotated or completely unannotated.

12.3.2   Formulation

Formally, we want to learn a structured prediction model from a *partially* annotated training set $\{(x_n, y_n^*) \in \mathcal{X}_n \times \mathcal{Y}_n\}_{n \in [N]}$. Here, x_n is a structured input from a space $\mathcal{X}_n$. (Note that the cardinality of the spaces $\mathcal{X}_n$, $\mathcal{Y}_n$ is typically different for each input n.) y^* is a *partially* annotated structured output that induces a partitioning of the structured output space $\mathcal{Y}$ into two sets: $\mathcal{Y}^* \cap \mathcal{Y}^\circ = \emptyset$, and $\mathcal{Y}^* \cup \mathcal{Y}^\circ = \mathcal{Y}$. $\mathcal{Y}^*$ comprises all outputs that *are* compatible with a partial annotation y^*, whereas $\mathcal{Y}^\circ$ encompasses all those structured outputs that are *not* compatible with the partial annotation.

Structured learning needs to discriminate a correct structured output from an exponential number of wrong ones. We follow the max-margin argument (Tsochantaridis et al., 2006; Taskar et al., 2003) by constructing a loss function that penalizes small margins between the current prediction inferred from the partial annotation and the second best output, which, coupled with margin rescaling, leads to the following loss:

$$l^{\text{partial}}(x, y^*; \boldsymbol{w}) \;=\; \left| \max_{y \in \mathcal{Y}^{\text{P}}} \left[f(x, y; \boldsymbol{w}) + \Delta(y^*, y) \right] - \max_{y \in \mathcal{Y}^{\text{R}}} \left[f(x, y; \boldsymbol{w}) \right] \right|_+$$

Here, $\mathcal{Y}^{\text{P}}$ is a "Penalty" space because its members make a positive contribution to the loss. On the contrary, $\mathcal{Y}^{\text{R}}$ denotes a "Reward" space because it contains the correct configuration and brings a negative contribution. This loss resembles a generic structure for a number of other losses proposed in the literature (see a summary in Lou and Hamprecht, 2012). For example, if $\mathcal{Y}^{\text{P}} = \mathcal{Y}^\circ$ and $\mathcal{Y}^{\text{R}} = \mathcal{Y}^*$, then $l^{\text{partial}}(x, y^*; \boldsymbol{w})$ becomes the **bridge loss** proposed in Lou and Hamprecht (2012), which is used in this chapter.

Given the loss for partial annotations, we define the learning objective as

$$\min_{\boldsymbol{w}} \quad \lambda\Omega(\boldsymbol{w}) + \underbrace{\sum_n \max_{y \in \mathcal{Y}_n^{\mathrm{P}}} \left[f(x_n, y_n; \boldsymbol{w}) + \Delta(y_n^*, y)\right]}_{P(\boldsymbol{w}), \text{ convex}} - \underbrace{\sum_n \max_{y \in \mathcal{Y}_n^{\mathrm{R}}} \left[f(x_n, y; \boldsymbol{w})\right]}_{R(\boldsymbol{w}), \text{ convex}}.$$

$$\text{s.t.} \quad \text{each loss must be non} - \text{negative.} \tag{12.5}$$

(12.5) is a subtraction of two convex functions, namely, $\lambda\Omega(\boldsymbol{w}) + P(\boldsymbol{w}) - R(\boldsymbol{w})$. Note that this formulation is equivalent to the canonical form with slack variables and (exponentially many) constraints. We keep this form to emphasize the structure of the objective that we will elaborate next. Note that for max loss and bridge loss, the non-negativity constraints can be achieved by ignoring the gradients of the samples that violate them during model update, as in usual SVM.

12.3.3 Optimization

In the sequel we will discuss the algorithmic aspects of solving (12.5).

The subtraction of two convex functions forms a convex-concave optimization problem that can be solved by the CCCP procedure (Yuille and Rangarajan, 2003). Briefly, CCCP iterates between:
Step 1: At iteration t, estimate a linear upper bound on the concave function $-R(\boldsymbol{w})$ using its subgradient at $\boldsymbol{w}_t$ (i.e., $\boldsymbol{v}_t = -\partial_{\boldsymbol{w}} R(\boldsymbol{w}_t)$).
Step 2: Update the model by $\operatorname{argmin}_{\boldsymbol{w}} \tilde{J}(\boldsymbol{w}) := \lambda\Omega(\boldsymbol{w}) + P(\boldsymbol{w}) + \langle \boldsymbol{v}_t, \boldsymbol{w} \rangle$.

However, structured learning is computationally expensive due to the repetitive maximization problems one has to solve at every iteration to compute the subgradients. This becomes even worse in the CCCP framework because a complete run of structured learning is performed largely from scratch per iteration. We now introduce a novel method for speeding up CCCP when structured learning is required.

The learning objective $\tilde{J}(\boldsymbol{w})$ in (12.5) has two important properties:
Complexity: $\tilde{J}(\boldsymbol{w})$ consists of three terms with different complexity: a regularizer $\lambda\Omega(\boldsymbol{w})$ (e.g., quadratic when using L2 regularization) and a linear term $\langle \boldsymbol{v}, \boldsymbol{w} \rangle$, both smooth and easy to solve, and a complicated, possibly non-smooth term $P(\boldsymbol{w})$.
Consistency: $\tilde{J}(\boldsymbol{w})$ changes at each CCCP iteration due to the update of $\boldsymbol{v}$; however, the difficult function $P(\boldsymbol{w})$ remains the same.

These two observations lead to two ideas for speedup. Firstly, we construct a piece-wise linear lower bound on the difficult $P(\boldsymbol{w})$ only, rather than on the entire objective $\tilde{J}(\boldsymbol{w})$ as in Yu and Joachims (2009). Because the $P(\boldsymbol{w})$ part of $\tilde{J}(\boldsymbol{w})$ remains the same, we can reuse these bounds across multiple CCCP

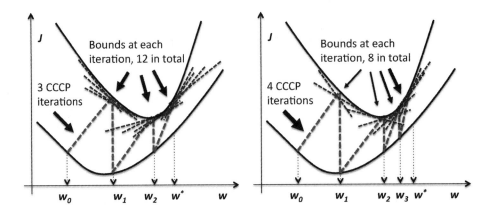

Figure 12.3: CCCP procedure: starting from $\boldsymbol{w}_0$, iteratively match points in the two curves that have the same subgradient, until convergence to the optimal $\boldsymbol{w}^*$. CCCP with fixed precision (left) requires fewer iterations but more bounds than CCCP with adaptive precision (right).

iterations and avoid recomputing them from scratch. When some "good" linear approximation for $P(\boldsymbol{w})$ is provided at each iteration, solving $\tilde{J}(\boldsymbol{w})$ is easy because the other two terms are simple. We name this technique *bounds recycling*, because the bounds will be reused to compute the approximation gap between the original objective and its linear approximation.

Secondly, CCCP iteratively matches points on the two convex functions (i.e., $\lambda\Omega(\boldsymbol{w}) + P(\boldsymbol{w})$ and $R(\boldsymbol{w})$), which have the same subgradient (see Figure 12.3, left). Because we usually start with some $\boldsymbol{w}_0$ far from the optimum, it is not sensible to solve $\tilde{J}(\boldsymbol{w})$ to high precision at early iterations. Otherwise, many bounds need be computed to achieve this precision at some immature $\boldsymbol{w}$, which are mostly not reused at later iterations when precision really matters. Therefore, we propose to adaptively increase the precision of CCCP iteration until reaching the required precision. This procedure, named *adaptive precision*, is shown in Figure 12.3 (right). Because the training precision is controlled by the approximate gap ϵ, this means we gradually decrease ϵ per CCCP iteration (see line 5, Algorithm 12.1).

To construct a lower bound approximation for $P(\boldsymbol{w})$, we follow the bundle minimization method from Teo et al. (2010). Briefly, at some $\boldsymbol{w}_t$, we compute the subgradient of $P(\boldsymbol{w})$ and the corresponding offset, denoted as $\boldsymbol{a}$ and b, respectively.

Now, this lower bound sitting at $\boldsymbol{w}_t$ can be expressed as $\langle \boldsymbol{a}, \boldsymbol{w}\rangle + b \leq P(\boldsymbol{w}), \forall\boldsymbol{w}$. We store all subgradients $\boldsymbol{a}$ as column vectors in set $\boldsymbol{A} = \{\boldsymbol{a}_0, \boldsymbol{a}_1, \ldots\}$ and the offsets b in set $\boldsymbol{b} = \{b_0, b_1, \ldots\}$. Given $\boldsymbol{A}$ and $\boldsymbol{b}$, solving

---

Algorithm 12.1 Structured learning from partial annotations

1: **Input:** $\{x_n, y_n^*\}$, $\boldsymbol{w}_0$, η, $\{\epsilon, \epsilon_{min}, \rho\}$
2: Initialize $t \leftarrow 0, k \leftarrow 0, \boldsymbol{A} \leftarrow \emptyset, \boldsymbol{b} \leftarrow \emptyset, \boldsymbol{w} \leftarrow \boldsymbol{w}_0$
3: **repeat**
4:     Compute $\boldsymbol{v}_t$ as the upper bound of the concave function
5:     Set adaptative precision $\epsilon \leftarrow \max(\epsilon \times \rho, \epsilon_{min})$
6:     **repeat**
7:         Compute gradient $\boldsymbol{a}_k$ and offset b_k
8:         Set $\boldsymbol{A} \leftarrow \boldsymbol{A} \cup \boldsymbol{a}_k$ and $\boldsymbol{b} \leftarrow \boldsymbol{b} \cup \boldsymbol{b}_k$
9:         Update $\boldsymbol{w}$ using Eq. 12.7 with $\boldsymbol{A}$, $\boldsymbol{b}$ and $\boldsymbol{v}_t$
10:        Compute approximation gap $\hat{\epsilon}$ (see Teo et al., 2010)
11:         Set $k \leftarrow k + 1$
12:     **until** $\hat{\epsilon} \leq \epsilon$
13:     Set $\boldsymbol{w}_{t+1} \leftarrow \boldsymbol{w}$
14:     Set $t \leftarrow t + 1$
15: **until** $\tilde{J}(\boldsymbol{w}_{t-1}) - \tilde{J}(\boldsymbol{w}_t) \leq \eta$
16: **Output:** $\boldsymbol{w}$

$\tilde{J}(\boldsymbol{w})$ in (12.5) becomes

$$\min_{\boldsymbol{w}} \quad \lambda\Omega(\boldsymbol{w}) + \underbrace{\max_{(\boldsymbol{a},b)\in(\boldsymbol{A},\boldsymbol{b})} (\langle \boldsymbol{a}, \boldsymbol{w} \rangle + b)}_{\text{Linearly lower bounded } P(\boldsymbol{w})} + \langle \boldsymbol{v}, \boldsymbol{w} \rangle. \tag{12.6}$$

Given regularizer $\Omega(\boldsymbol{w}) = \frac{1}{2}\|\boldsymbol{w}\|^2$, this can be solved in its dual by

$$\max_{\boldsymbol{\alpha}} \quad -\frac{1}{2\lambda}\boldsymbol{\alpha}'\boldsymbol{A}'\boldsymbol{A}\boldsymbol{\alpha} + \left(b' - \frac{1}{\lambda}v'\boldsymbol{A}\right)\boldsymbol{\alpha}$$
$$\text{s.t.} \quad \boldsymbol{\alpha}'\boldsymbol{1} = 1, \boldsymbol{\alpha} \geq \boldsymbol{0}. \tag{12.7}$$

Note that the particular $\boldsymbol{A}$ in (12.7) is a matrix representation of the set of gradients $\boldsymbol{A}$ obtained by concatenating the (column) vectors $\boldsymbol{a} \in \boldsymbol{A}$. Similarly, the variable $\boldsymbol{b}$ in (12.7) is a column vector of the offsets $b \in \boldsymbol{b}$. The primal variable $\boldsymbol{w}$ is connected to $\boldsymbol{\alpha}$ by $\boldsymbol{w} = -\frac{1}{\lambda}(\boldsymbol{v} + \boldsymbol{A}\boldsymbol{\alpha})$. It is possible to collapse the previous lower bounds to a small number without loss of accuracy or convergence guarantees (Do and Artieres, 2012).

12.3.4 Theoretical Analysis

In this section, we show a generalization bound for the proposed method of structured learning with partially annotated outputs. This establishes the theoretical guarantee that the algorithm will not overfit, given sufficiently many training examples.

Theorem 12.1 (Generalization Bound for Structured Learning With Partially Annotated Outputs). *Let $D = (x_n, y_n^*)_{1 \leq n \leq N}$ be an i.i.d. family of* *random variables with $y_n^* \in \mathcal{Y}^p \supset \mathcal{Y}$, such that there exist $B > 0$ such that $\mathbb{P}\left(\|\Phi(x, y)\| \leq B\right) = 1$. Let $\Delta^{\max} := \sup_{y, y'} \Delta(y, y')$. Put $l(x_n, y_n^*, \boldsymbol{w}) := \left| \max_{y \in \mathcal{Y}_n^\circ} \left(\langle \boldsymbol{w}, \Phi(x, y) \rangle + \Delta(y_n, y) \right) - \max_{y \in \mathcal{Y}_n^*} \langle \boldsymbol{w}, \Phi(x, y) \rangle \right|_+$. Denote $\boldsymbol{w}^* \in \operatorname{argmin}_{\boldsymbol{w}:\|\boldsymbol{w}\| \leq \mu} \mathbb{E}[l(x, y, \boldsymbol{w})]$ and $\widehat{\boldsymbol{w}}_N \in \operatorname{argmin}_{\boldsymbol{w}:\|\boldsymbol{w}\| \leq \mu} \widehat{\mathbb{E}}[l(x, y, \boldsymbol{w})]$. Then, with probability at least $1 - \delta$, the generalization error of structured prediction with partially annotated outputs is bounded by:*

$$\mathbb{E}[l(x, y, \widehat{\boldsymbol{w}}_N)|D] - \mathbb{E}[l(x, y, \boldsymbol{w}^*)] \leq \frac{(\mu B + \Delta^{\max}) \left(8 |\mathcal{Y}^p| |\mathcal{Y}| + \sqrt{2 \log(2/\delta)} \right)}{\sqrt{N}}.$$

Due to the chapter space constraint, the detailed proof is available online at `http://raetschlab.org/suppl/mitbookstruct`. The proof follows similar ideas in multiclass classification (Koltchinskii and Panchenko, 2002). We observe that the bound depends quadratically on the size of the output space, which can be large and render the value of the bound high. For specific structures such as hidden Markov models, it might be possible to obtain a tighter bound (cf. Bakır et al., 2006, Chapter 11). The above bound establishes consistency in the sense that $\mathbb{E}[\widehat{\boldsymbol{w}}_N] - \mathbb{E}[\boldsymbol{w}^*] \to 0$, when $N \to \infty$. Another interesting question is whether the formulation fulfills consistency with respect to the discrete loss function Δ. Such an analysis was presented in McAllester and Keshet (2011), who showed asymptotic consistency of the update direction of a perception-like structured prediction algorithm. Whether such a result also holds for an analog perceptron-like algorithm using partially annotated labels is unknown at the present time.

12.3.5 Results

We use training data (DCellIQ from Li et al., 2010) and test data (Mitocheck from `www.mitocheck.org`) from two different labs for a realistic demonstration.

Firstly, on the running example, our structured learning from partial annotations is compared against bundle method for risk minimization (Lou and Hamprecht, 2011) using full annotations and structured perceptron with partial annotations (Fernandes and Brefeld, 2011). To make all experiments comparable, the same (training) precision (i.e., the approximation gap) (Teo et al., 2010) was used for bundle method and the method proposed here. The structured perceptron with partial annotations was trained until the task loss (i.e., the true loss $\Delta(\cdot, \cdot)$) became zero or stopped improving, using early stopping.

Figure 12.4 shows a comparison of the average test loss (specifically, the task loss $\Delta(\cdot, \cdot)$). Firstly, the tracking model trained using 25% partial annotation is comparable to a model training using fully annotated data. Secondly, the proposed method consistently outperforms the structured perceptron with partial annotation. We attribute this to the perceptron's lack of regularization and resulting overfitting. Figure 12.5 shows a comparison of training times. Once the proportion of partial annotation exceeds 20%, our method requires roughly twice as much time as the bundle method for risk minimization that is working on full annotations only. Training the structured perceptron appears to be more expensive.

Secondly, we compare our optimization strategy to the CCCP procedure from Yu and Joachims (2009), which does not use the bounds recycling and adaptive precision proposed here. We also study the effect of omitting either bounds recycling or/and adaptive precision. Figure 12.6 shows the convergence of the objective function. All optimization methods converge to the same objective value. Using both bounds recycling and adaptive precision, we achieve a speed-up of a factor of approximately 5. Note that we implemented Yu and Joachims (2009)'s CCCP procedure using the BMRM method (Teo et al., 2010) whose complexity $\mathcal{O}(\frac{1}{\epsilon})$ is actually better than that of the proximal bundle method used in the original paper, $\mathcal{O}(\frac{1}{\epsilon^3})$. Figure 12.7 shows the total number of bounds computed across the CCCP iterations. By using bounds recycling, our method only requires ca. 100 bounds until convergence, whereas Yu and Joachims (2009)'s approach computes almost 100 bounds at its first iteration.

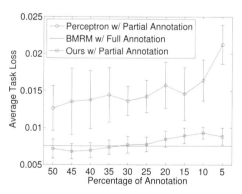

Figure 12.4: Comparison of average test loss. The model training using 25% partial annotation is comparable to a model training using fully annotated data.

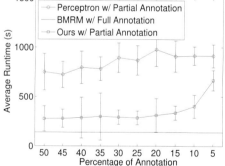

Figure 12.5: Comparison of training time. Training time is doubled compared with BMRM, yet this is much more affordable than the annotation cost.

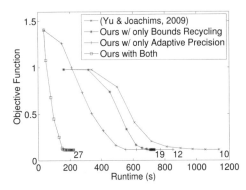 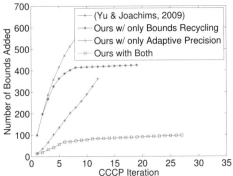

Figure 12.6: Decrease of the objective function. Using both bounds recycling and adaptive precision, we achieve a speed-up of a factor of approximately five compared to Yu and Joachims (2009).

Figure 12.7: Total number of bounds before convergence. We need ca. 100 bounds until convergence, whereas Yu and Joachims (2009) already computed almost 100 bounds at its first iteration.

12.4   Strategy II: Structured Data Retrieval via Active Learning

In the previous chapter, we described a strategy in which we can take advantage of partial annotation that is typically easier to obtain than a complete annotation. In many cases, the annotation is produced in a manual effort. This section describes an alternative strategy based on *active learning*, in which the annotator is guided through the data set and asked to label only specific parts. This can lead to significant reductions of the labeling efforts.

12.4.1   Motivation

The concept of active learning is to guide users to annotate samples that are pivotal to improving the predictor and avoid wasting efforts on already well-covered cases. One principled way is to estimate the uncertainty of each parameter in the model after structured learning and then identify that (part of a) training sample that will lead to the greatest reduction in uncertainty (Anderson and Moore, 2005). Unfortunately, such an endeavor is extremely costly (Krause and Guestrin, 2009) and not pursued here. Another good approach is to find that part of a training annotation whose inclusion in the training set minimizes the expected risk. Additional strategies of active learning for detecting rare positives were discussed (Warmuth et al., 2003). Even in unstructured prediction, such criteria are only tractable for specific classifiers such as Naive Bayes which allow efficient evaluation. In structured prediction, one possibility is to estimate the expected change of the predictions instead.

This section discusses a simple alternative, namely, to break the large training instances into parts (a violation of their structure) and then identify those parts that look most informative according to a variety of criteria. The parts selected by the algorithm can then be annotated by the human expert, added to the training set, and so on. Our method consists of the following core components: uncertainty measure, model update, and stopping criteria. In what follows, we elaborate on the details following the pseudo-code shown in Algorithm 12.2.

Algorithm 12.2 Active structured learning with perceptron

1:   **Input:** $\boldsymbol{D} \leftarrow \{x_n\}_{n \leftarrow 1}^{N}, \boldsymbol{w}, \hat{\eta}$
2:   Initialize $\boldsymbol{D}_{\mathrm{L}} \leftarrow \emptyset, \boldsymbol{D}_{\mathrm{U}} \leftarrow \boldsymbol{D}, t \leftarrow 1$
3:   **repeat**
4:       Find $\tilde{x} \leftarrow \arg\max_{x \in \boldsymbol{D}_{\mathrm{U}}} q(x, \boldsymbol{w})$
5:       Annotate $\tilde{y}^*$
6:       Set $\boldsymbol{D}_{\mathrm{U}} \leftarrow \boldsymbol{D}_{\mathrm{U}} \setminus \tilde{x}$
7:       Set $\boldsymbol{D}_{\mathrm{L}} \leftarrow \boldsymbol{D}_{\mathrm{L}} \cup \{(\tilde{x}, \tilde{y})\}$
8:       **for all** $(x, y^*) \in \boldsymbol{D}_{\mathrm{L}}$ **do**
9:           Compute the best assignment $\hat{y}$
10:          Update $\boldsymbol{w} \leftarrow \boldsymbol{w} + \Phi(x, y^*) - \Phi(x, \hat{y})$
11:      **end for**
12:      Compute average uncertainty $\bar{q}_t \leftarrow \dfrac{1}{|\boldsymbol{D}_{\mathrm{U}}|} \sum_{x \in \boldsymbol{D}_{\mathrm{U}}} q(x, \boldsymbol{w})$
13:      Compute convergence measure $\eta(\bar{q}_{t-T:t})$ according to (12.8)
14:      Set $t \leftarrow t + 1$
15: **until** $\eta(\bar{q}_{t-T:t}) \leq \hat{\eta}$ or $\boldsymbol{D}_{\mathrm{U}} \equiv \emptyset$
16: **Output:** $\boldsymbol{w}$

12.4.2   Algorithm

In this section, we will discuss the algorithmic aspects of our approach.

Firstly, proper means for measuring prediction uncertainty is vital to the uncertainty-based active learning framework (Settles, 2012). We propose to use four different uncertainty measures described in Table 12.2. They are direct extensions of uncertainty measures for flat data (Tong and Koller, 2002; Schohn and Cohn, 2000) to structured data as in this chapter. As lines 4–6 of Algorithm 12.2 shows, at each iteration, we find the most uncertain sample (i.e., pair of patches) from all unlabeled samples $\boldsymbol{D}_{\mathrm{U}}$ and demand annotation from the annotator. We will compare the learning curves of those uncertainty measures in Section 12.4.4.

Name	Formulation and Description
Random	$q(x, \boldsymbol{w}) \sim \mathrm{uniform}(0,1)$
Scoring	$q(x, \boldsymbol{w}) = \exp\left(-\max_{y \in \mathcal{Y}} \boldsymbol{w}' \Phi(x, y)\right)$
	Higher value of $\max_{y \in \mathcal{Y}} \boldsymbol{w}' \Phi(x, y)$ indicates higher confidence on the predicted tracking using existing parameter $\boldsymbol{w}$.
Best vs. Worst	$q(x, \boldsymbol{w}) = \exp\left(-\left(\max_{y \in \mathcal{Y}} \boldsymbol{w}' \Phi(x, y) - \min_{y \in \mathcal{Y}} \boldsymbol{w}' \Phi(x, y)\right)\right)$
	Larger margin between those two terms indicates higher confidence toward the best predicted tracking w.r.t the worst one.
Best vs. 2nd	$q(x, \boldsymbol{w}) = \exp\left(-\left(\max_{y \in \mathcal{Y}} \boldsymbol{w}' \Phi(x, y) - \max_{y \in \mathcal{Y}^{\circ}} \boldsymbol{w}' \Phi(x, y)\right)\right)$
	$\max_{y \in \mathcal{Y}^{\circ}} \boldsymbol{w}' \Phi(x, y)$ means computing the second best scoring and larger margin between those two terms indicates higher confidence toward the best predicted tracking w.r.t the second best one.

Table 12.2: List of uncertainty sampling strategy for comparison. *Random* assumes a uniform distribution of uncertainty on all samples. The rest are direct extensions of uncertain measures proposed in the literature on flat data (Tong and Koller, 2002; Schohn and Cohn, 2000).

Secondly, at each iteration, the model parameter $\boldsymbol{w}$ needs to be properly updated after receiving a newly annotated sample. Given a labeled training set $\boldsymbol{D}_{\mathrm{L}}$, a naïve way is to invoke max-margin structured learning from Section 12.2.3. However, this turns out to be inefficient in practice: max-margin structured learning is known to be expensive (Tsochantaridis et al., 2006), which means that the annotator has to wait a few minutes before proceeding to the next sample. Therefore, we resort to structured perceptron (Collins, 2002) for a model update (Algorithm 12.2, line 8–11). Briefly, it makes a one-pass run through all labeled samples and updates the parameter by incrementally (and locally) adding the gradient (i.e., $\boldsymbol{w} = \boldsymbol{w} + \partial_{\boldsymbol{w}} \left(L(x, y^*; \boldsymbol{w}) - L(x, \hat{y}; \boldsymbol{w})\right)$) (equivalent to line 10).

Thirdly, to decide when to terminate the entire active learning iteration, we chose a popular measure proposed in Vlachos (2008) — the average uncertainty over all remaining unlabeled samples (cf. Table 12.2). This does not require any holdout validation data set. At iteration t, given a sequence of computed average uncertainty $\bar{q}_{t-T:t}$ (incl. previous ones), we compute the convergence measure η from Laws and Schätze (2008) (Algorithm 12.2, lines 12–13) using

$$\eta(\bar{q}_{1:T+1}) = |\widehat{\mathrm{mean}}(\bar{q}_{2:T+1}) - \widehat{\mathrm{mean}}(\bar{q}_{1:T})|, \tag{12.8}$$

where $\widehat{\text{mean}}(\cdot)$ is the robust mean (i.e., mean of the elements within the 10% and 90% quantile). This convergence measure drops low when the improvement on average uncertainty remains minor for several iterations. We stop the active learning when the convergence measure is below a given threshold or all samples are labeled (line 15, Algorithm 12.2).

Finally, we propose a *combined* learning strategy. Although gaining speed, using structured perceptron for model update has two drawbacks: lack of regularization and local (thus noisy) gradient update (Algorithm 12.2, line 10). This makes the learned model prone to overfitting and also unstable in convergence. Therefore, in practice, we use a combined approach: we use active structured perceptron *only* for training data retrieval, and, after its convergence, we use max-margin structured learning to obtain a regularized and globally optimized model. It is also possible to call max-margin training multiple times during the active learning procedure, which is in spirit related to the hybrid training procedure in the latent-SVM (LA-SVM) (Bordes et al., 2005).

12.4.3 Complexity Analysis

Assuming a pool of N unannotated samples, the complexity of the proposed Algorithm 12.2 is $\mathcal{O}(N^2)$, whereas the complexity of using dual max-margin structured learning for model update is at least $\mathcal{O}(N^3)$.

In Algorithm 12.2, at iteration t $(1 \leq t \leq N)$, we need N predictions in total, among which $N - t$ predictions are for uncertainty estimation on unlabeled samples (line 4) and the rest t for model update using the newly labeled sample (lines 8–11). This gives $t \cdot N$ predictions overall after t iterations. Because t is a fraction of N, the overall complexity is $\mathcal{O}(N^2)$.

In the case of dual max-margin structured learning (cf. Section 12.2.3), for a model update, Bottou (2007) shows that, in the dual SVM (and max-margin structured learning), the number of support vectors scales at least linearly with the number of training samples. Thus, the complexity of max-margin structured learning using the dual is at least quadratic because we need to compute the inner-product of each support vector and each sample. The complexity is at least $\sum_t \left[(N - t) + t^2 \right]$, which amounts to $\mathcal{O}(N^3)$.

12.4.4 Results

We train on the DCellIQ data set from Li et al. (2010) and test on the Mitocheck data set. We first applied patchification on the training data (DCellIQ), namely, a pair of full images is divided into pairs of local patches used for training. We consider patchification a necessary and viable pre-processing step for active learning. Otherwise, annotating a single sample with many patches is already too tedious and time-consuming, and part of the effort is wasted on similar and repeated event patterns.

We first evaluate the uncertainty measures and stopping criteria. Using 660 patchified training samples from the DCellIQ data set, in Figure 12.8, we compare the learning curves (i.e., average uncertainty) of the four uncertainty measures up to 50% of the total training samples. *Best vs. Worst* is stably converging at the beginning but has a second wave of significant changes after 16% of total training samples. The same applies to *Scoring* but the changes of average uncertainty are more drastic. *Best vs. 2nd* appears to be the best performing one: it converges to a stable state after 17% of total training samples.

Regarding stopping criteria, *Random* is excluded because it is not suitable for the uncertainty convergence measure η according to (12.8). To compute η, we chose $T = 80$ and used 10^{-4} as the stopping threshold. As the embedded figure in Fig. 12.8 shows, they all stop at around 17% of training data.

To further understand the learning curve in a practical setting, we evaluated all intermediate $\boldsymbol{w}$ by the active learning on the test data, respectively, for all uncertainty measures. The result in Figure 12.9 further supports our choice of *Best 2nd* not only because of its superiority in stability but also because of its lower test error.

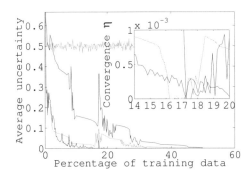

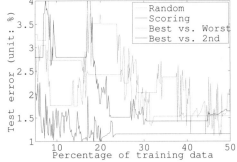

Figure 12.8: Comparison of uncertainty measures: average uncertainty *vs.* percentage of training data. The embedded figure shows the uncertainty convergence η *vs.* the percentage of training data.

Figure 12.9: Comparison of uncertainty measure: test error *vs.* percentage of training data. *Best vs. 2nd* shows superior performance in terms of convergence speed and stability.

Regarding practical run time, using the structured perceptron for model update yields pleasant run time. Across iterations, it requires (stably) less than nine seconds to perform model update and uncertainty computation.

Pct. of Training Data	17%		30%		40%	
Active or Combined Learning	AL	CL	AL	CL	AL	CL
Random	1.77	1.66	2.14	1.53	2.43	1.31
Scoring	3.72	1.78	2.79	1.73	1.80	1.11
Best vs. Worst	2.73	2.23	2.73	3.06	3.72	1.36
Best vs. 2nd	1.33	**1.08**	1.26	1.06	1.29	1.09
Baseline	1.07					

Table 12.3: Comparison of average test loss between active learning (AL) and combined learning (CL) on different percentages of training data. Among those uncertainty measures, *Best vs. 2nd* reaches a performance comparable to the baseline method (trained on all data) using 17% of the entire training data. The unit of the average loss is %.

We consider this a tolerable delay for interactive labeling. Note that this run time is dependent on the hardware specification of the computer because the underlying solver CPLEX can run the branch-and-bound ILP algorithm in parallel. We used a 2.40 GHz Intel Xeon machine with 12 cores.

Finally, Table 12.3 shows the result of the proposed combined learning (CL) strategy, using 17% (i.e., the stopping point by the convergence measure) and 30% and 40% of training samples, compared against the active learning (AL) output. This affords the following observations. Firstly, using the same amount of training samples, regularized max-margin learning generally improves the output of active learning. Secondly, *Best vs. 2nd* performs better than the rest uncertainty measures. Finally (and most importantly), using *Best vs. 2nd* as an uncertainty measure and using only 17% of the training samples, we can train a tracking model as competent as the baseline model learned from all samples (*baseline* in Table 12.3).

12.5 Strategy III: Structured Transfer Learning

12.5.1 Motivation

The previous strategies are designated for settings in which one has to construct training data completely from scratch. This section focuses on a different setting in which rich annotations are available for some datasets while we need to analyze another one that is different yet closely related. Typical examples include machine translation across similar languages and experimental data analysis with varying experimental conditions. Intuitively, we can reduce the extra effort on annotating the new data set by exploiting its connection to those well-annotated data sets. Such problems fall into the category of *transfer learning* which in essence is an embodiment of the notion "extra data for better regularization." This section presents an extension of transfer learning to structured data.

Transfer learning (Caruana, 1997; Evgeniou and Pontil, 2006) has been successfully applied to many real-world problems, such as sequence labeling in NLP (Pan and Yang, 2010) and mRNA splicing site recognition in computational biology (Schweikert et al., 2008). For the particular case of structured data, Görnitz et al. (2011) considered transfer learning for hierarchical tasks for gene finding across species.

12.5.2 Formulation

Formally, we want to jointly learn from D data sets $\{\boldsymbol{D}^1, \ldots, \boldsymbol{D}^D\}$, where $\boldsymbol{D}^d = \{(x_n, y_n^{*d})\}_{n \in [N^d]}, d \in [D]$. A naïve approach is to train on the union of all data sets, which is referred to as *Union*. Obviously, the *Union* formulation treat all data sets *identically*, and the learning objective is to achieve a balanced performance over all data sets. This may help but is limited, particularly regarding the fact that data sets are not likely identical. To this end, we propose a second strategy that drops this condition:

$$\min_{\substack{\boldsymbol{w}, \boldsymbol{w}^1, \boldsymbol{w}^2, \ldots \\ \boldsymbol{\xi}^1, \boldsymbol{\xi}^2, \ldots}} \quad \frac{\lambda}{2}\|\boldsymbol{w}\|^2 + \frac{\rho}{2}\sum_{d=1}^{D}\|\boldsymbol{w}^d - \boldsymbol{w}\|^2 + \sum_{d=1}^{D}\sum_{n=1}^{N^d}\xi_n^d \qquad (12.9)$$

$$\text{s.t.}$$

$$\forall n \in [N^1], \forall y \in \boldsymbol{\mathcal{Y}}_n^1, \langle \Psi(x_n^1, y_n^{*1}, y), \boldsymbol{w}^1 \rangle \geq \Delta(y_n^{*1}, y) - \xi_n^1$$

$$\vdots$$

$$\forall n \in [N^D], \forall y \in \boldsymbol{\mathcal{Y}}_n^D, \langle \Psi(x_n^D, y_n^{*D}, y), \boldsymbol{w}^D \rangle \geq \Delta(y_n^{*D}, y) - \xi_n^D$$

As (12.9) shows, we first regularize each data set d using separate parameter vector $\boldsymbol{w}^d$ (left term). This avoids the "averaging" effect in *Union*. Secondly, to still encode similarity between data sets, we add the middle regularization term that penalizes the difference between $\boldsymbol{w}^d$ and the shared component $\boldsymbol{w}$. The overall contribution of the middle term is controlled by ρ. After all, we introduced a higher degree of freedom to the model that allows to capture the similarity between data sets while respecting their distinction.

The optimization formulation stated in (12.9) is quite generic and resembles several different strategies when parametrized accordingly. When $\rho = 0$, each $\boldsymbol{w}^d$ is learned for data set d independently, which means no learning transferred across data sets. When $\rho = \infty$, all $\boldsymbol{w}^d$ are forced to be identical to each other, which exactly leads to *Union*.

12.5.3 Optimization

For the *union*, the learning objective can be solved using the bundle method (cf. Section 12.2.3). For the more complicated *transfer learning*, we provide an extension of the bundle method (Teo et al., 2010). Briefly, like in max-margin structured learning, we iteratively construct piece-wise linear lower bounds for the empirical loss, respectively, for each data set (i.e., domain). This leads to the following update rule for $\boldsymbol{w}$:

$$\min_{\boldsymbol{w},\boldsymbol{w}^1,\boldsymbol{w}^2,\ldots} \frac{\lambda}{2}\|\boldsymbol{w}\|^2 + \frac{\rho}{2}\sum_{d=1}^{D}\|\boldsymbol{w}^d - \boldsymbol{w}\|^2 + \sum_{d=1}^{D}\max_{(a,b)\in(\boldsymbol{A}^d,\boldsymbol{b}^d)}\{\langle \boldsymbol{a}, \boldsymbol{w}^d\rangle + b\},$$

where $(\boldsymbol{A}^d, \boldsymbol{b}^d)$ denote the set of gradients and offsets that form the linear lower bounds for the empirical loss of domain d.

Using Lagrange multipliers, we can eventually obtain the dual form for the above formulation:

$$\max_{\boldsymbol{\alpha}^1,\boldsymbol{\alpha}^2,\ldots} \quad -\frac{1}{2}\begin{bmatrix}\boldsymbol{\alpha}^1\\\vdots\\\boldsymbol{\alpha}^D\end{bmatrix}'\begin{bmatrix}\frac{1}{\tau}\boldsymbol{Q}^{11} & \cdots & \frac{1}{\lambda}\boldsymbol{Q}^{1D}\\\vdots & \vdots & \vdots\\\frac{1}{\lambda}\boldsymbol{Q}^{D1} & \cdots & \frac{1}{\tau}\boldsymbol{Q}^{DD}\end{bmatrix}\begin{bmatrix}\boldsymbol{\alpha}^1\\\vdots\\\boldsymbol{\alpha}^D\end{bmatrix} + \begin{bmatrix}\boldsymbol{b}^1\\\vdots\\\boldsymbol{b}^2\end{bmatrix}'\begin{bmatrix}\boldsymbol{\alpha}^1\\\vdots\\\boldsymbol{\alpha}^D\end{bmatrix}$$

$$\text{s.t.} \qquad \forall d \in 1,\ldots,D, \|\boldsymbol{\alpha}^d\|_1 \leq 1 \text{ and } \boldsymbol{\alpha}^d \geq 0.$$

Here, $\boldsymbol{Q}^{ij} = (\boldsymbol{A}^i)'\boldsymbol{A}^j$ and $\tau = \frac{\rho\lambda}{\rho+\lambda}$. Furthermore, the primal and dual variables are connected by

$$\boldsymbol{w} = -\frac{1}{\lambda}\sum_{d=1}^{D}\boldsymbol{A}^d\boldsymbol{\alpha}^d \text{ and } \boldsymbol{w}^d = \boldsymbol{w} - \frac{1}{\rho}\boldsymbol{A}^d\boldsymbol{\alpha}^d, \forall d \in 1,\ldots,D. \qquad (12.10)$$

Note that, similar to (12.7), the variable $\boldsymbol{A}^d$ and $\boldsymbol{b}^d$ in the above optimization formulation are also the matrix/vector representation of the set of gradients/offsets, respectively.

12.5.4 Results

We experimented on the same DCellIQ and Mitocheck data set. Our objective was to leverage the fully annotated DCellIQ data (e.g., *source*, 1188 samples) to ease the training of a model for the Mitocheck data (e.g., *target*, assumed newly acquired and lacking annotation, 2166 samples for training). The test data derive from a hold-out data set sampled from Mitocheck

(2165 samples). We compared five different learning strategies as given in Table 12.4. As Figure 12.10 shows, when annotation in the target increases, *Transfer* converges to the baseline strategy (*All Target*) faster than the rest methods and achieved a comparable performance at 20% target annotation. Afterwards *Transfer* shows similar performance to *Union*, and they both outperform *All Target* after adding 30% target annotation, which is an indication of the advantage of leveraging extra data for better regularization.

Strategy	**Formulation**	**Parameters**	**Trained on**
All Source	BMRM	$\lambda = 1$	All DCellIQ
All Target	BMRM	$\lambda = 1$	All Mitocheck
Partial Target	BMRM	$\lambda = 2.5$	Partial Mitocheck
Union	BMRM	$\lambda = 1$	All DCellIQ & partial Mitocheck
Transfer	(12.9)	$\lambda = 0.5, \rho = 2.5$	All DCellIQ & partial Mitocheck

Table 12.4: Comparison of learning strategies – Unit %. The approximate gap parameter ϵ (see Teo et al., 2010) is set to 10^{-2} throughout all strategies. The other parameters are selected using cross-validation.

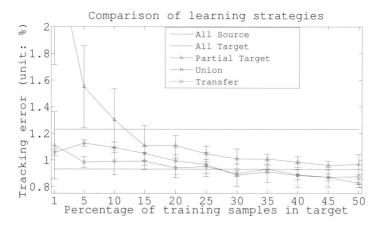

Figure 12.10: Comparison of learning strategies listed in Table 12.4. *Transfer* converges to the baseline strategy (*All Target*) faster than the rest methods and achieved a comparable performance at 20% target annotation.

12.6   Discussion and Conclusions

We have explored three different approaches for training structured prediction models with significant less annotations while maintaining a similar generalization performance.

We have proposed and theoretically as well as experimentally analyzed a method for structured output learning based on partial annotations. In many cases, it is much easier to annotate only a part of an image or a sequence or to provide incomplete information about the structure. We proposed a novel algorithm based on bundle methods for solving a CCCP problem. Theoretically, we have shown that the proposed algorithm is consistent, and we provided its generalization bound. Our experimental results show that we only need a tiny fraction (approximately 5%) of the complete label information to achieve almost the same generalization performance as with full labels.

We have described and proposed two additional strategies for the same purpose. First, we considered a hybrid active learning strategy in which the algorithm quickly performs prediction and estimates its prediction uncertainty of many yet unlabeled patches. The annotator then iteratively labels the most uncertain patches. We have analyzed a few estimators for uncertainty and have shown that the *Best vs. 2nd* best predictor performs best in our experiments. With less then 10% of the labeled training data, the active learning algorithm predicts almost as well as with the full training data. We have also shown work on using transfer learning to reuse model information from prior experiments to train more accurate models with limited information in a new setting. Again with only approximately 5% of the data in the target domain, the accuracy is almost as good as with all data.

Depending on the prediction problem at hand and the specific difficulties of obtaining annotation data, different combinations of the presented and above-mentioned methods will lead to the best results. What we have described is a set of essentially orthogonal strategies of how to deal with costly annotations in practice.

12.7   References

B. Anderson and A. Moore. Active learning for hidden markov models: Objective functions and algorithms. In *International Conference on Machine Learning (ICML)*, 2005.

G. Bakır, T. Hofmann, B. Schölkopf, A. J. Smola, B. Taskar, and S. Vishwanathan. *Predicting Structured Data*. MIT Press, 2006.

A. Bordes, S. Ertekin, J. Weston, and L. Bottou. Fast kernel classifiers with online and active learning. *Journal of Machine Learning Research*, 6:1579–1619, 2005.

L. Bottou. *Large-Scale Kernel Machines*. The MIT Press, 2007.

R. Caruana. Multitask learning. *Machine Learning*, 28:41–75, 1997.

M. Collins. Discriminative training methods for hidden markov models: Theory and experiments with perceptron algorithms. In *Meeting of the Association for Computational Linguistics (ACL)*, 2002.

T. Cour, B. Sapp, and B. Taskar. Learning from partial labels. *Journal of Machine Learning Research*, 12:1225–1261, 2011.

T.-M.-T. Do and T. Artieres. Regularized bundle methods for convex and non-convex risks. *Journal of Machine Learning Research*, 2012.

A. A. T. Evgeniou and M. Pontil. Multi-task feature learning. In *Neural Information Processing Systems (NIPS)*, 2006.

E. Fernandes and U. Brefeld. Learning from partially annotated sequences. In *European Conference on Machine Learning (ECML)*, 2011.

N. Görnitz, C. Widmer, G. Zeller, A. Kahles, S. Sonnenburg, and G. Rätsch. Hierarchical multitask structured output learning for large-scale sequence segmentation. In *Advances in Neural Information Processing Systems*, 2011.

R. Jin and Z. Ghahramani. Learning with multiple labels. In *Neural Information Processing Systems (NIPS)*, 2002.

T. Joachims, T. Finley, and C.-N. Yu. Cutting-plane training of structural svms. *Machine Learning*, 77(1):27–59, 2009.

V. Koltchinskii and D. Panchenko. Empirical margin distributions and bounding the generalization error of combined classifiers. *Annals of Statistics*, 30(1):1–50, 2002.

A. Krause and C. Guestrin. Optimal value of information in graphical models. *Journal of Artificial Intelligence Research*, 35:557–591, 2009.

F. R. Kschischang, B. J. Frey, and H. A. Loeliger. Factor graphs and the sum-product algorithm. *IEEE Transactions on Information Theory*, 47(2):498–519, 2001.

F. Laws and H. Schätze. Stopping criteria for active learning of named entity recognition. In *International Conference on Computational Linguistics (COLING)*, 2008.

F. Li, X. Zhou, J. Ma, and S. Wong. Multiple nuclei tracking using integer programming for quantitative cancer cell cycle analysis. *IEEE Transactions on Medical Imaging*, 29(1):96, 2010.

X. Lou and F. A. Hamprecht. Structured learning for cell tracking. In *Neural Information Processing Systems (NIPS)*, 2011.

X. Lou and F. A. Hamprecht. Structured learning from partial annotations. In *International Conference on Machine Learning (ICML)*, 2012.

X. Lou, F. O. Kaster, et al. DELTR: Digital Embryo Lineage Tree Reconstructor. In *IEEE International Symposium on Biomedical Imaging: From Nano to Macro (ISBI)*, 2011.

D. McAllester and J. Keshet. Generalization bounds and consistency for latent structural probit and ramp loss. In *Neural Information Processing Systems (NIPS)*, 2011.

E. Meijering, O. Dzyubachyk, I. Smal, and W. A. van Cappellen. Tracking in cell and developmental biology. *Seminars in Cell & Developmental Biology*, 20(8): 894–902, 2009.

D. Padfield, J. Rittscher, and B. Roysam. Coupled minimum-cost flow cell tracking for high-throughput quantitative analysis. *Medical Image Analysis*, 15(4):650–668, 2011.

S. J. Pan and Q. Yang. A survey on transfer learning. *IEEE Transactions on Knowledge and Data Engineering*, 22(10):1345–1359, 2010.

G. Rätsch, A. Demiriz, and K. Bennett. Sparse regression ensembles in infinite and finite hypothesis spaces. *Machine Learning*, 48(1-3):189–218, 2002.

G. Schohn and D. Cohn. Less is more: Active learning with support vector machines. In *International Conference on Machine Learning (ICML)*, 2000.

G. Schweikert, C. Widmer, B. Schölkopf, and G. Rätsch. An empirical analysis of domain adaptation algorithms for genomic sequence analysis. In *Advances in Neural Information Processing Systems (NIPS)*, 2008.

B. Settles. *Active Learning*. Morgan & Claypool, 2012.

B. Taskar, C. Guestrin, and D. Koller. Max-margin markov networks. In *Neural Information Processing Systems (NIPS)*, 2003.

C. H. Teo, S. V. N. Vishwanthan, A. J. Smola, and Q. V. Le. Bundle methods for regularized risk minimization. *Journal of Machine Learning Research*, 11: 311–365, 2010.

S. Tong and D. Koller. Support vector machine active learning with applications to text classification. *The Journal of Machine Learning Research*, 2:45–66, 2002.

I. Tsochantaridis, T. Joachims, T. Hofmann, and Y. Altun. Large Margin Methods for Structured and Interdependent Output Variables. *Journal of Machine Learning Research*, 6(2):1453, 2006.

A. Vlachos. A stopping criterion for active learning. *Computer Speech & Language*, 22(3):295–312, 2008.

M. Warmuth, G. Rätsch, M. Mathieson, J. Liao, and C. Lemmen. Active learning in the drug discovery process. In *Advances in Neural Information Processing Systes (NIPS)*, 2003.

C. N. J. Yu and T. Joachims. Learning structural svms with latent variables. In *International Conference on Machine Learning (ICML)*, 2009.

A. L. Yuille and A. Rangarajan. The concave-convex procedure. *Neural Computation*, 15(4):915–936, 2003.

T. Zhang. Statistical analysis of some multi-category large margin classification methods. *Journal of Machine Learning Research*, 5:1225–1251, 2004.

A. Zien, U. Brefeld, and T. Scheffer. Transductive support vector machines for structured variables. In *International Conference on Machine Learning (ICML)*, 2007.

13   Dynamic Structured Model Selection

David Weiss   djweiss@cis.upenn.edu
University of Pennsylvania
Philadelphia, PA

Ben Taskar   taskar@cs.washington.edu
University of Washington
Seattle, WA

In many applications of structured prediction, feature extraction—rather than inference—takes up the bulk of computation time. In this chapter, we investigate methods for learning to allocate feature extraction computation adaptively at test time.

13.1   Introduction

Effective models in complex computer vision and natural language problems try to strike a favorable balance between accuracy and speed of prediction. One source of computational cost is inference in the model, which can be addressed with a variety of approximate inference methods. However, in many applications, computing the scores of the constituent parts of the structured model (i.e., *feature computation*) is the primary bottleneck. For example, when tracking articulated objects in video, optical flow is an informative feature that often requires many seconds of computation time per frame, whereas inference for an entire sequence typically requires only fractions of a second per frame (Sapp et al., 2011).

In this chapter, we show that large gains in the speed/accuracy trade-off can be obtained by departing from the traditional "one-size-fits-all" model and feature selection, in which a static set of features are computed for all inputs uniformly. Instead, we employ an *adaptive* approach: we select a structured model at test time specifically for each particular instance. This model can be constructed in a piece-wise fashion, for example, at the level of individual video frames. There are several key distinctions of this approach.

No generative model. One approach to feature selection is to assume a joint probabilistic model of the input and output variables and a utility function measuring payoffs. The expected value of information measures the increase in expected utility after observing a given variable (Lindley, 1956; Howard, 1966). Unfortunately, the problem of computing optimal conditional observation plans is computationally intractable even for simple graphical models like Naive Bayes (Krause and Guestrin, 2009). Moreover, assuming and learning a joint model of input and output is typically quite inferior to discriminative models of output given input (Lafferty et al., 2001; Collins, 2002; Taskar et al., 2003; Altun et al., 2003).

Richly parametrized, conditional value function. The central component of our method is an approximate value function that utilizes a set of *meta-features* to estimate future changes in value of information given a predictive model and a proposed feature set as input. The critical advantage here is that the meta-features can incorporate valuable properties beyond confidence scores from the predictive model, such as long-range input-dependent cues that convey information about the self-consistency of a proposed output.

Non-myopic reinforcement learning. We frame the control problem in terms of finding a *feature extraction policy* that sequentially adds features to the models until a budget limit is reached, and we show how to learn approximate policies that result in accurate structured models that are dramatically more efficient. Specifically, we learn to weigh the meta-features for the value function using linear function approximation techniques from reinforcement learning, where we utilize a deterministic model that can be approximately solved with a simple and effective sampling scheme.

In particular, we describe a two-tier architecture that provides dynamic speed versus accuracy trade-offs through a simple type of *introspection*. The key idea is a division of labor between a hierarchy of models/inference algorithms (tier one) and meta-level model selector (tier two), which decides when to use expensive models adaptively, where they are most likely to improve the accuracy of predictions. The two tiers have complementary strengths: Tier one models provide increasingly accurate and more expensive inference over structured outputs. Tier two model selectors use arbitrary sparsely computed features and long-range dependencies, which would make inference intractable, to evaluate the outputs of the first tier and decide when to stop. While the first tier optimizes over a combinatorial set of possibilities using inference over densely computed features, the second tier simply evaluates proposals of the first. The advantage of this division is that both tiers are efficient, and the second tier has more information than the first that allows it to reason about the success of the first. This approach is called *Dynamic Structured Model Selection* (DMS).

We describe two versions of this two-tier framework. The first is based on a simple goal: at test time, we selectively apply different models to different examples. Each model is pre-trained off-line and utilizes its own set of features and inference algorithm. Given a batch of test examples, we wish to allocate models to examples in order to maximize accuracy within an overall budget constraint. The DMS approach is to learn a selector that estimates the change in error rate when switching from one model to the next; we allocate budget according to priority determined by these estimated improvements in error rate. In the articulated pose tracking application, applying DMS in this way corresponds to making feature and modeling decisions at the level of individual videos and empirically yields improvements in efficiency with little or no cost to accuracy.

However, one might expect to achieve even greater efficiency on the same problem by reasoning about features at the level of individual frames, and this motivates further development of the DMS approach in subsequent sections. Continuing with the same basic framework—estimating the change in error rate as more features are added—we assume the model hierarchy uses increasingly expensive feature sets within a single unified graph structure. We then pose the problem of feature extraction for edges and nodes in the graph as a reinforcement learning problem. Rather than choose a model *selector*, we non-myopically learn a feature extraction *policy* π that allocates computation to specific unary or pairwise terms within individual examples. The resulting approach is known as DMS-π and yields significant improvements compared with the baselines and the basic DMS approach.

13.1.1   Problem Setting: Structured Prediction

We now briefly review the notation and setting used in this chapter. We consider the problem of *structured prediction*, in which our goal is to learn a hypothesis mapping inputs $\boldsymbol{x} \in \mathcal{X}$ to outputs $\boldsymbol{y} \in \mathcal{Y}(\boldsymbol{x})$, where $|\boldsymbol{x}| = \ell$ and $\boldsymbol{y}$ is a ℓ-vector of K-valued variables (i.e., $\mathcal{Y}(\boldsymbol{x}) = \mathcal{Y}_1 \times \cdots \times \mathcal{Y}_\ell$ and each $\mathcal{Y}_i = \{1, \ldots, K\}$). We consider linear hypotheses of the form

$$h(\boldsymbol{x}; \boldsymbol{w}) = \operatorname*{argmax}_{\boldsymbol{y} \in \mathcal{Y}(\boldsymbol{x})} \psi_{\boldsymbol{w}}(\boldsymbol{x}, \boldsymbol{y}), \tag{13.1}$$

Algorithm 13.1 Dynamic structured model selection (DMS)

1:   Given a test set $\{\boldsymbol{x}^j\}_1^n$ and budget B
2:   Let $B' \leftarrow 0$, $\tau_j \leftarrow 1$, $\boldsymbol{y}^j \leftarrow h_1(\boldsymbol{x}^j)$
3:   Initialize priority queue Q with priority-value pairs $\langle \nu(h_2, \boldsymbol{x}^j), j \rangle$
4:   **while** $B' < B$ and Q is not empty **do**
5:       Pop value j from Q with max priority
6:       **if** $c_{\tau_j+1} \leq (B - B')$ **then**
7:           $\tau_j \leftarrow \tau_j + 1$, $B' \leftarrow B' + c_{\tau_j}$
8:           $\boldsymbol{y}^j \leftarrow h_{\tau_j}(\boldsymbol{x})$
9:           Insert $\langle \nu(h_{\tau_j+1}, \boldsymbol{x}^j), j \rangle$ into Q
10:      **end if**
11: **end while**

---

where $\psi_{\boldsymbol{w}} = \boldsymbol{f}(\boldsymbol{x}, \boldsymbol{y}) \cdot \boldsymbol{w}$ is a linear scoring function of a weight vector $\boldsymbol{w}$ and feature vector $\boldsymbol{f}(\boldsymbol{x}, \boldsymbol{y})$. Note that because there are exponentially many $\boldsymbol{y} \in \mathcal{Y}(\boldsymbol{x})$, in order for the inference problem (13.1) to be computationally feasible, we assume $\boldsymbol{f}$ is decomposed into a piece-wise sum over *unary* and *pairwise* terms:

$$\boldsymbol{f}(\boldsymbol{x}, \boldsymbol{y}) = \sum_{i=1}^{\ell} \boldsymbol{f}_u(\boldsymbol{x}, y_i) + \sum_{(i,j) \in \mathcal{E}} \boldsymbol{f}_e(\boldsymbol{x}, y_i, y_j) \tag{13.2}$$

where $\mathcal{E}$ is a set of edges linking variables (i, j) for each $(i, j) \in \mathcal{E}$. In this chapter, we will assume a tree structure for $\mathcal{E}$ so that standard dynamic programming (message-passing; e.g., Koller and Friedman (2009)) will suffice for inference.

We learn models using the standard structured max-margin framework (Taskar et al., 2005). Given a set of n training pairs $\{(\boldsymbol{x}^j, \boldsymbol{y}^j)\}_{j=1}^n$, we learn $\boldsymbol{w}$ by minimizing the following structured max margin objective,

$$\min_{\boldsymbol{w}} \frac{\lambda}{2} \|\boldsymbol{w}\|_2^2 + \frac{1}{n} \sum_{j=1}^{n} \max_{\boldsymbol{y}} \left[\psi_{\boldsymbol{w}}(\boldsymbol{x}^j, \boldsymbol{y}) + \Delta(\boldsymbol{y}^j, \boldsymbol{y}) - \psi_{\boldsymbol{w}}(\boldsymbol{x}^j, \boldsymbol{y}^j) \right], \tag{13.3}$$

where the latter term in (13.3) is the standard structured Hinge loss on the jth example. In our applications, we set $\Delta(\boldsymbol{y}, \boldsymbol{y}')$ to be the Hamming loss to measure distance between two sequences.

13.2   Meta-Learning a Myopic Value-Based Selector

In this section, we introduce our approach to dynamic model selection and provide an overview of the algorithm. The core idea behind our approach is simple: we learn to predict the *value* of choosing a more expensive model over a cheaper one using introspective *meta-features*, and we use these predicted values to allocate computational resources at test time. In this fashion, we only apply the computationally expensive models to those examples where we will receive the most benefit.

For the dynamic model selection problem we consider here, we assume that we are given a *set* of models, $h_1, \ldots, h_T$, that require some amortized cost $c_1, \ldots, c_T$ to evaluate on any given example $\boldsymbol{x}$. Given a fixed ordering of the models, we define the *value* of evaluating model h_i on example $\boldsymbol{x}$,

$$V(h_i, \boldsymbol{x}, \boldsymbol{y}) = \mathcal{L}(h_{i-1}(\boldsymbol{x}), \boldsymbol{y}) - \mathcal{L}(h_i(\boldsymbol{x}), \boldsymbol{y}), \tag{13.4}$$

where $\mathcal{L}(\boldsymbol{y}, \boldsymbol{y}')$ is a non-negative loss function. Note that a positive value signifies a decrease in loss, whereas a negative value signifies an increase is loss. (While more expensive models usually increase accuracy on *average*, in practice we find that there are many examples where the more expensive features hurt performance.) Furthermore, this definition is *myopic*—it takes into account only one selection step regardless of how much budget remains in the inference process. Nonetheless, our proposed goal for meta-learning is to learn a *selector* $\nu(h_i, \boldsymbol{x})$ to approximate this value function.

Given a set of pre-trained models $h_1, \ldots, h_T$, a selector ν, and a test set $\{\boldsymbol{x}^1, \ldots, \boldsymbol{x}^n\}$, we perform inference using Algorithm 13.1. The algorithm is simple: we greedily optimize the total predicted value,

$$J(\tau_1, \ldots, \tau_n, \eta) = \sum_{j=1}^{n} \sum_{i=1}^{\tau_j} \nu(h_i, \boldsymbol{x}^j), \tag{13.5}$$

where τ_j is the stopping point on the jth example. This can be implemented easily using a single priority queue. The value for selecting the next model for each example is put in the queue, and resources are allocated by repeatedly extracting the highest value element from the queue and computing the next model's predictions to update the value. Note that even if all predicted $\nu(h_i, \boldsymbol{x}^j)$ are negative, Algorithm 13.1 continues to greedily choose more expensive models as long as budget is available.

13.2.1   Learning the Selector

For Algorithm 13.1 to succeed, the selector ν must provide a useful estimate of the value V. We formulate the selector as a linear function of *meta-features* computed on the output of the models. The key idea is that, while the feature generating function $\boldsymbol{f}$ for a structured prediction model decomposes over subsets of $\boldsymbol{y}$ in order to maintain feasible inference, the meta-features ϕ need only be computed efficiently for the specific outputs $h_1(\boldsymbol{x})$ through $h_{i-1}(\boldsymbol{x})$.

We provide detail on the specific meta-features used in each application in Section 13.3.

We learn the selector by learning a weight vector β to approximate the value function. On the training set, we first compute the value for every model on every training example. We then minimize the following ℓ_2-regularized squared loss over a training set,

$$\frac{\lambda}{2}\|\beta\|_2^2 + \sum_{i=1}^{m}\sum_{j=1}^{n}\left(V(h_i, \boldsymbol{x}^j, \boldsymbol{y}^j) - \beta^\top \phi(\boldsymbol{x}^j, h_{1:i-1})\right)^2, \tag{13.6}$$

where the function ϕ is a function generating *meta-features* that takes all predictions $h_1, \ldots, h_{i-1}$ as input and λ is a regularization parameter chosen via cross-validation.

Some care is needed when learning the selector in order to avoid re-using the same training set for learning both the models and the selector (i.e., if h_i was trained on example $(\boldsymbol{x}^j, \boldsymbol{y}^j)$, we expect $\mathcal{L}(h_i(\boldsymbol{x}^j), \boldsymbol{y}^j)$ to be unrealistically low, and thus the value may be unrepresentative of the test distribution). However, a simple N-fold cross-validation scheme suffices to prevent this. We train N different models $h_i^1, \ldots, h_i^N$ in the standard way and use the model not trained on example j when evaluating (13.6).

13.3   Applications to Sequential Prediction

In the next sections, we discuss two applications of Algorithm 13.1 to computer vision problems: handwriting recognition and human pose estimation from two-dimensional video. In both settings, DMS provides a far more efficient structured prediction model.

13.3.1   Linear-Chain Model

In both settings, we use the standard linear-chain model for structured prediction. Given an input $\boldsymbol{x}$ of length ℓ, we wish to predict a sequence of discrete K-valued outputs $y_1, \ldots, y_\ell$, where $y_i \in \{1, \ldots, K\}$. For the handwriting recognition problem, each y_i corresponds to one letter of the written word; for human pose estimation, each y_i corresponds to one of K possible predicted poses. For any given sequence $y_1, \ldots, y_\ell$, the combined score of the sequence is the sum of unary and pairwise potentials,

$$\psi_{\boldsymbol{w}}(\boldsymbol{x}, \boldsymbol{y}) = \sum_{i=1}^{\ell} \boldsymbol{w}^\top \boldsymbol{f}(\boldsymbol{x}, y_i) + \sum_{i=2}^{\ell} \boldsymbol{w}^\top \boldsymbol{f}(\boldsymbol{x}, y_{i-1}, y_i), \tag{13.7}$$

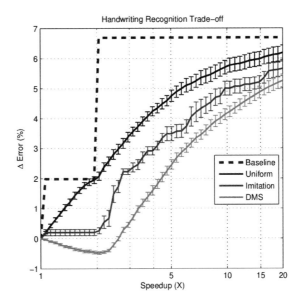

Figure 13.1: Trade-off on handwriting recognition task, displayed as a function of the efficiency speedup w.r.t the final model (Speedup) versus the change in error rate w.r.t the final model (ΔError). To draw each curve, we sweep the budget B or tradeoff parameter η until we find a point with at least the target speedup and record the error rate. Our approach (DMS) significantly outperforms imitation learning, yielding an error rate *below* that of the final model. The Uniform method consists of picking which element to expand uniformly at random until all examples use the same model, and the Baseline method consists of picking a single entire fixed stage of models a priori.

where $\boldsymbol{w}$ is a (learned) weight vector and $\boldsymbol{f}$ is a feature generating function. At test time, we can efficiently make predictions using the Viterbi algorithm to find the state sequence that maximizes (13.7).

13.3.2 Imitation Learning Baseline

We compare to an alternative method for dynamic model selection inspired by imitation learning methods for feature selection (He et al., 2012). For this baseline, we first pick a trade-off parameter η and then for each example $(\boldsymbol{x}^j, \boldsymbol{y}^j)$ in the training set independently decide the optimal stopping point,

$$\tau_j^\star = \operatorname*{argmin}_\tau \mathcal{L}(h_\tau(\boldsymbol{x}^j), \boldsymbol{y}^j) + \eta \cdot c_\tau. \tag{13.8}$$

These stopping points define an optimal policy $\pi^\star(i, \boldsymbol{x}^j) = \mathbf{1}[\tau_j^\star < i]$, where the policy $\pi^\star(i, \boldsymbol{x}^j)$ is 1 if computation should continue on example $\boldsymbol{x}^j$ after model i and 0 otherwise. We then learn an approximate policy $\pi(i, \boldsymbol{x}^j)$ using a linear SVM classifier trained with the same meta-features as the selector uses; we generated training data points by sampling all trajectories generated by the optimal policy on the training set. Note that for each η, we obtain one error/cost trade-off point. For all experiments, we swept η across many values to generate all possible unique optimal policies for each fold of cross-validation.

13.3.3 Handwriting Recognition

We first apply our method to the handwriting recognition data set of Taskar et al. (2003). For our purposes, this data set represents a "best case"-type of scenario: while there are thousands of examples of handwritten words in the data set, examples were generated by enlisting many different people to rewrite the same list of less than a hundred unique words. Therefore, we expect high-order features (e.g., five-grams) to be informative, but these features are computationally infeasible to include in the linear-chain model directly. Instead, they are ideally suited as informative meta-features for the selector. In this way, the selector is ideally suited to direct computation at test time, and a fast and effective method is the result.

We use three different models for the handwriting recognition problem, differing only in the unary term features of the sequence model. In each model, we have K^2 binary pairwise features $\boldsymbol{f}_{k,k'}(y_{i-1}, y_i) = \mathbf{1}[y_{i-1} = k, y_i = k']$ as well as a unary feature for every binary pixel activation in the 16×8 image. The second model h_2 computes a coarse Histogram of Gradients (HoG) in 3×3 bins, and the third model h_3 additionally computes HoG in smaller 2×2 bins. Because the pixels are given as in the input and HoG takes constant time for fixed input size, we have $c_1 = 0$, $c_2 = 1$, and $c_3 = 1$.

We use two sets of meta-features for the selector. The first are computed from the output of $h_i(\boldsymbol{x})$, consisting of the relative difference in the scores of the top two outputs and the average of the mean, min, and max entropies of the marginal distributions predicted by h_i at each position in the sequence.[1] The second set of meta-features count the number of times an n-gram was predicted in $h_i(\boldsymbol{x})$ that occured zero times in the training set, computed for $n = 3, 4, 5$. Both of these features take negligible time to compute compared with the HoG computation.

---

1. In addition to Viterbi, we also ran sum-product inference to compute probabilistic marginals to obtain entropies.

13.3.4 Results

We visualize the trade-off between error rate and computation time on the handwriting recognition task in Figure 13.1. All results are plotted in terms relative to the third, most expensive model. Our approach significantly outperforms imitation learning, and both imitation learning and our approach provide a significant increase in efficiency over choosing one of the models a priori or uniformly at random. Most significantly, the model/selector approach leads to a predictor that is more accurate than the final model (due to choosing the most accurate models first) while yielding a roughly 2.5× speedup compared with the most expensive model. Note that we also computed a different uniform baseline where examples were advanced to the next model uniformly at random without ensuring that all examples reached the same stage; we found this performed equivalent or worse than the baseline shown.

Besides the improvement in accuracy and speedup, there are several practical advantages of DMS over the imitation learning baseline. Unlike DMS, each choice of η yields a different policy; to sweep a curve, we must re-run learning for every point we wish to generate on the curve. Furthermore, imitation learning as defined using (13.8) does not guarantee that computation over a batch of test examples will run within a fixed budget; each choice of η yields a fixed trade-off that will approximately run at some budget that is a function of the interaction between computation and accuracy on the given training set.

13.3.5 Human Pose Estimation in Video

We use the MODEC+S model first introduced by Weiss et al. (2013). This approach to video pose estimation can be summarized as follows. MODEC+S utilizes a linear-chain model, one per arm. The model consists of 32 states per frame, corresponding to one of 32 mode predictions by the state-of-the-art MODEC pose model (Sapp and Taskar, 2013). Given the set of states for each clip in our training database, the MODEC+S model computes high-level features between subsequent poses such as color and optical flow consistency. For more details on the state space and training of the MODEC+S model, see Weiss et al. (2013).

As in the handwriting recognition task, we use a fixed hierarchy of features to create a series of four increasingly complex base models. The first model uses unary features consisting of a prior term and the normalized MODEC score for each mode and binary features consisting of a (mode, mode) transition prior and several kinematic terms (angular joint and limb velocities and

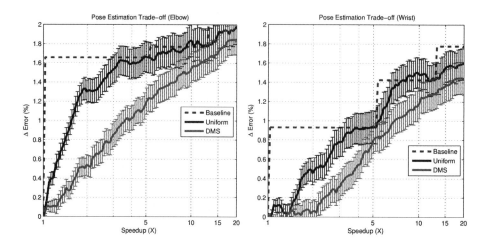

Figure 13.2: Dynamic model selection on the CLIC data set. See caption of Figure 13.1 for explanation of axes/baselines. DMS provides a significant increase in speedup with little accuracy cost compared to picking elements uniformly at random (e.g., for elbows, a 2× speedup can be obtained for hardly any accuracy cost, while a 5× speedup with DMS can be obtained for the same accuracy of a 3× speedup when picking uniformly at random).

x, y joint location velocities). The second model adds an image-dependent pairwise term, the χ^2-distance between color histograms of the predicted arm locations from one frame to the next. The third model adds an image-dependent unary term; each image is quickly segmented into superpixels using the algorithm of Felzenszwalb and Huttenlocher (2004), and we compute the intersection-over-union (IoU) score between the predicted arm rectangles and superpixels selected by the rectangles. Finally, the fourth model computes a fast and coarse optical flow using the method of Liu (2009); we obtain an estimate of the *foreground* flow by subtracting the median flow outside the target bounding box. We then compute a flow-based pairwise feature as follows: for each predicted arm location in the first frame, we shift each arm pixel by its estimated flow to produce a predicted arm location in the next frame, and we compute the IoU between the flow-shifted arm and each possible predicted arm location in the next frame. Although the computational cost depends on the size of the input images, for the data set we used, we compute the per-frame amortized costs of each model (in seconds)^2 to be $c_1 = 0, c_2 = 0.41$, $c_3 = 1$, and $c_4 = 5.2$ (optical flow is by far the most expensive feature of MODEC+S).

---

2. All computation was carried out on an AMD Opteron 4284 CPU @ 3.00 GHz with 16 cores.

We use similar meta-features as in the handwriting recognition setting (n-gram occurrences and distribution and entropy of the sequence model marginals) with one set of additional image-dependent features. For every n-gram in the image, where $n = 2k$, we compute the mean and max χ^2 distance between a center frame predicted arm location and the k frames before and after. The feature is then the average number of times these distances exceed 0.5, indicating a significant difference between the predicted arm color of the center frame and the surround frames. For $k = 1, 2, 3$, these features yield a total of 40 features for the selector. Finally, for computing meta-features at model level i, we also compute the features of level $i - 1$ and the change in these features from $i - 1$ to i. The per-frame amortized cost of evaluation is 0.014 seconds.

We use the Clips Labeled in Cinema (CLIC) data set from Weiss et al. (2013). This data set consists of 362 annotated clips from the same movies as the Frames Labeled in Cinema (FLIC) data set from Sapp and Taskar (2013), for a total of roughly 15,000 individual frames. Each clip is between 10 and 61 frames in length, with a median clip length of 46 frames. Following Weiss et al. (2013), we selected half of the clips that contained the most arm motion to provide for a more challenging data set. We evaluated our dynamic model selection framework on the CLIC data set with 200 random partitions of the data set. For each partition, we used 70% of the data for training, 10% as development, and 20% as test. Within the training set, we ran three-fold cross-validation to generate model predictions for learning the selector as described in Section 13.2. When learning the selector, we focused on minimizing wrist test error, counting as an error any frame that the wrist was not localized to within 20 pixels. We also smoothed the predictions of each model before passing them to the selector because we found this improved the overall accuracy of the system.

13.3.6 Results

The results are shown in Figure 13.2. For wrist localization, our approach was able to obtain a $2\times$ speedup for little to no accuracy cost and maintain a significant speedup compared to the uninformed model selection baseline. For elbow localization, our approach yields a speedup of $5\times$ at the same accuracy cost as an uninformed $2\times$ speedup, a significant improvement. Note that these improvements include the slight additional cost of evaluating the DMS meta-features.

To further shed light on the difference between DMS and the uniform expansion, we investigated whether Algorithm 13.1 was choosing models to use by simply choosing the cheapest first. We found this not to be the

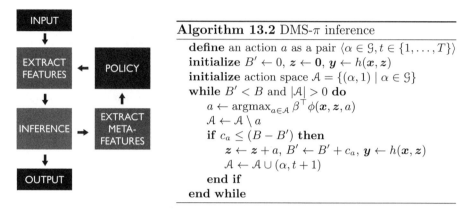

Algorithm 13.2 DMS-π inference

> **define** an action a as a pair $\langle \alpha \in \mathcal{G}, t \in \{1, \dots, T\} \rangle$
> **initialize** $B' \leftarrow 0$, $\boldsymbol{z} \leftarrow \boldsymbol{0}$, $\boldsymbol{y} \leftarrow h(\boldsymbol{x}, \boldsymbol{z})$
> **initialize** action space $\mathcal{A} = \{(\alpha, 1) \mid \alpha \in \mathcal{G}\}$
> **while** $B' < B$ and $|\mathcal{A}| > 0$ **do**
> $a \leftarrow \operatorname{argmax}_{a \in \mathcal{A}} \beta^\top \phi(\boldsymbol{x}, \boldsymbol{z}, a)$
> $\mathcal{A} \leftarrow \mathcal{A} \setminus a$
>   **if** $c_a \le (B - B')$ **then**
> $\boldsymbol{z} \leftarrow \boldsymbol{z} + a$, $B' \leftarrow B' + c_a$, $\boldsymbol{y} \leftarrow h(\boldsymbol{x}, \boldsymbol{z})$
> $\mathcal{A} \leftarrow \mathcal{A} \cup (\alpha, t + 1)$
>   **end if**
> **end while**

Figure 13.3: Overview of the DMS-π approach. (Left) A high-level summary of the processing pipeline: as in standard structured prediction, features are extracted and inference is run to produce an output. However, information may optionally feedback in the form of extracted meta-features that are used by a control policy to determine another set of features to be extracted. (Right) Detailed algorithm for factor-wise inference for an example $\boldsymbol{x}$ given a graph structure $\mathcal{G}$ and budget B. The policy repeatedly selects the highest valued action from an action space $\mathcal{A}$ that represents extracting features for each part of the graph structure $\mathcal{G}$.

case; instead, the most expensive model is assigned to examples early on in the budget-allocation process. This suggests that the computational gains of DMS stem from being able to allocate resources to difficult examples quickly.

13.4   Meta-Learning a Feature Extraction Policy

We now turn to extending the DMS framework to model the *feature extraction* problem within a single structured model. We start by introducing an additional *explicit* feature extraction state vector $\boldsymbol{z}$:

$$h(\boldsymbol{x}, \boldsymbol{z}) = \underset{\boldsymbol{y} \in \mathcal{Y}(\boldsymbol{x})}{\operatorname{argmax}} \, \boldsymbol{w}^\top \boldsymbol{f}(\boldsymbol{x}, \boldsymbol{y}, \boldsymbol{z}). \tag{13.9}$$

Above, $\boldsymbol{f}(\boldsymbol{x}, \boldsymbol{y}, \boldsymbol{z})$ is a sparse vector of D features that takes time $\boldsymbol{c}^\top \boldsymbol{z}$ to compute for a non-negative cost vector $\boldsymbol{c}$ and binary indicator vector $\boldsymbol{z}$ of length $|\boldsymbol{z}| = F$. Intuitively, $\boldsymbol{z}$ indicates which of F sets of features are extracted when computing $\boldsymbol{f}$; $\boldsymbol{z} = \boldsymbol{1}$ means every possible feature is extracted, whereas $\boldsymbol{z} = \boldsymbol{0}$ means that only a minimum set of features is extracted.

Note that by incorporating $\boldsymbol{z}$ into the feature function, the predictor h can learn to use different linear weights for the same underlying feature value by conditioning the feature on the value of $\boldsymbol{z}$. As we discuss in Section 13.4.4, adapting the weights in this way is crucial to building a predictor h that works well for *any* subset of features. We will discuss later how to construct such features in more detail.

Suppose we have learned such a model h. At test time, our goal is to make the most accurate predictions possible for an example under a fixed budget B. Specifically, given h and a loss function $\mathcal{L} : \mathcal{Y} \times \mathcal{Y} \mapsto \mathbb{R}^+$, we wish to find the following:

$$H(\boldsymbol{x}, B) = \underset{\boldsymbol{z}}{\arg\min} \, \mathbb{E}_{\boldsymbol{y}|\boldsymbol{x}}[\mathcal{L}(\boldsymbol{y}, h(\boldsymbol{x}, \boldsymbol{z}))]. \tag{13.10}$$

In practice, there are three primary difficulties in optimizing (13.10). First, the distribution $P(Y|X)$ is unknown. Second, there are exponentially many $\boldsymbol{z}$ to explore. Most important, however, is the fact that we do not have free access to the objective function. Instead, given $\boldsymbol{x}$, we are optimizing over $\boldsymbol{z}$ using a *function oracle* because we cannot compute $\boldsymbol{f}(\boldsymbol{x}, \boldsymbol{y}, \boldsymbol{z})$ without paying $\boldsymbol{c}^\top \boldsymbol{z}$, and the total cost of all the calls to the oracle must not exceed B. Our approach to solving these problems is outlined in Figure 13.3; we learn a *control model* (i.e., a policy) by posing the optimization problem as an MDP and using reinforcement learning techniques.

We model the budgeted prediction optimization as the following Markov Decision Process (MDP). The state of the MDP is the tuple $s = (\boldsymbol{x}, \boldsymbol{z})$, defined for an input $\boldsymbol{x}$ and feature extraction state $\boldsymbol{z}$ (for brevity we will simply write s). The start state is $s_0 = (\boldsymbol{x}, \boldsymbol{0})$, with $\boldsymbol{x} \sim P(X)$ and $\boldsymbol{z} = \boldsymbol{0}$ indicating only a minimal set of features have been extracted. The action space $\mathcal{A}(s)$ is $\{i \mid z_i = 0\} \cup \{0\}$, where z_i is the ith element of $\boldsymbol{z}$; given a state-action pair (s, a), the next state is deterministically $s' = (\boldsymbol{x}, \boldsymbol{z} + \mathbf{e}_a)$, where $\mathbf{e}_a$ is the indicator vector with a 1 in the ath component or the zero vector if $a = 0$. Thus, at each state we can choose to extract one additional set of features or none at all (at which point the process terminates). Finally, for fixed h, we define the shorthand $\eta(s) = \mathbb{E}_{\boldsymbol{y}|\boldsymbol{x}}\mathcal{L}(\boldsymbol{y}, h(\boldsymbol{x}, \boldsymbol{z}))$ to be the expected error of the predictor h given state $\boldsymbol{z}$ and input $\boldsymbol{x}$.

We now define the expected reward to be the adaptive value of information of extracting the ath set of features given the system state and budget B:

$$R(s, a, s') = \begin{cases} \eta(s) - \eta(s') & \text{if } \boldsymbol{c}^\top \boldsymbol{z}(s') \leq B \\ 0 & \text{otherwise.} \end{cases} \tag{13.11}$$

Intuitively, (13.11) says that each time we add additional features to the computation, we gain reward equal to the decrease in error achieved with the new features (or pay a penalty if the error increases). Note that this is essentially the myopic definition of value given in Section 13.2. However, if we ever exceed the budget, then any further decrease does not count; no more reward can be gained. Furthermore, assuming $f(x, y, z)$ can be cached appropriately, it is clear that we pay only the additional computional cost c_a for each action a, so the entire cumulative computational burden of reaching some state s is exactly $c^\top z$ for the corresponding z vector.

Given a trajectory of states $s_0, s_1, \ldots, s_T$, computed by some deterministic policy π, it is clear that the final cumulative reward $R_\pi(s_0)$ is the difference between the starting error rate and the rate of the last state satisfying the budget:

$$R_\pi(s_0) = \eta(s_0) - \eta(s_1) + \eta(s_1) - \cdots = \eta(s_0) - \eta(s_{t^\star}), \qquad (13.12)$$

where $t^\star$ is the index of the final state within the budget constraint. Therefore, the optimal policy $\pi^\star$ that maximizes expected reward will compute $z^\star$ minimizing (13.10) while satisfying the budget constraint.

13.4.1 Q-Learning a Non-Myopic Policy

We focus on a straightforward method for learning an approximate policy: a batch version of least-squares policy iteration (Lagoudakis and Parr, 2003) based on Q-learning (Watkins and Dayan, 1992). We parametrize the policy as the greedy optimization of a linear function of *meta-features* ϕ computed from the current state $s = (x, z)$: $\pi_\beta(s) = \text{argmax}_a \beta^\top \phi(x, z, a)$. The meta-features (which we abbreviate as simply $\phi(s, a)$ henceforth) need to be rich enough to represent the value of choosing to expand feature a for a given partially computed example (x, z). Note that we already have computed $f(x, h(x, z), z)$, which may be useful in estimating the confidence of the model on a given example. However, we have much more freedom in choosing $\phi(s, a)$ than we had in choosing f; f is restricted to ensure that inference is tractable, whereas we have no such restriction for ϕ. We therefore compute functions of $h(x, z)$ that take into account large sets of output variables, and because we need only compute them for the particular output $h(x, z)$, we can do so efficiently. As before in the DMS framework, we typically use meta-features that measure the self-consistency of the output as a surrogate for the expected accuracy.

We now show how to learn a policy with off-policy least-squares Q-learning. To simplify the notation, we will assume given current state s, taking action a deterministically yields state s'. Given a policy π, the value of a policy is recursively defined as the immediate expected reward plus the discounted value of the next state:

$$Q_\pi(s, a) = R(s, a, s') + \gamma Q_\pi(s', \pi(s')). \qquad (13.13)$$

The goal of Q-learning is to learn the Q for the optimal policy $\pi^\star$ with maximal $Q_{\pi^\star}$; however, it is clear that we can increase Q by simply stopping early when $Q_\pi(s, a) < 0$ (the future reward in this case is simply zero). Therefore, we define the *off-policy* optimized value $Q_\pi^\star$ as follows:

$$Q_\pi^\star(s_t, \pi(s_t)) = R(s_t, \pi(s_t), s_{t+1}) + \gamma \left[Q_\pi^\star(s_{t+1}, \pi(s_{t+1})) \right]_+ . \tag{13.14}$$

The DMS-π approach uses the following one-step algorithm for learning Q from data. Suppose we have a finite trajectory $s_0, \ldots, s_T$. Because both π and the state transitions are deterministic, we can unroll the recursion in (13.14) and compute $Q_\pi^\star(s_t, \pi(s_t))$ for each sample using simple dynamic programming. For example, if $\gamma = 1$ (there is no discount for future reward), then we obtain $Q_\pi^\star(s_i, \pi(s_i)) = \eta(s_i) - \eta(s_{t^\star})$, where $t^\star$ is the optimal stopping time that satisfies the given budget.

We therefore learn parameters $\beta^\star$ for an approximate Q as follows. Given an initial policy π, we execute π for each example $(\boldsymbol{x}^j, \boldsymbol{y}^j)$ to obtain trajectories $s_0^j, \ldots, s_T^j$. We then solve the following least-squares optimization,

$$\beta^\star = \operatorname*{argmin}_\beta \lambda ||\beta||^2 + \frac{1}{nT} \sum_{j,t} \left(\beta^\top \phi(s_t^j, \pi(s_t^j)) - Q_\pi^\star(s_t^j, \pi(s_t^j)) \right)^2 , \tag{13.15}$$

using cross-validation to determine the regularization parameter λ.

13.4.2   Policy Iteration

We perform a simple form of policy iteration as follows. We first initialize β by estimating the expected reward function (this can be estimated from pairs (s, s'), which are more efficient to compute than Q-functions on trajectories). We then compute trajectories under π_β and use these trajectories to compute $\beta^\star$ that approximates $Q_\pi^\star$. We found that additional iterations of policy iteration did not noticeably change the results.

13.4.3   Modified Reward for Any-Time Budgets

One potential drawback of the approach just described is that we must learn a different policy for every desired budget. A more attractive alternative is to learn a single policy that is tuned to a range of possible budgets. One solution is to set $\gamma = 1$ and learn with $B = \infty$ so that the value $Q_\pi^\star$ represents the best improvement possible using some optimal budget $B^\star$. However, at test time, it may be that $B^\star$ is greater than the available budget B and $Q_\pi^\star$ is an over-estimate. By choosing $\gamma < 1$, we can trade off between valuing reward for short-term gain with smaller budgets $B < B^\star$ and longer-term gain with the unknown optimal budget $B^\star$.

In fact, we can further encourage our learned policy to be useful for smaller budgets by adjusting the reward function. Note that two trajectories that start at s_0 and end at $s_{t^\star}$ will have the same reward, yet one trajectory might be more useful if the process were to stop earlier: for example, the other trajectory might introduce a large mistake early on before correcting the mistake later. If the budget were smaller, the trajectory that does not introduce higher error would be a better choice. We therefore add a shaping component to the expected reward in order to favor the more useful trajectory as follows:

$$R_\alpha(s, a, s') = \eta(s) - \eta(s') - \alpha \left[\eta(s') - \eta(s)\right]_+. \tag{13.16}$$

This modification introduces a term that does not cancel when transitioning from one state to the next, *if the next state has higher error than our current state*. Thus, we can only achieve optimal reward $\eta(s_0) - \eta(s_{t^\star})$ when there is a sequence of feature extractions that never increases the error rate.[3] If such a sequence does not exist, then the parameter α controls the trade-off between the importance of reaching $s_{t^\star}$ and minimizing any errors along the way. Note that we can still use the procedure described above to learn β when using R_α instead of R. We use a development set to tune α as well as γ to find the most useful policy when sweeping B across a range of budgets.

13.4.4   Design of the Information-Adaptive Predictor h

We now address the problem of learning $h(\boldsymbol{x}, \boldsymbol{z})$ from n labeled data points $\{(\boldsymbol{x}^j, \boldsymbol{y}^j)\}_{j=1}^n$. Because we do not necessarily know the test-time budget during training (nor would we want to repeat the training process for every possible budget), we formulate the problem of minimizing the *expected* training loss according to a uniform distribution over budgets:

$$\boldsymbol{w}^\star = \underset{\boldsymbol{w}}{\operatorname{argmin}} \, \lambda ||\boldsymbol{w}||^2 + \frac{1}{n} \sum_{j=1}^n \mathbb{E}_{\boldsymbol{z}}[\mathcal{L}(\boldsymbol{y}^j, h(\boldsymbol{x}^j, \boldsymbol{z})]. \tag{13.17}$$

Note that if $\mathcal{L}$ is convex, then (13.17) is a weighted sum of convex functions and is also convex. Our choice of distribution for $\boldsymbol{z}$ will determine how the predictor h is calibrated. In our experiments, we used the following generative process: (1) first sample a budget $B \in [0, |\boldsymbol{c}|_1]$ uniformly at random, and (2) then sample $\boldsymbol{z}$ uniformly from $\{\boldsymbol{z} \mid \boldsymbol{c}^\top \boldsymbol{z} = B\}$ by greedily adding feature sets to $\boldsymbol{z}$ in random order. To learn $\boldsymbol{w}$, we use Pegasos-style

---

3. While adding features decreases training error on average, even on the training set, additional features may lead to increased error for any particular example.

(Shalev-Shwartz et al., 2007) stochastic subgradient descent; we approximate the expectation (13.17) by re-sampling z every time we pick up a new example (x^j, y^j). We set λ and a stopping-time criterion through cross-validation onto a development set.

We now turn to the question of designing $f(x, y, z)$. In the standard pair-wise graphical model setting (before considering z), we decompose a feature function $f(x, y)$ into unary and pairwise features as in (13.2). We consider several different schemes of incorporating z of varying complexity. The simplest scheme is to use several different feature functions $\{f^i\}_1^T$. Then $|z| = F$, and $z_a = 1$ indicates that f^a is computed. Thus, we have the following expression, where we use $z(a)$ to indicate the ath element of z:

$$f(x, y, z) = \sum_{a=1}^{T} z(a) \left[\sum_{i=1}^{\ell} f_u^a(x, y_i) + \sum_{(i,j) \in \mathcal{E}} f_e^a(x, y_i, y_j) \right]. \quad (13.18)$$

Note that in practice we can choose each f^a to be a sparse vector such that $f^a \cdot f^{a'} = 0$ for all $a' \neq a$; that is, each feature function f^a "fills out" a complementary section of the feature vector f. Note that this feature extraction scheme is essentially equivalent to the series of linear models of the standard DMS scheme, because adding features sequentially in this way corresponds to using entirely different feature functions.

A much more powerful approach—the entire purpose of moving to the DMS-π framework—is to create a feature vector as the composite of different extracted features for each vertex and edge in the model. In this setting, we set $z = [z_u \ z_e]$, where $|z| = (\ell + |\mathcal{E}|)T$, and we have

$$f(x, y, z) = \sum_{i=1}^{\ell} \sum_{a=1}^{T} z_u(a, i) f_u^a(x, y_i) + \sum_{(i,j) \in \mathcal{E}} \sum_{a=1}^{T} z_e(a, ij) f_e^a(x, y_i, y_j).$$

$$(13.19)$$

We refer to this latter feature extraction method as a *factor-level* feature extraction and the former as as *example-level*. As we will show empirically, the factor-level extraction method allows for much finer-grained control of computation and therefore much more favorable trade-offs. However, these gains come at the cost of increased inference time; inference is re-run many more times per equivalent budget increase for the factor-level extractions as compared with the example-level extractions. This is because each action taken by the controller uses up smaller chunks of the budget and computes far fewer features when features are only added to a single factor at a time.

Algorithm 13.3 Quiescent forward-backward algorithm

Given forward/backward messages α/β, target position p, scores $\psi_{\boldsymbol{w}}$, tolerance $q \in [0,1]$
Let $\alpha' \leftarrow \alpha$, $\beta' \leftarrow \beta$, $i \leftarrow p, j \leftarrow p, \Delta\alpha \leftarrow 1, \Delta\beta \leftarrow 1$
Let $\tau(i) = \max_k\{\alpha_{ik} + \beta_{ik}\} - \min_k\{\alpha_{ik} + \beta_{ik}\}$
while $i \leq L$ and $\Delta\alpha > q$ **do**
$\quad \forall k: \quad \alpha'_{ik} \leftarrow \psi_{\boldsymbol{w}}(i,k) + \max_{k'} \alpha'_{i-1,k'} + \psi_{\boldsymbol{w}}(i,k',k)$
$\quad \Delta\alpha \leftarrow \max_k |\alpha'_{ik} - \alpha_{ik}|/\tau(i)$
end while
while $j \geq 1$ and $\Delta\beta > q$ **do**
$\quad \forall k: \quad \beta'_{jk} \leftarrow \max_{k'} \beta'_{j+1,k'} + \psi_{\boldsymbol{w}}(j+1,k,k') + \psi_{\boldsymbol{w}}(j+1,k')$
$\quad \Delta\beta \leftarrow \max_k |\beta'_{jk} - \beta_{jk}|/\tau(j)$
end while

13.4.5   Reducing Inference Overhead

Although for reasons of simplicity we only consider low tree-width models in this work for which (13.9) can be efficiently solved via a standard max-sum message-passing algorithm, the meta-features $\phi(s,a)$ require access to $h(\boldsymbol{x}, \boldsymbol{z})$, and therefore we must run message-passing every time we compute a new state s in order to compute the next action. Using the factor-level feature definition thus leads to many repeated runs of the inference algorithm, despite the fact that only a small subset of scores change when features are added to only a subset of the model.

Therefore, we can save time by running message passing *once* and then performing less expensive local updates using saved messages from the previous iteration. We define a simple algorithm for such *quiescent* inference; we refer to this inference scheme as *q*-inference. The intuition is that we stop propagating messages once the magnitude of the update to the max-marginal decreases below a certain threshold q; we define q in terms of the margin of the current MAP decoding at the given position, because that margin must be surpassed if the MAP decoding will change as a result of inference.

The algorithm for local updates to message passing is in Algorithm 13.3. This algorithm is similar to the standard forward-backward max-sum message passing algorithm for linear-chain models, but it assumes that messages have already been precomputed. Based on these precomputed messages, computation stops if the new message does not change by a specified fraction q of the amount needed to change the argmax at a given position in the sequence. Furthermore, it begins computation at a position p (where scores have presumably changed) and propagates the changes outward from that position.

13.4.6   Batch Mode Inference

We now have all the elements in place to define the final DMS-π algorithm. We once again assume a *test set* of n examples rather than a single example. Thus, we extend our framework just described to concatenate the states of all n examples $s = (\boldsymbol{x}^1, \ldots, \boldsymbol{x}^n, \boldsymbol{z}^1, \ldots, \boldsymbol{z}^n)$. The action consists of choosing an example and then choosing an action within that example's substate; our policy searches over the space of *all* actions for *all* examples simultaneously. Because of this, we impose additional constraints on the action space, specifically:

$$z(a, \ldots) = 1 \implies z(a', \ldots) = 1, \quad \forall a' < a. \tag{13.20}$$

(13.20) states that there is an inherent *ordering* of feature extractions, such that we cannot compute the ath feature set without first computing feature sets $1, \ldots, a-1$. This greatly simplifies the search space in the batch setting while preserving enough flexibility to yield significant improvements in efficiency.

Finally, we further note that (13.20) also allows us to increase the complexity of the feature function $\boldsymbol{f}$ as follows; when using the ath extraction, we allow the model to re-weight the features from extractions 1 through a. In other words, we condition the value of the feature on the current set of features that have been computed; because there are only T sets in the restricted setting, this is a feasible option. We simply define $\hat{\boldsymbol{f}}^a = [0 \ \ldots \ \boldsymbol{f}^1 \ \ldots \ \boldsymbol{f}^a \ \ldots \ 0]$, where we add duplicates of features $\boldsymbol{f}^1$ through $\boldsymbol{f}^a$ for each feature block a. Thus, the model can learn different weights for the same underlying features based on the current level of feature extraction; we found that this was crucial for optimal performance.

A precise form of the algorithm is given in Algorithm 13.2. Note that we use the factor-level feature extraction scheme given in Section 13.4.4; an action chooses an element α from a graph structure $\mathcal{E}$ and a feature tier level t (assuming T tiers) and computes that specific feature tier of features for the specific factor corresponding to the graph element α. Thus, for a set of edges $\{\mathcal{E}\}$, there are $(\ell + |\mathcal{E}|)T$ (unary and pairwise) possible actions per example.

13.5   Applications to Sequential Prediction Revisited

We revisit the experiments of the DMS framework, applying the finer-grained DMS-π. We once again use linear-chain models and apply the ap-

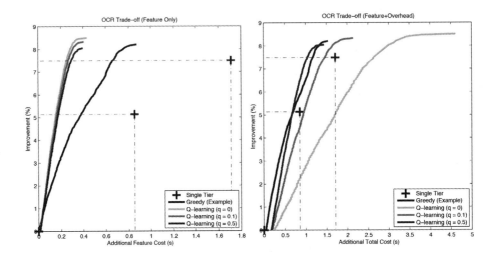

Figure 13.4: **Controlling overhead on the handwriting data set.** (Left) Accuracy improvement as a function of additional feature costs. (Right) Accuracy improvement as a function of total cost. While the DMS-π approach is extremely efficient in terms of how many features are extracted (Left), the additional overhead of inference is prohibitively expensive for the handwriting recognition task without applying q-inference (Right) with a large threshold. Furthermore, although the example-wise strategy is less efficient in terms of features extracted, it is more efficient in terms of overhead.

proach to the handwriting and pose estimation data sets, and we find empirically that DMS-π provides a superior trade-off of accuracy and efficiency.

13.5.1   Imitation Learning Baseline

As before, we define a baseline using an imitation learning scheme. As an alternative to the DMS-π approach, we consider an imitation learning scheme in which we learn a classifier to reproduce a target policy given by an oracle. We use the same trajectories as used to compute $Q_\pi^\star$, but instead we create a classification data set of positive and negative examples given a budget B by assigning all state/action pairs along a trajectory within the budget as positive examples and all budget violations as negative examples. We tune the budget B using a development set to optimize the overall trade-off when the policy is evaluated with multiple budgets.

13.5.2   Handwriting Recognition

For this problem, we re-use the same three sets of features: the original pixels (free) and two sets of Histogram-of-Gradient (HoG) features computed on the images for different bin sizes. However, this time we are concerned

| Feature | | Time (s) | | |
Tier (T)	Error (%)	Fixed	Entropy	Q-Learn
4	44.07	16.20s	16.20s	**8.91s**
3	46.17	12.00s	8.10s	**5.51s**
2	46.98	5.50s	6.80s	**4.86s**
1	51.49	2.75s	—	—
Best	**43.45**	—	—	**13.45s**

Table 13.1: Trade-off between average elbow and wrist error rate and total runtime achieved by our method on the pose data set; each row fixes an error rate and determines the amount of time required by each method to achieve the error. Unlike using entropy-based confidence scores, our Q-learning approach always improves runtime over a priori selection and even yields a faster, more accurate model (final row).

with inference as a potential bottleneck: the features are fast to compute compared with inference. Thus, we evaluate the effectiveness of q-inference with various thresholds to minimize inference time.

We define the meta-features $\phi(s, a)$ in terms of the targeted position in the sequence i and the current predictions $\boldsymbol{y}^{\star} = h(\boldsymbol{x}, \boldsymbol{z})$. Specifically, we concatenate the already computed unary and edge features of $y_i^{\star}$ and its neighbors (conditioned on the value of $\boldsymbol{z}$ at i), the margin of the current MAP decoding at position i, and a measure of self-consistency computed on $\boldsymbol{y}^{\star}$ as follows. For all sets of m positions overlapping with position i, we extract the corresponding m-gram and use a binary indicator to specify whether the specific m-gram occurred in the training set or not; we repeat for $m = 2, \dots, 5$. We also add several bias terms for which sets of features have been extracted around position i.

13.5.3 Results

The results are summarized in Figure 13.4. Regardless of the value of q, our method is extremely efficient in terms of the features computed for h; however, in this case, the overhead of inference is on par with the feature computation. Thus, we obtain a more accurate model with $q = 0.5$ that is $1.5\times$ faster than baseline, even though it uses only $1/5$ of the features; if the implementation of inference were improved, we would expect a speedup much closer to $5\times$. Notably, however, the factor-level features are far more efficient in terms of features extracted than the example-wise policy (an equivalent to the vanilla DMS framework).

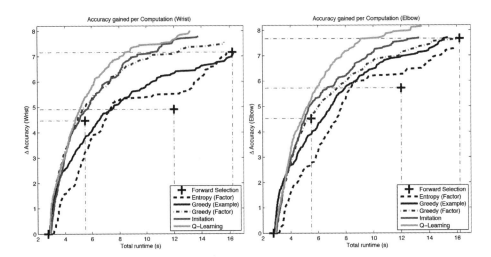

Figure 13.5: **Trade-off performance on the pose data set for wrists (Left) and elbows (Right).** The curve shows the increase in accuracy over the minimal-feature model as a function of total runtime per frame (including all overhead). We compare to two baselines that involve no learning: forward selection and extracting factor-wise features based on the entropy of marginals at each position ("Entropy") (i.e., extracting the positions with greatest uncertainty). The learned policy results are either greedy ("Greedy" example-level and factor-level) or non-myopic (either our "Q-learning" or the baseline "Imitation"). Note that the example-wise method is far less effective than the factor-wise extraction strategy. Furthermore, Q-learning in particular achieves higher accuracy models at a fraction of the computational cost of using all features and is more effective than imitation learning.

13.5.4 Tracking of Human Pose in Video

We next revisit the pose problem from Section 13.3.5. Unlike the handwriting recognition case, the overhead of inference is far less compared with the cost of computing features, so we expect to achieve larger runtime speedups.

In these experiments, we present cross-validation results averaged over 50 replicates, each being 80/20 train/test splits of the same data set; we also measure localization performance for both elbow and wrists in terms of percentage of times the predicted locations fall within 20 pixels of the ground truth. For meta-features, we use the same construction as for handwriting recognition, but we compute inter-frame χ^2-distances for each frame in the m-gram and take the maximum distance from the first frame to any other frame; we use a binary indicator as to whether each of these maximum distances exceeds 0.5. Furthermore, incrementally compute poses and features to minimize the total runtime, starting with a model with eight poses before eventually computing all 32 poses as input to MODEC+S, and evaluate the total runtime of the approach (compared with the previous section, where we evaluated only the runtime of additional feature computation for MODEC+S). Finally, we also include in these results a simple entropy-based baseline. The entropy-based approach simply computes probabilistic marginals and extracts features for whichever portion of the output space has highest uncertainty (as measured by entropy) in the predicted distribution.

13.5.5 Results

We present a short summary of our pose results in Table 13.1 and compare to various baselines in Figure 13.5. We found that our Q-learning approach is consistently more effective than all baselines; Q-learning yields a model that is both more accurate and faster than the baseline model trained with all features. Furthermore, while the feature extraction decisions of the Q-learning model are significantly correlated with the error of the starting predictions ($\rho - 0.23$), the entropy-based are not ($\rho = 0.02$), indicating that our learned reward signal is much more informative.

13.6 Conclusion

We presented *dynamic structured model selection* (DMS), a simple but powerful meta-learning algorithm that leverages typically intractable features in structured learning problems in order to automatically determine which of several models should be used at test time to maximize accuracy under a fixed budgetary constraint. We have also described DMS-π, a framework for learning feature extraction policies and predictive models that adaptively select features for extraction in a factor-wise, online fashion. In two domains, we found significant improvements in accuracy and efficiency compared with alternative or uninformed approaches.

13.6.1   Further Reading and Related Work

This chapter is based on preliminary work of Weiss et al. (2013) and Weiss and Taskar (2013). However, the idea of learning a feature extraction policy is not inherently new. Much prior work takes a generative approach that models the distribution of feature values, and the policy chooses individual features to evaluate. This generative setting differs greatly from the discriminative setting studied in this chapter; in the generative approach, one models a distribution $P(\boldsymbol{f}(X), Y)$ and uses Bayes rule to make predictions. One approach to feature extraction given a generative model is to maximize the *value of information*, which is a measure of the information about $P(Y \mid \boldsymbol{f}(X))$ gained by observing new features, subject to cost constraints. Although generally infeasible, approximations exist given graphical models of the data or for special cases (Krause and Guestrin, 2005, 2009; Bilgic and Getoor, 2007). The policies can also be learned using reinforcement learning techniques; for example Ji and Carin (2007) formulate the feature extraction problem as a Partially Observable MDP (POMDP) and use Gaussian Mixture Models (GMMs) to model the features, whereas Bayer-Zubek (2004) use discrete distributions in a standard MDP framework. It's noteworthy that in both cases, the best empirical policies are defined myopically, greedily optimizing a heuristic, despite formulating the problem using the standard reinforcement learning frameworks.

Another core component of the DMS/DMS-π approach is the idea of using meta-features to evaluate the progress of a structured model; this basic idea of predicting the accuracy of a model has been studied before, albeit in different contexts. Bedagkar-Gala and Shah (2010) attempt to predict various video analysis algorithms' performance (similar in spirit to the selector we propose) but based on measures of image quality rather than properties of model output. Jammalamadaka et al. (2012) propose an evaluator for human pose estimators, but only for single-frame images, and they propose only learning "correct or not" coarse-level distinctions, whereas we attempt to predict a measure of the error of each model directly. In the speech community, Lanchantin and Rodet (2010) propose a parallel method of "dynamic model selection," in which several models are continually reevaluated in an online fashion using a generative model, which is a different setting than the one we analyze here.

Acknowledgments

The authors were partially supported by ONR MURI N000141010934, NSF CAREER 1054215, and STARnet, a Semiconductor Research Corporation program sponsored by MARCO and DARPA.

13.7 References

Y. Altun, I. Tsochantaridis, and T. Hofmann. Hidden Markov support vector machines. In *Proc. ICML*, 2003.

V. Bayer-Zubek. Learning diagnostic policies from examples by systematic search. In *UAI*, 2004.

A. Bedagkar-Gala and S. Shah. Joint modeling of algorithm behavior and image quality for algorithm performance prediction. In *BMVC*, 2010.

M. Bilgic and L. Getoor. Voila: Efficient feature-value acquisition for classification. In *AAAI*, 2007.

M. Collins. Discriminative training methods for hidden Markov models: Theory and experiments with perceptron algorithms. In *Proc. EMNLP*, 2002.

P. Felzenszwalb and D. Huttenlocher. Efficient graph-based image segmentation. *IJCV*, 59(2), 2004.

H. He, H. Daumé III, and J. Eisner. Imitation learning by coaching. In *NIPS*, 2012.

R. A. Howard. Information value theory. *Systems Science and Cybernetics, IEEE Transactions on*, 2(1):22–26, 1966.

N. Jammalamadaka, A. Zisserman, M. Eichner, V. Ferrari, and C. Jawahar. Has my algorithm succeeded? An evaluator for human pose estimators. In *ECCV*, 2012.

S. Ji and L. Carin. Cost-sensitive feature acquisition and classification. *Pattern Recognition*, 2007.

D. Koller and N. Friedman. *Probabilistic Graphical Models: Principles and Techniques*. The MIT Press, 2009.

A. Krause and C. Guestrin. Near-optimal value of information in graphical models. In *UAI*, 2005.

A. Krause and C. Guestrin. Optimal value of information in graphical models. *Journal of Artificial Intelligence Research (JAIR)*, 35:557–591, 2009.

J. Lafferty, A. McCallum, and F. Pereira. Conditional random fields: Probabilistic models for segmenting and labeling sequence data. In *Proc. ICML*, 2001.

M. G. Lagoudakis and R. Parr. Least-squares policy iteration. *Journal of Machine Learning Research*, 4:1107–1149, 2003.

P. Lanchantin and X. Rodet. Dynamic model selection for spectral voice conversion. In *Interspeech*, 2010.

D. V. Lindley. On a measure of the information provided by an experiment. *The Annals of Mathematical Statistics*, pages 986–1005, 1956.

C. Liu. *Beyond Pixels: Exploring New Representations and Applications for Motion Analysis*. PhD thesis, MIT, 2009.

B. Sapp and B. Taskar. MODEC: Multimodal decomposable models for human pose estimation. In *CVPR*, 2013.

B. Sapp, D. Weiss, and B. Taskar. Parsing human motion with stretchable models. In *CVPR*, 2011.

S. Shalev-Shwartz, Y. Singer, and N. Srebro. Pegasos: Primal estimated subgradient solver for SVM. In *ICML*, 2007.

B. Taskar, C. Guestrin, and D. Koller. Max-margin Markov networks. In *NIPS*, 2003.

B. Taskar, V. Chatalbashev, D. Koller, and C. Guestrin. Learning structured prediction models: A large margin approach. In *ICML*, 2005.

C. Watkins and P. Dayan. Q-learning. *Machine Learning*, 8(3–4), 1992.

D. Weiss and B. Taskar. Learning adaptive value of information for structured prediction. In *NIPS*, 2013.

D. Weiss, B. Sapp, and B. Taskar. Dynamic structured model selection. In *ICCV*, 2013.

14 Structured Prediction for Event Detection

Minh Hoai   minhhoai@robots.ox.ac.uk
University of Oxford
Oxford, UK

Fernando de la Torre   ftorre@cs.cmu.edu
Carnegie Mellon University
Pittsburgh, PA, USA

This chapter describes Segment-based SVMs (SegSVMs), a framework for event detection. SegSVMs combine energy-based structured prediction, maximum margin learning, and Bag-of-Words (BoWs) representation. Unlike traditional approaches for event detection based on Dynamic Bayesian Networks, the learning formulation of SegSVMs is convex, and the inference over multiple events can be efficiently done in linear time. Beyond detecting a single event, SegSVMs can be extended to solve two relatively unexplored problems in computer vision: early event detection and sequence labeling of multiple events. We illustrate the benefits of SegSVMs in several computer vision applications, namely, facial action unit detection, early recognition of hand gestures, early detection of facial expressions, and sequence labeling of human actions.

14.1 Introduction

Event detection (ED) is a cornerstone in many important applications, from video surveillance (Piciarelli et al., 2008) to motion analysis (Aggarwal and Cai, 1999) and psychopathology assessment (Cohn et al., 2009). ED refers to the task of localizing and recognizing the occurrences of temporal patterns that belong to some predefined target classes. Examples of target event classes are human actions (Ke et al., 2005), sport events (Efros et al., 2003; Xu et al., 2003), and facial expressions (Lucey et al., 2006; Bartlett et al., 2006; Zhu et al., 2009; Valstar and Pantic, 2007). ED is different from and harder than event recognition. ED in continuous time series involves both localization and recognition. Event recognition systems, such as those from Yamato et al. (1992), Brand et al. (1997), Gorelick et al. (2007), Sminchisescu et al. (2005), and Laptev et al. (2008), only need to classify pre-segmented subsequences that correspond to coherent events.

ED in video is a challenging problem. Several highly important challenges are to: (1) accommodate large variability of human behavior across subjects; (2) train classifiers when relatively few examples for each event are present; (3) recognize events with subtle human motion; (4) model the temporal dynamics of events, which can be highly variable; and (5) determine the beginnings and ends of the events.

Existing approaches for ED are typically based on segment classification or Dynamic Bayesian Networks (DBNs). Segment classification works by classifying candidate temporal segments (e.g., Piciarelli et al. (2008); Vassilakis et al. (2002); Nowozin et al. (2007); Shechtman and Irani (2007)). Although segment classification has been widely used for ED, it has several limitations. First, this approach classifies each candidate segment independently; it makes myopic decisions (Wang et al., 2006) and requires post-processing (e.g., to handle overlapping detections). Second, the segment classification approach often has difficulties for accurate localization of event boundaries (Wang et al., 2006) due to the ineffective use of negative examples in training. Negative examples are segments that misalign with target events, and they are either ignored (e.g., Shechtman and Irani (2007); Bobick and Wilson (1997)) or required to be disjoint from the positive training examples (e.g., Ke et al. (2005); Laptev and Perez (2007)). In both cases, segments that partially overlap with positive examples are not used in training; those segments, however, are candidates for inaccurate localization at test time. Another popular approach for ED is to use a variant of DBNs. However, DBNs typically lead to a high-dimensional optimization problem with multiple local minima. Furthermore, generative models such as HMMs and variants have limited ability to model the *null* class (no event or unseen events) due to the large variability of the null class.

In this chapter, we propose Segment-based SVMs (SegSVMs) to address the limitations of existing ED methods. SegSVMs combine structured prediction, maximum margin learning, and Bag-of-Words (BoW) representation. SegSVMs have several benefits for ED. First, SegSVMs use energy-based structured prediction because detecting semantic events in continuous time series is inherently a structured prediction task. Given a time series, the desired output is more than a binary label indicating the presence or absence

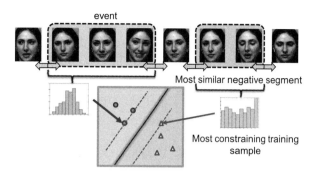

Figure 14.1: During testing, the events are found by efficiently searching over the segments (position and length) that maximize the SVM score. During training, the algorithm searches over all possible negative segments to identify those hardest to classify, which improves classification of subtle events.

of target events. It must predict the locations of target events and their associated class labels, and energy-based structured prediction provides a principled mechanism for concurrent top-down recognition and bottom-up temporal localization (see Figure 14.1). Second, SegSVMs model temporal events using the BoW representation (Lewis, 1998; Sivic and Zisserman, 2003). The BoW representation requires no state transition model, eliminating the need for detailed annotation and manual definition of event dynamics. This representation can model and detect events of different lengths, removing the necessity of multi-size templates or multi-scale processing. BoW representation is not as rigid as template matching or dynamic time warping; it tolerates errors in misalignment, and it is robust to the impreciseness in human annotation. Finally, SegSVMs are based on the maximum margin training (Taskar et al., 2003; Tsochantaridis et al., 2005), which learns a discriminative model that maximizes the separating margin between different event classes. Maximizing the separating margin yields classifiers that are less prone to over-fitting. Furthermore, the learning formulation of SegSVMs is convex and extendable.

Beyond ED, SegSVMs can be extended to address the problems of early event detection and sequence labeling of multiple events. A temporal event has a duration, and by early detection, we mean to detect the event as soon as possible, *after it starts but before it ends*. Figure 14.2 illustrates the problem of early detection of smile facial event. While ED has been studied extensively, little attention has been paid to early detection, even in the broader literature of computer vision. In Section 14.3, we will describe an extension of SegSVMs for early event detection by training them to recognize partial events.

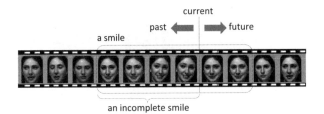

Figure 14.2: How many frames do we need to detect a smile reliably? Can we even detect a smile before it finishes? Existing event detectors are trained to recognize complete events only; they require seeing the entire event for a reliable decision, preventing early detection. We propose a learning formulation to recognize partial events, enabling early detection.

Figure 14.3: Sequence labeling factorizes a time series into a set of non-overlapping segments and recognizes their classes. In this figure, a facial video is labeled as a sequence of expressions.

The last section of this chapter presents another extension of SegSVMs for sequence labeling of multiple events. Sequence labeling factorizes a time series into a set of non-overlapping segments and assigns a class label to each segment. Recall that a sequence labeling system assigns a unique semantic label to each frame, whereas an ED system may assign none or multiple labels. Figure 14.3 shows an example of sequence labeling. While the problems are slightly different, SegSVMs can be extended to solve the sequence labeling problem too.

14.2 Structured Prediction for Event Detection

This section formulates ED as a structured prediction problem.

14.2.1 Event Detection as a Structured Prediction Problem

Consider a time series $\mathbf{X}$ and suppose that we need to detect a target event of which the length is bounded by l_{min} and l_{max}. We denote $\mathcal{Z}(t)$ be the set of length-bounded time intervals from the 1st to the tth frame:

$$\mathcal{Z}(t) = \{[s,e] \in \mathbb{N}^2 | 1 \le s \le e \le t, l_{min} \le e - s + 1 \le l_{max}\} \cup \{\emptyset\}.$$

Here $|\cdot|$ is the length function. For a time series $\mathbf{X}$ of length l, $\mathcal{Z}(l)$ (or $\mathcal{Z}$ for brevity) is the set of all possible locations of an event. The empty segment, $\mathbf{z} = \emptyset$, indicates no event occurrence. For an interval $\mathbf{z} = [s, e] \in \mathcal{Z}$, let $\mathbf{X_z}$ denote the subsegment of $\mathbf{X}$ from frame s to e inclusive.

Let $g(\mathbf{X})$ denote the output of the detector. We will learn the mapping g as in the structured prediction framework (Tsochantaridis et al., 2005; Bakır et al., 2007; Blaschko and Lampert, 2008) as:

$$g(\mathbf{X}) = \underset{\mathbf{z} \in \mathcal{Z}(l)}{\text{argmax}} \, f(\mathbf{X_z}; \boldsymbol{\theta}). \tag{14.1}$$

Here, $f(\mathbf{X_z}; \boldsymbol{\theta})$ is the detection score of segment $\mathbf{X_z}$, and $\boldsymbol{\theta}$ is the parameter vector of the score function. The output of the detector is defined as the segment that maximizes the detection score. We assume here that each sequence contains at most one occurrence of the event to be detected. This can be extended to k-or-fewer occurrences (Nguyen et al., 2010). The detector searches over all locations and temporal scales from l_{min} to l_{max}. The output of the detector may be the empty segment, and if it is, we report no detection.

14.2.2 Learning and Inference

Let $(\mathbf{X}^1, \mathbf{z}^1), \cdots, (\mathbf{X}^n, \mathbf{z}^n)$ be the set of training time series and their associated ground truth annotations for the events of interest. We assume each training sequence contains at most one event of interest, as a training sequence containing several events can always be divided into smaller subsequences of single events. Thus, $\mathbf{z}^i = [s^i, e^i]$ consists of two numbers indicating the start and end of the event in time series $\mathbf{X}^i$.

We consider a linear detection score function, where the detection score is a linear combination of the features:

$$f(\mathbf{X_z}; \boldsymbol{\theta}) = \begin{cases} \mathbf{w}^T \varphi(\mathbf{X_z}) + b & \text{if } \mathbf{z} \neq \emptyset, \\ 0 & \text{otherwise.} \end{cases} \tag{14.2}$$

Here, $\varphi(\mathbf{X_z})$ is the feature vector for segment $\mathbf{X_z}$ and $\boldsymbol{\theta} = [\mathbf{w}^T, b]$. For brevity, hereafter we use $f(\mathbf{X_z})$ instead of $f(\mathbf{X_z}; \boldsymbol{\theta})$ to denote the score of segment $\mathbf{X_z}$. The function parameters can be learned using Structured Output SVM (SOSVM) (Taskar et al., 2003; Tsochantaridis et al., 2005):

$$\underset{\mathbf{w}, \{\xi^i\}}{\text{min.}} \frac{1}{2} ||\mathbf{w}||^2 + \frac{C}{n} \sum_{i=1}^{n} \xi^i, \tag{14.3}$$

$$\text{s.t. } f(\mathbf{X}_{\mathbf{z}^i}^i) \geq f(\mathbf{X_z}^i) + \Delta(\mathbf{z}^i, \mathbf{z}) - \xi^i \ \forall \mathbf{z} \in \mathcal{Z} \text{ and } \xi^i \geq 0 \ \forall i.$$

Here, $\Delta(\mathbf{z}^i, \mathbf{z})$ is a loss function that decreases as a label $\mathbf{z}$ approaches the ground truth label $\mathbf{z}^i$. Intuitively, the constraints in (14.3) force the score of $f(\cdot)$ to be higher for the ground truth label $\mathbf{z}^i$ than for any other value of $\mathbf{z}$ and, moreover, to exceed this value by a margin equal to the loss associated with labeling $\mathbf{z}$.

This optimization problem is convex, but it has an exponentially large number of constraints. A typical optimization strategy is *constraint generation* (Tsochantaridis et al., 2005), which is theoretically guaranteed to produce a global optimal solution. Constraint generation is an iterative procedure that optimizes the objective w.r.t. a smaller set of constraints. The constraint set is expanded at every iteration by adding the most violated constraint. Thus, at each iteration of constraint generation, given the current value of $\mathbf{w}$, we need to solve:

$$\hat{\mathbf{z}} = \operatorname*{argmax}_{\mathbf{z} \in \mathcal{Z}} \{\Delta(\mathbf{z}^i, \mathbf{z}) + f(\mathbf{X}_{\mathbf{z}}^i)\}. \tag{14.4}$$

Thus, for the feasibility of the training phase, it is necessary that (14.4) can be solved effectively and efficiently at every iteration. It is worth noting that this inference problem is different from the one for localizing an event:

$$\hat{\mathbf{z}} = \operatorname*{argmax}_{\mathbf{z} \in \mathcal{Z}} f(\mathbf{X}_{\mathbf{z}}^i). \tag{14.5}$$

The optimization of (14.4) and (14.5) depends on the feature representation $\varphi(\mathbf{X}_{\mathbf{z}})$. In the next section, we describe two types of signal representation that render fast optimization.

14.2.3   Segment Features Using Bag-of-Words Representation

We consider the feature mapping $\varphi(\mathbf{X}_{\mathbf{z}})$ as the histogram of temporal words (Nguyen et al., 2009). A temporal dictionary is built by applying a clustering algorithm to a set of feature vectors sampled from the training data (Sivic and Zisserman, 2003). Subsequently, each feature vector is represented by the ID of the corresponding vocabulary entry. Finally, the feature mapping $\varphi(\mathbf{X}_{\mathbf{z}})$ is taken as the histogram of IDs associated with the frames inside the interval $\mathbf{z}$. Let $\mathbf{x}_i$ be the feature vector associated with the ith frame of signal $\mathbf{X}$, and let $\mathcal{C}_j$ denote the cluster j of the temporal dictionary. The feature mapping is defined as:

$$\varphi(\mathbf{X}_{\mathbf{z}}) = [\varphi_1, \cdots, \varphi_d, \operatorname{len}(\mathbf{z})]^T; \quad \varphi_j = \sum_{i \in \mathbf{z}} \varphi_{ji}; \quad \varphi_{ji} = \delta(\mathbf{x}_i \in \mathcal{C}_j). \tag{14.6}$$

Here d is the number of clusters, and $[\varphi_1, \cdots, \varphi_d]^T$ is the histogram of temporal words located within segment $[s, e]$ of signal $\mathbf{X}$.

In this work, instead of using hard quantization where each frame is associated with only one cluster, we propose to use *soft quantization* instead:

$$\varphi(\mathbf{X_z}) = [\varphi_1, \cdots, \varphi_d, \text{len}(\mathbf{z})]^T; \;\; \varphi_j = \sum_{i \in \mathbf{z}} \varphi_{ji}; \;\; \varphi_{ji} = k(\mathbf{x}_i, \mathbf{c}_j). \quad (14.7)$$

Here $\{\mathbf{c}_j\}$ are cluster centers, and $k(\cdot, \cdot)$ is the kernel function that measures the similarity between the frame $\mathbf{x}_i$ to the cluster center $\mathbf{c}_j$. φ_j measures the total similarity of the frames inside the segment $\mathbf{z}$ to the cluster center $\mathbf{c}_j$.

Notably, the vectors $\{\mathbf{c}_j\}$ do not need to be the cluster centers. They can be chosen to be any set of representative vectors. For example, $\{\mathbf{c}_j\}$ can be taken as the support vectors of a frame-based SVM trained to distinguish between individual positive and negative frames. In this case, our method directly improves the performance of frame-based SVM by relearning the weights to incorporate temporal constraints. To see this, consider the score function of frame-based SVM. For a frame $\mathbf{x}_i$ of a given signal $\mathbf{X}$, the SVM score is of the form $\mathbf{v}^T \varphi(\mathbf{x}_i) + b$. It has been shown that $\mathbf{v}$ can be expressed as a linear combination of the support vectors: $\mathbf{v} = \sum_{j=1}^{d} \alpha_j \varphi(\mathbf{c}_j)$. Thus, the SVM score for frame $\mathbf{x}_i$ is: $\mathbf{v}^T \varphi(\mathbf{x}_i) + b = \sum_{j=1}^{d} \alpha_j k(\mathbf{x}_i, \mathbf{c}_j) + b$. Meanwhile, the decision function of structured learning is: $\mathbf{w}^T \varphi(\mathbf{X_z}) + b = \sum_{i=s}^{e} \sum_{j=1}^{d} w_j k(\mathbf{x}_i, \mathbf{c}_j) + w_{d+1} \cdot \text{len}(\mathbf{z}) + b$.

For both feature mappings defined in (14.6) and (14.7), let a_i denote $\sum_{j=1}^{d} w_j \varphi_{ji} + w_{d+1}$. Thus, $\mathbf{w}^T \varphi(\mathbf{X_z}) = \sum_{i=s}^{e} a_i$. The label $\hat{\mathbf{z}}$ that maximizes $\mathbf{w}^T \varphi(\mathbf{X_z})$ is: $\hat{\mathbf{z}} = [\hat{s}, \hat{e}] = \text{argmax}_{1 \le s \le e} \sum_{i=s}^{e} a_i$. There exists a linear time algorithm (Nguyen et al., 2009) for this optimization problem. Similarly, the label $\hat{\mathbf{z}}$ that maximizes $\Delta(\mathbf{z}^i, \mathbf{z}) + \mathbf{w}^T \varphi(\mathbf{X}_\mathbf{z}^i)$ can be found as:

$$\hat{\mathbf{z}} = [\hat{s}, \hat{e}] = \underset{1 \le s \le e}{\text{argmax}} \left\{ \Delta(\mathbf{z}^i, [s, e]) + \sum_{t=s}^{e} a_t \right\}. \quad (14.8)$$

This can be conveniently solved using an exhaustive search, or it can be efficiently optimized by means of a branch-and-bound algorithm (Lampert et al., 2008; Chu et al., 2012).

14.3 Early Event Detection

The ability to make reliable early detection of temporal events has many potential applications in a wide range of fields, ranging from security (e.g., pandemic attack detection), environmental science (e.g., tsunami warning) to health care (e.g., risk-of-falling detection) and robotics (e.g., affective computing). While temporal ED has been extensively studied, early detection is a relatively unexplored problem. By early detection, we mean to detect the event as soon as possible, *after it starts but before it ends*, as illustrated in Figure 14.2. To see why it is important to detect events before they finish, consider a concrete example of building a robot that can affectively interact with humans. Arguably, a key requirement for such a robot is its ability to accurately and rapidly detect human emotional states from facial expressions so that appropriate responses can be made in a timely manner. More often than not, a socially acceptable response is to imitate the current human behavior. This requires facial events such as smiling or frowning to be detected even before they are complete; otherwise, the imitation response would be out of synchronization. However, the learning formulation provided in Section 14.2 does not train detectors to recognize partial events. Consequently, using this formulation for Early Event Detection (EED) would lead to unreliable decisions as we will illustrate in the experimental section.

This section proposes Max-Margin Early Event Detectors (MMED), a novel formulation for training event detectors that recognize partial events, enabling early detection. MMED is based on SOSVM (Taskar et al., 2003; Tsochantaridis et al., 2005) but extends it to accommodate the nature of sequential data. In particular, we simulate the sequential frame-by-frame data arrival for training time series and learn an event detector that correctly classifies partially observed sequences. Figure 14.4 illustrates the key idea behind MMED: partial events are simulated and used as positive training examples. It is important to emphasize that we train a *single* event detector to recognize *all* partial events. But MMED does more than augment the set of training examples; it trains a detector to localize the temporal extent of a target event, even when the target event has not yet finished. This requires monotonicity of the detection function with respect to the inclusion relationship between partial events—the detection score (confidence) of a partial event cannot exceed the score of an encompassing partial event. MMED provides a principled mechanism to achieve this monotonicity, which cannot be assured by a naive solution that simply augments the set of training examples.

14.3.1   Learning with Sequential Data

To support early detection of events in time series data, we propose to use partial events as positive training examples (Figure 14.4). In particular, we simulate the sequential arrival of training data as follows. Suppose the length of $\mathbf{X}^i$ is l^i. For each time $t = 1, \cdots, l^i$, let $\mathbf{z}_t^i$ be the part of event $\mathbf{z}^i$ that has already happened (i.e., $\mathbf{z}_t^i = \mathbf{z}^i \cap [1, t]$), which is possibly empty. Ideally, we want the output of the detector on time series $\mathbf{X}^i$ at time t to be the

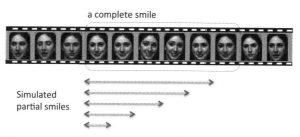

a complete smile

Simulated
partial smiles

Figure 14.4: Given a training time series that contains a complete event, we simulate the sequential arrival of training data and use partial events as positive training examples. The red segments indicate the temporal extents of the partial events. We train a *single* event detector to recognize *all* partial events, but our method does more than augment the set of training examples.

partial event (i.e., $g(\mathbf{X}^i_{[1,t]}) = \mathbf{z}^i_t$). Note that $g(\mathbf{X}^i_{[1,t]})$ is not the output of the detector running on the entire time series $\mathbf{X}^i$. It is the output of the detector on the subsequence of time series $\mathbf{X}^i$ from the first frame to the tth frame only, that is,

$$g(\mathbf{X}^i_{[1,t]}) = \underset{\mathbf{z} \in \mathcal{Z}(t)}{\operatorname{argmax}} f(\mathbf{X}^i_\mathbf{z}). \tag{14.9}$$

The desired property of the score function is: $f(\mathbf{X}^i_{\mathbf{z}^i_t}) \geq f(\mathbf{X}^i_\mathbf{z}) \ \forall \mathbf{z} \in \mathcal{Z}(t)$. This constraint requires the score of the partial event $\mathbf{z}^i_t$ to be higher than the score of any other time series segment $\mathbf{z}$ that has been seen in the past, $\mathbf{z} \subset [1,t]$. This is illustrated in Figure 14.5. Note that the score of the partial event is not required to be higher than the score of a future segment.

As in the case of SOSVM, the previous constraint can be required to be well satisfied by an adaptive margin. This margin is $\Delta(\mathbf{z}^i_t, \mathbf{z})$, the loss of the detector for outputting $\mathbf{z}$ when the desired output is $\mathbf{z}^i_t$ (in our case, $\Delta(\mathbf{z}^i_t, \mathbf{z}) = 1 - \frac{2|\mathbf{z}^i_t \cap \mathbf{z}|}{|\mathbf{z}^i_t| + |\mathbf{z}|}$). The desired constraint is $f(\mathbf{X}^i_{\mathbf{z}^i_t}) \geq f(\mathbf{X}^i_\mathbf{z}) + \Delta(\mathbf{z}^i_t, \mathbf{z}) \ \forall \mathbf{z} \in \mathcal{Z}(t)$. This constraint should be enforced for all $t = 1, \cdots, l^i$. As in the formulations of SVM, constraints are allowed to be violated by introducing slack variables, and we obtain the following learning formulation:

$$\underset{\mathbf{w}, b, \xi^i \geq 0}{\operatorname{minimize}} \frac{1}{2}||\mathbf{w}||^2 + \frac{C}{n}\sum_{i=1}^{n}\xi^i, \tag{14.10}$$

$$\text{s.t. } f(\mathbf{X}^i_{\mathbf{z}^i_t}) \geq f(\mathbf{X}^i_\mathbf{z}) + \Delta(\mathbf{z}^i_t, \mathbf{z}) - \frac{\xi^i}{\mu\left(\frac{|\mathbf{z}^i_t|}{|\mathbf{z}^i|}\right)} \ \forall i, \forall t = 1 \cdots l^i, \forall \mathbf{z} \in \mathcal{Z}(t). \tag{14.11}$$

Here, $|\cdot|$ denotes the length function, and $\mu\left(\frac{|\mathbf{z}^i_t|}{|\mathbf{z}^i|}\right)$ is a function of the proportion of the event that has occurred at time t. $\mu\left(\frac{|\mathbf{z}^i_t|}{|\mathbf{z}^i|}\right)$ is a

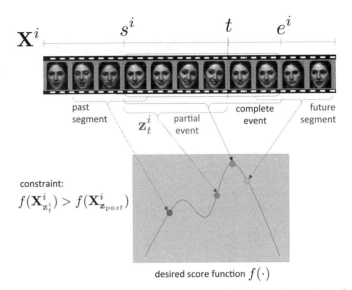

Figure 14.5: The desired score function for early event detection: the complete event must have the highest detection score, and the detection score of a partial event must be higher than that of any segment that ends before the partial event. To learn this function, we explicitly consider partial events during training. At time t, the score of the partial event is required to be higher than the score of any past segment; however, it is not required to be higher than the score of any future segment.

slack variable rescaling factor and should correlate with the importance of correctly detecting at time t whether the event $\mathbf{z}^i$ has happened. $\mu(\cdot)$ can be any arbitrary non-negative function, and in general, it should be a non-decreasing function in $(0, 1]$. In our experiments, we found the following piece-wise linear function a reasonable choice: $\mu(0) = 1$; $\mu(x) = 0$ for $0 < x \leq \alpha$; $\mu(x) = (x - \alpha)/(\beta - \alpha)$ for $\alpha < x \leq \beta$; and $\mu(x) = 1$ for $\beta < x \leq 1$. Here, α and β are tunable parameters. $\mu(0) = \mu(1)$ emphasizes that true rejection is as important as true detection of the complete event.

This learning formulation is an extension of SOSVM. From this formulation, we obtain SOSVM by not simulating the sequential arrival of training data (i.e., to set $t = l^i$ instead of $t = 1, \cdots, l^i$) in Constraint (14.11). Notably, our method does more than augment the set of training examples; it enforces the monotonicity of the detector function as shown in Figure 14.6.

For a better understanding of Constraint (14.11), let us analyze the constraint without the slack variable term and break it into three cases: (i) $t < s^i$ (event has not started); (ii) $t \geq s^i$, $\mathbf{z} = \emptyset$ (event has started; compare the partial event against the detection threshold); and (iii) $t \geq s^i$, $\mathbf{z} \neq \emptyset$ (event has started; compare the partial event against any non-empty segment). Recall $f(\mathbf{X}_\emptyset) = 0$ and $\mathbf{z}_t^i = \emptyset$ for $t < s^i$, cases (i), (ii), and (iii)

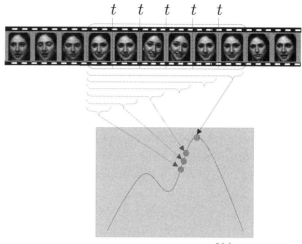

desired score function $f(\cdot)$

Figure 14.6: Monotonicity requirement—the detection score of a partial event cannot exceed the score of an encompassing partial event. MMED provides a principled mechanism to achieve this monotonicity, which cannot be assured by a naive solution that simply augments the set of training examples.

lead to Constraints (14.12), (14.13), and (14.14), respectively:

$$f(\mathbf{X}_{\mathbf{z}}^{i}) \leq -1 \; \forall \mathbf{z} \in \mathcal{Z}(s^{i}-1) \setminus \{\emptyset\}, \tag{14.12}$$

$$f(\mathbf{X}_{\mathbf{z}_{t}^{i}}^{i}) \geq 1 \; \forall t \geq s^{i}, \tag{14.13}$$

$$f(\mathbf{X}_{\mathbf{z}_{t}^{i}}^{i}) \geq f(\mathbf{X}_{\mathbf{z}}^{i}) + \Delta(\mathbf{z}_{t}^{i}, \mathbf{z}) \; \forall t \geq s^{i}, \mathbf{z} \in \mathcal{Z}(t) \setminus \{\emptyset\}. \tag{14.14}$$

Constraint (14.12) prevents false detection when the event has not started. Constraint (14.13) requires successful recognition of partial events. Constraint (14.14) trains the detector to accurately localize the temporal extent of the partial events.

The proposed learning formulation (14.10) is convex, but it contains a large number of constraints. As in Section 14.2.2, we propose to use constraint generation in optimization (Tsochantaridis et al., 2005). In our experiments described in Section 14.5, constraint generation usually converges within 20 iterations. Each iteration requires minimizing a convex quadratic objective. This objective is optimized using Cplex[1] in our implementation.

---

1. www-01.ibm.com/software/integration/optimization/cplex-optimizer/

14.3.2 Loss Function and Empirical Risk Minimization

In Section 14.3.1, we have proposed a formulation for training early event detectors. This section provides further discussion on what exactly is being optimized. First, we briefly review the loss of SOSVM and its surrogate empirical risk. We then describe two general approaches for quantifying the loss of a detector on sequential data. In both cases, what (14.10) minimizes is an upper bound on the loss.

As previously explained, $\Delta(\mathbf{z}, \hat{\mathbf{z}})$ is the function that quantifies the loss associated with a prediction $\hat{\mathbf{z}}$ if the true output value is $\mathbf{z}$. Thus, in the setting of offline detection, the loss of a detector $g(\cdot)$ on a sequence-event pair $(\mathbf{X}, \mathbf{z})$ is quantified as $\Delta(\mathbf{z}, g(\mathbf{X}))$. Suppose the sequence-event pairs $(\mathbf{X}, \mathbf{z})$ are generated according to some distribution $P(\mathbf{X}, \mathbf{z})$, the loss of the detector g is

$$\mathcal{R}^{\Delta}_{true}(g) = \int_{\mathcal{X} \times \mathcal{Z}} \Delta(\mathbf{z}, g(\mathbf{X})) dP(\mathbf{X}, \mathbf{z}). \qquad (14.15)$$

However, P is unknown so the performance of $g(.)$ is described by the empirical risk on the training data $\{(\mathbf{X}^i, \mathbf{z}^i)\}$, assuming they are generated i.i.d according to P. The empirical risk is $\mathcal{R}^{\Delta}_{emp}(g) = \frac{1}{n} \sum_{i=1}^{n} \Delta(\mathbf{z}^i, g(\mathbf{X}^i))$. It has been shown that SOSVM minimizes an upper bound on the empirical risk $\mathcal{R}^{\Delta}_{emp}$ (Tsochantaridis et al., 2005).

Due to the nature of continual evaluation, quantifying the loss of an online detector on streaming data requires aggregating the losses evaluated throughout the course of the data sequence. Let us consider the loss associated with a prediction $\mathbf{z} = g(\mathbf{X}^i_{[1,t]})$ for time series $\mathbf{X}^i$ at time t as $\Delta(\mathbf{z}^i_t, \mathbf{z}) \mu\left(\frac{|\mathbf{z}^i_t|}{|\mathbf{z}^i|}\right)$. Here, $\Delta(\mathbf{z}^i_t, \mathbf{z})$ accounts for the difference between the output $\mathbf{z}$ and true truncated event $\mathbf{z}^i_t$. $\mu\left(\frac{|\mathbf{z}^i_t|}{|\mathbf{z}^i|}\right)$ is the scaling factor; it depends on how much the temporal event $\mathbf{z}^i$ has happened. Two possible ways for aggregating these loss quantities is to use their maximum or average. They lead to two different empirical risks for a set of training time series:

$$\mathcal{R}^{\Delta,\mu}_{max}(g) = \frac{1}{n} \sum_{i=1}^{n} \max_t \left\{ \Delta(\mathbf{z}^i_t, g(\mathbf{X}^i_{[1,t]})) \mu\left(\frac{|\mathbf{z}^i_t|}{|\mathbf{z}^i|}\right) \right\},$$

$$\mathcal{R}^{\Delta,\mu}_{mean}(g) = \frac{1}{n} \sum_{i=1}^{n} \max_t \left\{ \Delta(\mathbf{z}^i_t, g(\mathbf{X}^i_{[1,t]})) \mu\left(\frac{|\mathbf{z}^i_t|}{|\mathbf{z}^i|}\right) \right\}.$$

In the following, we state and prove a proposition that establishes that the learning formulation given in (14.10) minimizes an upper bound of the above two empirical risks.

Proposition: Denote by $\boldsymbol{\xi}^*(g)$ the optimal solution of the slack variables in (14.10) for a given detector g, then $\frac{1}{n}\sum_{i=1}^n \xi^{i*}$ is an upper bound on the empirical risks $\mathcal{R}_{max}^{\Delta,\mu}(g)$ and $\mathcal{R}_{mean}^{\Delta,\mu}(g)$.

Proof: Consider Constraint (14.11) with $\mathbf{z} = g(\mathbf{X}_{[1,t]}^i)$ and together with the fact that $f(\mathbf{X}_{g(\mathbf{X}_{[1,t]}^i)}^i) \geq f(\mathbf{X}_{\mathbf{z}_t^i}^i)$, we have $\xi^{i*} \geq \Delta(\mathbf{z}_t^i, g(\mathbf{X}_{[1,t]}^i))\mu\left(\frac{|\mathbf{z}_t^i|}{|\mathbf{z}^i|}\right) \; \forall t$. Thus, $\xi^{i*} \geq \max_t\{\Delta(\mathbf{z}_t^i, g(\mathbf{X}_{[1,t]}^i))\mu\left(\frac{|\mathbf{z}_t^i|}{|\mathbf{z}^i|}\right)\}$. Hence $\frac{1}{n}\sum_{i=1}^n \xi^{i*} \geq \mathcal{R}_{max}^{\Delta,\mu}(g) \geq \mathcal{R}_{mean}^{\Delta,\mu}(g)$. This completes the proof of the proposition. This proposition justifies the objective of the learning formulation.

14.4   Sequence Labeling

Another important problem in time series analysis is sequence labeling, which factorizes a time series into a set of non-overlapping segments and assigns a class label to each segment. Sequence labeling is related to ED and is often used for ED. But these two problems are different. A sequence labeling system assigns a unique semantic label to each frame, whereas an ED system may assign no or multiple labels. Sequence labeling has been shown to be useful in a wide range of applications, from natural language processing (Rabiner, 1989) to office activity understanding (Brand and Kettnaker, 2000) and animal behavior analysis (Oh et al., 2008).

Most existing techniques for sequence labeling are based on probabilistic hidden-state models, and labeling a time series is equivalent to finding the sequence of event labels that yields the highest probability. Brand and Kettnaker (2000) use Hidden Markov Models (HMMs) (Rabiner, 1989) for understanding office activities. Xu et al. (2003) use multi-layer HMMs (Rabiner, 1989) to analyze baseball and volleyball videos. Oh et al. (2008) and Fox et al. (2009) use variants of Switching Linear Dynamical Systems (SLDS) (Pavlovic et al., 2000; Pavlovic and Rehg, 2000) to analyze human and animal behavior. Valstar and Pantic (2007), Koelstra and Pantic (2008), Tong et al. (2007), and Shang and Chan (2009); Chang et al. (2009) use Dynamic Bayesian Networks (DBNs) for detecting facial events, whereas Laxton et al. (2007) designed a hierarchical structure based on DBNs to decompose complex activities. Although these generative methods have been shown to be effective in their respective scenarios, they have limited ability to model the null class (i.e., no event, unseen event, or anything that we do not have a label for) due to the large variability of the null class. Conditional Random Fields (CRFs) (Lafferty et al., 2001) are the discriminative alternatives to HMMs, and they have been successfully used for a number

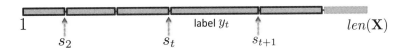

Figure 14.7: Joint segmentation and recognition process—we need to find the events' boundary points $s_1, \cdots, s_{k+1}$ and the class labels $y_1, \cdots, y_k$.

of applications such as detection of highlight events in soccer videos (Wang et al., 2006). CRFs, however, cannot model long-range dependencies between labels (Sarawagi and Cohen, 2005), disabling the use of segment-level features. CRFs can be extended to account for higher-order dependencies, but the computational cost increases exponentially with the clique size. Semi-Markov CRFs (Sarawagi and Cohen, 2005) have lower computational cost, but they also require short segment lengths (Okanohara et al., 2006). Nevertheless, CRF-based models, like HMMs or any other hidden-state model, suffer the drawbacks of needing either an explicit definition of the latent state of all frames or the need to simultaneously learn a state sequence and state transition model that fits the data, resulting in a high-dimensional minimization problem with typically many local minima. This section develops a multi-class extension of Seg-SVMs for sequence labeling, which simultaneously performs temporal segmentation and event recognition in time series.

14.4.1   Structured Prediction for Sequence Labeling

Our goal is to factorize a time series into a sequence of events and recognize their classes. Suppose there are m classes of events. We will discuss how to learn the detectors in Section 14.4.2, but assume for now that the detectors $\{\mathbf{w}_j\}_{j=1}^m$ have been learned. These detectors can be used independently to detect each class of target events in turn. This works well for many applications such as facial Action Unit (AU) detection. In many other applications, however, knowledge about the presence or absence of a particular event constrains on those of any other events, just like drinking and kissing do not occur together. This constraint can be incorporated in the joint segmentation and recognition process by finding a set of change points $s_1, \cdots, s_{k+1}$ (see Figure 14.7) that:

$$\underset{k, s_t, y_t, \xi_t \geq 0}{\text{minimize}} \sum_{t=1}^{k} \xi_t, \tag{14.16}$$

$$\text{s.t. } l_{min} \leq s_{t+1} - s_t \leq l_{max} \ \forall t, \ s_1 = 0, s_{k+1} = len(\mathbf{X}),$$

$$(\mathbf{w}_{y_t} - \mathbf{w}_y)^T \varphi(\mathbf{X}_{(s_t, s_{t+1}]}) \geq 1 - \xi_t \ \forall t, y \neq y_t.$$

Observe that the number of segments k is not known in advance and, therefore, needs to be optimized over. In the above formulation, l_{min} and l_{max} are the minimum and maximum lengths of segments, which can be inferred from training data. Here, $\mathbf{X}_{(s_t,s_{t+1}]}$ denotes the segment of time series $\mathbf{X}$, taken from frame $s_t + 1$ to frame s_{t+1} inclusive. $len(\mathbf{X})$ denotes the length of time series $\mathbf{X}$. $\mathbf{w}_y^T \varphi(\mathbf{X}_{(s_t,s_{t+1}]})$ is the SVM score for assigning segment $\mathbf{X}_{(s_t,s_{t+1}]}$ to class y. What we propose is to maximize the difference between the SVM score of the winning class y_t and that of any other class $y \neq y_t$, filtering through the Hinge loss. The idea is to seek a segmentation in which each resulting segment is assigned a class label with high confidence. This is different from what was proposed by Shi et al. (2008), who maximize the total SVM scores:

$$\underset{k,s_t,y_t}{\text{maximize}} \sum_{t=1}^{k} \mathbf{w}_{y_t}^T \varphi(\mathbf{X}_{(s_t,s_{t+1}]}), \text{ s.t.} \tag{14.17}$$

$$l_{min} \leq s_{t+1} - s_t \leq l_{max} \; \forall t, \; s_1 = 0, s_{k+1} = len(\mathbf{X}),$$

Different from the above formulation, our segmentation criterion, (14.16), requires suppressing the non-maximum classes. To see the difference between these two criteria, consider breaking a time series AB in Figure 14.8 at either M or N. For simplicity, suppose there are only two classes, and the SVM scores of the first and second class for some segments in Figure 14.8 are in printed in underlined and overlined, respectively. The segmentation criterion of (14.17) would prefer to divide AB at M because it leads to higher total SVM scores of the winning classes (total score of $3.5 = \underline{2.0} + \overline{1.5}$, $\underline{2.0}$ from segment AM and $\overline{1.5}$ from MB). In contrast, our segmentation criterion does not prefer to cut at M because it cannot confidently classify the resulting segments. To see this, consider the segment AM, even though the SVM score of the winning class, class 1, is high, the SVM score of the alternative, class 2, is also similarly high. Our proposed criterion seeks the optimal segmentation that maximizes the difference between the SVM scores of the winning class and the next best alternative, filtering through the robust Hinge loss. As we will show in Subsection 14.4.2, our segmentation criterion optimizes the same objective as that of the training formulation.

14.4.2 Maximum-Margin Learning for Sequence Labeling

We now describe how to learn $\mathbf{w}_1, \cdots, \mathbf{w}_m$ from a collection of training time series $\mathbf{X}^1, \cdots, \mathbf{X}^n$ with known segmentation and class labels, i.e., the change points between actions $0 = s_1^i < \cdots < s_{k_i+1}^i = len(\mathbf{X}^i)$ and the associated class labels $y_1^i, \cdots, y_{k_i}^i \in \{1, \cdots, m\}$ are provided (see Figure 14.7). We

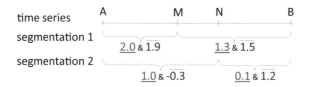

Figure 14.8: Which segmentation is preferred, breaking time series AB at M or N? Suppose there are only two classes; SVM scores of the first and second class for corresponding segments are printed in red and blue, respectively. Our segmentation criterion prefers to cut at N because the resulting segments can be confidently classified.

can use multi-class SVM Crammer and Singer (2001) to train a model for temporal actions:

$$\underset{\mathbf{w}_j, \xi_t^i \geq 0}{\text{minimize}} \ \frac{1}{2m} \sum_{j=1}^{m} \|\mathbf{w}_j\|^2 + \frac{C}{n} \sum_{i=1}^{n} \sum_{t=1}^{k_i} \xi_t^i, \tag{14.18}$$

$$\text{s.t.} \ (\mathbf{w}_{y_t^i} - \mathbf{w}_y)^T \varphi(\mathbf{X}_{(s_t^i, s_{t+1}^i)}^i) \geq 1 - \xi_t^i \ \forall i, t, y \neq y_t^i. \tag{14.19}$$

Constraint (14.19) requires segment $\mathbf{X}_{(s_t^i, s_{t+1}^i)}^i$ to belong to class y_t^i with high confidence; in other words, the SVM score for class y_t^i should be relatively higher than that of any other class by a large margin. $\{\xi_t^i\}$ are slack variables that allow for penalized constraint violation. C is the parameter controlling the trade-off between a large margin and less constrained violation.

14.4.3 Dynamic Programming Algorithm for Sequence Labeling

Given the parameters $\{\mathbf{w}_j\}_{j=1}^{m}$, the inference for (14.16) can be solved using a dynamic programming algorithm, which makes two passes over the time series $\mathbf{X}$. In the forward pass, at frame u $(1 \leq u \leq len(\mathbf{X}))$, it computes the best objective value for segmenting and labeling truncated time series $\mathbf{X}_{(0,u]}$ (ignoring frames from $u + 1$ onward), that is,

$$h(u) = \min_{k, s_t, y_t, \xi_t \geq 0} \sum_{t=1}^{k} \xi_t, \tag{14.20}$$

$$\text{s.t.} \ l_{min} \leq s_{t+1} - s_t \leq l_{max} \ \forall t, \ s_1 = 0, s_{k+1} = u,$$

$$(\mathbf{w}_{y_t} - \mathbf{w}_y)^T \varphi(\mathbf{X}_{(s_t, s_{t+1}]}) \geq 1 - \xi_t \ \forall t, y \neq y_t.$$

The forward pass computes $h(u)$, as well as $l(u)$, for $u = 1, \cdots, len(\mathbf{X})$ using the recursive formulas:

$$h(u) = \min_{l_{min} \leq l \leq l_{max}} \{\xi(u, l) + h(u - l)\},$$

$$l(u) = \operatorname*{argmin}_{l_{min} \leq l \leq l_{max}} \{\xi(u, l) + h(u - l)\}.$$

Here, $\xi(u, l)$ denotes the slack value of segment $\mathbf{X}_{(u-l,u]}$, that is,

$$\xi(u, l) = \max\{0, 1 - (\mathbf{w}_{\hat{y}} - \mathbf{w}_{\tilde{y}})^T \varphi(\mathbf{X}_{(u-l,u]})\}, \tag{14.21}$$

where

$$\hat{y} = \operatorname*{argmax}_{y} \mathbf{w}_y^T \varphi(\mathbf{X}_{(u-l,u]}), \text{and } \tilde{y} = \operatorname*{argmax}_{y \neq \hat{y}} \mathbf{w}_y^T \varphi(\mathbf{X}_{(u-l,u]}). \tag{14.22}$$

The backward pass of the algorithm finds the best segmentation for $\mathbf{X}$, starting with $s_{k+1} = len(\mathbf{X})$ and using the backward-recursive formula: $s_t = s_{t+1} - l(s_{t+1})$. Once the optimal segmentation has been determined, the optimal assignment of class labels can be found using $y_t = \operatorname{argmax}_y \mathbf{w}_y^T \varphi(\mathbf{X}_{(s_t,s_{t+1}]})$. The total complexity for the forward and backward passes of this dynamic programming algorithm is $O(m(l_{max} - l_{min} + 1)len(\mathbf{X}))$. This is linear in the length of the time series.

14.5 Experiments

This section describes experimental results on the detection of facial Action Units (AUs) from video, early detection of facial expressions and sign language, and sequence labeling of human actions from video.

14.5.1 Detection of Facial AUs

This section describes the experiments on detecting AUs in video. The experiments were performed on the RU-FACS-1 data set (Bartlett et al., 2006), a relatively large corpus of FACS coded videos. Recorded at Rutgers University, subjects were asked to either lie or tell the truth under a false opinion paradigm in interviews conducted by police and FBI members who posed around 13 questions. These interviews resulted in 2.5-minute continuous 30-fps video sequences containing spontaneous AUs of people of varying ethnicity and sex. Ground truth FACS coding was provided by expert coders. Data from 28 of the subjects were available for our experiments. In particular, we divided this data set into 17 subjects for training (97,000 frames) and 11 subjects for testing (67,000 frames).

The AUs for which we present results were selected by requiring at least 100 event occurrences in the available RU-FACS-1 data, resulting in the following set of AUs: $1, 2, 12, 14, 15, 17, 24$. Additionally, to test performance on AU combinations, AU1+2 and AU6+12 were selected due to the large number of occurrences.

Following Zhu et al. (2009), we extracted fixed-scale-and-orientation SIFT descriptors (Lowe, 1999) anchored at several points of interest at the tracked landmarks for frame-level feature representation. Intuitively, the histogram of gradient orientations calculated in SIFT has the potential to capture much of the information that is described in FACS (e.g., the markedness of the naso-labial furrows, the direction and distribution of wrinkles, the slope of the eyebrows). At the same time, the SIFT descriptor has been shown to be robust to illumination changes and small errors in localization.

After the facial components have been tracked in each frame, a normalization step registers each image with respect to an average face (Zhu et al., 2009). An affine texture transformation is applied to each image so as to warp the texture into this canonical reference frame. This normalization provides further robustness to the effects of head motion. Once the texture is warped into this fixed reference, SIFT descriptors are computed around the outer outline of the mouth (11 points for lower face AU) and on the eyebrows (5 for upper face AU). Due to the large number of resulting features (128 by number of points), the dimensionality of the resulting feature vector was reduced using PCA to keep 95% of the energy, obtaining 261 and 126 features for lower face and upper face AU, respectively.

We compared our method against a frame-based SVM and dynamic methods using HMM (Rabiner, 1989). The frame-based SVM (Bartlett et al., 2006) (referred to as SVM) is trained to distinguish between positive (AU) and negative (non-AU) frames and uses a radial basis kernel $k(\mathbf{x}, \mathbf{z}) = \exp(-\gamma||\mathbf{x}-\mathbf{z}||^2)$. Our method (*SegSVM*) is based on soft clustering, with the cluster centers chosen to be the support vectors (SVs) of frame-based SVMs with a radial basis kernel. Because for several AUs the number of SVs can be quite large (2000–4000), we apply the idea proposed by Avidan (2003) to reduce the number of SVs for faster training time and better generalization. However, instead of using a greedy algorithm for subset selection, we used LASSO regression (Tibshirani, 1996). In our experiments, the sizes of the reduced SV sets ranges from 100 to 500 SVs.

We also compared the performance of our method with dynamic approaches using HMMs, which have been used with success in the facial expression literature (Valstar and Pantic, 2007). In this experiment, we will limit ourselves to a basic generative HMM model where the observations for each state are modeled as a Gaussian distribution using a full covariance matrix with ridge regularization (i.e., $\hat{\mathbf{\Sigma}} = \mathbf{\Sigma} + \lambda\mathbf{I}$, where $\mathbf{I}$ is the identity matrix) and consider the same feature set used for all other experiments. Two different state mappings were tried, resulting in HMM2 and HMM4. HMM2 is a two-state model, where state-0 corresponds to a neutral face (no AU present) and state-1 corresponds to frames where the AU is present. HMM4 is a 4-state model, where state-0 is mapped to neutral face frames, state-1 corresponds to AU onset frames, state-2 corresponds to peak frames, and state-3 corresponds to offset frames.

Following Bartlett et al. (2005), positive samples were taken to be frames where the AU was present and negative samples where it was not. To evaluate performance, we used the precision-recall values and the maximum $F1$ score. The precision and recall measures were computed on a frame-by-frame basis by varying the bias or threshold of the corresponding classifier. The $F1$ score is defined as $F1 = \frac{2 \cdot Recall \cdot Precision}{Recall + Precision}$, summarizing the trade-off between high recall rates and accuracy among the predictions. $F1$ score is a better performance measure than the more common ROC metric because the latter is designed for balanced binary classification rather than detection tasks, and it fails to reflect the effect of the proportion of positive to negative samples on classification performance.

Parameter tuning is done using three-fold subject-wise cross-validation on the training data. For the frame-based SVM, we need to tune C and γ, the scale parameter of the radial basis kernel. For SegSVM, we need to tune C only. The kernel parameter γ of SegSVM could also potentially be tuned, but for simplicity it was set to the same γ used for frame-based SVM.

Table 14.1 shows the experimental results on the RU-FACS-1 data set. As can be seen, SegSVM, based on structured prediction, consistently outperforms frame-based SVM and HMM, achieving the highest $F1$ score on 7 out of 10 test cases. Figure 14.9 depicts the precision-recall curves of AU12 and AU15. These curves clearly show superior performance for SegSVM. For example, at 70% recall, the precision of SVM and SegSVM are 0.79 and 0.87, respectively. At 50% recall for AU15, the precision of SVM is 0.48 compared to 0.67, roughly $\frac{2}{3}$ that of SegSVM.

14.5.2 Early Detection of Facial Expression

The experiment for early detection of facial expression was performed on CK+, the Extended Cohn-Kanade data set (Lucey et al., 2010). This data set contains 327 facial image sequences from 123 subjects performing one of seven discrete emotions: anger, contempt, disgust, fear, happiness, sadness, and surprise. Each of the sequences contains images from onset (neutral

352 *Structured Prediction for Event Detection*

Methods	Action Units									
	1	2	6	12	14	15	17	24	1+2	6+12
SVM	0.48	0.42	0.50	0.74	0.20	0.50	0.55	0.15	0.36	0.55
HMM2	0.43	0.42	0.62	0.76	0.18	0.26	0.38	**0.18**	0.31	**0.64**
HMM4	0.39	0.18	**0.63**	0.77	0.12	0.25	0.28	0.05	0.31	0.63
SegSVM	**0.59**	**0.56**	0.59	**0.78**	**0.27**	**0.59**	**0.56**	0.08	**0.56**	0.62

Table 14.1: Max F1-score on the RU-FACS-1 data set. Higher numbers indicate better performance, and best results are printed in bold.

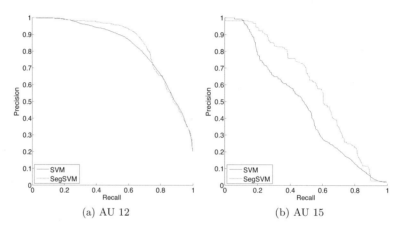

(a) AU 12   (b) AU 15

Figure 14.9: Precision-recall curves for AU 12 and AU 15. Our method significantly outperforms Frm-SVM.

frame) to peak expression (last frame). We considered the task of detecting negative emotions: anger, disgust, fear, and sadness.

We used the canonical normalized appearance feature, CAPP (Lucey et al., 2010). For comparison purposes, we implemented two frame-based SVMs: *Frm-peak* was trained on peak frames of the training sequences, whereas *Frm-all* was trained using all frames between the onset and offset of the facial action. Frame-based SVMs can be used for detection by classifying individual frames. In contrast, SOSVM and MMED are segment-based. Because a facial expression is a deviation of the neutral face, we represented each segment of an emotion sequence by the difference between the end frame and the start frame. Even though the start frame was not necessarily a neutral face, this representation led to good recognition results.

We used the area under the ROC curve for accuracy comparison and Normalized Time to Detection (NTtoD) for benchmarking the timeliness of detection. The ROC and AMOC curves are defined below.

ROC area: Consider testing a detector on a set of time series. The False Positive Rate (FPR) of the detector is defined as the fraction of time series that the detector fires before the event of interest starts. The True Positive Rate (TPR) is defined as the fraction of time series that the detector fires during the event of interest. A detector typically has a detection threshold that can be adjusted to trade off high TPR for low FPR and vise versa. By varying this detection threshold, we can generate an ROC curve, which is a function of TPR against FPR. We used the area under the ROC for evaluating the detector accuracy.

AMOC curve: To evaluate the timeliness of detection, we use Normalized Time to Detection (NTtoD), which is defined as follows. Given a testing time series where the event of interest occurs from s to e, suppose the detector starts to fire at time t. For a successful detection, $s \leq t \leq e$, we define the NTtoD as the fraction of event that has occurred (i.e., $\frac{t-s+1}{e-s+1}$). NTtoD is defined as 0 for a false detection ($t < s$) and ∞ for a false rejection ($t > e$). By adjusting the detection threshold, one can achieve smaller NTtoD at the cost of higher FPR and vice versa. For a complete characteristic picture, we vary the detection threshold and plot the curve of NToD versus FPR. This is referred as the Activity Monitoring Operating Curve (AMOC) (Fawcett and Provost, 1999).

We randomly divided the data into disjoint training and testing subsets. The training set contained 200 sequences with equal numbers of positive and negative examples. For reliable results, we repeated our experiment 20 times and recorded the average performance. Regarding the detection accuracy, segment-based SVMs outperformed frame-based SVMs. The ROC areas (mean and standard deviation) for Frm-peak, Frm-all, SOSVM, and MMED are 0.82 ± 0.02, 0.84 ± 0.03, 0.96 ± 0.01, and 0.97 ± 0.01, respectively. Comparing the timeliness of detection, our method was significantly better than the others, especially at low false-positive rates, which is what we care about. For example, at 10% false-positive rate, Frm-peak, Frm-all, SOSVM, and MMED can detect the expression when it completes 71%, 64%, 55%, and 47%, respectively. Figure 14.11a plots the AMOC curves, and Figure 14.10 displays some qualitative results. We used a linear SVM with $C = 1000$, $\alpha = 0$, and $\beta = 0.5$.

14.5.3 Early Detection of Sign Language

This section describes our experiments on a publicly available data set (Kadous, 2002) that contains 95 Auslan signs, each with 27 examples. The signs were captured from a native signer using position trackers and instrumented gloves; the location of the two hands, the orientation of the

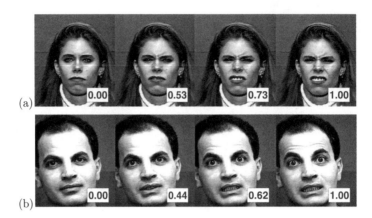

Figure 14.10: Disgust (a) and fear (b) detection on CK+ data set. From left to right of each sequence are the onset frame, the frame at which MMED fires, the frame at which SOSVM fires, and the peak frame. The number in each image is the corresponding NTtoD.

palms, and the bending of the fingers were recorded. We considered detecting the sentence "I love you" in monologues obtained by concatenating multiple signs. In particular, each monologue contained an I-love-you sentence, which was preceded and succeeded by 15 random signs. The I-love-you sentence was ordered concatenation of random samples of three signs: "I," "love," and "you." We created 100 training and 200 testing monologues from disjoint sets of sign samples; the first 15 examples of each sign were used to create training monologues, whereas the last 12 examples were used for testing monologues. The average lengths and standard deviations of the monologues and I-love-you sentences were 1836 ± 38 and 158 ± 6, respectively.

Previous work (Kadous, 2002) reported high recognition performance on this data set using Hidden Markov Models (HMMs) (Rabiner, 1989). Following their success, we implemented a continuous density HMM for I-love-you sentences. Our HMM implementation consisted of 10 states, each was a mixture of four Gaussians. To use the HMM for detection, we adopted a sliding window approach; the window size was fixed to the average length of the I-love-you sentences.

Inspired by the high recognition rate of HMM, we constructed feature representation for SVM-based detectors (SOSVM and MMED) as follows. We first trained a Gaussian Mixture Model of 20 Gaussians for the frames extracted from the I-love-you sentences. Each frame was then associated with a 20×1 log-likelihood vector. We retained the top three values of this vector, zeroing out the other values, to create a frame-level feature representation. This is the soft quantization approach. To compute the feature vector for a given window, we divided the window into two roughly equal halves, the

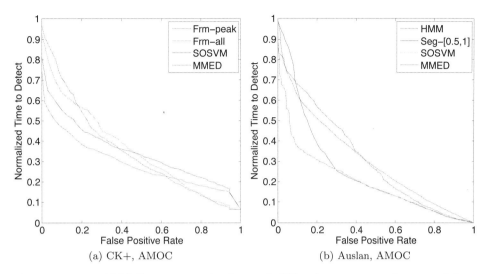

(a) CK+, AMOC   (b) Auslan, AMOC

Figure 14.11: AMOC curves on Auslan and CK+ data sets; at the same false-positive rate, MMED detects target events sooner than the other methods.

mean feature vector of each half was then calculated, and the concatenation of these mean vectors was then used as the feature representation of the window.

A naive strategy for early detection is to use truncated events as positive examples. For comparison, we implemented *Seg-[0.5,1]*, a binary SVM that used the first halves of the I-love-you sentences in addition to the full sentences as positive training examples. Negative training examples were random segments that had no overlapping with the I-love-you sentences.

We repeated our experiment 10 times and recorded the average performance. Regarding the detection accuracy, all methods except SVM-[0.5,1] performed similarly well. The ROC areas for HMM, SVM-[0.5,1], SOSVM, and MMED were 0.97, 0.92, 0.99, and 0.99, respectively. However, when comparing the timeliness of detection, MMED outperformed the others by a large margin. For example, at 10% false-positive rate, our method detected the I-love-you sentence when it observed the first 37% of the sentence. At the same false-positive rate, the best alternative method required seeing 62% of the sentence. The full AMOC curves are depicted in Figure 14.11b. In this experiment, we used linear SVM with $C = 1$, $\alpha = 0.25$, and $\beta = 1$.

14.5.4   Sequence Labeling of Human Actions

The experiments on sequence labeling of human actions were performed on the Weizmann data set (Gorelick et al., 2007). This data set contains

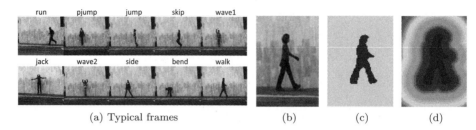

(a) Typical frames   (b)   (c)   (d)

Figure 14.12: (a) Weizmann data set, (b–d) computing frame-level features: (b) original frame, (c) binary mask, and (d) Euclidean distance transform.

90 video sequences (180×144 pixels, deinterlaced 50fps) of nine people, each performing 10 actions. Figure 14.12(a) displays several typical frames extracted from the data set. Each video sequence in this data set only consists of a single action.

To evaluate the segmentation and recognition performance of our method, we performed experiments on longer video sequences that were created by concatenating existing single-action sequences. Specifically, we created nine long sequences, each composed of 10 videos for 10 different actions (each original video sample was used only once). To evaluate the performance of the proposed method in the presence of the null class, background clutter with large variability, we considered the last five classes of actions (side, skip, walk, wave1, and wave2) as the null class. Following Gorelick et al. (2007), we extracted binary masks (Figure 14.12c) and computed Euclidean distance transform (Figure 14.12d) for frame-level features. We built a codebook of temporal words with 100 clusters using k-means.

We measured the leave-one-out joint segmentation and recognition performance as follows. We ran our algorithm on long video sequences to find the optimal segmentation and class labels. At that point, each frame was associated with a particular class, and the overall frame-level accuracy against the ground truth labels was calculated as the ratio between the number of agreements over the total number of frames. This evaluation criterion is different from recognition accuracy of algorithms that require pre-segmented video clips (Gorelick et al., 2007).

Table 14.2 shows the confusion matrix for five actions and the null class. Our method yielded the average accuracy of 93.3%. The variant of our method, MaxScoreSeg (Shi et al., 2008), which performed temporal segmentation by maximizing the total SVM scores (14.17), obtained an average accuracy of 77.9%. This relatively low accuracy is due to the mismatch between the segmentation criterion and the training objective, as explained in Section 14.4.1. Figure 14.13 displays side-by-side comparison of

	bend	jack	jump	pjump	run	Null
bend	.96	.01	.01	.00	.00	.01
jack	.00	.97	.00	.01	.00	.02
jump	.00	.00	.88	.06	.04	.02
pjump	.00	.00	.01	.98	.00	.01
run	.00	.00	.01	.00	.91	.08
Null	.01	.03	.00	.03	.03	.90

Table 14.2: Results on Weizmann data set. Confusion matrix for segmentation and recognition of five different actions: bend, jack, jump, pjump, and run. The null class is the combination of all other classes. The average accuracy is 93.3%.

the prediction result and the human-labeled ground truth. Except for several cases, the majority of error occurs at the boundaries between actions. Error at the boundaries does not necessarily indicate the flaw of our method as human labels are often imperfect (Satkin and Hebert, 2010).

14.6   Summary

This chapter proposed SegSVMs, a structured prediction framework for ED, early ED, and sequence labeling. SegSVMs have convex learning formulations and efficient inference algorithms. We illustrated the benefits of our approaches in a number of existing and new problems in computer vision.

In this chapter, we have addressed the problems of ED, early ED, and sequence labeling using supervised learning. However, other important problems arise in the context of weakly supervised and unsupervised settings. For instance, in weakly supervised learning, we need to localize the discriminative events from a set of time series annotated with binary labels indicating the presence of the event but not its location (Nguyen et al., 2009). This has many important applications (e.g., for analyzing times series with or without a particular medical condition). Similarly, unsupervised clustering of time series is important for learning taxonomies of human behavior (Hoai and de la Torre, 2012a). These tasks can also be formulated as extensions of SegSVMs, and we refer the reader to Nguyen et al. (2009), Hoai et al. (2011), Hoai and de la Torre (2012a), and Hoai and de la Torre (2012b) for more details.

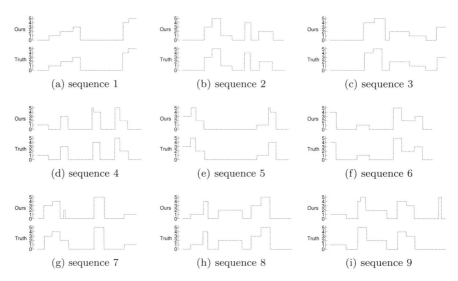

Figure 14.13: Automatic segmentation-recognition versus human-labeled ground truth for Weizmann data set. The segments at values 0, 1, 2, 3, 4, and 5 correspond to null, bend, jack, pjump, jump, and run, respectively.

Acknowledgments

This work was supported by the National Science Foundation (NSF) under Grant No. RI-1116583. Any opinions, findings, conclusions, or recommendations expressed in this material are those of the author(s) and do not necessarily reflect the views of the NSF. The authors would like to thank Jeffrey Cohn and Tomas Simon for their contribution on the experiment 14.5.1 and many helpful discussions.

14.7   References

J. Aggarwal and Q. Cai. Human motion analysis: A review. *Computer Vision and Image Understanding*, 73(3):428–440, 1999.

S. Avidan. Subset selection for efficient SVM tracking. In *Proc. CVPR*, 2003.

G. Baklr, T. Hofmann, B. Schölkopf, A. Smola, B. Taskar, and S. Vishwanathan, editors. *Predicting Structured Data*. MIT Press, 2007.

M. Bartlett, G. Littlewort, M. Frank, C. Lainscsek, I. Fasel, and J. Movellan. Recognizing facial expression: Machine learning and application to spontaneous behavior. In *Computer Vision and Pattern Recognition*, 2005.

M. Bartlett, G. Littlewort, M. Frank, C. Lainscsek, I. Fasel, and J. Movellan. Automatic recognition of facial actions in spontaneous expressions. *Journal of Multimedia*, 1(6):22–35, 2006.

M. B. Blaschko and C. H. Lampert. Learning to localize objects with structured output regression. In *Proc. ECCV*, 2008.

A. F. Bobick and A. D. Wilson. A state-based technique for the summarization and recognition of gesture. *IEEE PAMI*, 19(12):1325–1337, 1997.

M. Brand and V. Kettnaker. Discovery and segmentation of activities in video. *IEEE PAMI*, 22(8):844–851, 2000.

M. Brand, N. Oliver, and A. Pentland. Coupled hidden Markov models for complex action recognition. In *Proc. CVPR*, 1997.

K. Chang, T. Liu, and S. Lai. Learning partially-observed hidden conditional random fields for facial expression recognition. In *Computer Vision and Pattern Recognition*, 2009.

W.-S. Chu, F. Zhou, and F. de la Torre. Unsupervised temporal commonality discovery. In *Proc. ECCV*, 2012.

J. Cohn, T. Simon, I. Matthews, Y. Yang, M. H. Nguyen, M. Tejera, F. Zhou, and F. de la Torre. Detecting depression from facial actions and vocal prosody. In *Proceedings of International Conference on Affective Computing and Intelligent Interaction*, 2009.

K. Crammer and Y. Singer. On the algorithmic implementation of multiclass kernel-based vector machines. *J. Machine Learning Research*, 2:265–292, 2001.

A. Efros, A. Berg, G. Mori, and J. Malik. Recognizing action at a distance. In *Proc. ICCV*, 2003.

T. Fawcett and F. Provost. Activity monitoring: Noticing interesting changes in behavior. In *Proceedings of the SIGKDD Conference on Knowledge Discovery and Data Mining*, 1999.

E. B. Fox, E. B. Sudderth, M. I. Jordan, and A. S. Willsky. Nonparametric Bayesian learning of switching linear dynamical systems. In *NIPS*. 2009.

L. Gorelick, M. Blank, E. Shechtman, M. Irani, and R. Basri. Actions as space-time shapes. *IEEE PAMI*, 29(12):2247–2253, 2007.

M. Hoai and F. de la Torre. Maximum margin temporal clustering. In *Proceedings of International Conference on Artificial Intelligence and Statistics*, 2012a.

M. Hoai and F. de la Torre. Max-margin early event detectors. In *Proc. CVPR*, 2012b.

M. Hoai, Z.-Z. Lan, and F. De la Torre. Joint segmentation and classification of human actions in video. In *Proc. CVPR*, 2011.

M. Kadous. *Temporal classification: Extending the classification paradigm to multivariate time series*. PhD thesis, The University of New South Wales, 2002.

Y. Ke, R. Sukthankar, and M. Hebert. Efficient visual event detection using volumetric features. In *Proc. ICCV*, 2005.

S. Koelstra and M. Pantic. Non-rigid registration using free-form deformations for recognition of facial actions and their temporal dynamics. In *International Conference on Automatic Face and Gesture Recognition*, 2008.

J. Lafferty, A. McCallum, and F. Pereira. Conditional random fields: Probabilistic models for segmenting and labeling sequence data. In *Proc. ICML*, 2001.

C. H. Lampert, M. B. Blaschko, and T. Hofmann. Beyond sliding windows: Object localization by efficient subwindow search. In *Proc. CVPR*, 2008.

I. Laptev and P. Perez. Retrieving actions in movies. In *Proc. ICCV*, 2007.

I. Laptev, M. Marszalek, C. Schmid, and B. Rozenfeld. Learning realistic human actions from movies. In *Proc. CVPR*, 2008.

B. Laxton, J. Lim, and D. Kriegman. Leveraging temporal, contextual and ordering constraints for recognizing complex activities in video. In *Proc. CVPR*, 2007.

D. Lewis. Naive (Bayes) at forty: The independence assumption in information retrieval. In *Proc. ECML,* 1998.

D. Lowe. Object recognition from local scale-invariant features. In *Proc. ICCV*, 1999.

P. Lucey, J. F. Cohn, T. Kanade, J. Saragih, Z. Ambadar, and I. Matthews. The extended Cohn-Kanade dataset (CK+): A complete dataset for action unit and emotion-specified expression. In *CVPR Workshop on Human Communicative Behavior Analysis*, 2010.

S. Lucey, I. Matthews, C. Hu, Z. Ambadar, F. de la Torre, and J. Cohn. AAM derived face representations for robust facial action recognition. In *International Conference on Automatic Face and Gesture Recognition*, 2006.

M. H. Nguyen, L. Torresani, F. De la Torre, and C. Rother. Weakly supervised discriminative localization and classification: a joint learning process. In *Proc. ICCV*, 2009.

M. H. Nguyen, T. Simon, F. de la Torre, and J. Cohn. Action unit detection with segment-based SVMs. In *Proc. CVPR*, 2010.

S. Nowozin, G. BakIr, and K. Tsuda. Discriminative subsequence mining for action classification. In *Proc. ICCV*, 2007.

S. M. Oh, J. M. Rehg, T. Balch, and F. Dellaert. Learning and inferring motion patterns using parametric segmental switching linear dynamic systems. *IJCV*, 77(1–3):103–124, 2008.

D. Okanohara, Y. Miyao, Y. Tsuruoka, and J. Tsujii. Improving the scalability of semi-Markov conditional random fields for named entity recognition. In *Proceedings of International Conference on Computational Linguistics*, 2006.

V. Pavlovic and J. M. Rehg. Impact of dynamic model learning on classification of human motion. In *Proc. CVPR*, 2000.

V. Pavlovic, J. M. Rehg, and J. MacCormick. Learning switching linear models of human motion. In *NIPS*, 2000.

C. Piciarelli, C. Micheloni, and G. L. Foresti. Trajectory-based anomalous event detection. *IEEE Transactions on Circuits and System for Video Technology*, 18 (11):1544–1554, 2008.

L. R. Rabiner. A tutorial on hidden Markov models and selected applications in speech recognition. *Proceedings of the IEEE*, 77(2):257–286, 1989.

S. Sarawagi and W. Cohen. Semi-Markov conditional random fields for information extraction. In *NIPS*, 2005.

S. Satkin and M. Hebert. Modeling the temporal extent of actions. In *Proc. ECCV*, 2010.

L. Shang and K. Chan. Nonparametric discriminant HMM and application to facial expression recognition. In *Conference on Computer Vision and Pattern Recognition*, 2009.

E. Shechtman and M. Irani. Space-time behavior based correlation—or—how to tell if two underlying motion fields are similar without computing them? *IEEE PAMI*, 29(11):2045–2056, 2007.

Q. Shi, L. Wang, L. Cheng, and A. Smola. Discriminative human action segmentation and recognition using semi-Markov model. In *Proc. CVPR*, 2008.

J. Sivic and A. Zisserman. Video Google: A text retrieval approach to object matching in videos. In *Proc. ICCV*, 2003.

C. Sminchisescu, A. Kanaujia, Z. Li, and D. Metaxas. Conditional models for contextual human motion recognition. In *Proc. ICCV*, 2005.

B. Taskar, C. Guestrin, and D. Koller. Max-margin Markov networks. In *NIPS*. 2003.

R. Tibshirani. Regression shrinkage and selection via the LASSO. *Journal of the Royal Statistical Society, Series B*, 58(267–288), 1996.

Y. Tong, W. Liao, and Q. Ji. Facial action unit recognition by exploiting their dynamic and semantic relationships. *Transactions on Pattern Analysis and Machine Intelligence*, pages 1683–1699, 2007.

I. Tsochantaridis, T. Joachims, T. Hofmann, and Y. Altun. Large margin methods for structured and interdependent output variables. *Journal of Machine Learning Research*, 6:1453–1484, 2005.

M. Valstar and M. Pantic. Combined support vector machines and hidden markov models for modeling facial action temporal dynamics. In *ICCV Workshop on Human Computer Interaction*, 2007.

H. Vassilakis, A. J. Howell, and H. Buxton. Comparison of feedforward (TDRBF) and generative (TDRGBN) network for gesture based control. In *Proceedings of Revised Papers From the International Gesture Workshop on Gesture and Sign Languages in Human-Computer Interaction*, 2002.

T. Wang, J. Li, Q. Diao, W. Hu, Y. Zhang, and C. Dulong. Semantic event detection using conditional random fields. In *CVPR Workshop*, 2006.

G. Xu, Y.-F. Ma, H.-J. Zhang, and S. Yang. A HMM based semantic analysis framework for sports game event detection. *International Conference on Image Processing*, 2003.

J. Yamato, J. Ohya, and K. Ishii. Recognizing human action in time sequential images using hidden Markov model. In *Proc. CVPR*, 1992.

Y. Zhu, F. de la Torre, and J. Cohn. Dynamic cascades with bidirectional bootstrapping for spontaneous facial action unit detection. In *Affective Computing and Intelligent Interaction*, 2009.

15   Structured Prediction for Object Boundary Detection in Images

Sinisa Todorovic   sinisa@eecs.oregonstate.edu
School of EECS, Oregon State University
Corvallis, OR, USA

This chapter presents an overview of our recent work on boundary detection in images using structured prediction. Our input are image edges that are noisy responses of a low-level edge detector. The edges are labeled as belonging to either a boundary or background clutter, thus producing the structured output. The labeling is based on photometric and geometric properties of the edges, as well as evidence of their perceptual grouping. We consider two structured prediction algorithms. First, the policy iteration algorithm, called SLEDGE, sequentially labels the edges, where every labeling step updates features of unlabeled edges based on previously detected boundaries. Second, Heuristic-Cost Search (HC-Search) uncovers high-quality boundary predictions based on a heuristic function and then selects the prediction with the smallest cost as structured output. On the benchmark Berkeley Segmentation Dataset 500, both algorithms prove robust and effective and compare favorably with the state of the art in terms of recall and precision. HC-Search outperforms SLEDGE but at the cost of higher complexity.

15.1   Introduction

This chapter presents an overview of our recent work on detecting object boundaries in an arbitrary image. We consider boundary detection that is uninformed about specific objects and their numbers, scales, and layouts in the scene.

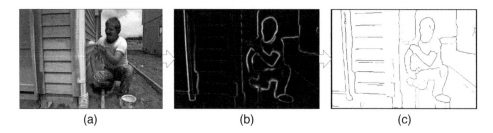

(a)   (b)   (c)

Figure 15.1: Overview: (a) The input image. (b) Edge detectors typically output a probability edge map, which can be thresholded into a set of image edges. (c) Our structured prediction labels every edge as being on or off an object boundary. The darker the boundaries, the higher prediction confidence.

This problem can be cast within the structured prediction framework, where image edges comprising the structured input are mapped to boundary detections comprising the structured output. We use image edges as features suitable for boundary detection. This is because boundaries typically coincide with a sub set of edges, and edges provide rich information about the spatial extent and layout of objects in the image. Thus, our structured prediction labels image edges as belonging to either a boundary or background clutter, as illustrated in Figure 15.1.

In this chapter, we consider two structured prediction algorithms aimed at optimally combining intrinsic and layout properties of image edges for boundary detection. First, SLEDGE is a policy iteration algorithm, presented in Payet and Todorovic (2013). It sequentially labels the edges, where in each labeling step, evidence about the Gestalt grouping of the edges is updated based on previously detected boundaries. Training of SLEDGE is iterative. In each iteration, SLEDGE labels a sequence of edges extracted from each training image. This induces loss with respect to the ground truth. The training sequences are then used as training examples for re-learning SLEDGE in the next iteration, such that the total loss is minimized.

Second, Heuristic-Cost Search (HC-Search) is a structured prediction algorithm based on search in the space of structured outputs (Doppa et al., 2012, 2013). HC-Search uncovers high-quality labelings of image edges (i.e., structured outputs) and represents them as nodes of a rooted tree. Links in the tree correspond to moves from one candidate output to another. The goal of HC-Search is to effectively search this tree in order to quickly find an optimal output. To this end, we train a heuristic function to evaluate the moves throughout the search tree and a cost function to select an optimal node in the tree among the candidates.

Both algorithms prove robust and effective and compare favorably with the state-of-the-art structured prediction methods, in terms of recall and precision, on the following benchmark data sets: Berkeley segmentation data sets BSD300 and BSD500 (Martin et al., 2001; Arbelaez et al., 2010), Weizmann Horses (Borenstein and Ullman, 2002), and LabelMe (B.Russell et al., 2008). HC-Search gives higher recall and precision but at the cost of higher complexity than SLEDGE.

Section 15.2 reviews prior work, Section 15.3 describes the edge detector and edge properties used in this chapter, Section 15.4 specifies SLEDGE, Section 15.5 presents HC-Search, and Section 15.6 presents our experimental evaluation.

15.2   Related Work

This section focuses on reviewing prior work on structured prediction and closely related work on edge-based boundary detection in images.

A standard approach to structured prediction is to learn a cost function $\mathcal{C}(\boldsymbol{x}, \boldsymbol{y})$ for scoring a structured output, $\boldsymbol{y}$, given a structured input, $\boldsymbol{x}$. Computing $\mathcal{C}(\boldsymbol{x}, \boldsymbol{y})$ involves solving the "Argmin" problem, which is to find the minimum cost output for a given input:

$$\text{Argmin:} \quad \hat{\boldsymbol{y}} = \operatorname*{argmin}_{\boldsymbol{y}} \mathcal{C}(\boldsymbol{x}, \boldsymbol{y}). \tag{15.1}$$

Prior work has demonstrated that log-distributions of graphical models — namely, Markov Random Fields (MRFs) (Zhu, 1999) or Conditional Random Fields (CRFs) (Ren et al., 2008; Maire et al., 2008) — can be used to suitably define $\mathcal{C}(\boldsymbol{x}, \boldsymbol{y})$ in (15.1) for boundary detection. In general, exactly solving the Argmin problem of (15.1) is intractable, including the cases when $\mathcal{C}(\boldsymbol{x}, \boldsymbol{y})$ is defined using MRFs or CRFs. This has been addressed using heuristic optimization methods, such as, loopy belief propagation or variational inference. While such methods have shown some success in practice, the effect of their approximation on learning parameters of the original models of $\mathcal{C}(\boldsymbol{x}, \boldsymbol{y})$ (i.e., MRFs or CRFs) is poorly understood. This is because learning of $\mathcal{C}(\boldsymbol{x}, \boldsymbol{y})$ on training examples typically involves inference as one of the necessary steps.

Another group of methods considers solving the Argmin problem via cascading (Felzenszwalb and McAllester, 2007; Weiss and Taskar, 2010; Munoz et al., 2010), where inference is run in stages from a coarse to fine level of abstraction. These methods, however, have a number of limitations. They place restrictions on the form of $\mathcal{C}(\boldsymbol{x}, \boldsymbol{y})$ to facilitate cascading, which may not be suitable for boundary detection. In particular, they typically ignore the loss function of a problem (e.g., by assuming the Hamming loss) or require that the loss function be decomposable in a way that supports loss augmented inference. In contrast, HC-Search makes minimal assumptions about the loss function, requiring only a "black-box" evaluation of a candidate structured output.

SLEDGE is related to classifier-based methods, including SEARN (III et al., 2009), SMiLe (Ross and Bagnell, 2010), and DAGGER (Ross et al., 2011). They avoid directly solving the Argmin problem by assuming that structured outputs can be generated by making a series of discrete decisions. Decisions are usually made in a greedy manner using classifiers to produce structured outputs. As a key advantage, these approaches do not make any assumptions about the underlying structure and statistical dependencies of the output variables. However, some decisions in the series are difficult to predict by a greedy classifier, and any intermediate errors may lead to error propagation. SLEDGE mitigates this issue by classifying first those edges that have higher confidence to help make decisions in subsequent ambiguous cases. HC-Search, in contrast leverages efficient search spaces over complete outputs, which allows decision making by comparing multiple complete outputs and choosing the best.

HC-Search is also related to Re-Ranking (Collins, 2002), which uses a generative model to propose a k-best list of outputs, which are then ranked by a separate ranking function. Rather than restricting to a generative model for producing candidate outputs, HC-Search leverages generic search over efficient search spaces guided by a learned heuristic function that has minimal representational restrictions and employs a learned cost function to rank the candidate outputs.

There is a large volume of prior work on edge-based boundary detection. These approaches extract a clutter of image edges and then use the Gestalt-grouping principles to select and link a sub set of the edges into boundaries (Zhu, 1999; Sharon et al., 2001; Zhu et al., 2007; Ren et al., 2008; Kokkinos, 2010a,b). Due to accounting for more global visual information carried by edges as mid-level features, these methods typically outperform patch-based approaches. Another group of related methods track image edges for boundary detection (Guy and Medioni, 1996; Williams and Thornber, 1999; Mahamud et al., 2003; Felzenszwalb and McAllester, 2006). They usually resort to heuristic: (i) assumptions about the total number of boundaries, (ii) protocols for tracking (e.g., where to start), and (iii) definitions of edge affinities for tracking. SLEDGE and HC-Search use training examples to estimate these heuristic functions.

15.3   Edge Extraction and Properties

Any low-level edge detector can be used for feature extraction in our approach. In our experiments, we use: (a) Canny edge detector (Canny, 1986), or (b) gPb detector (Maire et al., 2008). gPb produces a probability map of edge saliences. This map is thresholded at all probability levels, and edges are extracted using the standard non-maximum suppression. Given a set of image edges, we extract their intrinsic properties and evidence about their Gestalt grouping. In this chapter, we use the same edge properties as those described in Payet and Todorovic (2013). Below, we give a brief overview of these properties for completeness.

15.3.1   Intrinsic Edge Properties

The intrinsic edge properties, $\boldsymbol{\psi}_i = [\psi_{i1}, \psi_{i2}]$, include: (a) saliency, ψ_{i1}; and (b) repeatability, ψ_{i2}. Salient edges are likely to belong to boundaries, and repeating edges are more likely to arise from clutter and texture than boundaries.

ψ_{i1} is computed as the mean Pb value along an edge, $\boldsymbol{\psi}_{i1} = \text{mean}_i(Pb)$, for the gPb detector, or the mean of magnitude of intensity gradient along the edge, $\boldsymbol{\psi}_{i1} = \text{mean}_i(\text{gradient})$, for the Canny detector.

For computing ψ_{i2}, we match all pairs of edges in the image. We estimate the dissimilarity of two edges, s_{ij}, as a difference between their Shape Context descriptors (Belongie et al., 2002). After linking all pairs of edges and computing their dissimilarities, Page Rank (Brin and Page, 1998; Kim et al., 2008; Lee and Grauman, 2009) iteratively estimates the degree of repetition of each edge as $\psi_{i2} = (1 - \rho) + \rho \sum_j \frac{\psi_{j2}}{\sum_j s_{ik}}$, where $\rho = 0.85$ is the residual probability and j and k the indices of neighboring edges to edge i. For estimating the neighbors, we construct the Delaunay Triangulation (DT) of all endpoints of the edges. If a pair of endpoints is connected in the DT and directly "visible" to each other without crossing any other edge, then their edges are declared as neighbors. This allows us to estimate proximity and good continuation between even fairly distant edges in the image.

15.3.2   Layout Edge Properties

Layout properties are defined between pairs of neighboring image edges, $\boldsymbol{\phi}_{ij} = [\phi_{ij1}, \ldots, \phi_{ij5}]$, and include standard formulations of the Gestalt principles of grouping (Lowe, 1985; Zhu, 1999; Ren et al., 2008). Let Q_i and Q_j denote the 2D coordinates of the closest endpoints of edges i and j. We estimate:

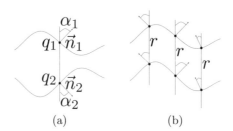

Figure 15.2: (a) The line between symmetric points q_1 and q_2 lying on two distinct edges subtends the same angle $\alpha_1 = \alpha_2$ with the respective edge normals $\vec{n}_1$ and $\vec{n}_2$. (b) Constant distance r between symmetric points of two distinct edges indicates parallelism of the edges.

1. Proximity as $\phi_{ij1} = \frac{2\pi\|Q_i - Q_j\|^2}{\min(\mathrm{len}(i), \mathrm{len}(j))^2}$, where $\mathrm{len}(\cdot)$ measures the length of an edge.

2. Collinearity as $\phi_{ij2} = \left|\frac{d\theta(Q_i)}{dQ_i} - \frac{d\theta(Q_j)}{dQ_j}\right|$. $\theta(Q) \in [0, 2\pi]$ measures the angle between the x-axis and the tangent of the edge at endpoint Q, where the tangent direction is oriented toward the curve.

3. Co-Circularity as $\phi_{ij3} = \left|\frac{d^2\theta(Q_i)}{dQ_i^2} - \frac{d^2\theta(Q_j)}{dQ_j^2}\right|$.

4. Symmetry as $\phi_{ij5} = \mathrm{mean}_{q \in i}\left|\frac{d^2 r(q)}{dq^2}\right|$. As illustrated in Figure 15.2(a), two points $q_1 \in i$ and $q_2 \in j$ are symmetric iff angles $\alpha_1 = \alpha_2$, where α_1 is subtended by line (q_1, q_2) and normal to i, and α_2 is subtended by line (q_1, q_2) and normal to j.

5. Parallelism as $\phi_{ij4} = \mathrm{mean}_{q \in i}\left|\frac{dr(q)}{dq}\right|$. As illustrated in Figure 15.2(b), parallelism is estimated as the mean of distance variations $r(q)$ between points q along edge i and their symmetric points on edge j.

To find symmetric points on two edges, we consider all pairs of points (q_1, q_2), where q_1 belongs to edge 1 and q_2 belongs to edge 2, and compute their cost matrix as a function of α_1 and α_2. We then use the standard Dynamic Time Warping to find the best symmetric points.

By definition, we set $\phi_{ij} = \mathbf{0}$ for all edge pairs (i, j) that are not neighbors.

15.3.3   Helmholtz Principle of Edge Grouping

The Helmholtz principle of grouping (Helmholtz, 1962) is also used as one of the edge properties. It is formalized as the entropy of a layout of edges. When this entropy is low, the edges are less likely to belong to background clutter.

The layout of edges can be characterized using the Voronoi diagram, as presented in Ahuja and Todorovic (2008). Given a set of edges, we first compute the Voronoi tessellation for all pixels along the edges. Then, for each edge i, we find a union of the Voronoi polygons γ_q of the edge's pixels q, resulting in a generalized Voronoi cell, $U_i = \cup_{q \in i} \gamma_q$. The Voronoi cell of edge i defines the relative area of its influence in the image, denoted as $P_i = \text{area}(U_i)/\text{area}(\text{image})$. For n edges, we define the entropy of their layout, H, as

$$H = -\sum_{i=1}^{n} P_i \log P_i. \tag{15.2}$$

Note that P_i depends on the length of i and its position and orientation relative to the other edges in the image. Because background clutter consists of edges of different sizes, which are placed in different orientations and at various distances from the other edges, H of the clutter is likely to take larger values than H of object boundaries. From our experiments presented in Payet and Todorovic (2013), H of boundary layouts are in general lower than those of background clutter.

15.3.4   Edge Descriptors

Without losing generality, we assume that from every image we can extract a set of n edges $V = \{i : i = 1, \ldots, n\}$. In our experiments, we set $n = 200$. With every edge $i \in V$, we associate the descriptor $\boldsymbol{x}_i$ defined as

$$\boldsymbol{x}_i = [\boldsymbol{\psi}_i, [\boldsymbol{\phi}_{i1}, \ldots, \boldsymbol{\phi}_{ij}, \ldots], H], \tag{15.3}$$

where $j \in V \setminus \{i\}$. The edge descriptors are used in our structured prediction for boundary detection, as explained in the next two sections.

15.4   Sequential Labeling of Edges

This section describes how to conduct boundary detection as a sequential labeling of image edges.

Let $\boldsymbol{x} = (\boldsymbol{x}_1, \boldsymbol{x}_2, \ldots, \boldsymbol{x}_n) \in \mathcal{X}$ denote a sequence of edge descriptors that are sequentially labeled in n steps and $\boldsymbol{y} = (y_1, y_2, \ldots, y_n) \in \mathcal{Y}$ denote their corresponding binary labels, $\mathcal{Y} \in \{0, 1\}^n$. SLEDGE sequentially uses a ranking function to select an edge k to be labeled $\hat{y}_k = f(\boldsymbol{x}_k)$ and then updates the descriptors of unlabeled edges, $\boldsymbol{x}_i, i = k+1, \ldots, n$, because they depend on the layout of previously detected boundaries.

SLEDGE uses iterative batch-learning for estimating the structured prediction $f : \mathcal{X} \to \mathcal{Y}$, as summarized in Algorithm 15.1. The structured prediction f is defined as

$$f^{(\tau+1)} = \begin{cases} h^{(\tau+1)} & , \text{ with probability } \beta \in [0,1], \\ f^{(\tau)} & , \text{ with probability } (1-\beta). \end{cases} \tag{15.4}$$

In every learning iteration τ, the result of classification $\hat{\boldsymbol{y}}^{(\tau)} = f^{(\tau)}(\boldsymbol{x})$ is compared with ground truth $\boldsymbol{y}$. This induces loss $l(\hat{\boldsymbol{y}}^{(\tau)}, \boldsymbol{y})$, which is then used to learn a new classifier $h^{(\tau+1)}$ and update $f^{(\tau+1)}$ as in (15.4) with probability $\beta \in (0,1]$. This definition of $f^{(\tau)}$ amounts to a probabilistic sampling of individual classifiers $h^{(1)}, h^{(2)}, \ldots, h^{(\tau)}$. The classifier sampling is governed by the multinomial distribution. From (15.4), the probability of selecting classifier $h^{(\tau)}$ in iteration T is

$$\alpha_T^{(\tau)} = \beta^\tau (1-\beta)^{T-\tau}, \quad \tau = 1, 2, \ldots, T. \tag{15.5}$$

After τ reaches the maximum allowed number of iterations, T, the output of learning is the last policy $f^{(T)}$ from which $h^{(1)}$ is eliminated, that is, the output is $\{h^{(2)}, h^{(3)}, \ldots, h^{(T)}\}$ and their associated sampling probabilities $\{\kappa\alpha_T^{(2)}, \kappa\alpha_T^{(3)}, \ldots, \kappa\alpha_T^{(T)}\}$. The constant κ re-scales the αs, such that $\sum_{\tau=2}^{T} \kappa\alpha_T^{(\tau)} = 1$.

In the following, we specify two loss functions that can be used for learning SLEDGE.

15.4.1   Two Loss Functions of SLEDGE

SLEDGE learns a labeling policy, f, that minimizes the expected loss over all loss-sequences of sequential edge labeling in all training images. In this section, we define two alternative loss functions.

First, we use the standard Hamming loss that counts the total number of differences between predicted and ground-truth labels, $\hat{\boldsymbol{y}} = (\hat{y}_1, \ldots, \hat{y}_n)$ and $\boldsymbol{y} = (y_1, \ldots, y_n)$, as

$$L_H(\hat{\boldsymbol{y}}, \boldsymbol{y}) = \sum_{i=1}^{n} \mathbf{1}\left[\hat{y}_i \neq y_i\right], \tag{15.6}$$

where $\mathbf{1}$ is the indicator function.

Because an error made at any edge carries the same relative weight, the Hamming loss may guide SLEDGE to try to correctly label all small, non-salient edges. To address this problem, we specify another loss function, L_F, that uses the F-measure of recall and precision associated with a specific edge. F-measure is one of the most common performance measures for boundary detection (Martin et al., 2004). It is defined as the harmonic mean of recall and precision of all image pixels that are detected as lying along

---

Algorithm 15.1 Iterative Batch-Learning of SLEDGE

1: Input:
2: The set of edges V_t of training images $t = 1, 2, \ldots$
3: Ground-truth labels of edges $\boldsymbol{y}_t \in \mathcal{Y}$
4: Loss-sensitive classifier h and initial $h^{(1)}$
5: Loss function l
6: Interpolation constant $\beta = 0.1$
7: Maximum number of learning iterations T
8: Output:
9: Learned policy $f^{(T)}$
10:
11: $f^{(1)} = h^{(1)}$
12: **for** all training images t **do**
13:      **for** all edges $i \in V_t$ **do**
14:          Compute $\boldsymbol{x}_{t,i}^{(1)}$ using intrinsic edge properties
15:          Set layout edge properties in $\boldsymbol{x}_{t,i}^{(1)}$ to 0
16:      **end for**
17: **end for**
18: **for** $\tau = 1 \ldots T$ **do**
19:      **for** all training images t **do**
20:          **for** unlabeled edges in V_t **do**
21:              Select unlabeled edge $k \in V_t$ such that $k = \operatorname{argmax}_{i \in V_t} f^{(\tau)}(\boldsymbol{x}_{t,i}^{(\tau)})$
22:              Compute prediction $\hat{\boldsymbol{y}}_{t,k}^{(\tau)} = f^{(\tau)}(\boldsymbol{x}_{t,k})$
23:              Update layout properties of unlabeled edges $\boldsymbol{x}_{t,i}^{(\tau)}$
24:          **end for**
25:      **end for**
26:      Estimate loss over all training images $l(\hat{\boldsymbol{y}}_t^{(\tau)}, \boldsymbol{y}_t)$
27:      Learn a new classifier $h^{(\tau+1)} \leftarrow h(\mathcal{X}; l)$
28:      Compute $f^{(\tau+1)}$ as in (15.4).
29: **end for**
30: Return $f^{(T)}$ without $h^{(1)}$.

---

an object boundary. A large value of $F(\hat{\boldsymbol{y}}, \boldsymbol{y})$ indicates good precision and recall, and corresponds to a low loss. Thus, we specify

$$L_F(\hat{\boldsymbol{y}}, \boldsymbol{y}) = 1 - F(\hat{\boldsymbol{y}}, \boldsymbol{y}). \tag{15.7}$$

Note that L_H coarsely counts errors at the edge level, while L_F is estimated finely at the pixel level.

15.4.2 Majority Voting of SLEDGE

SLEDGE iteratively learns an optimal policy f given by (15.4) which represents a probabilistic mixture of classifiers $\{h^{(\tau)} : \tau = 2, 3, \ldots, T\}$. Edges of a new image are sequentially labeled by weighted majority voting of $\{h^{(\tau)}\}$ as described below. Voting decisions of several classifiers have been shown to improve performance and reduce overfitting of each individual classifier (Kittler et al., 1998; Dieterich, 2000; Freund et al., 2001).

For a given edge descriptor $\boldsymbol{x}_i$, we first run all classifiers $\{h^{(\tau)}(\boldsymbol{x}_i)\}$ and then estimate the confidence of edge labeling $\hat{y}_i \in \{0, 1\}$ as

$$P(f(\boldsymbol{x}_i) = \hat{y}_i) = \sum_{\tau=2}^{T} \kappa \alpha_T^{(\tau)} P(h^{(\tau)}(\boldsymbol{x}_i) = \hat{y}_i), \qquad (15.8)$$

where the constant κ and αs are given by (15.5), and $P(h^{(\tau)}(\boldsymbol{x}_i) = y')$ is the confidence of classifier $h^{(\tau)}$ when predicting the label of edge i. Finally, SLEDGE classifies the edge as

$$\hat{y}_i = \operatorname*{argmax}_{y' \in \{0,1\}} P(f(\boldsymbol{x}_i) = y'). \qquad (15.9)$$

15.5 HC-Search

HC-Search (Doppa et al., 2012, 2013) performs a search-based structured prediction for a given structured input. Given a set of edges and their descriptors $\boldsymbol{x} = \{\boldsymbol{x}_i : i = 1, \ldots, n\}$, HC-Search generates a number of candidate outputs $\tilde{y}$, where input/output pairs $\boldsymbol{s} = (\boldsymbol{x}, \tilde{\boldsymbol{y}})$ represent states of a search space, $\boldsymbol{s} \in \mathcal{S}$, and then selects an optimal state $\hat{\boldsymbol{s}} = (\boldsymbol{x}, \hat{\boldsymbol{y}})$ as the solution. For exploring the search space, HC-Search conducts a search procedure, π, guided by a heuristic function $\mathcal{H}$, whereby new states are generated based on the best previously visited state selected by $\mathcal{H}$. The generation of new states is specified by a generation function, $\boldsymbol{s}' = \mathcal{G}(\boldsymbol{s})$, which is designed to flip low-confidence labels of edges in $\boldsymbol{s}$ and thus generate the new states $\boldsymbol{s}'$. Finally, HC-Search uses a cost function $\mathcal{C}(\boldsymbol{x}, \boldsymbol{y})$ to return the least cost output $\hat{\boldsymbol{y}}$ that is uncovered during the search.

The key elements of HC-Search include:

- Search space over input/output pairs $(\boldsymbol{x}, \hat{\boldsymbol{y}}) \in \mathcal{S}$;
- Search strategy π;
- Heuristic function, $\mathcal{H} : \mathcal{X} \times \mathcal{Y} \mapsto \mathbb{R}$, for guiding the search toward high-quality outputs;
- Cost function, $\mathcal{C} : \mathcal{X} \times \mathcal{Y} \mapsto \mathbb{R}$, for scoring the candidate outputs generated by the search.

Advantages of HC-Search relative to other structured prediction approaches, including CRFs, are as follows. First, it scales gracefully with the complexity of the dependency structure of features. In particular, we are free to increase the complexity of $\mathcal{H}$ and $\mathcal{C}$ (e.g., by including higher-order features) without considering its impact on the inference complexity. The work of Doppa et al. (2012, 2013) shows that the use of higher-order features results in significant improvements. Second, the terms of the error decomposition in (15.16) can be easily measured for a learned $(\mathcal{H}, \mathcal{C})$ pair, which allows for an assessment of which function is more responsible for the overall error. Third, HC-Search makes minimal assumptions about the loss function, requiring only that we have a "black-box" evaluation of any candidate output. HC-Search can work with non-decomposable loss functions, such as F1 loss mentioned in Section 15.4.1.

In the following, we explain all these elements and then describe how to learn the heuristic and cost functions.

15.5.1   Key Elements of HC-Search

Search Space. A search space $\mathcal{S}$ is defined in terms of two functions: (i) *Initial state function*, $I(\boldsymbol{x})$, returns an initial state in $\mathcal{S}$ for input $\boldsymbol{x}$; and (ii) *Generator function*, $\mathcal{G}(\boldsymbol{s})$, returns for any state $\boldsymbol{s}$ a set of new states $\{(\boldsymbol{x}, \tilde{\boldsymbol{y}}_1), \ldots, (\boldsymbol{x}, \tilde{\boldsymbol{y}}_k)\}$ that share the same input $\boldsymbol{x}$.

The specific search space that we investigate leverages boundary predictions made independently for every image edge by the logistic regression classifier. Specifically, our $I(\boldsymbol{x})$ corresponds to the logistic-regression predictions of edge labels. $\mathcal{G}$ generates a set of next states in two steps. First, it identifies a sub set of image edges where the classifier has confidence lower than a threshold. When gPb edges are used as input, the threshold is set to 0.5. Second, it generates one successor state for each low-confidence edge i with the corresponding $\tilde{y}_i$ value flipped. We use the conditional probability of the logistic regression as the confidence measure:

$$P(\tilde{y}_i = 1|\boldsymbol{x}_i; \boldsymbol{w}_{\mathrm{LR}}) = 1/(1 + \exp(-\boldsymbol{w}_{\mathrm{LR}}^\top \boldsymbol{x}_i)), \qquad (15.10)$$

where $\boldsymbol{w}_{\mathrm{LR}}$ are parameters of the logistic regression. Note that a particular state may have a large number of successors depending on $P(\tilde{y}_i = 1|\boldsymbol{x}_i; \boldsymbol{w}_{\mathrm{LR}})$ values, whereas some other states may have only a few successors.

Search Strategy. The role of the search procedure π is to uncover high-quality outputs guided by the heuristic function $\mathcal{H}$. Prior work of Doppa et al. (2012, 2013) has shown that greedy search works quite well when used with an effective search space. We investigate HC-Search with greedy search. Given an input $\boldsymbol{x}$, greedy search traverses a path of length τ through the search space, selecting as the next state the best successor of the current state according to $\mathcal{H}$. Specifically, if $\boldsymbol{s}^{(\tau)}$ is the state at search step τ, π selects $\boldsymbol{s}^{(\tau+1)} = \operatorname{argmin}_{\boldsymbol{s} \in \mathcal{G}(\boldsymbol{s}^{(\tau)})} \mathcal{H}(\boldsymbol{s})$, where $\boldsymbol{s}^{(0)} = I(\boldsymbol{x})$. We define the maximum allowed number of search steps from one state to another as time bound $\tau_{\max}$. Note that $\tau_{\max}$ is equal to the number of good candidate states, selected by $\mathcal{H}$ as parents for generating a number of successor states. Thus, the total number of generated states during the search can be much larger than τ.

In this work, we define $\mathcal{H}$ following the standard formulation of CRF in terms of unary and pairwise potential functions, Φ_1 and Φ_2, as

$$\mathcal{H}(\boldsymbol{x},\boldsymbol{y}) = \sum_{i\in V} \boldsymbol{w}_{\mathcal{H},1}^{\top}\Phi_1(\boldsymbol{x}_i,y_i) + \sum_{i,j\in V} \boldsymbol{w}_{\mathcal{H},2}^{\top}\Phi_2(\boldsymbol{x}_i,\boldsymbol{x}_j,y_i,y_j), \qquad (15.11)$$

where V is the set of input image edges, and $\boldsymbol{w}_{\mathcal{H}}^{\top} = [\boldsymbol{w}_{\mathcal{H},1}^{\top},\boldsymbol{w}_{\mathcal{H},2}^{\top}]$ are parameters of $\mathcal{H}$. As standard, $\Phi_{\mathrm{un}}(\boldsymbol{x}_i,y_i)$ has non-zero elements in the segment that corresponds to label y_i (i.e., $\Phi_{\mathrm{un}}(\boldsymbol{x}_i,0) = [\boldsymbol{x}_i,\boldsymbol{0}]$ or $\Phi_{\mathrm{un}}(\boldsymbol{x}_i,1) = [\boldsymbol{0},\boldsymbol{x}_i]$). The pairwise potential function is defined as

$$\Phi_2(\boldsymbol{x}_i,\boldsymbol{x}_j,y_i,y_j) = \begin{cases} \boldsymbol{0} & , \text{ if } y_i = y_j, \\ \exp(-\lambda|\boldsymbol{x}_i-\boldsymbol{x}_j|^2) & , \text{ if } y_i \neq y_j, \end{cases} \qquad (15.12)$$

where λ is a parameter set to $\lambda = 1$ in our experiments. Φ_2 encourages neighboring edges to take the same label. A similar formulation of the CRF model for boundary detection is specified in Ren et al. (2008) and Maire et al. (2008).

Making Predictions. Given $\boldsymbol{x}$ and a prediction time bound τ, HC-Search traverses the search space starting at $I(\boldsymbol{x})$, using the search procedure π, guided by the heuristic function $\mathcal{H}$, until the time bound is exceeded. It then scores each visited state $\boldsymbol{s}$ according to $\mathcal{C}(\boldsymbol{s})$ and returns the $\hat{\boldsymbol{y}}$ of the lowest-cost state as the predicted output.

In this work, we define $\mathcal{C}$ to take the same form as $\mathcal{H}$. In particular, we specify

$$\mathcal{C}(\boldsymbol{x},\boldsymbol{y}) = \sum_{i\in V} \boldsymbol{w}_{\mathcal{C},1}^{\top}\Phi_1(\boldsymbol{x}_i,y_i) + \sum_{i,j\in V} \boldsymbol{w}_{\mathcal{C},2}^{\top}\Phi_2(\boldsymbol{x}_i,\boldsymbol{x}_j,y_i,y_j), \qquad (15.13)$$

where $\boldsymbol{w}_{\mathcal{C}}^{\top} = [\boldsymbol{w}_{\mathcal{C},1}^{\top},\boldsymbol{w}_{\mathcal{C},2}^{\top}]$ are parameters of $\mathcal{C}$.

15.5.2   Learning Heuristic and Cost Functions

Learning is aimed at training $\mathcal{H}$ and $\mathcal{C}$ such that the error of HC-Search, $\epsilon_{\mathcal{HC}}$, is minimized over training data. $\epsilon_{\mathcal{HC}}$ can be decomposed into two parts: (i) *Generation error*, $\epsilon_{\mathcal{H}}$, due to $\mathcal{H}$ not generating high-quality outputs; and (ii) *Selection error*, $\epsilon_{\mathcal{C}|\mathcal{H}}$, conditional on $\mathcal{H}$, due to $\mathcal{C}$ not selecting the best loss output generated by $\mathcal{H}$. Our learning seeks to minimize $\epsilon_{\mathcal{HC}}$ on training data in a greedy stage-wise manner by first training $\mathcal{H}$ to minimize $\epsilon_{\mathcal{H}}$ and then training $\mathcal{C}$ to minimize $\epsilon_{\mathcal{C}|\mathcal{H}}$ conditioned on $\mathcal{H}$. Below, we specify the error functions minimized in learning.

Let $\boldsymbol{y}_{\mathcal{H}}^*$ denote the best output that HC-Search could possibly return when using $\mathcal{H}$, let $\hat{\boldsymbol{y}}$ denote the output that it actually returns, let $\tilde{\boldsymbol{y}}$ denote candidate outputs, and let $\boldsymbol{y}$ denote the ground-truth output. Also, let $\mathcal{Y}_{\mathcal{H}}(\boldsymbol{x})$ be the set of candidate outputs generated using $\mathcal{H}$ for a given input $\boldsymbol{x}$. Then, we define

$$\boldsymbol{y}_{\mathcal{H}}^* = \operatorname*{argmin}_{\tilde{\boldsymbol{y}} \in \mathcal{Y}_{\mathcal{H}}(x)} L(\boldsymbol{x}, \tilde{\boldsymbol{y}}, \boldsymbol{y}), \tag{15.14}$$

$$\hat{\boldsymbol{y}} = \operatorname*{argmin}_{\tilde{\boldsymbol{y}} \in \mathcal{Y}_{\mathcal{H}}(x)} \mathcal{C}(\boldsymbol{x}, \tilde{\boldsymbol{y}}), \tag{15.15}$$

where $L(\cdot)$ is a loss function. For HC-Search, we use only the Hamming loss specified in (15.6).

We decompose the error of HC-Search as

$$\epsilon_{\mathcal{H}\mathcal{C}} = \underbrace{L\left(\boldsymbol{x}, \boldsymbol{y}_{\mathcal{H}}^*, \boldsymbol{y}\right)}_{\epsilon_{\mathcal{H}}} + \underbrace{L\left(\boldsymbol{x}, \hat{\boldsymbol{y}}, \boldsymbol{y}\right) - L\left(\boldsymbol{x}, \boldsymbol{y}_{\mathcal{H}}^*, \boldsymbol{y}\right)}_{\epsilon_{\mathcal{C}|\mathcal{H}}}. \tag{15.16}$$

$\mathcal{H}$ is trained by imitating search decisions made by the true loss available for training data. We run the search procedure π for a time bound of τ for input $\boldsymbol{x}$ using a heuristic equal to the true loss function (i.e., $\mathcal{H}(\boldsymbol{x}, \tilde{\boldsymbol{y}}) = L(\boldsymbol{x}, \tilde{\boldsymbol{y}}, \boldsymbol{y})$). In addition, we record a set of ranking constraints that are sufficient to reproduce the search behavior. For greedy search, at every search step τ, we include one ranking constraint for every state $(\boldsymbol{x}, \tilde{\boldsymbol{y}}) \in \mathcal{C}^{(\tau)} \setminus (\boldsymbol{x}, \tilde{\boldsymbol{y}}_{\text{best}})$, such that $\mathcal{H}(\boldsymbol{x}, \tilde{\boldsymbol{y}}_{\text{best}}) < \mathcal{H}(\boldsymbol{x}, \tilde{\boldsymbol{y}})$, where $(\boldsymbol{x}, \tilde{\boldsymbol{y}}_{best})$ is the best state in the candidate set $\mathcal{C}^{(\tau)}$ (ties are broken by a random tie breaker). The aggregate set of ranking examples is given to a rank learner — namely, SVM-Rank (Joachims, 2006) – to learn $\mathcal{H}$.

$\mathcal{C}$ is trained to score the outputs $\mathcal{Y}_{\mathcal{H}}(\boldsymbol{x})$ generated by $\mathcal{H}$ according to their true losses. Specifically, this training is formulated as a bi-partite ranking problem to rank all the best loss outputs $\mathcal{Y}_{\text{best}}$ higher than all the non-best loss outputs $\mathcal{Y}_{\mathcal{H}}(\boldsymbol{x}) \setminus \mathcal{Y}_{\text{best}}$. For more details, the reader is referred to Doppa et al. (2013).

15.6 Results

This section presents qualitative and quantitative evaluation of SLEDGE and HC-Search on images from the BSD (Martin et al., 2001; Arbelaez et al., 2010), Weizmann Horses (Borenstein and Ullman, 2002), and LabelMe (B.Russell et al., 2008) data sets. BSD300 and BSD500 consist of 300 and

500 natural-scene images, respectively. They are manually segmented by a number of different human annotators. The Weizmann Horses data set consists of 328 side-view images of horses that are also manually segmented. For the LabelMe data set, we select the 218 annotated images of the Boston houses 2005 sub set. The challenges of these data sets have been extensively discussed in the past and include, but are not limited to, clutter, illumination variations, and occlusion. Below, we present our default training and testing setups.

Training. We train SLEDGE and HC-Search on the 200 training images of BSD300. For each image, we compute the edge probability map gPb (Maire et al., 2008) and threshold the map so as to extract top 200 edges. We compute edge intrinsic and layout properties as described in Section 15.3. For training, we convert the manually annotated boundaries to ground-truth labels for all edges in the training images: if more than 50% of an edge length overlaps with a boundary, then the ground-truth label of that edge is 1; otherwise, the label is 0.

For SLEDGE, the initial classifier $h^{(1)}$ is a fully grown C4.5 decision tree that chooses the split attribute based on the normalized information gain. The attributes considered for $h^{(1)}$ are only the intrinsic parameters ψ_i specified in Section 15.3.1. In further iterations of SLEDGE, the classifiers $h^{(\tau)}$ are pruned C4.5 decision trees, which are learned on all edge properties. C4.5 pruning uses the standard confidence factor of 0.25. The interpolation constant β, defined in Section 15.4, is set to $\beta = 0.1$. We use F1 loss function and voting to combine the output of the decision tree classifiers as described in Section 15.4.2.

For HC-Search, we use SVM-Rank (Joachims, 2006) to learn $\mathcal{H}$ and $\mathcal{C}$ functions. The HC-Search results are obtained for the number of search steps (i.e., time bound) $\tau = 100$.

Testing and Comparison. Performance is measured as the average, pixel-level precision and recall of the boundary map produced by SLEDGE or HC-Search, as defined in Martin et al. (2004). We compare SLEDGE and HC-Search with the latest work that uses standard structured-prediction methods for boundary detection. Namely, for comparison, we use the CRF-based method presented in Maire et al. (2008) and the F^3 boosting method presented in Kokkinos (2010b). For fair comparison, we use the same set of input image edges extracted using the Berkeley segmentation algorithm, as described in Maire et al. (2008).

In the following, we first illustrate a few sample qualitative results of boundary detection by SLEDGE and HC-Search on the BSD data set. Then we evaluate SLEDGE and HC-Search using different initial conditions, edge labeling strategy, classifier type, and loss function.

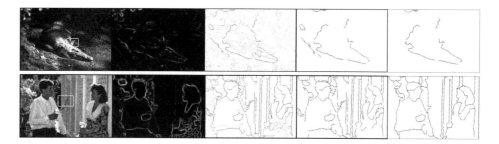

Figure 15.3: **Boundary detection on BSD.** From left to right: input image; edge probability map gPb (Maire et al., 2008); boundary map output by SLEDGE; boundaries detected by SLEDGE for best F-measure; boundary map output by HC-Search. The highlighted windows in the original images do not contain salient edges in the input gPb edge map. Yet both SLEDGE and HC-Search successfully label these non-salient edges as boundaries. SLEDGE and HC-Search perform well on challenging object boundaries amid texture or low-contrast ramps (e.g., tip of the alligator's mouth is correctly labeled as boundary, and many salient edges on the woman's dress are correctly labeled as non-boundary).

15.6.1   Qualitative Results

Figure 15.3 shows high accuracy of boundary detection on two sample images from the BSD data set by SLEDGE and HC-Search. As can be seen, both approaches perform well on challenging object boundaries amid texture or low-contrast ramps (e.g., tip of the alligator's mouth is correctly labeled as boundary, and many salient edges on the woman's dress are correctly labeled as non-boundary). Boundary detection is good even in the following cases: (i) when objects have complex textures, e.g., many salient edges on the woman's dress in Figure 15.3(right); (ii) when the boundaries are blurred or jagged, e.g., the tip of the alligator's mouth in Figure 15.3(left); and (iii) when boundaries form complex layouts, e.g., the man's hand in Figure 15.3(right). Filter-based methods, or approaches based on image decimation and smoothing, would typically fail to accurately delineate topologically complex layouts of edges where several texture boundaries meet. We are also able to detect boundaries where there is no strong gradient in the input gPb map, e.g., the woman's white collar in Figure 15.3(right).

Figure 15.4 shows the 50 most confident boundaries found by SLEDGE and HC-Search in two example images from the BSD data set. The boundary detection confidence is color-coded in the HSV space, where "warmer" colors mark higher confidence, and "colder" colors indicate lower confidence. As can be seen, both SLEDGE and HC-Search generally are able to find boundaries for non-salient image edges in the gPb map (e.g., see the back of the kangaroo). However, in some cases, SLEDGE wrongly labels salient

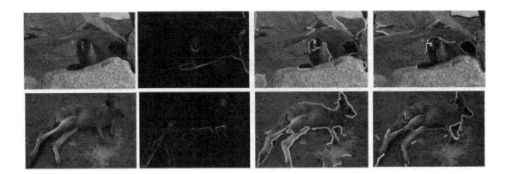

Figure 15.4: **Confidence of boundary detection**. From left to right: Sample image from the BSD data set; edge probability map gPb (Maire et al., 2008); 50 most confident boundaries labeled by SLEDGE; 50 most confident boundaries labeled by HC-Search. The confidence of boundary detection is color-coded in the HSV space, where "warm" colors indicate high confidence, and "cold" colors mark low confidence.

edges as boundaries when they group well under a certain Gestalt principle. For example, the edges on the rock texture in Figure 15.4(top) are wrongly labeled as boundaries, because they continue each other well, and thus reinforce their joint labeling as boundaries. HC-Search does not make that mistake on these edges.

Figure 15.5 illustrates the order in which SLEDGE selects edges to label edges in an example image from the BSD data set. As can be seen, SLEDGE typically first selects to label long, salient edges. Then SLEDGE seeks to group unlabeled edges with previously identified boundaries. The figure caption explains the underlying Gestalt principle that SLEDGE uses for edge grouping in this example.

SLEDGE and HC-Search compute for every input edge the confidence that it lies on a boundary. Figure 15.6 shows confidence results of SLEDGE and HC-Search on example images from the Weizmann and Labelme data sets. The higher confidence of boundary detection is marked by darker edges. BothSLEDGE and HC-Search accurately assign high confidence to the boundaries of elongated objects (e.g., the electric pole, which are typically challenging for existing approaches). SLEDGE might confuse highly salient edges for boundaries (e.g., the shadow on the horse's neck and the shadow on the paved area). This is typically because these edges perceptually group well with boundaries (e.g., represent a valid continuation of the horse's front leg). As can be seen, HC-Search gives better results on these two images.

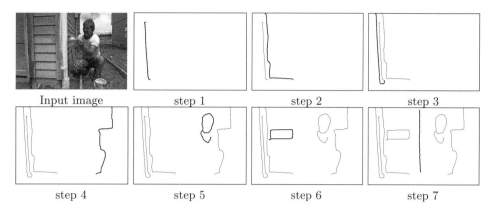

Figure 15.5: Initial sequential labeling steps of SLEDGE for an example image from the BSD data set. We show only edges from the gPb map (Maire et al., 2008) labeled as boundaries. At step 1, SLEDGE selects a long, prominent edge. At steps 2–4, it selects edges that are parallel to the first boundary, using the grouping principle of parallelism.

15.6.2   Quantitative Evaluation

Following the standard evaluation method of Martin et al. (2004), we convert confidence of boundary detection produced by SLEDGE or HC-Search to a boundary probability map and use the map for performance evaluation.

First, we evaluate the boundary map output by SLEDGE and HC-Search using different types of input edges. We use the same type of input edges for training and testing of our algorithms. Figure 15.7 shows our precision and recall for image edges obtained with the Canny detector (Canny, 1986), and the gPb detector (Maire et al., 2008). Sequential labeling significantly improves performance for all edge detectors, especially in the high-recall-low-precision regime. This demonstrates that SLEDGE does not require a good initial set of edges for good performance. We note, however, that the higher the precision of original input edges, the higher the precision of output boundaries. For example, Figure 15.7 shows that the precision of gPb+SLEDGE is higher than the precision of Canny+SLEDGE. HC-Search also improves boundary detection over the performance of edge detectors, and outperforms SLEDGE.

Figure 15.8 shows the average precision and recall of gPb+SLEDGE, gPb+HC-Search, gPb of (Maire et al., 2008), and the F^3 boosting method of (Kokkinos, 2010b) on the following data sets: BSD 300, BSD 500, Weizmann Horses and LabelMe. SLEDGE and HC-Search are trained on the standard 200 training images from the BSD as the competing approaches. As can be seen, both SLEDGE and HC-Search outperform the standard structured prediction methods — namely, the CRF-based gPb (Maire et al., 2008)

Figure 15.6: Boundary detection on the Weizmann data set (top) and the LabelMe data set (bottom). From left to right: input image; edge probability map gPb (Maire et al., 2008); boundary detection confidence map output by SLEDGE; boundary detection confidence map output by HC-Search.

and F^3 boosting (Kokkinos, 2010b) — on all the data sets. HC-Search outperforms SLEDGE.

15.6.3 Evaluating Particular Aspects of SLEDGE

This section presents the effect of different design choices on the performance of SLEDGE.

Initial conditions. The early errors of SLEDGE in the sequence might be critical because they could sequentially propagate to the entire sequence. To test this aspect of our algorithm, we compare our default setup with the following variant of SLEDGE. We create 100 different initial configurations by randomly picking b true boundaries as the initial set of correctly labeled edges. The randomization serves to eliminate any bias in picking certain boundaries (e.g., long ones). Then we let SLEDGE continue labeling the remaining edges. The pairwise and global features are computed based on the initial set of randomly selected true boundaries. Finally, we compute recall and precision averaged over these 100 distinct initializations. These tests serve to evaluate SLEDGE performance when there is no error at the beginning of the labeling sequence. Table 15.1 shows the average increase in recall and precision, at equal error rate, relative to those of our default setup, for $b = 2, 4, 6$. As can be seen, when errors at the beginning of the labeling sequence are manually eliminated, our performance gain is relatively small. This suggests that our default setup is relatively insensitive to initial labeling errors.

Edge Labeling Strategy. We test how performance varies when we allow SLEDGE to continue relabeling edges after all the edges have already

	$b = 2$	$b = 4$	$b = 6$
Increase in recall [%]	21 ± 2.3	33 ± 2.4	61 ± 1.84
Increase in precision [%]	23 ± 3.5	25 ± 1.9	49 ± 2.1

Table 15.1: **Initial conditions.** Increase in recall and precision in %, at equal error rate, relative to those of our default setup, averaged over 100 random initializations consisting of $b \in \{2, 4, 6\}$ true boundaries as the initial set of correctly labeled edges.

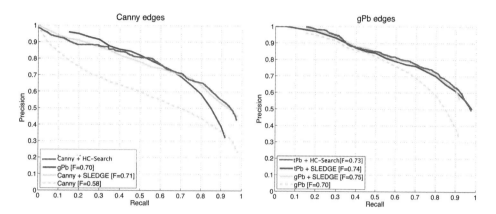

Figure 15.7: **Improvement in boundary detection.** We evaluate boundary detection on the BSD300 data set in two cases: outputs of edge detectors are input to SLEDGE and HC-Search (solid lines), and outputs of edge detectors are simply declared as boundary detection without using our algorithms (dashed line). The detectors include: (top) Canny (Canny, 1986), and (bottom) gPb (Maire et al., 2008). Training and testing are performed with the same type of edges (e.g., for testing SLEDGE on Canny edges, we trained SLEDGE on Canny edges). Both SLEDGE and HC-Search improve the precision of the input set of edges. HC-Search outperforms SLEDGE.

been labeled once. Specifically, after all edges have been visited, we remove them from the labeled set and send them to the unlabeled set. The pairwise and global features are still computed based on the current labeling of boundaries. We iterate SLEDGE until it reaches convergence (i.e., no edge changes the label). On the 100 test images of the BSD300, at equal error rate, SLEDGE with relabeling improves by 0.2% in precision, and by 0.5% in recall relative to the performance of the default SLEDGE with just one labeling pass. Thus, allowing edges to be relabeled, in our approach, only marginally improves precision and recall, but increases complexity. Therefore, it seems that the iterative relabeling of edges is not justified in our approach.

Classifiers. From our experiments, a non-linear classifier is more suitable than a linear one for separating boundaries from background edges. Classification accuracy of SLEDGE with decision trees compared to that of

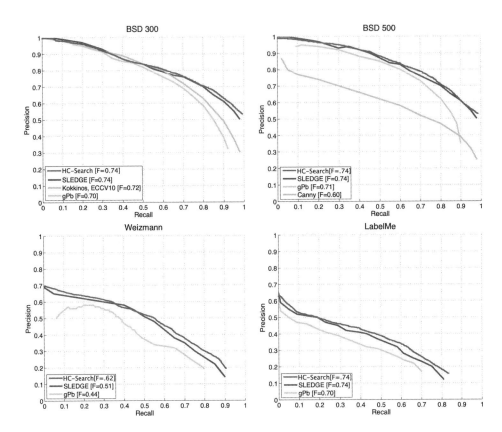

Figure 15.8: **Boundary detection.** Precision and recall of gPb+SLEDGE, gPb+HC-Search, and gPb (Maire et al., 2008) on the data sets: BSD 300 (Martin et al., 2001), BSD 500 (Arbelaez et al., 2010), Weizmann Horses (Borenstein and Ullman, 2002), and LabelMe (B.Russell et al., 2008). For BSD 300, we also show a comparison with the method of Kokkinos (2010b). We outperform gPb on all four data sets and obtain a better F-measure than Kokkinos (2010b) on the BSD 300.

SLEDGE with a linear SVM-type classifier is 91% versus 72%. For training SVMs (as in the case of decision trees), we use a balanced number of positive and negative examples — the under-sampling procedure mentioned in Section 15.4.2-Remark — with the complexity parameter $C = 1.0$. When more sophisticated classifiers are used (e.g., SVM with RBF and random forests), we observe only a relatively small gain in accuracy over the decision tree, which does not justify the increase in complexity. Indeed, the total computation time primarily depends on the complexity of the chosen classifier as all classifiers have to be run at each iteration of SLEDGE.

Loss Functions. Figure 15.9(a) shows the performance of SLEDGE when using the loss function L_H or L_F, specified in Section 15.4.1. L_H coarsely counts errors at the edge level, whereas L_F is a loss estimated finely at the pixel level. SLEDGE with L_F produces boundaries with slightly better

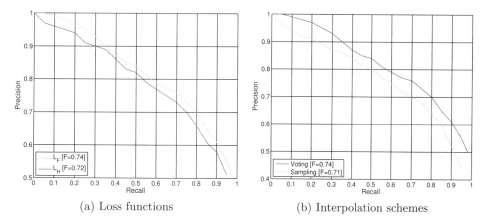

(a) Loss functions   (b) Interpolation schemes

Figure 15.9: Performance of SLEDGE on the BSD 300. (a) Using the loss function L_H or L_F, given by (15.6) and (15.7); L_H coarsely counts errors at the edge level, while L_F is a loss estimated finely at the pixel level. (b) Making decisions using classifier sampling or voting.

precision than SLEDGE with L_H. SLEDGE with L_F also runs about three times faster than SLEDGE with L_H.

Interpolation Scheme. We stop learning new classifiers when the average performance on the training data does not change. For the BSD 300, this happens after about 10 iterations. Figure 15.9(b) compares the performance of SLEDGE with these 10 classifiers for two types of making decisions by: (i) Sampling the classifiers, and (ii) Weighted voting of the classifiers as described in Section 15.4.2. As can be seen, voting outperforms sampling.

15.6.4   Evaluating Particular Aspects of HC-Search

This section presents the effect of different design choices on the performance of HC-Search. We evaluate our sensitivity to the time bound, $\tau_{\max}$ (i.e., the number of search steps that are allowed before making the final prediction). Recall that $\tau_{\max}$ is equal to the number of states selected by the heuristic function $\mathcal{H}$ as parents for generating successor states, as described in Section 15.5.1. The total number of generated states during HC-Search can be much larger than $\tau_{\max}$.

Figure 15.10 shows the plots of precision and recall of HC-Search for increasing time bound $\tau_{\max}$. The plots show four types of curves: LL-Search, HL-Search, LC-Search, and HC-Search. LL-Search uses the loss function as both the heuristic and the cost function, and thus serves as an upper bound on the performance. HL-Search uses the learned heuristic function and the loss function as cost function, and thus serves to illustrate how well the learned heuristic $\mathcal{H}$ performs in terms of the quality of generated

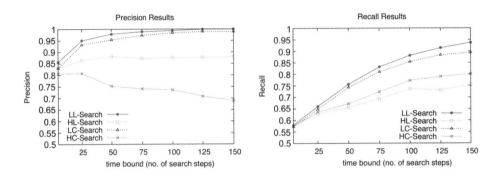

Figure 15.10: The plots of precision and recall of HC-Search on the BSD 300 versus the allowed number of search steps.

outputs. LC-Search uses the loss function as an oracle heuristic and learns a cost function to score the outputs generated by the oracle heuristic. From Figure 15.10, for HC-Search, we see that as τ_{max} increases, precision drops, but recall improves up to a certain point before decreasing. This is because as τ_{max} increases, the generation error ($\epsilon_{\mathcal{H}}$) will monotonically decrease because strictly more outputs will be encountered. Simultaneously, difficulty of cost function learning can increase as τ_{max} grows because it must learn to distinguish among a larger set of candidate outputs. In addition, we can see that the LC-Search curve is close to the LL-Search curve wheras the HL-Search curve is far below the LL-Search curve. This suggests that the overall error of HC-Search, $\epsilon_{\mathcal{HC}}$, is dominated by the heuristic error $\epsilon_{\mathcal{H}}$. A better heuristic is thus likely to lead to better performance overall. One could try to improve the heuristic error in several ways, including flipping multiple patch labels, training heuristic function with more advanced imitation learning algorithms (e.g., DAgger), and learning non-linear ranking functions (e.g., Boosted Regression Trees). We plan to investigate these directions in the future.

15.6.5 Running Time

Training SLEDGE on 200 BSD training images takes about 24 hours on a 2.66GHz, 3.4GB RAM PC. Computing the boundary probability map by SLEDGE for a new image takes 20 to 40 seconds, depending on the image content.

Training heuristic $\mathcal{H}$ and cost $\mathcal{C}$ functions on 200 BSD training images takes 3 to 4 hours on the same PC. For the maximum allowed number of search steps $\tau_{max} = 100$, boundary detection by HC-Search in a new image takes about 2 minutes.

Our code is implemented in MATLAB and is not fully optimized for efficiency.

15.7 Conclusion

We have presented two structured prediction approaches to boundary detection in arbitrary images: SLEDGE and HC-Search. Both approaches take as input salient edges and label these edges as belonging to a boundary. SLEDGE is a sequential labeling algorithm, which learns how to optimally combine Gestalt grouping cues and intrinsic edge properties for boundary detection. HC-Search is a search-based algorithm, which greedily explores the space of candidate solutions guided by the heuristic function and then selects the minimum cost solution from all the candidates.

Our empirical evaluation demonstrates that both SLEDGE and HC-Search outperform standard structured prediction approaches to boundary detection on the benchmark data sets — specifically, the CRF-based method gPb (Maire et al., 2008) and F^3 boosting (Kokkinos, 2010b). This is, in part, because both SLEDGE and HC-Search avoid directly solving the Argmin problem of structured prediction by generating structured outputs through: (i) Making a series of discrete decisions in the case of SLEDGE, or (ii) Searching the output space in the case of HC-Search. Both SLEDGE and HC-Search employ training data to explicitly *learn how to conduct inference* through making sequential decisions or searching the output space. This learning for inference seems to improve on common practice to use heuristic approximations for solving the NP-hard Argmin problem. As a key advantage over the other structured prediction methods, SLEDGE and HC-Search do not make strong assumptions about the underlying structure and statistical dependencies of the output variables.

We have observed that SLEDGE tends to favor good continuation of strong edges, which works well in most cases but fails when there is an accidental alignment of object and background edges (e.g., shadows).

Our experimental results indicate that the overall error of the HC Search approach is dominated by the heuristic error. One could try to further improve our current results with HC-Search by improving the heuristic function. We are currently investigating this direction by employing more effective search spaces, advanced imitation learning algorithms, and nonlinear representations (e.g., Boosted Regression Trees) for the heuristic and cost functions. A better search space can be constructed by flipping the labels of multiple edges rather than one at a time, thereby reducing the search depth for imitation learning. In this chapter, we have used exact imitation to generate training examples for learning the heuristic function. Perhaps using DAGGER (Ross et al., 2011) would be a better method. Finally, we have used SVM Rank to learn the heuristic and cost functions, but one could try to use other rank learners such as boosting and trees.

Acknowledgments

This research has been sponsored in part by grant NSF IIS 1302700.

15.8 References

N. Ahuja and S. Todorovic. Connected segmentation tree — a joint representation of region layout and hierarchy. In *Conf. Computer Vision Pattern Recognition*, 2008.

P. Arbelaez, M. Maire, C. Fowlkes, and J. Malik. Contour detection and hierarchical image segmentation. *IEEE Trans. PAMI*, 99(RapidPosts), 2010.

S. Belongie, J. Malik, and J. Puzicha. Shape matching and object recognition using shape contexts. *IEEE Trans. PAMI*, 24(4):509–522, 2002.

E. Borenstein and S. Ullman. Class-specific, top-down segmentation. In *European Conf. Computer Vision*, volume 2, pages 109–124, 2002.

S. Brin and L. Page. The anatomy of a large-scale hypertextual web search engine. In *Seventh International World-Wide Web Conference (WWW 1998)*, 1998.

B.Russell, A. Torralba, K. Murphy, and W. Freeman. LabelMe: A database and web-based tool for image annotation. *Int. J. Computer Vision*, 77(1-3):157–173, 2008.

J. Canny. A computational approach to edge detection. *IEEE Trans. PAMI*, 8(6): 679–698, 1986.

M. Collins. Ranking algorithms for named entity extraction: Boosting and the voted perceptron. In *Proceedings of Association for Computational Linguistics*, 2002.

T. Dietterich. Ensemble methods in machine learning. In *Lecture Notes in Computer Science*, pages 1–15, 2000.

J. Doppa, A. Fern, and P. Tadepalli. Output space search for structured prediction. In *Int. Conf. Machine Learning*, 2012.

J. Doppa, A. Fern, and P. Tadepalli. HC-Search: Learning heuristics and cost functions for structured prediction. In *AAAI Conference on Artificial Intelligence*, 2013.

P. Felzenszwalb and D. McAllester. A min-cover approach for finding salient curves. In *Conf. Perceptual Organization Computer Vision*, 2006.

P. Felzenszwalb and D. McAllester. The generalized A* architecture. *Journal of Artificial Intelligence Research*, 29:153–190, 2007.

Y. Freund, Y. Mansour, and R. Schapire. Why averaging classifiers can protect against overfitting. In *Int. Workshop on Artificial Intelligence and Statistics*, 2001.

G. Guy and G. Medioni. Inferring global perceptual contours from local features. *Int. J. Computer Vision*, 20(1-2):113–133, 1996.

H. Helmholtz. *Treatise on physiological optics*. New York: Dover (first published in 1867), 1962.

H. D. III, J. Langford, and D. Marcu. Search-based structured prediction. *Machine Learning Journal*, 75(3):297–325, 2009.

T. Joachims. Training linear SVMs in linear time. In *Int. Conf. Knowledge Discovery and Data Mining*, pages 217–226, 2006.

G. Kim, C. Faloutsos, and M. Hebert. Unsupervised modeling of object categories using link analysis techniques. In *Conf. Computer Vision Pattern Recognition*, June 2008.

J. Kittler, M. Hatef, R. Duin, and J. Matas. On combining classifiers. *IEEE Trans. PAMI*, 20:226–239, 1998.

I. Kokkinos. Highly accurate boundary detection and grouping. In *Conf. Computer Vision Pattern Recognition*, 2010a.

I. Kokkinos. Boundary detection using F-measure-, Filter- and Feature- (F^3) boost. In *European Conf. Computer Vision*, 2010b.

Y. Lee and K. Grauman. Shape discovery from unlabeled image collections. In *Conf. Computer Vision Pattern Recognition*, 2009.

D. Lowe. *Perceptual Organization and Visual Recognition*. Kluwer Academic Publishers, 1985.

S. Mahamud, L. Williams, K. Thornber, and K. Xu. Segmentation of multiple salient closed contours from real images. *IEEE Trans. PAMI*, 25(4):433–444, 2003.

M. Maire, P. Arbelaez, C. Fowlkes, and J. Malik. Using contours to detect and localize junctions in natural images. In *Conf. Computer Vision Pattern Recognition*, 2008.

D. Martin, C. Fowlkes, D. Tal, and J. Malik. A database of human segmented natural images and its application to evaluating segmentation algorithms and measuring ecological statistics. In *Int. Conf. Computer Vision*, 2001.

D. Martin, C. Fowlkes, and J. Malik. Learning to detect natural image boundaries using local brightness, color, and texture cues. *IEEE Trans. PAMI*, 26:530–549, 2004.

D. Munoz, A. Bagnell, and M. Hebert. Stacked hierarchical labeling. In *European Conf. Computer Vision*, 2010.

N. Payet and S. Todorovic. SLEDGE: Sequential labeling of image edges for boundary detection. *Int. J. Computer Vision*, 104(1):15–37, 2013.

X. Ren, C. Fowlkes, and J. Malik. Learning probabilistic models for contour completion in natural images. *Int. J. Computer Vision*, 77(1-3):47–63, 2008.

S. Ross and A. Bagnell. Efficient reductions for imitation learning. *Journal of Machine Learning Research — Proceedings Track*, 9:661–668, 2010.

S. Ross, G. Gordon, and A. Bagnell. A reduction of imitation learning and structured prediction to no-regret online learning. *Journal of Machine Learning Research — Proceedings Track*, 15:627–635, 2011.

E. Sharon, A. Brandt, and R. Basri. Segmentation and boundary detection using multiscale intensity measurements. In *Conf. Computer Vision Pattern Recognition*, pages 469–476, 2001.

D. Weiss and B. Taskar. Structured prediction cascades. *Journal of Machine Learning Research — Proceedings Track*, 9:916–923, 2010.

L. Williams and K. Thornber. A comparison of measures for detecting natural shapes in cluttered backgrounds. *Int. J. Computer Vision*, 34(2-3):81–96, 1999.

Q. Zhu, G. Song, and J. Shi. Untangling cycles for contour grouping. In *Int. Conf. Computer Vision*, pages 1–8, 2007.

S.-C. Zhu. Embedding Gestalt laws in Markov random fields. *IEEE Trans. PAMI*, 21(11):1170–1187, 1999.

16 Genome Annotation with Structured Output Learning

Jonas Behr   jonas.behr@bsse.ethz.ch
Sloan-Kettering Institute & ETH Zurich, D-BSSE
New York City, USA & Basel, Switzerland

Gabriele Schweikert   G.Schweikert@ed.ac.uk
University of Edinburgh
Edinburgh, UK

Gunnar Rätsch   raetsch@cbio.mskcc.org
Sloan-Kettering Institute
New York City, USA

This chapter describes an important application of structured output prediction to the problem of computational genome annotation. The genome codes for genes, and the gene products are the results of multiple complex biochemical processing steps. Based on prior knowledge and accurate detectors of specific sequence elements, one can predict the gene products and processing steps. The problem setting, available data, and common approaches will be discussed in sufficient detail. Two inference methods are presented. The first one is based on Hidden Semi-Markov Models, and the second one uses Mixed Integer Programming. Subsequently, the learning approach is described and four essential strategies are given to make learning and inference scalable to thousands of training sequences and predictions on genomes with more than three billion letters. Finally, results obtained from different systems participating in two competitions are presented.

16.1   Introduction: The Genome Annotation Problem

Important applications of structured prediction arise in the ever-growing field of computational genome annotation (e.g., Do et al., 2006; Rätsch et al., 2007; DeCaprio et al., 2007; Bernal et al., 2007; Zeller et al., 2008a; De Bona et al., 2008; Zeller et al., 2008b; Schweikert et al., 2009; Görnitz et al., 2011). Biological sequence analysis was already pioneered in the 1970s, and it recently gained new impact in the time of the "genomic revolution." It is one of the application areas where expert knowledge of the underlying problem is particularly important. The following section will therefore give a basic introduction to genome biology, experimental techniques employed, and typical computational systems used to tackle the genome annotation problem.

16.1.1   Genome Biology

An organism's complete hereditary information, its genome, is stored in the double-stranded helices of the Deoxyribonucleic acid (DNA). In a simplistic view, these long biopolymers can be thought of as linear strings consisting of many basic units called nucleotides or base pairs. The strands have an orientation, and many important cellular processes work in a unique direction along the strand, that is, from its 5' to its 3' end. For simplication, we will also refer to the start (5' end) and the end (3' end) of the strand sequence. There are merely four different types of nucleotides, called adenine, cytosine, guanine, and thymine (abbreviated A, C, G, and T). Within one strand, successive nucleotides are linked by strong covalent bonds. Therefore, DNA has the potential to form arbitrary sequences using the four "letters," thus storing complex genetic information over millions of years.

In recent years, the complete genomes of many diverse organisms have been reconstructed by sequencing, most notably the human genome (Lander et al., 2001; Venter et al., 2001). In stark contrast, the hidden meaning of these *instructions* are far from being deciphered. For example, it is assumed that parts of the genome might merely contain "junk," whereas other subsequences are functionally relevant. One of the most important and best studied genomic elements are protein-coding genes (see Figure 16.1). These are defined portions of the DNA sequence that are *transcribed* nucleotide by nucleotide into *pre-messenger RNAs* (pre-mRNAs). They are subsequently processed, with some parts, called *introns*, being removed and the remaining parts, called *exons*, being *spliced* to form *mature mRNAs*. (Other steps involve adding a cap and a tail to these mature mRNAs.) Mature mRNAs

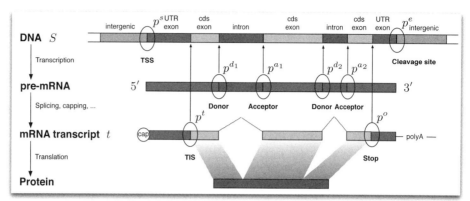

Figure 16.1: **The Central Dogma of Molecular Biology:** "DNA makes RNA, RNA makes proteins, proteins make us" (Leavitt and Nirenberg, 2010): DNA is first transcribed to pre-mRNA. Subsequent processing involves splicing, adding a cap and a tail to form the mature mRNA or RNA transcript, denoted by t. mRNAs are translated into proteins, which are an essential component of life. Signals that are needed for the machinery to work are marked with an ellipsoid. While acceptor and donor splice sites are required on the pre-mRNA sequence for splicing, their characteristic sequence is also found in the genome sequence as the pre-mRNA is a RNA copy of a part of the DNA molecule. Similarly for translation start and stop sites.

are also referred to as (RNA) *transcripts* and will be denoted with t in the following. Eventually, the processed RNAs are *translated* according to the genetic code into chains of *amino acids*, which in turn fold into functional proteins. Proteins are important building blocks of living organisms and key players in almost every process in the cell. Apart from protein-coding genes there are other classes of genes including structural or long non-coding RNA genes which are transcribed and processed but not translated. The prediction of those genes will not be addressed in this chapter.

An important aspect of the genome annotation problem is to detect and define those parts of the genome that are functionally important (e.g., code for proteins). The problem of predicting a non-overlapping set of transcripts can be considered as a segmentation problem where, in addition to the hidden location of genes, their exon-intron structures have to be predicted from the DNA sequence. Such a segmentation is illustrated in Figure 16.1. In many cases, competing but often highly regulated molecular processes during transcription and processing lead to *multiple, different transcripts* being generated from the same gene (see, e.g., Gerstein et al., 2007, for an in-depth discussion of what defines a *gene*). Hence, one has to predict multiple segmentations simultaneously (see considerations in Zien et al., 2006). By solving this problem, one establishes an initial *static view of the genome*.

For a detailed understanding of cellular processes, it is important to adopt a more dynamic perspective: For instance, any multi-cellular organism consists of many different cell types that all contain identical copies of the individual's genomic DNA sequence. Nevertheless, different cell types can exhibit widely varying morphologies and functions. What distinguishes, for instance, a human liver cell from a heart cell is the set of genes that are expressed in one cell versus the other and also the quantitative scale of this activity in the respective cells. An important second step in the genome annotation problem is therefore to reconstruct and determine the abundance of all intermediate and mature gene products. The *cell-* or *sample-specific* set of RNA transcripts is called the *transcriptome*, and the set of proteins is called the *proteome* of a cell.

Apart from the complex nature of the problem, computational challenges arise from the scale of the genome and the complexity of the biochemical processes. For example, the human genome consists of three billion nucleotides. However, a mere, dispersed 1% of the total DNA sequence codes for all of the 20,000 protein-coding genes with more than 100,000 alternative RNA transcripts. A significantly larger part of the genome, however, is assumed to have some yet unknown function (ENCODE Project Consortium et al., 2012).

16.1.2   Experimental Evidence

For this work, it is assumed that the genome sequence is given. There exist many different technologies to analyze the RNA or protein content of a biological sample (e.g., a cell or population of cells), and these technologies have revolutionized molecular biology over the last 10 years. Important technologies include Sanger sequencing, (Tiling) Micro Arrays, Deep RNA sequencing, and Tandem Mass-Spectrometry. Reviewing all of them in detail goes beyond the scope of this work. Instead we focus on the description of one method, namely, Deep RNA sequencing—also called RNA-seq. In RNA-seq, one starts with a mixture of RNA transcripts/molecules that are extracted from a biological sample. These molecules are sheared, and the fragments are then sequenced using a deep sequencing technology (e.g., from Illumina Inc.). The results are the sequences of millions of relatively short fragments of RNA (one experiment often has 100 million fragments, each 100-200 bp long). These fragments are then *aligned* to the genome, such that the genomic coordinates of their origin can, with some uncertainty, be extracted. In many cases, RNA-seq measurements can be represented as a density of *read* fragments over the genome (see Figure 16.2 for an illustration). A detailed description of the format, advantages, and limitations of this information goes beyond the scope of this work. Instead it is abstractly assumed that the quantitative measurements of the transcribed DNA sequences is given as $\boldsymbol{x}$. In addition, we assume:

Assumption 16.1 (Additivity of Experimental Evidence). *If we have a measurement $\boldsymbol{x}_a$ that corresponds to transcript t_a and another $\boldsymbol{x}_b$ that corresponds to another transcript t_b, then the superposition of both transcripts would lead to a measurement*

$$\boldsymbol{x}_{a\&b} = \boldsymbol{x}_a + \boldsymbol{x}_b. \tag{16.1}$$

This assumption is illustrated in Figure 16.2 for two overlapping transcripts. It is relatively well satisfied for RNA-seq and tiling arrays (if saturation can be ignored). For Sanger sequencing, the number of fragments is typically too small, such that one often only observes either a or b (or neither). In mass spectrometry, the assumption is less well satisfied due to interactions of the analyzed peptides. While this assumption may be satisfied for some experimental evidence, it is not (even closely) satisfied for evidence encoded into the DNA (e.g., sequence signals do not add up if there is more than one transcript).

It is important to note that if sequencing technologies were perfect, the problem of genome annotation as defined above would be solved. The problem is therefore dependent on the limitations of these techniques, which include that (i) typically only relatively short pieces of sequences are obtained and hence whole transcripts are rarely observed in a single read; (ii) one usually observes a mixture of reads stemming from multiple, overlapping transcripts, which makes the reconstruction more challenging; and (iii) that experimental artifacts lead to quantitative and qualitative variation in the data, which requires robust prediction algorithms.

16.1.3   Existing Annotations and Training Data

Annotations of genomes are typically large consortial efforts in which experimental data of one or multiple types described above are collected, and based on that and previously developed computational models, an initial annotation is produced. These annotations then develop over time and are improved by manual curation, a process that is time consuming and can lead to biologically more plausible and complete annotations. However, the generation of complete and accurate labels for training a gene-finding system can be said to be challenging.

16.1.4   Formalization of the Problem

The genome sequence $S = \Sigma^L$ of length L, with $\Sigma = \{A, C, G, T\}$, contains regions that encode G genes. The boundaries (p_g^s, p_g^e) of genes are typically unknown, and genes may overlap. The genomic sequence $S_g \in \Sigma^{L_g}$ associated with a gene $g = 1, \ldots, G$ of length L_g encodes all transcripts $t_i, i = 1, \ldots, T_g$, that can be produced at any time by any cell. A transcript t is given by its start and end positions, p_t^s and p_t^e, respectively, translation start and stop positions, p_t^t and p_t^o, as well as a list of J_t acceptor/donor splice site positions $(p_t^{d_j}, p_t^{a_j}), j = 1, \ldots, J_t$ (see Figure 16.1 for illustration).

Problem 16.1 (*Ab initio* Gene Prediction). The aim of *ab initio* gene prediction is to predict the boundaries (p_g^s, p_g^e) of *all* genes $g = 1, \ldots, G$ and *all* transcripts $t_i, i = 1, \ldots, T_g$, that are encoded in these genes in the given genome sequence S. Hence, we seek a prediction algorithm as follows:

$$\mathcal{A}_{ai} : S \mapsto \left\{ (p_g^s, p_g^e), \{t_i\}_{i=1}^{T_g} \right\}_{g=1}^{G}.$$

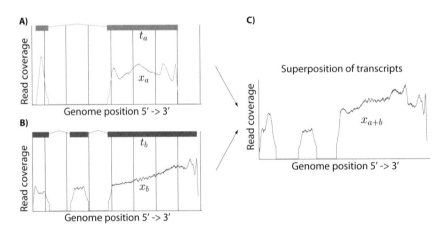

Figure 16.2: Additivity of Experimental Evidence and Measurement Noise: A given gene may give rise to two different types of transcripts, t_a and t_b. In a given cell, these two types of transcripts are present in different amounts, and RNA-seq can be used to estimate their abundance. For example, in a certain cell type, only t_a may be transcribed (**A**). Ideally, the measured read coverage should be uniform across the two transcribed exons and 0 everywhere else. In reality, the read coverage varies strongly over the transcribed regions. (**B**) shows the read coverage for a cell in which only transcripts of the type t_b are present, and **C** shows a cell state in which both transcripts are generated. The aim of the Transcriptome Reconstruction Problem is to determine the complete set of transcripts in a given cell (i.e., t_a in [**A**], t_b in [**B**], and (t_a, t_b) in [**C**]) and in addition to estimate their relative abundance. Figure appeared similarly in Bohnert and Rätsch (2010).

While it would be nice to predict the transcript abundance from the genomic sequence, it is hard and, to our knowledge, has not been done with reasonable accuracy. Also, most algorithms are not able to predict multiple transcripts and only report transcript per gene (with few exceptions).

Experimental evidence is typically associated with a cell (or mixture of cells) in one or more specific conditions. In *de novo* gene prediction, the experimental evidence is used to improve gene prediction:[1]

Problem 16.2 (*De novo* Gene Prediction). As in Problem 16.1, one attempts to predict *all* genes and transcripts. In addition to the genome sequence, there is genome-wide experimental evidence X (possibly of a different type and of a heterogeneous origin) that can be taken advantage of to solve the problem. Hence, we seek a prediction algorithm as follows:

$$\mathcal{A}_{dn} : (S, X) \mapsto \left\{ (p_g^s, p_g^e), \{t_i\}_{i=1}^{T_g} \right\}_{g=1}^{G}.$$

Ultimately, one is interested in reconstructing the transcriptome and proteome of a single cell or a collection of cells in a specific state. Here it is important to predict not the transcripts that could potentially be produced, but to predictively reconstruct transcripts that are present in a given cell and determine their abundance:

Problem 16.3 (Transcriptome Reconstruction). As in Problem 16.2, one attempts to predict genes and transcripts, however, in a sample-specific manner. In transcriptome reconstruction, one additionally has to predict the abundance α_i of transcripts t_i in a biological sample. Hence, we seek a prediction algorithm as follows:

$$\mathcal{A}_{tr} : (S, X) \mapsto \left\{ (p_g^s, p_g^e), \{t_i, \alpha_i\}_{i=1}^{T_g} \right\}_{g=1}^{G}.$$

If the set of genes and transcripts is already known (e.g., by solving Problem 16.1 or 16.2), then it will be sufficient to solve a simpler problem.

Problem 16.4 (Transcriptome Quantification). Given a complete set of genes and transcripts, in transcriptome quantification one predicts the abundance α_i of transcripts t_i in a biological sample. Hence, we seek a prediction algorithm as follows:

$$\mathcal{A}_{tr} : \left(S, X, \left\{ (p_g^s, p_g^e), \{t_i\}_{i=1}^{T_g} \right\}_{g=1}^{G} \right) \mapsto \left\{ \{\alpha_i\}_{i=1}^{T_g} \right\}_{g=1}^{G}.$$

---

1. The term "*de novo* gene finding" has typically been used for gene finding using the genome sequence and conservation. We use it in a broader sense.

To solve the latter problem, one typically exploits Assumption 16.1, which leads to the following implied relationship: $X_g = \sum_{i=1}^{T_g} \alpha_i \boldsymbol{x}_{t_i}$, where X_g is the measurement for the mixture that we observe for gene g and $\alpha_i \mathbf{x}_{t_i}$ is the measurement that we would observe if only transcript t_i would be expressed at level α_i. Because we know the structure of a transcript t and how the experimental evidence is generated, we can infer what data $\boldsymbol{x}_t$ can be expected for that transcript (see coverage pattern $\boldsymbol{x}_a$ and compare with t_a in Figure 16.2). We assume this is given as $\boldsymbol{x} = \psi(t)$. A straightforward way to quantify the transcripts is by solving the following optimization problem for each gene g:

$$\{\alpha_i\}_{i=1}^{T_g} = \operatorname*{argmin}_{\alpha \in \mathbb{R}^{T_g}} \ell^{\boldsymbol{x}}\left(X_g, \sum_{i=1}^{T_g} \alpha_i \psi(t_i)\right), \tag{16.2}$$

where $\ell^{\boldsymbol{x}}(\cdot, \cdot)$ is an appropriate loss function.

16.1.5   Related Work

Gene Finding Systems   Most early gene finders were designed to solve a simplified version of Problem 16.1, that is predicting a single transcript per gene from DNA sequence. These systems were based on Hidden Markov Models (HMMs) (Durbin et al., 1998; Majoros, 2007) and include, for example, GeneMark.hmm (Lukashin and Borodovsky, 1998; Borodovsky et al., 2003), HMMgene (Krogh, 2000), and Unveil (Majoros et al., 2003). A first substantial improvement was achieved when generalized HMMs (gHMM) were introduced to gene finding (Rabiner, 1990; Kulp et al., 1996). This allowed systems like Fgenesh (Salamov and Solovyev, 2000) and AUGUS-TUS (Stanke et al., 2006) to accurately model segment length distributions and segmental sequence content. Another major advancement was observed when discriminatively trained methods were first introduced; these include mSplicer (Rätsch et al., 2007), Conrad (DeCaprio et al., 2007), Contrast (Gross et al., 2007), and mGene (Schweikert et al., 2009). The latter will be the basis of the work presented here.

Transcriptome Reconstruction Methods   Several methods solve the transcriptome reconstruction problem by first enumerating all paths in a graph (see Section 16.2.2) generated directly from RNA-seq data and then solving the transcript quantification problem. The main distinctive feature is the regularization employed to induce sparsity. These methods include *iReckon* (Mezlini et al., 2012), *NSMAP* (Xia et al., 2011), *IsoLasso* (Li et al., 2011) using the l_1 norm, and *CLIIQ* (Lin et al., 2012) employing the l_0-norm. *Scrip-*

ture (Guttman et al., 2010) does not use any regularization. Few methods avoid the expensive enumeration of all paths by computing a graph coverage, for instance, Cufflinks (Trapnell et al., 2010) and heuristic search strategies (e.g., Hiller and Wong, 2012). *MiTie* (Behr et al., 2013) uses the l_0 norm to regularize the transcript abundance prediction and avoids the path enumeration using an inference method discussed later in this chapter.

16.2   Inference

For inference, performing prediction to obtain an annotation, we assume we are given a scoring function $G_{\boldsymbol{\theta}}(\boldsymbol{x}, y)$ that measures the consistency of a label sequence y with the observed data given our model parametrized with $\boldsymbol{\theta}$. Learning the parameters $\boldsymbol{\theta}$ is discussed in Section 16.3. We will now introduce two inference methods to compute

$$\boldsymbol{y}^* = \operatorname*{argmax}_{\boldsymbol{y}} G_{\boldsymbol{\theta}}(\boldsymbol{x}^n, \boldsymbol{y})$$

for a given training example $\boldsymbol{x}^n$. To keep the notation uncluttered, from now on $\boldsymbol{x}^n$ summarizes all input data including the genomic sequence and, if available, any associated experimental evidence. In case of the first inference method, the predicted label $\boldsymbol{y}$ will be a single segmentation of a piece of DNA. The segmentation specifies the location of genes, including a single transcript per gene. In the second case, the prediction $\boldsymbol{y}$ for a gene can correspond to multiple transcripts simultaneously.

16.2.1   Hidden Semi-Markov Models

Assume the scoring function $G_{\boldsymbol{\theta}}$ can be decomposed as

$$G_{\boldsymbol{\theta}}(\boldsymbol{x}^n, \boldsymbol{y}) = \sum_{i=1}^{|\boldsymbol{x}^n|} g(\boldsymbol{x}^n_{i-1,i}, \boldsymbol{y}_{i-1,i}), \tag{16.3}$$

where g is some atomic scoring function and $\boldsymbol{x}_{i-1,i}$ denotes a part of the input data associated with region $(i-1, i)$. Similarly, $\boldsymbol{y}_{i-1,i}$ denotes the label in the same region. Then the maximal scoring label sequence $\boldsymbol{y}^*$ can be computed efficiently using the Viterbi algorithm for Hidden Markov Models (Rabiner, 1990).

In generalized Hidden Markov Models, the states are associated with variable length d sequences (different from [16.3], where the state duration $d = 1$). Within the state the scoring can be non-Markovian, but transitions between states are scored in a Markovian manner. Therefore, such models

Algorithm 16.1 Extended Viterbi-like decoding in mGene. $\mathcal{Q}$ is the set of states, T is the state transition matrix, and $pos(p)$ is the genomic position of index position p. We assume signal prediction per state q and index position p precomputed and given by $\mathbf{FSX}_{p,q}$. Also, region-based scoring is assumed to be precomputed cumulatively, such that $\mathbf{FCX}_{p,q} - \mathbf{FCX}_{p-d,q}$ scores the region $(pos(p-d), pos(p))$ for state q. κ is a scoring function for lengths and region scores (that cannot be precomputed). The routines *stopcodons* and *checkORF* are helper functions that deal with avoiding specific sequence elements (stop codons) in the produced sequences. See main text for further explanations.

```
1    Input: Sequence label pair, precomputed sequence signals
2         (x, y, pos, FSX, FCX)
3
4    # Precompute list of stop codons:
5    pos_stop ← stopcodons(x)
6
7    # Initialize V with -∞ and T1, T2 with -1
8    for p = 1, . . . , P
9        for q = 1, . . . , |Q|
10           if FSX_{p,q} = -∞: break
11           # Get allowed predecessor states for state q: 𝒥_q
12           # Compute segment loss, for all states q' ∈ 𝒥_q and
13           #     all positions, p - 1, . . . , p - D_max:
14           Δ ← comploss(y, p, D_max, 𝒥_q)
15           for q' ∈ 𝒥_q
16               while pos(p) - pos(p - d) ≤ D_max(q, q')
17                   if FSX_{p-d,q'} = -∞: break
18                   ok ← checkORF(x, q, q', pos(p), pos(p - d), pos_stop)
19                   if !ok: break
20                   trans ← T(q, q')
21                   len ← κ^{l(q,q')}(pos(p) - pos(p - d))
22                   cont ← κ^{c(q,q')}(FCX_{p,q} - FCX_{p-d,q'})
23                   loss ← Δ(d, q')
24                   score ← V(p - d, q') + trans + len + cont + loss
25                   if score > V(p, q):
26                       V(p, q) ← score
27                       T1(p, q) ← q'
28                       T2(p, q) ← p - d
29                   d ← d + 1
30           V(p, q) ← V(p, q) + FSX_{p,q}
31
32   y* ← traceback(T1, T2)
```

are also often called Hidden Semi-Markov Models. The decoding problem is computationally more expensive to solve as one has to track multiple variable segment lengths. The *dynamic programming* (DP) matrix is then given by:

$$V(i,k) = \max_{l=1,\ldots,|\mathcal{Q}|} \max_{d=1,\ldots,i-1} \left(V(i-d,l) + g(q_l, q_k, \boldsymbol{x}, i-d, i)\right) \qquad (16.4)$$

if $i > 1$ and $V(i,k) = 0$ otherwise, where $\mathcal{Q}$ is the set of states. The optimal label sequence can be obtained as in the HMM case by backtracking. However, to do so, saving the states of the optimal predecessor alone is not sufficient, but additionally the respective positions $i - d$ have to be remembered (see lines $27 - 28$ in Algorithm 16.1) in two additional variables:

$$T_1(i,k) = \underset{l=1\ldots|\mathcal{Q}|}{\operatorname{argmax}} \max_{d=1\ldots i-1} \left(V(i-d,l) + g(q_l, q_k, \boldsymbol{x}, i-d, i)\right) \qquad (16.5)$$

$$T_2(i,k) = i - \underset{d=1\ldots i-1}{\operatorname{argmax}} \max_{l=1\ldots|\mathcal{Q}|} \left(V(i-d,l) + g(q_l, q_k, \boldsymbol{x}, i-d, i)\right) (16.6)$$

for $i > 1$ and $T_{1,2}(i,k) = 0$ otherwise.

Without any further assumptions, the run time becomes quadratic in the length of the sequence $\mathcal{O}(|\mathcal{Q}|^2 \times L^2)$ as for each cell in the DP matrix, g has to be evaluated $|\mathcal{Q}| \times L$ times. In practice, the maximal look-back is determined by the maximal segment length D, leading to a run time $\mathcal{O}(|\mathcal{Q}|^2 \times L \times D)$. This can still be problematic in gene finding, as some segments, like intergenic or intronic regions, can be of great length (e.g., > 400 *kbp* for human introns).

Approximations   The DP described above needs to be solved many times during training. Therefore, it is important to use fast approximations of the solution of the DP. One way is to exploit the fact that state transitions only occur at few positions in the sequence. In addition, if one restricts the number of positions (cf. variable *pos* in Algorithm 16.1) by a factor λ, then the complexity of the algorithm reduces by a factor of λ^2 (because the sequence is effectively shorter and fewer steps need to be tracked back). Because the algorithm runs repeatedly on the same sequence during training, one can build a set of *positions of interest* at which the algorithm is allowed to switch state. This strategy leads to drastic speedups and is essential for the practicability of training the model (more on this topic in Section 16.3.2).

16.2.2   Mixed Integer Optimization for Predicting Multiple Transcripts

In this section, we introduce a second inference algorithm solving the transcript identification and quantification simultaneously (Problem 16.3). Therefore, we assume we are given RNA-seq reads in addition to the genomic sequence. The information obtained from alignments of RNA-seq reads against the genome can be compiled into a directed acyclic graph such that, assuming a sufficient amount of RNA-seq observations, transcripts correspond to paths in the graph. In this graph, nodes correspond to parts of exons (segments) and edges correspond to connections between segments (see Behr et al., 2013, for more details). We denote $\mathcal{P}$ as the set of all paths in this graph.

The mixed integer inference algorithm may be formalized as:

$$
\min_{\{t_i, \alpha_i\}_{i=1}^{T_g}} \quad \ell^{\boldsymbol{x}} \left(X_g, \sum_{i=1}^{T_g} \alpha_i \psi(t_i) \right) + \gamma_1 \sum_{i=1}^{T_g} G_{\boldsymbol{\theta}}(t_i) + \gamma_2 \|\boldsymbol{\alpha}\|_0 \tag{16.7}
$$
$$
\text{s.t.} \quad t_i \in \mathcal{P} \quad \forall i \in \{1, .., T_g\}
$$
$$
\boldsymbol{\alpha} \in \mathbf{R}^{T_g}
$$
$$
\alpha_i \geq 0 \quad \forall i \in \{1, .., T_g\}
$$
$$
T_g \leq T_{\max},
$$

where γ_1, γ_2, and $\boldsymbol{\theta}$ are parameters of the model, $\ell^{\boldsymbol{x}}$ is an appropriately chosen loss function (see also [16.2]), and $\psi(.)$ computes the expected measurement as defined in Problem 16.4 (see Figure 16.3 for an example). $G_{\boldsymbol{\theta}}$ is a scoring function for sequence features (as for the Hidden Semi-Markov Model in the previous section). Using the l_0-norm to regularize $\boldsymbol{\alpha}$, denoted by $\|\boldsymbol{\alpha}\|_0$, leads to sparse solutions (ℓ_1-norm regularization as done in Bohnert and Rätsch, 2010, does not lead to sparse enough solutions). While combinatorial optimization in general is intractable, the problem above can typically be solved within minutes for most cases (e.g., using IBM's CPLEX). One instance of this optimization problem is illustrated in Figure 16.3 and described in detail in Behr et al. (2013).

Approximations   The optimization Problem 16.7 can be approximated by iterative solving for one additional transcript at a time. This approximation is not accurate in general, but it is empirically successful and several orders of magnitude faster than finding the exact solution.

16.3   Learning

16.3.1   Large Margin Structure Learning

Given a $\boldsymbol{\theta}$-parametrized scoring model $G_{\boldsymbol{\theta}} : \mathcal{X} \times \mathcal{Y} \to \mathbf{R}$ that measures the compatibility of a prediction $\boldsymbol{y} \in \mathcal{Y}$ with the observed data $\boldsymbol{x} \in \mathcal{X}$ and an

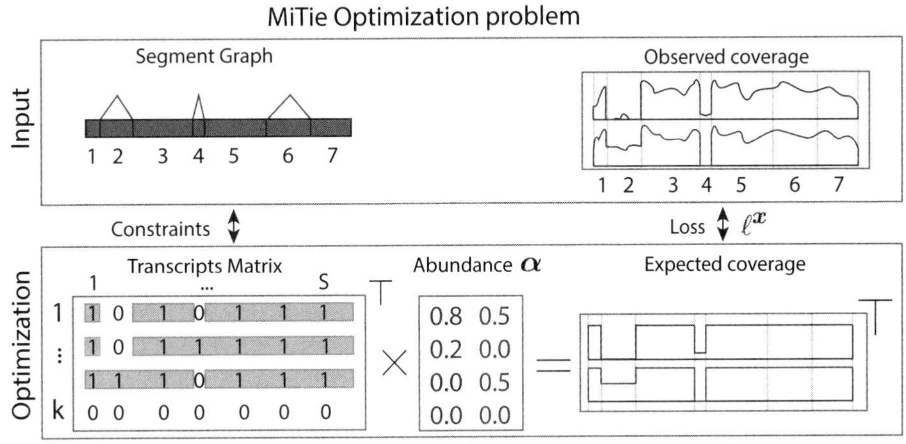

Figure 16.3: Illustration of the core optimization problem of *MiTie*. The transcript matrix U (bottom left) and abundance matrix $\boldsymbol{\alpha}$ (bottom center) will be optimized such that the implied expected read coverage of the k valid transcripts (bottom right) matches the observed coverage (top right) well. For this illustration, we chose a simplistic implementation of $\psi(.)$, where the i-th row of U corresponds to $\psi(t_i)$, ignoring bias models (Bohnert and Rätsch, 2010) and evidence for introns (Behr et al., 2013). Validity of the transcripts is ensured by appropriate constraints derived from the segment graph (top left). We illustrate the case of two samples. For each sample, we have abundance estimates $\boldsymbol{\alpha}$ for each of the $k = 4$ transcripts. The identity of the transcripts (i.e., the rows of U) is shared among the samples. By *Occam's razor* principle, we implement a trade-off between loss between the observed and expected coverages and the number of used transcripts (i.e., number of rows in $\boldsymbol{\alpha}$ with non-zero abundances).

inference method to compute

$$\tilde{y}^n = \underset{\boldsymbol{y}}{\operatorname{argmax}} \, G_{\boldsymbol{\theta}}(\boldsymbol{x}^n, \boldsymbol{y}),$$

we will now present a maximum margin-based algorithm to learn the model parameters $\boldsymbol{\theta}$. The algorithm is based on the framework of Hidden Markov Support Vector Machines introduced by Altun et al. (2003), Taskar et al. (2004), and Tsochantaridis et al. (2005). The semi-Markov extension and additional aspects were first described in Rätsch and Sonnenburg (2007) and Rätsch et al. (2007).

The parameters $\boldsymbol{\theta}$ of the scoring function are learned on a set of labeled training examples $\left\{ (\boldsymbol{x}^n, \boldsymbol{y}^n) \right\}_{n=1}^N$, such that for each instance $(\boldsymbol{x}^n, \boldsymbol{y}^n)$, the true labeling $\boldsymbol{y}^n$ scores higher than all other possible labelings $\boldsymbol{y} \in \mathcal{Y}^n$, that is, $G_{\boldsymbol{\theta}}(\boldsymbol{x}^n, \boldsymbol{y}^n) \gg G_{\boldsymbol{\theta}}(\boldsymbol{x}^n, \boldsymbol{y})$. In analogy to the SVM architecture, the correct labeling should not only score maximal, but should additionally be separated from all other labelings by a *large margin* (Vapnik, 1979). This leads to the following soft-margin optimization problem (Altun and Hofmann, 2003):

$$\min_{\boldsymbol{\xi} \in \mathbb{R}^N, \boldsymbol{\theta}} \quad \frac{1}{2} P[\boldsymbol{\theta}] + C \sum_{n=1}^{N} \boldsymbol{\xi}^n \tag{16.8}$$

$$\text{s.t.} \quad G_{\boldsymbol{\theta}}(\boldsymbol{x}^n, \boldsymbol{y}^n) - G_{\boldsymbol{\theta}}(\boldsymbol{x}^n, \boldsymbol{y}) \geq \ell^{\boldsymbol{y}}(\boldsymbol{y}^n, \boldsymbol{y}) - \boldsymbol{\xi}^n \tag{16.9}$$

$$\boldsymbol{\xi}^n \geq 0 \quad \forall \, n = 1, \dots, N, \ \boldsymbol{y} \in \mathcal{Y}^n,$$

where $P[\cdot]$ is a regularizer and C is a hyper-parameter. With a problem-specific loss function $\ell^{\boldsymbol{y}}(.,.)$ the margin is rescaled, hence enforcing a larger margin if $\boldsymbol{y}^n$ and $\boldsymbol{y}$ are very different (Taskar et al., 2004; Crammer and Singer, 2003; Tsochantaridis et al., 2005). The choice of $\ell^{\boldsymbol{y}}$ is important and should resemble the evaluation criterion one seeks to optimize.

The large number of possible wrong label sequences results in an exponential number of constraints, and this problem cannot be solved directly in an efficient manner, but the optimal solution can be found in polynomial time using column generation (Crammer and Singer, 2003; Tsochantaridis et al., 2005), where we iterate between solving the optimization problem for a subset of constraints and finding the most informative new constraints (see also Hettich and Kortanek, 1993, and references therein).

16.3.2 Large-Scale Learning

A typical application scenario has thousands of labeled sequences of length $10^3 - 10^6$ bp. If one were to use string kernels to characterize the sequence elements in the genome sequence (as necessary for gene finding), then computing $G_{\boldsymbol{\theta}}(\boldsymbol{x}, \boldsymbol{y})$ quickly becomes intractable. We therefore designed a two-layer learning strategy to separate the kernel computations from the structure predictions (Rätsch and Sonnenburg, 2007; Rätsch et al., 2007). However, even with this strategy, solving the problem would take weeks of computing time on a medium-sized compute cluster even for relatively small genomes. We therefore developed multiple strategies that each led to significant speedups. The resulting algorithm is described in Algorithm 16.2.

The column-generation procedure involves the steps of (ii) finding informative constraints, and (ii) solving the optimization problem, which are both computationally costly. The speedup strategies are as follows.

a) Two-layered architecture We drastically reduce the computational costs of step (1) by introducing a two layered design. All features that are computationally costly to compute are encapsulated into sub-models. The sub-model features can then be precomputed for all positions, where their prediction may be needed. Here we use large-scale SVMs developed for

Algorithm 16.2 The HM-SVM training algorithm. In each iteration, constraint generation (lines 15-28) is alternated with solving of an intermediate optimization problem (lines 32-36).

1	**Input:** labeled training examples, $\{\boldsymbol{x}^n, \boldsymbol{y}^n\}_1^N$
2	
3	**Initialization:**
4	objective function $\quad$ **O**
5	arbitrary parametrization $\quad$ $\boldsymbol{\theta}_0$
6	slack variables $\quad$ $\boldsymbol{\xi}_0^n = \{0\}^n$
7	constraints $A \cdot \boldsymbol{\theta} \leq b$
8	init constraints empty $\quad$ $A = \{\}, b = \{\}$ and $\epsilon > 0$
9	
10	**for** $t = 1, 2, \ldots$
11	$\quad$ # decide on approximation of the inference method
12	$\quad$ # based on the number of constraints from iteration $t - 1$
13	$\quad$ $a = \text{useapprox}()$
14	
15	$\quad$ **parallel for** training example $(\boldsymbol{x}^n, \boldsymbol{y}^n)$
16	
17	$\quad\quad$ # run inference algorithm
18	$\quad\quad$ **if** $\quad$ a
19	$\quad\quad\quad$ $\boldsymbol{y}^{n*} = \widetilde{\text{argmax}}_{\boldsymbol{y}} \, G_{\boldsymbol{\theta}_t}(\boldsymbol{x}^n, \boldsymbol{y}) + \ell(\boldsymbol{y}^n, \boldsymbol{y})$
20	$\quad\quad$ **else**
21	$\quad\quad\quad$ $\boldsymbol{y}^{n*} = \text{argmax}_{\boldsymbol{y}} \, G_{\boldsymbol{\theta}_t}(\boldsymbol{x}^n, \boldsymbol{y}) + \ell(\boldsymbol{y}^n, \boldsymbol{y})$
22	$\quad\quad$ **end if**
23	
24	$\quad\quad$ # add maximal margin violator to the active set
25	$\quad\quad$ **if** $G_{\boldsymbol{\theta}_{t-1}}(\boldsymbol{x}^n, \boldsymbol{y}^n) - G_{\boldsymbol{\theta}_{t-1}}(\boldsymbol{x}^n, \boldsymbol{y}^{n*}) \leq \ell(\boldsymbol{y}^n, \boldsymbol{y}^{n*}) - \boldsymbol{\xi}_{t-1}^n$
26	$\quad\quad\quad$ $A \leftarrow A \cup \nabla_{\boldsymbol{\theta}_{t-1}} G_{\boldsymbol{\theta}_{t-1}}(\boldsymbol{x}^n, \boldsymbol{y}^n) - \nabla_{\boldsymbol{\theta}_{t-1}} G_{\boldsymbol{\theta}_{t-1}}(\boldsymbol{x}^n, \boldsymbol{y}^{n*})$
27	$\quad\quad\quad$ $b \leftarrow b \cup \ell(\boldsymbol{y}^n, \boldsymbol{y}^{n*}) - \boldsymbol{\xi}_{t-1}^n$
28	$\quad\quad$ **end if**
29	
30	$\quad$ **end for**
31	
32	$\quad$ # select active and violated constraints
33	$\quad$ $\mathbf{m} = b - A \cdot \boldsymbol{\theta}_{t-1}$
34	
35	$\quad$ # solve the intermediate training problem
36	$\quad$ $\boldsymbol{\theta}_t, \boldsymbol{\xi}_t^n \leftarrow solve(\mathbf{O}, \{A_i, b_i | \mathbf{m}_i < \epsilon\})$
37	
38	**until** no more margin violators found

genomic signal prediction (Sonnenburg et al., 2007b, 2006, 2007a). They can be trained on millions and predict on billions of examples efficiently (e.g., implemented in the *Shogun Toolbox*, Sonnenburg et al., 2010). This allows us to learn a simple linear G_θ, which is fast to compute. Optimized encoding of the parameters, as described in Section 16.3.3, keeps the model flexible enough to learn sufficiently complex relationships between features.

b) Parallel constraint generation   We may reduce the number of times we need to solve the optimization problem by generating a large batch of constraints with the same parameter vector $\boldsymbol{\theta}^t$ in the t-th column-generation iteration. This allows us to distribute step (ii) for parallel computation at the cost that some of the generated constraints might not be informative.

c) Approximations of the inference method   For both inference methods introduced in Section 16.2, we provide approximate solutions that radically reduce the computational costs. These approximations may, however, not provide the most violated constraints. We have noticed that we can speed up the training process drastically by performing column-generation iterations using the approximate inference in turn with iterations where we solve the exact inference problem. The constraints generated by the approximate inference methods turn out to be inactive at the optimal solution but effectively guide the search for the optimal solution.

d) Constraint selection   Both above-mentioned speedups significantly increase the number of constraints we have to consider in step (ii). We therefore make use of the previous solution $\boldsymbol{\theta}^{t-1}$ when solving the optimization problem. For all N inequality constraints of the form $A_i \cdot \boldsymbol{\theta} \leq b_i$, $i = 1, \ldots N$, including the constraints accumulating in step (i), we compute the margin $m_i = b_i - A_i \cdot \boldsymbol{\theta}^{t-1}$. By definition, m_i is negative for all violated constraints generated in iteration t. We then solve step (ii) with respect to constraints $A_i \cdot \boldsymbol{\theta} \leq b_i$, $i \in \{i|m_i \leq \epsilon, i = 1, \ldots, N\}$, $\epsilon > 0$ to obtain $\boldsymbol{\theta}^t$. Constraints not satisfied by solution $\boldsymbol{\theta}^t$ will be accounted for in iteration $t + 1$. For the final solution we make sure that all constraints are satisfied. With this trick, we speed up layer two of this two-layered learning strategy by one order of magnitude and still guarantee optimality.

16.3.3   Joint Feature Map and Two-Layered Architecture

In this section, we will turn our attention to the construction of the scoring function $G_\theta(\boldsymbol{x}^n, \boldsymbol{y})$. As mentioned in the previous sections, the computational constraints in our domain of application restrict the scoring function

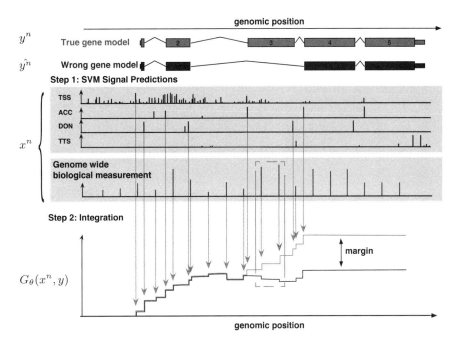

Figure 16.4: We illustrate the integration of several SVM-based signal predictions (Transcription Start Site; ACCeptor splice site; DONor splice site; Transcription Termination Site) and biological measurements. The biological measurement symbolizes an expression measurement with large values indicating exonic regions. Therefore, large values should be scored high in exons and low (or negative) outside of exons (see dashed box). To implement this, the model includes distinct parameters for expression measurements in each segment type (e.g., exon, intron, etc.). The true label sequence y^n is distinct from another label sequence $\hat{y}^n$ by the usage of exon number 3. SVM predictions for the acceptor and donor splice site as well as the expression measurement give good indication for the presence of exon 3. Therefore, the fully trained model scores y^n higher than $\hat{y}^n$ with a large margin.

to be linear. Thus, we can write the scoring function as a product of a *joint feature map* $\Phi(\boldsymbol{x}, \boldsymbol{y})$ and the parameters $\boldsymbol{\theta}$:

$$G_{\boldsymbol{\theta}}(\boldsymbol{x}, \boldsymbol{y}) = \langle \Phi(\boldsymbol{x}, \boldsymbol{y}), \boldsymbol{\theta} \rangle$$

The feature representation Φ is a function of $\boldsymbol{x}$ and $\boldsymbol{y}$ because elements of $\boldsymbol{x}$ need to be scored differently depending on the label sequence (see Figure 16.4 for an illustration).

The choice of joint feature representation $\Phi(\boldsymbol{x}, \boldsymbol{y})$ is clearly crucial for the performance of the model. In the simplest case of a quantitative feature f, we define $\Phi_f(\boldsymbol{x}, \boldsymbol{y}) \to \mathbf{R}$ to be scalar and learn a parameter $\boldsymbol{\theta}_f$ weighting this feature in a prediction. This formulation assumes that the predictive power of a feature scales linear with the value of the feature. In practice, this assumption is often violated, where changes of a feature in a certain range may be much more informative than in another range.

To account for this potential non-linearity in the predictive capability of a feature, we implement *piecewise linear transformations* to approximate arbitrary non-linear transformations of a feature f as follows:

We define $\pi_f \in \mathbf{R}^b$ as a fixed set of b thresholds, given by percentiles of the empirical distribution of f and

$$[\Phi_f(\boldsymbol{x}, \boldsymbol{y})]_{i \in \{1,\ldots,b\}} = \begin{cases} 1 & \text{if } x_f^n \leq [\pi_f]_1 \wedge i = 1 \\ 1 & \text{elif } x_f^n \geq [\pi_f]_b \wedge i = b \\ d_i & \text{elif } x_f^n \geq [\pi_f]_i \wedge x_f^n \leq [\pi_f]_{i+1} \\ (1 - d_{i-1}) & \text{elif } x_f^n \leq [\pi_f]_i \wedge x_f^n \geq [\pi_f]_{i-1} \\ 0 & \text{else,} \end{cases}$$

where $d_i = \frac{[\pi_f]_{i+1} - x_f^n}{[\pi_f]_{i+1} - [\pi_f]_i}$. For each threshold, we learn a separate parameter.

This increases the total number of parameters by a factor of b, which we counter by introducing additional regularization terms. In addition to l_2 penalties on each parameter, we couple the parameters of neighboring thresholds by adding an l_1 or l_2 penalty on the difference.[2]

This design allows us to incorporate arbitrary non-probabilistic predictors as sum models in the system and learn to integrate the predictions by learning arbitrary transformations of the predictor outputs. More details are given in Rätsch and Sonnenburg (2007).

Moreover, the model may leverage any amount of additional information sources such as expression measurements (or other information based on RNA-seq) without having to make independence assumptions.

16.4   Experiments

In this section, we will demonstrate three algorithms: (i) *mGene*, which uses the two-layered large margin parameter estimation approach described in Section 16.3 (without experimental evidence) using the dynamic programming-based inference algorithm described in Section 16.2.1; (ii) *mGene.ngs*, which is like *mGene* but uses experimental evidence in addition to the genomic sequence; and (iii) the more sophisticated inference algorithm based on Mixed Integer Programming described in Section 16.2.2 for

---

2. Empirically, both penalties behave similarly, although the training convergence is slightly more fast with the l_2 penalty.

multiple transcript detection when applied to RNA-seq data. This algorithm uses extensive prior information on the structure of the RNA-seq data and does not need to be trained.

16.4.1   *Ab initio* Predictions with *mGene* and the nGASP Challenge

We participated in the nGASP challenge (Coghlan et al., 2008) for genome annotation. Based on a fixed training set of 500 genes, the task was to perform predictions of a given set of evaluation regions of the *C. elegans* genome.[3] No further information was allowed to be used.

The evaluation was then performed based on a curated version of the genome annotation, which was not available to the participants prior to submission. The evaluation was carried out in different levels. For the nucleotide-level evaluation, the sensitivity is computed as the number of nucleotides in the test region that are part of a coding exon in at least one annotated transcript and in at least one predicted transcript, divided by the number of nucleotides being part of any coding exon of any annotated transcript. Specificity is computed accordingly. Similarly, the exon/transcript level evaluation requires entire coding exons/transcripts to be correctly predicted.

The results of the methods comparison are given in Table 16.1. The submitted predictions based on the developmental version of *mGene* (mGene.init (dev)) outperforms all other methods in terms of mean of sensitivity and specificity for all evaluation criteria. Further improvements on *mGene* (mGene.init; see Schweikert et al., 2009, not part of the competition) resulted in additional significant improvements especially on transcript level. The increased accuracy was mainly due to an improved loss function that also took transcript-level deviations into account.

16.4.2   *De novo* Predictions with *mGene.ngs* and the rGASP Challenge

We participated in a similar competition called rGASP (Steijger et al., 2013), where participants were given RNA-seq data for three different organisms (*H. sapiens*, *D. melanogaster*, and *C. elegans*) to perform transcript predictions. Participants were allowed to use the genome annotation for training. This is the ideal application scenario for learning the integration of genomic sequence features and transcriptome measurements.

The evaluation was performed genome-wide based on the same genome annotation. This evaluation procedure may favor submissions based on a

---

3. This translucent worm, a few millimeters long, serves as a model organism and has considerable impact in biological research.

Method	Nucleotide			Exon			Transcript		
	Sn	Sp	$\frac{Sn+Sp}{2}$	Sn	Sp	$\frac{Sn+Sp}{2}$	Sn	Sp	$\frac{Sn+Sp}{2}$
mGene.init	96.78	90.87	**93.83**	85.11	80.17	**82.64**	49.59	42.25	**45.92**
mGene.init (dev)	96.85	91.59	**94.22**	84.17	78.63	81.40	44.30	38.69	41.50
Craig	95.54	90.92	93.23	80.17	78.15	79.16	35.70	35.44	35.57
Eugene	93.96	89.47	91.72	80.28	73.00	76.64	49.09	28.19	38.64
Fgenesh	98.20	87.11	92.65	86.37	73.55	79.96	47.11	34.11	40.61*
Augustus	97.01	89.01	93.01	86.12	72.55	79.34	52.89	28.64	40.77*

Table 16.1: Comparison of top-performing gene-finding systems that participated in the nGASP challenge (Coghlan et al., 2008). Shown are sensitivity (Sn), specificity (Sp), and their average (each in percent) on nucleotide, exon, and transcript level (see Schweikert et al., 2009, for the full table). The prediction of mGene.init was generated after the deadline but according to the rules of the nGASP challenge. The results within 0.5% of the best performing method within a category and according to each of the evaluation levels are set in boldface.

larger training set. For *mGene* and *AUGUSTUS* (Mario Stanke, personal communication), a set of $\leq 3,000$ training genes for each organisms was used. Otherwise, the evaluation criteria were similar to those in the nGASP challenge (see Section 16.4.1).

The results of the comparison are given in Table 16.2. They show excellent performance in terms of mean of sensitivity and specificity of *mGene* for *D. melanogaster* and *C. elegans*. *AUGUSTUS* and *GSTRUCT* showed similarly good performance on *C. elegans* and *D. melanogaster*, respectively.

For the *H. sapiens*, *AUGUSTUS* and other methods perform significantly better than *mGene*. This has two main reasons: *mGene*'s signal predictions for human were less tuned and less accurate as for the other organisms, and *mGene* did not use genomic conservation information for its predictions, which is informative for predicting exons correctly.

Approaches such as *Cufflinks* that ignore the information of the genomic DNA sequence perform significantly worse than the gene-finding approach for this task. This difference is the smallest for *H. sapiens*, where *ab initio* gene prediction is harder due to multiple factors (e.g., genome is larger, genetic code more complex).

16.4.3   Transcriptome Reconstruction with *MiTie*

We implemented a version of the Mixed Integer Inference algorithm described in (16.7) in a tool called *MiTie* (Behr et al., 2013). Here we use a loss function that is a piece-wise quadratic approximation of the negative log-likelihood of the negative binomial distribution between observed and expected read counts (see Behr et al., 2013, for more details). The negative

Method	H. sapiens			D. melanogaster			C. elegans		
	Sn	Sp	$\frac{Sn+Sp}{2}$	Sn	Sp	$\frac{Sn+Sp}{2}$	Sn	Sp	$\frac{Sn+Sp}{2}$
AUGUSTUS all	**16.27**	39.26	27.77	**42.66**	61.14	51.90	**59.28**	44.09	51.69
AUGUSTUS high	**16.27**	44.41	30.34	n.a.	n.a.	n.a.	**59.21**	51.96	**55.59**
Exonerate high	13.23	41.92	27.58	30.98	66.02	48.50	39.98	50.42	45.20
GSTRUCT	14.10	**59.85**	**36.98**	28.21	**76.77**	**52.49**	39.03	**59.92**	49.48
mGene	10.83	8.98	9.90	38.02	67.02	**52.52**	55.27	50.73	53.00
mGene graph	14.90	14.89	14.90	40.00	64.82	**52.41**	55.78	54.68	**55.23**
NextGeneid	11.30	36.99	24.15	36.30	62.23	49.27	37.04	44.55	40.80
Cufflinks	**16.03**	19.29	17.66	36.18	46.32	41.25	39.75	37.53	38.64
mTim	10.14	22.66	16.40	20.59	40.70	30.65	31.86	37.72	34.79

Table 16.2: Comparison of top-performing gene-finding systems that participated in the rGASP challenge (*AUGUSTUS* (Stanke et al., 2008), *Exonerate* (Slater and Birney, 2005), *GSTRUCT*, *NextGeneid*) as well as the commonly used tool *Cufflinks* (Trapnell et al., 2010) and another margin-based predictor called *mTim* (Zeller et al., 2013), which uses a simpler statement. See Steijger et al. (2013) (Supplementary Table 5) for the full table. Both *Cufflinks* and *mTIM* are almost solely based on RNA-seq features. Shown are sensitivity (Sn), specificity (Sp), and their average (in %) on transcript level for three organisms. The results within 0.5% of the best performing method within a category and according to each of the evaluation levels are set in boldface.

binomial distribution is frequently used to model read count distributions (see, e.g., Drewe et al., 2013; Anders et al., 2013). Also, *MiTie* does not use the term G_θ to take genome sequence information into account. This simplified model does not have many free parameters, and the few remaining ones were tuned by model selection (see details and references in Behr et al., 2013). Furthermore, we used an important feature of *MiTie*, namely, to take known transcripts during the inference step into account. This is done by not penalizing the known transcript in the ℓ_0 regularizer in (16.7). The rationale is that *MiTie* will only predict new transcripts if the read data sufficiently supports it but can predict a known transcript with much less evidence.

We compare *MiTie* to the well-established tool *Cufflinks* (Trapnell et al., 2010), which has proven in previous studies (see Section 16.4.2) to perform well when compared with other solely RNA-seq based methods. *Cufflinks* can also take known transcripts into account.

To evaluate the ability of both methods to find additional transcripts in already well-annotated organisms, we utilized an extensive RNA-seq data set compiled as part of the modENCODE project (Celniker et al., 2009). We performed a retrospective experiment where we removed one transcript at random from the annotation of a gene. Based on this incomplete annotation and the RNA-seq data, we then ran the algorithm and computed the sensitivity of detecting the omitted transcript. The specificity was measured with respect to all transcripts. More details of the evaluation metric can be found in Behr et al. (2013).

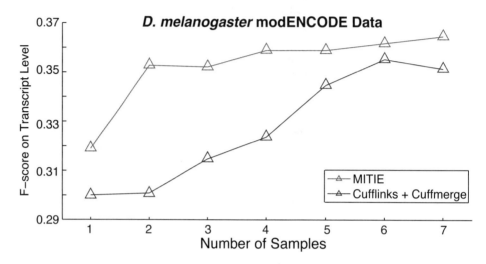

Figure 16.5: Comparison of *MiTie* to *Cufflinks* of RNA-seq data for seven developmental stages of *D. melanogaster*. See main text and Behr et al. (2013) for details.

Figure 16.5 shows that *MiTie* outperforms *Cufflinks* by a large margin. Especially when considering multiple RNA-seq samples from different developmental stages at the same time, the performance of *MiTie* increases. To achieve a similar performance, *Cufflinks* needs significantly more samples.

16.5   Conclusions

We have presented a unified framework for structured output prediction applied to the large-scale biological problem of genome annotation. The application of the learning framework of HM-SVMs to this task is computationally challenging. We discussed the strategies to scale up the framework with respect to both the learning as well as the inference aspects in this chapter.

The strategy has been implemented in the gene-finding system *mGene* and two international competitions have shown that this framework performs well in different practical applications.

However, as mentioned earlier, the traditional inference method based on dynamic programming, also employed in *mGene*, has the shortcoming that it cannot predict several overlapping transcripts. Therefore, this inference method is not ideal for integration of the new, informative RNA-seq data. *MiTie* implements a more general and flexible inference algorithm based on mixed integer programming (MIP) that outperforms commonly used approaches.

We have formalized the learning framework such that it allows us to replace the dynamic programming-based inference algorithm with the MIP inference. This strategy may eliminate one of the most severe restrictions of traditional computational gene finding, which is the limitation to predict only one transcript per gene. However, statistical models for RNA-seq data so far were not able to utilize information from the genomic DNA sequence due to a lack of suitable methods to learn the massively increasing number of parameters. Therefore, we think that this unified framework will further the field of transcriptome reconstruction. However, for practical application of the combination of the two technologies, significant technical issues will need to be faced.

Within the next decade, we may expect that the task of transcriptome reconstruction will be largely solved due to improvements in sequencing technology. Nevertheless, the learned models will still be of great importance, for instance, to predict the outcome of perturbations of the system. The perturbations of a system are often crucial to obtain clues about the internal mechanisms. While many perturbation experiments can also be carried out in the real world, there are often technical and/or ethical constraints that leave predictive models as the only option.

Acknowledgments

We gratefully acknowledge funding from the German Research Foundation under grants RA1894/1 and RA1894/2 (to G.R.) as well as core funding from the Max Planck Society (to G.R.) and the Sloan-Kettering Institute (to G.R.). We also acknowledge the following people for preparing the rGASP submission: Andre Kahles and Geraldine Jean for RNA-seq alignments, Peter Niermann for preparing the human signal predictions, Regina Bohnert for quantifying transcripts in *mGene graph*, and Georg Zeller for conceptual and technical advice on *mGene.ngs*. Finally, we thank Theofanis Karaletsos for carefully reading the manuscript.

16.6 References

Y. Altun and T. Hofmann. Large margin methods for label sequence learning. In *Proceedings of 8th European Conference on Speech Communication and Technology (EuroSpeech)*, 2003.

Y. Altun, I. Tsochantaridis, and T. Hofmann. Hidden Markov support vector machines. In *Proceedings of the 20th International Conference on Machine Learning*, pages 3–10, 2003.

S. Anders, D. J. McCarthy, Y. Chen, M. Okoniewski, G. K. Smyth, W. Huber, and M. D. Robinson. Count-based differential expression analysis of RNA sequencing data using R and Bioconductor. *Nature Protocols*, 8(9):1765–1786, September 2013.

J. Behr, A. Kahles, Y. Zhong, V. T. Sreedharan, P. Drewe, and G. Rätsch. MITIE: Simultaneous RNA-Seq-based transcript identification and quantification in multiple samples. *Bioinformatics*, page btt442, 2013. URL http://bioinformatics.oxfordjournals.org/content/early/2013/08/25/bioinformatics.btt442.short.

A. Bernal, K. Crammer, A. Hatzigeorgiou, and F. Pereira. Global discriminative learning for higher-accuracy computational gene prediction. *PLoS Computational Biology*, 3(3):e54, 2007.

R. Bohnert and G. Rätsch. rQuant.web: A tool for RNA-Seq-based transcript quantitation. *Nucleic Acids Research*, 38(Web Server issue):W348–351, July 2010.

M. Borodovsky, A. Lomsadze, N. Ivanov, and R. Mills. Eukaryotic gene prediction using GeneMark.hmm. *Current Protocols in Bioinformatics*, Chapter 4:Unit4.6, May 2003. ISSN 1934–340X (Electronic); 1934–3396 (Linking).

S. Celniker, L. Dillon, M. Gerstein, K. Gunsalus, S. Henikoff, G. Karpen, M. Kellis, E. Lai, J. Lieb, D. MacAlpine, G. Micklem, F. Piano, M. Snyder, L. Stein, K. White, R. Waterston, and modENCODE Consortium. Unlocking the secrets of the genome. *Nature*, 459(7249):927–930, 2009.

A. Coghlan, T. J. Fiedler, S. J. McKay, P. Flicek, T. W. Harris, D. Blasiar, The nGASP Consortium, and L. D. Stein. nGASP–the nematode genome annotation assessment project. *BMC Bioinformatics*, 9:549, 2008. ISSN 1471–2105 (Electronic); 1471–2105 (Linking).

K. Crammer and Y. Singer. Ultraconservative online algorithms for multiclass problems. *Journal of Machine Learning Research*, 3:951–991, 2003. ISSN 1532-4435.

F. De Bona, S. Ossowski, K. Schneeberger, and G. Rätsch. Optimal spliced alignments of short sequence reads. *Bioinformatics*, 24(16):i174–i180, 2008.

D. DeCaprio, J. Vinson, M. Pearson, P. Montgomery, M. Doherty, and J. Galagan. Conrad: Gene prediction using conditional random fields. *Genome Research*, 17:1389–1398, 2007.

C. B. Do, D. A. Woods, and S. Batzoglou. CONTRAfold: RNA secondary structure prediction without physics-based models. *Bioinformatics*, 22(14):e90–e98, July 2006.

P. Drewe, O. Stegle, L. Hartmann, A. Kahles, R. Bohnert, A. Wachter, K. Borgwardt, and G. Rätsch. Accurate detection of differential RNA processing. *Nucleic Acids Research*, 41(10):5189–5198, May 2013.

R. Durbin, S. Eddy, A. Krogh, and G. Mitchison. *Biological Sequence Analysis: Probabilistic Models of Proteins and Nucleic Acids.* Cambridge University Press, 1998.

ENCODE Project Consortium, B. E. Bernstein, E. Birney, I. Dunham, E. D. Green, C. Gunter, and M. Snyder. An integrated encyclopedia of DNA elements in the human genome. *Nature*, 489(7414):57–74, September 2012.

M. B. Gerstein, C. Bruce, J. S. Rozowsky, D. Zheng, J. Du, J. O. Korbel, O. Emanuelsson, Z. D. Zhang, S. Weissman, and M. Snyder. What is a gene, post-ENCODE? history and updated definition. *Genome Research*, 17(6):669–681, June 2007.

N. Görnitz, C. Widmer, G. Zeller, A. Kahles, S. Sonnenburg, and G. Rätsch. Hierarchical multitask structured output learning for large-scale sequence segmentation. In *Advances in Neural Information Processing Systems (NIPS)*, 2011.

S. Gross, C. Do, M. Sirota, and S. Batzoglou. CONTRAST: A discriminative, phylogeny-free approach to multiple informant de novo gene prediction. *Genome Biology*, 8(12):r269, 2007.

M. Guttman, M. Garber, J. Z. Levin, J. Donaghey, J. Robinson, X. Adiconis, L. Fan, M. J. Koziol, A. Gnirke, C. Nusbaum, J. L. Rinn, E. S. Lander, and A. Regev. Ab initio reconstruction of cell type-specific transcriptomes in mouse reveals the conserved multi-exonic structure of lincRNAs. *Nature Biotechnology*, 28(5):503–510, May 2010. ISSN 1087-0156. doi: 10.1038/nbt.1633. URL http://dx.doi.org/10.1038/nbt.1633.

R. Hettich and K. Kortanek. Semi-infinite programming: Theory, methods and applications. *SIAM Review*, 3:380–429, September 1993.

D. Hiller and W. Wong. Simultaneous isoform discovery and quantification from RNA-Seq. *Statistics in Biosciences*, pages 1–19, 2012. ISSN 1867-1764. doi: 10.1007/s12561-012-9069-2. URL http://dx.doi.org/10.1007/s12561-012-9069-2.

A. Krogh. Using database matches with HMMGene for automated gene detection in *Drosophila. Genome Research*, 10(4):523–528, April 2000. ISSN 1088-9051 (Print); 1088-9051 (Linking).

D. Kulp, D. Haussler, M. Reese, and F. Eeckman. A generalized hidden Markov model for the recognition of human genes in DNA. *ISMB 1996*, pages 134–141, 1996.

E. S. Lander et al. Initial sequencing and analysis of the human genome. *Nature*, 409(6822):860–921, February 2001.

S. Leavitt and M. Nirenberg. Deciphering the genetic code: Marshall Nirenberg. Office of NIH History, June 2010.

W. Li, J. Feng, and T. Jiang. Isolasso: A LASSO regression approach to RNA-Seq based transcriptome assembly. In V. Bafna and S. Sahinalp, editors, *Research in Computational Molecular Biology*, volume 6577 of *Lecture Notes in Computer Science*, pages 168–188. Springer Berlin Heidelberg, 2011. ISBN 978-3-642-20035-9. doi: 10.1007/978-3-642-20036-618. URL http://dx.doi.org/10.1007/978-3-642-20036-6_18.

Y.-Y. Lin, P. Dao, F. Hach, M. Bakhshi, F. Mo, A. Lapuk, C. Collins, and S. Sahinalp. CLIIQ: Accurate comparative detection and quantification of expressed isoforms in a population. In B. Raphael and J. Tang, editors, *Algorithms in Bioinformatics*, volume 7534 of *Lecture Notes in Computer Science*, pages 178–189. Springer Berlin Heidelberg, 2012. ISBN 978-3-642-33121-3. doi: 10.1007/978-3-642-33122-014. URL http://dx.doi.org/10.1007/978-3-642-33122-0_14.

A. V. Lukashin and M. Borodovsky. GeneMark.hmm: New solutions for gene finding. *Nucleic Acids Research*, 26(4):1107–1115, February 1998. ISSN 0305-1048 (Print); 0305-1048 (Linking).

W. Majoros. *Methods for Computational Gene Prediction*. Cambridge University Press, 2007.

W. Majoros, M. Pertea, C. Antonescu, and S. L. Salzberg. GlimmerM, Exonomy and Unveil: Three ab initio eukaryotic genefinders. *Nucleic Acids Research*, 31 (13):3601–3604, July 2003. ISSN 1362-4962 (Electronic); 0305-1048 (Linking).

A. M. Mezlini, E. J. Smith, M. Fiume, O. Buske, G. Savich, S. Shah, S. Aparicion, D. Chiang, A. Goldenberg, and M. Brudno. iReckon: Simultaneous isoform discovery and abundance estimation from RNA-Seq. *Genome Research*, 2012.

L. R. Rabiner. A tutorial on hidden Markov models and selected applications in speech recognition. In *Readings in speech recognition*, pages 267–296, San Francisco, CA, USA, 1990. Morgan Kaufmann Publishers Inc. ISBN 1-55860-124-4.

G. Rätsch and S. Sonnenburg. Large scale hidden semi-Markov SVMs. In B. Schölkopf, J. Platt, and T. Hoffman, editors, *Advances in Neural Information Processing Systems (NIPS'06)*, volume 19, pages 1161–1168. MIT Press, 2007.

G. Rätsch, S. Sonnenburg, J. Srinivasan, H. Witte, K.-R. Müller, R.-J. Sommer, and B. Schölkopf. Improving the *Caenorhabditis elegans* genome annotation using machine learning. *PLoS Computational Biology*, 3(2):e20, February 2007. ISSN 1553-7358 (Electronic).

A. Salamov and V. Solovyev. Ab initio gene finding in *Drosophila* genomic DNA. *Genome Research*, 10(4):516–522, 2000. URL http://genome.cshlp.org/cgi/content/abstract/10/4/516.

G. Schweikert, A. Zien, G. Zeller, J. Behr, C. Dieterich, C. S. Ong, P. Philips, F. De Bona, L. Hartmann, A. Bohlen, N. Krüger, S. Sonnenburg, and G. Rätsch. mGene: Accurate SVM-based gene finding with an application to nematode genomes. *Genome Research*, 19(11):2133–2143, Nov 2009. ISSN 1549-5469 (Electronic).

G. S. C. Slater and E. Birney. Automated generation of heuristics for biological sequence comparison. *BMC Bioinformatics*, 6:31, 2005.

S. Sonnenburg, A. Zien, and G. Rätsch. ARTS: Accurate recognition of transcription starts in human. *Bioinformatics*, 22(14):e472–e480, 2006. URL http://bioinformatics.oxfordjournals.org/content/22/14/e472.short.

S. Sonnenburg, G. Rätsch, and K. Rieck. Large-scale learning with string kernels. In L. Bottou, O. Chapelle, D. DeCoste, and J. Weston, editors, *Large-Scale Kernel Machines*, chapter 4, pages 73–104. MIT Press, Cambridge, MA, 2007a.

S. Sonnenburg, G. Schweikert, P. Philips, J. Behr, and G. Rätsch. Accurate splice site prediction using support vector machines. *BMC Bioinformatics*, 8 Suppl 10: S7, 2007b.

S. Sonnenburg, G. Rätsch, S. Henschel, C. Widmer, J. Behr, A. Zien, F. de Bona, A. Binder, C. Gehl, and V. Franc. The SHOGUN machine learning toolbox. *Journal of Machine Learning Research*, 11:1799–1802, June 2010. URL `http://www.shogun-toolbox.org`.

M. Stanke, O. Schoffmann, B. Morgenstern, and S. Waack. Gene prediction in eukaryotes with a generalized hidden Markov model that uses hints from external sources. *BMC Bioinformatics*, 7(1):62, 2006. ISSN 1471-2105. URL `http://www.biomedcentral.com/1471-2105/7/62`.

M. Stanke, M. Diekhans, R. Baertsch, and D. Haussler. Using native and syntenically mapped cDNA alignments to improve de novo gene finding. *Bioinformatics*, 24(5):637–644, March 2008. URL `http://dx.doi.org/10.1093/bioinformatics/btn013`.

T. Steijger, J. Abril, P. Engström, F. Kokocinski, The RGASP Consortium, T. Hubbard, R. Guigo, J. Harrow, and P. Bertone. Assessment of transcript reconstruction methods for RNA-seq. *Nature Methods*, accepted, 2013.

B. Taskar, D. Klein, M. Collins, D. Koller, and C. D. Manning. Max-margin parsing. In *In Proceedings of EMNLP*, pages 1–8. Association for Computational Linguistics, 2004.

C. Trapnell, B. A. Williams, G. Pertea, A. Mortazavi, G. Kwan, M. J. van Baren, S. L. Salzberg, B. J. Wold, and L. Pachter. Transcript assembly and quantification by RNA-Seq reveals unannotated transcripts and isoform switching during cell differentiation. *Nature Biotechnology*, 28(5):511–515, May 2010. ISSN 1087-0156. URL `http://dx.doi.org/10.1038/nbt.1621`.

I. Tsochantaridis, T. Joachims, T. Hofmann, and Y. Altun. Large margin methods for structured and interdependent output variables. *Journal of Machine Learning Research*, 6:1453–1484, 2005. ISSN 1532-4435.

V. Vapnik. *Estimation of Dependences Based on Empirical Data [in Russian]*. Nauka, Moscow, 1979. (English translation: Springer Verlag, 1982).

J. C. Venter et al. The sequence of the human genome. *Science*, 291(5507):1304–51, Feb 2001.

Z. Xia, J. Wen, C. C. Chang, and X. Zhou. NSMAP: A method for spliced isoforms identification and quantification from RNA-Seq. *BMC Bioinformatics*, 12(1):162+, 2011. ISSN 1471-2105. doi: 10.1186/1471-2105-12-162. URL `http://dx.doi.org/10.1186/1471-2105-12-162`.

G. Zeller, R. M. Clark, K. Schneeberger, A. Bohlen, D. Weigel, and G. Rätsch. Detecting polymorphic regions in *arabidopsis thaliana* with resequencing microarrays. *Genome Research*, 18(6):918–929, June 2008a.

G. Zeller, S. R. Henz, S. Laubinger, D. Weigel, and G. Rätsch. Transcript normalization and segmentation of tiling array data. *Pacific Symposium on Biocomputing*, pages 527–538, 2008b.

G. Zeller, N. Görnitz, A. Kahles, J. Behr, P. Mudragarta, S. Sonnenburg, and G. Rätsch. mTIM: Rapid and accurate transcript reconstruction from RNA-Seq data. Technical report, arXiv:1309.5211, 2013.

A. Zien, G. Rätsch, and C. Ong. Towards the inference of graphs on ordered vertices. Technical report, Max-Planck-Institut für biologische Kybernetik, August 2006.